## FEELING HURT IN CLOSE RELATIONSHIPS

*Feeling Hurt in Close Relationships* presents a synthesis of cutting-edge research and theory on hurt feelings. People hurt each other even in the closest, most satisfying relationships. What varies from one relationship to another is not whether partners hurt each other but how their relationship is affected by hurtful events. Given the potential influence of hurt feelings on people's interpersonal relationships, it is not surprising that scholars have begun to study the antecedents, processes, and outcomes associated with hurt. This collection integrates the various issues addressed by researchers, theorists, and practitioners who study the causes of hurt feelings, the interpersonal events associated with hurt, and the ways people respond to hurting and being hurt by others. To capture the breadth and depth of the literature in this area, the work of scholars from a variety of disciplines – including social psychology, communication, sociology, and family studies – is highlighted.

Anita L. Vangelisti is the Jesse H. Jones Centennial Professor of Communication at the University of Texas at Austin. Her work focuses on the associations between communication and emotion in the context of close, personal relationships. She has published numerous articles and chapters and has edited or authored several books. Vangelisti has served on the editorial boards of more than a dozen scholarly journals. She has received recognition for her research from the National Communication Association, the International Society for the Study of Personal Relationships, and the International Association for Relationship Research.

# Feeling Hurt in Close Relationships

Edited by

Anita L. Vangelisti

*University of Texas at Austin*

CAMBRIDGE UNIVERSITY PRESS
Cambridge, New York, Melbourne, Madrid, Cape Town, Singapore, São Paulo, Delhi

Cambridge University Press
32 Avenue of the Americas, New York, NY 10013-2473, USA

www.cambridge.org
Information on this title: www.cambridge.org/9780521866903

© Cambridge University Press 2009

This publication is in copyright. Subject to statutory exception
and to the provisions of relevant collective licensing agreements,
no reproduction of any part may take place without the written
permission of Cambridge University Press.

First published 2009

Printed in the United States of America

*A catalog record for this publication is available from the British Library.*

*Library of Congress Cataloging in Publication data*

Feeling hurt in close relationships / edited by Anita L. Vangelisti.
    p.   cm. – (Advances in personal relationships)
Includes bibliographical references and index.
ISBN 978-0-521-86690-3 (hbk.)
1. Interpersonal relations – Psychological aspects.   2. Emotions.   I. Vangelisti, Anita L.
II. Title.   III. Series.
HM1106.F45   2010
155.9′–dc22       2009013035

ISBN   978-0-521-86690-3 hardback

Cambridge University Press has no responsibility for the persistence or
accuracy of URLs for external or third-party Internet Web sites referred to in
this publication and does not guarantee that any content on such Web sites is,
or will remain, accurate or appropriate. Information regarding prices, travel
timetables, and other factual information given in this work are correct at
the time of first printing, but Cambridge University Press does not guarantee
the accuracy of such information thereafter.

## Advances in Personal Relationships

Harry T. Reis
*University of Rochester*

Mary Anne Fitzpatrick
*University of South Carolina*

Anita L. Vangelisti
*University of Texas at Austin*

Although scholars from a variety of disciplines have written and conversed about the importance of personal relationships for decades, the emergence of personal relationships as a field of study is relatively recent. *Advances in Personal Relationships* represents the culmination of years of multidisciplinary and interdisciplinary work on personal relationships. Sponsored by the International Association for Relationship Research, the series offers readers cutting-edge research and theory in the field. Contributing authors are internationally known scholars from a variety of disciplines, including social psychology, clinical psychology, communication, history, sociology, gerontology, and family studies. Volumes include integrative reviews, conceptual pieces, summaries of research programs, and major theoretical works. *Advances in Personal Relationships* presents first-rate scholarship that is both provocative and theoretically grounded. The theoretical and empirical work described by authors will stimulate readers and advance the field by offering new ideas and retooling old ones. The series will be of interest to upper division undergraduate students, graduate students, researchers, and practitioners.

## Other Books in the Series

*Attribution, Communication Behavior, and Close Relationships*
Valerie Manusov and John H. Harvey, editors

*Stability and Change in Relationships*
Anita L. Vangelisti, Harry T. Reis, and Mary Anne Fitzpatrick, editors

*Understanding Marriage: Developments in the Study of Couple Interaction*
Patricia Noller and Judith A. Feeney, editors

*Growing Together: Personal Relationships Across the Life Span*
Frieder R. Lang and Karen L. Fingerman, editors

*Communicating Social Support*
Daena J. Goldsmith

*Communicating Affection: Interpersonal Behavior and Social Context*
Kory Floyd

*Changing Relations: Achieving Intimacy in a Time of Social Transition*
Robin Goodwin

# CONTENTS

| | |
|---|---|
| *List of Contributors* | *page* xi |
| *Foreword* | xv |
| *Daniel Perlman* | |

### PART I: INTRODUCTION

1. Hurt Feelings: Distinguishing Features, Functions, and Overview    3
   *Anita L. Vangelisti*

### PART II: CONCEPTUALIZING HURT

2. The Nature of Hurt Feelings: Emotional Experience and Cognitive Appraisals    15
   *Mark R. Leary and Sadie Leder*

3. Thinking the Unthinkable: Cognitive Appraisals and Hurt Feelings    34
   *Julie Fitness and Wayne Warburton*

4. Adding Insult to Injury: The Contributions of Politeness Theory to Understanding Hurt Feelings in Close Relationships    50
   *Daena J. Goldsmith and Erin Donovan-Kicken*

5. Rejection Sensitivity: A Model of How Individual Difference Factors Affect the Experience of Hurt Feelings in Conflict and Support    73
   *N. Jan Kang, Geraldine Downey, Masumi Iida, and Sylvia Rodriguez*

6. Understanding and Altering Hurt Feelings: An Attachment-Theoretical Perspective on the Generation and Regulation of Emotions    92
   *Phillip R. Shaver, Mario Mikulincer, Shiri Lavy, and Jude Cassidy*

## PART III: HURTFUL ACTS

7. Rejection: Resolving the Paradox of Emotional Numbness after Exclusion — 123
   *C. Nathan DeWall, Roy F. Baumeister, and E. J. Masicampo*

8. Conflict and Hurt in Close Relationships — 143
   *John P. Caughlin, Allison M. Scott, and Laura E. Miller*

9. When the Truth Hurts: Deception in the Name of Kindness — 167
   *Bella M. DePaulo, Wendy L. Morris, and R. Weylin Sternglanz*

10. Affairs and Infidelity — 191
    *Graham Allan and Kaeren Harrison*

11. Aggression, Violence, and Hurt in Close Relationships — 209
    *Brian H. Spitzberg*

## PART IV: HURT IN RELATIONAL CONTEXTS

12. Aggression and Victimization in Children's Peer Groups: A Relationship Perspective — 235
    *Noel A. Card, Jenny Isaacs, and Ernest V. E. Hodges*

13. Haven in a Heartless World? Hurt Feelings in the Family — 260
    *Rosemary S. L. Mills and Caroline C. Piotrowski*

14. Hurt Feelings in Adult Friendships — 288
    *Beverley Fehr and Cheryl Harasymchuk*

15. When Love Hurts: Understanding Hurtful Events in Couple Relationships — 313
    *Judith A. Feeney*

16. Hurt in Postdivorce Relationships — 336
    *Sandra Metts, Dawn O. Braithwaite, and Mark A. Fine*

## PART V: HURT IN APPLIED CONTEXTS

17. The Physiology of Feeling Hurt — 359
    *Timothy J. Loving, Benjamin Le, and Erin E. Crockett*

18. Hurt and Psychological Health in Close Relationships — 376
    *Scott R. Braithwaite, Frank D. Fincham, and Nathaniel M. Lambert*

19. Technology and Hurt in Close Relationships — 400
    *Monica Whitty*

20. Hurt Feelings and the Workplace — 417
    *Michael R. Cunningham, Anita P. Barbee, and Eshita Mandal*

21. Cultural Influences on the Causes and Experience of Hurt Feelings  457
    Robin M. Kowalski

22. Hurt Feelings: The Last Taboo for Researchers and Clinicians?  479
    Luciano L'Abate

Author Index  499

Subject Index  519

# LIST OF CONTRIBUTORS

GRAHAM ALLAN
School of Sociology and Criminology
Keele University

ANITA P. BARBEE
Kent School of Social Work
University of Louisville

ROY F. BAUMEISTER
Department of Psychology
Florida State University

DAWN O. BRAITHWAITE
Department of Communication
 Studies
University of Nebraska–Lincoln

SCOTT R. BRAITHWAITE
Family Institute
Florida State University

NOEL A. CARD
Department of Family Studies and
 Human Development
University of Arizona

JUDE CASSIDY
Department of Psychology
University of Maryland

JOHN P. CAUGHLIN
Department of Communication
University of Illinois

ERIN E. CROCKETT
Department of Human Ecology
University of Texas at Austin

MICHAEL R. CUNNINGHAM
Department of Psychology and Brain
 Sciences
University of Louisville

BELLA M. DePAULO
Department of Psychology
University of California at Santa
 Barbara

C. NATHAN DeWALL
Department of Psychology
University of Kentucky

ERIN DONOVAN-KICKEN
Department of Communication
 Studies
University of Texas at Austin

GERALDINE DOWNEY
Department of Psychology
Columbia University

JUDITH A. FEENEY
School of Psychology
University of Queensland

BEVERLEY FEHR
Department of Psychology
University of Winnipeg

FRANK D. FINCHAM
Family Institute
Florida State University

MARK A. FINE
Department of Human Development
  and Family Studies
University of Missouri

JULIE FITNESS
Department of Psychology
Macquarie University

DAENA J. GOLDSMITH
Department of Communication
Lewis and Clark College

CHERYL HARASYMCHUK
Department of Psychology
University of Manitoba

KAEREN HARRISON
Department of Social Work
Southampton Solent University

ERNEST V. E. HODGES
Department of Psychology
St. John's University

MASUMI IIDA
Department of Psychology
Kent State University

JENNY ISAACS
Department of Psychology
Yeshiva University

N. JAN KANG
Department of Psychology
Columbia University

ROBIN M. KOWALSKI
Department of Psychology
Clemson University

LUCIANO L'ABATE
Department of Psychology
Georgia State University

NATHANIEL M. LAMBERT
Family Institute
Florida State University

SHIRI LAVY
Department of Behavioral Sciences
Ariel University Center

BENJAMIN LE
Department of Psychology
Haverford College

MARK R. LEARY
Department of Psychology and
  Neuroscience
Duke University

SADIE LEDER
Department of Psychology
State University of New York at Buffalo

TIMOTHY J. LOVING
Department of Human Ecology
University of Texas at Austin

ESHITA MANDAL
Private Practice
Mumbai, India

E. J. MASICAMPO
Department of Psychology
Florida State University

SANDRA METTS
School of Communication
Illinois State University

MARIO MIKULINCER
New School of Psychology
Interdisciplinary Center (IDC)
  Herzliya

LAURA E. MILLER
Department of Communication
University of Illinois

## List of Contributors

ROSEMARY S. L. MILLS
Department of Family Social Sciences
University of Manitoba

WENDY L. MORRIS
Department of Psychology
McDaniel College

DANIEL PERLMAN
Department of Human Development and Family Studies
University of North Carolina at Greensboro

CAROLINE C. PIOTROWSKI
Department of Family Social Sciences
University of Manitoba

SYLVIA RODRIGUEZ
Department of Psychology
Columbia University

ALLISON M. SCOTT
Department of Communication
University of Illinois

PHILLIP R. SHAVER
Department of Psychology
University of California

BRIAN H. SPITZBERG
School of Communication
San Diego State University

R. WEYLIN STERNGLANZ
Division of Social and Behavioral Sciences
Nova Southeastern University

ANITA L. VANGELISTI
Department of Communication Studies
University of Texas at Austin

WAYNE WARBURTON
Department of Psychology
Macquarie University

MONICA WHITTY
Division of Psychology
Nottingham Trent University

# FOREWORD

## DANIEL PERLMAN

> Hurt feelings are at the bottom of our existence. If left covered, pushed down, and avoided they can produce dangerous personal and interpersonal outcomes. It is doubtful whether scholars and clinicians in psychology can continue to ignore these feelings.
> L. L'Abate, this volume

Think about it: When was the last time you were hurt in a close relationship? Who was it who hurt you? What led up to it? How severe was the hurt you experienced? What interpretations and explanations did you have for what the other person did? How did you feel initially? What did you do? How did the other person respond? Did your feelings change? Was the incident resolved? Questions of this sort are what this book is all about: It examines the feelings of hurt that we experience in our relationships.

### HURT: ITS NATURE AND PREVALENCE

Throughout the book, there are several definitions of hurt. A useful starting point for several contributors is editor Anita Vangelisti's statement that hurt is "a feeling that occurs as a result of a person being emotionally injured by another" (Vangelisti, Young, Carpenter-Theune, & Alexander, 2005, p. 446). Thus the hurt of concern in this volume is a reaction to the interaction between two people. The reaction is in the negative part of the emotional spectrum, with the outcomes often – but not necessarily – being negative.

There are multiple views of what constitutes the core of relational hurt. Vangelisti (2001) used the notion of relational transgression, a person's sense that their partner has violated relational norms or rules, victimized them in some way, or heightened their sense of vulnerability. Leary and Leder (this volume) contend that a central aspect of hurt is relationship devaluation, wanting a partner to value the relationships more than he or she does. Attachment theorists see hurt as stemming from the threats that interpersonal events pose for one's positive views of self (e.g., "I'm not worthy of love") and others

("My partner isn't available," "My partner isn't trustworthy") (Feeney, this volume). It is not too far of a stretch to imagine that these views may have complementary aspects (e.g., when relational transgressions occur, people feel their relationship is being devalued). Furthermore, at an underlying process level, all these authors share in common the assumption that the experience of hurt is filtered through people's perceptions and appraisals rather than a direct response to the other person's actions per se.

Reports of the frequency of hurt vary depending on the population, the definition of hurt used, the data collection method employed, and so on. At the higher end, Mills and Piotrowski (this volume) report that mothers interacting with preschool children experience an aversive event every few minutes, with major events occurring up to three times an hour. At the lower end, over the course of a 3-week diary study, Feeney (see Chapter 15) found that dating and married couples reported an average of about four hurtful events, with more of those events being reported from the victim's than the perpetrator's perspective. Whatever the exact count, hurt is common in close relationships.

## THE PLACE OF HURT IN THE STUDY OF RELATIONSHIPS

The study of hurt fits into the larger landscape of research on close relationships. With intellectual roots that can be traced back to antiquity and empirical roots dating back to the late 1800s, the area of personal relationships has flourished during the past 30 years. As in this volume, it is a multidisciplinary, multinational endeavor. Contributor Lu L'Abate published an early comment on the value of confronting hurt as a means of achieving intimacy (L'Abate, 1977). Vangelisti's 1994 chapter "Messages that Hurt" was a seminal contribution that triggered contemporary interest in hurt within relationships. This was in Cupach and Spitzberg's *The Dark Side of Interpersonal Communication*, a volume that awakened concern with the aversive, negative aspect of relationships. Thus, the study of hurt is part of a more general thrust of recent scholarly work on the problematic aspects of relationships such as abuse, bereavement, betrayal, conflict, deception, divorce, infidelity, jealousy, loneliness, peer rejection, stalking, and unrequited love. As chapters in the current volume testify, there are links among these phenomena (DeWall, Baumeister, & Masicampo; Caughlin, Scott, & Miller; DePaulo, Morris, & Sternglanz; Allan & Harrison; Spitzberg; Card, Isaacs, & Hodges). For example, infidelity typically leads to hurt, whereas lies are often told to spare the feelings of others.

Despite the interwoven aspects of the dark side of relationships, hurt is important in its own right for at least three reasons: its functions, its role in relationships, and its implications for individuals. First, Vangelisti (this volume) argues that hurt functions as an indicator of the quality of a relationship, as a means of influencing others (cf. Metts, Braithwaite, & Fine, this volume), and paradoxically as a form of support. Second, hurt is important throughout the life cycle of relationships. In the early, less certain stage of initiating relationships, hurtful words and deeds are likely important in whether relationships evolve (Feeney, this volume). Dealing with hurt is important in maintaining relationships. Hurtful messages undermine relationship satisfaction (Vangelisti & Crumley, 1998) and therefore are likely implicated in the dissolution of many relationships. Third, beyond their role in relationships, hurtful messages are also important for the individuals in those relationships. Loving, Le, and Crockett (this volume) indicate that being in what they presume are hurtful relations affects endocrine responses as well as immune system functioning. They conclude "it is clear that living with an emotionally abusive partner is a risk factor for long-term poor health." Similarly, Braithwaite, Fincham, and Lambert (this volume) sum up by saying that "the hurt that can be experienced in marriage and other close relationships is significant and can exert significant influence on the mental health of those involved."

## A PREVIEW OF THE BOOK'S CONTENTS

This volume provides a synthesis of current research and theory on hurt feelings in relationships. Following the Introduction in Part I, the book includes four main parts: conceptualizing hurt, hurtful acts, relational contexts, and applied contexts. In conceptualizing hurt in Part II, Leary and Leder ask: Is hurt a blend of other emotions, part of a common core of negative affect that is shared by all negative emotions, or a distinct emotion in its own right? This question reverberates throughout the volume. Working within the social cognition tradition, Fitness and Warburton discuss appraisal processes: cognitive processes leading to the experience of hurt feelings. (In Part IV, Card, Isaacs, and Hodges work from a similar perspective.) Rooted in Goffman's symbolic interaction, self-presentation position, Goldsmith and Donovan-Kicken link hurt to face threats. The final two chapters in this part stem from the personality tradition within psychology: Kang, Downey, Iida, and Rodriguez illuminate the role of rejection sensitivity (individual differences in the thoughts and feelings of individuals in the presence of cues of potential rejection) whereas Shaver, Mikulincer, Lavy, and Cassidy apply their influential attachment perspective. (In Part IV, Feeney also employs this perspective in discussing hurt in couple relationships.)

The third part of the volume identifies acts that often lead to hurt; the fourth part examines the special aspects of hurt in different types of relationships. These parts confirm that a range of antecedents lead to hurt and that hurt is a significant aspect of various types of relationships.

The fifth part of book starts with chapters on the physical and mental health correlates of hurt. In the second of these, Braithwaite, Fincham, and Lambert suggest that forgiveness can ameliorate the impact of hurt. The next three chapters in this part focus on hurt in a broader context. In her chapter on technology, Whitty examines hurt inflicted via the Internet. She considers views on whether the lack of social context cues available via the

Internet promulgate hurtful communication (e.g., flaming). She also discusses electronically enacted relationship behaviors that might cause hurt (e.g., lying, cyberstalking, monitoring someone's behavior, revenge Web sites, infidelity). Cunningham, Barbee, and Mandal consider multiple aspects of hurt in the workplace (e.g., in job interviews, in exchange processes, in the process of unionization, as a result of leaders' behaviors, incivility). A capstone of their chapter is an application of Cunningham and Barbee's social allergy model, the idea that sensitivity to behaviors that are initially only minor irritants becomes stronger as repetitions of the behaviors increase. In the following chapter, Kowalski examines hurt in a cultural perspective. She especially draws on Mesquita's (2003) theory of emotions that acknowledges the neurological and physiological aspects of emotions but believes that emotional experience and expression is heavily influenced by the sociocultural context. Thus factors such as the interdependent, collective vs. independent nature of a culture are seen as important in the antecedent events, appraisals, physiological changes, action tendencies, and emotional regulation surrounding hurt. This part concludes with a chapter in which a distinguished senior contributor, Lu L'Abate, provides a multilayered theoretical model of hurt rooted in clinical work and Tomkins' (1962, 1963) notion that affect amplifies drives. L'Abate also makes suggestions for how practitioners can help people deal positively with their hurt feelings.

## INTERNATIONAL ASSOCIATION FOR RELATIONSHIP RESEARCH SPONSORSHIP

The International Association for Relationship Research (IARR) is the leading professional organization concerned with the scientific study of personal relationships. This volume is sponsored by IARR and was developed under the oversight of IARR's publication committee to meet the Association's expectations for excellence and importance. It is an exemplary addition to their *Advances in Personal Relationship Series*. This volume admirably achieves the standards and orientation of the series in presenting:

> first-rate scholarship that is both provocative and theoretically grounded. The theoretical and empirical work described by authors will stimulate readers and advance the field by offering up new ideas and retooling old ones. The series will be of interest to upper division undergraduate students, graduate students, researchers, and practitioners.

## STRENGTHS OF THE VOLUME

As noted in IARR's sponsorship statement, IARR volumes are characterized by presenting the best in current empirical work and theoretical thinking. An asset of the current volume is that it provides the broad picture of research on hurt, presented in a less technical way that will be easily accessible to a wide range of readers. In terms of theory, the book is rich in conceptual viewpoints (e.g., social cognitive, attachment, script, prototype, politeness, the social allergy model, L'Abate's multilayered amplification model). Collectively, these perspectives offer a fuller, more comprehensive view of hurt than any one theoretical perspective would by itself.

For me, other strengths of this volume include:

- It is the first book-length treatment of hurt. It is being published at a moment when work in this area has matured to where having a compendium is very timely both to synthesize the now substantial body of what is known and to serve as a foundation for the next generation of knowledge and practice.
- The set of contributors is outstanding in terms of the quantity and quality of the work they have been doing on hurt.
- The book is well edited in terms of both introductory and concluding pieces and of the parts fitting together. Contributors were aware of each others' writing so several core issues (e.g., is hurt a discrete emotion?) are addressed by multiple authors. Editor Vangelisti gave authors a set of useful guidelines to add consistency across chapters. Thus, the chapters regularly offer integrative reviews, comments on relevant approaches to studying hurt, identification of major conflicts in the literature, and directions for future research.

I have studied relationships throughout my professional career. Like many other people, I have perpetrated hurt and been its victim. *Feeling Hurt in Close Relationships* has given me a comprehensive tour of work on hurt that has taught me new information, expanded my thinking about this key phenomenon, and made me consider how to conduct my own relationships. Reading the manuscript stimulated my insights into researchable questions and practical implications for mental health professionals and our everyday lives. While reading, I was teaching a graduate course and immediately changed my syllabus to include a section on hurt. I wanted my students (and others) to have the experience of reading *Feeling Hurt in Close Relationships* to explore this phenomenon.

In sum, for me this is an excellent book on an important and relevant topic. I am grateful to the book's authors. I enthusiastically recommend their work to you. Read on – you will be glad you did!

### REFERENCES

Cupach, W. R., & Spitzberg, B. H. (Eds.). (1994). *The dark side of interpersonal communication*. Hillsdale, NJ: Lawrence Erlbaum.

L'Abate, L. (1977). Intimacy is sharing hurt feelings: A reply to David Mace. *Journal of Marriage and Family Counseling, 3,* 13–16.

Mesquita, B. (2003). Emotions as dynamic cultural phenomena. In R. J. Davidson, K. R. Scherer, & H. H. Goldsmith (Eds.), *Handbook of affective sciences* (pp. 871–890). New York: Oxford University Press.

Tomkins, S. S. (1962). *Affect, imagery, and consciousness: Vol. 1. The positive effects.* New York: Springer-Verlag.

Tomkins, S. S. (1963). *Affect, imagery, and consciousness: Vol. 2. The negative effects.* New York: Springer-Verlag.

Vangelisti, A. L. (1994). Messages that hurt. In W. R. Cupach & B. H. Spitzberg (Eds.), *The dark side of interpersonal communication* (pp. 53–82). Hillsdale, NJ: Lawrence Erlbaum.

Vangelisti, A. L., & Crumley, L. P. (1998). Reactions to messages that hurt: The influence of relational contexts. *Communication Monographs, 65,* 173–196.

Vangelisti, A. L. (2001). Making sense of hurtful interactions in close relationships. In V. Manusov & J. H. Harvey (Eds.), *Attribution, communication behavior, and close relationships* (pp. 38–58). New York: Cambridge University Press.

Vangelisti, A. L., Young, S. L., Carpenter-Theune, K., & Alexander, A. L. (2005). Why does it hurt?: The perceived causes of hurt feelings. *Communication Research, 32,* 443–477.

# PART I

# INTRODUCTION

# 1

# Hurt Feelings: Distinguishing Features, Functions, and Overview

### ANITA L. VANGELISTI

Hurt feelings are powerful. They can influence relational partners' behavior, the thoughts that partners have about their relationship, and the attitudes they hold toward each other. Over time, the way people interpret and respond to their hurt feelings can affect the decisions they make about initiating, maintaining, and terminating relationships. Some who have been hurt repeatedly opt to avoid close relationships altogether, whereas others anxiously search for a partner who will shield them from emotional pain. Yet others find ways to cope with their experiences that enable them to initiate and maintain relatively secure, satisfying partnerships.

Given the potential influence of hurt feelings on people's close relationships, it is not surprising that researchers and theorists have begun to turn their attention to understanding the antecedents, processes, and outcomes associated with the emotion. Indeed, the study of hurt feelings has flourished over the past decade. Scholars have examined issues such as the phenomenology of hurt (Leary, Springer, Negel, Ansell, & Evans, 1998), the perceived causes of hurt feelings (Vangelisti, Young, Carpenter, & Alexander, 2005), the influence of intentionality on hurt (Vangelisti & Young, 2000), factors that affect the way people evaluate hurtful communication (Young, 2004), distancing responses to hurt (McLaren & Solomon, 2008), the effects of hurtful events on romantic relationships (Feeney, 2004), individuals' willingness to confront hurtful messages from romantic partners (Miller & Roloff, 2005), parent and child perceptions of hurtful interactions (Mills, Nazar, & Farrell, 2002), and hurtful family environments (Vangelisti, Maguire, Alexander, & Clark, 2007). The current volume offers a synthesis of extant research on hurt feelings, presents new conceptions of how the emotion operates, and provides directions for future theoretical and conceptual work on hurt.

### DISTINGUISHING FEATURES OF HURT

Most researchers and theorists who have studied hurt agree that hurt feelings involve emotional injury or harm (Folkes, 1982; L'Abate, 1977). Hurt occurs when people believe that the communication or behavior of an individual, or group of individuals, caused them emotional pain. Indeed, one of the first empirical studies to examine hurt supported the notion that emotional injury is linked to hurt feelings. Specifically, a prototype analysis of emotion concepts conducted by Shaver, Schwartz, Kirson, and O'Connor (1987) indicated that hurt was associated with emotion terms such as anguish and agony and that hurt was linked to sadness. Shaver and his colleagues argued that the emotion terms that clustered with hurt all involved suffering or, put differently, the endurance of emotional pain.

Although defining hurt in terms of emotional injury provided researchers with a starting point for investigating the possible causes, correlates, and outcomes associated with hurt feelings, it did little to situate hurt – conceptually or theoretically – with regard to other emotions. Specifying the nature of the relationship between hurt and other emotions has been a challenging task for researchers and theorists. Part of the reason this task has been challenging is that hurt feelings are difficult to isolate. They usually occur in concert with other emotions (Feeney, 2005; Leary et al., 1998). In fact, some argue that hurt feelings typically are expressed via emotions such as anger, fear, or even jealousy (see L'Abate, Chapter 22, this volume). The intermingling of hurt with other emotions is one factor that initially led Vangelisti and her colleagues to suggest that hurt is an emotion "blend" (e.g., Vangelisti & Young, 2000). These researchers argued that hurt is the result of combining feelings of sadness (that occur when individuals believe they have been emotionally injured) and fear (that is elicited when people perceive they are vulnerable to harm). The idea put forth was that the blending of sadness and fear creates a separate emotion, "hurt," that often is paired with and defensively masked by emotions characterized by less vulnerability (e.g., anger).

Whereas Vangelisti and her colleagues conceptualized hurt as an emotion blend, others created a case for defining hurt as a unique emotion. Leary and Springer (2001) were among the first to champion this idea. They examined a wide variety of negative emotions and found that those emotions did not account for all of the variance in hurt feelings. Based on these results, they argued that hurt is a distinct emotion in and of itself. Feeney (2005) concurred with Leary and Springer. In addition to conceptualizing hurt as a unique emotion, she offered a way for researchers to predict which emotions are likely to accompany hurt. Feeney suggested that the type of experience or event that evokes individuals' hurt feelings affects the negative emotions that are paired with hurt. She found, for example, that terms related to the loss of hopes or ideals were associated with both hurt and sadness, whereas terms related to exploitation were associated with both hurt and anger. The evidence presented by Leary and Springer and by Feeney suggests that the emotional pain people refer to when they describe their hurt feelings is different from other emotions.

Although often accompanied by other negative emotions, and perhaps even sharing a common source, hurt is distinct and should be treated as such by researchers and theorists.

In addition to characterizing the nature of the relationship between hurt and other emotions, researchers have made substantial strides in identifying factors that differentiate hurt from other emotions. For instance, Fine and Olson (1997) distinguished hurt from anger by suggesting that hurt is elicited when people believe a provocation they experienced is deserved, whereas anger is evoked when a provocation is perceived to be undeserved or unwarranted. By contrast, Leary and his colleagues (1998) argued that the feature that differentiates hurt from other emotions is relational devaluation. Analyzing people's descriptions of hurtful events, they found that those events typically involved "the perception that another individual does not regard his or her relationship with the person to be as important, close, or valuable as the person desires" (p. 1225). Vangelisti and her colleagues (e.g., Vangelisti, 2001; Vangelisti & Young, 2000) similarly examined individuals' accounts of hurtful events and found that hurt feelings typically are a result of a relational transgression. They noted that relational transgressions can elicit a range of negative emotions, but argued that those that evoke hurt are marked by a sense of vulnerability (Kelvin, 1977). Feeney (2005) adopted aspects of Leary et al.'s and Vangelisti's arguments to suggest that hurt feelings are evoked by relational transgressions and that those transgressions usually imply low relational evaluations. She also argued that the sense of personal injury typically associated with hurt feelings is a consequence of damage or threats to individuals' positive mental models of self and others. For Feeney, then, hurt involves a threat to people's attachments to others.

Chapter 6, written by Shaver, Mikulincer, Lavy, and Cassidy, may provide the most useful, elegant description to date of the distinguishing features of hurt. These researchers suggest that:

> A core feature of hurtful events is their capacity to destroy a person's sense of safety and security, which is related to, but not exactly the same as, the person's positive views of self and others... deeply hurt feelings are likely to occur only when a partner's actions or words pierce one's deep, visceral, generally unconscious sense of safety and security. (p. 99)

The description put forth by Shaver and his colleagues touches on several features of hurt feelings that have been discussed by other researchers. First, and most broadly, it suggests that the emotional pain people experience when they are hurt is an interpersonal phenomenon. People feel hurt because of something they perceive another individual said or did. Their feelings are elicited and defined by their interpersonal relationship with the person who hurt them. Second, hurt feelings are evoked in part as a consequence of a relational loss or the threat of a relational loss. This loss may take any one of several forms. It may involve a partner engaging in behavior that devalues the relationship, the willingness of a partner to violate relational norms, one partner's tendency to degrade the other's positive views of him- or herself, or the inability of one or both partners to create a safe, secure relational environment. The third feature underlined by Shaver et al.'s description is a sense of vulnerability. People feel hurt when they believe someone said or did something that caused them harm – "when a partner's actions or words pierce... [their] deep, visceral, generally unconscious sense of safety and security" (Shaver et al., p. 99). Individuals can only feel hurt if they are vulnerable to emotional pain. Further, once they have been hurt by a relational partner, they understand that they may be hurt again. Thus, hurt feelings are characterized both by a sense of current vulnerability and by a sense of impending vulnerability.

## FUNCTIONS OF HURT

Although researchers' views concerning the features that distinguish hurt from other emotions are beginning to converge, their perspectives on the functions of hurt feelings have yet to be clearly articulated. A review of extant literature as well as some of the more recent thinking reflected in the current volume suggests that hurt serves at least three functions. First, hurt feelings act as a relational indicator – they provide people with information about the quality of their association with the person who evoked their emotional pain. Hurt feelings emerge in part as a consequence of individuals' evaluations of their partner's attitudes toward them as well as their own attitudes toward their partner. When these assessments indicate that their partner does not value their relationship as much as they would like (Leary et al., 1998; MacDonald & Leary, 2005), when they yield threatening information about individuals' mental models of self or others (Feeney, 2005), or when they indicate that the relational context is unsafe (Shaver et al., Chapter 6, this volume), people feel hurt. Hurt, thus, serves an *informative* function.

A second function of hurt is *persuasive*. Hurt feelings may serve as a means of influence or behavioral control. Hurtful influence strategies can be relatively direct and obvious, or they may be more indirect and subtle. Direct strategies are those that involve explicit negative statements about individuals, their behavior, or their attitudes and that are employed with the intent to exert control. For example, when people describe events that hurt their feelings, they often report incidents involving accusations, evaluations, or criticisms (Feeney, 2004; Leary et al., 1998; Vangelisti, 1994). These sorts of communication behaviors can be used as techniques to influence others. By identifying a characteristic, behavior, or attitude as negative or undesirable, they suggest that it should be changed.

Whereas accusations, evaluations, and criticisms are relatively direct, obvious influence strategies, other techniques are more subtle. For instance, as previously suggested, people describing hurtful events often note that they were hurt by statements that are informative. In addition to conveying information, these statements – particularly those that involve active or passive relational devaluation (e.g., "I don't know how I feel about our relationship anymore," "I'm going to apply for jobs out of state") – can be used as strategies to indirectly influence others' behavior. The relational threats inherent in these sorts of statements can make them powerful tools. Such threats can imply that a change in some characteristic, behavior, or attitude is necessary to prevent a negative relational outcome. Partners who are invested in the relationship and who interpret these threats seriously may be willing to change their behavior to eliminate or at least minimize the threats.

A third function of hurt feelings is *supportive*. Although this function may not be as common or as easily recognizable as the other two, it is one that has emerged repeatedly in our research on hurt feelings. In particular, people describe times when an individual they trust – such as a coach, a parent, a teacher, or even a close friend – said something to them that was hurtful but was intended to be, and was interpreted as, supportive. For example, participants sometimes report interactions when a coach or teacher expressed disappointment in their performance (e.g., "That is the worst performance I've ever seen!" or "You should be doing better than that!") or when a friend or family member voiced disapproval of their behavior (e.g., "You're really stupid to start smoking!" or "Boy, you need to quit eating so much!"). Even though participants say they were hurt by these interactions, they also describe the interactions as functioning in supportive ways. They note that the other person's statement was well-intended, describe it as helpful, and often report that it showed how much the other person cared about them. In colloquial terms, these hurtful but supportive statements sometimes are interpreted by recipients as displays of "tough love."

It is important to note that the three functions described herein are not mutually exclusive. While it is certainly possible for hurt feelings to function in only one of these three ways, it is more likely that they serve multiple functions simultaneously. Thus, for example, a person who is hurt by a romantic partner's threat (e.g., "I can't stand your drinking anymore. I'm leaving if you don't stop.") might be simultaneously informed about the status of the relationship and persuaded to change his or her behavior. Similarly, someone who is hurt by a coach's harsh comments ("You're not trying at all – you're just lazy!") might be persuaded to work harder because he or she sees the coach as supportive.

Whether operating separately or together, the functions of hurt feelings illustrate the broad range of circumstances in which hurt is elicited as well as the potential impact of hurt on individuals and their interpersonal relationships. The functions suggest not only that hurt feelings are ubiquitous but also that they have impact. They can provide people with information about themselves and their relationships, they can persuade individuals to change their attitudes or behaviors, and they can convey caring and support.

## OVERVIEW: THE CURRENT VOLUME

The research and theory described in the current volume reflect the range of contexts and relationships that can be affected by hurt feelings. Because scholars who have studied hurt bring different theoretical and disciplinary assumptions to their work, the literature on hurt feelings is quite diverse.

### General Description

The purpose of this volume is to advance the study of hurt feelings by synthesizing current research and theory on hurt and offering new ideas about how hurt feelings operate. This book is the first to integrate the various perspectives addressed by researchers, theorists, and practitioners who study the causes of hurt feelings, the interpersonal events associated with hurt, and the ways people respond to hurting and being hurt by others.

In Part II, the following part of the book, various definitions of hurt are examined and both theoretical and methodological issues that influence current conceptions of hurt are described. Chapters explore the phenomenology of hurt feelings, appraisal processes and their associations with hurt, and the influence of politeness or "facework" on hurtful interactions. Individual differences and their role in the elicitation and experience of hurt also are examined. The theoretical and methodological concerns raised in Part II provide a foundation for examining hurt feelings – they set the baseline for the ways researchers observe, explain, and evaluate hurtful behavior and hurtful interactions.

Hurtful acts are described in the third part of the volume. Research conducted over the past decade indicates that a number of different acts or events are deemed by individuals as hurtful (e.g., Feeney, 2004; Leary et al., 1998; Vangelisti, 1994). Chapters in Part III elaborate on several of these acts or events and, in doing so, highlight the cognitive and behavioral processes associated with the way people experience and respond to hurt.

The fourth part focuses on the manifestation of hurt in various relational contexts. Hurt feelings do not occur in a vacuum. They are elicited within interpersonal relationships. The types of hurtful events that individuals are likely to experience and the meanings associated with those events vary from one relationship to another. Chapters in Part IV cover hurt as it occurs in children's peer relationships, family relationships, adult friendships, romantic relationships, and postdivorce relationships.

The fifth and final part of the book demonstrates that hurt feelings both influence and are influenced by social, cultural, physiological, and psychological variables. Chapters address issues associated with the experience of hurt in the workplace, cultural differences in the experience and expression of hurt, physical and psychological effects of hurt, and the influence of technology on the elicitation of hurt.

To provide consistency across the volume's different parts, contributors were provided with some general guidelines. More specifically, they were instructed to offer integrative reviews of existing theoretical and empirical literature, to comment on relevant approaches to studying hurt, and to critically evaluate methods used to assess hurt and its related constructs. They also were asked to delineate major conflicts in the literature and to discuss directions for future research.

## Authors

The authors who contributed to *Feeling Hurt in Close Relationships* are internationally known scholars from a variety of disciplines, including psychology, communication, family studies, and sociology. They approach the study of hurt from a number of different perspectives and focus on topics ranging from the influence of cognition on the experience of hurt to behaviors that elicit hurt feelings in the context of romantic relationships. They were selected as authors for this volume because they are recognized for the theoretical and empirical contributions they have made to the study of emotion and personal relationships.

## Audience

Because this book spotlights the recent work of first-rate scholars, many researchers and theorists who study emotion and personal relationships will want to read it. These individuals will be able to use the findings and the ideas that are presented in the volume to further their own work. Graduate students in psychology, communication, family studies, and sociology comprise another group who will want to read *Feeling Hurt in Close Relationships*. Advanced students who study emotions will need to know the material covered in the book. In addition, counselors and therapists who want to keep up with the literature on emotion and personal relationships will find the theory and research included in this volume relevant to their practices.

### ACKNOWLEDGMENTS

I am indebted to a number of people for the contributions they have made to this book. *Feeling Hurt in Close Relationships* was made possible by a superlative group of authors. The expertise and care they brought to the task of writing their chapters made my work a pleasure. I also am thankful for my editors,

Philip Laughlin, Eric Schwartz, and Simina Calin. Each of them patiently responded to my questions and provided me with the grounding that I needed to complete this project.

Studying hurt feelings has made me acutely aware of both the pain and the joy that accompany close relationships. I am especially grateful to the relational partners who bring far more joy to my life than I ever thought possible. I would like to thank John, who always makes sure that I have an extra hot latte available when I need one. I also would like to thank Abigail and Patrick, who remind me every day that studying close relationships isn't half as important as embracing them.

### REFERENCES

Feeney, J. A. (2004). Hurt feelings in couple relationships: Toward integrative models of the negative effects of hurtful events. *Journal of Social and Personal Relationships, 21*, 487–508.

Feeney, J. A. (2005). Hurt feelings in couple relationships: Exploring the role of attachment and perceptions of personal injury. *Personal Relationships, 12*, 253–271.

Fine, M. A., & Olson, K. (1997). Hurt and anger in response to provocation: Relations to aspects of adjustment. *Journal of Social Behavior and Personality, 12*, 325–344.

Folkes, V. S. (1982). Communicating the causes of social rejection. *Journal of Experimental Social Psychology, 18*, 235–252.

Kelvin, P. (1977). Predictability, power, and vulnerability in interpersonal attraction. In S. Duck (Ed.), *Theory and practice in interpersonal attraction* (pp. 355–378). New York: Academic Press.

L'Abate, L. (1977). Intimacy is sharing hurt feelings: A reply to David Mace. *Journal of Marriage and Family Counseling, 3*, 13–16.

Leary, M. R., & Springer, C. A. (2001). Hurt feelings: The neglected emotion. In R. M. Kowalski (Ed.), *Behaving badly: Aversive behaviors in interpersonal relationships* (pp. 151–175). Washington, DC: American Psychological Association.

Leary, M. R., Springer, C., Negel, L., Ansell, E., & Evans, K. (1998). The causes, phenomenology, and consequences of hurt feelings. *Journal of Personality and Social Psychology, 74*, 1225–1237.

MacDonald, G., & Leary, M. R. (2005). Why does social exclusion hurt? The relationship between social and physical pain. *Psychological Bulletin, 131*, 202–223.

McLaren, R. M., & Solomon, D. H. (2008). Appraisals and distancing responses to hurtful messages. *Communication Research, 35*, 339–357.

Miller, C. W., & Roloff, M. E. (2005). Gender and willingness to confront hurtful messages from romantic partners. *Communication Quarterly, 53*, 323–337.

Mills, R. S. L., Nazar, J., & Farrell, H. M. (2002). Child and parent perceptions of hurtful messages. *Journal of Social and Personal Relationships, 19*, 731–754.

Shaver, P., Schwartz, J., Kirson, D., & O'Connor, C. (1987). Emotion knowledge: Further exploration of a prototype approach. *Journal of Personality and Social Psychology, 52*, 1061–1086.

Vangelisti, A. L. (1994). Messages that hurt. In W. R. Cupach & B. H. Spitzberg (Eds.), *The dark side of interpersonal communication* (pp. 53–82). Hillsdale, NJ: Lawrence Erlbaum.

Vangelisti, A. L. (2001). Making sense of hurtful interactions in close relationships. In V. Manusov & J. H. Harvey (Eds.), *Attribution, communication behavior, and close relationships* (pp. 38–58). New York: Cambridge University Press.

Vangelisti, A. L., Maguire, K. C., Alexander, A. L., & Clark, G. (2007). Hurtful family environments: Links with individual, relationship, and perceptual variables. *Communication Monographs, 74*, 357–385.

Vangelisti, A. L., & Young, S. L. (2000). When words hurt: The effects of perceived intentionality on interpersonal relationships. *Journal of Social and Personal Relationships, 17*, 393–424.

Vangelisti, A. L., Young, S. L., Carpenter, K., & Alexander, A. L. (2005). Why does it hurt?: The perceived causes of hurt feelings. *Communication Research, 32*, 443–477.

Young, S. L. (2004). Factors that influence recipients' appraisals of hurtful communication. *Journal of Social and Personal Relationships, 21*, 291–303.

# PART II

# CONCEPTUALIZING HURT

2

# The Nature of Hurt Feelings: Emotional Experience and Cognitive Appraisals

MARK R. LEARY AND SADIE LEDER

A prevailing question in the study of emotion has involved the number and identity of human emotions. Theorists have sliced the emotional pie in a variety of ways, but most fall into one of two camps. Advocates of categorical approaches have identified a relatively small number of "basic" emotions – such as anger, fear, joy, sadness, disgust, and surprise – that cannot be reduced to other, more fundamental states (e.g., Ekman, 1992; Izard, 1991; Plutchik, 1980; Tomkins, 1962). These theorists suggest that all emotional experiences can be defined as mixes, blends, or hybrids of these basic emotions.

In contrast, proponents of dimensional models have argued that emotions are not divisible into discrete units. Rather, they suggest that much of the variance in emotional experience can be captured by a small number of primary dimensions. Some theorists endorse two-dimensional models characterized by the valence of the emotion (pleasant vs. unpleasant) and the degree of arousal or activation involved (aroused vs. tranquil; see Larsen & Diener, 1992; Russell, 1980; Watson & Tellegen, 1985). Others suggest that the data are better explained by a three-dimensional model defined by dimensions of valence, potency, and activity (Shaver, Schwartz, Kirson, & O'Conner, 1987).

For our purposes, the important point is that none of the common ways of parsing emotions includes mention of the experience that people colloquially call hurt feelings. Despite the importance and prevalence of hurt, none of the theorists advocating the existence of primary emotions has either suggested that hurt is a basic emotion or has identified the blend of emotions that produces the feeling of being hurt. Moreover, none of the dimensional models has located hurt feelings along the valence and arousal dimensions. Nor have theorists devoted much attention to the cognitive appraisals that may characterize hurt feelings, despite mapping out appraisals for many other emotions (see Scherer, Schorr, & Johnstone, 2001).

Our goal in this chapter is to address two fundamental issues regarding hurt feelings. The first involves the best way to conceptualize the emotional experience of hurt. Is hurt best regarded as a distinct emotion, as a blend of other emotions, or as something else? The second issue involves the cognitive underpinnings of hurt feelings – the appraisals that lead people to feel hurt. As we show, these two questions have received virtually no research attention. Therefore, we present new and currently unpublished data that bear on these issues.

## WHAT KIND OF AN EMOTION IS HURT?

Although hurt feelings have received little attention in their own right, two studies involving how people structure and think about emotions provide insight into the nature of "hurt." In a hierarchical cluster analysis of 135 emotion names, Shaver et al. (1987) found that the item *hurt* fell within a subcategory of the sadness cluster, being closely associated with items such as *agony, suffering,* and *anguish*. In a more comprehensive study of 525 emotion terms, Storm and Storm (1987) found that the item *hurt* grouped with the items *betrayal, neglected, rejected, unwanted, let down, unwelcome, misunderstood, reproachful, self-pity, different,* and *isolated* as a subcategory of emotions that were associated with sadness, shame, and pain.

Leary, Springer, Negel, Ansell, and Evans (1998) shed further light on the nature of hurt by explicitly examining the emotional concomitants of hurt feelings. In their study, participants described an event in which their feelings had been hurt and then rated the experience using 18 emotion adjectives. Not surprisingly, participants' ratings of how hurt they felt correlated highly with feelings of general distress (e.g., upset, distressed) and moderately with anxiety and positive affect (in a negative direction). Regression analyses suggested that the experience of hurt is characterized primarily by undifferentiated negative affect – both the core negative affect shared among distinct emotions such as anxiety, hostility, and guilt and general but discernible negative feelings such as those associated with feeling "upset." Unfortunately, it was unclear whether the 18 emotion items used in this study adequately covered the emotional territory in which hurt dwells.

We report here for the first time two additional studies that were designed to compare three conceptual models of hurt – the blended emotion, common negative affect, and distinct emotion models. The *blended emotion model* suggests that hurt feelings arise from the combined experience of other discrete emotions such as anxiety, sadness, and anger. According to this model, people feel hurt when they experience certain other negative emotions simultaneously, perhaps in some particular proportion. For example, Vangelisti (2001; Vangelisti & Young, 2000) suggested that hurt is a blend of sadness and fear. The blended emotion model would be supported by evidence that all of the reliable variance in hurt feelings could be accounted for by measures of other emotions.

In contrast, the *common negative affect model* proposes that hurt feelings reflect the common core of negative affect that is shared by all negative emotions

(Barrett, Mesquita, Ochsner, & Gross, 2007). Rather than being related to any specific emotion, this model holds that hurt feelings involve the undifferentiated negative affect that accompanies all negative emotional states. This model would be supported if hurt feelings were accounted for by the common variance shared among other negative emotions rather than by the unique variance contributed by each. The results of Leary et al. (1998) were partly consistent with the common negative affect model, but as noted, these findings were based on only a small number of emotion items.

Finally, the *distinct emotion model* regards hurt as a distinct emotional experience. Although hurt feelings are sometimes accompanied by other emotions, this model predicts that some aspect of the experience of being hurt is unique and, thus, cannot be accounted for by either the specific or the shared variance associated with other emotions. The distinct emotion model would be supported if one measure of hurt feelings could account for residual variance in another measure of hurt feelings after removing both shared and unique variance attributable to other emotions. Anecdotally, people's personal experiences appear to support this model, as being "hurt" typically feels quite different from other emotions such as sadness and anger (Leary et al., 1998).

## Retrospective Reports of Hurt Feelings

In our first study to compare these models, 120 university students wrote a brief account of a time when someone hurt their feelings and then rated how hurt they had been by the incident on a 12-point scale. Participants also completed items from the four basic negative emotion subscales of the Positive and Negative Affect Schedule (PANAS-X; Watson & Clark, 1994): fear (*afraid, scared, frightened, nervous, jittery, shaky*), hostility (*angry, hostile, irritable, scornful, disgusted, loathing*), guilt (*guilty, ashamed, blameworthy, angry at self, disgusted with self, dissatisfied with self*), and sadness (*sad, blue, downhearted, alone, lonely*), as well as the items *upset, distressed,* and *sluggish*. In addition, the items *hurt, injured,* and *wounded* were added specifically to measure the experience of hurt.[1]

Overall, the average incident was rated as very hurtful ($M = 10.1$ on a 12-point scale), suggesting that we were dealing with relatively hurtful events. Multiple regression analyses were used to partition the variance in ratings of hurt feelings into three components that reflected variance due to other discrete

---

[1] In trying to develop measures of hurt feelings, we have been struck by the absence of English synonyms for feeling psychologically hurt. Most negative emotions have many synonyms (for example, anxiety is reflected by terms such as afraid, scared, frightened, anxious, nervous, tense, and fearful), but even the closest synonyms for hurt feelings (such as injured and wounded) do not connote precisely the same experience. Similarly, the words that cluster with hurt in analyses of emotion labels do not seem to capture the subjective experience of hurt per se (e.g., rejected, isolated, let down, misunderstood; see Storm & Storm, 1987).

negative emotions as measured by the PANAS-X, undifferentiated negative affect (i.e., variance shared by other negative emotions), and feelings unique to being hurt (see Watson & Clark, 1992, for a similar strategy). Results revealed that the 26 ratings from the PANAS-X accounted for 63% of the variance in hurt feelings (as measured by the 12-point rating). Then, when the three items specifically measuring hurt (hurt, injured, and wounded) were entered into the regression analysis, they accounted for an additional 16% of the variance in hurt feelings. This pattern suggests that the experience of feeling hurt involves a unique subjective quality that goes beyond the rather comprehensive list of 26 feelings assessed by the PANAS-X. Thus, these results are consistent with the notion that hurt is a distinct emotional experience, albeit one that also shares features with other negative emotions.

To more thoroughly understand the emotional characteristics of hurt, we partitioned the variance in hurt feelings to distinguish the unique and shared contributions of each of the specific emotion ratings. Approximately 55% of the variance in the 12-point measure of hurt involved negative affect that was shared with other specific ratings. Importantly, when all of the ratings were entered simultaneously into a regression analysis to predict the 12-point rating of hurt feeings, only four other emotion ratings contributed unique variance to the prediction of hurt – *sad, shaky, sluggish,* and *hurt* – with hurt contributing the most unique variance.

The results of this study are consistent with the notion that hurt is a distinct emotional experience. Although self-reported hurt feelings correlated with other varieties of negative emotion, such as sadness, an alternative measure of hurt accounted for residual variance in the 12-point measure of hurt feelings after other emotions were partialed out. Thus, some aspect of feeling hurt is unique.

However, this study was limited by its use of participants' retrospective ratings of how they felt as the result of a previous hurtful event. Not only are such ratings subject to memory distortions and other biases, but people's recollections of past emotional events may be influenced by emotional prototypes or schemas (Niedenthal & Halberstadt, 2001; Shaver et al., 1987). To address the concerns associated with retrospective ratings, a second study used an experimental paradigm to assess participants' feelings in response to an actual hurtful event.

## Contemporaneuous Reports of Hurt Feelings

This study extended the previous research in several ways; it used alternative and more comprehensive measures of negative emotion, including hurt, and employed an experimental induction of hurt feelings. The procedure employed to induce hurt was analogous to how children often select teams on the playground by having two team captains alternate in choosing members for their teams. We assumed that individuals who are selected last by this procedure perceive that they are being included as team members only reluctantly and begrudgingly and would experience mild hurt feelings.

Undergraduate participants were studied in groups of 10 to 12 that also included a male and a female confederate. Participants were told that two of them would be randomly selected to serve as team captains who would then choose teams to work on an unspecified laboratory task. On the basis of a rigged drawing, the confederates were designated as the team captains. Each participant then met individually with the captains for a brief getting-acquainted conversation and received an identifying letter of the alphabet. Following this, the captains ostensibly chose their respective teams and gave their selections to the researcher.

The researcher explained that she would announce the members of each team by their identifying letters in the order in which the team captains had selected them. She then announced the first-chosen participants for each team, followed by the captains' second choices, third choices, and so on, until the last-chosen members were announced. Half of the participants were led to believe that they were picked first by one of the team captains, and the other half were told that they were picked last by one of the captains. (Because several participants in each session had received the same identifying letter, it was possible to have half of the participants in each session believe that they were picked first and half believe they were picked last.)

To obtain broad, comprehensive measures of emotions, we used both the Multiple Affect Adjective Check List-Revised (MAACL-R; Zuckerman & Lubin, 1985; Zuckerman, Lubin, & Rinck, 1983) and the full version of the PANAS-X (Watson & Clark, 1994). The MAACL-R consists of 25 emotion terms and provides subscale scores for anxiety, hostility, depression, and positive affect (Hunsley, 1990). Four ad hoc items were mixed among the MAACL-R items to measure hurt feelings: *hurt, not hurt, devastated,* and *traumatized*. The PANAS-X consists of 60 items that assess affect using a 5-point scale, providing higher order scales for positive and negative affect as well as lower order scales that assess specific emotions (e.g., fear, sadness, hostility). Additionally, five items were mixed among those on the PANAS-X to assess hurt feelings: *hurt, not hurt, emotionally injured, wounded,* and *psychologically pained*. To make the response format for the MAACL-R items different from that of the PANAS-X, participants checked one of seven responses beside each emotion to indicate how they felt.

To facilitate description of the results, we identify subscales with the suffix *-P* if they were derived from the PANAS-X and by *-M* if they were based on items on the MAACL-R. (For example, *Fear-P* is the Fear subscale from the PANAS-X, whereas *Hurt-M* is the ad hoc Hurt subscale included with the MAACL-R). Two-step multiple regression analyses were conducted in which the emotion scales were entered as predictors of one of the measures of hurt

TABLE 2.1. *Shared and unique variance in hurt feelings: Separate PANAS and MAACL analyses*

| Analysis 1: Predicting Hurt-P (Hurt items mixed with the PANAS items) | | | |
|---|---|---|---|
| Step | Variables entered | $R^2$ | $R^2$ change |
| 1 | All PANAS-X and MAACL-R subscales | .75 | .75** |
| 2 | Hurt-M | .86 | .10** |
| Analysis 2: Predicting Hurt-M (Hurt items mixed with the MAACL items) | | | |
| Step | Variables entered | $R^2$ | $R^2$ change |
| 1 | All PANAS-X and MAACL-R subscales | .86 | .86** |
| 2 | Hurt-P | .91 | .06** |

*Note:* In Step 1 all emotion subscales were included – Fear-P, Sadness-P, Hostility-P, and Guilt-P (the basic negative emotion scales on the PANAS-X) and Anxiety-M, Depression-M, and Hostile-M (the negative affect subscales on the MAACL-R). Hurt-P is the sum of the hurt feelings items embedded on the PANAS-X; Hurt-M is the sum of the hurt feelings items included on the MAACL-R.

(either *Hurt-P* or *Hurt-M*) on Step 1 and the alternative measure of hurt was entered on Step 2. In this way, we could see whether one measure of hurt could account for residual variance in another measure of hurt after we removed variance due to a wide array of negative emotions. If so, we would have additional evidence that the experience of feeling hurt differs qualitatively from other aversive emotions.

In the analyses of *Hurt-P* (see the upper portion of Table 2.1), the PANAS-X and MAACL-R subscales accounted for 75% of the variance in *Hurt-P*, and *Hurt-M* contributed an additional 10% of the variance when it was entered in Step 2. In the analysis predicting *Hurt-M* (shown in the lower portion of Table 2.1), the PANAS-X and MAACL-R subscales accounted for 86% of the variance in *Hurt-M* on Step 1, and *Hurt-P* accounted for another 6% on Step 2. Thus, 10% of the variance in *Hurt-P* and 6% of the variance in *Hurt-M* were due to unique variance in hurt feelings that was not explained by the other negative emotions.[2] These results further support the distinct emotion model by showing that other negative emotions cannot account for all of the experience of feeling hurt. As in the retrospective study of hurt feelings discussed earlier, participants' ratings of hurt could not be explained by other negative emotions.

---

[2] The PANAS-X items, *upset* and *distressed*, do not fall on any of the four subscales. Thus, we conducted two additional analyses in which these two items were also entered on Step 1 in the prediction of *Hurt-P* and *Hurt-M*. Although these items contributed to the prediction of both *Hurt-P* and *Hurt-M* (3% and 2% of the variance, respectively), the alternative measure of hurt continued to account for a significant portion of unique variance.

Given the findings of the first study, we also examined the degree to which hurt feelings included unique and shared contributions of other negative emotions in addition to *hurt* per se. The subscales *Sadness-P, Hostility-P,* and *Guilt-P* each made significant unique contributions to scores on *Hurt-P,* but taken together, these emotions contributed only 3% unique variance to hurt feelings. However, the common variance shared by these emotions – their common core of negative affect – accounted for 67% of the variance in hurt feelings. Then, after the unique and shared variance contributed by the four emotions were accounted for, *Hurt-M* accounted for an additional 13% of the variance in *Hurt-P.*

The pattern for the prediction of *Hurt-M* was similar. *Hostility-M* and *Depression-M* made significant unique contributions to the variance in *Hurt-M*. These emotions contributed approximately 10% unique variance to *Hurt-M* (due mostly to *Depression-M*), and the common variance shared by the three added an additional 72%. As before, *Hurt-P* still accounted for an additional, unique portion of the variance (8%) in *Hurt-M*.

## Summary

Taken together, these two studies show that the reliable variance in self-reported hurt feelings is attributable to (a) undifferentiated negative affect that is common to all negative emotions, (b) small contributions of specific discrete emotions, such as sadness and guilt, and, importantly, (c) the unique experience of feeling hurt. It appears that all negative emotions, including hurt feelings, share a common core of negative affect that contributes to the unpleasantness of the experience ("core affect"; Barrett et al., 2007). Presumably, this undifferentiated negative affect is also partly responsible for the correlations that are typically obtained between different negative emotions. Our data suggest that a substantial portion of the variance in hurt feelings reflects this general and nonspecific negative affect.

The proportion of nonspecific emotional variance may be larger with hurt feelings than with other negative emotions. For example, Watson and Clark (1992) found that nonspecific variance among emotions such as fear, hostility, sadness, and guilt tended to be between 20% and 30%. One explanation for the large role that core negative affect plays in hurt compared to other emotions is that hurt feelings hurt in a more diffuse way than many other negative emotions, possibly because hurt shares some of the neural pathways that are associated with the negative affect that accompanies physical pain (Eisenberger, Lieberman, & Williams, 2003; MacDonald & Leary, 2005).

Specific discrete emotions, such as sadness and guilt, contributed relatively little variance to hurt feelings (between 5% and 12% depending on the subscale). What remains unclear is whether the experience of hurt feelings involves subjective features that inherently resemble other emotions or whether the interpersonal events that cause hurt feelings may tend to trigger other discrete emotions as well. These two studies offer little to address this question, and we return to this issue later in the chapter.

Most noteworthy is the fact that, after both specific and nonspecific variance associated with other discrete negative emotions were accounted for, a portion of reliable variance remained that appeared to be unique to the experience of hurt. Although the amount of unique variance was small (ranging from 6% to 13%), its magnitude is comparable to the emotion-specific variance obtained for other negative emotions such as fear, hostility, sadness, and guilt (Watson & Clark, 1992). Our data suggest that there are reasons to consider hurt as a discrete emotional experience that cannot be reduced entirely to one or more other emotions or to blends of other emotions. Although hurt feelings share variance with other negative emotions, feeling hurt includes a distinct subjective quality that is unique to being hurt.

Of course, the possibility exists that the PANAS-X and MAACL-R are not sufficiently comprehensive and, thus, did not measure all negative emotional states that might account for the residual variance in hurt feelings. Although this is possible, the negative emotion items on the PANAS-X and MAACL-R, when taken together, capture a tremendous amount of variance in emotional experience. Specifically, the MAACL-R provides subscale scores for anxiety, hostility, depression, and positive affect, and the PANAS-X consists of 60 items that assess both higher order scales for positive and negative affect as well as lower order scales of specific emotions like fear, sadness, and hostility. In fact, the scales tap into a broader array of affective experiences than their labels suggest. For example, the sadness subscale on the PANAS-X includes items that assess not only sadness (e.g., sad, downhearted) but also loneliness (e.g., lonely, alone), and the hostility subscale includes items such as disgusted and scornful. Given the size and breadth of the item pools used in these studies, we doubt that partialing out additional self-reported emotions would eliminate the unique contribution of hurt.

Further support for the distinct emotion model can be found in research on hurt feelings within the context of romantic relationships. Both retrospective accounts in which participants describe hurtful events perpetrated by a romantic partner and a word-sorting task based on the hurtful emotional accounts provide evidence that, although hurt may share a common negative core and be elicited along with other negative emotions, it is indeed a distinct emotional experience (Feeney, 2005).

## Is Hurt a Basic Emotion?

Although hurt feelings can be distinguished phenomenologically from other emotions, the question remains whether hurt should be regarded as a fundamental or basic emotion. Emotion theorists have discussed various criteria by which to judge whether a particular emotion should be regarded as fundamental and indeed whether the concept of a basic emotion is tenable (Frijda, 1986; Izard, 1991; Ortony & Turner, 1990). The two studies described earlier, along with work conducted on hurt feelings in close relationships, show that hurt clearly meets one of the common criteria – that fundamental emotions possess a distinct and specific feeling (Izard, 1991).

Other criteria that have been suggested for basic emotions are more equivocal. For example, at present we do not have evidence regarding whether the experience of hurt feelings has a distinct and specific neural substrate or is associated with distinct and specific facial expressions or other movements (see, however, Eisenberger et al., 2003; MacDonald & Leary, 2005). It seems likely that an emotion that is subjectively distinct has a distinct neural substrate, and collective experience suggests that people often "look hurt." However, empirical investigations of these questions remain to be conducted. It seems more obvious that hurt feelings organize and motivate behavior (another often-cited criterion for concluding that an emotion is fundamental), but the specific action tendencies that are associated with feeling hurt require further investigation as well. One possible action tendency associated with feeling hurt is relational distancing (Vangelisti & Young, 2000; Vangelisti, Young, Carpenter-Theune, & Alexander, 2005). Because hurt involves feeling vulnerable to emotional harm, it is associated with a tendency to disengage from the context in which the hurt was elicited. Related research on rejection shows that people do indeed distance themselves from others if they feel that rejection and hence hurt feelings are likely (Bourgeois & Leary, 2001; Feeney, Noller, & Roberts, 2001; Murray, Holmes, MacDonald, & Ellsworth, 1998; Vangelisti, 2001). Thus, current evidence suggests that hurt may qualify as a basic emotion, but future research is clearly needed.

## WHAT IS THE FUNDAMENTAL CAUSE OF HURT FEELINGS?

The second question that we address here involves the immediate cause of hurt feelings. According to appraisal theories, specific emotions are accompanied by cognitive evaluations or appraisals of situations and events. Although differing in details, these theories assume that each emotion is elicited by a distinct pattern of appraisals and that the same pattern of appraisals will elicit the same emotion in all situations (e.g., Frijda, 1986; Lazarus, 1991; Ortony, Clore, & Collins, 1988; Smith & Ellsworth, 1985). For example, appraisals involving threat may induce fear, whereas appraisals involving an unrecoverable loss induce sadness. What, then, is the specific appraisal that is associated with the experience that people call hurt feelings?

### The Relational Evaluation Hypothesis

Elsewhere, we have suggested that hurt feelings arise when a person perceives that one or more other people do not value their relationship with him or her to the degree that the person desires. Thus, hurt is related to the discrepancy between how much people want others to value their relationship and the degree to which they believe the relationship is actually valued (Leary & Springer, 2001; Leary et al., 1998). Importantly, a discrepancy between desired and perceived relational value is associated with the sense that one is not valued, liked, or accepted regardless of the actual level of perceived relational value. Thus, even when people know that a friend or romantic partner values them greatly, they will nonetheless experience a sense of low relational value – and feel hurt – when they perceive that the other person does not value their relationship as much as they desire. Hurt is particularly strong when people experience relational *devaluation* – the perception that one's relational value in another's eyes has declined relative to some earlier time – because the sense of being insufficiently valued is more salient. In brief, framed in terms of appraisal theory, we could say that hurt feelings occur from appraisals of low relational evaluation that arise from a perceived discrepancy between one's desired and perceived relational value.

The relational evaluation hypothesis suggests that hurt feelings should be highly related to the *discrepancy* between how much people wish a particular person to value their relationship and the degree to which they believe the relationship is actually valued. To test this hypothesis, 60 male and 60 female undergraduate participants were asked to think of people in their lives who represented each of 10 relationships – a good same-sex friend, same-sex best friend, teacher they like, person to whom they are secretly attracted, current or former roommate, friend of the other sex, sales clerk in a store, student they do not know well, parents, and a person they formerly dated. After thinking of each person, participants reported their desired relational value (e.g., how much they wanted that particular person to value their relationship with them).

Then, for each of the 10 target individuals, respondents read about a potentially hurtful situation. For example, one scenario asked participants to imagine that their parents canceled a planned visit for a trivial reason:

> Imagine that your parents promised to come to visit you for a weekend, and you are really looking forward to their visit. However, a few days beforehand, they call to say that they are not coming because they are going to a neighborhood barbeque that weekend.

Other scenarios involved a former romantic partner going out of his or her way to avoid interacting with the participant, a best friend telling other people embarrassing stories about the participant, and a romantic partner breaking up with the participant to date someone else (see Table 2.2 for a list of the 10 scenarios). Participants were asked to imagine each situation as vividly as possible and then to answer two questions: "How much would this person's

TABLE 2.2. *Correlations between hurt feelings and the discrepancy between desired and perceived relational evaluation*

| Zero-order | Zero-order correlation | Semipartial correlation[a] |
|---|---|---|
| Parents cancel visit | .62 | .58 |
| Best friend tells embarrassing stories | .54 | .42 |
| Romantic partner breaks up with you | .41 | .15 |
| Friend of other sex never calls or writes | .47 | .35 |
| Good friend cancels plans with you | .61 | .51 |
| Person to whom you are secretly attracted ignores you | .41 | .33 |
| Favorite teacher is not interested in talking to you | .45 | .46 |
| Former dating partner goes out of way to avoid you | .67 | .71 |
| Sales clerk in expensive store ignores you | .25 | .34 |
| Student acquaintance fails to say "hi" | .56 | .56 |

[a] This is the correlation between hurt feelings and the discrepancy between desired and perceived relational evaluation with ratings of desired relational evaluation partialed out.

behavior hurt your feelings?" and "If this happened, how much would you feel that this person valued his or her relationship with you?" (perceived relational value).

As noted, hurt feelings should be related to the discrepancy between how much people wish a particular person to value their relationship and the degree to which they believe the person actually values the relationship. Thus, each measure of perceived relational value was subtracted from its respective measure of desired relational value. As seen in Table 2.2, a moderate to strong correlation was obtained between this discrepancy and hurt feelings for all 10 hurtful scenarios. The greater the discrepancy between desired and perceived relational evaluation, the more hurt participants indicated they would feel.

Because the magnitude of the discrepancy was correlated with ratings of desired relational value (e.g., higher ratings of desired relational value inherently allowed greater discrepancies), desired relational value was partialed out of the relationship between the discrepancy scores and hurt feelings. As shown by the semipartial correlations in the last column of Table 2.2, the discrepancy between desired and perceived relational evaluation significantly predicted hurt feelings in all 10 situations even with the influence of desired relational value partialed out. This finding is important because it shows that hurt feelings are associated specifically with the difference between how much a person desires another individual to value their relationship and perceptions of the degree to which the other individual actually values it. Thus, hurt feelings are not the result of another person placing a low value on their relationship but rather the result of wanting others to value the relationship more than seemed to be the case.

### Additional Support for the Relational Evaluation Hypothesis

Several other pieces of indirect evidence also support the notion that appraisals of low relational evaluation underlie hurt feelings. First, the major categories of events that cause hurt feelings involve things that connote that other people do not value their relationship with the person as much as he or she would like. In a study of retrospective accounts of hurtful experiences, Leary et al. (1998) identified six primary categories of hurtful events – active disassociation (explicit rejection), passive disassociation (being ignored or avoided), criticism, betrayal, teasing, and feeling unappreciated or taken for granted – all of which connote low relational evaluation. Similarly, investigations of hurt within the context of romantic relationships have provided support for the link between low relational evaluation and hurt feelings (Feeney, 2004, 2005). Based on participants' accounts of instances when a partner had hurt their feelings, Feeney (2004) adapted Leary et al.'s (1998) typology to reveal five categories of hurtful events in romantic relationships: active disassociation, passive disassociation, criticism, infidelity, and deception (misleading acts, such as lying and breaking promises). Again, each of these categories of events connotes that another individual does not adequately value the person's relationship.

An analysis of perceived causes for feeling hurt by Vangelisti et al. (2005) also revealed low relational evaluation as a pervasive theme. Although respondents did not always explicitly mention "rejection" or "low relational evaluation" in their explanations, virtually all of the 14 categories of causes of hurt feelings revealed in the study involved actions that convey low relational evaluation. Some of the categories identified by Vangelisti et al. (such as rejection, behavioral criticism, betrayal, relational depreciation, indifference, personal attack, and humiliation) clearly connote that another person does not value his or her relationship with the target. For other categories, low relational evaluation may be less explicit but is nonetheless present. For example, being the target of inappropriate or spiteful humor, having someone shatter one's hopes, being told hurtful truths about oneself, suffering moral affronts or insults, being subjected to inappropriate communication, or having one's self-concept undermined all would reasonably raise questions regarding how much one was relationally valued by the perpetrator of such actions.

Likewise, experimental studies that lead participants to believe that others do not wish to interact with or get to know them – that is, manipulations that induce low relational evaluation – reliably elicit hurt feelings. For example, participants have been excluded from a ball-tossing game (Eisenberger et al., 2003), told that they were selected first versus last for a laboratory team (Bourgeois & Leary, 2001), led to believe that another participant was not interested in what they had to say (Snapp & Leary, 2001), and given feedback that others did not want to work with them (Buckley, Winkel, & Leary, 2003). In all instances, the experimental manipulation, which presumably induced a perception of low relational evaluation, led participants to report feeling hurt.

Mills, Nazar, and Farrell (2002) looked at hurt feelings within the context of parent–child relationships. In their study, children were asked to recall a time when their mother or father did something that hurt their feelings, whereas mothers were asked to describe a time when their child had hurt their feelings. Consistent with previous research (Feeney, 2005; Leary et al., 1998), many of the events that children and mothers considered hurtful involved low relational evaluation, specifically being disparaged or disregarded. Thus, not only are low relational evaluation and hurt feelings an important aspect of adult relationships involving friends, romantic partners, acquaintances, supervisors, and strangers, but they are seen in parent–child relationships as well.

## DISTINGUISHING HURT FEELINGS FROM OTHER EMOTIONS

As we have seen, several avenues of research conducted by multiple investigators converge on the idea that hurt results from perceptions of low relational evaluation. Yet, as noted, hurt is often accompanied by other negative emotions such as sadness or anger, raising the question of whether perceived low relational evaluation can elicit other emotions as well. Although it is tempting to conclude that low perceived relational evaluation can lead to a number of emotions, we believe that only hurt results from appraisals of low relational evaluation per se and that other emotions that often accompany hurt arise from other features of the social context.

Situations in which people feel that others do not value their relationships as much as desired are often complex, involving many possible outcomes for the individual in addition to low relational evaluation or rejection. We suggest that these other features of such situations are responsible for the other emotions that people who are hurt sometimes feel. For example, if an interpersonal rejection involves the loss of an existing or potential relationship, the person may feel not only hurt but also sad because sadness involves appraisals of irrevocable loss (Lazarus, 1991). Similarly, if an event that connotes low relational evaluation also frustrates the person's efforts to obtain other outcomes, particularly in an unjustified manner, the person might feel both hurt and angry. Furthermore, an incident in which a rejection puts the person in danger of harm (for example, when a romantic rejection leaves one without adequate financial support) might elicit both hurt and anxiety (Leary & Springer, 2001). Although it might appear that the person is hurt, sad, angry, or afraid because he or she was devalued or rejected, only the feelings of hurt are due to perceived low relational value per se.

To examine the links between appraisals and rejection-related emotions, 120 university students were asked to write a brief description of a time when someone hurt their feelings. After describing the event and why they thought it occurred, participants rated the degree to which they had wanted the rejecting individual to regard their relationship as valuable or important (desired relational evaluation) and how valuable or important they thought the other person regarded their relationship after the hurtful event (perceived relational evaluation). They also rated how they had felt on items from the Positive and Negative Affect Schedule-Expanded Form (PANAS-X; Watson & Clark, 1994) as well as on ad hoc items that measured hurt feelings.

As in the study described earlier, the difference between desired and perceived relational value correlated with emotion scales from the PANAS-X, specifically with hurt, anger, sadness, anxiety, guilt, and general distress. (These correlations were virtually unchanged when desired relational value was partialed out.) Furthermore, only hurt was uniquely related to the discrepancy between desired and perceived relational value, supporting the hypothesis that low relational evaluation is the source of hurt but not other negative emotions.

Two raters independently coded participants' narratives of the hurtful episodes with respect to appraisal dimensions hypothesized to underlie fear, sadness, hostility, guilt, and hurt feelings (see Ellsworth & Smith, 1988; Leary, Koch, & Hechenbleikner, 2001; Smith, 1991; Smith & Ellsworth, 1985). For each essay, raters noted whether the situation described by the participant involved (a) any threat of physical, social, occupational, or financial harm (appraisals associated wth fear); (b) a partial or total loss of a relationship they previously had (sadness); (c) a potential barrier or obstacle to the satisfaction of their goals or desires (anger); (d) a situation in which the participant violated an important moral, ethical, or normative standard (guilt); and (e) a situation in which other people did not value their relationship with him or her as much as the participant desired or as much as they did previously (hurt).

These appraisal ratings were regressed simultaneously on the participants' ratings of fear, sadness, hostility, guilt, hurt feelings, and general distress. As predicted by appraisal theories of emotion, the threat of harm was related to ratings of anxiety, barriers to goal satisfaction were related to anger, and violations of standards were related to guilt. Most importantly, ratings of hurt were uniquely related to appraisals involving the belief that others did not value their relationship with the individual as much as desired.

## Factors Predicting Hurt vs. Anger

As noted, hurt and anger may co-occur when an event that connotes low relational evaluation also frustrates the individual or leads people to perceive that they have been treated unfairly. In a further effort to understand differences between hurt and anger, we conducted a study of 119 participants who were in romantic relationships. Each participant rated how hurt and how angry they would feel if their partner engaged in 30 possible relational transgressions that ranged from relatively trivial misdeeds (e.g., your partner makes a joke at your expense) to serious relationship threats (e.g., your partner cheats on you). Consistent with both Leary et al. (1998) and Feeney (2004, 2005), factor analyses of the ratings of hurt revealed five factors that connoted low relational evaluation: active disassociation (e.g., partner tells you that he is not sure if he loves you), passive disassociation (e.g., partner gives you the "silent treatment"), criticism (e.g., partner makes a joke at your expense), betrayal (e.g., partner lies to you), and feeling unappreciated (e.g., partner doesn't say "thank you" when you do something nice).

Importantly, different features of participants' relationships moderated the degree to which they indicated that they would feel hurt versus angry by these partner transgressions. For example, participants who were most in love with their partners reported that they would feel more hurt after active disassociation and betrayal than participants who reported less love for their partners, but love did not moderate reactions to other kinds of hurtful misdeeds. For anger, participants who reported less love for their partners were most angered by transgressions that connoted low relational priority. In addition, relationship satisfaction moderated the experience of hurt but not anger. Participants who were more satisfied with their relationships reported that they would feel more hurt after active dissociation (i.e., explicit rejection) compared to those who were less satisfied with their relationships.[3]

The fact that relationship variables differently moderate hurt and anger provides additional evidence for the distinct nature of hurt feelings. Event that convey that one has low relational value may elicit several emotions depending on the particular features of the precipitating event, the nature of one's relationship with the people involved, and the kinds of threats that the events entail. Hurt appears to be the most basic response to feeling that one is not valued to the degree that one desires, and whether people also experience anger, sadness, anxiety, guilt, or other emotions depends on other features of the situation.

## CONCLUSIONS

Our review of the literature, supported by the new findings reported here, converge to suggest that hurt is an important and impactful emotional experience that is distinct from other negative emotions. In our view, the relational evaluation hypothesis provides a viable and parsimonious explanation of the events that cause people to feel hurt, although it remains to be seen whether instances of hurt feelings can be found that do not involve a discrepancy between desired and perceived relational evaluation.

---

[3] Overall, women reported feeling more hurt than men by all six categories of hurtful events. Women also reported feeling greater anger than men after a transgression that connoted lack of appreciation. However, male participants reported greater anger than women after active disassociation and disparagement.

As we have seen, studies consistently find that hurt is typically accompanied by one or more other emotions, particularly sadness and anger. Although we believe that these other emotions are linked to different appraisals from those involved in hurt, the fact that rejection episodes often evoke multiple emotions raises the question of whether hurt ever occurs by itself without other accompanying emotions and, if so, what it feels like when it does. We have the sense that the subjective experience of hurt feelings is more diffuse and less phenomenologically distinct than other common emotions, possibly because hurt involves a larger component of core negative affect than other negative emotions. If, as MacDonald and Leary (2005) proposed, hurt feelings involves the same neural circuitry as that involved in "pain affect" – the emotional distress that accompanies physical pain – hurt may feel broadly painful and unpleasant without the distinctive emotional signature that characterizes many other emotional states. More research is needed on the experience of hurt feelings and how it resembles and differs from other emotions.

Another question raised by this chapter is whether the discrepancy between desired and perceived relational evaluation predicts hurt feelings equally across all levels of desired and perceived relational evaluation. When people perceive that their relationship is insufficiently valued, do their reactions differ as a function of the degree to which they desire it to be valued and how valued they believe it to be? As noted earlier, people may perceive their relational value to be lower than desired (and, thus, feel hurt) even when they know that others value their relationship at some nonzero level. Will people in such a situation feel more or less hurt than those who detect an identical discrepancy between desired and perceived relational evaluation but do not feel valued at all? If we imagine a graph with desired relational value on the x-axis and perceived relational value on the y-axis, what does the curve look like that describes when hurt feelings will occur? We have assumed in this chapter that hurt feelings arise whenever perceived relational value falls below desired relational value, but it is quite possible that the relationship is curvilinear, such that greater discrepancies are needed to evoke hurt feelings when desired relational value is low rather than high. This is an intriguing topic for future research.

Finally, although we know a great deal about how appraisals of low relational evaluation relate to hurt feelings, we have virtually no information regarding how people assess their relational value in other people's eyes. What are the cues that people use to judge whether other people value having a relationship with them? How accurately can people infer their relational value? Do people differ in their ability to assess their relational value to others? Moreover, is there, as we suspect, a built-in bias to err on the side of inferring lower rather than higher realational value than actually exists? (Such a bias would be consistent with other psychological systems that are biased toward false positives in detecting potential threats.) Given that assessments of one's relational value are central to the experience of hurt feelings, research is needed on the processes by which people determine the degree to which other people value having relationships with them.

ACKNOWLEDGMENTS

We thank Nancy Hechenbleikner, Kristine Borgeois, Karen Stiles, and Katherine Higgins with their assistance on aspects of the research reported in this chapter.

REFERENCES

Barrett, L. F., Mesquita, B., Ochsner, K. N., & Gross, J. J. (2007). The experience of emotion. *Annual Review of Psychology, 58,* 373–403.

Baumeister, R. F., & Leary, M. R. (1995). The need to belong: Desire for interpersonal attachments as a fundamental human motivation. *Psychological Bulletin, 117,* 497–529.

Bourgeois, K. S., & Leary, M. R. (2001). Coping with rejection: Derogating those who choose us last. *Motivation and Emotion, 25,* 101–111.

Buckley, K. E., Winkel, R. E., & Leary, M. R. (2003). Reactions to acceptance and rejection: Effects of level and sequence of relational evaluation. *Journal of Experimental Social Psychology, 40,* 14–28.

Eisenberger, N. I., Lieberman, M. D., & Williams, K. D. (2003). Does rejection hurt? An fMRI study of social exclusion. *Science, 302,* 290–292.

Ekman, P. (1992). Are there basic emotions? *Psychological Review, 99,* 550–553.

Ellsworth, P. C., & Smith, C. A. (1988). From appraisal to emotion: Differences among unpleasant feelings. *Motivation and Emotion, 12,* 271–302.

Feeney, J. A. (2004). Hurt feelings in couple relationships: Toward integrative models of the negative effects of hurtful events. *Journal of Social and Personal Relationships, 21,* 487–508.

Feeney, J. A. (2005). Hurt feelings in couple relationships: Exploring the role of attachment and perceptions of personal injury. *Personal Relationships, 12,* 253–271.

Feeney, J. A., Noller, P., & Roberts, N. (2001). Attachment and close relationships. In C. Hendrick & S. Hendrick (Eds.), *Close relationships: A sourcebook* (pp. 185–201). Thousand Oaks, CA: Sage.

Frijda, N. (1986). *The emotions.* Cambridge: Cambridge University Press.

Hunsley, J. (1990). Dimensionality of the Multiple Affect Adjective Check List-Revised: A comparison of factor analytic procedures. *Journal of Psychopathology and Behavioral Assessment, 12,* 81–101.

Izard, C. E. (1991). *The psychology of emotions.* New York: Plenum Press.

Larsen, R. J., & Diener, E. (1992). Promises and problems with the circumplex model of emotion. In M. S. Clark (Ed.), *Emotion* (pp. 25–59). Newbury Park, CA: Sage.

Lazarus, R. S. (1991). Cognition and motivation in emotion. *American Psychologist, 46,* 352–367.

Leary, M. R., Koch, E. J., & Hechenbleikner, N. R. (2001). Emotional responses to interpersonal rejection. In M. R. Leary (Ed.), *Interpersonal rejection* (pp. 145–166). New York: Oxford University Press.

Leary, M. R., & Springer, C. S. (2001). Hurt feelings: The neglected emotion. In R. M. Kowalski (Ed.), *Aversive behaviors and interpersonal transgressions: The underbelly of social interaction* (pp. 151–175). Washington, DC: American Psychological Association.

Leary, M. R., Springer, C., Negel, L., Ansell, E., & Evans, K. (1998). The causes, phenomenology, and consequences of hurt feelings. *Journal of Personality and Social Psychology, 74*, 1225–1237.

MacDonald, G., Kingsbury, R., & Shaw, S. (2005). Adding insult to injury: Social pain theory and response to social exclusion. In K. Williams, J. Forgas, & W. von Hippel (Eds.), *The social outcast: Ostracism, social exclusion, rejection, and bullying* (pp. 77–90). New York: Psychology Press.

MacDonald, G., & Leary, M. R. (2005). Why does social exclusion hurt? The relationship between social and physical pain. *Psychological Bulletin, 131*, 202–223.

Mills, R. S. L., Nazar, J., & Farrell, H. M. (2002). Child and parent perceptions of hurtful messages. *Journal of Social and Personal Relationships, 19*, 731–754.

Murray, S. L., Holmes, J. G., MacDonald, G., & Ellsworth, P. E. (1998). Through the looking glass darkly: When self-doubts turn into relationship insecurities. *Journal of Personality and Social Psychology, 75*, 1459–1480.

Niedenthal, P. M., & Halberstadt, J. B. (2000). Grounding categories in emotional response. In J. P. Forgas (Ed.), *Feeling and thinking: The roles of affect in social cognition* (pp. 357–386). Cambridge: Cambridge University Press.

Ortony, A., Clore, G. L., & Collins, A. (1988). *The cognitive structure of emotions*. Cambridge: Cambridge University Press.

Ortony, A., & Turner, T. J. (1990). What is basic about basic emotions? *Psychological Review, 97*, 315–331.

Plutchik, R. (1980). *Emotions: A psychoevolutionary synthesis*. New York: Harper & Row.

Russell, J. A. (1980). A circumplex model of affect. *Journal of Personality and Social Psychology, 39*, 1161–1178.

Scherer, K. R., Schorr, A., & Johnstone, T. (2001). *Appraisal processes in emotion*. New York: Oxford University Press.

Shaver, P. R., Schwartz, J., Kirson, D., & O'Conner, C. (1987). Emotion knowledge: Further exploration of a prototype approach. *Journal of Personality and Social Psychology, 52*, 1961–1086.

Smith, C. A. (1991). The self, appraisal, and coping. In C. R. Snyder & D. R. Forsyth (Eds.), *Handbook of social and clinical psychology* (pp. 116–137). New York: Pergamon.

Smith, C. A., & Ellsworth, P. C. (1985). Patterns of cognitive appraisal in emotion. *Journal of Personality and Social Psychology, 48*, 813–838.

Snapp, C. M., & Leary, M. R. (2001). Hurt feelings among new acquaintances: Moderating effects of interpersonal familiarity. *Journal of Personal and Social Relationships, 18*, 315–326.

Storm, C., & Storm, T. (1987). A taxonomic study of the vocabulary of emotion. *Journal of Personality and Social Psychology, 53*, 805–816.

Tomkins, S. S. (1962). *Affect, imagery, consciousness: Vol. 1. The positive affects*. New York: Springer-Verlag.

Vangelisti, A. L. (2001). Making sense of hurtful interactions in close relationships: When hurt feelings create distance. In V. Manusov & J. Harvey (Eds.), *Attribution, communication behavior, and close relationships: Advances in personal relations* (pp. 38–58). New York: Cambridge University Press.

Vangelisti, A. L., & Young, S. L. (2000). When words hurt: The effect of perceived intentionality on interpersonal relationships. *Journal of Social and Personal Relationships, 17*, 393–424.

Vangelisti, A. L., Young, S. L., Carpenter-Theune, K. E., & Alexander, A. L. (2005). Why does it hurt? The perceived causes of hurt feelings. *Communication Research, 32*, 443–477.

Watson, D., & Clark, L. A. (1992). Affects separable and inseparable: On the hierarchical arrangement of the negative affects. *Journal of Personality and Social Psychology, 62*, 489–505.

Watson, D., & Clark, L. A. (1994). *The PANAS-X: Manual for the Positive and Negative Affect Schedule–Expanded Form.* Unpublished manuscript, University of Iowa.

Watson, D., & Tellegen, A. (1985). Toward a consensual structure of mood. *Psychological Bulletin, 98*, 219–235.

Zuckerman, M., & Lubin, B. (1985). *Manual for the Multiple Affect Adjective Check List Revised.* San Diego: Educational and Industrial Testing Service.

Zuckerman, M., Lubin, B., & Rinck, C. M. (1983). Construction of new scales for the Multiple Affect Adjective Check List. *Journal of Behavioral Assessment, 5*, 119–129.

# 3

# Thinking the Unthinkable: Cognitive Appraisals and Hurt Feelings

JULIE FITNESS AND WAYNE WARBURTON

INTRODUCTION

"A man is hurt not so much by what happens to him as by his opinion of what happens."

Montaigne, 16th century

As a rule, human beings neither seek nor enjoy the experience of pain. By definition, pain involves suffering, and given the choice, we would rather go through life without it. Fortunately, we have no such choice – fortunately, because pain is critical to our survival. Without the felt experience of pain, we would fail to notice injuries. Only the smell of burning flesh would alert us to the fact that we were on fire, and we would have no inkling that our leg was shattered until we noticed that walking was difficult. Pain, then, is adaptive and helps keep us alive. However, pain is not just a physical phenomenon; it is also psychological. Experiences of heartache and loneliness involve psychological suffering, and this too is adaptive. As social creatures, humans are dependent on their relationships with others – in particular, parents, siblings, partners, and friends – for their survival. Just as physical pain alerts individuals to physical harm, so too does psychological pain alert them to social harm such as rejection or abandonment (MacDonald & Leary, 2005). The pain of appendicitis and the pain of social loss, then, serve similar functions: they let us know we are in trouble, they motivate us to cry out in protest, and they motivate others to come to our aid.

In Western culture, people frequently refer to the experience of psychological pain in terms of *feeling hurt* or as having *hurt feelings*. Such experiences can range from a twinge of discomfort in response to a perceived slight from a friend to the deepest anguish in response to a loved one's betrayal. Until recently, however, psychologists have paid remarkably little attention to the features and functions of hurt and have done relatively little empirical work, in particular, on the links between people's cognitive appraisals, or interpretations, of social interactions and their feelings of hurt. In part, this is because few emotion researchers have conceptualized hurt as an emotion in its own right. Rather, they have tended to subsume hurt within larger emotion families such as sadness (e.g., see Shaver, Collins, & Clark, 1996). There is growing evidence, however, that hurt is a distinct emotion with its own cognitive and motivational profile (Feeney, 2005; Leary & Springer, 2001). Further, hurt is an intrinsically relational emotion that can be conceptualized as the flipside of love; that is, to the extent that we love others, so too are we vulnerable to being hurt by them.

The focus of this chapter is on the cognitions that elicit the experience of hurt feelings. Our position is that hurt is a discrete emotion that is different from emotions like anger, sadness, and anxiety and that hurt can be distinguished from these emotions, at least in part, by its cognitive elicitors. We begin the chapter with a discussion of cognitive appraisal theory and review the evidence supporting the role of appraisals in the elicitation of different emotions. We then detail the kinds of cognitive appraisals that are particularly salient to hurt and discuss how individuals may, over time, develop cognitive schemas in which hurt-eliciting appraisals become a habitual way of (mis-)interpreting their relational worlds. Finally, we point the way to future research on the cognitive features of psychological hurt in close relationships.

## COGNITION AND EMOTION: THE ROLE OF APPRAISAL

The notion that our thoughts or cognitions are inextricably linked to our feelings and emotions has a long history, reaching back at least as far as the ancient Greek and Roman philosophers. Epictetus, for example, in the 1st century CE, claimed, "It is not the things themselves that disturb men, but their judgments about things." Shakespeare, too, noted that "there is nothing either good or bad in the world but thinking makes it so."

Within psychology, the idea that emotions are generated by cognitive appraisals of stimuli was introduced in 1960 by Magda Arnold, "the mother of appraisal theory" (Kappas, 2006, p. 955). According to Arnold (1960), cognitive appraisals are direct and immediate and do not require conscious, or reflective, thinking about the object being appraised. Further, Arnold argued that "to arouse an emotion, the object must be appraised as affecting me in some way, affecting me personally as an individual with my particular experience and my particular aims" (p. 171). Thus, the primary function of direct and immediate cognitive appraisals is to ascertain whether a particular stimulus, such as a surprise gift from a lover or the discovery of a love letter from our spouse to another, is relevant to us and in line with our needs, goals, and desires. If we appraise the stimulus as irrelevant to us, then we experience no emotion. However, if we appraise the stimulus as relevant to us and as facilitating or obstructing our needs, goals, and desires, then we will experience physiological arousal and a "felt tendency" either to approach or avoid the stimulus. This felt tendency, along with our positive or negative appraisals, constitutes the experience of emotion. Thus, for example, we might experience a felt tendency to approach a stimulus appraised as relevant and positive, such as a gift-giving partner, and experience positive emotion, or we might experience a felt tendency to avoid a stimulus appraised as relevant and negative, such as an unfaithful spouse, and experience negative emotion.

Arnold's theory has been described as a monumental event in the history of the study of emotion (Ellsworth, 1991). However, it was also somewhat sketchy, with its failure to account for the ways in which different emotions, as opposed to global positive or negative emotional states, might come about. For example, a woman might appraise evidence of her husband's infidelity as personally relevant and not at all in line with her goals and desires and then experience physiological arousal. However, she might not experience a felt tendency to avoid her husband. Rather, she might feel urges to abuse him verbally and physically, and her emotional state might be better described as angry than as negative. Or, a husband may experience a felt tendency to closely guard his unfaithful wife and prevent her from leaving the house. Again, his emotional state may be better described as anxious, angry, or jealous than as simply negative. Clearly, basic distinctions between appraisals of "good for us" and "bad for us," along with tendencies to approach and avoid appraised stimuli, do not go nearly far enough to explain the richness of our emotional experiences.

Following Arnold's (1960) exposition of the cognitive appraisal approach to emotion, several theorists have attempted to delineate the kinds of cognitive appraisals that, either singly or in combination, elicit various kinds of emotions (e.g., see Roseman, 1984, 2004; Scherer, 1984; Smith & Ellsworth, 1985). In essence, these theorists agree with Arnold that emotion results from cognitive appraisals of environmental stimuli. However, they also argue that such appraisals are not simply concerned with determining whether a personally relevant stimulus is good or bad for us (or, as defined by Roseman [1984], motivationally congruent or incongruent; that is, in line or not in line with our needs, goals, and desires). Rather, we appraise stimuli that are relevant to us along a number of different dimensions, including their novelty or unexpectedness; their perceived cause (self, other, or external circumstances); their legitimacy, or compatibility with social or personal norms; and our coping potential power, to deal with them (see Ellsworth & Scherer, 2003).

According to this more complex view, different emotions are elicited as a function of the different ways in which a stimulus may be appraised. Thus, for example, if I perceive that a personally relevant, motivationally incongruent event has occurred (I have been criticized in front of friends), has been caused by another (my spouse), and is illegitimate (not compatible with my norms for loving spouse behavior), then I am likely to feel angry. Further, and in broad agreement with Arnold's (1960) concept of felt tendency, different emotions involve different states of "action readiness," including desires such as to attend, care for, withdraw, oppose, and amend (Frijda, 2007). Anger, for example, motivates and energizes individuals to attack a motivationally incongruent stimulus – to yell at offending spouses and make them see the error of their ways. However, if individuals' power to take such remedial action is appraised as low (the offending spouse is likely to retaliate violently), then they may experience hate rather than anger and a corresponding urge to reject or escape from the stimulus (Fitness & Fletcher, 1993).

The cognitive appraisal approach has been criticized for its apparent assumption that people do so much thinking before experiencing emotions, but this is not what is argued. Rather, and in line with Arnold's initial explication of appraisal theory, so-called primary appraisals (e.g., Lazarus, 1991) may be immediate, direct, and not necessarily accessible to conscious awareness. These direct perceptions may rapidly generate emotional states such as shock or upset that hit us "out of the blue." Secondary appraisals, in contrast, are deliberative, reflective, and potentially accessible to consciousness and self-report (Kappas, 2006). Depending on the outcomes of secondary appraisals, different kinds of emotions such as anger, joy, or sadness may be elicited. Thus, the cognitive appraisal process is a sequential one that takes place over time, with even the most subtle shifts in appraisal shaping corresponding shifts in feelings and emotions (Ellsworth, 2007). Further, feelings and emotions have the capacity to shape ongoing appraisals, as when an appraisal of threat (I think my spouse is having an affair) generates anxiety. This emotion, in turn, shapes ongoing cognitive appraisals (my spouse appears to be acting suspiciously) that in turn, generate further anxiety. In this sense, feelings and emotions become emotional lenses through which individuals (accurately or otherwise) appraise their social worlds (Planalp & Fitness, 1999).

Clearly, cognitive appraisal analysis is a powerful tool for teasing apart and better understanding people's experiences of even such closely related emotions as anger, sadness, and fear. This teasing apart is important because individuals frequently report experiencing many emotions in relation to the same stimulus. For example, if asked how they remembered feeling about a romantic partner's infidelity, individuals may say they felt upset, frightened, angry, and sad. Further questioning, however, reveals the cognitive appraisals that generated these different emotions in turn. For example, people may report they felt upset when they discovered the infidelity, frightened when they realized the situation was beyond their control, angry when they ruminated on the injustice of what their partner had done, and sad when they reflected on the irreparable damage that had been done to the relationship. Individuals may also report that they felt deeply hurt by their spouse's actions, but the kinds of cognitive appraisals that generate this emotion and the ways in which such appraisals differ from those that elicit, for example, anger or sadness are less clear. In the next section of this chapter we review what is currently known about the cognitive aspects of the powerful yet poorly understood emotion called hurt and describe the results of a study that explicitly examined individuals' appraisals of hurt-, anger-, and sadness-eliciting events.

## COGNITIVE APPRAISALS AND HURT FEELINGS

As noted previously, of all the different emotions humans are capable of experiencing, there is possibly none so intrinsically relational as hurt. Some emotions, such as anger, frequently involve other people, but they can also be experienced in response to nonrelational stimuli, such as when an individual screams at the computer that has swallowed and lost her files. However, although our computers may infuriate us they do not hurt our feelings.[1] Other so-called self-conscious emotions are relational in that they require both a sense of self and other (Leary & Baumeister, 2001). Shame and pride, for example, are elicited by cognitive appraisals that we are being evaluated by others. Further, the audience need not be an actual other; we can feel ashamed or proud of ourselves. However, we do not and, we would argue, cannot hurt our own feelings – only other people have the power to do that. Discovering that you forgot your own birthday a week ago might make you feel surprised or foolish, but it is the fact that your family and friends also forgot that makes you feel hurt.

The crux of hurt feelings, then, derives from our attachments to others and our expectations of the extent to which they will care for us and value their relationships with us (Leary, Springer, Negel, Ansell, & Evans, 1998; Vangelisti & Young, 2000). When the people on whom we depend reject us or behave in ways that imply they do not, after all, value their relationships with us as much as we want, we experience psychological pain or hurt. This pain may be severe. As noted by Leary et al. (1998), the psychological hurt elicited by rejection and perceived relational devaluation "can be as acute and aversive as the physical pain of bodily injury, and... sometimes lasts longer" (p. 1225; see also Fitness, 2001). Further, relational devaluation and rejection carry an even more basic message than "you do not matter to me." Specifically, and as Murray, Holmes, and Collins (2006) have argued, the symbolic meaning of rejection is that we are currently and will be in the future "unconnected and uncared for" (p. 651). Essentially, we are alone and therefore fundamentally unsafe in the world.

This observation again underscores the functional nature of hurt feelings. If, over the course of evolutionary history, humans had failed to react with alarm to the threatened or actual loss of attachment figures, they would not have survived to adulthood. However, evolution has equipped humans with powerful psychological mechanisms that generate strong positive emotions

---

[1] It has been pointed out to us that some individuals do develop parasocial relationships with their computers in much the same way as some individuals become fond of their cars. However, we would still argue that, although a computer crash or car breakdown may be distressing and infuriating, neither is likely to hurt one's feelings.

(joy and love) when attachment figures are available and strong negative emotions (pain and distress) when humans lose or perceive they may lose those attachment figures (Mikulincer & Shaver, 2005). We are wired for pain, then, because we love, and we must love and be loved to survive.

What is the empirical evidence supporting the theory that appraisals of relational devaluation and rejection generate feelings of hurt? In a seminal paper on the cognitive appraisals that underpin hurt feelings, Vangelisti, Young, Carpenter-Theune, and Alexander (2005) asked respondents to describe an interpersonal event that caused them to experience hurt feelings and to explain what it was about the incident that had caused their hurt. Vangelisti et al. coded the appraised causes of hurt into eight categories: relational denigration; humiliation; being spoken to or treated aggressively by a relationship partner; intrinsic flaw, whereby a relationship partner focused on a personal defect that participants could not change; shock, reflecting participants' surprise at the hurtful interaction; ill-conceived humor; mistaken intent, whereby a relationship partner assumed the worst about participants' motives or behaviors; and discouragement, where the hurtful interaction made participants feel their hopes or efforts were unimportant.

Interestingly, reported hurtful interactions involving either relational denigration or humiliation generated feelings of hurt that were relatively more intense than the hurt generated by any other kind of event. Thus it appears that it is not only appraisals of relational devaluation that are important in generating hurt feelings but also appraisals of self-devaluation, involving the perception that one is literally "worth less" to one's partner. This perception is a bitter blow from someone we trust to care about us and our welfare. Such shaming messages metaphorically "gut" or "crush" us; they "slap us in the face" and "cut us down to size." All such descriptions suggest painful injuries that damage our psychological well-being. In line with this observation, Feeney (2005) has argued that the key to hurt is, in fact, a sense of personal injury, defined as "damage to the victim's view of self as worthy of love, and/or to core beliefs about the availability and trustworthiness of others" (p. 256).

Feeney (2005) conducted a study in which university students wrote brief accounts of hurtful events with their romantic partners. Feeney found that respondents used a range of injury-related terms such as "cut to the quick," "pierced," and "torn apart" to describe what had happened to them. However, this begs the question – what is it, exactly, that can so injure an individual and generate such psychological pain? Feeney found that the core cognitions underpinning individuals' feelings of personal injury involved perceptions that important (and frequently unspoken) relational rules had been broken or violated. In particular, and drawing on Bowlby's theory of attachment (see Bowlby, 1969, 1973, 1980), Feeney argued that relational rule violations (also described as relational transgressions; see Vangelisti, 2001) that threaten people's perceptions of themselves as worthwhile and lovable (i.e., their positive self-schemas), or that threaten their perceptions of their partners as responsive and trustworthy (i.e., their positive other-schemas) are the ones that cut the deepest and cause the most severe pain. To reiterate the point previously made, the intensity of this pain functions to let us know that we are uncared for and thus unsafe.

The crucial question, here, however, is why the kinds of appraisals described above generate hurt, rather than anger, fear, or sadness. After all, relational transgressions are, by definition, perceived as illegitimate, which should generate anger, and as potentially threatening, which should generate fear; they also imply loss of self-esteem or of a partner's love or both, which should generate sadness. Indeed, some researchers have argued that hurt feelings are essentially a mix of such basic emotions, with any one emotion becoming salient depending on the aspect of the situation under scrutiny (e.g., see Vangelisti, 2001). Others, however, speculate that hurt may be a discrete emotion in its own right, distinct from emotions such as anger, fear, and sadness (e.g., Feeney, 2005). One way to investigate this issue is to examine the cognitive appraisals that generate each of the different emotions and to identify the appraisals that are most strongly associated with people's reports of hurt, as opposed to other salient emotions. An attempt to identify such hurt-eliciting appraisals is described in the next section of this chapter.

## HURT: A DISCRETE EMOTION?

Emotion researchers have always found it difficult to generate and study examples of "pure" emotions in laboratory settings. Typically, people report experiencing mixed emotions, not necessarily simultaneously, but certainly sequentially, depending on how they are appraising a particular stimulus at any one time. Leary and Springer (2001), for example, found that different types of interpersonal events described globally as "hurtful" produced different emotional and cognitive responses: appraisals of relationship loss were associated with sadness; appraisals of unjustified attack were associated with anger; and perceived threats to an individual's sense of security were associated with anxiety.

In a recent attempt to examine more systematically the cognitive appraisals associated with hurt-eliciting events, 115 university students were asked to recall and write three separate accounts of emotion-eliciting events in their romantic relationships: one focused on a hurt event, one on an anger event, and one on a sadness event (Fitness, under review). The students were asked to try very hard to relive each of the events as if it were currently happening and to concentrate on feeling the emotions that were most strongly associated with each event (i.e., hurt, anger, or sadness). While recalling each event, students rated their cognitive appraisals along 18 Likert-type scales previously identified as important in the elicitation of emotions such as anger, hate, and jealousy (Fitness & Fletcher, 1993; Roseman, 1984; Smith & Ellsworth, 1985).

The kinds of emotion-eliciting events described by respondents could be readily (though not exclusively) classified into three broad themes: illegitimate partner behavior (e.g., being unjustly accused, being lied to, having goals and desires obstructed or frustrated); loss or longing (e.g., breaking up with the partner, being separated from the partner over holidays, falling out of love with the partner, losing contact with friends because of the developing relationship with the partner); and uncaring partner behavior (e.g., not having needs taken seriously, being compared unfavorably to a previous partner, partner implying the individual was a nuisance or stupid, forgotten birthdays, partner scoffing at a marriage proposal). Not surprisingly, the first category of events characterized anger accounts; the second, sadness accounts; and the third, hurt accounts.

With respect to cognitive appraisals, participants' ratings for hurt were significantly different from ratings for the other two emotions on three dimensions. Specifically, hurt-eliciting events were appraised as significantly more unexpected, effortful, and difficult to understand than anger- or sadness-eliciting events. They were also associated with strong feelings of confusion and distress, and the most frequently reported action tendencies involved urges to cry and to leave the situation (e.g., "I had an urge to run but there was nowhere to go"; "I felt like running away but was also unable to move"). Further, and in contrast to what might have been expected on the basis of literary accounts of broken-heartedness (see also MacDonald & Leary, 2005), the physical symptoms most frequently reported in respondents' accounts were stomach, rather than heart, related. For example, respondents reported feeling "sick," as if they were "going to be sick"; they described a "tight feeling in stomach," feeling "physically sore in the stomach as if I'd been punched," "stomach in knots," "butterflies in stomach," and "stomach turning over." Respondents also reported feeling weak, shaky, and disoriented, as if they were in shock. Many reported having disbelieving, questioning cognitions such as "Why, why? Why has this happened? Why has he or she done this to me? How can this have happened to me?" In particular, the experience of hurt appeared to force respondents to think the unthinkable – that they were not loved as much as they wanted or needed. The following verbatim extract comes from a 24-year-old male student:

> Feeling loving and playful, I asked my partner if she was happy being married to me (only married 6–7 months).... She hesitated and then she said, "Danny... you are kind of difficult." Boom! The kind of honesty I always say I want but not the adoring answer I was expecting... my stomach turned over... what?!... doesn't she appreciate how wonderful I am?!... I felt an urge to howl, to run away.

In contrast to hurt-related events, anger events were characterized by appraisals of injustice, unfairness, and high levels of perceived obstacles to respondents obtaining what they wanted or needed. Partners were perceived to be responsible for these obstacles, and respondents reported having blaming, derogatory thoughts about them. They also described feelings of tension and energy, and they experienced urges to protest, argue, and punish their partners for their transgressions. Finally, and in contrast to both anger- and hurt-related events, the key cognitive appraisals for sadness events involved low perceived control and low unexpectedness. It was in the sadness accounts that respondents were most likely to report heart-related symptoms such as "feeling broken-hearted" and having "an ache in my chest," along with self-pitying thoughts and feelings of yearning, loneliness, and emptiness. As one respondent reported, "All I wanted was to be hugged and cared for but I knew this was never going to happen again."

Overall, the results of this study demonstrated that, despite some inevitable overlap, laypeople can distinguish hurt from anger and sadness, and the most salient cognitive appraisals generating hurt involved high unexpectedness, effort, and lack of understanding. These findings are in line with theoretical speculations that humans may rapidly register relationally threatening events at an affective or emotional level before much conscious cognitive processing has had a chance to occur (e.g., Leary & Baumeister, 2001; Planalp & Fitness, 1999). In this sense, the emotional state of hurt described by respondents in the current study resembles what other theorists have described as a relatively undifferentiated state of distress. For example, Roseman (2004) characterized distress as having "a distinct phenomenology (thinking you do not know what to do to make things less upsetting) and action tendency (feeling like moving away from something"; p. 146). Distress is also strongly associated with crying, in both children and adults (Tomkins, 1963). However, distress may be elicited by the experience of any kind of aversive stimulus, including physical pain, hunger, or thirst, whereas hurt requires us to have developed expectations about others and the extent to which they care for us. Further, the results of a study examining laypeople's abilities to discriminate between hurt and a range of other emotional states found that hurt could be distinguished from upset and distress (Leary & Springer, 2001). Clearly, and as noted also by Feeney (2005), hurt is predicated on attachment relationships and our perceptions of ourselves as lovable and of others as trustworthy. Perceiving that we may be "worth less" to someone we trust and love or that they do not value their relationship with us as much as we assumed is therefore shocking, threatening, and painful.

At some point, however, and once the initial shock of experiencing a self or relationally threatening event has been assimilated, individuals must begin to appraise the situation in more complex ways to make sense of it and deal with it. Some kinds of cognitive appraisals seem to intensify hurt feelings. For example, Vangelisti et al. (2005) found that hurtful partner-caused behaviors appraised as intentional were reported to be more painful than behaviors that could be excused as unintentional and nonmaliciously motivated. Clearly, to the extent that your partner appears to have hurt you deliberately, you can be confident of having "got the message" that you and your relationship with this person are not as important as you wanted or assumed them to be. Other kinds of cognitive appraisals of the situation may, in turn, generate a range of different emotions such as anger (this situation is unfair and my partner is solely to blame), anxiety (does this mean our relationship is in trouble?), and sadness (I've lost my faith in my partner.... I'll never be able to trust him again). Over time, individuals may also develop cognitive-affective schemas or "hot-wired" cognitive responses to hurtful events, such that appraisals of relational devaluation or rejection immediately trigger hurt-anger (I'm in pain and it's your fault), hurt-anxiety (I'm in pain and it's terrifying), or hurt-sadness (I'm in pain and the situation is hopeless). In the next section of this chapter, we discuss some features and functions of such "hot and hurtful" schemas and the ways in which they may shape ongoing cognitive appraisals of individuals' relational worlds.

## PERCEIVING THE WORLD THROUGH THE PRISM OF PAIN

When considering the role of cognitive appraisals in the generation of emotions, it is important to remember that, although cognitions clearly elicit emotions, once elicited, emotions also elicit cognitions. The cognition–emotion relationship is not a linear, two-step sequence, with a beginning and an end; rather, individuals are continually enmeshed in a complex weave of events, cognitions, and emotions that feed into and shape one another (Planalp & Fitness, 1999). Thus, for example, Keltner, Ellsworth, and Edwards (1993) found that sad individuals are more likely to blame uncontrollable circumstances for negative events than angry individuals, who are more likely to blame others for the same events. With respect to hurt and the ways in which it colors ongoing cognitive processing, there is no doubt that, just as physical pain leaves individuals bruised and scarred, so too does psychological pain leave them feeling sore, scarred, and sensitive to the prospect of further pain. However, there is something of a paradox here. The cognitive appraisals associated with hurt-eliciting events reported earlier suggest that hurt-sensitive individuals are vigilant for signals that their relationship partners do not value them or their relationships with them to the desired extent (see also Leary & Springer's [2001] work on hurt proneness). Yet, when relational events that appear to send such signals are detected (and detection thresholds for such events may be extraordinarily low), hurt-sensitive individuals are likely to appraise them, ironically, as unexpected and difficult to understand. To be hurt sensitive, then, suggests that individuals are simultaneously hoping for the best from their relationship partners yet expecting the worst – a cognitive conundrum that has been described in the psychological literature as being rejection sensitive (Downey & Feldman, 1996).

There is a growing body of empirical literature supporting the construct of rejection sensitivity (e.g., see Romero-Canyas & Downey, 2005). According to these authors, rejection sensitivity develops as a result of multiple experiences of childhood rejection or abandonment. Such experiences generate expectations that what is most feared (being alone, uncared for, and unsafe) is indeed likely to occur. For example, research confirms that when highly rejection-sensitive individuals enter into romantic relationships, they tend to appraise ambiguous partner-caused behaviors (e.g., inattentiveness) as motivated by hurtful intent (Downey & Feldman, 1996). Further, such rejection-ready expectations and appraisals may eventually elicit actual rejecting behaviors from romantic partners (Downey, Freitas, Michaelis, & Khouri, 1998).

One of the ways in which a rejection-sensitive disposition works its malevolent magic on individuals' ongoing cognitive appraisals of relationship interactions is by way of the so-called sociometer (see Leary et al., 1998). The sociometer is held to be an evolved, acutely sensitive, psychological mechanism that constantly and nonconsciously scans the environment for cues to social approval and acceptance. If the sociometer detects cues of social disapproval or rejection, the individual is alerted by way of a painful signal that motivates adaptive (or maladaptive) behaviors to deal with the threat. For individuals with a moderately secure sense of self-worth and a degree of trust in others (i.e., who have healthy self-esteem), the sociometer is effectively on "idle" until an unambiguously threatening cue is detected (e.g., a forgotten birthday). Such an event is likely to come as a shock to individuals with healthy self-esteem and to generate considerable hurt and cognitive searching for causes (see also Vangelisti et al., 2005). However, for individuals with chronically low self-esteem or low trust in others, a forgotten birthday may have been anticipated and appraised as confirming their gloomiest beliefs (if my partner forgets my birthday, then I am worthless) and expectations (my partner has forgotten my birthday, as I knew he or she would). Cognitive searching in this case is likely to focus on negative qualities of the self or the partner; that is, my partner meant to hurt me because I am not worth caring about; he or she is an uncaring person. Such appraisals, in turn, generate more hurt, along with anger and sadness, and further reinforce individuals' maladaptive beliefs about themselves and others.

There is a growing body of empirical evidence in support of such links among chronically negative beliefs about the self, negative appraisals of partner-caused behaviors, and hurt feelings. For example, Vangelisti (2001) reported a significant negative association between self-esteem and individuals' reports of hurtful events having been caused by relational denigration, perceived humiliation, or the partner's focus on an unchangeable personal defect. There is a clear link here with findings from the attachment literature. As noted previously, Feeney (2005) argued that individuals hold schemas, or working models, about themselves and their partners that may be positive or negative (see also Mikulincer & Shaver, 2005). Such schemas develop from birth as a function of interactions with caregivers and comprise sets of beliefs, many of which are affectively charged or emotionally laden, about the self and others and what can be expected from relationships. Thus, for example, like the rejection-sensitive individual, individuals with anxious-ambivalent attachment schemas tend to be hopeful that they will be loved and cared for, yet they also fear and expect that they will be betrayed or let down. Accordingly, they are hypervigilant for signs of rejection and tend to appraise their partners' ambiguous behaviors as hurtful or hostile. They also tend to respond to hurt in ways that further damage their relationships (e.g., by retaliation or dependent behaviors). Individuals with avoidant attachment styles, in contrast, tend to deal with the rejection they have learned to expect as inevitable in relationships by rejecting intimacy and relational closeness altogether. The primary function of such emotional distancing is to protect avoidant individuals from experiencing further hurt. Accordingly, and in contrast to anxious-ambivalent individuals, avoidant individuals may be relatively insensitive to ambiguous or mild rejection cues. However, they may also respond to unequivocally hurtful partner behaviors by retreating even further from intimacy and connection.

In summary, the cognitive appraisals that generate hurt in what social psychologists call the proximal, or immediate, context are driven by the learned beliefs and expectations held by individuals in the distal, or background, context (e.g., see Fitness, Fletcher, & Overall, 2003). Moreover, frequent experiences of hurt in the proximal context feed back into the distal context, further reinforcing the message that an individual is uncared for. In this way, an individual may develop a hurt-prone disposition that, in turn, motivates dysfunctional behaviors toward others (who respond, naturally, with defensiveness and rejection). Little wonder that such individuals may feel despairing and trapped in a never-ending vicious cycle of hurt and pain.

## FUTURE RESEARCH DIRECTIONS

Clearly, cognitive appraisal research has much to contribute to our understanding of psychological hurt. However, there has been some criticism of the reliance of cognitive appraisal researchers on self-reported (and necessarily, reflective) appraisals of remembered or hypothetical events (e.g., see Parkinson, 1997). It is encouraging, then, to note recent findings from more naturalistic studies that corroborate the self-report data. For example, Tong et al. (2007) recently had police officers in Singapore rate their ongoing cognitive appraisals and emotions on personal digital assistants (PDAs) during work hours and analyzed the data with an ecological momentary assessment program. Their findings were in line with previous cognitive appraisal–emotion research, with different emotions associated with distinct appraisal profiles. A similar methodology could be applied to the study of hurt by, for example, providing PDAs to married partners and asking them to record their ongoing appraisals and emotions during a difficult relationship period.

There is also scope for further work on distinguishing the emotions involved in the experience of hurt. In particular, the role of shame and humiliation seems to be important. Indeed, Feeney (2005) found that 10 of the 11 terms describing a cognitive appraisal of the self during a hurtful incident were related to shame (inadequate, embarrassed, worthless, stupid, foolish, unattractive, unimportant, blameworthy, naïve, ugly); only one term (alone) was related to another category (sadness). There is ample evidence from the shame literature attesting to the propensity for shamed individuals to behave in hostile, dysfunctional ways (Tangney & Salovey, 1999). Accordingly, and to the extent that relational devaluation, rejection, and humiliation experiences elicit both hurt and shame, individuals may respond to hurtful experiences with vengeful, retaliatory behaviors – responses that may disguise the extent to which they are, in fact, appraising themselves as worthless, threatened, and uncared for (see also Warburton & Williams, 2005). In a similar vein, there is more research to be conducted on the kinds of "hot" cognitive-affective schemas described earlier that may automatically generate emotions such as anger, fear, and sadness in response to psychological pain.

Finally, an important avenue for future research is to explore the cognitive appraisals associated with hurt in non-Western cultures. As social animals, all humans must deal with the same survival-related problems including frustration, threat, and loss. Further, empirical research confirms that humans universally recognize and experience the same basic emotions in response to such situations (i.e., anger, fear, and sadness). However, there are also historical and cross-cultural differences in beliefs and value systems that shape cognitive appraisals and emotions (Scherer, 1994). For example, in contrast to Western individualistic societies, many non-Western societies emphasize the importance of interconnectedness and the "relational" self (Andersen & Chen, 2002). Given that hurt is a quintessentially relational emotion, it might also be a highly salient and cognitively elaborated emotion in cultures where one's first responsibility is to family and community, rather than to the self (see Planalp & Fitness, 1999). This, in turn, may mean that non-Western cultures have complex rules and systems for avoiding and dealing with potentially hurt-eliciting situations in particular kinds of relationships. This is a vast and virtually untapped area for future research.

CONCLUSIONS

Clearly, and as proposed by the Stoic philosophers and by Shakespeare, psychological hurt, like other emotions, is a function of how we appraise our social worlds. Being ignored by a fellow traveler on the bus is not hurtful; being ignored by one's spouse is unexpected and hard to understand and signals a lack of care that hurts. Further, like physical pain, emotional pain seems to be crucial to our survival – humans need to be cared for by others, and it is our relationships with those who care for us that sustain us, both physically and psychologically.

The research reported in this chapter demonstrates that hurt is intimately intertwined with cognition: with perceptions, appraisals, expectations, and beliefs. It is our hope that over the coming years we will achieve a deeper understanding of this primal, excruciating, yet indispensable emotion. After all, hurt is what makes us human.

### REFERENCES

Andersen, S. M., & Chen, S. (2002). The relational self: An interpersonal social-cognitive theory. *Psychological Review, 109,* 619–645.

Arnold, M. (1960). *Emotion and personality: Vol. 1. Psychological aspects.* New York: Columbia University Press.

Bowlby, J. (1969). *Attachment and loss: Vol. 1. Attachment.* New York: Basic Books.

Bowlby, J. (1973). *Attachment and loss: Vol. 2. Separation, anxiety, and anger.* New York: Basic Books.

Bowlby, J. (1980). *Attachment and loss: Vol. 3. Loss, sadness, and depression.* New York: Basic Books.

Downey, G., & Feldman, S. I. (1996). Implications of rejection sensitivity for intimate relationships. *Journal of Personality and Social Psychology, 70,* 1327–1343.

Downey, G., Freitas, A. L., Michaelis, B., & Khouri, H. (1998). The self-fulfilling prophecy in close relationships: Rejection sensitivity and rejection by romantic partners. *Journal of Personality and Social Psychology, 75,* 545–560.

Ellsworth, P. (1991). Some implications of cognitive appraisal theories of emotion. In K. T. Strongman (Ed.), *International review of studies on emotion* (Vol. 1, pp. 143–162). New York: Wiley.

Ellsworth, P. (2007). Appraisals, emotions, and adaptation. In J. P. Forgas, M. Haselton, & W. von Hippel (Eds.), *Evolution and the social mind* (pp. 71–88). New York: Psychology Press.

Ellsworth, P., & Scherer, K. R. (2003). Appraisal processes in emotion. In R. J. Davidson, H. Goldsmith, & K. R. Scherer (Eds.), *Handbook of affective sciences* (pp. 572–595). New York: Oxford University Press.

Feeney, J. A. (2005). Hurt feelings in couple relationships: Exploring the role of attachment and perceptions of personal injury. *Personal Relationships, 12,* 253–271.

Fitness, J. (2001). Betrayal, rejection, revenge, and forgiveness: An interpersonal script approach. In M. Leary (Ed.), *Interpersonal rejection* (pp. 73–104). New York: Oxford University Press.

Fitness, J., & Fletcher, G. J. O. (1993). Love, hate, anger, and jealousy in close relationships: A prototype and cognitive appraisal analysis. *Journal of Personality and Social Psychology, 65,* 942–958.

Fitness, J., & Fletcher, G. J. O., & Overall, N. (2003). Interpersonal attraction and intimate relationships. In J. Cooper & M. Hogg (Eds.), *Sage handbook of social psychology* (pp. 258–278). Thousand Oaks, CA: Sage.

Frijda, N. H. (2007). *The laws of emotion.* Mahwah, NJ: Erlbaum.

Kappas, A. (2006). Appraisals are direct, immediate, intuitive, and unwitting and some are reflective. *Emotion, 20,* 952–975.

Keltner, D., Ellsworth, P., & Edwards, K. (1993). Beyond simple pessimism: Effects of sadness and anger on social perception. *Journal of Personality and Social Psychology, 64*, 740–752.

Lazarus, R. S. (1991). *Emotion and adaptation*. New York: Oxford University Press.

Leary, M. R., & Baumeister, R. F. (2001). The nature and function of self-esteem: Sociometer theory. In M. Zanna (Ed.), *Advances in experimental social psychology* (Vol. 32, pp. 1–62). San Diego: Academic Press.

Leary, M. R., & Springer, C. A. (2001). Hurt feelings: The neglected emotion. In R. Kowalski (Ed.), *Behaving badly: Aversive behaviors in interpersonal relationships* (pp. 151–175). Washington DC: American Psychological Association.

Leary, M. R., Springer, C., Negel, L., Ansell, E., & Evans, K. (1998). The causes, phenomenology and consequences of hurt feelings. *Journal of Personality and Social Psychology, 74*, 1225–1237.

MacDonald, G., & Leary, M. R. (2005). Why does social exclusion hurt? The relationship between social and physical pain. *Psychological Bulletin, 131*, 202–223.

Mikulincer, M., & Shaver, P. R. (2005). Attachment theory and emotions in close relationships: Exploring the attachment-related dynamics of emotional reactions to relational events. *Personal Relationships, 12*, 149–168.

Murray, S. L., Holmes, J. G., & Collins, N. L. (2006). Optimizing assurance: The risk regulation system in relationships. *Psychological Bulletin, 132*, 641–666.

Parkinson, B. (1997). Untangling the appraisal-emotion connection. *Personality and Social Psychology Review, 1*, 62–79.

Planalp, S., & Fitness, J. (1999). Thinking/feeling about social and personal relationships. *Journal of Social and Personal Relationships, 16*, 731–750.

Romero-Canyas, R., & Downey, G. (2005). Rejection sensitivity as a predictor of affective and behavioral responses to interpersonal stress. In K. D. Williams, J. P. Forgas, & W. von Hippel (Eds.), *The social outcast: Ostracism, social exclusion, rejection, and bullying* (pp. 131–154). New York: Psychology Press.

Roseman, I. J. (1984). Cognitive determinants of emotion: A structural theory. In P. Shaver (Ed.), *Review of personality and social psychology* (Vol. 5, pp. 11–36). Beverly Hills, CA: Sage.

Roseman, I. (2004). Appraisals, rather than unpleasantness or muscle movements, are the primary determinants of specific emotions. *Emotion, 4*, 145–150.

Scherer, K. (1984). On the nature and function of emotion: A component process approach. In K. Scherer & P. Ekman (Eds.), *Approaches to emotion* (pp. 293–318). Hillsdale, NJ: Erlbaum.

Scherer, K. (1994). Evidence for both universality and cultural specificity of emotion elicitation. In P. Ekman & R. J. Davidson (Eds.), *The nature of emotion* (pp. 172–175). New York: Oxford University Press.

Shaver, P. R., Collins, N., & Clark, C. L. (1996). Attachment styles and internal working models of self and relationship partners. In G. J. O. Fletcher & J. Fitness (Eds.), *Knowledge structures in close relationships: A social psychological approach* (pp. 25–61). Mahwah, NJ: Erlbaum.

Smith, C., & Ellsworth, P. (1985). Patterns of cognitive appraisal in emotion. *Journal of Personality and Social Psychology, 48*, 813–838.

Tangney, J., & Salovey, P. (1999). Problematic social emotions: Shame, guilt, jealousy and envy. In R. Kowalski & M. Leary (Eds.), *The social psychology of emotional and behavioral problems* (pp. 167–195). Washington: American Psychological Association.

Tomkins, S. S. (1963). *Affect, imagery, and consciousness, Vol. 2*. New York: Springer.

Tong, E. M. W., Bishop, G. D., Enkelmann, H. C., Why, Y. P., Diong, S. M., Khader, M., & Ang, J. (2007). Emotion and appraisal: A study using ecological momentary assessment. *Cognition and Emotion, 21,* 1361–1381.

Vangelisti, A. L. (2001). Making sense of hurtful interactions in close relationships. In V. Manusov & J. H. Harvey (Eds.), *Attribution, communication behavior, and close relationships* (pp. 38–58). New York: Cambridge University Press.

Vangelisti, A. L., & Young, S. L. (2000). When words hurt: The effects of perceived intentionality on interpersonal relationships. *Journal of Social and Personal Relationships, 17,* 393–424.

Vangelisti, A. L., Young, S. L., Carpenter-Theune, K. E., & Alexander, A. L. (2005). Why does it hurt? The perceived causes of hurt feelings. *Communication Research, 32,* 443–477.

Warburton, W. A., & Williams, K. D. (2005). Ostracism: When social motives collide. In J. P. Forgas, K. D. Williams, & W. von Hippel (Eds.), *Social motivation: Conscious and unconscious processes* (pp. 294–313). London: Cambridge University Press.

# 4

## Adding Insult to Injury: The Contributions of Politeness Theory to Understanding Hurt Feelings in Close Relationships

DAENA J. GOLDSMITH AND ERIN DONOVAN-KICKEN

A clerk in a clothing and jewelry store told one of us about an incident in which a customer said to her, "You aren't helping me at all here." The clerk reported that, normally, this comment would have hurt her feelings, but it did not because several other customers and coworkers rolled their eyes, smiled, shrugged, and gave other signs that the clerk interpreted as indicating that the customer was being unreasonable and the comment should be ignored. On another occasion, one of us overheard a group of teenage girls talking. In front of the group, one of the girls said to another, "It hurt my feelings when you blew me off last weekend. You're supposed to be my best friend," to which the other girl responded, "We're not *best* friends. Why are you being such a drama queen?" In both examples, feeling hurt was not only a matter of an individual's internal state but also involved performances in which roles and hurt were interactively negotiated.

Why might the same event or comment be more hurtful if others witness it or if it is stated bluntly rather than tactfully? How is hurt related to embarrassment, and how do others' reactions to a hurtful event shape the experience? What is accomplished by retelling the story of one's own or another's hurt? These anecdotes and questions remind us that sometimes we suffer not only injury to our internalized sense of self but also insult to our public image. Likewise, we may be hurt not just by a threat to a particular valued relationship but also by a breach in the contract of civility we enact in all interactions. Some emotions have to do with personal injury and others with social insult, but often hurt feelings are a blend of both. The nature and magnitude of the insult may be negotiated in interaction with the person who hurts us and in talk with and by others after the incident has concluded.

Recognizing these social, public, and symbolic facets of hurt feelings is one contribution of Brown and Levinson's politeness theory (1987) and of Goffman's conceptualization of face (1967) on which politeness theory is based. These theorists remind us that often it is not just the action that hurts but also the ceremonial import of the action, the rending of the social order, and, with it, the profaning of the sacred self. This approach reveals aspects of hurt feelings not considered from the perspective of theories focused on the individual and his or her self-image, vulnerabilities, personal tendencies, and particular relationships. It also has practical import for reconciliation because how you repair hurt depends on what needs fixing.

We do not present politeness theory as a master explanation or as a competing explanation – there are facets of hurt feelings best left to other kinds of theories. As Vangelisti (2007) observed, exploring multiple conceptualizations of hurt "does not necessarily imply that one of the approaches should or will emerge as superior to others" (p. 124). Rather, we propose that Goffman's (1967) conceptualization of face and Brown and Levinson's (1987) elaboration of the verbal features that attend to face provide a complementary conceptualization of one important facet of hurt feelings. Feelings may be attached to many things, but face is one important kind of thing to which feelings are attached and from which hurt can result. Face is intrinsically social and exists in interactions, so a focus on hurt feelings that result from face threats provides an appropriate explanation for those instances when hurt feelings arise from social, rather than strictly personal, affront.

Politeness theory has generated much research as well as controversies and reformulations (for a brief summary, see Goldsmith, 2007, 2008), and there are other theories of politeness (e.g., see Watts, 2003). Nonetheless, politeness theory remains a widely known theory with proven heuristic power, and in this chapter we demonstrate the fruitfulness of applying it to hurt feelings. We begin by summarizing elements of politeness theory (and the conceptualization of face that preceded it) that are germane to hurt feelings. We then describe five implications of considering hurt feelings through the lens of face and politeness theory. We conclude with directions for future research on hurt feelings and on politeness.

## POLITENESS THEORY

For many readers, the word *politeness* may connote formal etiquette at ritual events or being on our best behavior among strangers. In contrast, Brown and Levinson's politeness theory (1987) is intended to account for the many ways we show consideration for others in all of our everyday interactions, including those with close relational partners. Politeness theory builds on the concepts of "face" and "facework" as articulated by sociologist Erving Goffman in *Interaction Ritual* (1967), so it is useful to begin there before proceeding to a summary of politeness theory.

### Goffman on Face and Facework

Goffman (1967) observed that, in any social encounter, our verbal and nonverbal actions are enacting a "line" (p. 5). That is, we are expressing our view of the type of interaction in which we are engaged and the corresponding types of participants who are interacting together. So, for example, if two couples are having dinner together, each person's behavior shows that he or she is having dinner and not, at that moment, giving a lecture to students in a class or disciplining a child on the playground or revealing doubts to his or her partner in private. Likewise, participating in the episode, "having dinner with another couple," implies various kinds of identities for each person and for their relationships, such as coupled, convivial, befriended, and so on. Goffman defines "face" as "the positive social value a person effectively claims for [her]self[1] by the line others assume [she] has taken during a particular contact" (p. 6). It is "an image of self delineated in terms of approved social attributes" (p. 6). To return to our dinner episode example, a participant might see herself as witty or shy, relationally faithful or flirtatious, intellectually superior or equal, or as any number of things, but her face has to do with the line she enacts and the responses of others toward that line in this particular social context.

Several features of face are worth explicating. First, face is performed. In contrast to an individual's cognitive self-image, face is a line enacted in observable behaviors. One's face comprises one's own self-presentation and others' response to it. As Goffman (1967) explains, "The individual must rely on others to complete the picture of him which he himself is allowed to paint only in certain parts" (p. 84). Second, face has to do with positive social value. In contrast to self-esteem, which may be based on personally preferred identities, face involves valued attributes associated with socially recognized lines in encounters. In any given encounter, only some capacities or statuses are relevant. Third, face is claimed. Unlike stable personal attributes, face must be acted out in a particular interaction, and it depends on others picking up on the line and acting in ways that are more or less compatible with it. Face is lost, saved, or sustained by the actions people take in a particular interaction:

> A person may be said to have, or be in, or maintain face when the line [s]he effectively takes presents an image of [her] that is internally consistent, that is supported by judgments and evidence conveyed by other participants, and that is confirmed by evidence conveyed through impersonal agencies in the situation. At such times, the person's face clearly is something that is not lodged in or on [her] body, but rather something that is diffusely located in the flow of events in the encounter

---

[1] Goffman (writing in 1967) and Brown and Levinson (whose monograph was originally published in 1978 and then rereleased unchanged in 1987) use masculine pronouns generically to refer to the experience of all humans, men and women. Were they writing these same texts today, we suspect these authors would find eloquent ways to use gender-neutral language, but the original texts were not written with this in mind and so when we simply added "she," "her," "herself" and the like to sentences not structured to accommodate those additions, it often detracted from the very eloquence we hoped to capture by using direct quotation. We therefore opted to alternate the use of masculine and feminine pronouns in direct quotations. When we have changed an author's masculine pronouns to feminine pronouns, we indicate this by the use of brackets.

and becomes manifest only when these events are read and interpreted for the appraisals expressed in them. (Goffman, 1967, pp. 6–7)

The concept of face draws attention to interactional processes. As Goffman states clearly at the outset of *Interaction Ritual*, "I assume that the proper study of interaction is not the individual and his psychology, but rather the syntactical relations among the acts of different persons mutually present to one another.... Not, then, men and their moments. Rather moments and their men" (1967, pp. 2–3).

The interactions Goffman (1967) studied, however, are not just empty rituals or acts we put on with little felt consequence. On the contrary, Goffman believed we are emotionally attached to face. The type and intensity of feeling vary. When interactions go as expected and face is maintained, we feel confident and secure. When we can pull off an image better than ordinarily expected, we may feel pleasantly surprised, even elated. In contrast, when our ordinary expectations are not fulfilled, we feel hurt (p. 6). It is not only the lack of identity validation that hurts but also disruption of a performance. We may be taken aback, confused, and even "momentarily incapacitate[d]" when our line is not taken up by others in quite the way we had anticipated (p. 8). If we can conceal our hurt, shame, and confusion, this constitutes acting with poise; if we cannot, this failure adds further injury. Not only have we failed to sustain a line to which we are emotionally attached but we have also failed to react with poise, falling into the unfavorable role of one who is embarrassed, chagrined, or shamefaced.

For Goffman (1967), "while [one's] social face can be [her] most personal possession and the center of [her] security and pleasure, it is only on loan to [her] from society; it will be withdrawn unless [s]he conducts [herself] in a way that is worthy of it" (p. 9). Because face can only be achieved in interaction with others, there is an implicit social contract to "sustain a standard of considerateness ... to go to certain lengths to save the feelings and the face of others present" and to do so "willingly and spontaneously because of emotional identification with the others and with their feelings" (p. 10). When others lose face, our reaction reflects on us too, and we must take steps to avoid looking cruel, incompetent, or unfeeling.

In this way, the potential for hurt feelings provides motivation for social order, a reason for us to buy into a system that constrains us: "approved attributes and their relation to face make of every [wo]man [her] own jailer; this is a fundamental social constraint even though each [wo]man may like [her] cell" (Goffman, 1967, p. 10). However, Goffman clarifies that he wishes to understand the social order itself and not individual motivation. Individuals may save their own face for a variety of internal motives, including emotional attachment to the image of self expressed, a felt duty to self or others to uphold an image, or the influence over others enabled by an image. Likewise, we may act to save others' face because we feel they have a moral right to face protection, we are emotionally attached to *their* image, we desire to avoid the hostility that would result from failing to uphold their face, or we want to sustain our own image as someone who is compassionate and well behaved toward others. The study of face is like the study of traffic rules: "one learns about the code the person adheres to in his movement across the paths and designs of others, but not where he is going, or why he wants to get there" (Goffman, p. 12).

Goffman (1967) also speaks of social interaction as ritual, which he defined as "the senses in which the person in our urban secular world is allotted a kind of sacredness that is displayed and confirmed by symbolic acts" (p. 47). Demeanor includes all the ways we show ourselves to be a person of worth, such as by displaying discretion, sincerity, modesty, sportsmanship, command of speech and physical movement, self-control over emotions and appetites, and poise under pressure (p. 77). Deference is directed toward honoring an object of special value – the other's face – and celebrating and confirming our relationship to others. It includes avoidance rituals through which we show respect for privacy, formality, and appropriate distance as well as presentational rituals through which we notice and appreciate others. Although he calls them "rituals," Goffman is referring to ordinary and often subtle features of everyday interaction such as space, touch, eye contact, terms of address, greetings, asking questions, making inquiries, reciprocating favors, and giving compliments. He concludes, "Many gods have been done away with, but the individual himself stubbornly remains as a deity of considerable importance" (p. 95). The ways we show care for our own and others' face are not only linked to our personal feelings but also to the value our society places on the self.

In addition to discussing "face" and its relation to feelings and the social order, Goffman also takes up "facework," defined as "actions taken by a person to make whatever he is doing consistent with face" (1967, p. 12). Facework may avoid threatening our own or another's face (e.g., showing respect, politeness, discretion, courtesy) or may display poise or do repair when face is lost (e.g., tactfully ignoring a faux pas, apologizing, defending). Facework also becomes habitual and standardized within social groups: Goffman claims that "almost all acts involving others are modified, prescriptively or proscriptively, by considerations of face" (p. 13).

Goffman (1967) acknowledges that face-saving practices can be used strategically or aggressively. If others can be counted on to perform or accept facework, their actions can be used for personal gain. For example, if we know that others are prepared to overlook some kinds of face threats or accept apologies for them, their actions can be a basis for "safely offending them" (p. 24). We could even arrange for others to hurt our feelings so as to make them feel bad (p. 24). Attribution of intention and responsibility figures into facework as well. Some threats to face occur unwittingly, some are undesired byproducts of other actions, and some are undertaken maliciously. There is a difference in the hurt we experience (and in the reparations required) when we overhear a hurtful comment that was not intended for our ears, when we infer a hurtful intention from an otherwise innocent-seeming utterance, or when we are directly confronted with a hurtful statement.

When a face threat cannot plausibly be overlooked, Goffman (1967) proposes that a corrective interchange will occur in a structure designed to mend the breach in the social order. The interchange includes a challenge that calls attention to the misconduct, an offering by the offender to correct for the offense (e.g., an excuse, justification, or apology), an acceptance or rejection of that offer by the offended party, and, eventually, a terminal move that signals restoration of order. Goffman characterizes the interchange as a ritual because it deals with "acts through whose symbolic component the actor shows how worthy [s]he is of respect or how worthy [s]he feels others are of it" (p. 19). Although it is a ritual rich in symbolic meaning, it is also a site of feelings, including hurt feelings. As Goffman observes,

> It is plain that emotions play a part in these cycles of response, as when anguish is expressed because of what one has done to another's face, or anger because of what has been done to one's own. I want to stress that these emotions function as moves, and fit so precisely into the logic of the ritual game that it would seem difficult to understand them without it. In fact, spontaneously expressed feelings are likely to fit into the formal pattern of the ritual interchange more elegantly than consciously designed ones. (p. 23)

For Goffman, hurt feelings have social as well as personal significance. The presentation of feelings is just as important as the feelings themselves. Sometimes when face threat hurts our feelings, we can avoid further damage to face by concealing the hurt and acting with poise. On other occasions, we might display hurt as we take the role of the aggrieved party. Similarly, the feelings we show when others lose face reflect on our own face. We do experience hurt feelings when face is threatened, but Goffman's interest is less in the feelings than in the face. Part of saving or recovering face (our own or others') is putting on a display of feelings, whether true to the felt experience of the participants or not. Thus, feelings are socially constructed in two senses – some of the things that count as hurtful are derived from the social order, and we also sometimes display or conceal hurt in particular ways because of our participation in that order.

## Brown and Levinson's Politeness Theory

Penelope Brown and Stephen Levinson are sociolinguists whose politeness theory (1987) uses Goffman's notion of face to explain how and why we use various linguistic forms. They begin by noticing that we do not always say what we mean in the most explicit and efficient way possible. Instead, we add verbal tokens that express solidarity or respect, or we imply what we mean "between the lines" of what we actually say. For example, if I need to criticize a colleague's work, I might try to do it in a friendly way to reduce the sting. Alternatively, I might hedge or minimize the criticism or try to distance the problem from the person (e.g., "the proposal kind of rambles a little," instead of "you ramble" or "I think it rambles"). I might decide to hint at the problem or to equivocate if asked for an opinion. Brown and Levinson observed that these kinds of linguistic options are present in three quite different languages and so they reasoned that there must be some fundamental social principles that explain their existence. Showing regard for face is one of those principles.

Brown and Levinson (1987) differentiate two kinds of face wants. Negative face wants refer to "the want of every 'competent adult member' that his actions be unimpeded by others," and positive face wants refer to "the want of every member that [her] wants be desirable to at least some others" (p. 62). Although Brown and Levinson acknowledge face threats and facework directed to our own face wants (Goffman's demeanor), their theory focuses primarily on others' face wants (Goffman's deference).

Many actions we undertake in everyday life have the potential to threaten face; Brown and Levinson term these face-threatening actions (FTAs). For example, orders, requests, suggestions, advice, reminders, threats, and warnings all potentially impede someone else's actions (negative face threat). Likewise, expressing disapproval, criticism, complaints, insults, disagreements, or challenges may disaffirm the other person's desirable self-image (positive face threat). Brown and Levinson reiterate Goffman's claims when they say,

> Face is something that is emotionally invested, and that can be lost, maintained, or enhanced, and must be constantly attended to in interaction. In general, people cooperate (and assume each other's cooperation) in maintaining face in interaction, such cooperation being based on the mutual vulnerability of face. (1987, p. 61)

This creates a dilemma when we need to commit a FTA: how can we act while still showing regard for the other person's face?

One option is to commit the FTA "bald on record"; that is, to state it explicitly (on record) and with little attempt to honor face (bald). To return to the example of criticizing a colleague's work, we might say, "Page four of your draft has errors you must correct." Alternatively, we could do the act using language forms that mitigate threat to face. Positive face redress uses solidary language to soften the blow (e.g., using informal language, claiming common ground, using in-group language or jokes, presenting both parties as cooperators, or recognizing the other's wants for goods, compliments, or services). Negative face redress employs respectful language such as avoiding sounding presumptuous or coercive, communicating a desire not to impose, or addressing wants for freedom. A positively redressed criticism might be

"Bill, I have some feedback to help us make this proposal as strong as it can be. I found some problems around page four and I've marked them. I know we're all under the gun so I hope this helps." In contrast, a negatively redressed message might be, "I hope you won't be offended by my saying this but there were just a few minor problems on page four that you might want to change." Both positive and negative redress entail committing FTAs on record (in this example, "I found some problems" or "there were ... problems"). In contrast, we can try to get the other person to infer the FTA without our having to actually say it. Indirect or "off-record" FTAs rely on hints or ambiguity to make a point while minimizing face threat. For example, we might criticize our colleague indirectly by saying, "Did you get a chance to proofread this yet?" or "You might want to take a look at page four and just be sure it's getting at what you mean." Neither is technically a criticism, but most people would take the hint that something is wrong. A final option, of course, is to decide not to make the criticism at all.

These options – bald on record, positive redress, negative redress, off record, and do not do the FTA – vary in the degree to which they take into account the other person's face, and this accounting for face is what Brown and Levinson (1987) mean by "politeness." Bald on record is least polite, positive redress and negative redress are more polite but still threatening by virtue of being on record, indirect strategies are more polite because they do not say the FTA, and not doing the act is the most polite. Each option has advantages and disadvantages. If you are too direct you may threaten face, but if you are too indirect the other person may not get the point. Positive redress is friendly, but sometimes that oversteps a boundary and inappropriately insinuates closeness. Negative redress is respectful, but can come off as distant, powerless, or uncertain. Different strategies are optimal for different kinds of situations, and Brown and Levinson propose a rational calculus for determining which approach should be optimally appropriate and effective: the greater the face threat, the more polite one should be.

Degree of face threat is determined by three features of the social context: the power of the speaker relative to the hearer, the distance between speaker and hearer, and the rank of the FTA. Those who have more power typically have greater authority to impose on others or evaluate their behavior. Likewise, in closer (i.e., less distant) relationships, we may intrude on one another and assume positive regard for one another. The more powerful the speaker and the closer the relationship, the less face threat is posed by a particular act and the less polite a speaker will need to be. Rank refers to culturally specific ideas about the relative amount of threat entailed by various acts. For example, among many Americans, it would be considered more threatening to criticize a colleague's personality than to point out errors in a particular part of a specific proposal, and it might be more acceptable for coworkers to comment on one another's work than on one another's child-rearing practices or dietary habits.

For acts of greater rank, one should be more polite. The combination of power, distance, and rank suggests how much face threat is involved in some action, which, in turn, directs attention to the appropriateness of more or less polite ways of expressing that act in that particular situation.

Politeness theory focuses on how to avoid face threat, and so there is little talk about hurt feelings. Still, the prospect of hurt feelings looms as the rationale for how and why we speak in a particular fashion. The theory also points to two different ways that feelings might be hurt. Positive face threats entail all the actions that suggest others do not find us as desirable as we might have hoped. In contrast, negative face threats hurt by making unreasonable impositions or restraints that disrespect the honor that is due our line in a particular interaction. Condescension or acting overly formal or distant can hurt as much as saying or implying we are undesirable.

The theory also explains how face can be threatened and, correspondingly, how feelings can be hurt: an action itself can be face threatening, but we may also react negatively to an unexpected way of doing the action. For example, even if I know that there is a problem on page four of the proposal, I might be hurt by my colleague's way of raising the criticism. If I feel the criticism is justified and not very face threatening (for example, if I frame this as a work document, produced under pressure, for which we are all responsible) and if my colleague is equal or superior to me in rank and someone I know fairly well, I might expect the criticism to be given fairly directly, perhaps in the style of friendly positive redress. If, instead, my colleague beats around the bush, I might be hurt by the implication that my ego is too fragile to take a more direct message. Conversely, if my colleague is quite junior to me and someone I do not know well, and if I am highly invested in the document, then I might expect a more respectful or indirect way of broaching any criticism. For a colleague in this situation to state the criticism baldly or in a solidary way might hurt my feelings by conveying a lack of respect for my position, authority, and experience. In other words, knowing the expected patterns of politeness alerts us to the implications and attributions we may reach when those patterns are violated. It may not be only (or even) the action that hurts, but an unexpected way of expressing it.

## CONCEPTUALIZING HURT FEELINGS AS THREATS TO FACE

Face and politeness theory have several implications for understanding hurt feelings. The assumptions of these frameworks draw attention to hurt feelings as social affront. They lead us to examine the social contexts of hurt and how hurt is communicated. These theories suggest that the perpetrator of hurt feelings may also be harmed, and they focus attention on the social accountability of hurt feelings.

## Hurt as Social Affront

Types of hurtful actions parallel closely the types of FTAs, and face threat may account for the link between some actions and hurt feelings. For example, in their study of criticisms from a relational partner, Cupach and Carson (2002) found that, as the perceived degree of positive and negative face threat increased, so did the magnitude of hurt feelings. Episodes that were coded as threatening to the victim's social desirability were among the most frequent and hurtful types of incidents in a study by Leary, Springer, Negel, Ansell, and Evans (1998). Vangelisti (1994) identified accusations, evaluations, directives, advice, expressions of desire, disclosures of information, questions, threats, jokes, and lies as types of hurtful speech acts. Directives and advice threaten negative face and can also threaten positive face when they imply one has acted incorrectly. Accusations threaten positive face, and expressing information, desires, or evaluations can threaten positive face if what is expressed reflects negatively on the other (as in the examples of hurt reported in Vangelisti's study). Face-related themes echo through many of the explanations for why actions are hurtful (Vangelisti, Young, Carpenter-Theune, & Alexander, 2005), including rejection, behavioral criticism, moral affront, indifference to one's feelings, personal attack, undermining self-concept, and humiliation.

Although there is overlap between actions that hurt and actions that threaten face, and evidence that perceived face threat predicts hurt, it is nonetheless useful to differentiate hurt that derives from face threat from hurt that derives from other sources. For example, hurt has been conceptualized as relational devaluation (see Leary and Leder, Chapter 2, this volume), relational transgression (Vangelisti, 2007), or damage to mental models of attachment (see Feeney, Chapter 15, this volume). In contrast, face theories focus on hurt that comes from violating a basic social contract to facilitate one another's identity performance in particular social interactions and on the vulnerability we feel in awkward interactional moments. When a hurtful action threatens face, we must ask, "Who am I now in this interaction and how can I regain a viable identity with some degree of poise?"

Hurt can arise from violated expectations in a close relationship, but it can also arise when the general cooperation that is prerequisite to any interaction is not forthcoming. Although it is a generic courtesy that is violated, that does not necessarily make it less painful – in fact, it may be especially hurtful when a close relational partner fails to show us the basic consideration he or she would show to a stranger. Consideration for face is expected, and the affront to this basic principle may compound a violation of particular close relational standards.

Other theories have explored the overlap between hurt and sadness, anger, and fear; face theories may be particularly useful for understanding the intersection of hurt with embarrassment. For example, a partner's infidelity may be hurtful because it is a relational transgression or devaluation or failure of a working model. However, whether it is face threatening depends on whether it disrupts valued performances. Do the partners confront the collapse of their performance as loyal partners, or do they collude to ignore the violation so that each can continue to "face" the other as if nothing happened? Do others find out about the infidelity, so that instead of playing the proud spouse at the company picnic, you are the target of gossip, or instead of being the ideal family in your social circle, you are now a family who "has been having some problems"? The significance of social affront is revealed in Vangelisti and colleagues' (2005) finding that "humiliation" is especially hurtful.

Vangelisti (2007) classifies the factors that affect how we evaluate hurtful interactions into those associated with the self (e.g., self-esteem, attachment style), the other (evaluations of the other's intent), and the relationship (e.g., quality). We might add that self, other, and relationship have both personal and social components. That is, there may be a difference between hurt that threatens my sense of self and hurt that comes from the embarrassment I suffer from not being able to claim a particular social identity before some audience (at a minimum, the partner who has hurt me but also others who might witness the incident or find out about it). When we evaluate others' intentions, we may differentiate between what they "really meant" and "how they seemed" in the interaction – to us and potentially to others who see or hear about the incident. Relationships have both private standards and public displays and expectations.

Conceptualizing hurt as social affront explains the finding that attributions of hurt and negative reactions tend to be magnified when an incident occurs in public rather than in private. For example, children may appraise the hurtfulness of a parent's comments differently if they are made in public rather than in private (Vangelisti & Maguire, 2002), and relational partners perceive more face threat and feel more hurt when criticism is delivered publicly rather than privately (Cupach & Carson, 2002). Relationships may suffer less damage, and people may be most likely to forgive, when cheaters disclose the infidelity privately to the person compared to if the person finds out more publicly (e.g., catching the partner or hearing about it from someone else; Afifi, Falato, & Weiner, 2001). It will probably always feel bad to be criticized by others or to find out that your partner is cheating on you, but because face is social, that threat (and the hurt that results from it) is magnified when a larger audience sees your failed identity performance.

Social affront can also explain why some types of comments are especially hurtful. To the degree that an individual can regain face and respond with poise, some of the hurtfulness may be mitigated. Messages are more hurtful when they leave recipients with very limited possibilities for responding (Feeney, 2004; Vangelisti, 2007). For example, Vangelisti (1994) suggested that informative statements (e.g., I don't love you anymore) were rated as especially hurtful because they are difficult to challenge, defend, and repair. A statement of how I feel is not something you can contest, whereas the presentation of selves is more negotiable. Other types of hurtful comments (e.g., accusations, jokes) may leave room for a remedial interchange to occur.

## Contexts of Hurt

Politeness theory leads us to consider whether the same action or comment might be more or less hurtful in different social contexts. The magnitude of face threat is a function of the power and distance of the relationship between speaker and hearer and the cultural rank of the particular action. By this reasoning, close peer relationships offer the greatest latitude for committing FTAs with little consequence; however, even in close relationships, actions of high rank may nonetheless threaten face, and variability in partners' power may also influence what counts as hurtful. For example, evaluations and directives concerning hygiene may be acceptable and even benevolent from a mother to a young child; the same comment might be hurtful when made to an adolescent child or adult partner.

Most studies of hurt feelings have focused on close relationships such as romantic partners, family members, and friends. In addition, study designs usually solicit from participants a report of a hurtful incident and then inquire about the relationship so we cannot tell whether the same action would be more or less threatening in a different relational context. Studies have examined perceptions of closeness (e.g., Vangelisti & Young, 2000) and powerlessness (e.g., Feeney, 2004), but these have been measured as outcomes of hurtful incidents rather than as preconditions that might influence the degree to which an action is considered hurtful.

Arguably, close relationships provide a distinctive environment for hurt to occur. However, we know comparatively little about how hurt occurs in less close relationships or how relational partners determine when actions they would not tolerate from less close others are acceptable or when some actions are unforgivable in any relational context. Leary and colleagues (1998) found that most hurtful episodes involved close friends (39%), romantic partners (32%), and family members (10%), but hurt also occurred among acquaintances (12%) and authority figures such as teachers or bosses (4%). One episode involved hurt by a stranger, and strangers were present (though not necessarily the source of hurt) in 16% of the episodes.[2] Snapp and Leary (2001) conducted one of the few studies that compared the hurtfulness of the same action

---

[2] Leary et al. did find that hurt was significantly greater in episodes with romantic partners compared to acquaintances, but this does not reveal whether the same acts were evaluated differently in different relationships.

in different relational contexts. Their participants became acquainted with a confederate prior to an experimental rejection. Those who became more familiar with the confederate were less hurt by the subsequent rejection experience than those who had low familiarity with the confederate.

Rather than focusing on how our closest relational partners can hurt us, politeness theory reminds us that we tolerate quite a lot in close relationships that would simply be unacceptable from anyone else. In fact, our willingness to tolerate criticism, teasing, or joking insults without feeling hurt may be one sign that a relationship is becoming closer, and it can be a tribute to relational strength when we are able to come back from deceptions and betrayals that would end a weaker relationship.

## The Hurt Is in the How

Hurt feelings can stem not only from what someone did but also from how they did it, and hurt may come from violating normative expectations about status or consideration owed. There is, for example, the common complaint, "It wasn't what you said that hurt me, it was how you said it." Vangelisti (1994) suggested that when a conversational partner is not cooperative and polite, it produces arousal; appraisal of the experience as a violation causes the arousal to be labeled with a negative emotion. What counts as "cooperative and polite" may have as much to do with the form of a message as its content, a central idea in politeness theory. The same content (e.g., a negative evaluation of someone's appearance) could be conveyed in different message forms (e.g., different wording, different use of humor or directness). Politeness theory offers useful ways of distinguishing one form from the other.

The few studies that have examined variation in how hurtful content is expressed suggest that this variation does shape the degree of hurt that is experienced. Intensely expressed hurtful messages (i.e., more harshly worded or using more extreme language) were less likely to be seen as having any positive intention to help, comfort, or express concern (Young, 2004). Both Leary and colleagues (1998) and Feeney (2004) differentiate between passive disassociation (being excluded, ignored) and active disassociation (explicitly being rejected by a partner) and find active to be more hurtful than passive disassociation.[3] Politeness theory suggests this is because active association is an on-record threat to face, whereas passive disassociation is likely to be more ambiguous.

Politeness theory provides a useful set of concepts for examining teasing and joking, behaviors that have been identified as hurtful acts in some studies

---

[3] The difference is statistically significant in Feeney's study of 224 participants, but not in Leary et al.'s study of 168 participants, though the means are in the expected direction in Leary et al.

(Kowalski, 2000; Vangelisti, 1994) but not in others (e.g., Feeney, 2004, who reports teasing did not appear, and Leary et al., 1998, who report it occurred infrequently). Politeness theory suggests teasing can be an ambiguous, off-record way of committing FTAs; in other words, though teasing can be an FTA, it may be relatively less hurtful than expressing the same content as criticism, accusation, evaluation, or the like. Playful, off-record linguistic devices can actually mitigate the amount of face loss and hurt, at least when compared to expressing the same hurtful comment in a serious style or frame. Although teasing can hurt, it may hurt less than the alternatives because it simultaneously signals relational closeness. It also allows face-saving ways for the target to respond, such as joining in the fun, teasing back, or shrugging off the hurtful comment as "just a joke." Teasing also affords face protection for the teaser who can deny the intent to hurt, claim to be "only kidding," and accuse the other of "not being able to take a joke." Of course, as Goffman (1967) noted, moves that can function to save face can also be used aggressively for self-serving motives. Face and politeness theories suggest greater attention to how and when teasing may be hurtful and to the facework that may be negotiated when a hurtful comment is delivered in a joking fashion.

The "how" of hurt feelings also entails the sequence of moves that precede or follow a hurtful act. For example, Goffman's (1967) remedial interchange is a type of conversational sequence that has the potential to restore face and perhaps mitigate hurt. Vangelisti and Crumley (1998) found that victims of hurt responded with active verbal responses (attacking the other, defending the self, reacting sarcastically, and asking for/providing an explanation), acquiescent responses (crying, conceding, and apologizing), and invulnerable responses (e.g., ignoring the act, laughing, or being silent). Those who responded with active verbal responses reported the highest levels of relational satisfaction, perhaps because some of these responses challenged the hurtful act and launched a conversation in which face could be regained.

Theories of face and politeness also suggest alternative interpretations of previous findings on response to hurt. For example, Vangelisti and Crumley (1998) found that acquiescent responses became more likely as the hurtfulness of the incident increased (cf. Leary et al., 1998, who found the likelihood of crying correlated with the magnitude of hurt). They suggested this pattern may have occurred because intense hurt overwhelmed the victim and made it difficult to marshal a response. Alternatively, we might consider whether the type of response shapes how hurtful an action is when reported retrospectively. Face threat and hurt may be compounded when acquiescence is the only viable line open in an unfolding interaction. A similar kind of reinterpretation can be suggested for Waldron and Kelley's (2005) findings regarding how people communicated forgiveness for a relational transgression. As the severity of the transgression increased, people were less likely to show forgiveness by acting affectionate or minimizing the offense and more likely to offer only conditional forgiveness (e.g., "I'll forgive you if you promise to act differently.") One way to interpret the findings is to presume that the severity of the transgression drives the response. Alternatively, we might speculate that when relational partners are able to enact a sequence that involves affection and minimization of offense, they end up seeing the transgression as less serious. In other words, we may expect that a sense of hurt will be magnified when injury to one's personal sense of self or a valued relationship is compounded by disruption of the *presentation* of that self and relationship and when there is little opportunity to redeem that performance. Rather than assuming that the individual experience of hurt causes an individual choice of response, we may consider the ways that both parties shape an unfolding hurtful incident and the impact this shaping can have on one or both parties' construction and recall of the hurtfulness of the incident after the fact.

In short, the hurtfulness of an action may be mitigated by its form. Criticism, betrayal, and rejection are likely hurtful no matter how they are conveyed, but some ways of communicating these FTAs show that the perpetrator is at least trying to soften the blow, and some ways of communicating after a hurtful act allow the victim (or the victim and perpetrator together) to save or restore face. Politeness strategies offer one way of categorizing hurtful messages – for example, the perception that a message is "harsh" may result from a failure to engage in appropriate facework. We may also ask what features of an act, message, incident, or conversation open up or shut down opportunities to save face. Rather than viewing responses to hurtful actions as individual moves prompted by internal, individual processes, we might also view responses to hurtful actions as moves in a sequence that is socially structured and dynamically enacted by both parties to the interaction.

## The One Who Hurts May Also Suffer Harm

Hurt feelings have implications not only for the one hurt but also for the one who hurts. To hurt others may also be hurtful (at least in a social sense) to the one who does the hurting. Being perceptive and considerate is part of being a well-demeaned social interactant. Victims frequently view the person who hurt them as inconsiderate and insensitive (Leary et al., 1998), and hurtful incidents can result in short- and long-term relational harm (e.g., Leary et al., 1998; Vangelisti & Young, 2000).

Individuals who have hurt others often engage in self-presentational strategies. Several studies have asked participants to describe a time when they were either the perpetrator or victim of a hurtful incident (Baumeister, Stillwell, & Wotman, 1990; Leary et al., 1998) or have asked both partners in a relationship to report on the same hurtful incident (Cameron, Ross, & Holmes, 2002; Mikula, Athenstaedt, Heschgl, & Heimgartner, 1998; Schütz, 1999). Both victims and perpetrators give face-saving accounts. For example, compared to victims' stories, perpetrator narratives are more likely to say the event was more accidental, less intentional, more a function of something the victims did, and more likely to be deserved by the victim. Perpetrators are also more likely to downplay negative consequences, to say they apologized, and to report feeling regret. Even when describing the same incident, victim and perpetrator stories differ and are marked by a tendency to see the other's behavior as the source of the problem. Although these narratives are produced for researchers, some of the same tendencies toward positive self-presentation likely occur between partners and with other audiences such as friends and family. Partners, friends, and family often have knowledge of the incident that could constrain a perpetrator's (or victim's) positive self-presentation. Theories of face direct our attention to the ways these issues may be negotiated and the implications these presentations have not only for construing episodes but also for the identities of the players in the drama.

Saving face matters not only for the perpetrator but also for the relationship. For example, in their study of infidelity among college dating partners, Afifi and colleagues (2001) found that when the cheating partner disclosed the infidelity unsolicited there was less damage to the relationship and a greater chance of forgiveness than when the disclosure was solicited or heard from a third party or the partner was discovered in the act. Infidelity ranks high among hurtful relational actions (e.g., Feeney, 2004) yet an unsolicited disclosure may afford the most opportunity for face saving, both for the victim and for the perpetrator (who can at least appear forthright and repentant even as he or she confesses a transgression). Zechmesiter and Romero (2002) found that narratives of forgiven offenses, compared to unforgiven offenses, were more likely to indicate that the incident was over, to describe the offender's apology and attempts to make amends, and to describe positive consequences and happy endings. Schütz (1999) found that, although partners tended to give self-serving narratives of hurtful incidents, those who had been hurt also included elements that saved face for their partners (e.g., they noted that the hurt was unintentional or caused by a difference of opinion). Similarly, children who reported being hurt by their mother's disparagement or disregard often attributed the event to external stress on their mothers (Mills, Nazar, & Farrell, 2002). Victims have a vested interest in saving face for the perpetrator so they do not look foolish for having a hurtful partner and so their relationship may be presented in a more positive light. Previous research has shown that individuals in satisfying relationships are more likely to see their partner's hurtfulness as unintentional (Vangelisti, 2007); it may also be that couples who succeed in constructing a version of a hurtful incident in a way that preserves face for both parties find this relationally satisfying.

Differences in victim and perpetrator perceptions and the tendency for both parties to engage in face-saving actions may yield differing accounts of who is victim and who is perpetrator and of what action constituted the hurt. For example, imagine that one partner is hurt, perceives the affront as intentional, and responds with relational distancing (a common pattern, according to Vangelisti & Young [2000]). If the offending partner did not perceive his or her action as intentional (a common pattern in several studies summarized earlier), then he or she may view the other's relational distancing as an unwarranted and hurtful instance of disassociation (perhaps active, perhaps passive). Relational distancing may be the outcome of a hurtful incident from one person's point of view, but the cause of hurt from the other's vantage point. Similarly, we can imagine that, when a victim responds with retaliation and accusation, this response may be hurtful to the perpetrator, particularly if he or she viewed the precipitating incident as unintentional. Vangelisti (2007) observed that some relationships are characterized by patterns of reciprocal hurtful behavior, and Leary and colleagues (1998) found that victims frequently reported responding to hurtful incidents with anger, accusations, criticism, and nasty remarks. If attempts to save one's own face intentionally or unintentionally threaten the other's face, a series of hurtful actions may follow. Conversely, to the extent that partners are able to construct and enact episodes in a way that saves face for both parties, hurtful spirals might be avoided (Metts, 2000).

## Hurt Is Socially Accountable

Hurt feelings include not only individual appraisal and emotional experience but also social accountability. When we focus attention on threats to face as a public, social performance, we may ask, does one have grounds for *acting* hurt? A recipient's right to act hurt and the kinds of repair that are socially obligated seem likely to vary, depending on how intention and responsibility are framed. Goffman (1967) proposed that the implications for face differ depending on whether an action is committed accidentally, intentionally and with malice, or as an incidental feature of some other action (e.g., expressing concern, helping). Similar dimensions have been identified in individuals' attributions for hurtful actions (Vangelisti, 1994; Vangelisti & Young, 2000; Young, 2004).

An act may be hurtful whether it is intended or not, but one's right to feel hurt and pursue remediation may differ, depending on whether the act was an accident or committed in the service of some positive intention. Vangelisti and Young (2000) found that hurtful messages that were perceived as intentional were associated with greater relational distancing, greater feelings of hurt, lower relationship satisfaction, and less feelings of closeness than those messages perceived as unintentional. Vangelisti (1994) found no significant difference in the hurtfulness of messages that were perceived as intentional versus unintentional, uttered in close versus less close relationships, or committed in family versus nonfamily relationships; however, intent, relational closeness, and family relationship did significantly influence the outcome of the hurtful action for the relationship. This is consistent with the idea that we may feel hurt, but whether we have a right to act hurt or to take action against the perpetrator may be contingent on social factors. Previous authors have given attributional explanations for this idea, but there may also be a social explanation for why the degree of hurt alone does not simply and straightforwardly predict the outcome: attributions of intent, relational status, and the like matter because they shape our grounds for responding. The salience of social support for hurt feelings is shown by Miller and Roloff's (2005) finding that social factors, including gender roles and perceived support from an audience (particularly when the audience was composed of one's own rather than the partner's friends), shaped the likelihood that a hurtful incident would be confronted openly. Willingness to confront a hurtful tease or insult increased as the victim perceived greater amounts of hurt and audience support.

Politeness theory reminds us that individuals are not unconstrained in the process of making attributions – at least those attributions that they intend to communicate to others. There are social conventions that influence when and how actions may be claimed to be accidental, malicious, or expected but undesired consequences. Patterns of response, such as defending oneself, attacking the perpetrator, asking for or providing an explanation, and conceding, resemble moves in Goffman's (1967) remedial interchange, suggesting that responses are shaped not only by individual perceptions and relationship specific factors but also by a socially shared interactional structure. Feeney (2004) found that relational harm in the wake of a hurtful incident was a function not only of an anxious attachment style but also of how the episode played out, including the victim's own behavior and the perpetrator's intent and remorse. Concern for saving and recovering face may also be behind Feeney and Hill's (2006) finding that, when couples were asked to track hurtful incidents in a diary, some minor episodes showed up in victim but not perpetrator reports. It may be that when the threat to face and resulting hurt are not too severe, we do not confront our partners because the risks of threatening our partner's face and perhaps compounding our own loss of face in a confrontation outweigh the likelihood of gaining recompense. Perhaps we pick our battles, confronting hurt when we can successfully play the role of maligned victim and avoiding confrontation when that role is untenable.

The literature on hurt feelings demonstrates variability in the magnitude of hurt, response to hurt, and outcome of hurt, depending on assessments of intent, responsibility, and relational states. A contribution of politeness theory is to suggest there are principled, socially shared norms for how we reach these conclusions. It is not just individual difference or the closeness of a particular relationship that shapes how we interpret a potentially hurtful act or message; there are also shared norms and public processes through which these interpretations may be reached.

## DIRECTIONS FOR RESEARCH

Conceptualizing hurt as arising from threats to face suggests several specific avenues for future research. First, it may be useful to disentangle public from private hurt and the different shades of feeling that may result. Whereas hurt has been associated with relational devaluation and interpersonal rejection, theories of face and politeness would call for attention to hurt that derives from disrupted social performances. Although the most immediate emotional reaction to such disruption may be embarrassment, an inability to redress the situation or respond with poise may also prompt sadness and anger. Researchers have acknowledged the blend of feelings that is associated with a lay person's perception of "hurt," and face theory provides a principled way of considering how the makeup of that blend may differ.

Second, politeness theory posits that the degree of face threat varies with elements of the social context, including the power and distance of the relationship between participants in an interaction as well as the culturally understood rank of the threatening action. Much of the work on hurt feelings has examined hurt in the context of personal relationships. Those studies that have compared relationships typically report how frequently hurtful incidents came from various relational types but do not shed light on whether the same action might be more or less hurtful in different relationships. In particular, politeness theory would have us expand our attention to consider hurt in impersonal relationships and in relationships of unequal power. For example, study of hurt feelings among coworkers would provide useful comparisons to the close relationships literature and would also coincide with organizational scholars' interest in emotion (for a review of research on emotion in the workplace, see Miller, Consadine, & Garner, 2007).

Likewise, research on hurt feelings has occurred largely among white, middle-class North Americans. Politeness theory predicts cultural variability in what acts threaten face and how much; correspondingly, hurt feelings may also vary cross-culturally. It seems likely that general categories of action such as "betrayal" or "humiliation" will occur and be hurtful in all cultures, but what pattern of action constitutes "betrayal" or "humiliation" is likely to vary and the same action might be more or less hurtful in different sociocultural groups, with important implications for intercultural communication.

Third, politeness theory is concerned with how one goes about committing FTAs. Subtle variations in language shape the degree to which an action threatens face. Although research on hurt feelings has shown that harshly worded comments may be seen as more hurtful, little attention has been given to gradations of "harshness," what linguistic features contribute to a perception of harshness or kindness, and how hurtful comments and actions can be mitigated by verbal and nonverbal cues. Research on hurt feelings frequently solicits recall of conversations, which is appropriate within an individual, attributional perspective on hurt. In contrast, politeness theory encourages us to examine how the form and sequence of interactions, variability in nonverbal tone, and other features of "how" something is said may be systematically linked to attributions of hurt. Politeness theory also provides a detailed catalog of language features that could be examined.

Fourth, theories of face and politeness emphasize the implicit cooperation that is built into all social interaction, directing our attention to the ways that hurtful actions may also harm the one who hurts. Research more often focuses on the point of view of the victim than the perpetrator, and when the perpetrator has been studied, the focus has been on how victim and perpetrator attributions differ. Although the perpetrator's desire to look good has been proposed as an explanation for differences in victim and perpetrator perspectives, we have not often examined how one who hurts may also suffer emotional repercussions by virtue of coming off as inconsiderate or mean. Considering the damage to image suffered by both parties could also lead us to consider how hurtful incidents do not necessarily end with the precipitating comment or action. Hurtful actions transpire in unfolding social interactions, sometimes with audiences whose reactions influence appraisals of, responses to, and outcomes of those actions. Hurtful incidents may also be talked about across a social network, which may mitigate or magnify hurt for both the victim and the perpetrator. Likely the types of hurt suffered will differ for victim and perpetrator, but examination of outcomes for the perpetrator is a clear implication of the social contract presumed in theories of face.

Fifth, face and politeness theories direct our attention to the social, as well as the individual, construction of hurt. Although the individual may be the ultimate arbiter of his or her feelings of hurt, social norms and the reactions of particular social others play a role in whether those feelings are seen as justifiable. Social expectations shape our understanding of what counts as hurtful. Negotiations occur in conversations about whether hurt is a warranted reaction to a particular comment or action, and individuals may mobilize social networks to justify their version of a hurtful incident. Whether an individual has a "right" to be hurt may play into the functionality of hurt, the options for remediation, and the impact on relationships. One implication of this view is to examine how a hurtful incident may ripple outward from a dyad. Although previous research has differentiated between hurtful incidents that occur in public and those in private, little attention has been given to how even private hurtful incidents may then be discussed within a family, a workplace, or some other social network. Hurt can also arise from patterns of network interaction (e.g., gossip, revealing confidences), such that the same information or action may not be hurtful within a dyad, but can be hurtful when others learn or talk about it (see Fehr and Harasymchuk Chapter 14, this volume).

Finally, applying politeness theory to hurt feelings also has implications for politeness theory. Research on face has often focused on the production or selection of strategies in response to situational variation or on interpretation of strategies as polite. A few studies have examined how attention to face may make an utterance more acceptable or effective (see Goldsmith, 2007, 2008, for reviews). However, there has been little attention to how we *feel* when face is saved or threatened. Likewise, when we have studied politeness in the context of personal relationships, it has often been to try to ascertain if people really are less polite in close relationships (as politeness theory predicted). This work focuses on how relationships shape the practice of politeness but has not focused attention on how threats to face (i.e., the failure of politeness) might have implications for relational well-being. Consequently, the application of politeness theory to hurt feelings in close relationships has the potential to expand the range of outcomes that have been associated with politeness to include individual feelings and relational distancing or satisfaction.

## CONCLUSION

Theories of face and politeness draw attention to the social drama of hurtful episodes. The expectations that are violated have social underpinnings. The selves that are hurt have public personas. The moves in the unfolding action improvise on well-learnt patterns. The audiences who see and hear about infractions weigh in. Whereas previous research has illumined individual emotion, cognition, motivation, personality, and perception in relation to hurt feelings, this chapter has focused on a complementary set of interactive, performed, communicative processes. Thinking about how face threat contributes to hurt feelings suggests a different emphasis in the study of hurt. We know individuals differ in their perception of and reaction to hurt and that this may be traced to personal factors such as self-esteem or attachment styles. Similarly, relationship-specific assessments of satisfaction or commitment can alter interpretations of and responses to hurt. One contribution of this chapter is to point out that running parallel to the individual and relationship-specific facets of hurt are also common social norms that create a shared frame of reference for interpreting hurtful acts and evaluating actors, as well as shared social structures for avoiding, engaging, or fixing hurtful incidents. Studies of hurt feelings have typically taken these shared social frames and structures as the ground against which the figure of individual and relational differences stands out for examination. Theories of face and politeness provide ways to conceptualize this common social ground and suggest the fruitfulness of making it the focus of future research.

### REFERENCES

Afifi, W. A., Falato, W. L., & Weiner, J. L. (2001). Identity concerns following a severe relational transgression: The role of discovery method for the relational outcomes of infidelity. *Journal of Social and Personal Relationships, 18,* 291–308.
Baumeister, R. F., Stillwell, A., & Wotman, S. R. (1990). Victim and perpetrator accounts of interpersonal conflict: Autobiographical narratives about anger. *Journal of Personality and Social Psychology, 59,* 994–1005.
Brown, P., & Levinson, S. (1987). *Politeness: Some universals in language usage.* Cambridge: Cambridge University Press.

Cameron, J. J., Ross, M., & Holmes, J. G. (2002). Loving the one you hurt: Positive effects of recounting a transgression against an intimate partner. *Journal of Experimental Social Psychology, 38*, 307–314.

Cupach, W. R., & Carson, C. L. (2002). Characteristics and consequences of interpersonal complaints associated with perceived face threat. *Journal of Social and Personal Relationships, 19*, 443–462.

Feeney, J. A. (2004). Hurt feelings in couple relationships: Towards integrative models of the negative effects of hurtful events. *Journal of Social and Personal Relationships, 21*, 487–508.

Feeney, J. A., & Hill, A. (2006). Victim-perpetrator differences in reports of hurtful events. *Journal of Social and Personal Relationships, 23*, 587–608.

Goffman, E. (1967). *Interaction ritual: Essays in face-to-face interaction.* Garden City, NY: Doubleday.

Goldsmith, D. J. (2007). Brown and Levinson's politeness theory. In B. B. Whaley & W. Samter (Eds.), *Explaining communication: Contemporary theories and exemplars* (pp. 219–236). Mahwah, NJ: Erlbaum.

Goldsmith, D. J. (2008). Politeness theory: How we use language to save face. In L. A. Baxter & D. Braithwaite (Eds.), *Engaging theories in interpersonal communication: Multiple perspectives* (pp. 255–267). Thousand Oaks, CA: Sage.

Kowalski, R. M. (2000). "I was only kidding!": Victims' and perpetrators' perceptions of teasing. *Personality and Social Psychology Bulletin, 26*, 231–241.

Leary, M. R., Springer, C., Negel, L., Ansell, E., & Evans, K. (1998). The causes, phenomenology, and consequences of hurt feelings. *Journal of Personality and Social Psychology, 74*, 1225–1237.

Metts, S. (2000). Face and facework: Implications for the study of personal relationships. In K. Dindia & S. Duck (Eds.), *Communication and personal relationships* (pp. 77–93). Chichester: Wiley.

Mikula, G., Athenstaedt, U., Heschgl, S., & Heimgartner, A. (1998). Does it only depend on the point of view? Perspective-related differences in justice evaluations of negative incidents in personal relationships. *European Journal of Social Psychology, 28*, 931–962.

Miller, C. W., & Roloff, M. E. (2005). Gender and willingness to confront hurtful messages from romantic partners. *Communication Quarterly, 53*, 323–337.

Miller, K. I., Consadine, J., & Garner, J. (2007). "Let me tell you about my job": Exploring the terrain of emotion in the workplace. *Management Communication Quarterly, 20*, 231–260.

Mills, R. S. L., Nazar, J., & Farrell, H. M. (2002). Child and parent perceptions of hurtful messages. *Journal of Social and Personal Relationships, 19*, 731–754.

Schütz, A. (1999). It was your fault!: Self-serving biases in autobiographical accounts of conflicts in married couples. *Journal of Social and Personal Relationships, 16*, 193–208.

Snapp, C. M., & Leary, M. R. (2001). Hurt feelings among new acquaintances: Moderating effects of interpersonal familiarity. *Journal of Social and Personal Relationships, 18*, 315–326.

Vangelisti, A. L. (1994). Messages that hurt. In W. R. Cupach & B. H. Spitzberg (Eds.), *The dark side of interpersonal communication* (pp. 53–82). Hillsdale, NJ: Erlbaum.

Vangelisti, A. L. (2007). Communicating hurt. In W. R. Cupach & B. H. Spitzberg (Eds.), *The dark side of interpersonal communication* (2nd ed., pp. 121–142). Mahwah, NJ: Erlbaum.

Vangelisti, A. L., & Crumley, L. P. (1998). Reactions to messages that hurt: The influence of relational contexts. *Communication Monographs, 65*, 173–196.

Vangelisti, A. L., & Maguire, K. (2002). Hurtful messages in family relationships: When the pain lingers. In J. H. Harvey & A. Wenzel (Eds.), *A clinician's guide to maintaining and enhancing close relationships* (pp. 43–62). Mahwah, NJ: Erlbaum.

Vangelisti, A. L., & Young, S. L. (2000). When words hurt: The effects of perceived intentionality on interpersonal relationships. *Journal of Social and Personal Relationships, 17,* 393–424.

Vangelisti, A. L., Young, S. L., Carpenter-Theune, K. E., & Alexander, A. L. (2005). Why does it hurt?: The perceived causes of hurt feelings. *Communication Research, 32,* 443–477.

Waldron, V. R., & Kelley, D. L. (2005). Forgiving communication as a response to relational transgressions. *Journal of Social and Personal Relationships, 22,* 723–742.

Watts, R. (2003). *Politeness.* Cambridge: Cambridge University Press.

Young, S. L. (2004). Factors that influence recipients' appraisals of hurtful communication. *Journal of Social and Personal Relationships, 21,* 291–303.

Zechmeister, J. S., & Romero, C. (2002). Victim and offender accounts of interpersonal conflict: Autobiographical narratives of forgiveness and unforgiveness. *Journal of Personality and Social Psychology, 82,* 675–686.

# 5

## Rejection Sensitivity: A Model of How Individual Difference Factors Affect the Experience of Hurt Feelings in Conflict and Support

N. JAN KANG, GERALDINE DOWNEY, MASUMI IIDA,
AND SYLVIA RODRIGUEZ

Everyone experiences hurt feelings in close relationships – a mother publicly criticizes her daughter, a boyfriend doesn't offer to pick his girlfriend up from the airport, or a woman chooses not to confide in her best friend. Although hurt feelings can be experienced in any interpersonal context, they are more likely to occur in close relationships. What leads to hurt feelings may differ for individuals, but studies highlight several commonalities. "Feeling hurt" has been conceptualized as an emotional interpersonal response (Leary, Springer, Negel, Ansell & Evans, 1998; Vangelisti, 1994) to a devaluation (Leary et al., 1998) or relational transgression (Vangelisti, 2001). One can respond to hurt feelings in both constructive (i.e., increasing understanding of one's partner) and unconstructive ways (e.g., lashing out in anger). Maladaptive responses to feeling hurt can have negative consequences including lower self-esteem and relational distancing (Vangelisti, 2001) or retaliation (Ayduk, Downey, Testa, Yen, & Shoda, 1999).

Hurtful events may occur more frequently to or be felt more intensely by some individuals than others. A teenager may interpret ridicule as the end of the world, whereas a 30-year-old may be more poised to shrug it off. The new kid in school may find himself the subject of bullying more often than his classmates. Individual differences in personality dispositions can also explain some of the variability in hurtful experiences and responses to them. This variability can have significant consequences for emotional and physical health (see Loving, Le, and Crockett, Chapter 17, this volume). Examining the link between various dispositional differences and feelings of hurt can lead to an understanding of this variability and illuminate the underlying dynamics that lead to hurt feelings. Adopting an interactionist perspective, we focus on dispositional characteristics of individuals that become activated by situational cues and take different forms over the life course.

This chapter focuses primarily on the individual difference termed *rejection sensitivity* (Downey & Feldman, 1996) and the theoretical model of the processes comprising this disposition and linking it with vulnerability to hurt feelings in close relationships. We also address relevant findings on other relational vulnerabilities – attachment style, self-esteem, and depressive symptoms – that dispose individuals to experience hurt in close relationships. All of these relatively enduring or, in the case of depressive symptoms, episodic individual differences affect what we attend to and how we think, feel, and behave in relational contexts. They may result in greater relationship anxiety or more maladaptive responses to feeling hurt, which in turn have been shown to lead to a longer term negative impact by hurtful events (Feeney, 2004).

Downey and Feldman (1996) conceptualized rejection sensitivity (RS) in cognitive-affective terms to account for the individual differences in the thoughts and feelings of individuals in the presence of cues of potential rejection. They proposed that understanding variability in these immediate psychological antecedents would help account for variability in people's responses to rejection cues. They viewed the immediate cognitive and affective antecedents as rooted in anticipatory anxiety about rejection and doubts about acceptance developed through prior exposure to rejection. Thus, they viewed these anxious expectations as what the person carries from a history of rejection into new relationships and specific social encounters. These expectations then shape what is attended to and perceived in the situation and the intensity of responses to the perceived rejection. Individuals high in rejection sensitivity are characterized by anxiously expecting rejection, readily perceiving it in situations where it is a possibility, and responding intensely to it. Rejection can take the form of personal devaluation, as proposed by Leary et al. (1998); for example, a man may feel like his proposal of marriage was turned down because the woman's parents did not think he was good enough for her. Rejection can also take the form of disrespect or a transgression of relational norms (Vangelisti, 2001), such as when a wife takes her mother's advice over her husband's. These types of rejection experiences in turn lead to hurt feelings. Although the RS model was developed to account for the link between rejection expectations and maladaptive responses to rejection, we believe that the basic cognitive-affective model can be effectively adapted to delineate the processes linking other dispositions, such as self-esteem, attachment style, neuroticism, and depressive symptoms, with vulnerability to hurt feelings in relationships.

We focus on two ways in which hurt can be conveyed. First, hurt may occur as a consequence of the presence of negative interpersonal interactions, such as those that arise out of criticism. For example, a man may tell his wife that he is embarrassed to be seen with her in public. These are hurts of commission, marked by the addition of negative actions. Second, hurt may also be caused by omission, a result of disappointment in a relationship. For example, a wife may forget to ask her husband how his big presentation went. We propose that the RS model applies to hurt feelings resulting from commission and from omission.

In this chapter we examine the association between individual differences and hurt feelings in close relationships by applying the RS model. First, we describe the three components of the RS model – anxious expectations, ready perceptions, and intense reactions. Second, we show how these three components operate to increase both perceived exposure and reactivity to rejection cues, thus leading to the experience of hurt feelings. We employ examples from studies of RS as well as of other individual differences that are associated with the experience of feeling hurt in close relationships, such as attachment style, self-esteem, and depression. We describe the RS model in relation to rejection in the form of commission, such as conflict, and present a study of rejection by omission. Specifically, we describe a study of the effects of RS on social support processes. Support seeking is a relationship process that tests expectations of the relationship and provides an occasion for the potential hurt of omission. We test the hypothesis that high RS individuals are especially vulnerable to feeling hurt when the support they seek is not provided.

## REJECTION SENSITIVITY

The RS model proposes that early rejection in the forms of exposure to family violence, emotional neglect, or conditional love from significant friends and family (Downey, Khouri, & Feldman, 1997) can heighten anxious expectations of rejection, which may influence interpersonal perceptions and behavior into adulthood. What develops is a lowered threshold for perceptions of negative social cues, a greater personalization of these cues, and a strong cognitive, emotional, and behavioral response to them. These cognitions, feelings, and behaviors may present as depression or hostility and influence those with whom a high rejection-sensitive person interacts to respond in a rejecting way, creating and perpetuating a cyclical self-fulfilling prophecy.

Anxious expectations encapsulate both the emotional and cognitive precursors to rejection. Emotionally, in anticipation of rejection, those high in rejection sensitivity are highly anxious before engaging in potentially rejecting interactions. Cognitively, those with high rejection sensitivity are more likely to endorse the belief that the interaction will result in being rejected. During interactions that hold the possibility of rejection, those high in rejection sensitivity are in a heightened state of readiness to perceive rejection and are more likely to focus on cues that could be interpreted as rejection and then imbue them with such meaning. After rejection is perceived, those high in rejection sensitivity react intensely, often experiencing greater levels of depressive symptoms and hostility.

The model of rejection sensitivity was initially introduced to help explain why some individuals are at greater risk for aggressive and depressive responses to rejection, but it can also clarify our understanding of why some individuals are at greater risk for experiencing hurt in relationships. Other individual differences may function in a comparable manner to rejection sensitivity by influencing expectations, perceptions, and reactions. Each of these in turn can influence the experience of hurt feelings by leading to greater exposure or reactivity to hurtful events or both. Insecure attachment style, low self-esteem, and depression have also been shown to be associated with hurt feelings in close relationships (i.e., Campbell, Simpson, Boldry, & Kashy, 2005; Joiner, Metalsky, Gencoz, & Gencoz, 2001; Murray, Rose, Bellavia, Holmes, & Kusche, 2002). We suggest that they operate similarly to rejection sensitivity by affecting an individual's expectations, perceptions, and reactions in potentially hurtful interactions.

## THE RS MODEL AND HURT FEELINGS

To study the underlying dynamics of how individual differences influence one's responses to rejection, it is helpful to conceptually frame individual differences as cognitive-affective processing systems (CAPS; Mischel & Shoda, 1995). The CAPS approach explains how and why an individual's behavior varies across situations, but is constant within situations. Each situation carries cues that activate cognitive-affective units – expectations, biases, goals, coping response patterns. These units in turn influence behavior. Individuals differ in their dispositions and attend differently to particular cues, imbuing them with different meanings that reflect differences in their biopsychosocial history. The activation of a specific pattern of cognitive-affective units by specific cues (e.g., a frowning face) leads to consistent behavioral outcomes. Across similar situations, the same pattern should be evident for a particular individual. Global dispositions such as rejection sensitivity or self-esteem emerge in each component of the cognitive-affective processing system.

Adopting Bolger and colleagues' framework to describe the association between stress and personality (Bolger & Schilling, 1991; Bolger & Zuckerman, 1995), we propose that expectations, perceptions, and reactions to social cues influence the likelihood of hurt feelings by (a) increasing exposure to hurtful events and (b) increasing reactivity to hurtful events (see Fig. 5.1). Greater exposure leads individuals to experience hurtful events with more frequency. Some personality characteristics, like jealousy, may create unreasonable expectations and a wider definition of what constitutes a hurtful event. Jealousy may lead a boyfriend to forbid his girlfriend to talk to all other men. Because the likelihood of her interacting with other men is high, he will feel hurt with greater frequency. Stronger reactivity leads individuals to respond to events with volatility in their reactions as a consequence of feeling hurt. The chronically jealous boyfriend, for example, may register much higher levels of anger than his nonjealous counterpart who may also be hurt when his girlfriend ignores a request.

## HURTS OF COMMISSION

Examples of potential hurts of commission include criticism, conflict, and revenge. Particular individuals may be more sensitive to the possibility of these

# Rejection Sensitivity

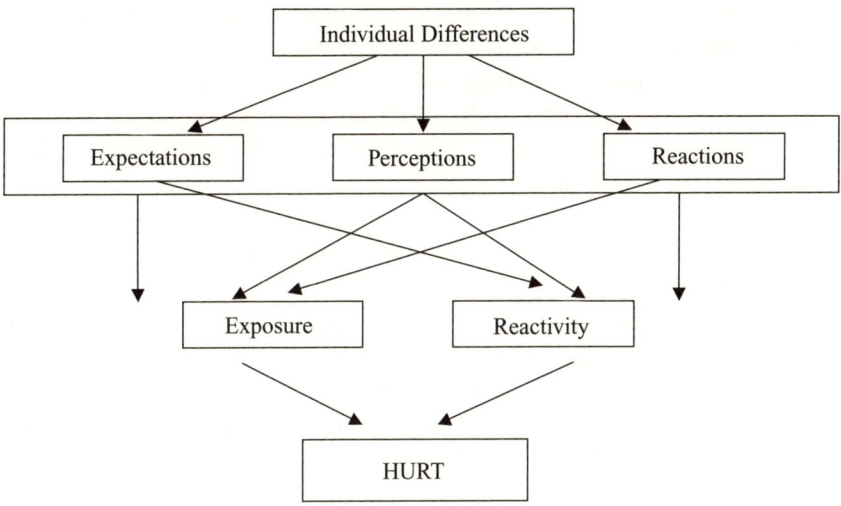

FIGURE 5.1. Using the RS model to explain how individual differences lead to experiences of hurt.

kinds of actions, anxiously expect them, more readily perceive them, and react more strongly to their presence.

## Anxious Expectations

The variability in people's experience of hurt feelings can be affected by, among other differences, their expectations that they will be hurt, even before anything hurtful happens. For instance, a man may dread going to social gatherings with his wife's family because he believes they will make racist comments as they have in the past. A woman may hyperventilate before a job interview because she is worried about what her potential employers will think of her. These expectations lead individuals to view and react to subsequent interactions through a negative lens. They may also lead to defensive behavior, resulting in a self-fulfilling prophecy in which people act in ways that lead their partner to reject them or act in hurtful ways (Downey, Freitas, Michaelis, & Khouri, 1998). This interaction of disposition and environment follows Coyne's (1976) finding that depressed people elicit rejection from their interaction partners via a contagion effect of their depression. Through this cycle, anxious expectations can lead to greater exposure to hurtful events.

According to the RS model, particular individuals may be more predisposed to being anxious about a potential rejection and more likely to believe a rejection will occur. In addition to biological predispositions of temperament that may shape people's beliefs, these anxious expectations may be formed by early and significant experiences with significant others such as parents, those in authority, or peers. High levels of rejection sensitivity involve both high anxiety and low expectations of acceptance. High rejection-sensitive individuals feel insecure about their partners, and their partners are more likely to perceive them as insecure (Downey & Feldman, 1996, study 4).

Research by Downey et al. (1998) supports the notion that greater exposure to hurtful events in close relationships may be a consequence of a self-fulfilling prophecy. In a 4-week diary study, couples were asked individually to answer questions about the presence of conflict and to write about their thoughts and feelings about the relationship. This format allowed the authors to establish that a conflict on a particular day predicted a greater likelihood of the partners of those high in rejection sensitivity acting in more rejecting ways on the subsequent day. A second study used videotaped interactions of women and their partners discussing an unresolved relationship issue. The videos were coded using the Marital Interaction Coding System-IV (Weiss & Summers, 1983). The coding revealed that women who were higher in rejection sensitivity were more likely to behave negatively during conflict. This negativity elicited anger and resentment about the relationship in the partner. Also, among women high rejection sensitivity predicted a greater likelihood of breaking up within a year, further illustrating the cyclical role that rejection sensitivity plays in people's expectations of hurt.

Negative interpersonal expectations are also associated with low self-esteem, insecure attachment styles, and depression. In one study on self-esteem in close relationships (Murray et al., 2002, study 1), participants in dating relationships were instructed to write down aspects of themselves that were less desirable – essentially, aspects of themselves that they kept secret. They were then told that the revelation of that information could lead to conflict and were asked to think about how their partner would feel about them if these secret parts were discovered. Those with low self-esteem were much less confident in their partner's continued acceptance of them, revealing anxious expectations.

Attachment style also was found to be associated with valence of interpersonal expectations (Baldwin, Fehr, Keedian, Seidel, & Thomson, 1993). Individuals who were anxious/ambivalent in attachment style had significantly more negative expectations in the domains of trust and closeness seeking compared to both securely attached and avoidant participants. Consistent with these findings, a lexical decision task revealed that participants with a secure attachment style more quickly recognized words associated with positive interpersonal outcomes and those with insecure attachment styles more quickly recognized words associated with negative interpersonal outcomes. Similarly, those who are depressed have been shown to be particularly attentive to appraisals that confirm their negative views of themselves. Receiving this feedback is likely to reinforce their depression (Swann, Wenzlaff, Krull, & Pelham, 1992). Depression has been shown to accentuate the effect of rejection and lead to behavior that may elicit responses that confirm negative expectations (Coyne, 1976; Joiner & Coyne, 1999; Joiner et al., 2001).

In short, individual differences such as self-esteem, attachment style, and depression account for some of the negative expectations that people may experience when they have interpersonal interactions with partners. There is evidence that these individual differences are also present in people's ready perceptions of hurt.

## Ready Perceptions

People have different thresholds as to what constitutes a relational transgression or devaluation. Having a partner who plays golf all weekend during a couple's first free weekend in months may bother one spouse but not another. Having a partner who spends a lot of time at work may lead to hurt feelings for one person but not another. According to the RS model, anxious expectations of rejection influence the degree to which individuals attend to negative social cues, thus increasing the likelihood of perceiving rejection and experiencing hurt. A similar process likely occurs in other individual differences such as self-esteem and insecure attachment.

In one experiment that examined the link between rejection sensitivity and ready perceptions of hurtful events, participants were informed that they were going to interact in two sessions with another participant. During these sessions they would have the opportunity to get acquainted with each other. Participants in the experimental group were told before the second session that their partner (a confederate) did not want to continue in the study. The control participants were told that there was not enough time to complete the second session. Those high in rejection sensitivity showed a significant increase in feelings of rejection compared to those low in rejection sensitivity (Downey & Feldman, 1996, study 2). In another study, people who indicated greater anxious expectations about their relationship were later found to be more likely to attribute a partner's insensitive behavior to hurtful intentions (Downey & Feldman, 1996, study 3).

The readiness to perceive negativity is also seen physiologically (Downey, Mougios, Ayduk, London, & Shoda, 2004). For individuals with higher levels of rejection sensitivity, the startle response to a loud noise, as assessed by magnitude of the eyeblink, was greater when they were viewing rejection-themed art (paintings by Hopper) than when they were viewing acceptance-themed art (paintings by Renoir), abstract negative-themed art (paintings by Rothko), or abstract positive-themed art (paintings by Miro). These findings imply that, in the presence of rejection cues, those high in rejection sensitivity are in a more negatively valenced, high-arousal physiological state. Physiologically they are perceiving more negativity and threat.

Other individual characteristics such as self-esteem and attachment style are also associated with differences in interpersonal perception. In a laboratory experiment, an emotional Stroop task (involving naming colors in which words of different meaning [e.g., rejection, acceptance] are printed) demonstrated that rejection words caused more interference in performance on the color naming task than acceptance words for those low in self-esteem (Dandeneau & Baldwin, 2004). Similarly, in a real-life close relationship context, married and dating couples were asked to report on a variety of positive and negative attributes regarding how they saw themselves, how they thought their partners saw them, and how they desired their partners to see them. Participants low in self-esteem greatly underestimated how positively their romantic partners viewed them (Murray, Holmes, & Griffin, 2000). In both of these studies; the perceptions of individuals with low self-esteem were skewed in a negative direction.

Attachment style also affects perception. In one study by Niedenthal, Brauer, and Innes-Ker (2002), participants viewed computerized movies depicting faces that started out happy, sad, or angry and gradually morphed to neutral. They were asked to indicate at what point the emotion was no longer displayed. Under conditions of distress, insecurely attached participants indicated a later point of offset for the negative faces than did securely attached participants. Using a different methodology, another study on attachment (Collins, 1996) gave participants a number of imaginary relationship scenarios and asked them to write how they would respond in each situation. The resulting open-ended responses demonstrated that insecurely attached participants were more likely to explain the scenarios in negative ways. These biased perceptions are likely to lead to a greater number of subjective experiences of hurt.

Individual differences not only influence perceptions of stimuli in lab studies but they also can affect the way people perceive interactions in ongoing relationships. Campbell et al. (2005) conducted a study with dating college couples and examined attachment style, conflict, and support within their romantic relationships through a 14-day diary study and a videotaped interaction of the couples discussing a recent major problem. They found that the anxious attachment style was related to reporting more frequent conflicts and that these conflicts were more likely to escalate. Additionally, among anxiously attached individuals these conflicts led to lower feelings of satisfaction and closeness, greater distress, and a more negative view of the future of the relationship.

Taken together, these studies indicate some of the ways in which people's interpersonal perceptions vary across individuals. The following section discusses how these differences are manifested in people's reactions to hurt.

## Intense Reactions

People's responses to hurtful events may be the clearest indicator of how individual differences influence the experience of hurt feelings. The same transgression or devaluation may elicit different levels of hurt in people. For women, higher levels of rejection sensitivity are associated with more hostility, greater negative evaluation of one's partner, and more conflict (Ayduk et al., 1999). Research examining the link between rejection sensitivity and hostility in women found that rejection sensitivity predicted a stronger association between rejection words and hostility words in a priming pronunciation paradigm (Ayduk et al., 1999, study 1). Study 2 reported in the same article used a computer-dating cover story and found that participants with greater rejection sensitivity rated a potential dating partner's profile more negatively after the fictitious partner exited the study without explanation. In study 3, a diary study, high rejection-sensitive women were more likely to report hostile conflict the day after feeling rejected. Other research has found that, when relationships ended in a partner-initiated breakup, women high in rejection sensitivity showed a significant increase in depressive symptoms compared to women low in rejection sensitivity (Ayduk, Downey, & Kim, 2001). Greater hostility was also found in the relationships of adolescent girls high in rejection sensitivity (Purdie & Downey, 2000). Greater rejection sensitivity in these girls predicted greater physical aggression and nonphysical hostility during romantic conflict, as well as greater agreement with statements that indicated insecurity within romantic relationships such as "I would do anything to keep my boyfriend with me even if it's things that I know are wrong." Rejection sensitivity is one of the ways in which intense reactions to hurt arise, though other individual differences such as self-esteem and attachment style are involved as well. Though women were the focus of these studies, similar processes may also occur among men.

For example, both men and women with low self-esteem tend to derogate their partners and feel less close to them after a felt rejection (Murray et al., 2002, study 2). Low self-esteem is also related to more jealousy (White, 1981). Similarly, attachment style captures some of the difference seen in individuals' reactions to hurt. Securely attached individuals report less frequent withdrawal and verbal aggression from their partner during marital conflict than do those who are insecurely attached (Senchak & Leonard, 1992). Other research has found that anxiously attached individuals report less relationship satisfaction, closeness to their partner, and optimism about the relationship's future on days in which there is relationship conflict (Campbell et al., 2005).

People's physiological reactivity to conflict can vary across attachment style as well. A study by Powers, Pietromonaco, Gunlicks, and Sayer (2006) had participants and their partners discuss a heated issue that had not been resolved in the past month. They found that individuals who were insecurely attached (anxious or avoidant) experienced more stress, which was marked by higher levels of cortisol, before and during the conflict negotiation task with their partner. Research on these factors indicates that some individuals are more likely to react intensely to potential instances of hurt than others.

Our review of studies on rejection sensitivity, self-esteem, and attachment suggests that, when there are hurtful acts of commission within a relational context, there exists a consistent link between individual differences and hurt feelings through the processing dimensions of anxious expectations, ready perceptions, and intense reactions that lead to increased exposure and reactivity to hurtful events. In the next section, we explore whether this is also true of hurt caused through disappointments experienced in positive relationship processes such as social support.

## HURTS OF OMISSION

Feelings of hurt can also result from actions of omission, the absence of a positive act. Do individual differences play out in hurts of omission in the same manner (via anxious expectations, ready perceptions, intense reactions) as in hurts involving the presence of negatives? To consider this question, we undertook a study of rejection sensitivity and social support.

Those high in rejection sensitivity are concerned about rejection because they desire to be accepted by close others. Acceptance in close relationships is communicated through responsiveness from one's partner in a variety of potentially rejecting situations, of which the dyadic process of social support is a prime example. Social support is a critical element of satisfying romantic relationships (Sarason, Pierce, & Sarason, 1990) and romantic partners typically expect to be supported. Support is broadly defined as responsiveness to stress in another's life (Cutrona, 1996) and willingness to be readily available in times of need for a partner (Wade, Howell, & Wells, 1994). The significance of support within couples is shown by its relation to increased levels of relationship trust (Cutrona, Russell, & Gardner, 2005); the development of effective coping strategies (Cutrona & Russell, 1987); an increased sense of being understood, cared for, and validated (Reis & Shaver, 1988); relationship commitment (Sprecher, 1988); psychological adjustment (Kurdek, 1988); and marital satisfaction (Bradbury, Fincham, & Beach, 2000). But alongside the potential of these numerous positive outcomes, there is the possibility of rejection, disappointment, and hurt.

Support, as a relationship process, is highly relevant to the fear of rejection. Needing support indicates that a person is going through a stressful experience and is vulnerable. During this time of need, seeking support is an act that may elicit potential rejection, whereas receiving support can be seen as a visible act of acceptance. We examined the association between rejection sensitivity and social support, asking whether the absence of social support results in greater feelings of hurt (sadness, anger) for those high in rejection sensitivity. We used data from a daily diary study of couples conducted by Niall Bolger and Patrick Shrout in which one partner was undergoing the stress of preparing for a highly important exam to enter the legal profession (e.g., Iida, Seidman, Shrout, Fujita,

& Bolger, 2008). Using this paradigm allowed us to examine the dynamics of social support in a controlled sample of participants sharing a major, known stressor that most directly affects one partner in the relationship. It is during stressful events such as preparing for the bar exam that social support has demonstrated the clearest buffering effects (Cohen & Wills, 1985).

We tested whether high rejection sensitivity predicted lower expectations of support, lower perceptions of support, and stronger emotional reactions both to the receipt and failure to receive requested support. Would individuals who were highly rejection sensitive expect and perceive receiving less support than they sought from their partner? We also predicted that examinees' reports of receiving support would increase their positive feelings within the relationship and that failing to receive support when it was sought would be associated with a decrease in positive feelings. Because of the potential weight given to social support actions by high rejection-sensitive individuals, we predicted an interaction effect between rejection sensitivity and support, such that support would have a magnified effect on relationship feelings for high rejection-sensitive individuals and a failure to receive sought support would be particularly devastating to high rejection-sensitive individuals because of its implication of rejection. Data were analyzed using multilevel modeling, which provides estimates within couples of the relationship between support actions and relationship feelings for each participant (Bolger, Davis, & Rafaeli, 2003).

Two hundred fifty-nine law students, in their final year of law school, participated in the study with their partners. To meet eligibility criteria, only one partner could be taking the bar examination in July 2003 and couples had to have been living together for at least 6 months. The median age of examinees was 28. Sixty-one percent of the examinees were married, 50% were female, and 17% percent were from racial or ethnic minorities.

Final-year law students and their relationship partners were recruited nationwide. Couples individually filled out background questionnaires that gathered demographic, personality and relationship information including rejection sensitivity. For the 5 weeks leading up to the bar exam, during the exam, and a week afterward, both partners completed diaries every morning and every evening. Examinees were asked if they had sought support from their partner and if they had received support from their partner. Partners were asked whether they provided support. Answers were given as dichotomous yes/no responses to each question of receiving, seeking, and providing support.

To examine support effects during this period of stress, analyses focused on reports of support and relationship feelings from the member of the couple preparing for the bar exam during the 4 weeks leading up to it. Relationship feelings were collected solely in the evenings; thus, only data from evening diaries were used for the current study, and all analyses control for the previous evening's feelings. All analyses are based on reports of emotional support

|  | **Received Support (Examinee)** |
| --- | --- |
| **Sought Support (Examinee)** | Expected Support (Examinee) |
| **Provided Support (Partner)** | Enacted Support (Examinee) |

FIGURE 5.2. Operationalizations of expected and enacted support.

actions; analyses of practical support actions failed to reveal significant effects on feelings of hurt.

## Expectations of Support

Whereas some individuals may expect to receive support during times of need, others are prone to believe that support will not be there when they need it. People's expectations about receiving support depend, in part, on the amount of support that they expect is available to them. For example, a boyfriend may think that his girlfriend probably will be too busy to help him review for the bar exam, given that she is a busy person. His belief that she will not provide the support he seeks reflects his low expectation of receiving support (from the pool of support that he perceives is available to him). In the present study, we operationalized participants' expectations of receiving support as days when they reported both seeking and receiving support on the same day (see Fig. 5.2). This operationalization is based on the finding that reporting receipt of support was much more highly correlated with seeking it than any actual provision from one's partner. Only rarely did individuals in this study report seeking support and not receiving it. They often saw support even if it was not there; hence, the overwhelming expectation of support. Ninety-four percent of the time that participants reported seeking support, they also reported receiving support. By this measure, there were high expectations of support receipt, and RS did not moderate support expectations. However, unmet expectations were operationalized as days when support was sought but not received. Those high in rejection sensitivity were more likely to report such days than those low in rejection sensitivity.

The somewhat surprising finding that rejection sensitivity was not associated with support expectations may be a result of a sample in which all the participants were preparing for the bar exam. There may be a ceiling effect of high expectations of support during this clearly delineated stressful event and the block of time leading up to it. The surprising finding may also reflect differences in methodology from most prior studies that showed an association between individual differences and support expectations. Such studies focused on measures of global expectations about the availability of support rather than a daily question about a specific support provider. For example, securely attached individuals expect responsiveness from those around them – this is borne out in studies reporting their beliefs that more support is available to them compared to the expectations of insecurely attached individuals (Kobak & Sceery, 1988). This is true for romantic partners, parents, and friends (Florian, Mikulincer, & Bucholtz, 1995). For these individuals, the global expectations of availability of support may be an important determinant of their daily expectations.

The link between global expectations of support and aspects of the Big Five Traits has also been examined. The Big Five Traits refer to the five basic dimensions of personality: agreeableness, conscientiousness, neuroticism, extraversion, and openness to experience (Goldberg, 1981). For adults within families there were strong associations between higher levels of agreeableness and extraversion and perceived support (Branje, van Lieshout, & van Aken, 2004). Social support expectations may even be an individual difference in and of itself (Lutz & Lakey, 2001).

Given the stress inherent in taking the bar exam, both global expectations of available support and situational expectations could potentially help explain why rejection sensitivity did not moderate daily expectations of support in the study. Examining the association between rejection sensitivity and global expectations of support (i.e., "I can always rely on support from my partner when I need it") may have shown an association between rejection sensitivity and lower levels of expected available support that the daily diary questions did not capture. The daily diary format forced participants to focus only on the current day rather than rely on global impressions. Situational expectations may also have come into play. Because the bar exam is a known stressor to both partners in a relationship, it may give "permission" to high rejection-sensitive individuals to expect support. Relational norms would also call for partners of bar examinees to be more supportive during this time.

## Ready Perceptions of Support

Individual differences may also lead people to perceive their partner is not acting responsively to their need for support. For example, a woman may come home and vent about her study group, but trail off when she sees her partner staring out the window. In our study, perception of enacted support was operationalized as a day when the examinee reported receiving support and the partner reported providing support (see Fig. 5.2). Overall, examinee reports of receipt and partner reports of provision correlated at a moderately high level. However, rejection sensitivity did not moderate this correlation.

Rejection sensitivity may not affect perceptions of enacted support because expectations of receiving support may have been particularly high and this ceiling effect may have seriously limited variation in perceptions of enacted support. These high expectations may also partially explain the acute hurt felt when a failure of requested support was experienced. It is important to note, however, that other studies have found that individual differences can affect perceptions of support. Although such studies focused only on the individual's own report of enacted support, they can still add insight into the perception of support. In a diary study of dating couples, experiences of support were reported as less positive by individuals high in avoidant attachment, and both anxiously attached participants and their partners predicted that supportive events would have more positive long-term consequences for the stability of their relationship relative to those of other attachment styles (Campbell et al., 2005). The Big Five have also been associated with types of support that are provided. A study of married and dating couples (Dehle & Landers, 2005) found that men lower in conscientiousness or emotional stability reported receiving more esteem support from their wives, a type of support that consisted of compliments and validation of one's abilities and worth. The study also found that wives who were high in consciousness/emotional stability were more satisfied with the support they received than women low in these traits. Bolger and Eckenrode (1991) found lower emotional stability/higher neuroticism to be associated with perceptions of inadequate support. It appears that perceptions can sometimes vary with dispositional characteristics of individuals.

## Intense Reactions to Support Omission

After feeling hurt because of a lack of support, some individuals may react more intensely than others. For example, a man whose study partner does not show up for an important review session may send a nasty, revealing e-mail to the study partner's future employer. In our study we expected that, after experiencing a lapse of sought support, those high in RS would have a more extreme reaction than those low in RS. We analyzed examinees' feelings about their relationship assessed on the evening of a given day as a function of their support interactions that day.[1] There was a main effect of rejection sensitivity on relationship feelings, such that higher levels of rejection sensitivity were associated with higher levels of hurt feelings across the diary period. There was also an interaction such that, compared to days when they reported neither seeking nor receiving support, participants reported significant increases in hurt feelings (relationship anger and sadness) on days when they experienced a failure of sought support (i.e., when they sought support but did not receive it). Reporting receiving support alone resulted in significantly lower levels of hurt feelings. There was also an interaction effect for high rejection sensitivity and decreased feelings of hurt on days when participants both sought and received support compared to days when they neither sought nor received support.

---

[1] Analyses were conducted using the support interaction for a given day as the predictor of that evening's level of hurt feelings. These analyses controlled for the prior evening's relationship feelings as well as gender, the linear effects of day in the study, and the linear effect of the particular day's troubles and tensions.

The findings from this study show that high rejection-sensitive individuals suffer particularly when there is a failure to respond to requests for support within their relationships. This type of situation is one in which they test the hypothesis that important others will not help them when they are in need and their hypothesis is confirmed. Collins and Feeney (2004) similarly found that attachment style affects perceptions of supportiveness. Using a laboratory paradigm, they gave participants high- or low-support messages. Insecurely attached participants (both anxious and avoidant) appraised the low-support messages more negatively. Insecure participants in the low support message condition also remembered the supportiveness of their partners in earlier spontaneous interactions as more negative. These studies provide evidence for the link between insecure attachment and more negative appraisals not only at the time of message production but also at later recall.

Findings from the current study and others provide tentative evidence for a link between individual differences and reactivity to hurtful events of omission but less evidence for frequency of exposure to them. However, the difference in the strength of association between RS and exposure and reactivity through expectations, perceptions, and reactions may be caused by the relative strength of each of these specific links. In their work with neuroticism, Bolger and his colleagues (Bolger & Schilling, 1991; Bolger & Zuckerman, 1995) found that higher levels of neuroticism were associated with both greater exposure and greater reactivity to stress. However, the reactivity of those high in neuroticism accounted for approximately twice as much of the difference in perceived distress as exposure, thus making it easier to detect. Given these findings, it seems that the effect of the relationship between a particular individual difference and people's expectations, perceptions, or reactions is not always uniform and that some of these aspects may be contributing more to the experience of support than others.

## CONCLUSION AND IMPLICATIONS

Rejection sensitivity, self-esteem, attachment style, and depression are examples of individual differences that are involved in the processes that generate hurt feelings in close relationships. These individual factors are important for situations involving hurts of both commission and omission. Using the rejection sensitivity model, the current chapter reviews and identifies processes through which some of these different individual factors can contribute to people's expectations, perceptions, and reactions to the experience of hurt by increasing their exposure to hurtful events and contributing to the reactivity of their response to them.

A young woman preparing for the bar exam may feel angry when her partner complains that she thinks the world revolves around her and feel sad when she comes home from a long night at the library to find that her partner has already gone to bed. If the woman is someone who is highly sensitive to rejection, she may feel even worse, and her preparation and performance on the exam may be compromised. Such turns of events may lead to more anger, resentment, or hurt in the relationship. Individuals who are insecurely attached or have low self-esteem may also expect, perceive, and react in ways that make them more vulnerable to experiencing hurt, which in time could reinforce a debilitating cycle.

Understanding how dispositional factors emerge in people's expectations, perceptions, and reactions to hurt may help clinicians identify and intervene with individuals who suffer in a relationship. Addressing the different aspects of the processes involved in the experience of hurt feelings can help lead to better relationships and fewer hurt feelings. For example, changing expectations could be one entry point of intervention; Baldwin and Keelan (1999) found that those with higher self-esteem had higher expectations of affiliation responses from others. Changing perceptions could be another – Cobb, Davila, and Bradbury (2001) found that positive perceptions of partners' attachment security were associated with more supportive behavior and greater relationship satisfaction. Work has shown that it is possible to create interventions that train individuals to change their social patterns via changing their attentional focus from socially threatening to socially benevolent cues (i.e., Dandeneau & Baldwin, 2004).

We all experience hurt feelings in close relationships; they are part and parcel of intimacy. The ways in which we differ in our orientation toward social relationships – whether our emphasis is on them as opportunities for threat or for fulfillment or some combination thereof – play an important role in explaining why and how we feel hurt. Hurt can have a variety of negative personal and interpersonal consequences. The RS model sheds light on the specific means by which this happens and reveals opportunities for intervention.

## REFERENCES

Ayduk, O., Downey, G., Kim, M. (2001). Rejection sensitivity and depressive symptoms in women. *Personality and Social Psychology Bulletin, 27,* 868–877.

Ayduk, O., Downey, G., Testa, A., Yen, Y., & Shoda, Y. (1999). Does rejection elicit hostility in rejection sensitive women? *Social Cognition, 17,* 245–271.

Baldwin, M. W., Fehr, B., Keedian, E., Seidel, M., & Thomson, D. W. (1993). An exploration of the relational schemata underlying attachment styles: Self-report and lexical decision approaches. *Personality and Social Psychology Bulletin, 19,* 746–754.

Baldwin, M. W., & Keelan, J. P. R. (1999). Interpersonal expectations as a function of self-esteem and sex. *Journal of Social and Personal Relationships, 16,* 822–833.

Berenson, K., Kang, N. J., & Downey, G. (2009). The adult rejection sensitivity questionnaire (A-RSQ). Manuscript in preparation.

Bolger, N., Davis, A., & Rafaeli, E. (2003). Diary methods: Capturing life as it is lived. *Annual Review of Psychology, 54,* 579–616.

Bolger, N., & Eckenrode, J. (1991). Social relationships, personality, and anxiety during a major stressful event. *Journal of Personality and Social Psychology, 61,* 440–449.

Bolger, N., & Schilling, E. A. (1991). Personality and the problems of everyday life: The role of neuroticism in exposure and reactivity to daily stressors. *Journal of Personality, 59,* 355–386.

Bolger, N., & Zuckerman, A. (1995). A framework for studying personality in the stress process. *Journal of Personality and Social Psychology, 69,* 890–902.

Bradbury, T. N., Fincham, F. D., & Beach, S. R. H. (2000). Research on the nature and determinants of marital satisfaction: A decade in review. *Journal of Marriage and the Family, 62,* 964–980.

Branje, S. J. T., van Lieshout, C. F. M., & van Aken, M. A. G. (2004). Relations between Big Five prsonality characteristics and perceived support in adolescents' families. *Journal of Personality and Social Psychology, 86,* 615–628.

Campbell, L., Simpson, J. A., Boldry, J., & Kashy, D. A. (2005). Perceptions of conflict and support in romantic relationships: The role of attachment anxiety. *Journal of Personality and Social Psychology, 88,* 510–531.

Cobb, R. J., Davila, J., & Bradbury, T. N. (2001). Attachment security and marital satisfaction: The role of positive perceptions and social support. *Personality and Social Psychology Bulletin, 27,* 1131–1143.

Cohen, S., & Wills, T. A. (1985). Stress, social support, and the buffering hypothesis. *Psychological Bulletin, 98,* 310–357.

Collins, N. L. (1996). Working models of attachment: Implications for explanation, emotion, and behavior. *Journal of Personality and Social Psychology, 71,* 810–832.

Collins, N. L., & Feeney, B. C. (2004). Working models of attachment shape perceptions of social support: Evidence from experimental and observational studies. *Journal of Personality and Social Psychology, 87,* 363–383.

Coyne, J. C. (1976). Toward an interactional description of depression. *Journal for the Study of Interpersonal Processes, 39,* 28–40.

Cutrona, C. E. (1996). *Social support in couples: Marriage as a resource in times of stress.* Thousand Oaks, CA: Sage.

Cutrona, C. E., & Russell, D. (1987). The provisions of social relationships and adaptation to stress. In W. H. Jones & D. Perlman (Eds.), *Advances in personal relationships* (pp. 37–67). Greenwich: JAI Press.

Cutrona, C. E., Russell, D. W., & Gardner, K. A. (2005). The relationship enhancement model of social support. In T. A. Revenson, K. Kayser, & G. Bodenmann (Eds.), *Couples coping with stress: Emerging perspectives on dyadic coping* (pp. 73–95). Washington, DC: American Psychological Association.

Dandeneau, S. D., & Baldwin, M. W. (2004). The inhibition of socially rejection information among people with high versus low self-esteem: The role of attentional bias and the effects of bias reduction training. *Journal of Social and Clinical Psychology, 23,* 584–602.

Dehle, C., & Landers, J. E. (2005). You can't always get what you want, but can you get what you need? Personality traits and social support in marriage. *Journal of Social and Clinical Psychology, 24,* 1051–1076.

Downey, G., & Feldman, S. (1996). Implications of rejection sensitivity for intimate relationships. *Journal of Personality and Social Psychology, 70,* 1327–1343.

Downey, G., Freitas, A. L., Michaelis, B., & Khouri, H. (1998). The self-fulfilling prophecy in close relationships: Rejection sensitivity and rejection by romantic partners. *Journal of Personality and Social Psychology, 75,* 545–56.

Downey, G., Khouri, H., & Feldman, S. I. (1997). Early interpersonal trauma and later adjustment: The mediational role of rejection sensitivity. In D. Cicchetti & S. L. Toth (Eds.), *Developmental perspectives on trauma: Theory, research, and intervention* (pp. 85–114). Rochester, NY: University of Rochester Press.

Downey, G., Mougios, V., Ayduk, O., London, B. E., & Shoda, Y. (2004). Rejection sensitivity and the defensive motivational system: Insights from the startle response to rejection cues. *Psychological Science, 15*, 668–673.

Feeney, J. A. (2004). Hurt feelings in close relationships: Towards integrative models of the negative effects of hurtful events. *Journal of Social and Personal Relationships, 21*, 487–508.

Florian, V., Mikulincer, M., & Bucholtz, I. (1995). Effects of adult attachment style on the perception and search for social support. *Journal of Psychology: Interdisciplinary and Applied, 129*, 665–676.

Goldberg, L. R. (1981). Language and individual differences: The search for universals in personality lexicons. In L. Wheeler (Ed.), *Review of personality and social psychology* (pp. 141–165). Beverly Hills, CA: Sage.

Iida, M., Seidman, G., Shrout, P. E., Fujita, K., & Bolger, N. (2008). Modeling support provision in intimate relationships. *Journal of Personality and Social Psychology, 94*, 260–278.

Joiner, T., & Coyne, J. C. (Eds). (1999). *The interactional nature of depression: Advances in interpersonal approaches.* Washington, DC: American Psychological Association.

Joiner, T. E., Metalsky, G. L., Gencoz, F., & Gencoz, T. (2001). The relative specificity of excessive reassurance-seeking to depressive symptoms and diagnoses among clinical samples of adults and youth. *Journal of Psychopathology and Behavioral Assessment, 23*, 35–41.

Kobak, R. R., & Sceery, A. (1988). Attachment in late adolescence: Working models, affect regulation, and representations of self and others. *Child Development, 59*, 135–146.

Kurdek, L. A. (1988). Perceived social support in gays and lesbians in cohabitating relationships. *Journal of Personality and Social Psychology, 54*, 504–509.

Leary, M. R., Springer, C., Negel, L. Ansell, E., & Evans, K. (1998). The causes, phenomenology, and consequences of hurt feelings. *Journal of Personality and Social Psychology, 74*, 1225–1237.

Lutz, C. J., & Lakey, B. (2001). How people make support judgments: Individual differences in the traits used to infer supportiveness in others. *Journal of Personality and Social Psychology, 81*, 1070–1079.

Mischel, W., & Shoda, Y. (1995). A cognitive-affective system theory of personality: Reconceptualizing situations, dispositions, dynamics, and invariance in personality structure. *Psychological Review, 102*, 246–268.

Murray, S. L., Holmes, J. G., & Griffin, D. W. (2000). Self-esteem and the quest for felt security: How perceived regard regulates attachment processes. *Journal of Personality and Social Psychology, 78*, 478–498.

Murray, S. L., Rose, P., Bellavia, G. M., Holmes, J. G., & Kusche, A. G. (2002). When rejection stings: How self-esteem constrains relationship-enhancement processes. *Journal of Personality and Social Psychology, 83*, 556–573.

Niedenthal, P. M., Brauer, M., Robin, L. & Innes-Ker, A. H. (2002). Adult attachment and the perception of facial expression of emotion. *Journal of Personality and Social Psychology, 82*, 419–33.

Powers, S. I., Pietromonaco, P. R., Gunlicks, M., & Sayer, A. (2006). Dating couples' attachment styles and patterns of cortisol reactivity and recovery in response to a relationship conflict. *Journal of Personality and Social Psychology, 90*, 613–628.

Purdie, V., & Downey, G. (2000). Rejection sensitivity and adolescent girls' vulnerability to relationship-centered difficulties. *Child Maltreatment: Journal of the American Professional Society on the Abuse of Children, 5*, 338–349.

Reis, H. T., & Shaver, P. (1988). Intimacy as an interpersonal process. In S. W. Duck (Ed.), *Handbook of personal relationships* (pp. 367–389). New York: Wiley.

Sarason, B. R., Pierce, G. R., & Sarason, I. G. (1990). Social support: The sense of acceptance and the role of relationships. In B. R. Sarason, I. G. Sarason, & G. R. Pierce (Eds.), *Social support: An interactional view* (pp. 97–128). Oxford: Wiley.

Senchak, M., & Leonard, K. E. (1992). Attachment styles and marital adjustment among newlywed couples. *Journal of Social and Personal Relationships, 9*, 51–64.

Sprecher, S. (1988). Investment model, equity, and social support determinants of relationship commitment. *Social Psychology Quarterly, 51*, 318–328.

Swann, W. B., Wenzlaff, R. M., Krull, D. S., & Pelham, B. W. (1992). Allure of negative feedback: Self-verification strivings among depressed persons. *Journal of Abnormal Psychology, 101*, 293–306.

Vangelisti, A. L. (1994). Messages that hurt. In W. R. Cupach & B. H. Spitzberg (Eds.), *The dark side of interpersonal communication* (pp. 53–82). Hillsdale, NJ: Erlbaum.

Vangelisti, A. L. (2001). Making sense of hurtful interactions in close relationships: When hurt feelings create distance. In V. E. Manusov & J. H. Harvey (Eds.), *Attribution, communication behavior, and close relationships* (pp. 38–58). New York: Cambridge University Press.

Wade, C. K., Howell, F. M., & Wells, J. G. (1994). Turning to family, friends or others: A model of social network usage during stressful events. *Sociological Spectrum, 14*, 385–407.

Weiss, R. L. & Summers, K. J. (1983). Marital Interaction Coding System III. In E. E. Filsinger (Ed.), *A sourcebook of marriage and family assessment* (pp. 85–115). Beverly Hills, CA: Sage.

White, G. L. (1981). Some correlates of romantic jealousy. *Journal of Personality, 49*, 129–1981.

# 6

## Understanding and Altering Hurt Feelings: An Attachment-Theoretical Perspective on the Generation and Regulation of Emotions

PHILLIP R. SHAVER, MARIO MIKULINCER, SHIRI LAVY, AND JUDE CASSIDY

It is exciting to see how far research on hurt feelings has progressed since 1987 as both affective science and relationship science have blossomed. Our own professional involvement with the study of hurt feelings began accidentally, in the late 1980s, when Shaver, Schwartz, Kirson, and O'Connor (1987) probed the semantic structure of the English emotion lexicon, finding five major clusters of emotion terms in Americans' everyday vocabularies – clusters labeled love, joy, anger, sadness, and fear. Because of the prominence in the late 1980s of Ekman and Izard's discrete emotions theories (e.g., Ekman, 1992; Izard, 1977), Shaver et al. (1987) viewed particular members of each of the five emotion clusters as either prototypical of that cluster or as "blends" of two or more basic emotions. One such blend, according to the authors, was *hurt*:

> The emotion *hurt*, for example, although it appears within the sadness [category], seems to be a blend of sadness and anger.... A person feels hurt, according to subjects' accounts, when he or she has been wronged in a way that warrants anger (i.e., in a way that is unfair [or] inappropriate given agreed-upon roles or rules) but believes that the offender does not care enough to rectify matters, even if a reasonable objection were to be raised (cf. de Rivera, 1977). Not surprisingly, hurt is... mentioned more frequently by people who perceive themselves to be the weaker... party in a relationship. (p. 1082)

Around the time when that passage was written, Hazan and Shaver (1987) published an influential paper arguing that romantic love could be conceptualized as an "attachment" process and hence could be understood at least partly in terms of Bowlby (1982) and Ainsworth's (Ainsworth, Blehar, Waters, & Wall, 1978) attachment theory. Since then, hundreds of studies stimulated by adult attachment theory have been published (see Mikulincer & Shaver, 2007, for a review), some of which (e.g., Bachman & Guerrero, 2006; Feeney, 2004, 2005, and Chapter 14, this volume) have focused specifically on *hurt feelings*, bringing the two issues tackled independently by Shaver and colleagues in 1987 into direct contact. As Feeney (2005) has shown, attachment theory is useful both in revealing why hurt feelings are so important in relationships and how individual differences in attachment security affect the experience and expression of such feelings.

In this chapter we consider how hurt feelings arise, using an adaptation of the process model devised by Shaver et al. (1987), and we examine hurt feelings within the framework of adult attachment theory (Mikulincer & Shaver, 2007). We begin by explaining how emotions in general, and hurt feelings in particular, work. We then provide a brief overview of attachment theory and consider how hurt feelings relate to its basic concepts and principles. Specifically, we outline an attachment-theoretical perspective on the nature of hurtful events, the cognitive appraisal of these events, the nature of hurt feelings, and the action tendencies associated with them. We also review some of the evidence concerning attachment-style differences in the generation and regulation of hurt feelings. Finally, we present preliminary findings from a new study exploring the effect of security priming on the experience of, and behavioral reactions to, being hurt by a relationship partner.

## A PROCESS MODEL OF EMOTIONS

In analyzing emotions and the regulatory processes associated with different attachment strategies, we rely on an updated version of Shaver et al.'s (1987) process model of emotion elicitation (see Fig. 6.1). This model has been used to conceptualize both emotions and emotional development (e.g., Fischer, Shaver, & Carnochan, 1990). In the model, emotions are conceptualized as organized sets of thoughts, feelings, and action tendencies supported and colored by physiological changes in the brain and body – changes that are generated by the appraisal of external or internal events in relation to a person's goals and concerns. The resulting emotions are experienced and expressed through changes in the mental accessibility of various cognitions, action tendencies, behaviors, and subjective feelings. Both the generation and expression of emotions are affected by regulatory efforts, which can alter, obstruct, or suppress appraisals, concerns, action tendencies, and subjective feelings.

According to Shaver et al. (1987), emotion generation depends on a perceived change in the internal or external environment, especially an unexpected, surprising, or personally relevant change. These changes are automatically, and often unconsciously, appraised in relation to a person's needs, goals, wishes, and concerns. If the perceived changes are favorable to goal attainment, the resulting emotions are hedonically positive. If the changes are unfavorable to goal attainment, the resulting emotions are hedonically negative. The particular emotion that arises depends on the specific pattern of concerns and appraisals that gets activated (e.g., Lazarus, 1991; Shaver et al., 1987). When a specific appraisal pattern occurs, a corresponding kind of emotion, including

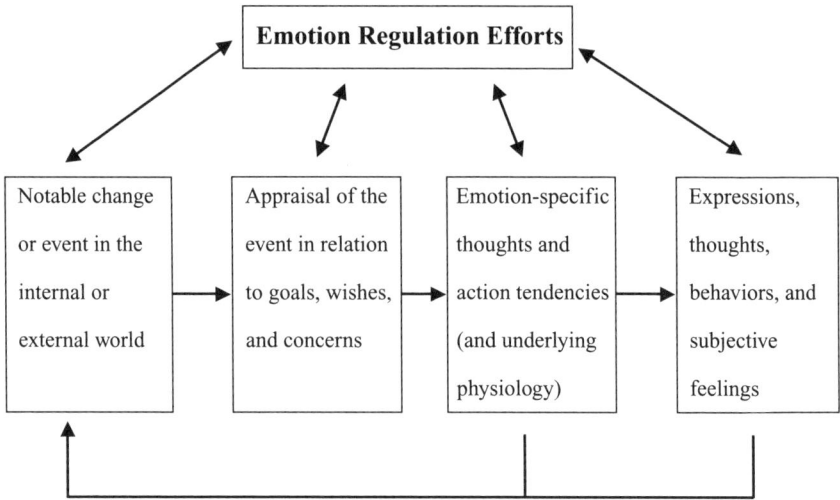

FIGURE 6.1. An updated process model of emotion elicitation.

its evolutionarily functional action tendencies and physiological substrates, follows automatically. These consequences can be manifested in thoughts, feelings, or actions; expressed both verbally and nonverbally; and measured in various ways.

Shaver et al. (1987) claimed, based partly on existing research and partly on their study of participants' emotion narratives, that regulatory efforts can alter the entire emotion process. If there is no reason to postpone, dampen, redirect, or deny the emerging emotion, the action tendencies are automatically expressed in congruent thoughts, feelings, and behaviors. However, when there are other goals in play (e.g., social norms, self-protective defenses) that make the experience or expression of a particular emotion undesirable, regulatory efforts are called into service to alter, obstruct, or suppress the emotion and bring about a more desirable mental state or at least the outward appearance of a more desirable state.

In this model, regulatory efforts can be directed at any or all of the various components or stages of the emotion process. The most direct regulatory strategy is to solve the problem or alter the conditions that elicited the emotion. Lazarus and Folkman (1984) called this "problem-focused coping." Regulatory maneuvers can also be directed at the appraisals linking provocative events to emotional reactions. Reappraisal can contribute to problem solving by calming a person and allowing him or her to deploy problem-solving resources more effectively ("The problem is not as difficult or troubling as I thought") or even eliminate the problem, rendering problem-solving efforts unnecessary ("I thought she was rejecting me, but in fact she wasn't"). However, when problem solving or reappraisal is insufficient to eliminate or weaken an aversive emotional reaction, regulatory efforts may be directed at the emotion itself. Alternatively, regulatory efforts can dissociate the emotion from its appearance in the stream of consciousness. The attempts to eliminate, weaken, or ignore the emotion without addressing the problem that caused it are examples of what Lazarus and Folkman (1984) called "emotion-focused coping."

When Shaver et al. (1987) first presented their emotion process model, they took for granted that there were only a few basic emotions of the kinds first discussed by Ekman (1992) and Izard (1977). These theories and the facial action coding systems they inspired suggested what might be called a cash register or typewriter model of emotion generation. When a particular key is struck (i.e., when a particular appraisal pattern occurs), a corresponding number pops up in the cash register's display window or a corresponding letter appears on the printed page. In the case of emotions, when a particular appraisal pattern is "struck" by perceived events, a corresponding expression appears on the face and a particular set of inner feelings occurs.

This discrete emotions model has repeatedly been challenged by dimensional models of emotion (e.g., Osgood, May, & Miron, 1975; Russell, 1980), which portray emotions as regions in a multidimensional space. Nevertheless, the discrete emotions approach has continued to be highly influential, sustaining the notion of "blended" discrete emotions. Shaver et al. (1987) showed that the same co-occurrence matrix, based on sorting named emotions into family resemblance groupings, can be statistically analyzed by either cluster analysis or multidimensional scaling, thereby producing either "basic" emotion categories or two- or three-dimensional spatial arrays. This demonstration suggests that different conceptual models – whether categorical or dimensional – are equally compatible with the data. We reconsider these issues in relation to hurt feelings after briefly presenting the core concepts of attachment theory.

## ATTACHMENT THEORY AS A FRAMEWORK FOR STUDYING EMOTIONS AND EMOTION REGULATION

Although Bowlby (1969/1982, 1973, 1980), the originator of attachment theory, did not devote much attention to the nature of emotions per se (only one brief chapter in Volume 1 of *Attachment and Loss*), he attempted to understand how attachment processes and emotional experiences are related. Specifically, he was interested in the course and consequences of emotions aroused by the availability and responsiveness of attachment figures in times of need (evoking, for example, love, joy, and relief); by threats of rejection, separation, or abandonment (anxiety, anger); and by the loss of a person to whom one is attached (grief, sadness, despair). Attachment theory is an attempt to explain how secure attachment relationships help a person resolve temporary bouts of negative emotion, including hurt feelings, and how attachment insecurities interfere with effective emotion regulation (Shaver & Mikulincer, 2007).

Bowlby (1982) claimed that human beings are born with an innate psychobiological system (the *attachment behavioral system*) that motivates them to seek proximity to significant others (*attachment figures*) in times of need.

He (Bowlby, 1973) also identified major individual differences in attachment system functioning, which arise in response to the behaviors of particular attachment figures. Interactions with attachment figures who are available and responsive in times of need facilitate the optimal functioning of the attachment system and promote a sense of *attachment security*. This sense of security is based on implicit beliefs that the world is generally safe, and it is rooted in positive mental representations of self and others, which Bowlby (1973) called *internal working models*.

However, attachment figures who are not reliably available and supportive cause whoever is dependent on them to form negative working models of self and others and to develop defensive *secondary attachment strategies* characterized by *hyperactivation* or *deactivation* of the attachment system (e.g., Cassidy & Kobak, 1988). Hyperactivation (which Bowlby [1982] called "protest") is characterized by intense efforts to attain security and protection and by insistent attempts to induce a relationship partner, viewed as insufficiently available or responsive, to provide more reassuring care. Hyperactivation includes clinging, controlling, and coercive behaviors; intense expressions of emotion; cognitive and behavioral efforts to establish physical or emotional contact; and overdependence on others for protection (Shaver & Mikulincer, 2002). In contrast, deactivation involves inhibition of proximity-seeking inclinations, actions, and emotional expressions and the determination to handle stress and distress alone (a defensive stance that Bowlby [1982] called "compulsive self-reliance").

When studying individual differences in attachment system functioning in adolescence and adulthood, attachment researchers have focused primarily on a person's *attachment style* – the chronic pattern of relational expectations, emotions, and behaviors that results from internalization of a particular attachment history (Fraley & Shaver, 2000). Beginning with Ainsworth et al.'s (1978) studies of infant–caregiver attachment and followed up by social and personality psychologists in many recent studies of adult attachment (reviewed by Mikulincer & Shaver, 2007), researchers have found that individual variations in attachment style can be measured along two orthogonal dimensions: *attachment anxiety* and *avoidance* (Brennan, Clark, & Shaver, 1998). The avoidance dimension reflects the extent to which a person distrusts others' goodwill and relies on deactivating strategies for coping with attachment insecurities. The anxiety dimension reflects the degree to which a person worries that relationship partners will be unavailable in times of need and relies on hyperactivating strategies for acting on these worries. People who score low on both dimensions enjoy a sense of felt security.

With Shaver et al.'s (1987) model of emotion generation in mind (Fig. 6.1), it is possible to characterize the attachment system as an innate emotion regulation device. Perceived threats automatically activate the system, which then causes the threatened individual to seek proximity to protective others (or evoke mental representations of them) as a means of managing the threat and restoring emotional balance. Moreover, perceived indications of reliable attachment figure availability have a powerful effect on the generation and regulation of emotions. An available attachment figure facilitates coping with threats and restoring emotional balance, whereas the unavailability of such a figure disrupts coping and increases the intensity of distress.

Beyond the normative role of attachment processes in emotion regulation, dispositional attachment styles can alter, obstruct, or suppress the generation, activation, and expression of emotions (Mikulincer & Shaver, 2007). Whereas a continuing sense of attachment security promotes the use of flexible, reality-attuned regulatory processes, which allow emotions to be experienced and expressed without defensive distortion, attachment insecurities contribute to the distortion or denial of emotional experience, unconscious suppression of potentially functional emotions, dysfunctional rumination on threats, and poor coping skills. For this reason, Bowlby (1988) viewed attachment insecurity as a risk factor for clinically significant emotional problems, a view that has been well supported by recent research. In the present chapter, we explore the role played by attachment style in the generation and regulation of *hurt feelings*.

## THE NATURE OF HURT FEELINGS IN LIGHT OF THE EMOTION GENERATION MODEL AND ATTACHMENT THEORY

Researchers who have been studying hurt feelings, including the authors of the chapters in this volume, have identified many of the pieces of the puzzle needed to conceptualize hurt feelings in terms of the emotion generation model shown in Figure 6.1. Some of them (especially Feeney, 2004, 2005, Chapter 15, this volume) have already demonstrated the relevance of attachment theory, especially the concept of internal working models, to an understanding of hurt feelings. They have also shown how individual differences in attachment style moderate hurt feelings. What we hope to do here is become more specific about the ways in which attachment theory and research can inform us about how hurt feelings are generated; how they become associated with other emotional reactions, including anger, sadness, shame, or fear; and how people react to these feelings. We also hope to elaborate the attachment perspective on hurt feelings, supplementing it with Kohut's (1977) self psychology. Our main goal with respect to Kohut is to explain briefly how what he called healthy narcissism depends on close relationships and why being hurt by an attachment figure is especially damaging to healthy narcissism. Finally, we raise the possibility that enhancing a person's attachment security can buffer him or her against hurt feelings. We have collected preliminary data to evaluate this possibility.

### The Nature of Hurtful Events

According to Shaver et al.'s (1987) emotion process model, emotion generation depends on a notable change in the internal or external environment that is appraised as relevant to one's wishes, goals, and concerns (see the first two modules in Fig. 6.1). In light of the model, it is important to ask what kinds of events or experiences generate hurt feelings and how attachment theory helps us understand the common denominator of these events.

Previous studies have provided valuable information about the nature of hurt feelings (e.g., Feeney, 2004; Leary, Springer, Negel, Ansell, & Evans, 1998; Vangelisti, Young, Carpenter-Theune, & Alexander, 2005). In these studies, participants were asked to recount situations in which their feelings were hurt. Their accounts were then content-analyzed to create major categories of hurtful events and experiences. For example, Leary et al.'s (1998) analysis of hurtful events in different kinds of relationships produced six major categories: active relationship denigration (rejection, abandonment, ostracism), passive relationship denigration (more implicit forms of rejection, such as being ignored), criticism, betrayal/infidelity, ill-conceived humor/teasing, and self-devaluation/self-humiliation (feeling unappreciated, misunderstood, used, or taken for granted). In Feeney's (2004) analysis of hurtful events in romantic relationships, she noted five major kinds of events: active relationship denigration, passive relationship denigration, criticism, sexual infidelity, and deception.

Based on the different categories of hurtful events, researchers have attempted to identify their common denominator. Leary (2001), for example, found the major defining feature of hurtful events to be *relationship devaluation* – the appraisal that a relationship partner regards the relationship as less valuable, important, or close than one had thought or would like. Vangelisti (2001) believed the defining feature to be *relationship transgression* – the appraisal that a relationship partner has violated relational norms or rules, victimized the injured person, or heightened his or her sense of vulnerability. Feeney (2005) challenged these claims, although acknowledging them as useful starting points, and offered a third perspective based on insights from attachment theory and research. In her view, relationship devaluations and transgressions generate hurt feelings only if they undermine or compromise a person's positive working models of self and others, signal a threat to one's safety and security, and are experienced as a personal injury. According to Feeney (2005),

> Hurt is an emotion elicited specifically by relational transgressions that evoke a sense of personal injury.... In this context, personal injury is defined as damage to the victim's view of the self as worthy of love and/or to core beliefs about the availability and trustworthiness of others. (p. 256)

In other words, the defining feature of hurtful events is the *sense of personal injury* caused by the threat these events pose to one's positive views of self and others. This approach to hurt feelings gives more prominence to the self than did the previous approaches.

We agree with Feeney's (2005) amendments to the previous conceptions of hurt feelings, which is not surprising given that we also rely on attachment theory. But we wish to suggest yet another amendment – namely that a core feature of hurtful events is their capacity to destroy a person's sense of safety and security, which is related to, but not exactly the same as, the person's positive views of self and others. The positive working models are, theoretically speaking, important pillars of the sense of attachment security (Bowlby, 1973, 1988), so events and experiences that challenge the models do undermine security. But we believe it is worthwhile to look first and foremost at the relation of hurt feelings to a person's fundamental sense of security and protection. That is, deeply hurt feelings are likely to occur only when a partner's actions or words pierce one's deep, visceral, generally unconscious sense of safety and security. In fact, there can be relational devaluations and transgressions that alter one's view of a relationship partner (e.g., "I won't trust him to keep my confidences") without necessarily endangering one's deeper sense of security. We suspect it is easier to handle relational difficulties and dangers without hurt feelings when the relationship in question is not an attachment relationship – that is, not a relationship with a person on whom one's fundamental safety and value depend.

Why is a threat or injury to one's sense of attachment security so painful? The attachment system evolved biologically because being close to loving and protective others, beginning immediately after birth, increases one's likelihood of survival and eventual success in reproducing and rearing offspring (Bowlby, 1982). This is, we believe, the most important reason for what Baumeister and Leary (1995) called the "need to belong." The issue in human infancy is not just belonging (a state that an infant can presumably not understand); it is to be protected, cared for, and helped to thrive. Hence, interactions with available and supportive caregivers in times of need not only generate feelings of warmth and love; they also enhance the sense that the world is a safe place, a good place, a welcoming place and that within the context of solid close relationships one can handle inevitable problems and hardships (Mikulincer & Shaver, 2007).

When we are brought up short by an attachment figure's hurtful words or deeds, we suddenly have our security blanket yanked away, and our nearness to the abyss of insecurity, vulnerability, unpredictability, and, yes, even injury or death is brought home with an emotional yelp (Mikulincer, Florian, Birnbaum, & Malishkevich, 2002). This association between hurtful comments, betrayals, and partner contempt, on the one hand, and the threat of injury and death, on the other, makes it more reasonable that hurt feelings and the insecurity with which they are linked are experienced almost as powerfully as physical injuries that threaten survival (Eisenberger, Lieberman, & Williams, 2003). We usually view biological survival and survival of one's self-image as two different things, with the latter being only metaphorically similar to the former. In fact, however, especially in infancy and childhood, having one's fundamental sense of safety and value threatened can literally be a matter of life or death.

This is not to say that the sense of attachment security is equivalent to being invulnerable. According to attachment theory and research, security-enhancing attachment figures help a child to articulate problems as well as hopes and to identify opportunities while increasing the child's ability to notice, understand, and act effectively in the face of concerns, worries, and vulnerabilities (e.g., Fonagy, Steele, Steele, Moran, & Higgitt, 1991). A secure person is not an emotionally bulletproof superhuman; he or she does not deny life's precariousness or finitude. But a secure person can deal more effectively than an insecure one with difficulties and frustrations because attachment figures have helped him or her identify, articulate, and deal with these tribulations. The "articulation" aspect of the process turns out to be important. A security-providing attachment figure's ability to coherently identify and discuss needs and emotions has proved to be one of the most important assets as far as the developing child is concerned. (See Hesse [1999] for a discussion of the role of discourse coherence and coherence of mind as assessed by the Adult Attachment Interview.)

A secure person benefits from having a continuing sense that other people are available to provide help, support, and encouragement when actual, correctly perceived conditions are threatening or painful. In other words, a sense of security can actually help people remain open to learning about needs and weaknesses and to acknowledge real threats when they arise as well as cope effectively with them. When this sense of security and solidity is violated, a person is forced to consider facing threats without a "protective shield," and the "pain" or "hurt" that arises is an accurate reflection of his or her lack of protection and support.

Recently, Beckes and Simpson (2007) provided noteworthy experimental evidence for the close connection between vulnerability and security. In the first part of their experiment, they implicitly conditioned people by pairing a subliminal frightening or neutral stimulus with one of two pictures of warmly smiling people (who were displaying authentic, or "Duchenne," smiles). In the second part of the experiment, participants performed a lexical decision task in which they saw security-related words, insecurity-related words, and non-attachment-related words. They were primed before each trial with one of the previously conditioned smiling faces, which were equally "warm." As it turned out, security-related words were recognized faster after priming with the face that had been previously associated with a frightening stimulus, but this did not happen in the presence of an equally accepting face that had previously been associated with a neutral stimulus. Thus, it seems that the sense of attachment security involves a connection between dangers, threats, and vulnerabilities, on the one hand, and feelings of protection and safety, on the other. An event or experience that violates a person's sense of security can momentarily break this connection, leaving the person unprotected from life's dangers. The visceral and anterior cingulate "pain" evoked by such experiences

(Eisenberger et al., 2003) is a strong signal that one's safety and survival are at risk.

Beyond signaling danger, an injury to one's sense of attachment security can produce what Kohut (1977) called "narcissistic wounds" – injuries to one's sense of self-integrity and personal value. Borrowing from Kohut's (1977) self psychology, we (Banai, Mikulincer, & Shaver, 2005; Mikulincer & Shaver, 2007) argued that the sense of attachment security is one of the building blocks of what Kohut called (1977) "healthy narcissism" – a cohesive self-structure that provides a sense of identity, value, and permanence and promotes the actualization of a person's potentialities (native talents and acquired skills). Interactions with loving and supportive attachment figures are an authentic source of personal value – thanks to being valued, loved, and viewed as special by caring relationship partners (Bowlby, 1973). These interactions also yield subjective feelings of solidity and stability even under threatening or unpredictable conditions, because the love and protection provided by attachment figures sustain one's ability to repair wounds to self-esteem inflicted by the inevitable disappointments and difficulties of life. Moreover, being confident that support is available when needed, a secure person can take calculated risks and accept important challenges that facilitate the actualization of his or her potentialities.

In our view, healthy narcissism is so closely wrapped up with the sense of security resulting from interactions with available and supportive attachment figures that when one source of strength is attacked the other suffers as well. According to Wolf (1988), "to maintain its cohesion, its vigour and its balance, the healthy self needs to be embedded in a milieu that is experienced as constantly supplying a self-sustaining selfobject ambience [i.e., regulatory functions provided by another, experienced as part of oneself]" (p. 28). According to the metaphors of self psychology, an attachment figure is a "container" that "holds" and sustains the self; it is also a safety net. In a related theoretical analysis, Gerzi (2005) characterized the "container" as a "membrane" that provides essential nutrients and protects a person from external dangers. Violation of the sense of security is therefore akin to an injury to this protective psychological membrane, which the brain represents as an almost physical pain (Eisenberger et al., 2003).

## The Appraisal of Hurtful Events

An attachment perspective on hurtful events helps us delineate the appraisals that generate hurt feelings (the second module of Fig. 6.1). There are at least two important aspects to these appraisals: (a) appraising a partner's actions, inaction, or words as endangering one's sense of attachment security and (b) appraising oneself as needing to maintain or restore such a sense. When being criticized, lied to, or betrayed, one is likely to feel hurt if one has been relying on the critic, liar, or cheater for a sense of safety, protection, and value. However, to the extent that a person never allows him- or herself to rely for safety and security on this relationship partner, the likelihood of being seriously hurt or wounded is greatly reduced. This is an example of the general emotional principle that if a person doesn't care, he or she need not experience so many negative emotions. If a person can find alternative defenses against feelings of helplessness and vulnerability, defenses that do not require close, loving attachment relationships (for example, through what Bowlby [1980] called "compulsive self-reliance"), he or she may be protected to a large extent from hurt feelings. In other words, the generation of hurt feelings depends both on *caring* about another person's availability and support and on appraising these qualities as either present or absent in that person's behavior toward oneself.

This analysis clarifies why transgressions and devaluations on the part of attachment figures generally "hurt" much more than similar behavior on the part of mere acquaintances. (In the hurt feelings studies published to date, the majority of studied narratives focus on parents, lovers, and close friends, not on mere acquaintances.) Moreover, the attachment-theoretical analysis helps us understand individual differences in the extent to which a partner's threatening behavior will generate hurt feelings. A person's dispositional attachment style should predict his or her appraisals of potentially hurtful events. Specifically, secure or avoidant attachment should reduce a person's tendency to appraise a partner's behavior as deeply hurtful, and attachment anxiety should make the occurrence of hurt feelings more likely. Security and avoidance are quite different from each other, however. Whereas dispositional security makes it less likely that any particular behavior on the part of a partner will undermine one's solid sense of security, dispositional avoidance includes the denial and suppression of needs for intimacy and support.

Through a long history of security-enhancing interactions with available and loving attachment figures, secure individuals develop a solid and stable sense of security and protection. Moreover, they construct increasingly strong, well-validated positive models of self as worthy of love and also positive models of others as available, sensitive, and trustworthy (Bowlby, 1973, 1988). Because of this solid, cohesive, and stable psychological foundation, secure people do not need to depend as much as insecure people on a partner's continuous support to maintain their sense of security. They are obviously not completely invulnerable to slights, relational devaluations, and relational transgressions, but they can usually withstand challenges to their well-grounded positive beliefs without being deeply hurt. Studies indicate that secure people are better able than insecure ones to excuse a partner's occasional negative or ambiguous behavior and not attribute it to evil intentions or an absence of love (e.g., Collins, 1996; Mikulincer & Shaver, 2007, Chapters 6 and 10). Moreover, they can more easily forgive a partner after occasional relational devaluations and transgressions (e.g., Mikulincer, Shaver, & Slav, 2006).

Securely attached adults' resilience in the face of relational perturbations is also made possible by the automatic activation of security-enhancing mental representations. Unlike infants and children, who are almost completely dependent on caregivers' sensitivity and responsiveness to repair hurt feelings and restore emotional balance, secure adults do not necessarily need to engage in actual proximity- or support-seeking behavior when coping with threats and dangers. Rather, they can activate soothing and comforting mental representations of relationship partners who regularly provide care and protection, or they can recall past supportive and loving interactions (e.g., Mikulincer, Gillath, & Shaver, 2002). Moreover, secure people can mobilize caring qualities within themselves – qualities modeled on those of their supportive attachment figures – as well as representations of being loved and valued (Mikulincer & Shaver, 2004). These cognitive-affective mental representations provide genuine comfort, bolster an inner sense of safety and security, and help a secure person remain unperturbed by threats and stressors. In other words, calling on a broad, deep set of security-enhancing mental representations when one is treated somewhat badly by a partner can reduce the damage to one's sense of security and thereby protect one, at least to some extent, from hurt feelings.

We do not mean to imply that secure people are completely free of hurt feelings or completely protected from relational devaluations and transgressions. Persistent relational devaluations from a principal attachment figure or traumatic relational transgressions (e.g., rape or physical abuse by a principal attachment figure) can surely shatter even a secure person's solid psychological foundation, and it would be maladaptive for anyone to put up with such relational injuries. As we discuss later, however, even under fairly extreme circumstances, dispositionally secure people are unlikely to be overwhelmed by hurt feelings. They tend to use constructive regulatory strategies aimed at resolving problems in a relationship, including ending the relationship if necessary, while continuing to maintain a strong sense of security.

Avoidant people are also relatively immune to hurt feelings, at least as judged by their own reports. However, unlike the case of the secure person, this immunity is not due to a solid, stable sense of security or to mentally accessible security-enhancing memories and positive working models of relationships. Rather, the avoidant person's immunity stems from the denial or dismissal of attachment needs. As explained earlier, avoidant people tend to deactivate attachment wishes, goals, and concerns and rely on themselves for protection in times of need (Bowlby, 1980). Research has consistently shown that avoidant people use diverse methods (e.g., getting sexually involved with more than one person at a time, keeping secrets from a partner) to maintain self-reliance while minimizing intimacy, emotional involvement, and interdependence (e.g., Feeney, 1999; Hazan & Shaver, 1987).

Moreover, avoidant individuals try not to depend on a partner's support, care, or love to make them feel safe and secure. Their deactivating strategies generally allow them to care less than other people about a relationship partner's complaints, relational devaluations, and relational transgressions, which they view as not very relevant to their own goals and concerns. They tend to exist in a self-created environment in which everyone is out for him- or herself and everyone is available for and interested in short-term sex if it promises to be rewarding (e.g., Schachner & Shaver, 2004). This protects them, at least much of the time, from experiencing hurt feelings and makes contempt a more likely response than hurt feelings to relational transgressions. As discussed later, this protection from hurt feelings is reinforced by a defensive tendency to direct attention away from information that might activate attachment needs (Fraley & Shaver, 1997).

Attachment anxiety, in contrast, renders a person more likely than usual to appraise a partner's behavior as hurtful and to react strongly with hurt feelings. Attachment-anxious people lack a stable psychological foundation, tend to expect the worst from their relationship partners, and tend to appraise relational devaluation and transgressions as major threats and sources of pain. As explained earlier, they have learned, through a history of interactions with self-preoccupied, unreliable, unpredictable caregivers, to hyperactivate their attachment system; be constantly vigilant for signs of impending separation or neglect; exaggerate the importance of a partner's approval, support, and protection; and maintain a high degree of dependence on a partner (Mikulincer & Shaver, 2007; Shaver & Mikulincer, 2007). As a result, attachment-anxious people are likely to notice a partner's potentially hurtful actions or comments and appraise them as discrepant from their intense needs for affection, safety, and security. Moreover, because attachment-anxious people have typically endured a history of frustrating interactions with unreliable attachment figures, they have ready mental access to painful memories, which tend to link a partner's present transgressions with past hurt feelings and thereby amplify their emotional effects (Mikulincer & Orbach, 1995).

Attachment-anxious people's vulnerability to hurt feelings is increased by their tendency to base their self-concepts on unstable, conditional sources of self-worth, such as others' immediate approval (e.g., Park, Crocker, & Mickelson, 2004). They tend not to view themselves as inherently competent or valuable. Although this stance makes sense for a healthy but helpless infant, it is maladaptive when continued into adolescence and adulthood, when self-esteem is better rooted in a history of evidence of one's actual competence and inherent value to self and others. Being overly reliant on others for a sense of personal value causes anxiously attached people constantly to seek reassurance and validation from relationship partners, leaving them overly susceptible to unkind partners' reactions. They feel exceptionally good, briefly, when a partner supplies praise and displays affection, but feel exceptionally bad when a partner is critical or neglectful (e.g., Campbell, Simpson, Boldry, & Kashy, 2005; Feeney, 2002).

There is good evidence that attachment-anxious people react with greater distress and stronger hurt feelings than less anxious people to a partner's hurtful behavior. Feeney (2004, 2005) asked people to recall and describe an event in which a romantic partner said or did something that hurt their feelings and found that attachment-anxious people reacted to these events with stronger than average distress, fear, and shame. In contrast, study participants who scored relatively high on avoidant attachment reported lower levels of hurt feelings and distress. Other researchers have also reported that attachment-anxious people experience strong negative emotions in response to either real or imagined partner infidelity. They are more suspicious, jealous, and worried about relationship exclusivity than secure and avoidant people, and they experience stronger feelings of fear, guilt, shame, sadness, inferiority, and anger (e.g., Guerrero, 1998; Knobloch, Solomon, & Cruz, 2001). There is also evidence that attachment-anxious people experience greater than average distress during relational conflicts (e.g., Feeney, 1994; Simpson, Rholes, & Phillips, 1996) and tend to be overwhelmed by negative feelings and catastrophic thoughts in response to real or imagined separation from or abandonment by a partner (e.g., Meyer, Olivier, & Roth, 2005; Mikulincer, Florian et al., 2002).

## The Nature of Hurt Feelings

With the foregoing attachment-theoretical framework in mind, we can consider in more detail what hurt feelings are like. Is "hurt" a unique emotion, a member of a broader basic emotion category, or a blend of basic emotions? Researchers have given different answers to this question, and their answers depend on their implicit or explicit theories of emotion. In their early study of the hierarchical organization of emotion concepts, Shaver et al. (1987) found that, although hurt was placed in a subcategory of sadness-related emotions reflecting pain and suffering (e.g., agony and anguish), a detailed analysis of participants' narratives suggested that "hurt" might be a blend of sadness and anger. Vangelisti (2001) and Vangelisti and Young (2000) also viewed hurt feelings as an amalgam or blend of other emotions, but they portrayed it mainly as a mixture of sadness and fear – sadness due to the loss of a loved one or a relationship and fear due to vulnerability caused by the loss. Other researchers have proposed that, although hurt feelings are often *accompanied* by other emotions, hurt is a fundamental, unique emotional experience in its own right and should be distinguished from other emotions. For example, Leary et al. (1998) found that people who described past situations in which their feelings were hurt had no difficulty distinguishing between their hurt feelings and the other negative emotions they experienced in relation to the described situations (e.g., "Eventually I became angry but initially it was just plain painful"). In addition, Leary and Springer (2001) found that hurt feelings (described in retrospective accounts as well as during laboratory studies) could not be fully accounted for by other negative emotions (anxiety, anger, and sadness).

In a recent study of retrospective accounts of being hurt by a romantic partner, Feeney (2005) concluded that being hurt is a unique emotional experience. It is marked by terms implying personal injury, such as "hurt," "in pain," or "damaged," that do not overlap completely with sadness, anger, or shame. However, Feeney also noticed that hurt feelings are often accompanied by other negative emotions, depending on the type of hurtful event. For example, whereas sexual infidelity and other forms of betrayal often elicit a combination of hurt and anger, a partner's disinterest, disapproval, or disengagement elicits a combination of hurt and sadness; and a partner's active attempts to end the relationship arouse a mixture of hurt, fear, and sadness. Feeney (2005) interpreted these results in terms of different appraisals of hurtful events.

We also view hurt feelings as unique emotional experiences. In fact, the entire notion of "basic emotions" needs to be reconsidered. Every emotion for which we have a unique name (i.e., a name that is not simply synonymous with some other emotion name, as some are in English because the language contains redundant borrowings from several other languages) differs from others either in intensity (e.g., annoyed, angry, enraged; disappointed, saddened, bereaved) or in the kind of situation that evokes it (righteous indignation, moral disgust, hatred). When we ask a person to recall an experience of some named emotion (such as "hurt"), he or she presumably enters memory with that label in mind and finds one or more examples that fit the label. In this circumstance, most people do dredge up events that caused an injury to their sense of security, which Eisenberger et al. (2003) recorded in the brain, and authors of the chapters in this book refer to, whether literally or metaphorically, as "painful." Other negative emotions do not share this particular painful quality, and not all are associated with wounded attachment security. Thus, "hurt" is distinct, and there is no convincing evidence for considering it to be a blend of other emotions (see also Leary and Leder, Chapter 2, this volume).

The emotions that often are mentioned in conjunction with hurt feelings are no more basic than hurt itself and are not necessarily "blended" with hurt to form an amalgam. More likely they are also distinct emotions that arise as a person appraises and reappraises, often in conjunction with thinking more about a hurtful event, the partner's motives that caused it, the partner's behavioral alternatives that were rejected or neglected in favor of the injurious behavior, a friend's perspective on the hurtful events, and so on. In most cases, when one person does something sufficiently powerful to deeply hurt another's feelings, the injured person will take more than a few milliseconds to encode the event – a few milliseconds being all that is required for the initial jab of pain to signal that the psychological/relational rug of security has been just been jerked out from under the hurt person's previously positive expectations and feelings. Thus, studies of the many emotions that arise in tandem with hurt or occur when a person reappraises a partner's hurtful actions are studies of all the different emotions these situations can evoke. They do not necessarily provide insights into the nature of hurt feelings themselves.

What matters, we assume, is how the hurtful event is appraised and reappraised over time (see also Fitness and Warburton, Chapter 3, this volume). As emotion researchers have shown, if the hurtful event is ascribed to a partner's hostile intentions, it is likely to elicit not just hurt feelings but also angry protest (e.g., Weiner, 1986). When attributed to one's own incompetence ("I've been so blind, so stupid"), the hurtful event can evoke shame and sadness (e.g., Abramson, Metalsky, & Alloy, 1989; Janoff-Bulman, 1979); if attributed to one's own destructive behavior, it may elicit guilt and remorse (Janoff-Bulman, 1979). If the person considers the long-term negative implications of the injury for self-esteem or one's primary relationship, it may arouse feelings of anxiety, depression, or despair (Feeney, 2004, 2005). In all such cases, the collateral emotions are not necessarily caused by the attachment injury itself and are not inherent aspects of the hurt feelings. We agree with Leary et al. (1998) that "the experience of hurt should be studied as a temporal phenomenon as opposed to a static experience" (p. 1235).

Attachment-style differences are likely to be involved in the reappraisal process that follows hurtful events and leads to the arousal of other emotions. We know, for example, that insecure people, whether anxious or avoidant, are more likely than secure ones to attribute a partner's undesirable behavior to hostile intentions (e.g., Collins, 1996; Mikulincer, 1998a). This attributional tendency, which reflects insecure people's negative working models of others, may predispose them to experience more anger in response to hurtful events. Indeed, there is evidence that insecure people react to their partners' negative behavior with stronger anger than is typically experienced or displayed by secure people (e.g., Mikulincer, 1998a).

In addition, attachment-anxious people's negative models of self often cause them to take some of the blame for their partner's destructive behavior (Mikulincer & Shaver, 2007), attributing it to their own negative behavior or qualities. This attributional tendency makes them vulnerable to shame, sadness, depression, and self-related worries. Feeney (2004) reported evidence for this hypothesized series of events. She found that people who scored higher on attachment anxiety were more likely to entertain negative self-views during hurtful events, which in turn exacerbated their self-relevant worries. Despite the value of these preliminary findings, more comprehensive research is needed to map out the major dimensions of the appraisal and reappraisal processes that evoke hurt feelings and explore their associations with the two major dimensions of attachment insecurity: anxiety and avoidance.

## Cognitive and Behavioral Responses to Hurtful Events

In this section, we focus on the third and fourth modules of Shaver et al.'s (1987) model of emotion generation and consider the specific action tendencies associated with hurt feelings and their manifestations in thought and behavior. According to Vangelisti and her colleagues (e.g., Vangelisti & Young, 2000; Vangelisti et al., 2005), hurt feelings increase a person's readiness to disengage from a painful relationship. That is, interpersonal avoidance or relational distancing is the prototypical action tendency associated with hurt feelings.

However, although most researchers who talk about emotion-guided action tendencies (e.g., Lazarus, 1991) seem to think there is a particular action tendency associated with each emotion (e.g., distancing because of being hurt), most emotions are associated with a broad array of action tendencies (as shown in Shaver et al.'s [1987] prototype or script diagrams), with each being a response to a particular aspect of the eliciting appraisal and each also being affected by the response possibilities available in a particular situation. For example, a frightened person is likely to run away from a charging elephant but toward a train that is pulling out of the station before he or she has managed to climb aboard.

Relational distancing is not the only tendency associated with hurt feelings. Like other action tendencies, relational distancing depends on how a person appraises the hurtful event. In fact, Vangelisti and Young (2000) and Vangelisti et al. (2005) noted that hurt feelings are associated with relational distancing mainly when a hurtful event is attributed to a partner's bad intentions or to the hurt person's own flaws. These are cases in which continuing the relationship may be perceived as difficult (given that at least one partner seems unsuited to a workable relationship). With other people or in other circumstances, there are alternative ways to react to the pain and injury caused by a relational devaluation or transgression (e.g., Leary et al., 1998). For example, the injured person can talk openly with the offending partner about the injury and the pain it caused and try to discourage further hurtful behavior and work toward a warm and satisfying relationship. In other cases, the injured person may decide to defer to the partner's needs and preferences, so as to avoid the breakup of the relationship (e.g., Davis et al., 2006).

Attachment-style differences also shape a person's cognitive and behavioral responses to hurtful events because, as reviewed earlier, people with different attachment styles differ in the way they appraise hurtful events, the importance they attach to close relationships, and the positivity of their working models of self and others. Moreover, they differ in the way they cope with stress and manage emotions (Mikulincer & Shaver, 2007; Shaver & Mikulincer, 2002, 2007). Attachment orientations include a variety of cognitive, affective, and behavioral strategies that guide emotion regulation and affect a person's appraisals, feelings, and action tendencies. These strategies can be expected to manifest themselves when a person reacts to hurtful events, including reacting behaviorally.

When managing emotions, securely attached people are able to direct most of their regulatory efforts to the emotion *generation* process – changing the emotion-eliciting event (e.g., by resolving a conflict or solving a problem) or reappraising it constructively – and they are therefore often able to sidestep or short-circuit painful experiences (Mikulincer & Shaver, 2007, Chapter 7). Specifically, they can place the negative event in perspective, making it seem less overwhelming, and can mobilize support from others. Secure people are also more likely to have developed self-soothing skills (Mikulincer & Shaver, 2004), calming themselves with implicit and explicit emotion-regulation techniques learned from security-enhancing attachment figures and maintaining attention on constructive alternatives rather than becoming victims of rumination or catastrophizing.

Having managed emotion-eliciting events or reappraised them in benign terms, secure people do not often have to alter or suppress other parts of the emotion process. They can remain open to their emotions and express and communicate feelings freely and accurately to others. A person with supportive attachment figures learns that distress can be expressed honestly without the relationship being at risk, and this realization fosters an increasingly balanced way of experiencing and expressing emotions – with a sensible goal in mind and without undue hostility, vengeance, or anxiety about losing control or being abandoned (Cassidy, 1994).

As a result, secure people should be willing and able to articulate and constructively express hurt feelings to an offending partner while trying to resolve the hurtful episode without damaging the relationship, finding a compromise between their own and their partner's needs, and bringing about a beneficial change in the partner's behavior. These constructive responses are likely to be supported by the secure person's positive models of self and others and his or her major goal of maintaining warm and mutually satisfying relationships (Shaver & Hazan, 1993).

In contrast, anxious attachment is likely to incline a person toward intense expressions of hurt, deference (though combined with bitterness and pouting) to a partner's demands, and sometimes uncontrollable anger and even violence (Bartholomew & Allison, 2006). Anxiously attached individuals are often guided by an unfulfilled wish to make attachment figures pay more attention and provide more reliable protection, which causes them to intensify their bids for love and care. As a result, attachment anxiety intensifies the expression of emotions such as jealousy and anger and exaggerates the expression of vulnerability, helplessness, and need. As already indicated, the anxious person's fear of rejection and overdependence on partners can ignite highly ambivalent reactions, running all the way from complete deference to a partner's needs, humiliation, and self-devaluation (e.g., Davis, 2006) to acts of violence against a partner (e.g., Bartholomew & Allison, 2006). Many of these reactions are likely to overwhelm or alienate the partner and provoke additional destructive behavior on the partner's part.

Avoidant defenses include interference with or suppression of emotional states that are incongruent with the goal of keeping one's attachment system deactivated. These defensive regulatory efforts are directed mainly at fear, anxiety, anger, sadness, shame, guilt, and distress because these emotions, like hurt feelings, are triggered by threats and can cause unwanted activation of the attachment system. Moreover, hurt, fear, anxiety, sadness, shame, and guilt can be interpreted as signs of weakness or vulnerability, which contradicts an avoidant person's sense of strength and independence (Cassidy, 1994). Like secure people, avoidant ones attempt to downregulate negative emotions. But whereas secure people's regulatory attempts usually promote accurate perception, good communication, and relationship maintenance, avoidant people's efforts are aimed at minimizing perceived threats, closeness, and interdependence, regardless of distorted perceptions or deleterious effects on the relationship.

The inability or unwillingness to deal openly with painful emotions constrains avoidant people to one or two narrow regulatory paths: suppressing emotion or dissociating themselves from its manifestations in experience and behavior. These regulatory efforts consist of denial or suppression of emotion-related thoughts and memories, diversion of attention from emotion-related material, and inhibition or masking of verbal and nonverbal expressions of emotion. As a result, avoidant people are often unwilling and unable to articulate and constructively express their feelings to a hurtful partner. Moreover, they are likely to avoid any forms of interaction with the offending partner that might reactivate hurt, pain, and distress. In fact, avoidant people are likely to view relational distancing and emotional disengagement as the most reasonable ways to back away from relational devaluations and transgressions.

There is considerable evidence concerning insecure people's maladaptive reactions to a romantic partner's transgressions (e.g., Gaines et al., 1997, 1999; Scharfe & Bartholomew, 1995). These studies generally find that attachment insecurities are associated with less "voice" (active attempts to solve a problem) and "loyalty" (understanding the temporary nature of a partner's behavior and waiting for improvement) – two constructive ways of dealing with hurt feelings. Attachment insecurities are associated with more "exit" responses (attempts to harm the partner or leave the relationship) and "neglect" responses (ignoring the partner and refusing to discuss the problem) – two kinds of relational distancing. Researchers have also found that attachment-anxious people tend to cope with even minor hints of a partner's infidelity by expressing strong disapproval and engaging in intense surveillance (e.g., Guerrero, 1998). In contrast, avoidant individuals prefer to avoid discussing the problem (e.g., Guerrero, 1998).

Conceptually similar findings were obtained in two studies of reactions to a relationship partner's betrayal of trust (e.g., Jang, Smith, & Levine, 2002; Mikulincer, 1998b). As compared with secure people, insecure ones were less likely to talk openly with their partner about his or her deception. In addition, more attachment-anxious people were likely to ruminate about their partner's betrayal, talk around and avoid discussing the partner's deception, and react with strong negative emotions. Avoidant people, in contrast, increased their distance from the transgressing partner and denied the importance of the threatening episode.

Two recent papers on the link between attachment style and forgiveness within couple relationships add to the evidence concerning insecure people's troubled reactions to a partner's transgressions (Kachadourian, Fincham, & Davila, 2004; Mikulincer et al., 2006). In two correlational studies of dating and married couples, Kachadourian et al. (2004) found that more attachment-anxious or avoidant people were less likely to forgive their romantic partners. In a diary study of daily fluctuations in the tendency to forgive a partner, Mikulincer et al. (2006) found that both attachment anxiety and avoidance predicted lower levels of daily forgiveness across 21 consecutive days. Moreover, whereas secure people were more inclined to forgive their spouse on days when they perceived more positive spousal behavior, more insecure people (either anxious or avoidant) reported little forgiveness even on days when they perceived their spouse to be available, attentive, and supportive.

## BUFFERING EFFECTS OF SECURITY-ENHANCING MENTAL REPRESENTATIONS: PRELIMINARY EVIDENCE

In addition to reviewing the attachment literature and speculating about the role played by felt security in regulating hurt feelings, we can offer some preliminary experimental data collected specifically for this chapter. If hurt feelings are generated by an assault on the sense of attachment security, an intervention that helps restore felt security – by providing a sense of love and support or experimentally activating security-enhancing mental representations (through cognitive priming) – should mitigate the pain caused by hurtful experiences and reduce the strength of action tendencies associated with the hurt feelings. In some of our previous experimental studies, we found that priming thoughts of love and support (by subliminally presenting security-related words), priming mental representations of an available and supportive attachment figure (by subliminally presenting the person's name or image), or evoking memories of supportive interactions with a loving partner can instill a temporary sense of security even in an otherwise insecure mind, with correspondingly positive effects on mood, mental health, compassionate and prosocial feelings and behaviors, and tolerance toward otherwise disliked outgroup members (see Mikulincer & Shaver, 2007, for a review). We wondered, while planning this chapter, whether this sort of security priming would have similar positive effects on a person's reactions to hurtful events.

The results were expected to be somewhat complicated, however. The buffering effect of security priming might be less evident among dispositionally secure people because, as explained earlier, they can mobilize security-enhancing mental representations and caring qualities within themselves even in the absence of external cues, and they are likely to have done so when a relationship partner hurt their feelings. We thought it likely that a security-priming intervention would have its most notable effects on insecure people, because they lack a reliable, stable sense of safety, security, and personal value. For attachment-anxious people, security priming might reduce the intensity of hurt feelings and other negative emotions after a hurtful experience. For avoidant people, security priming might not reduce self-reported pain and distress because these negative emotions might already have been blocked or suppressed by avoidant defenses (Feeney, 2004). However, an experimental infusion of stimuli related to safety and protection might allow them to acknowledge their hurt feelings and perhaps reduce their anger toward the offending party and their tendency to distance themselves from this person.

With this reasoning in mind, we conducted an experiment involving 70 undergraduates at a large state university (51 women and 19 men). The procedure included three parts. In the first part, participants completed the Experiences in Close Relationships inventory (ECR; Brennan et al., 1998), a measure of dispositional attachment anxiety and avoidance. Next, the participants described an incident in which a close relationship partner hurt their feelings (the typical procedure used in the studies reviewed earlier in this chapter, based on the assumed ability of young adults to find examples of hurt feelings in memory based on searching for them under that verbal label). The participants then completed a short computerized task in which they were asked to rate, for 20 pairs of pieces of furniture (e.g., table and chair), how similar or associated the two were. (This task was a "cover" for the subliminal security-priming procedure.) Before seeing each pair of named pieces of furniture, participants were exposed to either a secure prime (one of three words: love, secure, or affection) or a neutral prime roughly matched in length with the secure prime (one of three words: lamp, staple, or building). Each prime was presented subliminally (for 22 milliseconds). Based on random assignment to one of the two experimental conditions, 34 of the participants (25 women, 9 men) were exposed to the secure primes and 35 (26 women, 10 men) to the neutral primes. The subliminal priming procedure was similar to those used in our previous studies (e.g., Mikulincer, Gillath, & Shaver, 2002).

In the third part of the experiment, immediately after the priming trials, participants were asked to think again about the hurtful event they had described earlier and to rate on 7-point scales how hurtful this kind of event would be for them if it happened now (*not very hurtful* = 1, *extremely hurtful* = 7), how rejected they would feel (*not very rejected* = 1, *extremely rejected* = 7), how constructively they would handle the situation (*not very constructively* = 1, *extremely constructively* = 7), and how the event would cause them to feel about themselves on 6 positive and 10 negative self-relevant adjectives (used in a previous study of hurt feelings by Leary et al. [1998]).

A factor analysis of the adjective ratings, followed by varimax rotation, revealed two main factors (accounting for 57.4% of the explained variance). The first factor included the 10 negative feelings (stupid, undesirable, dislikable, humiliated, unattractive, helpless, foolish, incompetent, disrespected, and vulnerable). The second factor included the six positive feelings (intelligent, wise, likable, attractive, competent, and desirable). Based on this analysis we computed for each participant two scores by averaging ratings of the items that loaded higher than .40 on a factor (with alpha internal consistency coefficients of .88 and .91, respectively).

The participants were also asked to rate on a 7-point scale how much each of nine action descriptions fit the way they would react to the hurtful event. (This measure had been used in studies of hurt feelings by Leary et al. [1998].) The scale ranged from *I wouldn't do that at all* (1) to *That's pretty much exactly what I would do* (7). A factor analysis followed by varimax rotation of these reactions revealed three main factors (accounting for 66.2% of explained variance). The first factor included four items indicating defensive and hostile reactions (express anger, argue or defend myself, say something vengeful or nasty, distance myself from the person). The second factor included three items indicating more constructive reactions (tell the person I was hurt, try to discuss the matter calmly, and keep my feelings to myself [reverse-scored]). The third factor included two items about crying (cry in front of the person, cry later when I was alone). For each participant we computed three scores by averaging items that loaded higher than .40 on a particular factor. (The alpha coefficients for these scales were .69, .71, and .71, respectively.)

We conducted hierarchical regression analyses examining the unique and interactive effects of the attachment dimensions and security priming (a dummy variable, with 1 indicating security priming and −1 indicating neutral priming) on the various dependent variables. They revealed significant interactions between attachment anxiety and security priming in predicting feelings of rejection, $\beta = -.26$, $p < .05$; constructive reactions, $\beta = .30$, $p < .05$; and crying, $\beta = -.24$, $p = .05$. In addition, there was a marginally significant interaction between attachment anxiety and security priming in predicting negative emotions, $\beta = -.18$, $p = .10$. Simple slope tests clarified the meaning of the interactions. In the neutral priming condition, attachment anxiety was significantly associated with less constructive reactions and more intense feelings of rejection, more crying, and more negative emotions, with $\beta$s of −.42, .51, .38, and .64 (all $ps < .01$). These results are compatible with those from previous studies of the ways in which attachment-anxious people react to being hurt (e.g., Feeney, 2004, 2005). However, the parallel associations were weaker in the security-priming condition: $\beta$s of −.18, .01, .10, and .30 (except for the association between attachment anxiety and negative emotions, the $ps$ were significant at the .05 level). In other words, as expected, security priming buffered the tendency of attachment-anxious people to cope badly with a hurtful event, to experience strong feelings of rejection and other negative emotions, and to express vulnerability (i.e., by crying).

The regression analyses also revealed significant interactions between avoidant attachment and security priming in predicting feelings of rejection, $\beta = .35$, $p < .01$, and defensive/hostile reactions, $\beta = -.33$, $p < .01$. In addition, the avoidance x security-priming interaction approached statistical significance for the appraised severity of the hurtful event, $\beta = .20$, $p = .10$, and crying, $\beta = .23$, $p = .06$. Simple slope tests revealed the following pattern of effects. In the neutral priming condition, avoidant attachment was associated with less negative appraisals of the hurtful event, less intense feelings of rejection, less crying, and stronger defensive/hostile reactions, $\beta$s of $-.15$, $-.31$, $-.39$, $.48$ (except for the association with the appraised severity of the hurtful event, the remaining $p$s were less than .01). These findings fit previous results indicating that avoidant people tend to dismiss hurtful events, inhibit expressions of distress, and react hostilely to hurtful partners (e.g., Feeney, 2004, 2005).

However, security priming altered the associations with avoidant attachment. After security priming, avoidance was associated with greater appraised severity of the hurtful event, $\beta = .25$, $p < .05$; more intense feelings of rejection, $\beta = .40$, $p < .01$; and less defensive and hostile responses, $\beta = -.18$, $p = .10$. In addition, after security priming, the negative association between avoidant attachment and crying was no longer significant (and was even slightly positive), $\beta = .07$. Thus, as expected, security priming not only countered avoidant participants' usual tendency to dismiss hurtful events, inhibit negative feelings, and react hostilely to an offending partner. It seems that a small security boost allowed avoidant people to become more "open to the pain" (Cassidy, 2004) of hurtful events and give up some of their usual defenses.

Overall, this preliminary study supports our (and Feeney's, Chapter 14, this volume) emphasis on the role played by attachment security in buffering a person against hurt feelings. When a person is already secure, based on a security-bolstering attachment history, he or she can raise the threshold for hurt feelings and deal more effectively with them when they do occur. When a person has experienced a history of unreliable, unpredictable attachment figures and has become dispositionally anxious as a result, he or she is likely to react especially negatively to being hurt. But this habitual response can be notably reduced by a brief, simple, unconscious augmentation of neural circuits related to felt security. When a person has dealt with cool, abusive, or consistently unsupportive attachment figures and thereby developed a defensively avoidant pattern of relating to others, he or she is somewhat protected from being hurt but at the expense of rigid, distorting defenses and interpersonal distance. This protective armor can be at least temporarily softened by an infusion of felt security. This is dramatic, if still very preliminary, support for an attachment-theoretical analysis of hurt feelings, and it suggests ways in which clinical interventions might be structured differently for anxious and avoidant clients. The anxious ones need to feel supported so that their raw hurt feelings can be alleviated; the avoidant ones need to feel supported to an extent and in ways that allow them to experience and acknowledge their hurt feelings. They might then be amenable to therapeutic reconstruction of the kind used effectively with anxious clients (Mikulincer & Shaver, 2007, Chapter 14).

CONCLUDING REMARKS

Going back at least to 1987, it has been evident that hurt feelings are a rich source of ideas about emotions, the importance of appraisals in the emotion generation process, the complexity of human emotional reactions, the connections between emotions and emotion labeling in human memory, and the centrality of the social self in the mental processes that generate emotions. Hurt feelings are uniquely human, because no other animal can harbor such complex expectations about relationships, construct and maintain a symbolic self-concept, and generate such complex rules about relationships, and no other animal can talk about assaults on its symbolic self using the metaphor of physical pain.

At first, hurt feelings seemed to be "mixed" or "blended" emotions, because they often occurred in conjunction with anger, sadness, shame, and anxiety. But today the notion of blended emotions seems less useful. Every named emotion is understood, implicitly, by speakers of the naming language to designate a certain kind of emotional reaction, at a particular level of intensity, to a particular kind of situation. In the case of hurt feelings, the reaction is one of pain, narcissistic injury, and loss of love and security – often love and security that had been counted on and taken for granted (hence the possibility of violation and betrayal). This seems likely to make hurt feelings unique – and, at least when viewed by relationship scientists – as "basic" as any other human emotion.

Attachment theory helps us understand how intricately wrapped up each person's symbolic self is with his or her history of close relationships. Viewed developmentally, a social self is a product of thousands of social interactions in which a person has gradually learned whether he or she is socially valued, able to handle life's slings and arrows, and able to count on close others for protection, comfort, and encouragement. The symbolic self is therefore surrounded by a protective membrane, which for some people is quite secure and for others is highly vulnerable and either open to injury or shored up by rigid psychological defenses. The nature of the membrane determines the person's vulnerability to narcissistic wounds and hurt feelings. Research has greatly increased our understanding of hurt feelings. It now seems possible for further research to provide intervention techniques that buffer vulnerable people against future hurt feelings and help overly defended people open themselves to their feelings and vulnerabilities so their damaged selves can be reconstructed in more flexible ways. Until this is done, many avoidant individuals will remain rigidly guarded by protective barriers that rob them of the opportunity to experience the rewards of love, intimacy, and security.

ACKNOWLEDGMENTS

We are grateful to Omri Gillath for programming the software for the experiment described in this chapter and to Debbie Morales for running participants through the experimental procedure. The experiment and preparation of this chapter were facilitated by a grant from the Amini Foundation.

REFERENCES

Abramson, L. Y., Metalsky, G. I., & Alloy, L. B. (1989). Hopelessness depression: A theory-based subtype of depression. *Psychological Review, 96,* 358–372.

Ainsworth, M. D. S., Blehar, M. C., Waters, E., & Wall, S. (1978). *Patterns of attachment: Assessed in the strange situation and at home.* Hillsdale, NJ: Erlbaum.

Bachman, G. F., & Guerrero, L. K. (2006). Relational quality and communicative responses following hurtful events in dating relationships: An expectancy violations analysis. *Personal Relationships, 23,* 943–963.

Banai, E., Mikulincer, M., & Shaver, P. R. (2005). "Selfobject" needs in Kohut's self psychology: Links with attachment, self-cohesion, affect regulation, and adjustment. *Psychoanalytic Psychology, 22,* 224–260.

Bartholomew, K., & Allison, C. J. (2006). An attachment perspective on abusive dynamics in intimate relationships. In M. Mikulincer & G. S. Goodman (Eds.), *Dynamics of romantic love: Attachment, caregiving, and sex* (pp. 102–127). New York: Guilford.

Baumeister, R. F., & Leary, M. R. (1995). The need to belong: Desire for interpersonal attachments as a fundamental human motivation. *Psychological Bulletin, 117,* 497–529.

Beckes, L., & Simpson, J. A. (2007). *Social regulatory conditioning and the bonding power of fear: An attachment related learning mechanism?* Manuscript submitted for publication.

Bowlby, J. (1973). *Attachment and loss: Vol. 2. Separation: Anxiety and anger.* New York: Basic Books.

Bowlby, J. (1980). *Attachment and loss: Vol. 3. Sadness and depression.* New York: Basic Books.

Bowlby, J. (1982). *Attachment and loss: Vol. 1. Attachment* (2nd ed.). New York: Basic Books. (Originally published in 1969).

Bowlby, J. (1988). *A secure base: Clinical applications of attachment theory.* London: Routledge.

Brennan, K. A., Clark, C. L., & Shaver, P. R. (1998). Self-report measurement of adult romantic attachment: An integrative overview. In J. A. Simpson & W. S. Rholes (Eds.), *Attachment theory and close relationships* (pp. 46–76). New York: Guilford.

Campbell, L., Simpson, J. A., Boldry, J., & Kashy, D. A. (2005). Perceptions of conflict and support in romantic relationships: The role of attachment anxiety. *Journal of Personality and Social Psychology, 88,* 510–531.

Cassidy, J. (1994). Emotion regulation: Influences of attachment relationships. *Monographs of the Society for Research in Child Development, 59*, 228–283.

Cassidy, J. (2004). *Remaining open to the pain.* Presented at a research conference on attachment, University of California, Davis.

Cassidy, J., & Kobak, R. R. (1988). Avoidance and its relationship with other defensive processes. In J. Belsky & T. Nezworski (Eds.), *Clinical implications of attachment* (pp. 300–323). Hillsdale, NJ: Erlbaum.

Collins, N. L. (1996). Working models of attachment: Implications for explanation, emotion, and behavior. *Journal of Personality and Social Psychology, 71*, 810–832.

Davis, D. (2006). Attachment-related pathways to sexual coercion. In M. Mikulincer & G. S. Goodman (Eds.), *Dynamics of romantic love: Attachment, caregiving, and sex* (pp. 293–336). New York: Guilford.

Davis, D., Shaver, P. R., Widaman, K. F., Vernon, M. L., Follette, W. C., & Beitz, K. (2006). "I can't get no satisfaction": Insecure attachment, inhibited sexual communication, and sexual dissatisfaction. *Personal Relationships, 13*, 465–483.

de Rivera, J. (1977). A structural theory of the emotions. *Psychological Issues, 10*(4, Monograph no. 40).

Ekman, P. (1992). An argument for basic emotions. *Cognition and Emotion, 6*, 169–200.

Eisenberger, N. I., Lieberman, M. D., & Williams, K. D. (2003). Does rejection hurt? An fMRI study of social exclusion. *Science, 302*, 290–292.

Feeney, J. A. (1994). Attachment style, communication patterns, and satisfaction across the life cycle of marriage. *Personal Relationships, 1*, 333–348.

Feeney, J. A. (1999). Issues of closeness and distance in dating relationships: Effects of sex and attachment style. *Journal of Social and Personal Relationships, 16*, 571–590.

Feeney, J. A. (2002). Attachment, marital interaction, and relationship satisfaction: A diary study. *Personal Relationships, 9*, 39–55.

Feeney, J. A. (2004). Hurt feelings in couple relationships: Towards integrative models of the negative effects of hurtful events. *Journal of Social and Personal Relationships, 21*, 487–508.

Feeney, J. A. (2005). Hurt feelings in couple relationships: Exploring the role of attachment and perceptions of personal injury. *Personal Relationships, 12*, 253–271.

Fischer, K. W., Shaver, P. R., & Carnochan, P. (1990). How emotions develop and how they organize development. *Cognition and Emotion, 4*, 81–127.

Fonagy, P., Steele, M., Steele, H., Moran, G. S., & Higgitt, P. (1991). The capacity for understanding mental states: The reflective self in parent and child and its significance for security of attachment. *Infant Mental Health Journal, 12*, 201–218.

Fraley, R. C., & Shaver, P. R. (1997). Adult attachment and the suppression of unwanted thoughts. *Journal of Personality and Social Psychology, 73*, 1080–1091.

Fraley, R. C., & Shaver, P. R. (2000). Adult romantic attachment: Theoretical developments, emerging controversies, and unanswered questions. *Review of General Psychology, 4*, 132–154.

Gaines, S. O., Jr., Granrose, C. S., Rios, D. I., Garcia, B. F., Youn, M. S., Farris, K. R., & Bledsoe, K. L. (1999). Patterns of attachment and responses to accommodative dilemmas among interethnic/interracial couples. *Journal of Social and Personal Relationships, 16*, 275–285.

Gaines, S. O., Jr., Reis, H. T., Summers, S., Rusbult, C. E., Cox, C. L., Wexler, M. O., et al. (1997). Impact of attachment style on reactions to accommodative dilemmas in close relationships. *Personal Relationships, 4*, 93–113.

Gerzi, S. (2005). Trauma, narcissism, and the two attractors in trauma. *International Journal of Psychoanalysis, 86*, 1033–1050.

Guerrero, L. K. (1998). Attachment-style differences in the experience and expression of romantic jealousy. *Personal Relationships, 5*, 273–291.

Hazan, C., & Shaver, P. R. (1987). Romantic love conceptualized as an attachment process. *Journal of Personality and Social Psychology, 52*, 511–524.

Hesse, E. (1999). The Adult Attachment Interview: Historical and current perspectives. In J. Cassidy & P. R. Shaver (Eds.), *Handbook of attachment: Theory, research, and clinical applications* (pp. 395–433). New York: Guilford.

Izard, C. E. (1977). *Human emotions.* New York: Plenum.

Jang, S. A., Smith, S. W., & Levine, T. R. (2002). To stay or to leave? The role of attachment styles in communication patterns and potential termination of romantic relationships following discovery of deception. *Communication Monographs, 69*, 236–252.

Janoff-Bulman, R. (1979). Characterological versus behavioral self-blame: Inquiries into depression and rape. *Journal of Personality and Social Psychology, 37*, 1798–1809.

Kachadourian, L. K., Fincham, F., & Davila, J. (2004). The tendency to forgive in dating and married couples: The role of attachment and relationship satisfaction. *Personal Relationships, 11*, 373–393.

Knobloch, L. K., Solomon, D.-H., & Cruz, M. G. (2001). The role of relationship development and attachment in the experience of romantic jealousy. *Personal Relationships, 8*, 205–224.

Kohut, H. (1977). *The restoration of the self.* New York: International Universities Press.

Lazarus, R. S. (1991). *Emotion and adaptation.* New York: Oxford University Press.

Lazarus, R. S., & Folkman, S. (1984). *Stress, appraisal, and coping.* New York: Springer.

Leary, M. R. (2001). Toward a conceptualization of interpersonal rejection. In M. R. Leary (Ed.), *Interpersonal rejection* (pp. 3–20). New York: Oxford University Press.

Leary, M. R., & Springer, C. A. (2001). Hurt feelings: The neglected emotion. In R. M. Kowalski (Ed.), *Behaving badly: Aversive behaviors in interpersonal relationships* (pp. 151–175).Washington, DC: American Psychological Association.

Leary, M. R., Springer, C., Negel, L., Ansell, E., & Evans, K. (1998). The causes, phenomenology, and consequences of hurt feelings. *Journal of Personality and Social Psychology, 74*, 1225–1237.

Meyer, B., Olivier, L., & Roth, D. A. (2005). Please don't leave me! BIS/BAS, attachment styles, and responses to a relationship threat. *Personality and Individual Differences, 38*, 151–162.

Mikulincer, M. (1998a). Adult attachment style and individual differences in functional versus dysfunctional experiences of anger. *Journal of Personality and Social Psychology, 74*, 513–524.

Mikulincer, M. (1998b). Attachment working models and the sense of trust: An exploration of interaction goals and affect regulation. *Journal of Personality and Social Psychology, 74*, 1209–1224.

Mikulincer, M., Florian, V., Birnbaum, G., & Malishkevich, S. (2002). The death-anxiety buffering function of close relationships: Exploring the effects of separation reminders on death-thought accessibility. *Personality and Social Psychology Bulletin, 28*, 287–299.

Mikulincer, M., Gillath, O., & Shaver, P. R. (2002). Activation of the attachment system in adulthood: Threat-related primes increase the accessibility of mental representations of attachment figures. *Journal of Personality and Social Psychology, 83*, 881–895.

Mikulincer, M., & Orbach, I. (1995). Attachment styles and repressive defensiveness: The accessibility and architecture of affective memories. *Journal of Personality and Social Psychology, 68*, 917–925.

Mikulincer, M., & Shaver, P. R. (2004). Security-based self-representations in adulthood: Contents and processes. In W. S. Rholes & J. A. Simpson (Eds.), *Adult attachment: Theory, research, and clinical implications* (pp. 159–195). New York: Guilford.

Mikulincer, M., & Shaver, P. R. (2007). *Attachment in adulthood: Structure, dynamics, and change.* New York: Guilford.

Mikulincer, M., Shaver, P. R., & Slav, K. (2006). Attachment, mental representations of others, and gratitude and forgiveness in romantic relationships. In M. Mikulincer & G. S. Goodman (Eds.), *Dynamics of romantic love: Attachment, caregiving, and sex* (pp. 190–215). New York: Guilford.

Osgood, C. E., May, W. H., & Miron, M. S. (1975). *Cross-cultural universals of affective meaning.* Urbana: University of Illinois Press.

Park, L. E., Crocker, J., & Mickelson, K. D. (2004). Attachment styles and contingencies of self-worth. *Personality and Social Psychology Bulletin, 30,* 1243–1254.

Russell, J. A. (1980). A circumplex model of affect. *Journal of Personality and Social Psychology, 39,* 1161–1178.

Schachner, D. A., & Shaver, P. R. (2004). Attachment dimensions and motives for sex. *Personal Relationships, 11,* 179–195.

Scharfe, E., & Bartholomew, K. (1995). Accommodation and attachment representations in young couples. *Journal of Social and Personal Relationships, 12,* 389–401.

Shaver, P. R., & Hazan, C. (1993). Adult romantic attachment: Theory and evidence. In D. Perlman & W. Jones (Eds.), *Advances in personal relationships* (Vol. 4, pp. 29–70). London: Jessica Kingsley.

Shaver, P. R., & Mikulincer, M. (2002). Attachment-related psychodynamics. *Attachment and Human Development, 4,* 133–161.

Shaver, P. R., & Mikulincer, M. (2007). Adult attachment theory and the regulation of emotion. In J. J. Gross (Ed.), *Handbook of emotion regulation* (pp. 446–465). New York: Guilford.

Shaver, P. R., Schwartz, J., Kirson, D., & O'Connor, C. (1987). Emotion knowledge: Further exploration of a prototype approach. *Journal of Personality and Social Psychology, 52,* 1061–1086.

Simpson, J. A., Rholes, W. S., & Phillips, D. (1996). Conflict in close relationships: An attachment perspective. *Journal of Personality and Social Psychology, 71,* 899–914.

Vangelisti, A. L. (2001). Making sense of hurtful interactions in close relationships: When hurt feelings create distance. In V. Manusov & J. Harvey (Eds.), *Attribution, communication behavior, and close relationships: Advances in personal relations* (pp. 38–58). New York: Cambridge University Press.

Vangelisti, A. L., & Young, S. L. (2000). When words hurt: The effects of perceived intentionality on interpersonal relationships. *Journal of Social and Personal Relationships, 17,* 393–424.

Vangelisti, A. L., Young, S. L., Carpenter-Theune, K. E., & Alexander, A. L. (2005). Why does it hurt? The perceived causes of hurt feelings. *Communication Research, 32,* 443–477.

Weiner, B. (1986). *An attributional theory of motivation and emotion.* New York: Springer-Verlag.

Wolf, E. S. (1988). *Treating the self: Elements of clinical self-psychology.* New York: Guilford.

# PART III

HURTFUL ACTS

# 7

## Rejection: Resolving the Paradox of Emotional Numbness after Exclusion

C. NATHAN DeWALL, ROY F. BAUMEISTER,
AND E. J. MASICAMPO

The need for positive and stable relationships is among the most basic and fundamental of human needs. Like the need for food, shelter, and sleep, the need to belong is deeply rooted within evolutionary history and has a profound influence on contemporary psychological processes (Baumeister & Leary, 1995). Given the fundamental nature of the need to belong, it would seem somewhat straightforward that social exclusion would cause dramatic increases in emotional distress. This increased emotion distress after social exclusion should, in turn, cause various behavioral responses. Despite the intuitive appeal of this hypothesized model, converging evidence points to an altered perspective regarding how people respond to social exclusion. Multiple studies have shown that the behavioral effects of social exclusion are quite large (Baumeister, Twenge, & Nuss, 2002; Buckley, Winkel, & Leary, 2004), but the emotional effects are frequently small or nonexistent. Socially excluded participants often report emotional states that do not differ from those of participants in accepted or control conditions (Baumeister, DeWall, Ciarocco, & Twenge, 2005; Gardner, Pickett, & Brewer, 2000; Twenge, Baumeister, Tice, & Stucke, 2001; Zadro, Williams, & Richardson, 2004). Psychologists are therefore confronted with a paradox as to why people respond to such a momentous event as social exclusion with relative emotional detachment and numbness.

The purpose of this chapter is to discuss our recent efforts to resolve this paradox of emotional numbness after social exclusion. We contend that the hypothesized model of emotional distress mediating the behavioral effects of social exclusion was not inherently false; rather, the model was mistaken only in terms of the behavioral effects of social exclusion being contingent on emotional distress. Emotional numbness, in contrast, may prove more useful than emotional distress in explaining the behavioral consequences of social exclusion. Before considering the utility of emotional insensitivity as a predictor of behavioral responses to social exclusion, however, it is first necessary to address why social exclusion causes immediate emotional numbness.

We propose that social exclusion activates the body's pain system, which alters the manner in which excluded people experience physical pain and emotion (Eisenberger, Lieberman, & Williams, 2003). If this view is correct, then excluded people should show increases in both the physical pain threshold (i.e., sensitivity to pain) and pain tolerance (i.e., withstanding higher levels of pain). To the extent that physical and emotional pain share common neural mechanisms (MacDonald & Leary, 2005), deficits in physical sensitivity after social exclusion should be accompanied by reduced emotional sensitivity. These signs of emotional insensitivity should be domain-general, which is to say that excluded people should demonstrate reduced emotional sensitivity across a variety of contexts.

We organized the chapter into four main sections. The first section reviews evidence suggesting that social exclusion poses a serious threat to fundamental motives of social acceptance (Baumeister & Leary, 1995). Next, we review empirical evidence regarding the impact of social exclusion on physical and emotional insensitivity. Third, we review evidence showing that emotional insensitivity can help explain certain behavioral effects of social exclusion. Fourth, we discuss the possible relevance of the current findings to clinical research.

## UNDERSTANDING THE THREAT OF SOCIAL EXCLUSION

Forming and maintaining bonds with others can be considered among the most fundamental and pervasive of all human needs (Baumeister & Leary, 1995). It is likely that the need to belong formed in humans' evolutionary past as they became increasingly reliant on others for much of their well-being and survival. To be sure, humans are not well suited for living in complete solitude. It is therefore not entirely surprising that people would respond strongly to social exclusion. Evidence from our own and other laboratories has demonstrated that rejected people show reduced intellectual functioning (Baumeister et al., 2002), increased aggressiveness (Buckley et al., 2004; Twenge et al., 2001), reduced willingness to self-regulate (Baumeister et al., 2005), decreased helpfulness (Twenge, Baumeister, DeWall, Ciarocco, & Bartels, 2007), and increased likelihood of engaging in self-defeating behaviors such as procrastination and risk-taking (Twenge, Catanese, & Baumeister, 2002). A lack of stable relationships is associated with an increased incidence of psychopathology (Bloom, White, & Asher, 1979) and a variety of negative health consequences (Cacioppo, Hawkley, & Berntson, 2003; Hawkley, Burleson, Berntson, & Cacioppo, 2003; see Uchino, Cacioppo, & Kiecolt-Glaser, 1996, for a review).

These findings confirm that social exclusion has negative consequences for behavioral and health outcomes. Given these findings, it would seem plausible that such behaviors would be a direct result of the emotional distress that follows social exclusion. This distress might cause excluded people to make irrational decisions regarding the appropriate behavior for a given situation, such as behaving aggressively toward a person who was not at all involved in one's exclusion experience (e.g., Twenge et al., 2001). Psychologists have repeatedly shown that people experience anxiety and other negative emotional states after rejection and ostracism (Baumeister & Tice, 1990; Leary, 1990; Williams Cheung, & Choi, 2000). There has not yet been any empirical evidence, however, to suggest that the behavioral effects of social exclusion are mediated by emotional distress.

Why did this mediational model, which was based on previous theory and empirical evidence, fail to explain the causal mechanism underlying the effects of social exclusion for behavior? The simple answer is that, despite the effects of social exclusion on behavior, cognition, and health, people often respond to social exclusion with emotional numbness and detachment. Socially excluded participants frequently report emotional states that do not differ from those of participants who experience social acceptance or from participants in a variety of control conditions (Baumeister et al., 2002; Gardner et al., 2000; Twenge et al., 2001; Zadro et al., 2004). What is perhaps even more surprising, when differences in emotion are found, is that these differences do not mediate the behavioral effects of social exclusion. Researchers who have found that social exclusion produces emotional distress have not shown that the distress mediates the behavioral consequences of social exclusion (Buckley et al., 2004; Williams et al., 2000). Thus, psychologists are confronted with a paradox as to why emotional distress plays such a minor role in response to social exclusion.

A possible explanation why excluded people show signs of emotional insensitivity is that social exclusion causes a defensive state of cognitive deconstruction. Cognitive deconstruction has been used to describe presuicidal states (Baumeister, 1990) and is characterized by emotional numbness, lethargy, perceptions of meaninglessness, altered perception of time, and avoidance of self-focused attention. Social exclusion has been shown to cause each of these symptoms of cognitive deconstruction (Twenge, Catanese, & Baumeister, 2003). The deconstructed state may provide excluded people a temporary reprieve from the aversive emotional states that can result from threats to belongingness. Although the deconstructed state may have short-term benefits for excluded people (i.e., reduced emotional distress), emotional insensitivity has been linked to severe psychopathology in clinical populations (Bancroft, Skrimshire, & Simkin, 1976) and self-destructive behaviors in nonclinical samples (see Baumeister & Scher, 1988, for a review). If socially excluded people have natural defenses that protect them from emotional distress, then it is possible that such defenses temporarily impair the ability of excluded people to experience emotions in a normal fashion. As a result of the failure of the emotion system to function normally, the emotional numbness following social exclusion may be related to insensitivity to physical pain.

## SOCIAL EXCLUSION CAUSES PHYSICAL AND EMOTIONAL INSENSITIVITY

In this section we review theory and recent empirical evidence that supports the view that the emotional defenses after social exclusion result from a pervasive state of emotional numbness. We also provide evidence suggesting that this emotional numbness after social exclusion is further related to physical insensitivity to pain.

### Social Exclusion and Physical Pain

When describing emotional responses to events such as social exclusion, people frequently use words connoting physical pain. People may report feeling "hurt" or "crushed" after the dissolution of a friendship or romantic relationship (Leary & Springer, 2000). In a recent review, MacDonald and Leary (2005) proposed that the similarities in descriptions of socially and physically painful events extend beyond mere metaphor. They suggested that social pain and physical pain operate using the same neural mechanisms. These neural mechanisms include the anterior cingulate cortex, periaqueductal gray brain structures, and the opioid and oxytocin neuroendocrine systems.

Nearly 30 years ago, Panksepp and colleagues proposed a link between social and physical pain (Herman & Panksepp, 1978; Panksepp, Herman, Conner, Bishop, & Scott, 1978a; Panksepp, Vilberg, Bean, Coy, & Kastin, 1978b). These authors suggested that, instead of creating an entirely new system designed to respond to events such as social exclusion, evolution co-opted these responses onto the existing neural mechanisms designated for the detection and regulation of physical pain. Thus, social events might activate neural mechanisms originally designated for the detection and regulation of physical pain, which in turn might alter the manner in which the body responds to physical pain.

In recent years, there has been empirical support for the view that the pain of social exclusion shares many of the same neural and psychological mechanisms as experiences of physical pain. Eisenberger et al. (2003) demonstrated that the anterior cingulated cortex (ACC), which functions to warn people that factors in their environment threaten their goals (Bush, Luu, & Posner, 2000; Eisenberger & Lieberman, 2004; Nelson & Panksepp, 1998), is directly related to the detection of social exclusion. Participants in their study completed a virtual ball-tossing task ostensibly with two other participants while having their brain activity recorded using functional magnetic resonance imaging (fMRI). The results from this study indicated that participants who experienced ostracism showed increased activation of the dorsal ACC. Ostracized participants also showed increased activation in regions of the brain associated with the regulation of physical pain distress and negative affect (i.e., right ventral prefrontal cortex). Additional research has shown that the periaqueductal gray (PAG) brain structures, which are associated with the detection of physical pain, are involved in animal bonding behavior (Craig & Dostrovsky, 1999). Activation of the PAG has been shown to elicit separation distress cries from rats (Panksepp, 1998), whereas lesions to the PAG caused reductions in separation distress cries (Wiedenmayer, Goodwin, & Barr, 2000). Of particular relevance to the current chapter, short-term isolation from caregivers and conspecifics has been shown to cause reduced sensitivity to physical pain (i.e., analgesia) in a variety of animals (Kehoe & Blass, 1986; Naranjo & Fuentes, 1985; see MacDonald & Leary, 2005, for a review). Thus, threats to belongingness activate neural mechanisms hard-wired for the detection and regulation of physical pain.

Despite the large body of evidence showing that social and physical pain share neural pathways in animals, research testing whether a similar link exists in humans has been substantially more limited. We therefore set forth to conduct a series of experiments that sought to demonstrate that social exclusion alters the manner in which the body responds to physical pain, causing decreased sensitivity and increased tolerance to painful stimuli (DeWall & Baumeister, 2006). This research also aimed to show that the insensitivity to physical pain after social exclusion would have implications for emotional responding.

In these studies, social exclusion was manipulated by having participants complete a personality test and giving some participants bogus feedback that they had a personality type in which they could anticipate ending up alone later in life (Future Alone). This manipulation has been used in previous investigations to create a psychological state in which participants believe that something about their personality type will cause others to reject them in the future (e.g., Twenge et al., 2001). Three control groups were also used. The first condition (Future Belonging) involved participants receiving feedback stating that they had a personality type in which they could expect to have many lasting and fulfilling relationships. Participants in the second condition (No feedback control) were not given any feedback regarding their personality or the implications of their personality type for their future belongingness status. Participants in the third condition (Misfortune Control) were informed that their future would be marred by frequent accidents. The Misfortune Control condition was included to enable us to test the alternative hypothesis that the effects of the social exclusion manipulation were simply due to receiving a negatively valenced future diagnostic forecast, as opposed to being unique to social exclusion.

Using the current manipulation allowed us to provide a somewhat conservative test regarding the effects of social exclusion on physical and emotional insensitivity compared to the rejection experiences people might have in their everyday lives. Whereas many times people experience rejection from people with whom they have spent a great deal of time and about whom they care a great deal, participants in the current experiments received feedback from someone whom they had never met regarding the implications of their score on a personality test. The social exclusion that people experience in their everyday lives may also come in a more immediate form (e.g., "I don't want to work with you," "I'd like to end our relationship") than merely being told that one could anticipate experiencing social exclusion some time in the indeterminate future. If the current social exclusion manipulation causes immediate physical insensitivity to pain, it seems possible that the social exclusion that people experience in their everyday lives might have even more pronounced effects on the sensitivity to physical pain.

In a preliminary study, participants arrived at the laboratory and completed a series of baseline measures of physical pain sensitivity. These measurements of pain threshold and pain tolerance were taken using a pressure algometer (Type II, Somedic Inc.; Solletuna, Sweden). For the pain threshold measures, participants were instructed to say the word *now* at the first instant in which they felt pain caused by the pressure increase. Pain tolerance, in contrast, was measured by asking participants to say the word *stop* when they felt that they could no longer tolerate the pain caused by the pressure increase. The digital display showed the value of pressure applied at the moment the algometer was retracted. For more details regarding the physical pain sensitivity measurement, please see DeWall and Baumeister (2006).

After completing the baseline pain threshold and pain tolerance measurements, participants completed a personality test and were given bogus feedback regarding their personality profile. Following a procedure developed by Twenge et al. (2001), participants were randomly assigned to one of three conditions: Future Alone, Future Belonging, and No feedback control. The type of personality feedback participants received functioned as the social exclusion manipulation. Participants then completed a self-report measure of emotion and additional measurements of their pain threshold and pain tolerance.

The results from this study indicated that social exclusion decreased sensitivity to and increased tolerance for physical pain. Socially excluded participants had significantly higher pain threshold and pain tolerance scores than participants who anticipated a future filled with social acceptance and participants who received no personality feedback. Further analyses confirmed that this difference in pain threshold and tolerance scores among socially excluded participants was not merely relative to participants in the other two conditions, but was an absolute change from baseline measurements. The estimated effect sizes for the increases in pain threshold and pain tolerance among socially excluded participants exceeded a full standard deviation in each case, which exceeds criteria commonly used to describe large effects (Cohen, 1977). Thus, the results from this study provided initial evidence that social exclusion alters the manner in which the body responds to physical pain, with direct implications for pain threshold and pain tolerance.

We also tested for the possibility that emotional distress mediated the effects. Participants in the Future Alone condition did not differ significantly from participants in the other two conditions in their self-reported emotional response. These results speak strongly against the possibility that the current effects were mediated by emotional distress.

To test the alternative hypothesis that the results from this preliminary study were merely due to receiving a negatively valenced future diagnostic forecast (as opposed to being specific to social exclusion), we conducted another study that replaced the No feedback control condition from the initial study with a condition in which participants received negative feedback that was unrelated to their future belongingness. Participants in this condition (Misfortune Control) received feedback stating that they had a personality type in which they could anticipate a future filled with frequent accidents and injuries. Participants were therefore randomly assigned to one of three feedback conditions: Future Alone, Future Belonging, and Misfortune Control. The procedure for the second study was identical to the first study. Participants completed baseline measurements of pain threshold and pain tolerance, completed and received bogus feedback on a personality test, and then had their pain threshold and pain tolerance measured again.

The results from this second study were similar to those from the first study. Future Alone participants showed higher pain threshold and pain tolerance scores compared to both Future Belonging and Misfortune Control participants. The difference between baseline and postfeedback pain threshold and tolerance scores among socially excluded participants was an absolute change from baseline measurements. As in the first study, tests for mediation by self-reported emotion yielded no evidence that the increases in physical pain threshold and pain tolerance among socially excluded participants were due to differences in self-reported emotion. Thus, the results from this study provide further evidence that social exclusion produces insensitivity to physical pain. The results also contradict the alternative hypothesis that the observed effects were due merely to receiving a negatively valenced future diagnostic forecast as opposed to being unique to social exclusion. Misfortune Control participants, who anticipated a future marred by frequent physical injuries, did not differ in their pain threshold and pain tolerance scores from Future Belonging. If the decreases in sensitivity to physical pain were due to simply hearing bad news about one's future, then the pain threshold and pain tolerance scores of Future Alone and Misfortune Control participants should not have differed. Thus, the current findings contradict the alternative explanation that the results were simply due to hearing bad news about one's future and suggest that the effects relating to physical insensitivity were unique to social exclusion.

## IMPLICATIONS OF PHYSICAL INSENSITIVITY FOR EMOTIONAL RESPONDING

Having established that social exclusion causes increases in both physical pain tolerance and pain threshold, DeWall and Baumeister (2006) sought to test whether this physical insensitivity to pain would be related to emotional responding. If the neural mechanisms responsible for the detection and regulation of physical and emotional pain share a common physiological basis (MacDonald & Leary, 2005), then it seemed likely that physical insensitivity should be related to emotional insensitivity. What was less clear, however, was the best way to measure emotional insensitivity. We measured emotion using both self-report emotion measures and two types of emotional phenomena in which participants had to rely on their current emotional state and emotional simulation (imagining how oneself would feel) to make judgments about events distant from the present. The first type of emotional phenomenon measured was affective forecasting and the second type was empathy. If socially excluded people are unwilling to report their true emotional distress out of self-presentational concerns and are in reality full of emotion, it would seem likely that they would predict strong emotional responses and empathize with others' distress. But if social exclusion temporarily causes the emotion system to cease functioning normally, excluded people might find it difficult to predict strong emotional reactions to possible future events or to empathize with another person's suffering.

### Predicting Future Pain: Affective Forecasting

Affective forecasting refers to the tendency for people to predict the valence, intensity, and duration of their emotional responses to possible future events (see Wilson & Gilbert, 2003, for a review). Whereas people tend to predict the valence of their future emotional states quite accurately (e.g., "I will be sad if my marriage ends in divorce"), multiple experiments have demonstrated that people consistently overestimate the duration and intensity of their future emotional reactions (Gilbert, Pinel, Wilson, Blumberg, & Wheatley, 1998; Wilson, Wheatley, Kurtz, Dunn, & Gilbert, 2004). Of particular relevance to our study of social exclusion, research has also shown that a person's current emotional state can influence his or her predictions of future emotional responses (Gilbert, Gill, & Wilson, 2002; Van Boven & Loewenstein, 2003). If social exclusion causes people to experience temporary emotional numbness, then excluded people should make relatively unemotional affective forecasts compared to participants who have not experienced social exclusion.

To test this hypothesis, DeWall and Baumeister (2006) exposed participants to the same social exclusion manipulation used in the first study. Participants first completed baseline measures of pain threshold and pain tolerance, completed a personality test, and were either given bogus feedback regarding the implications of their personality type for their future belongingness (Future Alone, Future Belonging) or were not given any personality feedback (No feedback control). After completing a self-report emotion measure, participants were asked to predict their emotional reactions to possible future events. Specifically, participants (all registered students at Florida State University) were asked to predict their level of happiness if the Florida State University (FSU) football team was victorious in their game against a rival opponent (i.e., University of Florida) and their level of happiness if the FSU football team was defeated by the rival opponent. Thus, the design of this experiment allowed us to test whether social exclusion led to both physical insensitivity (as indicated by higher pain threshold and pain tolerance) and emotional insensitivity (as indicated by predictions of unemotional responses to a possible future event).

The results from this study indicated that social exclusion caused both physical and emotional insensitivity. Participants who anticipated a future filled with social exclusion showed increases in pain threshold and pain tolerance compared to participants who expected to have successful relationships and participants who received no personality feedback. In addition, socially excluded participants made less emotional affective forecasts compared to accepted and control participants. Accepted and control participants predicted high levels of happiness if their team was victorious and high levels of sadness if their football team was defeated, which replicated past research showing that people predict extreme emotional reactions to future events (Wilson & Gilbert, 2003). Socially excluded participants, in contrast, reported a neutral affective response to both a victory and a defeat. Notably, the physical and emotional insensitivities were highly correlated with each other. These findings provide support for the theory that physical and emotional pain share common neutral mechanisms (MacDonald & Leary, 2005).

As in our previous studies, there were no main effects for the self-reported emotion measure. Thus, there was no evidence that self-reported emotion mediated any of the affective forecasting or physical sensitivity effects.

Feeling Another Person's Pain: Empathy

Next, DeWall and Baumeister (2006) tested the hypothesis that social exclusion would cause emotional insensitivity as indicated by the amount of empathic concern participants reported in response to another person's distress. Excluded people tend to behave in a less prosocial manner compared to accepted and control participants (Twenge et al., 2007), and past research has demonstrated that high levels of empathy are related to increases in helping behavior (Batson, Klein, Highberger, & Shaw, 1995). Thus, it seemed possible that social exclusion might temporarily disable the capacity for strong empathic reactions to the distress of others.

This study used the same personality feedback exclusion paradigm used in the previous studies. Participants completed baseline measures of pain threshold and pain tolerance, completed a personality test, and received bogus feedback regarding the implications of their personality type for their future belongingness (Future Alone or Future Belonging) or received no personality feedback (No feedback control). After completing a short self-report emotion questionnaire (which yielded no differences among the three experimental conditions), participants completed an empathy measure. The experimenter explained that there was another experiment being conducted in the laboratory in which one participant writes an essay about a recent life event and another person, a rater, reads and responds to the essay. The participant was informed that the rater had not shown up for this other experiment and that because the amount of time required would not compromise the schedule of the current experiment, he or she would read and respond to the essay instead. Participants were then given a handwritten essay (in male or female handwriting, to match the participant's gender) and short questionnaire, both of which were adapted from Batson et al. (1995). The essay read (in part) as follows:

> Two days ago I broke up with my (girlfriend) boyfriend. We've been going together since our junior year in high school and have been really close, and it's been great being at FSU together. I thought (s)he felt the same, but things have changed. Now, (s)he wants to date other people. (S)He says (s)he still cares a lot about me, but (s)he doesn't want to be tied down to just one person. I've been real down. It's all I think about. My friends all tell me that I'll meet other (girls)guys and they say that all I need is for something good to happen to cheer me up. I guess they're right, but so far that hasn't happened.

Participants then reported the extent to which they felt compassionate, sympathetic, warm, softhearted, and tender toward the author of the essay. Responses to these adjectives have been used in previous investigations to measure empathy (Batson et al., 1995; Maner, Luce, Neuberg, Cialdini, Brown, & Sagarin, 2002). An empathy index was created by summing responses to the five empathy adjectives (compassionate, sympathetic, warm, softhearted, and tender). Higher scores therefore indicated higher levels of empathy for the author of the essay. After reading and responding to the essay, participants completed additional measures of pain threshold and pain tolerance.

The findings from this study provided additional support for the view that social exclusion causes the emotion system to temporarily cease functioning normally, with implications for physical pain and emotional responding. As in the previous experiments, socially excluded participants had higher pain threshold and pain tolerance scores than accepted and control participants. Socially excluded participants also expressed substantially less empathy toward the author of the essay than accepted and control participants. In fact, one participant in the Future Alone condition commented "tough shit" on reading the essay that described the other participant's sadness and despair. Additional analyses revealed that the physical pain threshold and tolerance scores were highly correlated with the empathy scores. Thus, socially excluded participants were insensitive to their own physical pain and the emotional pain experienced by another participant.

One possible limitation from this experiment was that participants were asked to empathize toward a person who had recently suffered romantic rejection. Socially excluded participants might have been unwilling to express empathy toward another rejected person because the person's rejection experience had possibly reminded them of their own recent social exclusion. We therefore conducted an additional study to investigate whether social exclusion causes reduced empathy toward many different forms of distress or if the reduced empathy is limited to people who have experienced recent social exclusion. For this study, we asked participants to empathize toward a person who had recently suffered a broken leg.

Because we had shown consistently that social exclusion causes increased physical pain threshold and pain tolerance, the current experiment did not include pain threshold and pain tolerance measurements. In the social exclusion manipulation used in the experiment, participants completed a vivid recall task: a brief autobiographical narrative recalling a time they experienced social rejection, social acceptance, or an unrelated event (i.e., the participant's previous daily activities). The manipulation was intended to prime participants with thoughts related to their experience, which would in turn influence their responses on a questionnaire designed to measure empathy. Past research has shown that vivid recall exclusion manipulations evoke responses that are similar to those found in manipulations of immediate rejection (Gardner et al., 2000; Pickett, Gardner, & Knowles, 2004). When participants finished writing their autobiographical narrative, they completed a short self-report emotion measure (which yielded no differences among the three experimental conditions) and additional materials aimed at measuring empathic responding. To evoke empathic responding, participants read a short vignette that described the recent suffering of a college student (of unknown gender). The vignette read (in part) as follows:

> Two days ago I broke my leg playing intramural sports. I've been playing on the same intramural team for the past three years and I'm upset that my season has been cut short. I'm experiencing pain because of my injury. I'm also having a tough time getting around campus, as there are lots of hills and stairs that make it hard to use my crutches on. The parking people won't let me get a handicapped permit because they said my injury was only temporary. I've been real down. It's all I think about.

Participants then rated the extent to which they felt compassionate, sympathetic, warm, softhearted, and tender toward the author of the essay. Responses to these items were then summed to create an empathy index, in which higher scores reflected higher levels of empathy.

The results from this study indicated that socially rejected participants expressed less empathy toward a person who had suffered a broken leg than accepted and control participants. These findings provide support for the view that social exclusion causes the emotion system temporarily to cease functioning normally, which causes reduced sensitivity to another person experiencing physical pain. Social exclusion appears to cause a widespread lack of empathy toward people experiencing various types of physical and psychological distress, as opposed to being a specific response toward other people who had also experienced social exclusion.

In sum, this series of studies demonstrated that the body reacts to social exclusion in the same manner as it does to physical injury (DeWall & Baumeister, 2006). Socially excluded participants showed decreased sensitivity and increased tolerance to physical pain compared to accepted and control participants. This physical numbness among socially excluded participants was related to their unemotional affective forecasts and reduced empathy for others' suffering.

## CAN EMOTIONAL INSENSITIVITY HELP EXPLAIN THE BEHAVIORAL EFFECTS OF SOCIAL EXCLUSION?

The studies reviewed in this chapter demonstrate that social exclusion causes a temporary cessation of normal emotional functioning, with direct implications for physical pain sensitivity and emotional responding. Participants who were led to anticipate a lonely future had higher pain threshold and pain tolerance scores than participants who did not experience social exclusion. Compared to participants in the accepted and control conditions, socially excluded participants also made relatively unemotional affective forecasts and expressed reduced empathy toward a person experiencing physical and mental suffering. The observed physical and emotional insensitivities among socially excluded participants were related, which suggests that both types of responses share common neural mechanisms (e.g., Eisenberger et al., 2003; MacDonald & Leary, 2005). The effects for both the physical and emotional insensitivity measures were in most cases substantial, exceeding criteria used to describe large effects (Cohen, 1977). These effects also appear to be unique to social exclusion. Participants who anticipated a future filled with frequent accidents and hospital stays (in the Misfortune Control condition) had pain threshold and pain tolerance scores that were indistinguishable from socially accepted participants. Thus, a direct threat to belongingness, and not merely a negatively valenced future diagnostic forecast, seemed necessary to alter the manner in which the body registered physical pain and emotion.

The broader implication from these studies is that socially excluded people use their impaired emotional faculties to understand their social world. Although the temporary emotional numbness after social exclusion might offer protection from severe emotional distress, it also might impair the ability of socially excluded people to relate to others and therefore behave in accordance with social standards for appropriate behavior. There is a growing body of research suggesting that reduced emotional capabilities have negative implications for effective decision making and other beneficial behaviors (e.g., Bechara, Damasio, Damasio, & Lee, 1999; Loewenstein, Weber, Hsee, & Welch, 2001). Thus, the disruption in normal emotional functioning after social exclusion may hamper an excluded person's ability to make decisions and interact with others in an effective an appropriate manner.

The next section reviews evidence from a recent study that investigated the role of emotional insensitivity in explaining the behavioral effects of social exclusion. Specifically, we tested the hypothesis that lack of empathy mediates the relationship between social exclusion and reduced prosocial behavior.

## WHY DOES SOCIAL EXCLUSION REDUCE PROSOCIAL BEHAVIOR?

Prosocial behavior is often contingent on the belief that one belongs to a group in which people are motivated to aid each other by providing mutual support and assistance. When people experience social exclusion, the rewards that follow from behaving in a prosocial manner may become reduced and not worth the effort. Correlational studies have shown that children who are rejected or excluded behave in a less prosocial manner (e.g., Asher & Coie, 1990; Coie & Dodge, 1988). In contrast, the tendency to experience social acceptance is highly correlated with behaving prosocially (e.g., Bukowski & Newcomb, 1984; Hartup, Glazer, & Charlesworth, 1967). Thus, social exclusion might decrease the motivation to behave prosocially.

Prosocial behavior relies on more than one's motivational state, however. The studies reviewed in this chapter suggest that social exclusion impairs inner responses that might have implications for prosocial behavior. Socially excluded people were less sensitive to physical pain, and this physical numbness was related to a lack of emotional sensitivity (DeWall & Baumeister, 2006). Specifically, socially excluded people were less empathic toward a person who had experienced recent romantic rejection or a physical injury. If the emotion system enables people to understand others, then social exclusion might impair prosocial behavior.

Empathy has been shown to play an integral role in shaping prosocial behavior (Batson, 1991). The capacity to empathize with another person depends heavily on a normally functioning emotion system, however. If social exclusion causes the emotion system to cease functioning normally, then the excluded person might be unable to simulate the feelings of another person. This lack of empathy might cause excluded people to behave in a less prosocial manner compared to participants who have not experienced social exclusion. We therefore conducted a study to test whether a temporary inability to empathize with others would mediate the hypothesized relationship between social exclusion and reduced prosocial behavior (Twenge et al., 2007).

Participants arrived at the laboratory, completed a personality test, and received bogus feedback regarding the implications of their personality type for their future belongingness (Future Alone or Future Belonging) or physical well-being (Misfortune Control; see earlier sections for more details). After receiving this feedback, participants completed a short self-report emotion measure (which showed no differences among the three experimental conditions) and materials designed to assess empathic concern. For the empathy measure, participants were asked to read and respond to an essay in which the author had experienced a recent romantic rejection. As in the previously reviewed studies (DeWall & Baumeister, 2006), participants reported the extent to which they felt various empathy-related emotions (i.e., compassionate, sympathetic) toward the author of the essay. Responses to the empathy items were summed to create an empathy index.

Participants were then given eight quarters ($2) as payment for their participation. The experimenter explained that the participants received their payment in quarters because participants in other conditions had their monetary payment doled out to them over the course of the experiment. The experimenter then said, "Before I go, I want to mention that we're taking up a collection for the Student Emergency Fund. It's a good cause. If you'd like to donate, that would be great. If not, that's totally fine too." Participants were shown a box that had a sign reading "Student Emergency Fund" and a short description of the fund as a resource for expenses that undergraduate students might not have anticipated. The experimenter then left the room for approximately 2 minutes, which allowed participants to donate as much or as little of their payment to the fund. The amount of money that participants donated served as the measure of prosocial behavior.

The results from this study indicated that socially excluded participants behaved in a less prosocial manner than accepted and control participants. Socially excluded participants donated almost one-third less to the Student Emergency Fund ($0.53) than accepted ($1.40) and control ($1.55) participants. Replicating the results from DeWall and Baumeister (2006), socially excluded participants also expressed less empathy toward another participant who had recently experienced romantic rejection than accepted and control participants. Most important, empathic concern mediated the link between social exclusion and prosocial behavior.

Thus, social exclusion temporarily impairs the emotion system from functioning properly, which has direct implications for prosocial behavior. Prosocial behavior is driven in part by empathic concern for others (e.g., Batson, 1991), and this decreased empathy led socially excluded participants to behave in a less prosocial manner compared to accepted and control participants.

### APPLICATION OF CURRENT FINDINGS TO CLINICAL RESEARCH

The research reviewed in the current chapter has begun to resolve the paradox as to why social exclusion produces emotional numbness. Social exclusion causes the emotion system to cease functioning normally, which renders the person insensitive to both physical pain and emotion. This final section offers a brief discussion as to how these findings might be applied to clinical research.

## Suicide

Suicide is a serious public health problem that claims the lives of approximately 30,000 Americans each year (Centers for Disease Control [CDC], 2003). Joiner (2006) has recently proposed a theory that seeks to differentiate between people who do and do not die by suicide. According to Joiner (2006), three necessary components must be present for a person to have the desire and capacity for completing suicide: (a) feelings of perceived burdensomeness (i.e., a sense of incompetence that affects others in a negative manner); (b) a thwarted sense of belongingness (i.e., a lack of positive and stable relationships with others); and (c) an acquired capacity to inflict lethal self-harm (i.e., prior exposure to painful/provocative stimuli). Feelings of burdensomeness and a thwarted sense of belongingness contribute to the desire for suicide, whereas the acquired ability to enact self-harm contributes to the ability to commit suicide (Joiner, 2006).

The findings from DeWall and Baumeister (2006) suggest that a thwarted sense of belongingess may contribute to the acquired ability for self-harm. In those studies, participants had their need to belong thwarted through social exclusion, and this thwarted belongingness caused them to exhibit decreased sensitivity and increased tolerance to physical pain. These findings suggest that the desire and capability for completing suicide may be related insofar as the body responds to social exclusion using neural mechanisms designed for the detection and regulation of physical pain (Eisenberger et al., 2003; MacDonald & Leary, 2005). Future research is needed to investigate the possibility that social exclusion contributes to both the desire and ability to complete suicide.

## Psychopathy

Psychopathy is a disorder that is characterized by elevated levels of antisocial behavior and emotional impairment such as lack of empathy and guilt (Blair, 2003). This emotional impairment among psychopathic individuals has been shown to interfere with appropriate social behaviors such as seeking money, sexual opportunities, or increases in social status (Cornell et al., 1996). The findings from the studies reviewed in this chapter demonstrated that social exclusion caused a physical and psychological state that may be similar to that found in psychopathic individuals. DeWall and Baumeister (2006) showed that socially excluded participants suffered from an emotional impairment that decreased their ability to empathize with another person's suffering. This lack of empathy caused socially excluded participants to behave in an unhelpful manner compared to participants who did not experience social exclusion (Twenge et al., 2007). Similar to individuals who meet the criteria for psychopathy, social exclusion disrupts the capacity for people to understand the emotions of others and to respond in a socially appropriate manner. Future research is needed to explore other possible similarities between the consequences of social exclusion and psychopathy.

## FUTURE RESEARCH

Future research may begin to apply the ideas reviewed in this chapter to the realm of everyday relationships, particularly close friendships, family relationships, and romantic couples. It is important to note that in our research we have been largely limited in the types of rejection and social exclusion we have been able to observe. The manipulations we have used involve, in some cases, only the threat of social exclusion. In experiments where we manipulated rejection in a direct manner (i.e., peer rejection), our participants knew each other for no longer than 15 minutes. Thus, it is plausible that the effects we observed in the laboratory are simply a weaker version of the toll rejection takes on individuals in everyday life. The effects of being rejected by those to whom we are much closer and have a much larger emotional and personal investment may be considerably stronger.

Another avenue for future research may be to investigate the role of repeated instances of rejection. The research we discussed in this chapter deals exclusively with isolated instances of social rejection. One feature of dysfunctional relationships is that relationship abuse and feelings of hurt occur much more frequently – often on a daily basis. It is possible that the defensive numbing response that we have shown may wear off over time, which may leave a person in a position to experience more physical and emotion distress after repeated rejection experiences.

## CONCLUDING REMARKS

Our program of research has begun to explain why people respond to such a momentous event as social exclusion with emotional numbness and detachment. The initial theory that emotional distress would mediate the behavioral consequences of social exclusion has not been supported. Multiple experiments have demonstrated that social exclusion causes large behavioral effects, but excluded people often do not report emotional states that differ from those of accepted and control participants. Even when socially excluded people report emotional distress, this distress does not mediate the behavioral effects. Thus, emotional distress does not seem to play a significant role in mediating the behavioral effects of social exclusion.

The findings reported in this chapter suggest that the body is equipped with natural defenses that respond to potential threats to belongingness, presumably as a means of minimizing the incipient distress after social exclusion. Evolution co-opted responses to events such as social exclusion onto the existing neural mechanisms designed for responding to physical pain (MacDonald & Leary, 2005; Panksepp et al., 1978). The result is that the emotion system temporarily ceases functioning normally after social exclusion, which has direct implications for responsiveness to physical pain and emotional responding. In our studies, socially excluded participants showed increased pain threshold and pain tolerance levels compared to participants who did not experience social exclusion. The insensitivity to physical pain was accompanied by unemotional affective forecasts and lack of empathy toward a person who suffered a recent romantic rejection or physical injury. Our findings also indicated that lack of empathy mediated the link between social exclusion and reduced prosocial behavior. Thus, the body responds to social exclusion in a way that protects the person from emotional distress but also impairs the capacity to respond to physical and emotion pain.

Social exclusion renders the person emotionally and hence socially impaired. The ability to simulate and understand another person's emotions enables people to feel connected with and care for others. Such a feeling of connectedness might motivate people to help others, to resist selfish temptations, and to curb their aggressive desires. Without a normally functioning emotion system, socially excluded people are therefore incapable of understanding and responding to the needs and emotions of others. The lack of interpersonal understanding following social exclusion prevents the person from enjoying many of the benefits of belonging to a group and reduces the willingness to behave in ways that promote interpersonal acceptance. The immediate relief from emotional numbness after social exclusion therefore comes with immense negative costs to the self and others.

### REFERENCES

Asher, S. R., & Coie, J. D. (1990). *Peer rejection in childhood.* New York: Cambridge University Press.

Bancroft, J. H., Skrimshire, A. M., & Simkin, S. (1976). The reasons people give for taking overdoses. *British Journal of Psychiatry, 128,* 538–548.

Batson, C. D. (1991). *The altruism question: Toward a social-psychological answer.* Hillsdale, NJ: Erlbaum.

Batson, C. D., Klein, T. R., Highberger, L., & Shaw, L. L. (1995). Immorality from empathy-induced altruism: When compassion and justice conflict. *Journal of Personality and Social Psychology, 68,* 1042–1054.

Baumeister, R. F. (1990). Suicide as escape from the self. *Psychological Review, 97,* 90–113.

Baumeister, R. F., DeWall, C. N., Ciarocco, N. J., & Twenge, J. M. (2005). Social exclusion impairs self-regulation. *Journal of Personality and Social Psychology, 88,* 589–604.

Baumeister, R. F., & Leary, M. R. (1995). The need to belong: Desire for interpersonal attachments as a fundamental human motivation. *Psychological Bulletin, 117,* 497–529.

Baumeister, R. F., & Scher, S. J. (1988). Self-defeating behavior patterns among normal individuals: Review and analysis of common self-destructive tendencies. *Psychological Bulletin, 104,* 3–22.

Baumeister, R. F., & Tice, D. M. (1990). Anxiety and social exclusion. *Journal of Social and Clinical Psychology, 9,* 165–195.

Baumeister, R. F., Twenge, J. M., & Nuss, C. K. (2002). Effects of social exclusion on cognitive processes: Anticipated aloneness reduces intelligent thought. *Journal of Personality and Social Psychology, 83,* 817–827.

Bechara, A., Damasio, H., Damasio, A., & Lee, G. P. (1999). Different contributions of the human amygdala ventromedial prefrontal cortex to decision-making. *Journal of Neuroscience, 19,* 5473–5481.

Blair, R. J. R. (2003). Neurological basis of psychopathy. *British Journal of Psychiatry, 182,* 5–7.

Bloom, B. L., White, S. W., & Asher, S. J. (1979). Marital disruption as a stressful life event. In G. Levinger (Ed.), *Divorce and separation: Context, causes and consequences* (pp. 184–200). New York: Basic Books.

Buckley, K. E., Winkel, R. E., & Leary, M. R. (2004). Reactions to acceptance and rejection: Effects of level and sequence of relational evaluation. *Journal of Experimental Social Psychology, 40,* 14–28.

Bukowski, W. M., & Newcomb, A. F. (1984). Stability and determinants of sociometric status and friendship choice: A longitudinal perspective. *Developmental Psychology, 20,* 941–952.

Bush, G., Luu, P., & Posner, M. I. (2000). Cognitive and emotional influences in anterior cingulated cortex. *Trends in Cognitive Sciences, 4,* 215–222.

Cacioppo, J. T., Hawkley, L. C., & Berntson, G. G. (2003). The anatomy of loneliness. *Current Directions in Psychological Science, 12,* 71–74.

Centers for Disease Control and Prevention. (2003). *Web-based injury statistics query and reporting system.* Retrieved August 14, 2006, from http://www.cdc.gov/ncipc/wisqars/default.htm.

Cohen, J. (1977). *Statistical power analysis for the behavioral sciences.* New York: Academic Press.

Coie, J. D., & Dodge, K. A. (1988). Multiple sources of data on social behavior and social status in the school: A cross-age comparison. *Child Development, 59,* 815–829.

Cornell, D. G., Warren, J., Hawk, G., Stafford, E., Oram, G., & Pine, D. (1996). Psychopathy in instrumental and reactive violent offenders. *Journal of Consulting and Clinical Psychology, 64,* 783–790.

Craig, A. D., & Dostrovsky, J. O. (1999). Medulla to thalamus. In P. D. Wall & R. Melzack (Eds.), *Textbook of pain* (pp. 183–214). Philadelphia: Lea & Febiger.

DeWall, C. N., & Baumeister, R. F. (2006). Alone but feeling no pain: Effects of social exclusion on physical pain tolerance and pain threshold, affective forecasting, and interpersonal empathy. *Journal of Personality and Social Psychology, 91,* 1–15.

Eisenberger, N. I., & Lieberman, M. D. (2004). Why rejection hurts: A common neural alarm system for physical and social pain. *Trends in Cognitive Sciences, 8,* 294–300.

Eisenberger, N. I., Lieberman, M. D., & Williams, K. D. (2003). Does rejection hurt? An fMRI study of social exclusion. *Science, 302,* 290–292.

Gardner, W. L., Pickett, C. L., & Brewer, M. B. (2000). Social exclusion and selective memory: How the need to belong influences memory for social events. *Personality and Social Psychology Bulletin, 26*, 486–496.

Gilbert, D. T., Gill, M. J., & Wilson, T. D. (2002). The future is now: Temporal correction in affective forecasting. *Organization Behavior and Human Decision Processes, 88*, 430–444.

Gilbert, D. T., Pinel, E. C., Wilson, T. D., Blumberg, S. J., & Wheatley, T. (1998). Immune neglect: A source of durability bias in affective forecasting. *Journal of Personality and Social Psychology, 75*, 617–638.

Hartup, W. W., Glazer, J. A., & Charlesworth, R. (1967). Peer reinforcement and sociometric status. *Child Development, 38*, 1017–1024.

Hawkley, L. C., Burleson, M. H., Berntson, G. G., & Cacioppo, J. T. (2003). Loneliness in everyday life: Cardiovascular activity, psychosocial context, and health behaviors. *Journal of Personality and Social Psychology, 85*, 105–120.

Herman, B. H., & Panksepp, J. (1978). Effects of morphine and naloxone on separation distress and approach attachment: Evidence for opiate mediation of social affect. *Pharmacology, Biochemistry, and Behavior, 9*, 213–220.

Joiner, T. (2006). *Why people die by suicide.* Cambridge, MA: Harvard University Press.

Kehoe, P., & Blass, E. M. (1986). Central nervous system mediation of positive and negative reinforcement in neonatal albino rats. *Developmental Brain Research, 27*, 69–75.

Leary, M. R. (1990). Responses to social exclusion: Social anxiety, jealousy, loneliness, depression, and low self-esteem. *Journal of Social and Clinical Psychology, 9*, 221–229.

Leary, M. R., & Springer, C. A. (2000). Hurt feelings: The neglected emotion. In R. Kowalski (Ed.), *Aversive behaviors and interpersonal transgression* (pp. 151–175). Washington, DC: American Psychological Association.

Loewenstein, G. F., Weber, E. U., Hsee, C. K., & Welch, N. (2001). Risk as feelings. *Psychological Bulletin, 127*, 267–286.

MacDonald, G., & Leary, M. R. (2005). Why does social exclusion hurt? The relationship between social and physical pain. *Psychological Bulletin, 131*, 202–223.

Maner, J. K., Luce, C. L., Neuberg, S. L., Cialdini, R. B., Brown, S., & Sagarin, B. J. (2002). The effects of perspective taking on helping: Still no evidence for altruism. *Personality and Social Psychology Bulletin, 28*, 1601–1610.

Naranjo, J. R., & Fuentes, J. A. (1985). Association between hypoalgesia and hypertension in rats after short-term isolation. *Neuropharmacology, 242*, 167–171.

Nelson, E. E., & Panksepp, J. (1998). Brain substrates of infant-mother attachment: Contributions of opioids, oxytocin, and norepinephrine. *Neuroscience & Biobehavioral Reviews, 22*, 437–452.

Panksepp, J. (1998). *Affective neuroscience: The foundations of human and animal emotions.* London: Oxford University Press.

Panksepp, J., Herman, B. H., Conner, R., Bishop, P., & Scott, J. P. (1978a). The biology of social attachments: Opiates alleviate separation distress. *Biological Psychiatry, 13*, 607–618.

Panksepp, J., Vilberg, T., Bean, N. J., Coy, D. H., & Kastin, A. J. (1978b). Reduction of distress vocalization in chicks by opiate-like peptides. *Brain Research Bulletin, 3*, 663–667.

Pickett, C. L., Gardner, W. L., & Knowles, M. (2004). Getting a cue: The need to belong and enhanced sensitivity to social cues. *Personality and Social Psychology Bulletin, 30*, 1095–1107.

Twenge, J. M., Baumeister, R. F., Tice, D. M., & Stucke, T. S. (2001). If you can't join them, beat them: Effects of social exclusion on aggressive behavior. *Journal of Personality and Social Psychology, 81*, 1058–1069.

Twenge, J. M., Baumeister, R. F., DeWall, C. N., Ciarocco, N. J., & Bartels, J. M. (2007). Social exclusion reduces prosocial behavior. *Journal of Personality and Social Psychology, 92*, 56–66.

Twenge, J. M., Catanese, K. R., & Baumeister, R. F. (2002). Social exclusion causes self-defeating behavior. *Journal of Personality and Social Psychology, 83*, 606–615.

Twenge, J. M., Catanese, K. R., & Baumeister, R. F. (2003). Social exclusion and the deconstructed state: Time perception, meaninglessness, lethargy, lack of emotion, and self-awareness. *Journal of Personality and Social Psychology, 85*, 409–423.

Uchino, B. N., Cacioppo, J. T., & Kiecolt-Glaser, J. K. (1996). The relationship between social support and physiological processes: A review with emphasis on underlying mechanisms and implications for health. *Psychological Bulletin, 119*, 488–531.

Van Boven, L., & Loewenstein, G. (2003). Social projection of transient drive states. *Personality and Social Psychology Bulletin, 29*, 1159–1168.

Wiedenmayer, C. P., Goodwin, G. A., & Barr, G. A. (2000). The effect of periaqueductal gray lesions on response to age-specific threats in infant rats. *Developmental Brain Research, 120*, 191–198.

Williams, K. D., Cheung, C. K. T., & Choi, W. (2000). CyberOstracism: Effects of being ignored over the Internet. *Journal of Personality and Social Psychology, 79*, 748–762.

Wilson, T. D., & Gilbert, D. T. (2003). Affective forecasting. In M. P. Zanna (Ed.), *Advances in experimental social psychology* (Vol. 35, pp. 345–411). San Diego: Academic Press.

Wilson, T. D., Wheatley, T., Kurtz, J., Dunn, E., & Gilbert, D. T. (2004). When to fire: Anticipatory versus post-event reconstrual of uncontrollable events. *Personality and Social Psychology Bulletin, 30*, 340–351.

Zadro, L., Williams, K. D., & Richardson, R. (2004). How low can you go? Ostracism by a computer is sufficient to lower self-reported levels of belonging, control, self-esteem, and meaningful existence. *Journal of Experimental Social Psychology, 40*, 560–567.

# 8

## Conflict and Hurt in Close Relationships

JOHN P. CAUGHLIN, ALLISON M. SCOTT,
AND LAURA E. MILLER

According to Vangelisti (2007), "whenever two people communicate, they risk hurting each other" (p. 121). Such risk is elevated when the communication involves conflict. Interactions involving conflicts tend to be more arousing and to elicit more negative emotions than do other conversations (Levenson & Gottman, 1985). The heightened affective intensity associated with conflict provides abundant occasions for hurt feelings. Indeed, the apparent connection between conflict and hurt is strong enough that some scholars treat being hurt as synonymous with interpersonal conflict (e.g., Wainryb, Brehl, & Matwin, 2005). Other scholars simply assume that conflict is inherently hurtful; for instance, one study examining the "most frequently used strategies of relational conflict resolution" was titled "You always hurt the one you love..." (Fitzpatrick & Winke, 1979, p. 3).

Despite the belief that conflict and hurt are closely related, there is surprisingly little research that systematically examines their association. This lack of focus on hurt and conflict is remarkable given that other emotions, like anger, are frequently linked to conflict (e.g., Notarius, Lashley, & Sullivan, 1997). Clearly, addressing this gap in the literature could be useful, potentially answering questions such as "How can individuals make their conflicts less hurtful?" and "Can (and should) people prevent hurt feelings from leading to interpersonal conflicts?" A single chapter can only begin to address such questions, but our goals are (a) to adumbrate the research that does exist on conflict and hurt and (b) to provide an initial framework for thinking about how the hurtful aspects of conflict can be reduced.

### ASSOCIATION BETWEEN CONFLICT AND HURT

Conflict and hurt feelings are connected, but the association is more complex than one of synonymy or even a direct correspondence. In fact, the literature suggests that hurt feelings may sometimes lead to conflict, but in other cases hurt feelings may lead one to avoid conflict. Similarly, conflict may frequently end with hurt feelings (Fitzpatrick & Winke, 1979), but this result is not inevitable. Some conflicts might even ameliorate hurt. We discuss each of these possible associations in turn.

### Hurt Can Lead to Conflict

The most obvious way in which hurt can lead to conflict is when a hurtful event also precipitates conflict. One commonly cited cause of hurt feelings in a close relationship is betrayal (Leary, Springer, Negel, Ansell, & Evans, 1998). There are distinct forms of betrayal, including engaging in extradyadic sexual relations, breaking promises, and divulging information that was meant to be confidential (Feeney, 2004). Regardless of the specific form, all betrayals involve the perception of a violated relational rule or expectation. If the aggrieved individual chooses to confront the other about this hurtful violation, conflict is likely to ensue. Indeed, once a person confronts a betrayer, numerous potential conflict issues become salient, including whether the rule or expectation is legitimate (e.g., was it reasonable to expect monogamy?), whether there were special circumstances that would excuse the transgression, and whether remediation is needed or sufficient (Newell & Stutman, 1988).

Along similar lines, conflict can be initiated by several types of messages that people find hurtful (Vangelisti, 2007). Accusations, orders, and negative disclosures can be hurtful, but they also may lead the person who was hurt to respond in a way that initiates conflict. It is even possible that a hurtful comment itself can be viewed as a conflict move. People sometimes believe that others who say hurtful things to them are justified because their own previous actions instigated the hurtful message (Vangelisti & Young, 2000). That is, some hurtful comments are viewed as part of aversive exchanges. Such exchanges certainly can lead to conflict and may even lead to ongoing conflicts with reciprocal complaining.

The aforementioned pathways to conflict involve a person who is hurt responding in a way that begins a conflict episode. Clearly, people do not always respond to hurt by instigating a conflict. Even events that are usually quite hurtful (e.g., relational infidelity; Feeney, 2004) only sometimes lead to overt conflict. What explains the variation in outcomes associated with hurt feelings? Given the scant literature specifically examining hurt and conflict, any answer to this question will be somewhat speculative and not exhaustive. Nevertheless, previous research suggests that other affective and cognitive factors associated with hurt likely influence whether hurt feelings lead to a conflict.

There has been some controversy about whether hurt is a blend of other emotions or a distinct experience in its own right (for a review, see Leary and Leder, Chapter 2, this volume). Regardless of how one conceptualizes hurt, however, there is widespread agreement that hurt feelings are often accompanied by other affective states, including sadness (Feeney, 2005; Shaver, Schwartz, Kirson, & O'Connor, 1987), anger (Feeney, 2005; Shaver et al., 1987), shame (Feeney, 2005), and anxiety (Leary et al., 1998). The degree to which various other emotions accompany hurt likely predicts whether a hurtful incident will lead to conflict. Anger, for instance, typically is associated with an impulse toward attacking or retaliation (Frijda, Kuipers, & ter Schure, 1989; Lazarus, 2006), and much of the conflict literature focuses on the need to manage the expression of anger (e.g., Carstensen, Gottman, & Levenson, 1995; Notarius et al., 1997). Thus, when the hurtful experience involves an amalgamation of hurt and anger, a person may be more likely to initiate conflict than if the experience involves little sense of anger.

In addition to the particular affective experience, individuals' cognitions can influence whether hurt feelings result in conflict. There is, for instance, a rich literature on the role of attributions in relationships (e.g., Bradbury & Fincham, 1990). Broadly speaking, attribution research suggests that individuals' reactions to negative events depend on their beliefs about why those events happened (Bradbury & Fincham, 1990). Consequently, people's attributions about their hurt feelings may predict whether the hurtful experience results in conflict. For example, people tend to view aversive behaviors more harshly if they attribute the behaviors to the other person's enduring qualities rather than temporary or situational conditions (Bradbury & Fincham, 1990). Blaming the other person (rather than circumstances) for a hurtful episode influences the hurt individual's emotional and behavioral reactions, likely increasing feelings of anger and the potential for conflict (Canary, 2003). Moreover, if conflict does begin, blaming the other person for an offense is associated with using uncooperative strategies during conflict (Canary, 2003).

Causal attributions provide just one example of how cognitions can determine whether hurt feelings lead to conflict. Many other perceptions and evaluations shape how conflict is experienced (for a review, see Roloff & Miller, 2006). For instance, the extent to which people view hurtful episodes as denigrating their relationship is positively associated with active responses, such as verbal attacks (Vangelisti, Young, Carpenter-Theune, & Alexander, 2005). A verbal attack, in turn, may lead to conflict.

## Hurt Can Lead to Conflict Avoidance

One reason why individuals sometimes avoid conflict is that they wish to manage or prevent aversive emotions that conflict can rouse (Roloff & Ifert, 2000). If people expect that another person will engage in punishing behaviors during conflict, they may decide not to confront that person. Indeed, research on the chilling effect suggests that expecting a punishing reaction often leads a person to withhold complaints (Cloven & Roloff, 1993). Of course, a person who has been hurt before in conflict may have good reason to believe that a confrontation about the hurtful act may only lead to more punishing behavior or an escalation of hurtful actions. Moreover, because vulnerability is a defining element of hurt (Vangelisti, 2007), a person currently experiencing hurt may be especially cautious about confronting the hurtful other. Concerns about being hurt again would be particularly acute if the hurtful acts are attributed to enduring characteristics of the partner: If the person "is selfish enough to hurt others, he or she may very well do so repeatedly" (Vangelisti, 2001, p. 49).

In addition to cognitive factors like attributions and expectations regarding the likelihood of being hurt, affective factors can also help explain when hurt does (and does not) result in conflict avoidance. As noted earlier, people who are hurt sometimes also experience associated affective states like sadness and anxiety (Feeney, 2005; Leary et al., 1998; Shaver et al., 1987). Hurtful experiences are probably more likely to result in conflict avoidance if they include elements of sadness or anxiety than if they do not. Sadness, for example, is related to appraising negative stimuli as uncontrollable. Sad people believe they are helpless because the aversive situation is not modifiable (Frijda et al., 1989). Given that the situation is viewed as unsolvable, a person experiencing sadness along with hurt may choose to avoid potential conflicts (Roloff & Ifert, 2000). Also, anxiety is associated with tendencies toward self-protection and avoiding the relevant stimulus (Frijda et al., 1989); thus, a hurtful experience with an element of anxiety may be especially likely to elicit avoidance of conflict.

## Conflict Can Lead to Hurt

The possibility of conflict leading to hurt feelings is implicit in a great deal of the research on interpersonal conflict. Much has been written about managing anger during conflict and – although there is usually no explicit mention of hurt feelings – hurt is an obvious risk of angry exchanges. In fact, people who are agitated with each other during conflict may say hurtful things purposefully (Vangelisti & Sprague, 1998).

Additionally, scholarly advice about productive conflict often seems aimed at preventing hurt feelings. One strategy for avoiding destructive conflict, for instance, is to focus on making complaints about a partner's behaviors rather than criticizing his or her character (e.g., Gottman, 1994b). Such strategies can be seen as attempts to allow a person to raise an issue while minimizing the chances that the other will feel personally hurt or vulnerable. Although there is no guarantee that one can prevent hurt during conflict, there is indirect evidence that spouses who avoid certain kinds of behaviors are less likely to hurt each other; for instance, interventions designed to teach couples to solve problems without enacting potentially hurtful behaviors (e.g., criticizing the other's character) can prevent marital distress and improve marital relationships (Hahlweg, Markman, Thurmaier, Engl, & Eckert, 1998; Markman, Floyd, Stanley, & Storaasli, 1988).

It is also important to note that behaviors that seem likely to induce hurt in particular conflict episodes are associated with undesirable long-term consequences. There is abundant research showing that poorly managed conflict presages poor outcomes (for reviews, see Caughlin & Vangelisti, 2006; Fincham & Beach, 1999). For example, conflict behaviors in families have been identified as a risk factor for poor physical and mental health (Repetti, Taylor, & Seeman, 2002; Whitson & El-Sheikh, 2003). Furthermore, frequent conflict with intense expressions of anger between parents and adolescents has been linked to adolescents' depression (Cole & McPherson, 1993; Jenkins, Goodness, & Buhrmester, 2002). In addition, the demand/withdraw pattern (when one person nags or criticizes while the other avoids) between parents and adolescents is related inversely to both parents' and adolescents' self-esteem (Caughlin & Malis, 2004).

Although such research does not directly connect hurt feelings during conflict with poor outcomes, many of the conflict behaviors that are consistent predictors of adverse consequences (e.g., intense expressions of anger, criticisms that happen as part of the demand/withdraw pattern) are also behaviors that have a high potential to hurt someone's feelings. This suggests that many of the negative outcomes associated with poor conflict management may be related to hurt feelings evoked during conflict episodes. Perhaps the accumulation of hurtful conflicts over time leads to a state of chronic hurt feelings that is detrimental to individuals' mental and physical health.

## Conflict Can Diminish Hurt

Although the functional utility of conflict is "not often realized" (Roloff & Miller, 2006, p. 97), the possibility exists for conflict to alleviate hurt feelings. In romantic relationships, conflict can result in increased certainty that the relationship will endure (Siegert & Stamp, 1994). Generally, events that decrease relational uncertainty tend to be associated with positive emotional reactions, such as happiness, rather than negative ones, such as sadness or anger (Knobloch & Solomon, 2003). Such findings suggest that conflict leading to increased relational certainty may alleviate feelings of hurt.

Additionally, conflicts sometimes elicit positive emotions (Schaap & Jansen-Nawas, 1987), particularly if the individuals exhibit positive and active conflict responses (Berry & Willingham, 1997). In fact, one study of thoughts and feelings during conflict suggested that positive emotions occur about as frequently as emotions like sadness and hurt (Sillars, Roberts, Leonard, & Dun, 2000). Such positive experiences in conflict may ameliorate hurt feelings.

Moreover, short-term hurt feelings in relationships occasionally could prevent long-term adverse outcomes. Sanford and Rowatt (2004), for instance, found that, when emotions like anger and fear are controlled, hurt is associated positively with relationship satisfaction. These researchers suggest that the ability to be hurt reflects "a core concern for maintaining an interpersonal relationship" (p. 330); consequently, hurt indicates a willingness to be invested in the relationship in ways that maintain positive functioning. Indeed, people who feel valued by their relational partner tend to draw closer to their partner when they feel hurt by him or her (Murray, Bellavia, Rose, & Griffin, 2003). For such individuals, being hurt during conflict can lead them to intensify relational maintenance efforts.

In short, the association between conflict and hurt is complex and bidirectional. Each can lead to the other, but the experience of one does not inevitably result in the other. Hurt feelings sometimes result in active avoidance of conflict, and some conflicts might alleviate hurt. Although the complexity of the association between conflict and hurt presents theoretical challenges, it also suggests important theoretical and practical opportunities. If conflict only sometimes leads to hurt, for example, how do we best understand the conditions when conflict does not lead to hurt? Also, can our knowledge of when conflict leads to hurt be used to help people prevent or minimize hurt feelings in conflict? The next section of this chapter addresses such questions.

## MANAGING CONFLICT AND HURT

The potential for experiencing hurt from conflict is great, and hurtful conflicts can have negative long-term effects. Thus, it is important to consider how hurt in conflict can be managed effectively. It is useful to conceptualize such management efforts in a temporal fashion, first theorizing about how hurt can be prevented and then discussing how hurt can be alleviated when it does occur in conflict.

### Conflict Strategies for Preventing Hurt

The literature on conflict strategies and behaviors is huge (for reviews, see Canary & Lakey, 2006; Sillars, Canary, & Tafoya, 2004). The current chapter cannot possibly provide a substantive review of the conflict literature, but a few statements about the most relevant aspects are warranted. First, common conflict behaviors can be categorized based on two broad distinctions. One distinction concerns the extent to which behaviors are considered cooperative versus competitive (Sillars et al., 2004), affectively positive versus negative (Sillars & Weisberg, 1987), or nice versus nasty (Canary, 2003). The other common distinction is engagement versus avoidance (Sillars & Weisberg, 1987) or directness versus indirectness (Canary & Lakey, 2006; Sillars et al., 2004).

Although such distinctions are broad, they are sufficient for making some general claims about conflict management strategies that are more or less likely to result in hurt. Typically, skills-based approaches to conflict management consider strategies that are direct and nice (i.e., affectively positive) to be constructive. This designation is based on the fact that such behaviors are often related to positive relational outcomes (Fincham & Beach, 1999). Not surprisingly, the types of behaviors usually considered constructive seem particularly unlikely to evoke hurt. Positive/direct tactics may acknowledge that conflict is a problem, show a willingness to deal with the problem, or display a positive regard for the other individual (Canary, 2003). People engaging in these cooperative strategies often accept (at least some) responsibility for causing the conflict or suggest a willingness to change personal behavior (Canary, 2003). Such strategies seem well suited for precluding a partner from feeling the vulnerability associated with hurt. Rather than blaming a partner for a negative event, for instance, a person using positive/direct tactics may offer an excuse for the partner's role or provide an assurance that the relationship remains on good terms.

Clearly, partners who deal with their conflicts using only positive/direct strategies generally run little risk of hurting each other's feelings. Indeed, it is possible that if couples are able to negotiate conflict issues using only nice strategies, they may not even recognize their interaction as a conflict (Fincham & Beach, 1999). Individuals would probably not experience much hurt if their conflict management was so pleasant that they did not realize they were engaging in conflict. Thus, people who wish to prevent hurt during conflict generally would be well advised to focus on using positive/direct strategies.

The conflict literature also suggests certain behaviors that should be avoided if hurt is to be prevented. Frequent negative/direct (i.e., nasty or competitive) behaviors are associated with poor relational outcomes like dissatisfaction and divorce (Canary, 2003; Gottman, 1994a; Karney & Bradbury, 1995). One reason why affectively negative conflict behaviors predict adverse relational outcomes is such behaviors can be hurtful. Some of the common nasty conflict behaviors, such as criticisms or disparaging remarks (Sillars, 1986), are also known to cause hurt feelings (Vangelisti et al., 2005). Thus, an obvious strategy for reducing the chances of hurting one's partner would be to minimize negative/direct behaviors. Additionally, Schroth, Bain-Chekal, and Caldwell (2005) examined specific types of statements that are viewed as hurtful in conflict. They reported that certain behaviors (e.g., labeling the motives of the other person, telling the partner what he or she should do) typically induce aversive feelings, including hurt. Again, such findings suggest behaviors that usually should be avoided to prevent hurt.

It is, of course, unrealistic to expect that relational partners would never engage in affectively negative behaviors during conflict. Even stable and happy married couples engage in some amount of criticisms and complaints (Gottman, 1994a; Huston, Caughlin, Houts, Smith, & George, 2001). Consequently, it is important to recognize that affectively negative behaviors vary in intensity. Relatively harsh negative behaviors tend to be better predictors of poor relational outcomes than are milder forms of negativity (Gottman,

Coan, Carrere, & Swanson, 1998). Moreover, the intensity or harshness of hurtful messages is associated with the extent to which such messages are seen as upsetting, uncaring, and harmful (Young, 2004). Such findings imply that there are normatively better and worse ways to deliver potentially hurtful messages. Gottman (1994b) suggested, for instance, that people raising complaints about someone's behavior should avoid criticizing his or her character. This advice may reduce the potential for hurt feelings by avoiding overtly negative evaluations of the partner.

In addition, research by Folkes (1982) on social rejection suggests that even the impact of inherently rejecting messages (such as declining a date or discontinuing a relationship) can be mitigated by attending to the other person's identity concerns. The same may be true with conflict behaviors that typically elicit hurt feelings. For instance, people can make accusations during conflict, and accusations often evoke hurt (Vangelisti, 2007). Yet, the extent to which a particular accusation is hurtful may be mitigated by any facework that accompanies it (see Goldsmith and Donovan-Kicken, Chapter 4, this volume). An accusation like "You are really insensitive," for example, probably would be more hurtful if stated by itself than if it were prefaced by statements like, "I know you don't mean to be, and you are dealing with a lot of stuff at work right now, but sometimes..." Even though the basic accusatory message remains the same, additional attention to identity issues probably would be viewed by most people as decreasing the intensity of the hurtful message, which in turn would likely diminish the experience of hurt (Young, 2004).

Attending to the other person's identity concerns when delivering a potentially hurtful remark is only one strategy for mitigating the hurtfulness of conflict behaviors; there are doubtlessly others. This particular example, however, illustrates a larger point: Preventing hurt during conflict is inevitably more complicated than simply listing types of behaviors that are (and are not) likely to lead to hurt. Even when someone engages in a conflict tactic that can be hurtful, the manner in which that person enacts the behavior and the messages surrounding it will help determine whether the message is seen as hurtful.

In sum, the conflict literature implies some fairly clear guidelines for preventing hurt in conflict. Generally, people who wish to avoid hurting each other should focus as much as possible on using positive (nice) strategies, and they should attempt to minimize negative (nasty) ones. Additionally, when engaging in a behavior that can be hurtful, they should recognize that there are normatively more and less hurtful ways of doing so. When wanting some sort of change in their relationship, for instance, criticizing a partner's character harms relationships more than does complaining about behaviors (Gottman, (1994b). Although Gottman (1994b) does not provide direct evidence regarding the hurtfulness of complaints versus criticisms, it is reasonable to suppose that complaining is viewed as generally less hurtful than criticisms of character. Future research should confirm that individuals typically find criticisms more hurtful than complaints, but in the interim it makes sense to deduce that a person wishing to avoid hurting a partner should use complaints rather than criticisms when attempting to change the partner's behavior.

## Limits to Conflict Strategies for Preventing Hurt

Whereas prescriptions concerning particular conflict strategies and behaviors are undoubtedly useful in many circumstances, they are also limited for at least two fundamental reasons. First, during conflict, people are not always motivated to avoid hurting the other person. Even if people begin a conflict with prosocial intentions, their goals for the interaction can shift (Fincham & Beach, 1999). If a conflict is not resolved quickly, the individuals may become frustrated (Roloff & Johnson, 2002) and more concerned about assigning blame than with the content of the argument (Fincham & Beach, 1999). In such cases, people's primary goal may be to attack the other's character (Fincham & Beach, 1999), and if they do so effectively, hurt feelings will probably result. If two individuals aim to attack one another, teaching them which sorts of behaviors are generally more and less hurtful is unlikely to reduce their use of hurtful behaviors. In fact, it may give them additional skills for hurting each other during conflict.

Second, although it is possible to describe normatively hurtful conflict strategies, there is not a finite and definable set of conflict behaviors that lead to experiences of hurt. Appraisal theories of emotion, for instance, imply that hurt is a subjective experience that could be triggered by apparently innocuous messages. Appraisals refer to people's beliefs about – and evaluations of – the extent to which their social context is consistent with their personal goals and well-being (Lazarus, 1991). There are several specific appraisal theories of emotion, but one commonality among them is they seek to explain why individuals have varying emotional responses to objectively similar circumstances (Lazarus, 2006; Smith & Kirby, 2001). According to such theories, appraisals produce and give meaning to our emotional experiences; consequently, individual differences in perceptions and evaluations of events explain the variability in emotional experiences in apparently comparable events (Lazarus, 2006).

With respect to conflict situations, there is considerable evidence that individuals differ substantially in their appraisals of given circumstances. For example, people tend to exhibit self-serving attribution biases: They judge their own conflict behaviors more favorably than they judge their partners' (Canary, 2003; Sillars, Roberts, Dun, & Leonard, 2001). One possible explanation for this bias is that people tend to be more outwardly focused on their partner's hurtful behaviors (Bradbury & Fincham, 1990). Accordingly, both relational partners tend to be more aware of the negative behaviors of the other person while thinking their behaviors are more positive and justified. Consequently, people engaged in conflict often overestimate the partner's responsibility for the conflict and underestimate their own (Canary, 2003; Sillars et al., 2001).

Research by Sillars and his colleagues (2001) provides a particularly compelling example of how such discrepancies can lead to hurt feelings. In this study, married couples engaged in a videotaped interaction about a disagreement in their relationship, and then the spouses separately viewed the recordings and reported on what they were thinking or feeling during the interaction. Many of the participants' thoughts involved inferences about the partner's behaviors or intentions (e.g. "she's trying to lie," p. 205), but these inferences were often quite different from what the partner reported. Sometimes spouses had fundamentally different understandings about what each other was doing; for example, whereas one husband reported he was trying to explain that his spouse "is always first to me," his wife thought, "I felt hurt because he wasn't really listening to what I said about my feelings" (p. 200). The husband reported that he was attempting to reassure his spouse, something that normally would not be hurtful. Nonetheless, the wife perceived his comments as hurtful. There may be a number of reasons why she was hurt, including personality traits and her particular experiences with her husband (see Lazarus, 2006). Regardless of the root reason, the wife appraised his (attempted) assurance as incompatible with her goal of being heard. What the husband actually was attempting to do was largely irrelevant in determining the wife's emotions: Her appraisals shaped the emotional experience. This example illustrates that even having good intentions and using strategies that are typically innocuous cannot always prevent hurt during conflict.

## Alleviating Hurt during Conflict

Given that hurt feelings during conflict cannot always be prevented, it is important to consider how hurt can be alleviated once it happens. We are not aware of any research that directly examines how to redress hurt feelings that arise in conflict. Still, the emotion and conflict literatures imply some suggestions for managing hurt feelings.

To begin, it is important to recognize that people may cope with hurt from conflicts in many of the same ways that they cope with hurt in other contexts. When people believe that they were hurt intentionally, for example, they may distance themselves from the offending individual (Vangelisti & Young, 2000). People can unilaterally add distance to their relationships, and this can be viewed as one coping strategy for dealing with hurt (McLaren & Solomon, 2006).

Because (overt) conflict is inherently dyadic, it is also reasonable to consider interactive strategies for coping, as in cases when the person who committed a hurtful act during conflict tries to alleviate the hurt. Most obviously, many of the same positive conflict behaviors that normatively prevent hurt could also be ones that often diminish hurt. If people recognize that they have hurt their partner, for instance, conciliatory remarks, such as "I can see why you'd be upset" (Sillars, 1986, p. 12) and "I think I could work on that more" (Sillars, p. 13), may be helpful in reducing hurt feelings.

However, the use of particular strategies to alleviate hurt is limited for the same reasons that no particular conflict strategies will always prevent hurt. Even if we were to assume that both individuals had good intentions, the cognitive discrepancies during conflict remain (see Sillars et al., 2001). Thus, strategies that typically ameliorate hurt may be ineffective or may even amplify hurt. A statement like "I can see why you'd feel that way," for instance, might be viewed as dismissive, which may magnify the existing hurt feelings. In short, because people can interpret particular strategies and behaviors in various ways, there is unlikely to be a set of strategies or behaviors that always adequately redresses hurt.

Burleson and Goldsmith (1998) make a similar argument in their discussion of comforting, suggesting that an adequate understanding of how emotional distress can be reduced requires a consideration of the factors contributing to it. Although their focus on emotional distress differs somewhat from the current topic of hurt feelings, some of Burleson and Goldsmith's broad points are relevant here. Most important, even though the precise connection between cognition and affect remains controversial (e.g., Forgas, 2001), appraisal theories of emotion provide a useful framework for understanding how negative emotions, such as hurt, can be alleviated (Burleson & Goldsmith, 1998).

Because emotions are shaped by appraisals, it follows that changing the way individuals perceive and evaluate a situation can change their emotions regarding that situation. Indeed, "there is substantial evidence that changing appraisals results in changed emotions" (Burleson & Goldsmith, 1998, p. 257). Changes in appraisals that alter affect are called reappraisals (Lazarus, 1991, 1999), and they provide a useful way of thinking about how to diminish aversive emotions like hurt. Specifically, Burleson and Goldsmith (1998) argue that the comforting process involves conversing in ways that prompt "useful appraisals" (p. 259) related to the aggrieved person's circumstances and goals. That is, interaction can serve "as a medium in which a distressed person can express, elaborate, and clarify relevant thoughts and feelings" (p. 260).

Recent research by Jones and Wirtz (2006) supports Burleson and Goldsmith's (1998) model of comforting. Jones and Wirtz asked participants to have a conversation about an upsetting event with a confederate. Confederates varied their level of person-centeredness, which involves the extent to which messages validate the other's feelings and encourage the other to talk about the events surrounding those feelings. As expected, higher levels of person-centered messages by the confederates led participants to greater verbalization of thoughts and emotions, including more use of positive emotion words. The use of positive emotion words, in turn, predicted reappraisals and improved emotional outlook regarding the upsetting events. Jones and Wirtz's findings suggest that one reason why some comforting messages are effective is they encourage distressed individuals to reappraise the situation themselves.

Some of Burleson and Goldsmith's (1998) advice for encouraging reappraisals may apply directly to encounters in which someone is attempting to alleviate hurt caused by a conflict. For instance, Burleson and Goldsmith caution against trying to comfort by simply telling the distressed person what to think about a particular event. Such behaviors are likely to be, at best, unhelpful. Pennebaker's (1997) research on the benefits of journaling about difficult experiences suggests that people benefit most when they are able to develop a coherent narrative for their situation, something that is unlikely to occur if another person simply provides them with proposed beliefs. The same advice seems plausible with respect to hurt feelings: substantive conversations in which the hurt individual is actively involved in bringing meaning to the hurtful events are more likely to encourage useful reappraisals than are simple directives for reappraising.

Although Burleson and Goldsmith's (1998) model of comforting is relevant to the problem of overcoming hurt, it is also important to recognize that there are some important differences between the type of distress usually examined in the comforting literature and hurt feelings in conflict. Comforting situations are usually conceptualized as ones in which the helper is not also the cause of the distress. Studies commonly examine comforting in response to situations like a death in the family, serious illness, or an important stressor experienced by a spouse or friend (Burleson & MacGeorge, 2002). Although the person providing the support could be the cause of a stressor, that is not the prototypical scenario.

In contrast, if an individual's feelings are hurt during conflict, the person who caused the hurt may be the same person who attempts to alleviate the hurt feelings, which could complicate efforts to mitigate hurt. One feature of generally helpful comforting, for example, is that it acknowledges the distressed person's emotional state and even encourages that person to elaborate on those feelings (Burleson & MacGeorge, 2002). The same strategy *could* be helpful for addressing hurt arising in conflict: It might help the hurt individual understand his or her feelings better, and it could allow the transgressor a chance to take some responsibility and make concessions. However, validating the hurt individual's emotions could also ossify those feelings or even add other negative emotions like anger. For instance, a person whose hurt feelings are validated after being criticized in a conflict may think, "You're right that it's reasonable for me to feel hurt, and now that I know you understand that, I'm not just hurt – I'm also angry!"

Moreover, messages designed to get the hurt individual to think about his or her feelings would be interpreted in the particular context, including the specific relational history. It is easy to imagine scenarios in which a message that would be seen as helpful in many comforting situations would be seen as disingenuous or even mocking if the same message were used with a partner who has been hurt during a conflict. In many comforting situations, a question like "Do you think you learned something about yourself and your reactions from this?" might help people explore and understand their feelings. The same question posed to a partner who was hurt during conflict could be seen as rude or condescending. Because it comes from the person who did the hurting, suggesting that the hurt be viewed in a larger context could imply that the hurt feelings are not legitimate or that they are the fault of the person who was hurt.

In short, Burleson and Goldsmith's (1998) comforting model provides a broad framework for theorizing about how to facilitate reductions in hurt feelings. However, alleviating hurt in conflict is different from the kinds of distress usually examined in the comforting literature; for instance, the person who tries to help mitigate the hurt may be the person who caused it. Such differences mean that the specific advice from the comforting literature will not always be useful with respect to managing hurt during conflict. Thus, it is also important to consider the literature that pertains specifically to hurt to glean some clues about strategies for encouraging reduced feelings of hurt.

Research on hurt in relationships suggests that the extent to which individuals find an interaction hurtful is related positively to the perception that the hurtful behavior or comment was intentional (McLaren & Solomon, 2006; Vangelisti et al., 2005). Additionally, perceptions that hurtful behaviors were intentional appear to amplify any negative impact on relationships. Vangelisti and Young (2000), for example, found that people were more likely to distance themselves from a person who hurt them when they believed that person hurt them intentionally. Given the importance of perceived intentionality to the experience of hurt, it may be productive to theorize about how to foster more useful beliefs about intentionality. Perceived intentions are a component of causal attributions (Bradbury & Fincham, 1990), and such attributions sometimes can be influenced (Fincham & Beach, 1999). In principle, it should be possible in some instances for people who have hurt someone during a conflict to encourage beliefs about intentionality that would mitigate hurt and its effects.

To conceptualize how the perceived intentionality of hurtful acts might be influenced, it is helpful to recognize that intentionality is not a unitary construct. Malle and Knobe (1997) found that five distinct components underlie folk concepts about intentionality: *desire* (doing the act in hopes of achieving an end), *belief* (thinking about the effect of the act before doing it), *intent* (performing the act on purpose), *awareness* (knowing that one is doing the act), and *skill* (perception that one has the ability to do the act at will). Perceptions of at least some of these components could be negotiated discursively during conflict. A wife who recognizes that she has made angry and hurtful comments, for instance, may attempt to provide an account for the hurtful behavior, such as, "Okay, let me calm down for a second. You know how I fly off the handle sometimes, and I am working on it, but sometimes I just can't help it." To the extent that such an account is accepted, it could shape perceptions of intentionality with respect to several of the pertinent components. This account is essentially a claim that a lack of skill led to actions that were not really intended or desired. Successfully conveying the impression that the hurtful behavior was not intentional may help provide remediation for the hurt feelings.

People also may attempt to foster certain perceptions of intentionality before engaging in a potentially hurtful conflict behavior. An unusually sophisticated individual might attempt to frame a potentially hurtful criticism in a way that encourages the other person to believe that hurt is not intended. One could, for example, allude to the cultural value placed on openness as a marker of good relationships (Caughlin, 2003; Parks, 1982). Imagine if a personal criticism were preceded by a statement like, "I want to tell you something that I normally would not tell another person, but I feel I can tell you because we have such a strong and open relationship." Even if that person proceeded to state a hurtful criticism, the previous message would encourage the recipient to consider the possibility that the primary intent was not to be hurtful.

Such examples suggest that it is possible to diminish hurt feelings during conflict interaction. We are not aware of any research that demonstrates this directly, and it is unclear how frequently even a skillful communicator is able and motivated to mitigate the effects of hurt during a particular conflict episode. This would certainly be an important area for future studies.

Even without more research, however, it is clear that individuals will not alleviate all hurt feelings during conflict. The examples of ameliorating hurt described in this section involve purposely shaping others' understanding of events, which treats the meaning of a hurtful comment or behavior as negotiable rather than inherent to the behavior. This sort of communication requires a high level of ability that most people do not display (e.g., O'Keefe, 1988). Moreover, even a very sophisticated communicator will not always be motivated to reduce hurt during conflict. People who hurt their partner's feelings during a conflict, for instance, may be experiencing their own negative emotions, such as anger (Carstensen, Gottman, & Levenson, 1995; Notarius et al., 1997). Rather than being concerned with alleviating their partner's hurt, people experiencing anger may be more focused on winning the argument (Fincham & Beach, 1999) or retaliating (Frijda et al., 1989; Lazarus, 2006). In short, although it is useful to consider what can be done during conflict episodes to mitigate hurt feelings, some conflicts will induce hurt feelings that are not diminished (and may even be exacerbated) over the course of the conflict episode. That is, people sometimes leave conflict encounters with hurt feelings. It is, therefore, important to consider how hurt caused by conflicts can be dealt with outside those particular episodes.

### Redressing Hurt outside Specific Conflict Episodes

The earlier sections have treated conflicts as if they are discrete events with recognizable beginnings and ends. This is a reasonable perspective because conflicts are recognized as a discernible speech event, which means that people often view them as distinct incidents (Goldsmith & Baxter, 1996). Still, the boundaries between conflict episodes and other relational interactions are not always clearly demarcated. Raush, Barry, Hertel, and Swain (1974) reported that married couples sometimes have a period of "postresolution comments" (p. 90) in which the spouses calm down and offer conciliatory gestures. Whereas Raush et al. viewed the postresolution comments as occurring outside the conflict episode, such remarks also provide a transition to other interaction and may shape the individuals' understandings of and feelings about the entire conflict. Thus, it is somewhat arbitrary to consider such comments as outside the boundary of the conflict.

Moreover, Roloff and Johnson (2002; Johnson & Roloff, 2000) point out that couples frequently have certain conflict issues that they discuss repeatedly. The serial nature of many arguments means that conflicts may not be resolved, even if a dyad stops explicitly discussing the issue for a period of time. In such cases, conflict is not only episodic; it also has an ongoing aspect.

Because conflicts are not entirely confined to discrete episodes, the particular events in a given episode are likely to be influenced by events that occur outside that specific encounter. With respect to hurt feelings, the extent to which an individual feels hurt from conflict will depend (in part) on the larger relational context in which the hurtful event occurs. Additionally, the meaning of hurtful events, and the reappraisals that are associated with potential reductions in hurt feelings, probably depend on interaction that may not be viewed as part of a certain conflict episode. Most obviously, discussions about a supposedly completed conflict can influence the appraisals of that conflict. In addition, other seemingly unconnected interactions – even interactions with third parties – may be important. Each of these possibilities is discussed in the following sections.

### Discussions about Hurtful Conflict Episodes

After conflict is putatively over, individuals may engage in "interplay involved in salving the real or potential injuries to the partner" (Raush et al., 1974, p. 90). This behavior can take various forms. Presuming that an individual is aware that he or she has done something hurtful during conflict, that person may offer an account for the hurtful behavior (Metts, 1994). From an appraisal theory perspective, various types of accounts can offer a way of judging events favorably. A justification, for instance, attempts to reframe a behavior so that it is viewed more positively (Metts, 1994). One possibility is attempting to recast the hurtful act as meaning something positive for the relationship (e.g., "I was not trying to be critical; I was trying to be honest because I love and respect you enough to tell you how I really feel"). This reframing could invite the hurt individual to focus on the beneficial elements of the relationship, perhaps diminishing feelings of vulnerability and hurt.

However, justifications will not always be successful at reducing hurt, and some may amplify hurt feelings. A transgressor may focus on justifying his or her own actions without suggesting anything positive about the relationship (e.g., "By the time I insulted you, I had just had enough of your whining, and I felt like I needed to say anything to get you to stop"). Such justifications would be unlikely to reduce hurt feelings and may exacerbate them by confirming that the hurtful message was intentional.

There are other types of accounts (see Metts, 1994), but as with justifications, the form of the account is probably less important than the way the events are implicitly framed. Accounts that are successful at encouraging the hurt individual to think about the generally positive qualities of the relationship, for instance, are likely to help reduce hurt feelings. There is no magic speech form that will inevitably eliminate hurt feelings when uttered after a conflict.

Nevertheless, it is likely that some strategies for discussing hurtful behaviors are generally more effective than others. Across a wide variety of relational transgressions (e.g., deception, infidelity), apologizing is often a particularly effective way to repair a relationship (Metts, 1994). Although a repaired relationship does not necessarily mean that hurt will be eliminated, messages that improve relationships can reduce feelings of being rejected, which in turn are related to the extent of hurt feelings (Feeney, 2005). The characteristics of an apology appear to encourage appraisals that would reduce hurt. A properly enacted apology, for instance, not only accepts responsibility for the negative action but also promises to avoid such actions in the future (Metts, 1994). Assuming a promise for better behavior is believable, it could encourage the hurt individual to assess the transgression as fairly infrequent or at least not ongoing. Whereas the particular event may have been quite hurtful at the time, believing that it was an isolated occurrence probably would minimize the impact of the hurt feelings on the relationship (see Vangelisti & Maguire, 2002). In short, if people want to remediate hurt from a conflict, apologizing is often a reasonable strategy.

Still, an apology (or any other behavior aimed at alleviating someone else's hurt) can only suggest a reappraisal of the events. There is no guarantee that the aggrieved individual will reappraise in the desired manner. The aforementioned research on comforting suggests that, rather than attempting to provide the hurt individual with a new appraisal, it may be more useful to encourage hurt individuals to discuss their experience in ways that enable them to reappraise the situation themselves (Burleson & Goldsmith, 1998; Jones & Wirtz, 2006). Although there is no research that specifically examines how to elicit useful reappraisals of hurt feelings, the clinical literature on forgiveness provides some clues that may be helpful. People who acknowledge their own hurtful behaviors in the past, for instance, tend to forgive transgressions (Wade & Worthington, 2005). Clearly, a transgressor who overtly asks the hurt individual to make such acknowledgments risks being seen as trying to justify his or her own hurtful behaviors. Still, it is theoretically possible to encourage the hurt individual to discuss the hurtful events. A transgressor might, for instance, attempt to treat the conflict in an analytical manner, asking for observations and comments in a nonevaluative way. Such analytical comments may look similar to the analytical conflict strategies that Sillars (1986) identified, with the difference being that participants view them as a recap to the conflict rather than as actually part of the conflict episode. Transgressors may, for instance, make nonhostile disclosures about their own thoughts and feelings leading up to the conflict. It is likely that such behaviors would be reciprocated (see Gottman, Markman, & Notarius, 1977; Pike & Sillars, 1985), which would effectively prompt hurt individuals to discuss their own feelings regarding the events, potentially leading to positive reappraisals.

## Other Relational Interaction

Overt conflict episodes are not particularly frequent in most relationships; for instance, married couples typically report less than one conflict per day (Caughlin & Vangelisti, 2006). Much relational talk involves speech events that are not directly related to conflict episodes (see Goldsmith & Baxter, 1996). The abundance of nonconflict interaction can be important to understanding conflicts. Indeed, the quality of couples' interaction outside of conflicts may moderate the potential impact of hurtful conflict. Caughlin and Huston (2002), for example, found that couples who are affectionate with each other in their daily interactions appear to be buffered from the adverse impact of the demand/withdraw pattern of conflict. That is, the negative impact of frequently hurtful conflict patterns can be diminished by positive interaction outside of conflict.

One possible explanation for why a warm relational climate would reduce the impact of hurt from conflict is that such a climate may reduce the frequency or intensity of hurt feelings in conflict. When relational partners are affectionate with each other, they tend to develop generally positive views of each other (Miller, Caughlin, & Huston, 2003). Such positive views are important because they shape the way people make appraisals pertaining to hurt. Murray and her colleagues (2003) found that spouses who believed their partner held them in positive regard were less vulnerable to hurt feelings on days with conflicts than were spouses who did not believe their partner viewed them positively. Murray et al. concluded that "intimates who felt less valued in a partner's eyes read more into signs of negativity, feeling more hurt and rejected [than did people who felt more valued]" (p. 142). Such findings suggest that the potential for hurt in conflict can be minimized by interacting in ways that foster an agreeable relationship in which both partners feel appreciated.

Even after a person experiences hurt during conflict, overall positive views of relational partners are still important. The likelihood of forgiving a partner for inflicting hurt feelings is positively related to the affection a person has for the partner and negatively related to ambivalent feelings about him or her (Kachadourian, Fincham, & Davila, 2005). Forgiveness is important in its own right, but one of its ancillary benefits may be particularly useful for managing hurt caused from conflict. The extent to which spouses forgive their partner for hurting them predicts constructive outcomes from subsequent conflict episodes (Fincham, Beach, & Davila, 2004). Being able to deal well with subsequent conflicts would diminish the chances of additional hurt feelings and would provide an opportunity for encouraging the reassessment of previous hurt (e.g., as an anomaly).

## Interaction with Third Parties

Although the primary focus of this chapter is on interaction between individuals in a relationship, an appraisal theory perspective on hurt implies that a broader lens also can be useful. Lazarus (2006) argued that a wide variety of factors, including personality characteristics and personal experiences, shape appraisal processes. Conversations with third parties are one type of experience that can influence appraisals of relational conflicts. It is common for people to talk with friends about the conflicts they have with romantic partners (Wilson, Roloff, & Carey, 1998), and these conversations affect people's views of their relational conflicts. For instance, individuals' beliefs in the legitimacy of their concerns during conflict are linked to whether people in their social network support their views (Klein & Milardo, 2000).

Such findings imply that ongoing feelings of hurt can be mitigated (or exacerbated) by discussions with people outside the relationship. When a hurt individual discusses a relational conflict with a third party, this may be similar to a classic comforting scenario because the transgressor is not the person attempting to redress the hurt. A third party may be able to encourage reappraisals by using person-centered messages as part of a larger discussion that validates the hurt individual's feelings and attempts to get that person to think of the larger context (Burleson & Goldsmith, 1998). In at least some cases, it may be more plausible for a third party to encourage positive reappraisals than it would be for the transgressor to do so. For instance, it may be helpful for a third party to ask the hurt individual about the transgressor's larger pattern of behavior (e.g., other positive tendencies that overshadow the hurtful act), but the same questions would be viewed quite differently if posed by the transgressor.

## FINAL THOUGHTS

There is surprisingly little research explicitly examining the connection between relational conflict and hurt feelings. The current chapter suggests that this is a significant omission in the literature. The association between conflict and hurt is complex but important. The majority of this chapter focuses on how hurt feelings that sometimes occur during conflict may be reduced through reappraisal processes. Although our discussion is rooted in the conflict literature and relevant aspects of appraisal theory, it is important to emphasize that systematic research is needed to demonstrate the utility of this reappraisal perspective on managing hurt. Such research could prove quite valuable because successfully managing hurt feelings in conflict is vital to individuals' well-being. People who do not manage hurt well (e.g., by becoming bitter or vengeful) typically exacerbate their problems (Wade & Worthington, 2005).

Despite the valid reasons for focusing on reducing hurt feelings through reappraisals, it is important to end with a caveat. As previously noted, hurt feelings sometimes serve useful functions, such as motivating a person to repair a relationship (Sanford & Rowatt, 2004). In other cases, hurt feelings are a useful indicator of a transgression that needs to be addressed. Simply reappraising such transgressions so they feel less hurtful would be counterproductive. A person whose partner repeatedly becomes violent during conflict, for instance, should do more than seek positive ways of conceptualizing the hurtful behavior. In such instances, reducing the feelings of hurt should not be used as a strategy for allowing or condoning unacceptable behaviors. Ultimately, it may still be useful for the victim to forgive abusive actions during conflict, but that should not be confused with "letting an offender off the hook" (Wade, Bailey, & Shaffer, 2005).

## REFERENCES

Berry, D. S., & Willingham, J. K. (1997). Affective traits, responses to conflict, and satisfaction in romantic relationships. *Journal of Research in Personality, 31,* 564–576.

Bradbury, T. N., & Fincham, F. D. (1990). Attributions in marriage: Review and critique. *Psychological Bulletin, 107,* 3–33.

Burleson, B. R., & Goldsmith, D. J. (1998). How the comforting process works: Alleviating emotional distress through conversationally induced reappraisals. In P. A. Andersen & L. K. Guerrero (Eds.), *The handbook of communication and emotion* (pp. 245–280). Thousand Oaks, CA: Sage.

Burleson, B. R., & MacGeorge, E. L. (2002). Supportive communication. In M. L. Knapp & J. A. Daly (Eds.), *Handbook of interpersonal communication* (3rd ed., pp. 374–424). Thousand Oaks, CA: Sage.

Canary, D. J. (2003). Managing interpersonal conflict: A model of events related to strategic choices. In J. O. Greene & B. R. Burleson (Eds.), *Handbook of communication and social interaction skills* (pp. 515–549). Mahwah, NJ: Erlbaum.

Canary, D. J., & Lakey, S. G. (2006). Managing conflict in a competent manner: A mindful look at events that matter. In J. G. Oetzel & S. Ting-Toomey (Eds.), *Sage handbook of conflict communication: Integrating theory, research, and practice* (pp. 185–210). Thousand Oaks, CA: Sage.

Carstensen, L. L., Gottman, J. M., & Levenson, R. W. (1995). Emotional behavior in long-term marriage. *Psychology and Aging, 10*, 140–149.

Caughlin, J. P. (2003). Family communication standards: What counts as excellent family communication and how are such standards associated with family satisfaction? *Human Communication Research, 29*, 5–40.

Caughlin, J. P., & Huston, T. L. (2002). A contextual analysis of the association between demand/withdraw and marital satisfaction. *Personal Relationships, 9*, 95–119.

Caughlin, J. P., & Malis, R. S. (2004). Demand/withdraw communication between parents and adolescents: Connections with self-esteem and substance use. *Journal of Social and Personal Relationships, 21*, 125–148.

Caughlin, J. P., & Vangelisti, A. L. (2006). Conflict in dating and marital relationships. In J. G. Oetzel & S. Ting-Toomey (Eds.), *Sage handbook of conflict communication: Integrating theory, research, and practice* (pp. 129–157). Thousand Oaks, CA: Sage.

Cloven, D. H., & Roloff, M. E. (1993). The chilling effect of aggressive potential on the expression of complaints in intimate relationships. *Communication Monographs, 60*, 199–219.

Cole, D. A., & McPherson, A. E. (1993). Relation of family subsystems to adolescent depression: Implementing a new family assessment strategy. *Journal of Family Psychology, 7*, 119–133.

Feeney, J. A. (2004). Hurt feelings in couple relationships: Towards integrative models of the negative effects of hurtful events. *Journal of Social and Personal Relationships, 21*, 487–508.

Feeney, J. A. (2005). Hurt feelings in couple relationships: Exploring the role of attachment and perceptions of personal injury. *Personal Relationships, 12*, 253–271.

Fincham, F. D., & Beach, S. R. H. (1999). Conflict in marriage: Implications for working with couples. *Annual Review of Psychology, 50*, 47–77.

Fincham, F. D., Beach, S. R. H., & Davila, J. (2004). Forgiveness and conflict resolution in marriage. *Journal of Family Psychology, 18*, 72–81.

Fitzpatrick, M. A., & Winke, J. (1979). You always hurt the one you love: Strategies and tactics in interpersonal conflict. *Communication Quarterly, 27*, 3–11.

Folkes, V. S. (1982). Communicating the causes of social rejection. *Journal of Experimental Social Psychology, 18*, 235–252.

Forgas, J. P. (Ed.). (2001). *Handbook of affect and social cognition*. Mahwah, NJ: Erlbaum.

Frijda, N. H., Kuipers, P., & ter Schure, E. (1989). Relations among emotion, appraisal, and emotional action readiness. *Journal of Personality and Social Psychology, 57*, 212–228.

Goldsmith, D. J., & Baxter, L. A. (1996). Constituting relationships in talk: A taxonomy of speech events in social and personal relationships. *Human Communication Research, 23*, 87–114.

Gottman, J. M. (1994a). *What predicts divorce? The relationship between marital processes and marital outcomes*. Hillsdale, NJ: Erlbaum.

Gottman, J. M. (1994b). *Why marriages succeed or fail.* New York: Simon & Schuster.

Gottman, J. M., Coan, J., Carrere, S., & Swanson, C. (1998). Predicting happiness and stability from newlywed interactions. *Journal of Marriage and the Family, 60,* 5–22.

Gottman, J. M., Markman, H., & Notarius, C. (1977). The topography of marital conflict: Sequential analysis of verbal and nonverbal behavior. *Journal of Marriage and the Family, 39,* 461–477.

Hahlweg, K., Markman, H. J., Thurmaier, F., Engl, J., & Eckert, V. (1998). Prevention of marital distress: Results of a German prospective longitudinal study. *Journal of Family Psychology, 12,* 543–556.

Huston, T. L., Caughlin, J. P., Houts, R. M., Smith, S., & George, L. J. (2001). The connubial crucible: Newlywed years as predictors of marital delight, distress, and divorce. *Journal of Personality and Social Psychology, 80,* 237–252.

Jenkins, S. R., Goodness, K., & Buhrmester, D. (2002). Gender differences in early adolescents' relationship qualities, self-efficacy, and depression symptoms. *Journal of Early Adolescence, 22,* 277–309.

Johnson, K. L., & Roloff, M. E. (2000). Correlates of the perceived resolvability and relational consequences of serial arguing in dating relationships: Argumentative features and the use of coping strategies. *Journal of Social and Personal Relationships, 17,* 677–687.

Jones, S. M., & Wirtz, J. G. (2006). How does the comforting process work? An empirical test of an appraisal-based model of comforting. *Human Communication Research, 32,* 217–243.

Kachadourian, L. K., Fincham, F. D., & Davila, J. (2005). Attitudinal ambivalence, rumination, and forgiveness of partner transgressions in marriage. *Personality and Social Psychology Bulletin, 31,* 334–342.

Karney, B. R., & Bradbury, T. N. (1995). The longitudinal course of marital quality and stability: A review of theory, method, and research. *Psychological Bulletin, 118,* 3–34.

Klein, R. C. A., & Milardo, R. M. (2000). The social context of couple conflict: Support and criticism from informal third parties. *Journal of Social and Personal Relationships, 17,* 618–637.

Knobloch, L. K., & Solomon, D. H. (2003). Responses to changes in relational uncertainty within dating relationships: Emotions and communication strategies. *Communication Studies, 54,* 282–305.

Lazarus, R. S. (1991). Cognition and motivation in emotion. *American Psychologist, 46,* 352–367.

Lazarus, R. S. (1999). *Stress and emotion: A new synthesis.* New York: Springer.

Lazarus, R. S. (2006). Emotions and interpersonal relationships: Toward a person-centered conceptualization of emotions and coping. *Journal of Personality, 74,* 9–46.

Leary, M. R., Springer, C., Negel, L., Ansell, E., & Evans, K. (1998). The causes, phenomenology, and consequences of hurt feelings. *Journal of Personality and Social Psychology, 74,* 1225–1237.

Levenson, R. W., & Gottman, J. M. (1985). Physiological and affective predictors of change in relationship satisfaction. *Journal of Personality and Social Psychology, 49,* 85–94.

Malle, B. F., & Knobe, J. (1997). The folk concept of intentionality. *Journal of Experimental Social Psychology, 33,* 101–121.

Markman, H. J., Floyd, F., Stanley, S., & Storaasli, R. (1988). Prevention of marital distress: A longitudinal investigation. *Journal of Consulting and Clinical Psychology, 56,* 210–217.

McLaren, R., & Solomon, D. (2006, November). *Applying appraisal theories of emotion to the experience of hurt.* Paper presented at the annual convention of the National Communication Association, San Antonio.

Metts, S. (1994). Relational transgressions. In W. R. Cupach & B. H. Spitzberg (Eds.), *The dark side of interpersonal communication* (pp. 217–239). Hillsdale, NJ: Erlbaum.

Miller, P. J., Caughlin, J. P., & Huston, T. L. (2003). Trait expressiveness and marital satisfaction: The role of idealization processes. *Journal of Marriage and Family, 65,* 978–995.

Murray, S. L., Bellavia, G. M., Rose, P., & Griffin, D. W. (2003). Once hurt, twice hurtful: How perceived regard regulates daily marital interactions. *Journal of Personality and Social Psychology, 84,* 126–147.

Newell, S. E., & Stutman, R. K. (1988). The social confrontation episode. *Communication Monographs, 55,* 266–285.

Notarius, C. I., Lashley, S. L., & Sullivan, D. J. (1997). Angry at your partner?: Think again. In R. J. Sternberg & M. Hojjat (Eds.), *Satisfaction in close relationships* (pp. 219–248). New York: Guilford.

O'Keefe, B. J. (1988). The logic of message design: Individual differences in reasoning about communication. *Communication Monographs, 55,* 80–103.

Parks, M. R. (1982). Ideology in interpersonal communication: Off the couch and into the world. In M. Burgoon (Ed.), *Communication yearbook 6* (pp. 79–107). Beverly Hills, CA: Sage.

Pennebaker, J. W. (1997). *Opening up: The healing power of expressing emotions* (Rev. ed.). New York: Guilford.

Pike, G. R., & Sillars, A. L. (1985). Reciprocity of marital communication. *Journal of Social and Personal Relationships, 2,* 303–324.

Raush, H. L., Barry, W. A., Hertel, R. K., & Swain, M. A. (1974). *Communication, conflict, and marriage.* San Francisco: Jossey–Bass.

Repetti, R. L., Taylor, S. E., & Seeman, T. E. (2002). Risky families: Family social environments and the mental and physical health of offspring. *Psychological Bulletin, 128,* 330–366.

Roloff, M. E., & Ifert, D. E. (2000). Conflict management through avoidance: Withholding complaints, suppressing arguments, and declaring topics taboo. In S. Petronio (Ed.), *Balancing the secrets of private disclosures* (pp. 151–163). Mahwah, NJ: Erlbaum.

Roloff, M. E., & Johnson, K. L. (2002). Serial arguing over the relational life course: Antecedents and consequences. In A. L. Vangelisti, H. T. Reis, & M. A. Fitzpatrick (Eds.), *Stability and change in relationships* (pp. 107–128). New York: Cambridge University Press.

Roloff, M. E., & Miller, C. W. (2006). Social cognition approaches to understanding interpersonal conflict and communication. In J. G. Oetzel & S. Ting-Toomey (Eds.), *Sage handbook of conflict communication: Integrating theory, research, and practice* (pp. 97–128). Thousand Oaks, CA: Sage.

Sanford, K., & Rowatt, W. C. (2004). When is negative emotion positive for relationships? An investigation of married couples and roommates. *Personal Relationships, 11,* 329–354.

Schaap, C., & Jansen-Nawas, C. (1987). Marital interaction, affect, and conflict resolution. *Sexual and Marital Therapy, 2,* 35–51.

Schroth, H. A., Bain-Chekal, J., & Caldwell, D. F. (2005). Sticks and stones may break bones and words can hurt me: Words and phrases that trigger emotions in negotiations and their effects. *International Journal of Conflict Management, 16,* 102–127.

Shaver, P., Schwartz, J., Kirson, D., & O'Connor, C. (1987). Emotion knowledge: Further exploration of a prototype approach. *Journal of Personality and Social Psychology, 52*, 1061–1086.

Siegert, J. R., & Stamp, G. H. (1994). "Our first big fight" as a milestone in the development of close relationships. *Communication Monographs, 61*, 345–360.

Sillars, A. L. (1986, April). *Procedures for coding interpersonal conflict (revised manual).* Missoula: University of Montana, Department of Interpersonal Communication.

Sillars, A., Canary, D. J., & Tafoya, M. (2004). Communication, conflict, and the quality of family relationships. In A. L. Vangelisti (Ed.), *Handbook of family communication* (pp. 413–446). Mahwah, NJ: Erlbaum.

Sillars, A., Roberts, L. J., Dun, T., & Leonard, K. (2001). Stepping into the stream of thought: Cognition during marital conflict. In V. Manusov & J. H. Harvey (Eds.), *Attribution, communication behavior, and close relationships* (pp. 193–210). New York: Cambridge University Press.

Sillars, A. L., Roberts, L. J., Leonard, K. E., & Dun, T. (2000). Cognition during marital conflict: The relationship of thought and talk. *Journal of Social and Personal Relationships, 17*, 479–502.

Sillars, A. L., & Weisberg, J. (1987). Conflict as a social skill. In M. E. Roloff & G. R. Miller (Eds.), *Interpersonal processes: New directions in communication research* (pp. 140–171). Newbury Park, CA: Sage.

Smith, C. A., & Kirby, L. D. (2001). Affect and cognitive appraisal processes. In J. P. Forgas (Ed.), *Handbook of affect and social cognition* (pp. 75–92). Mahwah, NJ: Erlbaum.

Vangelisti, A. L. (2001). Making sense of hurtful interactions in close relationships. In V. Manusov & J. H. Harvey (Eds.), *Attribution, communication behavior, and close relationships* (pp. 38–58). New York: Cambridge University Press.

Vangelisti, A. L. (2007). Communicating hurt. In B. H. Spitzberg & W. R. Cupach (Eds.), *The dark side of interpersonal communication* (2nd ed., pp. 121–142). Mahwah, NJ: Erlbaum.

Vangelisti, A. L., & Maguire, K. (2002). Hurtful messages in family relationships: When the pain lingers. In J. H. Harvey & A. Wenzel (Eds.), *A clinician's guide to maintaining and enhancing close relationships* (pp. 43–62). Mahwah, NJ: Erlbaum.

Vangelisti, A. L., & Sprague, R. J. (1998). Guilt and hurt: Similarities, distinctions, and conversational strategies. In P. A. Andersen & L. K. Guerrero (Eds.), *Handbook of communication and emotion* (pp. 123–154). San Diego: Academic Press.

Vangelisti, A. L., & Young, S. L. (2000). When words hurt: The effects of perceived intentionality on interpersonal relationships. *Journal of Social and Personal Relationships, 17*, 393–424.

Vangelisti, A. L., Young, S. L., Carpenter-Theune, K. E., & Alexander, A. L. (2005). Why does it hurt? The perceived causes of hurt feelings. *Communication Research, 32*, 443–477.

Wade, N. G., Bailey, D. C., & Shaffer, P. (2005). Helping clients heal: Does forgiveness make a difference? *Professional Psychology: Research and Practice, 36*, 634–641.

Wade, N. G., & Worthington, E. L., Jr. (2005). In search of a common core: A content analysis of interventions to promote forgiveness. *Psychotherapy: Theory, Research, Practice, Training, 42*, 160–177.

Wainryb, C., Brehl, B. A., & Matwin, S. (2005). Being hurt and hurting others: Children's narrative accounts and moral judgments of their own interpersonal conflicts. *Monographs of the Society for Research in Child Development, 70*, 1–114.

Whitson, S., & El-Sheikh, M. (2003). Marital conflict and health: Processes and protective factors. *Aggression and Violent Behavior, 8,* 283–312.

Wilson, L. L., Roloff, M. E., & Carey, C. M. (1998). Boundary rules: Factors that inhibit expressing concerns about another's romantic relationship. *Communication Research, 25,* 618–640.

Young, S. L. (2004). Factors that influence recipients' appraisals of hurtful communication. *Journal of Social and Personal Relationships, 21,* 291–303.

# 9

# When the Truth Hurts: Deception in the Name of Kindness

BELLA M. DePAULO, WENDY L. MORRIS, AND R. WEYLIN STERNGLANZ

Everyone lies. It would be impossible to prove that definitively, but we believe it to be so. But we also believe that it is truth-telling, rather than deception, that is the human default position. People typically prefer to tell the truth. They want to be honest, they want to see themselves as honest, and they want other people to see them that way.

Ordinary humans – that is, the vast majority, who are not pathological liars – usually need a reason to lie. Lying, then, often grows out of a conflict. On the one side is the desire to be truthful, and on the other is some goal that cannot be attained (or cannot easily be attained) by telling the truth. Something has to give. If the sought-after prize is sufficiently shiny and bright, then often it is the truth that is left by the wayside.

Lying has a bad reputation. When we think of instances in which people set aside the truth to get what they want, often what we envision as the prize is something rather seedy or at least self-serving. Boatloads of money, for example. Or an ill-deserved promotion. Or 15 minutes of unearned fame. And in fact, people do lie for such reasons. But lies told for crass, materialistic, self-serving reasons are just one slice of the lie-telling pie, and not even a very big one at that.

Sometimes what truth-telling bumps up against is not greed but graciousness. That, we think, is the most traveled intersection between lying and hurt feelings. People lie when they cannot both tell the truth *and* be kind and gracious at the same time. Something has to give, and what gives in these instances is usually the truth. In fact, we believe that, in situations in which the truth would hurt, our inclination to avoid causing emotional pain – even just a tiny bit of it – is so overlearned that the usual default is overridden. That is, when hurt feelings are at stake, our first inclination is to lie.

In this chapter, we examine the various types of lies people tell to spare the feelings of others. We explore both the kind-hearted lies that people tell on a daily basis without much forethought or discomfort as well as the most serious lies people have ever told or been told. When people must choose between truthfulness and kindness, what factors will tip the scale more heavily in one direction or the other? This chapter provides some answers to this question and also illustrates the tactics we use when we want to avoid hurting someone's feelings without telling an outright lie.

### LYING IN EVERYDAY LIFE: DO HURT FEELINGS PLAY A PART?

When we first set out to study the nature of lying in everyday life, there were only a few scattered studies of the phenomenon (e.g., Camden, Motley, & Wilson, 1984; Hample, 1980; Lippard, 1988; Metts, 1989; Turner, Edgley, & Olmstead, 1975). Most were limited in some ways. For example, in some the sample size was small. In others, participants described just one conversation or just one lie and could choose any conversation or lie they wished. In none of the studies did participants keep track of all of their social interactions (regardless of whether they had lied during them). Doing so is important in that it provides an indication of the number of opportunities the participants had to tell their lies.

So in the studies we conducted (DePaulo & Kashy, 1998; DePaulo, Kashy, Kirkendol, Wyer, & Epstein, 1996; Kashy & DePaulo, 1996), participants kept a record of all of their social interactions (lasting 10 minutes or longer) and all of the lies they told during their interactions every day for a week. Participants described, in their own words, each of the lies they told and the reason for telling the lie. In one of the two studies, the participants were 77 college students, and in the other, they were a more demographically diverse group of 70 people from the community.

First, the basics. Apart from any consideration of hurt feelings, just how deceitful were our participants? The 77 college students told a total of 1,058 lies. That amounted to an average of two lies a day for each participant, or about one lie in every three social interactions. The 70 community members told a total of 477 lies. That was about one lie a day, or one lie in every five social interactions.

With regard to the content of the lies, people in both studies lied about the same sorts of things and often in roughly similar proportions. For example, both the college students and the people from the community told many lies about their *achievements and knowledge*, often claiming greater accomplishments and more extensive learning than the facts of their lives could support. Participants in both studies lied often about their *actions, plans, and whereabouts*. They said that they had done things that they actually hadn't (such as giving to charity) and that they were planning to do things that they had no intention of ever doing (such as going to a boring social event). They made fanciful claims about being in a certain place at a certain time (home all night studying or meeting with a client from work). Study participants lied about the *explanations and reasons* for their actions or inactions. One college student, for example, told his roommate this lie: "I didn't take out the garbage because I didn't know where to take it." In both studies, participants lied about *facts and possessions* – claiming, for example, to own an impressive vehicle or to have a father who is an ambassador.

In both studies, though, lies about achievements and knowledge; actions, plans, and whereabouts; explanations and reasons; and facts and possessions were all less plentiful than lies about *feelings*. In everyday life, people lie about their emotions, opinions, and appraisals more often than they lie about anything else. They claim to like people they dislike, and they pretend to agree when in fact they disagree. They compliment others on their ugly sweaters and hairstyles and on their misguided taste in music and food. They act impressed with a coworker's holiday plans that they actually consider tacky. Sometimes they claim to dislike other people they actually do like. They also act emotionally unfazed when in fact they are torn up inside.

When people lied about their feelings, they overwhelmingly overstated their positivity (or understated their negativity). For instance, they faked positive emotions they really did not feel or hid their negative emotions. They exaggerated their liking for other people and places and things. They far more often faked agreement and interest than disagreement and disinterest. Feigning or exaggerating positive feelings and hiding or understating negative feelings are exactly what we would expect liars to do if they were telling at least some of their lies to avoid hurting another person's feelings.

We looked next at the referent of the lies – whether the lies referred to something about the liar, the target, another person, or an object or event. (Each lie could be sorted into as many referent categories as were relevant.) If participants were telling some of their lies about feelings to avoid hurting the target person's feelings, then feeling lies (compared to lies about other topics) should be especially likely to refer to the target of the lies. They were.

Finally, we examined the reasons our participants gave for telling their lies. Self-centered lies were motivated primarily by something the liars wanted for themselves, whether something psychological (such as making themselves look better or feel better) or something more concrete (such as a promotion or a better deal on a purchase). Other-oriented lies were told to accomplish the same sorts of goals on behalf of someone else – for example, to make someone else look better or feel better or to help someone attain a more concrete goal. If the participants in the diary studies were telling lies to spare other people's feelings, then the lies they told about feelings should have been told more often for other-oriented reasons than for self-centered ones. Again, in both studies, they were.

### Who Are the Targets of Self-Centered and Kind-Hearted Lies?

When we looked at all of the lies that our participants told, we found that most of them were self-centered. Only about 25% of lies were other-oriented (kind-hearted) lies. But the proportion of self-centered to other-oriented lies that people told depended importantly on the relationship they had with the target of their lies.

DePaulo and Kashy (1998) compared the ratio of self-centered to kindhearted lies that were told to best friends, friends, acquaintances, and strangers. The disproportionate telling of self-centered lies occurred mostly to targets who were strangers or acquaintances. Both the college students and the community members told relatively more kind-hearted lies than self-centered ones when the targets of their lies were best friends or friends.

The desire to be kind and gracious and to avoid causing pain is likely to be most intense with the people we care about the most. Perhaps the desire to be honest is also most compelling with regard to the people to whom we feel closest. When the clash between kindness and truthfulness is complicated by closeness, what gives then?

In addition to looking at discrete relationship categories (such as friends and strangers), DePaulo and Kashy also did analyses that included all relationship partners (for example, parents, children, other relatives, spouse). Participants had recorded their closeness to each of their interaction partners on the same rating scale. Participants told relatively more kind-hearted than self-centered lies to the targets to whom they felt closer. Emotionally closer relationship partners should be just the people whose feelings matter most and whose feelings liars would be most motivated to spare. That is what the results seemed to suggest.

## How Often Are Hurt Feelings Implicated in the Telling of Everyday Lies?

Because these studies were not originally designed specifically to examine the role of hurt feelings in the telling of lies, we did not initially code anything so precise as the telling of lies to avoid hurting another person's feelings. We revisited the original descriptions of the 1,535 lies (1,058 from the college students and 477 from the community members) in the participants' own words to see whether the participants framed the lies they told or the reasons for telling their lies in the language of hurt feelings. In 83 instances (5.4% of all lies), they did so unambiguously. As in the first example in Table 9.1, participants said they told their lies so as not to hurt the feelings of the other person. Another 20 gave reasons that seemed to amount to the same thing. As in the second example in Table 9.1, they said they told their lies so the other person would not feel bad. Six more said they were concerned about the level of caring that would have been conveyed to the other person if they had told the truth rather than a lie. As in the third example, they lied to communicate more caring than they really did feel. Finally, in 13 other instances, we inferred that participants were trying to avoid hurting the other person's feelings, though the participants did not say so directly (see the fourth example in Table 9.1). All told, then, 122 of the 1,535 lies (7.9%) were in some way about hurt feelings.

TABLE 9.1. *What counts as a lie about hurt feelings? Eight examples*

| | Content of lie | Reason given for lying |
|---|---|---|
| 1. | Said her hair looked great when it looked terrible. | So I wouldn't hurt her feelings. |
| 2. | Told her I liked her new sweater. (Really thought it was ugly.) | Didn't want her to feel bad. |
| 3. | I said I didn't send a birthday card because I couldn't get to the store when actually I could have if I had really tried. | I didn't want the person to think I didn't care about her birthday. |
| 4. | I lied and told her I wanted to see her more than I wanted to see my boyfriend. | I didn't want her to feel like our relationship is decreasing in importance to me because of my boyfriend. |
| 5. | I told him I didn't care that he had a date. | So I wouldn't appear vulnerable. |
| 6. | I said I wasn't hurt and that I wasn't ready to become involved with him. | In order to protect myself from getting hurt or receiving his sympathy. |
| 7. | Pretended not to mind that we couldn't carry out our plans for the afternoon when actually I was irritated. | Saw no reason to tell the truth, would only make us both feel bad. |
| 8. | Stated that I would like to plan a trip to Paris and Italy this summer. I know I can't plan a trip, since I can't afford a trip. | It was my way of, once again, saying I don't need you to make me happy. |

In nearly all of the lies about hurt feelings, participants said they were trying to spare the feelings of the other person. But there were a few exceptions. In nine instances, participants lied to cover their own wounded feelings with a veneer of invulnerability (as in the fifth example). In two more instances, participants explicitly said they were trying to avoid getting hurt (see the sixth example). In another two examples, participants said that they were trying to spare both their own feelings and the other person's (see example seven).

We found just two examples in which participants were not trying to spare anyone's feelings. Instead, they seemed to be trying deliberately to hurt another person (see example eight in Table 9.1). Of course, as in any self-report study, there is always the possibility that people may underreport socially undesirable behaviors – such as lying for the expressed purpose of hurting someone.

## Close Cousins to Lies about Hurt Feelings

We tried not to read too much into participants' descriptions of their lies or their reasons for telling their lies. We also refrained from stretching the hurt feelings category beyond what we perceived as its proper theoretical limits. The matter of discriminant validity, though, was not always straightforward.

In Table 9.2, we list the lies we regarded as close cousins of lies about hurt feelings. Ultimately, we did not count them in our tallies of hurt feelings lies, but we considered them. These close relatives of lies about hurt feelings included lies told to elicit sympathy or to keep sympathy far away. Lies told to

TABLE 9.2. *Examples of close cousins of lies about hurt feelings*

| | Content of lie | Reason given for lying |
|---|---|---|
| 1. | I said I had gained 5 pounds this weekend and I was fat. | So they would respond to make me feel better. |
| 2. | Lie about my relationship with her brother. | To make myself look nonchalant. |
| 3. | I said I didn't care about a car wreck. | To appear nonchalant. |
| 4. | I told her I was not depressed and I really was. | I didn't want her to feel sorry for me. |
| 5. | Told her I didn't feel any guilt over my mother's death. | She was worried about me and to reassure myself. |
| 6. | Told Trona my nightmares were about different subject. | My nightmares are about my mother's death and I didn't want her to feel sorry for me. |
| 7. | He was an old boyfriend and I told him I was glad he stopped going out. | Because I didn't want him to think I still liked him. |
| 8. | I told Ruth that I thought she had made the right decision about her boyfriend. | She was upset about her boyfriend and needed reassurance from me. |
| 9. | Said I would like to see him over Thanksgiving. | To make him feel good since he was depressed. |
| 10. | Deceived them about something that was going to happen in the future. | To make them worry. |
| 11. | I told her I thought this guy really liked her. | I didn't want to destroy her hopes. |
| 12. | I told her that her ex-boyfriend (my roommate) had not told me whether or not he still wanted to go out with her. (He does.) | I lied to protect my roommate – she can be a cold bitch, but I like her. |
| 13. | I told her I would call one of our friends because he was depressed. | To make myself feel better because I hadn't been keeping in touch. |
| 14. | I told her I hadn't been home and wasn't going home until Thanksgiving. | I had gone home last weekend and I didn't want her to know it because I didn't go and see her. If she found out she would get mad. |
| 15. | I told her I was not depressed and really I was. | I didn't want her to feel sorry for me. |
| 16. | She woke up late and I told her I didn't care if we were late to class. | So she wouldn't feel bad. |
| 17. | She told me about a personal problem and I said that I understood why she felt the way she did when actually I didn't agree with her feelings at all. | She was really upset so I wanted her to feel better by thinking someone understood. |
| 18. | I told her I love for her to stay with me and my family if she wanted to when I really wanted to be alone with them. | She was lonely and I didn't want her to have to stay in the dorm by herself. |
| 19. | I said I didn't know who my stranger date was and thought it didn't really matter when really it does matter to me. | I don't want to seem too worried about liking this guy since it's just one date. |
| 20. | Said this guy liked her when he really hates her guts. | To get back at her for setting me up with a pig. |

TABLE 9.3. *Lies about the valuing of relationships: Six examples*

| | Content of lie | Reason given for lying |
|---|---|---|
| 1. | Said I didn't know how I felt about him when I do. | I didn't want to hurt him. |
| 2. | Told her I would be back in a few weeks and that I'd stop by to see her and her mom. | I didn't want to hurt her feelings. |
| 3. | I said that some friends and I just recently started a project when it had been going on for weeks. | I thought he'd be hurt if he knew he'd been left out. |
| 4. | I sounded sorry she found another job, but I was actually glad. | Not to hurt her feelings. |
| 5. | Told him my roommate might go out with him when I knew she wouldn't. | I didn't want to hurt his feelings. |
| 6. | Pretended to like Doug when actually I thought he was a real geek! | Didn't want to hurt Kim's feelings. |

buoy another person's hopes or to refrain from angering someone are among the other examples.

### The Role of Hurt Feelings in Lying and Truth-Telling: Is It Mostly a Matter of Devalued Relationships?

Leary and his colleagues have proposed that at the heart of hurt feelings is "the sense that one's relationship is not sufficiently valued" (Leary, Springer, Negel, Ansell, & Evans, 1998, p. 1225). Relational devaluation, they explain, is "the perception that another individual does not regard his or her relationship with the person to be as important, close, or valuable as the person desires." Others have broadened or qualified the scope of the construct of hurt feelings, but because the Leary definition has been so influential, it is useful to start there and see how well it accounts for the experiences participants described in our studies of everyday lies.

When participants believed that they valued a relationship less than the other person did, they sometimes lied to spare the other person's feelings. Perhaps the prototypical version of this lie is the first example in Table 9.3. One person is interested in pursuing a relationship, but the other is not. Rather than expressing a lack of interest clearly and directly, the uninterested party lies. In the second example in Table 9.3, the liar promises a friend and her mom to come back to visit, with no actual intention of so doing. Again, the relationship is less important to the liar than it is to the liar's friend, and the liar hides that hurtful truth with a lie.

The third and fourth examples in Table 9.3 are also clear instances of lies told to shield another person from the painful awareness of being excluded or unwanted. In the third, the liar conceals from another person the fact that a group of friends has been working on a project without him for weeks. In the fourth, a liar who is glad to hear that her coworker has found another job claims instead to feel sorry.

Sometimes the liar is stuck in the role of the intermediary who knows that there is no way that Sally will go out with Harry, but tells Harry that she might. That was the case in the fifth example in Table 9.3. In still other instances, liars fake feelings not about the person they are deceiving but someone else who is important to that person. Mary, for instance, might tell Harry that she likes Sally (even though she actually loathes her) because she knows that Harry likes her. These are lies told in the pursuit of affective balance: If someone I like (Harry) cares about someone I dislike (Sally), then I will claim to like Sally. That way, I presume, Harry's feelings will not be hurt.

Another type of lie, though, was even more commonplace than the Table 9.3 lies that quite directly spared other people from learning that a particular relationship was not as prized by the other person as it was by them. Superficially, they are lies that do not appear to be about a relationship at all. As in the first two examples of Table 9.1, liars are hiding their opinion of something belonging to or created by the other person or something about that person's appearance, behavior, or skills. In the instances that seem relatively trivial, liars pretend to admire the other person's sweater, dress, earrings, hairstyle, ring, or Christmas ornament. Or they claim to like the other person's homemade bread, muffins, or meatballs. Liars claim to be enjoying parties, lunches, and ballets when in fact they are restless and bored. Other similar lies are about matters that may be a bit more significant. Liars offer the false reassurance that the other person seems to have lost weight, or looks just fine, or behaved reasonably and appropriately. They compliment the other person's field hockey skills or art work and act impressed by the person's enthusiastically described holiday plans.

All of the examples we just delineated, in which the relationship relevance is not immediately apparent, seem to fit under the category of shielding the other person from criticism. And in fact, in the Leary et al. (1998) research, participants said that they had their feelings hurt by criticism more than by any other event (such as being betrayed, rejected, ignored, unappreciated, or teased). Leary et al. (1998) suggest two ways in which criticism may convey a devalued relationship:

> First, criticism inherently indicates that the perpetrator holds some aspect of the victim in low regard. To the extent that the attribute being criticized is relevant to one's desirability as a friend, lover, employee, or acquaintance, the victim may infer that the perpetrator does not value the relationship as much as desired. [Also] the mere fact that the perpetrator has criticized them, often harshly, may suggest to the victim that the perpetrator does not value their relationship. (p. 1233)

Perhaps Leary and his colleagues are correct in suggesting that criticism of an aspect of another person is relationship relevant, at least indirectly. In another set of examples we found, though, the relationship relevance seems even less clear.

When people do better than others at a test or other performance, they sometimes understate their accomplishment. They claim that, in doing so, they are sparing the feelings of those who did not do as well. For example, one participant was studying in the library when a classmate asked how he had done on the exam. He lied and said "lousy." Here's the reason he cited: "Although I did well, I realized she had not; I wanted to prevent hurting her feelings." Liars give up something in telling these kind-hearted lies – their legitimate claim to a job well done.

Vangelisti and her colleagues (Vangelisti, Young, Carpenter-Theune, & Alexander, 2005) seemed to be describing a similar category of hurt feelings under the label "undermining of self-concept." Their participants said that their feelings were hurt when another person "made them doubt their competence or self-worth" (p. 449). Examples such as these, among others, were what led the researchers to suggest that the causes of hurt feelings needed to be expanded beyond just the devaluing of a relationship.

## TIPTOEING AROUND OTHER PEOPLE'S FEELINGS: HOW AND WHEN IS IT DONE?

In the diary studies of everyday lies, we relied on participants to tell us about their lies, the people to whom they told their lies, and their reasons for lying. By the participants' own accounts, they did indeed lie to avoid hurting other people's feelings. But our experimental hearts wanted to catch them in the act. We wanted to create the conditions that would cast participants in a clash between the desire to be honest and the wish to avoid hurting another person's feelings. The study we describe (DePaulo & Bell, 1996) is the only one we know of in which the motivation to avoid hurting another person's feelings was experimentally manipulated.

We started by collecting a set of paintings that were created by students in art classes. The paintings ranged widely in quality and style. We were hoping that the participants we recruited for our studies would have strong feelings about the paintings, really liking some and truly detesting others. Fortunately, they did.

When the participants first showed up for the study, the experimenter explained that the study was designed to help art students learn more about how art is perceived by people who are not experts. At that point, though, no art student was present.

The participants spent time in a room set up like a gallery. They chose their two favorite and two least favorite paintings in the collection and rated their degree of liking for each one. They also wrote, in their own words, what they liked and disliked about each of the paintings. They were assured, honestly, that the art student would never see what they had written about the paintings.

Theoretically, lies told to avoid hurt feelings should be about something personal. In the context of an art study, the artist who created the paintings might take another individual's opinions personally. Negative opinions, in particular, might hurt. The participants who disliked an artist's painting should be reluctant to say so to the artist. They should be sorely tempted to lie – especially because they knew that the art student would never see their descriptions of what they really did think of the paintings.

After the participants had committed their opinions of the paintings to writing, we introduced them to an art student. (The art student was actually a confederate. Three women alternated in that role.) Deeper into the study, the art student would point to one of the participant's least favorite paintings and say, "I painted this one myself. What do you think of it?"

This question should make the participant squirm both because the participant really disliked the painting and because it was the creation of the very person asking the question. If the painting were not the artist's own, then the participant should not be as tempted to lie. To test this, the artist also asked the participant about the other painting that the participant detested while making it clear that the painting was some other artist's work.

The artist also asked the participant about the participant's two most favorite paintings. Again, she claimed that one was a painting of her own and that the other was the work of some other artist. We expected very little lying in these conversations. Why hide your positive feelings about a painting, regardless of whether it is the creation of the artist in front of you or some other artist's work?

We could have left the study at that and looked for participants to lie most often when discussing paintings they disliked that were the work of the artist with whom they were conversing face to face. But we wanted even more evidence that participants were lying to avoid hurting the artist's feelings. So in one condition, the *polite* condition, we specifically instructed the participants not to hurt the artist's feelings. They were told that it was okay to admit to things they did not like about the paintings or to disagree with the artist, but that they should try to be nice about it. "This study is supposed to be a learning experience," they were told, "but we don't want any of [the artists] to end up feeling badly because of it." In the *no-instructions* condition, we gave participants no particular instructions.

Still, we were not quite finished. We thought that, in both the polite condition and in the no-instructions condition, participants would be tempted to lie about the artist's paintings that they disliked. So in a third condition, we turned up the pressure to tell the truth. In this *honest* condition, participants were urged to tell the artist "truthfully what you liked and what you disliked about each painting." They were reminded that, for the artists to learn what nonexperts really do think about art work, they would need to hear unbiased descriptions of the work.

Once the instructions were completed, the participant was introduced to the art student, who then proceeded to interview the participant about each of the four paintings – the participant's two favorite paintings (one of which was the art student's own work) and the participant's two least favorite paintings (again, one of which was the work of the art student). Each time, the art student began with a general question ("What do you think of this painting?") and then asked more specifically about what the participant liked and disliked.

### Rates of Clear Truth-Telling

We conducted this study to see whether people would tell outright lies to avoid hurting another person's feelings. We will get to the rates of lie-telling in the next section. First, though, as a comparison, we want to show how often our participants told the truth clearly and unambiguously.

What would a totally direct and honest answer sound like? In response to the artist's opening question – "What do you think of this painting?" – the participants could simply say "I like it" when they actually did like it and "I dislike it" when they did not. If only the truth mattered, it should make no difference whether the painting under discussion was the artist's own work or some other artist's creation. (In fact, the participants really did feel the same way about the paintings that were or were not the artist's own work. We learned that from their initial ratings of the paintings, before they knew anything about the artists.)

The top row of Table 9.4 shows what our data would have looked like had the participants told simple and direct truths in every condition. One hundred percent would say explicitly that they disliked the paintings that they really did dislike, and the same 100% would say explicitly that they liked the paintings that they really did like. No one (0%) would say that they liked the painting they disliked or that they disliked the painting they liked.

Let us look first at the condition in which it should have been easiest to tell the unvarnished truth – when the participants really did like the painting they were discussing. That is shown in the third column of the table. When participants were urged to be honest or when they were left to their own devices, they really did tell straightforward truths between 79% and 91% of the time. They liked these paintings, and that is exactly what they said. It did not much matter whether the paintings they liked were the artist's own work or some other artist's creation.

There was only one hint that participants may have been shying away from telling a simple truth when that truth should have been easy to tell. The

TABLE 9.4. *Percentage who were honest or dishonest in reporting whether they liked the paintings*

| True feelings: | Participant dislikes painting | | Participants likes painting | |
| --- | --- | --- | --- | --- |
| What they said: | "I like it" (dishonest) | "I don't like it" (honest) | "I like it" (honest) | "I don't like it" (dishonest) |
| Honest response (*hypothetical*) | 0 | 100 | 100 | 0 |
| Instructed to be honest | | | | |
| *Other artist's work* | 9 | 56 | 81 | 3 |
| *Artist's own work* | 3 | 62 | 91 | 0 |
| No instructions | | | | |
| *Other artist's work* | 0 | 64 | 83 | 0 |
| *Artist's own work* | 16 | 40 | 79 | 0 |
| Instructed to be polite | | | | |
| *Other artist's work* | 3 | 47 | 69 | 0 |
| *Artist's own work* | 16 | 22 | 81 | 0 |

participants instructed to be polite were the ones who showed a twinge of reluctance to say explicitly that they liked a painting they really did like. Their reluctance was evident when the painting they liked was the *other* artist's work: only 69% expressed unambiguous liking.

Now let us look at the more challenging condition, in which the participants actually detested the painting they were asked to discuss. (Those data are in the second column of Table 9.4.) Again, if they simply told the unvarnished truth, then 100% of them would have said that they disliked the paintings they truly did detest. A quick glance at that column shows that, regardless of the condition they were in, participants never even got close to telling high rates of simple truths when the truth was hard to tell.

The pressure to run from the truth was most intense for the participants who were discussing paintings they abhorred that were the art student's own work and who had been explicitly instructed to be polite and avoid hurting the artist's feelings. In that condition, only 22% of the participants straightforwardly told the artist that, in fact, they disliked her painting. When left to their own devices, 40% of the participants admitted that they disliked the artist's own work. But even in the condition in which the participants were urged to be honest, only 62% of them owned up to disliking the painting created by the artist sitting right in front of them.

When the paintings that the participants detested were the work of another artist, it was a bit easier for them to say explicitly that they disliked them. But even then, far fewer than 100% of them fessed up to their distaste. The participants who were instructed to be polite admitted to their disliking of the other artist's work only 47% of the time (compared to 22%, when the disliked painting was the artist's own work). In the no-instructions condition, the participants said they disliked the other artist's work 64% of the time (compared to 40% when it was the artist's own painting). Only in the condition in which participants were instructed to be honest did they own up to their disliking just as often when the painting was the artist's own as when it was the work of some other artist. Even then, the rates of explicit truth-telling were just 62% and 56% (not a significant difference).

Looking back at the middle two columns of Table 9.4, there is a pattern that is evident in every condition. Regardless of whether participants were told to be honest or polite or not given any particular instructions, and regardless of whether they were discussing the artist's own work or another artist's work, participants were always more willing to say explicitly that they liked a painting they really did like than to say that they disliked a painting they really did dislike.

Rates of Outright Lying

Bald-faced liars are those who would say "I liked it" when asked about a painting they despised. The relevant results are in the first column of Table 9.4. Clearly, the rate of outright lying was very low. The highest it ever got was in the challenging condition in which the disliked painting was the artist's own work. Then, 16% of the participants who were instructed to be polite and avoid hurting the artist's feelings and an identical 16% who were given no special instructions told an outright lie. They said explicitly and unambiguously that they liked the painting they disliked. Except when participants were instructed to be honest, the rates of telling outright lies about the disliked paintings were even lower when the paintings were the work of another artist. (In the honest condition, the difference was not significant.)

Unsurprisingly, the rates of telling perverse lies were nearly zero. That is, when the participants really did like the painting they were discussing, they almost never said that they disliked it.

## If They Are Not Lying and Not Telling the Truth, Then What Are They Doing?

### Stonewalling

When the participants were in the difficult situation of discussing a painting they disliked, they rarely told an outright lie and said that they liked it (first column of Table 9.4). But they did not often tell the unvarnished truth either (second column). So what were they doing? The unwillingness to offer any clear evaluation at all seemed to amount to *stonewalling*. When the going got tough, the participants simply stopped saying what they really did think – or at least they refrained from stating their opinions explicitly.

The participants were more likely to stonewall (refrain from saying explicitly that they disliked a painting or that they liked it) when they disliked the painting than when they liked it. They stonewalled most often when they were instructed to be polite and avoid hurting the artist's feelings and least often when they were instructed to be honest or were given no special instructions.

Stonewalling may have been a useful technique for participants who were trapped in a Catch-22 situation: they wanted to follow the instructions (be polite and avoid hurting the artist's feelings), and they wanted to be truthful. When they disliked the painting, these goals appear mutually exclusive; however, stonewalling may have provided participants with a way to avoid both rudeness and outright deception. Although there is always the danger that the artist may realize that stonewalling implies a lack of praise, at least participants can comfort themselves with the knowledge that they *tried* to avoid hurting the artist's feelings.

*Praising by Implication*
A close look at Table 9.4 reveals a very clever strategy that the participants seemed to use when trying not to hurt the artist's feelings. More so than the participants who were instructed to be honest or who got no particular instructions, the participants who were told to be polite were stingy in their compliments of the *other* artist's work, even when they liked that work. When they liked a painting, the polite participants were more likely to say so explicitly when the painting was the artist's own work. At the same time, when they disliked a painting, they were less likely to say so explicitly when the painting was the artist's own work than when it was created by another artist. The participants were conveying, by implication, a positive evaluation of the artist's own work. In comparison to how they discussed the other artist's work, the polite participants flattered the artist sitting right there with them. Yet they did so without telling an outright lie.

*Amassing Misleading Evidence*
We also looked in great detail at how participants responded when they were asked specifically what they liked and disliked about each painting. We compared every aspect they mentioned during the discussion with the artist to the aspects they wrote down on the forms before they met the artist. When pressed to say what they disliked about each of the paintings, participants on the average generated two more disliked aspects than they had originally written down. When pressed to say what they liked, they generated more than three additional liked aspects. They were not even-handed about this. They came up with more new aspects that they disliked when discussing the other artist's work and more new aspects that they liked when discussing the work of the artist in front of them. Participants in all three instructional conditions engaged in this strategy of amassing misleading evidence that flattered the artist's own work.

## DOES AFFECTION TILT THE SCALES TOWARD KIND-HEARTED LIES OR HURTFUL TRUTHS?

In the art study we just described, the participants were all strangers to the art student, and we did not nudge them one way or another with regard to their feelings of liking for her. In the next study (Bell & DePaulo, 1996), we deliberately tried to get half the participants to like the art student more than they may have on their own and the others to dislike her. We did so by leading half of the participants to believe that they agreed with the art student on most important issues and the other half to believe they disagreed with the art student on those issues. This attitude similarity technique has been a reliable way of influencing people's liking in past research, and it worked for us too. The other difference from the previous study was that, in this one, all of the participants were instructed to be polite and avoid hurting the art student's feelings.

Again, the most telling condition was the one in which the participants deeply disliked a painting that was created by the artist in front of them. To the usual clash between the desire to tell the truth (but then hurt the artist's feelings) and the desire to spare the artist's feelings (but then tell something other than the whole truth), we added the complication of the participant's liking for the artist. The key question was whether the participant's affection for the art student would tilt the scales toward truth-telling or toward lying when the truth was hard to tell.

As we had surmised, it was the truth, rather than kindness, that was sacrificed when the participants liked the art student. More so than when they disliked the art student, the participants stonewalled when asked directly what they thought of the painting they hated that the art student had created herself. Only 12% offered an explicit evaluation. In contrast, 23% were willing to say exactly what they thought of the wretched painting when they disliked the artist who created it, even though that artist was sitting right in front of them.

The sly game of evaluation by implication was also played out more clearly when the participants liked the art student than when they disliked her. Participants who liked the art student were significantly more likely to tell her exactly what they thought of the *other* artist's work (compared to her own work) when they disliked it (35% compared to 12%). When participants said explicitly that they disliked another artist's work and they did *not* express their dislike directly when talking about the work of the artist in front of them, they offered the artist an opportunity to draw an inaccurate but flattering inference. The artist just might have thought that the participants disliked the other artist's work more than they disliked her own. And, who knows – the artist might have even assumed that the participants didn't dislike her own work at all.

In contrast, when the participants disliked the art student, there was little difference in their willingness to spell out their disliking for the paintings, regardless of whether the loathed art work was created by the disliked artist (23%) or some other artist (27%).

As in the first study, participants amassed misleading evidence regardless of whether they liked or disliked the art student. In both conditions, they generated more new aspects of the paintings that they liked than disliked. But again, they tended to tilt the new evidence in an even more positive direction when the artist was someone they liked.

It was not surprising that the participants were kinder to the artist they liked than to the artist they disliked. What is noteworthy is that they achieved that extra increment in kindness at the expense of the truth. The flipside is that the disliked artists received more honest appraisals of their work.

### ARE SERIOUS LIES ABOUT HURT FEELINGS TOO?

In the diary studies of everyday lies, most of the lies that the participants described were little lies. On average, the participants described their lies as not very serious. They also said that they did not bother to plan most of their lies, and they did not worry much about the possibility of getting caught. They did feel a slight twinge of discomfort while they were telling their lies, and just afterward, but even these discomfort ratings were below the midpoint of the scale.

The people who recorded their everyday lies were undoubtedly concerned, in some instances, with the feelings of the persons to whom they told their lies. But the lies they described were not typically of the gut-wrenching variety. The same goes for the lies told in the art studies – surely, the situation we created was disconcerting, but it was not terribly consequential.

Do hurt feelings have a place in the most serious lies in people's lives, or are they confined to the lighter domain of little lies? To find out, we conducted another pair of studies to examine serious lies more directly (DePaulo, Ansfield, Kirkendol, & Boden, 2004).

As in the everyday lies studies, we recruited two samples of participants – one group of college students and another sample of people drawn from the community. Half of the lies described were the most serious lie the participant had ever told anyone. In these studies, though, we also included the target's perspective. The other half of the descriptions were of the most serious lie ever told to the participant.

As in the diary studies, we coded the content of the lies that participants told or were told. In contrast to the diary studies of lying in everyday life, in which lies about feelings were the most commonplace, in the serious lies studies, more lies were about affairs than about anything else (23% for the college students and 22% for the community members). Next in line were lies about misdeeds, such as stealing money or crashing the car (20% for the college students and 23% for the community members).

Lies about feelings were coded together with lies about personal facts. An example of a lie about feelings is a wedding vow that was made by a woman who did not really love the man she was marrying. An example of a lie about a personal fact was told by a woman who concealed from a friend that she had just had a miscarriage. Together, lies about personal facts and feelings accounted for 21% of the lies told by the college students and 16% of the lies told by the community members. Among the college students, no category of serious lies contents (other than affairs and misdeeds) was more common. Among the community sample, there was one more frequent category – lies about money and jobs accounted for 21% of the lies.

Based on the transcripts of the participants' descriptions of their serious lies, we also coded the motives for the lies. The two most basic categories were the same as in the everyday lies studies – self-centered lies and other-oriented lies. The other-oriented lies were told to protect the target or another person from harm or from distressing information. Usually, the upsetting information was about the serious illness or impending death of a loved one. College students were more likely than the community members to say that the most serious lie ever told to them was told to protect them from distressing news. Typically, it was their parents who told the protective lies.

The protective lies were told to shield the targets from distress. Still, they do not fit our usual understanding of lies told to spare another person's feelings. The people who told those lies (often parents) surely were not devaluing their relationship with their children. In fact, it was probably the intensity of their concern for their children that made it so difficult to tell them news that would be so distressing. Yet, from reading the targets's accounts of these lies, we think that their feelings often were hurt – not by the information that was withheld but by the fact that the bad news was kept from them. Participants seemed hurt that their parents regarded them as too emotionally vulnerable to hear the news at the same time as the adults. We did not design the study to test this interpretation directly though, so it remains speculative.

We separated the self-centered lies into those told for reasons of personal advantage (such as avoiding punishment or attaining ill-deserved material rewards) and those told for psychological reasons. Only a few serious lies (4%) were told for the expressed purpose of hurting the target person (rather than sparing that person from hurt). Some of the serious lies were told to protect the liars psychologically. Typically, though, the liars were ducking confrontation, embarrassment, or relationship conflict rather than trying to protect themselves from getting their feelings hurt. Some of these self-protective lies involved promises that were never kept. The liar is asked for a favor – sometimes a big one, such as to lend money for a mortgage – and cannot seem to decline in person. The promise becomes a lie (or is seen as such by the target) when the commitment is never honored. The final category of psychological reasons for telling serious lies involved lies told for reasons of identity management or self-presentation. For example, one woman told a man she was dating that she had some of her writings published in a prestigious magazine.

Because the serious lies studies included targets as well as tellers of serious lies, we were able to ask the targets directly the extent to which they felt hurt by the lies they were told. Targets' reports of acting hurt upon discovering the lie were correlated with their reports of crying and of feeling depressed and tense. Feeling angry and acting defiantly were correlated with each other and comprised a set of reactions that were distinct from the cluster that included hurt feelings. The hurt feelings reaction was also separate from three other reactions: acting relieved, acting forgiving, and feigning indifference.

The college students reported feeling most wounded by the lies that were told to protect them from distressing information. They felt the least hurt by lies told by people who were trying to impress them. Although the college students were pained by the lies that were told to protect them from emotional distress, the parents (and others) who told such lies seemed unaware of their impact. Not one of the participants describing the most serious lie they told to someone else mentioned a lie they told to protect a son or daughter from news of a death or serious illness.

### TAKING STOCK

Scholars have pointed out that people value openness and honesty in their close personal relationships and feel hurt when their partners do not honor these implicit relationship rules (e.g., Feeney, 2005). If the desire to be truthful never conflicted with other relationship expectations, such as kindness and loyalty, then the matter of honesty in relationships would be less complicated than it actually is. When one person has acted in a way that is not totally honorable (as all humans do now and then), an honest acknowledgment of that bad behavior – especially to a partner who expects so much more – can hurt. The temptation, then, is to lie (Millar & Tesser, 1988).

Sometimes people in relationships lie when they have done nothing wrong at all. They simply do not like something about the other person (maybe something as trivial as what the person is wearing) or do not agree with the person's judgment (about matters weighty or slight). Again, saying so can hurt, and so lying can seem preferable. At times, even exemplary behavior creates a risk of hurting the other person, as, for example, when one person in a relationship does particularly well at a task and the other does poorly. Once again, the dilemma can be resolved in favor of deceit, as when superior performers hide and deny their successes.

### Who Tilts the Scales toward Deceit and for Whom Are the Scales Tilted?

Based on our own research and on other reports in the literature, we believe that there are sex differences at the intersection of lying and hurt feelings, but the exact nature and account of those differences remain to be seen. Lippard (1988) reported that the women in her study were more likely than the men to say that they lied to protect another person's feelings. In our art studies, the women (more so than the men) conveyed even more liking for the paintings that were the art student's own work than for the other artist's work. (But because all of the artists were women, those results cannot be interpreted unambiguously.) In our everyday lies studies, we found that there was something special about the lying that took place between women. When women were interacting with other women, the rate at which they told kind-hearted lies was similar to the rate at which they told self-centered lies. In every other type of dyad (men with men, or women with men), self-centered lies clearly outnumbered other-oriented ones. In a study of lying in initial getting-acquainted conversations, Tyler and Feldman (2004) found that men and women lied equally when they did not expect to meet again, but that women lied more when they thought that they would interact with their partner again in the future.

Under some circumstances then, women may be more likely than men to tilt the scales toward deceit when hurt feelings are at stake. As for the people who seem especially likely to elicit kind lies, rather than hurtful truths, from other people, relationship closeness is important.

In our studies of the little lies of everyday life, we found that for best friends and friends, more so than for acquaintances and strangers, the desire to be kind trumped the motivation to be honest. People told more kind-hearted lies (relative to self-centered ones) to their best friends and other friends. In fact, they showed the same inclination with all of the people to whom they felt emotionally close. Lippard (1988) and Metts (1989) have reported similar findings.

In one of our art studies, we found that even when two people start out as total strangers, and one comes to like the other simply by virtue of learning that the two are in agreement on a variety of issues far more often than they are in disagreement, there is a shifting of the sands in the tug-of-war between truthfulness and kindness. Again, it is kindness that tends to win.

Compared to people who do not feel particularly close to each other, people in close relationships are not only more likely to lie to protect their partner's feelings but they are also less likely to notice certain forms of dishonesty in their partners. We have found that when one friend attempts to conceal negative emotions, the other friend is less likely to detect those emotions when the friendship is a particularly close one than when it is less close (Sternglanz & DePaulo, 2004). It appears that we often do not see the nonverbal cues that people do not want us to see if doing so could potentially damage a relationship (DePaulo, Wetzel, Sternglanz, & Walker Wilson, 2003).

## But Why?

In our studies of everyday lies, we asked our participants to rate the extent to which they were protecting themselves with their lies (i.e., they would have felt worse if they had told the truth) and the extent to which they were protecting the target of their lies (the target would have felt worse if the liar had instead told the truth). Participants generally said that they were protecting the other person with their lies more than they were protecting themselves. But telling lies, even for a supposedly good reason, is problematic, perhaps especially in close relationships.

Deception in relationships is contested territory. Hints of conflict emerge from people's claims about the motives for the lies. When Kaplar and Gordon (2004) asked participants to write two autobiographical narratives each, one from a time when they deceived a romantic partner and the other from a time when they were deceived by a romantic partner, the reasons they proffered for the lies were not the same. As liars, they claimed that they told their lies to avoid hurting and upsetting their partner. But as targets, they were more inclined to claim that their partner had deliberately hurt them with their lie and that the lie was not justified. Their results echoed our own findings from our study of serious lies that were not restricted to the domain of close relationships.

Claims that people lie to protect others rather than themselves are likely to elicit a predictable response among skeptical listeners – "sure, keep telling yourself that." It seems unlikely that liars have only the other person's interests at heart, even in the most defensible situations. Telling a painful truth is not just difficult for the person who hears it but also for the person who tells it and who then needs to deal with the reaction it creates in the target and the consequences that ensue. As Hrubes, Feldman, and Tyler (2004) have explained, regulation of the liar's own emotions is at the heart of the motivation for many lies.

It has become part of the conventional wisdom of our time that the cover-up is worse than the lie. The implication is that bad behaviors, if owned up to, are never as bad for a relationship as the lies told to conceal them. There is not much rigorous research on this matter, but the results of the one relevant study we know of do not bode well for our received wisdom. McCornack and Levine (1990) asked people to describe a recent instance in which a relationship partner had lied to them. They also asked the participants to rate the importance of the matter that was concealed and the importance of the lie itself. Then they looked at whether the relationship was still intact a month later. Whether the relationship survived depended more on the importance of the information that was hidden than on the importance to the target of the lie. When liars claim that they lied because they assumed the other person would be upset by the truth, sometimes their assumption was exactly right.

### The Lure of Lying to Avoid Hurtfulness – And the Costs

In the course of everyday life, when anger and vengeance are not at the fore, people are remarkably reluctant to give voice to their negative feelings and opinions or even to mention distressing news that they had no role in creating. A well-developed literature on the MUM effect (Tesser & Rosen, 1975) has shown that people are reluctant to convey bad news and prefer to pass it along to a third party than to tell it to the person to whom it applies and who is most in need of knowing it. Even in situations in which conveying critical feedback is in the job description and that critical feedback could be useful to the persons receiving it, people are still reluctant to pass along the negative evaluation. Supervisors, for example, do not like telling their employees that their work needs improvement and often put off doing so (Larson, 1989).

The favoring of kindness over truthfulness has its costs. People like to have others care about their feelings and say just what they want to hear. But sometimes they also value the person who will tell it like it is. Pontari and Schlenker (2006) illustrated this with their studies of intermediaries, who were caught between a friend who wanted to make a good impression on a potential suitor and the suitor whose preferences were not in line with the friend's actual characteristics. Sometimes the intermediary lied about the friend, making that person seem more compatible with the potential suitor. Those intermediaries were well liked. Other times, the intermediary was more honest. Those intermediaries were respected.

### Another Answer to the Choice between Kind Lies and Hurtful Truths: Neither

We started our exploration of the intersection of lying and hurt feelings by asking the question whether the truth or kindness would prevail when the two were at odds. That framing, we discovered, was too simplistic. As Bavelas and her colleagues pointed out (Bavelas, Black, Chovil, & Mullett, 1990), there is at least one other alternative. When caught between a hurtful truth and a kind lie, people prefer to choose neither. Instead, they equivocate. They try not to answer directly the question that was asked, they try to avoid stating their own opinion, and they deliberately make their statements unclear. In our art studies, we also found some strategies for dealing with the dilemma that did not involve outright lies. Our participants who did not want to say that they hated the painting they despised, but also did not want to say they liked it, amassed misleading evidence instead. They also stonewalled and implied a positive appraisal that they did not really feel.

A similar situation arises in the context of dating. How do people respond when asked on a date by someone they have no interest in dating? Here, again, the conflict between honesty and kindness rears its head. In this potentially hurtful situation, Folkes (1982) found that people tend to avoid providing truthful explanations to potential suitors, particularly if the real reason for rejection is based on stable physical or personality characteristics of the person about to be rejected. Instead, people cushion the blow by telling vulnerable suitors that they must decline the offer because of reasons that are impersonal ("it's not about you"), uncontrollable ("the circumstances make it impossible"), and unstable ("things could change in the future"). Similar to the tactic of amassing misleading evidence about paintings, these types of explanations are much less hurtful than a brutally honest rejection, and they imply a more positive appraisal of the person than is actually felt.

## The Bottom Line

Although lying is often considered a form of betrayal, it is frequently chosen as the lesser of two evils when the other option is hurting another person's feelings. Even parents and teachers who attempt to instill the value of honesty in children may urge children to commit lies of omission rather than hurt another person's feelings. Often the advice is stated in this familiar way: "If you don't have anything nice to say, don't say anything at all."

Honesty may well be an important foundation for any close relationship. Still, the research we have examined suggests that a certain degree of dishonesty in the service of sparing hurt feelings may have its place in close relationships. After all, even with those we care about the most, there may be times when we just don't have anything nice to say.

### REFERENCES

Bavelas, J. B., Black, A., Chovil, N., & Mullett, J. (1990). *Equivocal communication.* Newbury Park, CA: Sage.

Bell, K. L., & DePaulo, B. M. (1996). Liking and lying. *Basic and Applied Social Psychology, 18*, 243–266.

Camden, C., Motley, M. T., & Wilson, A. (1984). White lies in interpersonal communication: A taxonomy and preliminary investigation of social motivations. *Western Journal of Speech Communication, 48*, 309–325.

DePaulo, B. M., Ansfield, M. E., Kirkendol, S. E., & Boden, J. M. (2004). Serious lies. *Basic and Applied Social Psychology, 26*, 147–167.

DePaulo, B. M., & Bell, K. L. (1996). Truth and investment: Lies are told to those who care. *Journal of Personality and Social Psychology, 71*, 703–716.

DePaulo, B. M., & Kashy, D. A. (1998). Everyday lies in close and casual relationships. *Journal of Personality and Social Psychology, 74,* 63–79.

DePaulo, B. M., Kashy, D. A., Kirkendol, S. E., Wyer, M. M., & Epstein, J. A. (1996). Lying in everyday life. *Journal of Personality and Social Psychology, 70,* 979–995.

DePaulo, B. M., Wetzel, C., Sternglanz, R. W., & Walker Wilson, M. J. (2003). Verbal and nonverbal dynamics of privacy, secrecy, and deceit. *Journal of Social Issues, 59,* 391–410.

Feeney, J. A. (2005). Hurt feelings in couple relationships: Exploring the role of attachment and perceptions of personal injury. *Personal Relationships, 12,* 253–271.

Folkes, V. S. (1982). Communicating the causes of social rejection. *Journal of Experimental Social Psychology, 18,* 235–252.

Hample, D. (1980). Purposes and effects of lying. *Southern Speech Communication Journal, 46,* 33–47.

Hrubes, D., Feldman, R. S., & Tyler, J. M. (2004). Emotion-focused deception: The role of deception in the regulation of emotion. In P. Philippot & R. S. Feldman (Eds.), *The regulation of emotion* (pp. 227–249). Mahwah, NJ: Erlbaum.

Kaplar, M. E., & Gordon, A. K. (2004). The enigma of altruistic lying: Perspective differences in what motivates and justifies lie telling within romantic relationships. *Personal Relationships, 11,* 489–507.

Kashy, D. A., & DePaulo, B. M. (1996). Who lies? *Journal of Personality and Social Psychology, 70,* 1037–1051.

Larson, J. R., Jr. (1989). The dynamic interplay between employees' feedback-seeking strategies and supervisors' delivery of performance feedback. *Academy of Management Review, 14,* 408–422.

Leary, M. R., Springer, C., Negel, L., Ansell, E., & Evans, K. (1998). The causes, phenomenology, and consequences of hurt feelings. *Journal of Personality and Social Psychology, 74,* 1225–1237.

Lippard, P. V. (1988). "Ask me no questions, I'll tell you no lies": Situational exigencies for interpersonal deception. *Western Journal of Speech Communication, 52,* 91–103.

McCornack, S. A., & Levine, T. R. (1990). When lies are uncovered: Emotional and relational outcomes of discovered deception. *Communication Monographs, 57,* 119–138.

Metts, S. (1989). An exploratory investigation of deception in close relationships. *Journal of Social and Personal Relationships, 6,* 159–179.

Millar, K. U., & Tesser, A. (1988). Deceptive behavior in social relationships: A consequence of violated expectations. *Journal of Psychology, 122,* 263–273.

Pontari, B. A., & Schlenker, B. R. (2006). Helping friends manage impressions: We like helpful liars but respect nonhelpful truth tellers. *Basic and Applied Social Psychology, 28,* 177–183.

Sternglanz, R. W., & DePaulo, B. M. (2004). Reading nonverbal cues to emotions: The advantages and liabilities of relationship closeness. *Journal of Nonverbal Behavior, 28,* 245–266.

Tesser, A., & Rosen, S. (1975). The reluctance to transmit bad news. In L. Berkowitz (Ed.), *Advances in experimental social psychology* (Vol. 8, pp. 193–232). New York: Academic Press.

Turner, R. E., Edgley, C., & Olmstead, G. (1975). Informational control in conversations: Honesty is not always the best policy. *Kansas Journal of Sociology, 11,* 69–89.

Tyler, J. M., & Feldman, R. S. (2004). Truth, lies, and self-presentation: How gender and anticipated future interaction relate to deceptive behavior. *Journal of Applied Social Psychology, 34,* 2602–2615.

Vangelisti, A. L., Young, S. L., Carpenter-Theune, K. E., & Alexander, A. L. (2005). Why does it hurt?: The perceived causes of hurt feelings. *Communication Research, 32,* 443–477.

# 10

# Affairs and Infidelity

GRAHAM ALLAN AND KAEREN HARRISON

INTRODUCTION

This chapter is concerned with people's emotional responses to extradyadic relationships and in particular the hurt that is experienced when they occur. Given the enormous interest in popular culture about such relationships and the potential impact they have on family dynamics, including of course separation and divorce, surprisingly little research has been concerned directly with understanding the patterning and consequences of different forms of extrapartnership involvement. Some related topics have been researched more than others. For example, the incidence of extramarital sex has been examined in a number of studies (Haavio-Mannila & Kontula, 2003; Laumann, Gagnon, Michael, & Michaels, 1994; Treas & Giesen, 2000; Wellings, Fields, Johnson, & Wadsworth, 1994; Wiederman, 1997), as have feelings of jealousy in response to the discovery of a partner's infidelity (e.g., Buss, Larsen, Westen, & Semmelroth, 1992; Buunk & Dijkstra, 2006; Harris, 2003). But there has been limited research explicitly examining the social or psychological impact of extrapartnership involvement, particularly outside clinical settings (Olson, Russell, Higgins-Kessler, & Miller, 2002). Perhaps this is not surprising given the secret as well as sensitive nature of the topic, but as a consequence extensive or detailed information about people's actual experiences of extrapartnership involvement, including the hurt they experience, is not readily available.

The overall aim of this chapter is to raise questions about the nature of the hurt experienced during and after an affair. After briefly reflecting on the different elements that the concept of "hurt" entails, the chapter discusses some of the forms of hurt that being in an extradyadic relationship can generate. Most importantly it examines the different responses to the discovery of an affair. Although recognizing the complexity of these responses, it focuses particularly on three frequently interrelated themes: jealousy, betrayal, and loss. Before concluding with suggestions about key areas for future research, the chapter addresses the question of how recent changes in patterns of partnership formation and dissolution are likely to influence people's understandings of extradyadic sexual involvement.

Before proceeding to consider the notion of "hurt" more systematically, two other matters need to be raised. The first concerns the issue of terminology and language (Allen et al., 2005). The different terms used to describe extrapartnership sexual involvement are indicative of the changing understandings of these matters within Western culture. For many, terms like *adultery* and *infidelity* now seem both old-fashioned and overly moralistic. They were suitable for an era in which a traditional form of marriage was the key institution of partnership. They seem far less apposite now in an era when there is greater diversity and flexibility in the "rules" governing different partnerships. For some, even the term *affair* carries connotations linked too heavily to a form of marital commitment that is no longer appropriate to many partnerships. Within some of the research literature, the terms *extradyadic relationship* and *extradyadic sex* have come to be used as more value-free concepts, though clearly these terms do not have much cultural resonance.

Second, there is the question of what now constitutes "cheating," "infidelity," or an "affair." Under traditional "marital blueprints" (Cancian, 1987), infidelity was clearly premised on marriage and signified a breaking of the marital contract. Now with changes in the patterning of partnership, these issues are somewhat less straightforward. Being unfaithful (or whatever term is favored) implies a relational commitment, but that commitment is no longer synonymous with marriage. For example, couples cohabiting together can also be unfaithful, though whether they regard each other's extradyadic involvements as infidelity in part depends on the understandings they have mutually negotiated with each other. In addition to the circumstances of the couple, responses to extradyadic involvement are also likely to depend on the characteristics of the "infidelity." In general, the deinstitutionalization of marriage (Cherlin, 2004) and the concomitant individualization of partnerships mean that reactions to intimate/sexual involvement with others are likely to be more varied than they were in an era when marriage was more firmly embedded, both morally and structurally.

## HURT AND "INFIDELITY"

The idea of "hurt" has been discussed fully in different chapters in this book (see particularly the chapters in Part II). Although in comparison to other emotions, the idea of hurt has received relatively little scholarly attention, previous research has identified several processes that can generate feelings of hurt (e.g., Leary, Springer, Negel, Ansell, & Evans, 1998; Vangelisti, 1994). In Chapter 15 in the present volume, Feeney posits five forms of behavior that are liable to generate such feelings within romantic/sexual partnerships:

1. Active disassociation — behaviors that indicate disinterest in the partner, including denial of love and commitment

2. Passive disassociation — being ignored or excluded from activities, conversations, and disclosures
3. Criticism — negative comments about behavior, appearance, or personality
4. Infidelity — extrarelationship sexual involvement
5. Deception — misleading acts, lying, and breaking promises

The fourth of these, infidelity, is the central issue of this chapter, though it is also evident that extradyadic involvement can encompass the other categories, especially active disassociation, deception, and criticism. This complex of hurtful behaviors makes infidelity an intriguing topic for examining the character of hurt feelings.

Leary (2001) argued that the defining feature of hurtful events is perceived relational devaluation. In a similar vein, Vangelisti (2001) saw relational transgression as the central component of hurt feelings. Certainly the idea of relational transgression is core to any understanding of the hurt generated by involvement in extradyadic relationships. Feeney (2005 and Chapter 15, this volume) adds to this conception by noting that relational transgressions that evoke a sense of personal injury, as infidelity so frequently does, are particularly liable to generate feelings of hurt. As she writes (this volume, p. 316), "Hurt is associated with events that damage the victim's view of the self as worthy of love, or core beliefs about the availability and trustworthiness of others or both." Despite the evident connection between infidelity and these emotional reactions, little research has specifically examined the patterning of hurt consequent on extradyadic involvement.

Accordingly, in this chapter we are taking a broad perspective on "hurt." Its focus is on the range of painful emotional responses that direct or indirect involvement in extrapartnership intimate and sexual interactions generates. Rather than conceptualizing "hurt" as a specific emotional response (Leary & Springer, 2001), we are concerned with overlapping constructions of painful feelings (Feeney, 2005), some being well defined but others less clear-cut. Thus, although aspects of jealousy, betrayal, trust, emptiness, anger, abandonment, and the like could all in theory be distinguished, for our purposes a generic idea of "hurt" portrays well these different negative outcomes that may result from extrapartnership involvement. Of course, not all the negative emotional responses that can be subsumed under the term *hurt* necessarily arise in any particular instance, but nonetheless this broad conceptualization provides a useful framework for the discussion that follows.

There is one rider to add here. Intimate relationships by their nature are generally not "emotion-free." That is, although sexual interactions may at times be quite casual, relationships sustained for any period of time usually do entail a degree of emotional commitment. Consequently, they also have the potential to involve elements of hurt, particularly when they are in the process of ending. People can, for example, feel resentful or angry at the way they are or have been treated, upset, and mournful that the relationship is over and jealous of any new relationship that the ex-partner later forms. Consequently, in looking at hurt caused through extrapartnership involvement, it is important to separate out elements that are rooted in the circumstances of intimate and sexual relationships per se from those that stem from the fact of an extrapartnership liaison. Similarly, the hurt of extrapartnership involvement needs to be kept distinct from the pain consequent on any separation or divorce that may follow. Often in particular instances these elements are difficult to separate, but in what follows the focus is on the extrapartnership dimension.

## INVOLVEMENT IN AN "AFFAIR"

In this section we turn briefly to consider the experiences of those who have been directly involved in an extradyadic relationship, particularly in a sustained relationship, which is more likely to entail strong emotional feelings than an episodic sexual encounter. In addition to issues involved in any intimate relationship, a portion of the additional emotional strain experienced in significant, longer term affairs stems from their being clandestine. Only a proportion of infidelities and affairs ever become known to the established partner. Clearly the more short term the extrapartnership involvement and the less emotional attachment it entails, the more likely it is to remain hidden and the less likely it is to cause evident hurt for any of those involved.

At the early stages of the relationship, the "forbidden" character of the involvement may add an exciting *frisson* to the experience (Reibstein & Richards, 1992). However over time, feelings of anxiety and resentment are likely to come more to the fore as a consequence of having to be on guard against discovery. The need for secrecy, difficulties of arranging meetings, uncertainties about the timing of them, and limitations to spontaneity are liable to produce tensions in the relationship that would otherwise not be there. Although these tensions might be accepted as the cost of being involved in an extrapartnership liaison, at the same time they run somewhat counter to conventional conceptions of how romantic relationships are normally celebrated.

Many of those involved in sustained extrapartnership relationships experience feelings of guilt about their actions although these feelings are not always associated directly with ideas of "hurt" (Allan & Harrison, 2004; Allen et al., 2005; Lawson, 1988). Sometimes this guilt leads to a confession that brings the extrapartnership relationship into the open and changes its character. Other times, individuals devise ways of coping with these feelings, sometimes by framing their actions in ways that minimize any sense of betrayal they generate. This framing may involve emphasizing the lack of passion, love, or satisfaction in their regular partnership or taking the view that their partner is not being hurt so long as the affair remains secret. Further feelings of guilt may be experienced when the extrapartner relationship involves people who are known to each other as part of the same social group. In particular, the dynamics of affairs become particularly complex when the affair is between an individual and a friend of the spouse/partner. Here there is in effect a double betrayal as well as a greater need for monitoring and vigilance if the affair is to be kept clandestine.

As noted earlier, the ending of a significant extrapartnership relationship carries with it many of the problems associated with the ending of any emotionally close sexual attachment. However, it can also entail additional difficulties especially if the ending is undesired. In particular, if the relationship is discovered and becomes public, the person having the relationship is likely to have to deal with a wide range of emotional distresses – their own as well as those of the other people involved – and potentially conflicting pressures for action. In many cases he or she may be required to come to a decision as to which of the relationships to continue. For some, this decision may be a relief from the pressures of having a secret affair; for others, though, either decision will represent a significant loss, the costs of which may be borne over a lengthy period. As Amato and Previti (2003) among others indicate, a partner's knowledge of an affair is a prime ground for divorce. Moreover, the hurt felt by the uninvolved partner will often cause the person having the affair to experience a heightened sense of guilt and recrimination, as indeed may the hurt feelings of the other party to the affair.

Some of those involved in an affair will accept the "loyalty" of the other person in the relationship to their original partner – and may have a similar "loyalty" to their own long-term partner (Allan, 2004; Richardson, 1988). Others will feel more resentful and hurt at the ending of the relationship yet have few ways of challenging or channeling their distress. One important issue is the extent to which any grief or upset at the end of the relationship can be expressed socially. For some, the illicit and clandestine character of the relationship will mean that few others will be able to offer support. Being unable to express the hurt experienced to others or even talk through and reevaluate the events leading to the ending of the affair may make "closure" more difficult. This issue of social nonrecognition can be experienced particularly strongly in instances where the relationship ends through death. As Richardson (1985) notes, the bereaved lover in an affair is often unable to participate in the funeral or grieve publicly.

### RESPONSES TO DISCOVERY

The most obvious and extensive hurt arising from extrapartnership liaisons occurs when the liaison becomes known to the other partner. However, people's responses to a partner's unfaithfulness are not uniform; a wide range of factors will influence them. Although at an individual level any act of infidelity can cause hurt, it is likely that the nature of the involvement of the extradyadic pair will be of consequence. Thus, it is generally easier to accept a one-time encounter presented as an unfortunate and regrettable aberration than a continuing relationship based on emotional attraction. Similarly, a relationship that is now ended will be easier to reconcile than one that is known to be continuing. Moreover, as Vangelisti and Gerstenberger (2004) emphasize, the response of the partner who has been unfaithful is also likely to influence the reaction to the affair. Expressions of culpability and regret by the "guilty" partner for what has happened, especially if it is not part of a familiar cycle of infidelity within the relationship, are likely to generate different responses from those where no sense of remorse or guilt is expressed or where it seems evident an emotional attachment continues even if the relationship is "over" and sexual involvement has ceased.

Responses to infidelity will also be influenced by cultural understandings of partnership, marriage, and sexuality. In some cultural settings, exclusivity in marriage may play a less significant part than it does in others (Haavio-Mannila & Kontula, 2003). In particular, as part of normatively accepted sexual double standards in those societies, men's extramarital involvements may be seen as less damaging to marital commitment, especially where patriarchal control of economic and material resources is deeply embedded. Similarly among certain social groups, marriage may be more a mechanism for alliance and continuity of the lineage than for personal or romantic fulfillment. This would, for instance, appear to have been the case in aristocratic circles in Britain in the 19th and early 20th centuries. Some sexually libertarian groups may espouse an explicit ideology of open sexual relationships, as for example with the Bloomsbury set in Britain in the 1920s and Californian (and other) "swingers" in the 1960s and 1970s. In these and other such cases, emotional and social responses to a partner's sexual involvement with others are clearly going to be different than when sexual exclusivity is taken as the cornerstone of a successful partnership.

The form of emotional hurt that has received most attention in the research literature as a result of infidelity becoming "known" is jealousy. As White (1981, p. 24) indicates, jealousy itself comprises "a complex of thoughts, feelings and actions" that can be expressed in a wide variety of ways (cited in Vangelisti & Gerstenberger, 2004, p. 69; see also Guerrero, Spitzberg, & Yoshimura, 2004). But numerous other forms of hurt have also been reported in the literature, including betrayal, rejection, worthlessness, shame, and a sense of loss about self, relationship, and identity. Of course, such feelings are not experienced uniformly. Much depends on the history of the partnership, as well as on the dynamics of the infidelity and its aftermath.

## Jealousy

Buunk and Dijkstra (2006) provide a good summary of research into jealousy as a response to extrapartnership sexual involvement. As they point out, although there are indications that young women in Western societies are now beginning to behave more like men (Laumann et al., 1994; Wiederman, 1997), a double standard has applied around extrapartnership sexual activity in most societies, with men being far more open to engaging in such activity than women. Whatever its roots, the existence of such a double standard as part of normative understandings of masculinity and femininity are likely to have an impact on emotional responses to the discovery of a partner's infidelity. Given this, it is not surprising that gender differences in jealousy on the discovery of an affair have regularly been reported in the literature, though often this research has relied on the measurement of hypothetical, experimental responses among young populations rather than on people's actual responses to known extrapartnership involvement (e.g., Becker, Sagarin, Guadagno, Millevoi, & Nicastle, 2004; Buss et al., 1992; Cramer, Abraham, Johnson, & Manning-Ryan, 2001; Harris, 2003).

Women are often thought to be more jealous than men, though this may be because they are more liable to discuss their feelings openly. But equally they are given more cause to be jealous by their partners. In this, the operation of the double standard – its institutional incorporation into routine social relations and personal identities, based at least in part on men's greater control of economic and material resources – could be argued to result in jealousy being constructed differently for men and women. As Buunk and Dijkstra (2004) write,

> Men, more than women, seem to have a tendency to reduce the chances of their partner's infidelity by being possessive, by spending as much time with their partner as possible, by exhibiting controlling forms of jealousy, and by threatening their partner with undesirable consequences, such as desertion and violence if she were to be unfaithful, even when this would constitute only a single sexual act. (p. 108)

Thus, even if women appear to be more jealous than men, the consequence of men's jealousy with regard to partner unfaithfulness can be the more severe. Of relevance here are not only the punishments metered out by some religious groupings for wives' adultery, such as executions by stoning in some parts of the rural Muslim world, but also the acts of "patriarchal terrorism" (Johnson, 1995), including murder, that sometimes follow suspicion of unfaithfulness by jealous male partners (Harris, 2003). Clearly in these instances, the hurt involved in actual or suspected infidelity is more than just emotional.

Various researchers have also pointed out that there are differences in the degree to which different aspects of infidelity make men and women jealous (Becker et al., 2004; Buss et al., 1992). The prime argument has been that men's jealousy is aroused most by their partner's *sexual* involvement with another person, whereas women are more likely to experience strong feelings of jealousy when their partner is being *emotionally* unfaithful. That is, for men it is the act of sex itself that generates jealousy. Although sexual involvement may lead to jealousy in women too, they feel most threatened when their partners are involved with someone else at an emotionally intimate and not just a sexual level. Different explanations can be offered to account for this finding. Evolutionary psychologists have suggested that males' dominant concerns with potentially uncertain paternity lead them to focus most on sexual exclusivity, whereas females, for whom maternity is rarely an issue, focus instead on emotional commitment as a way of ensuring continued access to the material resources their partners control (Buss et al., 1992; Buunk & Dijkstra, 2006; Cann, Mangum, & Wells, 2001).

Others would agree that women often need to be concerned with relational commitment as a means of protecting their economic welfare, but would see this focus more as a consequence of socioeconomic structure than innate genetic drives. That is, in many societies, women's inferior economic position means that they (and their children) are materially dependent on their male partners, with separation and divorce generally resulting in significant economic deprivation. Consequently, within the normative blueprint of marriage/partnership in question, men's involvement in sexual activity with others may be tolerated, provided that they remain committed socially and economically to the original union. The threat, in other words, is not the sex – indeed culturally such infidelity may come to be expected of men as part of the routine construction of masculinity. The threat comes from the possibility that sexual involvement may lead to emotional commitment and from there to a more permanent alternative relationship. In contrast, men's status and honor as men, within the same normative blueprint, are likely to be more dependent on maintaining the sexual exclusivity – "purity" – of their committed partner. In line with other aspects of the sexual double standard, to be cuckolded is of itself threatening to their masculine identity.

Given this, we might expect gender differences in the facets of infidelity that generate jealousy to be less marked in societies like the United States in which women have greater economic opportunity. In this regard, the methodological criticisms of the evolutionary perspective made by researchers like DeSteno and Salovey (1996); DeSteno, Bartlett, Salovey, and Braverman (2002); and Harris (2003) seem particularly relevant. They argue that findings about gender differences on the impact of emotional or sexual infidelity are largely a consequence of respondents being required to select one or other of these possibilities through the use of forced-choice questions. In their own research, DeSteno and his colleagues (DeSteno, Bartlett, Salovey, & Braverman, 2002; DeSteno & Salovey, 1996) found that questions using continuous rating scales eliminated these differences. They suggest the reasons for this finding are that women are less likely to view sexual and emotional infidelity as independent events, instead usually assuming that emotional infidelity also implies sexual infidelity. In consequence, they argue that women select emotional infidelity as more jealousy provoking in forced-choice questions, as emotional infidelity signifies a "double-shot" infidelity, incorporating both emotional and sexual betrayal. In other words, at least for women in the United States, the apparent differences in jealousy response revealed in forced-choice studies arise as a result of such double-shot understandings of the different modes of infidelity specified rather than being valid reflections of gender differences in jealousy patterns.

## Betrayal

Jealousy is only one of the responses that people experience when they find out that their partners have been unfaithful (Allen et al., 2005; Becker et al., 2004; Boekhout, Hendrick, & Hendrick, 1999). Often people also experience a strong sense of betrayal and a feeling that trust has been broken, perhaps in a way that seems irreparable. As with other responses to a partner's infidelity, the extent to which these feelings arise obviously depends on the principles – implicit as well as explicit – around which the relationship has been negotiated. Where, as is usually the case with contemporary Western couples, there is an assumption of sexual exclusivity, knowledge that a partner has "cheated" can undermine the belief that the relationship is "special." However idealistic such a belief might be, part of the romantic construction of committed intimate relationships lies in the symbolism of the unity and bounded exclusivity of the couple. Thus, infidelity can represent a betrayal not just of a commitment to sexual exclusivity but more importantly of the essential "coupleness" that is the partners' relationship.

Such a betrayal can significantly undermine the degree of trust that is felt in the relationship. Frequently this undermining of trust is a consequence not just of betrayal but also a result of the lying and deceit that generally accompany an affair if it is prolonged over any period of time. Indeed sometimes the deliberate lies and planned deceits are felt most heavily. Whether suspicions have previously been raised matters little; deception is as damaging to trust as straightforward lies. Either way, the partner who finds out about the extradyadic relationship is left feeling deceived, often wondering how he or she could have been so foolish as not to recognize the tell-tale signs now so apparent with hindsight. Moreover, the erosion of trust is difficult to overcome. Many people whose partners have had an affair find themselves, willingly or otherwise, unable to trust again as fully as they did in the past. Determined not to repeat previous naivete, their default position is now suspicion rather than trust, a situation that over time can generate its own tensions and relationship deterioration (Knapp, 2006).

## Loss and Identity

Discovering a partner is involved in an extradyadic relationship also frequently leads to an undermining of the individual's sense of self (Olson et al., 2002).

In essence, the betrayal also comes to represent a personal rejection. In seeking to understand why the affair developed, what it was that led to it, and what made the attraction so great, questions about what is missing in the partnership inevitably get raised. And these questions about the relationship are themselves liable to be turned into questions about the self. In other words, individuals with partners who are involved in an extradyadic relationship end up doubting their own adequacy and pondering what it is they are lacking that makes the other person so compelling in comparison. This doubting can entail a range of different elements. It can certainly raise doubts about sexual performance and adequacy. But it can also cast doubts about other characteristics of the self, including physical attractiveness, personality, and overall worth. Thus within contemporary constructions of "coupledom," the evident desire of the partner for someone else, even if only temporarily, can represent personal rejection and significantly undermine confidence in the self.

Moreover, public knowledge of a partner's sustained involvement with another can lead to feelings of failure and even humiliation (Allen et al., 2005; Olson et al., 2002). Pride can suffer as a result of the rejection being known by others in the couple's social network. People may also experience a sense of shame in these circumstances. In part this stems from knowing others are gossiping about them. But this shame, in turn, can be compounded by a sense that people judge them as partially responsible for what has happened in their relationship. In other words, knowledge of an affair leaves partners open to public scrutiny and gossip issues that are normally bounded by privacy. In addition, similar feelings of shame can arise through awareness that others have known – or suspected – about the affair before they knew about it themselves. In these circumstances, they may feel anger at friends for not revealing what they suspected sooner. As above, individuals' pride may be further hurt through awareness of others perceiving them as gullible and foolish for not recognizing sooner what was happening.

Overall, people can experience a wide range of emotions when a partner's extradyadic involvement comes to light. However, many of them can be recognized as at least partially rooted in a significant sense of loss (Boekhout et al., 1999). As we have seen, there can be feelings of worthlessness and loss of self. There can also be a loss of "relationship," not so much through its ending but more through reinterpreting its meaning, though of course this loss is compounded if separation or divorce follows (Orbuch, 1992). That is, even if the relationship continues, it may no longer be seen as it was. In a sense its innocence may be lost in a way that is impossible to recapture. As a number of the respondents in the study reported by Allan and Harrison (2002) recognized, they felt they could possibly forgive but not forget. Their trust had been broken, their belief in their partner damaged. Even though they did not seek to dwell on whatever pain they had experienced at the time, it remained a vivid memory. For these people, this represented a consciousness of loss in their relationship, notwithstanding its continuation.

## EXCLUSIVITY IN LATE MODERNITY

People's expectations of partnerships have been changing in recent years throughout much of the Western world. One powerful indication of this change is the way in which patterns of partnership formation and dissolution have shifted, initially with increases in divorce and then with rises in cohabitation (Cherlin, 2004; Smock, 2004). These changes reflect, first, the demise of ideas of intimate partnerships necessarily being lifelong, "one-and-only" type relationships and, second, the increasing acceptance that individuals have the right to expect happiness and personal fulfillment through these partnerships (Giddens, 1992). Although symbolically marriage continues to be seen as a lifelong, "for better or worse" commitment, in reality cultural assumptions are increasingly informed by a belief that continuing personal happiness is the key rationale for any intimate partnership. Although there are religious and ethnic variations in this belief, staying unhappy in a long-term union for its own sake receives considerably less moral endorsement now than it did under previous marital blueprints.

A remaining question for this chapter concerns the impact of these changes in patterns of commitment on understandings of and responses to extrapartner sexual involvement. The increased emphasis on personal satisfaction in contemporary partnerships, along with the premise of increasing individualization generally, would suggest that partnerships are more fragile and less socially embedded than they once were. On this basis, emotional hurt stemming from partnership indiscretion or violation is liable to result more readily in the ending of the relationship. In other words, the expectation of achieving personal fulfilment and self-realization through one's intimate partnership may render sexual congress outside the partnership increasingly unacceptable. In line with this expectation, there is some evidence that younger cohorts are less accepting of infidelity than older ones, though obviously their views may change over time (Kontula & Haavio-Mannila, 2004; Laumann et al., 1994).

In contrast, it is conceivable that the emphasis on partnerships as individually negotiated relationships rather than socially prescribed sets of responsibilities and obligations will lead to partnership infidelity being understood within a different framework. In particular, although it seems likely that knowledge of a partner's involvement in another intimate relationship will be experienced as painful, it may be that particular episodes of infidelity come to be accepted as something that is liable to happen in long-term relationships. In other words, where there is an increasing emphasis on the *quality* of relationships, different understandings of sexual infidelity may emerge. This is not an argument about the liberalization of sexual mores. It is more a question of whether in certain circumstances contemporary forms of commitment lead to a readier acceptance that individuals may have competing "needs" or "desires" that cannot always be met within the confines of their established partnerships. Is it, for example, possible for people to become sexually involved with others in ways that, although painful, do not inevitably undermine their commitment to the existing partnership? What sort of tolerances are acceptable under what sorts of circumstances?

Given the high levels of ideological commitment to monogamy currently claimed, especially in the United States (Allen et al., 2005; Treas & Giesen, 2000), this changed conception may seem far-fetched, though clearly there have always been some couples who do not feel sexual exclusivity is important within their partnership. But many other shifts in sexual expression and behavior – including acceptance of "uncommitted" sexual relations, cohabitation, and gay marriage – would also have seemed far-fetched not that long ago. Moreover, there is a great deal more variation in the organization of coupledom now than was found in much of the 20th century. The growth of cohabitation is an example of this variation. So too, more couples are now choosing to have commitment without coresidence ("living apart together"), not solely for work reasons but also because this arrangement ensures a greater degree of personal autonomy than more standard couple arrangements. Similarly a significant number of gay couples have relationships that permit extrapartnership sexual involvement, with the proviso that such sexual involvements are just that – sexual rather than emotionally intimate. In these relationships, commitment requires emotional fidelity but not sexual exclusivity (Weeks, Heaphy, & Donovan, 2001).

A major demographic shift that may have some bearing here is the increased numbers of people experiencing more than one committed partnership over their life course. That is, the prevalence of remarriages and other forms of repartnering as a result of increased levels of separation and divorce may lead to some further reevaluation of monogamy and extrapartnership involvement. Clearly people's understandings of marriage as necessarily a lifelong commitment are shifting. In this context, it may be that acts of betrayal within partnerships are increasingly "resolved" through separation. It is possible though that there will be an increasing propensity for some people, perhaps especially those with greater relationship experience, to interpret some forms of extrapartnership sexual involvement as not necessarily indicative of an act of betrayal. Although such openness may not be regarded as routine or acceptable in the way some gay couples perceive it, the distinction between sexual and intimate involvement may come to have increased salience for heterosexual couples in the changed sexual climate of late modernity. Of course, this is highly speculative but understandings of partnership and commitment, and consequently feelings of emotional hurt in cases of known extrapartnership involvement, can be interpreted as culturally framed rather than psychologically or biologically given. At the very least, the ways in which such involvements are symbolically constructed and interpreted will be of consequence for the reactions generated.

### FUTURE RESEARCH

It is clear that we need a great deal more research on the emotional impact of different forms of extrapartnership involvement. As things stand, research knowledge is not only extremely limited but also frequently based on questionable methodologies. This applies to most aspects of extrapartnership involvement, including the emotional responses of those directly or indirectly party to it. Although we know that extrapartnership involvement is relatively common (despite high levels of expressed disapproval), knowledge of its patterning and consequences is largely missing. Clearly there are major methodological difficulties in generating high-quality information about people's experiences of the topic, largely as a result of its furtive and morally suspect character. Nonetheless if we are to understand the varied course of these events and the different responses they evoke, we need to find better ways of collecting appropriate data on them.

There are a number of different issues here. To begin with, there is the question of sampling. Much of the research concerned with people's responses to infidelity, including that on different aspects of jealousy, relies on samples drawn from undergraduate populations. Typically those involved are asked questions about how they would respond to a partner being unfaithful. From these types of data, extrapolations are made to a wider population. Although such an approach may be useful for many topics, it seems questionable with regard to extrapartnership sexual liaisons. Among the key issues here are the respondents' age and experience. Certainly it seems dubious to take the views and perspectives of people who have relatively little – and sometimes no – experience of long-term committed relationships as being indicative of the views of a wider population with its quite diverse histories of relationship commitment, especially about a subject matter that resonates with moral injunctive.

As important, research concerned with partnership infidelity that relies on hypothetical responses to presented scenarios, as much experimental research on undergraduate populations does, can also be questioned. Although this is an established and useful procedure for many topics, its utility for discerning people's actual responses to direct or indirect involvement in partnership infidelity is limited. What we undoubtedly need are more studies that focus on real rather than hypothetical extradyadic involvement. Obtaining an adequate sample of those with such experience is certainly difficult. In particular, why should those whose extrapartnership involvement remains covert choose to reveal their emotions, activities, and histories for the sake of scientific knowledge?

Even if the extrapartnership involvement is more openly known, not everyone would choose to share his or her experiences about such a personal and private issue. Paradoxically though, it is precisely because of the sensitive and morally charged nature of these experiences that reliance on data derived from hypothetical constructions of them is so questionable.

Data drawn from clinical populations are also problematic for a range of reasons, including the selectivity of those who end up undertaking some form of counseling after direct or indirect experience of extrapartnership involvement. However, studies based on clinical populations frequently have the advantage of being able to focus on process rather than relying on one-time accounts. It would seem imperative that we have fuller accounts of the processes involved in extrapartnership liaisons if we are to understand them adequately, not least when the focus is on hurt and other emotional impacts. To begin with, we need to know more than we currently do about the natural histories of different forms of extradyadic involvements, whether these be short lived or long term, emotionally empty or emotionally charged, known about or secret, a single episode/relationship or serial infidelity. We need to understand better the structural and contextual factors that influence their different pathways and how decisions are made by those involved about their relationships' continuation or ending.

In this regard, there would be many benefits from having a longitudinal research design, though the practical difficulties of ever conducting such studies, given the secrecy surrounding many extrapartnership liaisons, are huge. Such a longitudinal design could focus not only on the natural histories of the extradyadic relationships but also on the longer term consequences for the committed partnerships, including how successful couples are in their various attempts to repair any damage done to their relationship by the extradyadic liaison. The key issue here is that people's emotional responses to significant episodes in their lives are not static; their understandings change over time, for better or worse, as they reflect on the issues involved and gain further insight into them. Thus, whether directly or indirectly involved in the extradyadic relationship, their interpretation and emotional responses to the liaison are emergent over time and not necessarily consistent.

In particular, the emotions aroused when a partner comes to learn about an extradyadic involvement, the hurt and distress experienced, the arguments, rows, and discussions, as well as the resulting calm or resolution that follows, are dynamic and consequential. Frequently, especially when the infidelity has been prolonged and emotionally meaningful, the significance of past events and the accounts given of them are reconsidered, mulled over, and in the process reinterpreted (Olson et al., 2002). In turn, these emotionally charged musings and reinterpretations serve to generate new understandings of the infidelity, its history, and consequences for the existing relationship. Such account construction is central to the generally fluid process that informs future attitudes, decisions, and actions (Weber, 1992). Consequently we need to research individuals' emergent accounts of their experiences – whether direct or indirect – as they are key to the construction of whatever resolution is realized. A longitudinal design allows them to be studied as process rather than as single "fixed" accounts.

## CONCLUSION

If relational transgression is accepted as being a prime component of hurt feelings, then as noted earlier extradyadic involvement is a particularly apt phenomenon for examining processes of hurt. What makes it especially relevant is the fact that it involves actions as much as words. The hurt experienced is not just a consequence of people saying hurtful things; it arises from their behavioral acts transgressing their agreed relationship expectations. Although current research has focused on hurt experienced as a result of extradyadic involvement, much of it has been specifically concerned with jealousy, an important though partial aspect of the hurt feelings that can be provoked. And as discussed in the previous section, some of the studies investigating jealousy are open to question for drawing conclusions from what are effectively hypothetical data.

It would be valuable to have more analyses of the hurt experienced by all those involved in extradyadic relationships, despite the many methodological difficulties entailed in such research. Currently the focus tends to be on the betrayed party. In some cases those who are betrayed are the only ones who experience hurt as a result of the extradyadic liaison. But in other cases, those directly involved may also feel degrees of emotional pain. Whether this pain is defined as "hurt" depends on the breadth of definition used. But if the emotionally disruptive consequences of extradyadic relationships are to be understood properly, then the responses of the different actors as the events unfold all need to be studied. Although not discussed explicitly in this chapter, this would also include any hurt experienced by children as a consequence of parental discord arising from the extradyadic involvement.

From a social science perspective, it is important to research the bases of the hurt that extradyadic involvement creates, including its personal, cultural, and historical variations. But it is equally important that the resolutions to such hurt are better understood. Often, of course, the outcome is separation or divorce. In other cases though, the relationship is sustained, perhaps with renegotiated understandings of its framing. How long the hurt is experienced, how it is overcome, whether levels of trust are reestablished, what strategies are used to achieve a form of reconciliation, and the like are all key questions that warrant further research. Moreover in an era of rapid change in normative expectations of sexuality and intimacy, shifts in the patterning of hurt generated through extradyadic relationships also comprises an important topic for future research.

## REFERENCES

Allan, G. (2004). Being unfaithful: His and her affairs. In J. Duncombe, K. Harrison, G. Allan, & D. Marsden (Eds.), *The state of affairs: Explorations in infidelity and commitment* (pp. 121–140). Mahwah, NJ: Erlbaum.

Allan, G., & Harrison, K. (2002). Marital affairs. In R. Goodwin & D. Cramer (Eds.), *Inappropriate relationships* (pp. 45–63). Mahwah, NJ: Erlbaum.

Allen, E. S., Atkins, D. C., Baucom, D. H., Snyder, D. K., Gordon, K. C., & Glass, S. P. (2005). Intrapersonal, interpersonal, and contextual factors in engaging in and responding to extramarital involvement. *Clinical Psychology–Science and Practice, 12*, 101–130.

Amato, P. R., & Previti, D. (2003). People's reasons for divorcing: Gender, social class, the life course, and adjustment. *Journal of Family Issues, 24*, 602–626.

Becker, D. V., Sagarin, B. J., Guadagno, R. E., Millevoi, A., & Nicastle, L. D. (2004). When the sexes need not differ: Emotional responses to the sexual and emotional aspects of infidelity. *Personal Relationships, 11*, 529–538.

Boekhout, B. A., Hendrick, S. S., & Hendrick, C. (1999). Relationship infidelity: A loss perspective. *Journal of Personal and Interpersonal Loss, 4*, 97–123.

Buss, D. M., Larsen, R. J., Westen, D., & Semmelroth, J. (1992). Sex differences in jealousy: Evolution, physiology, and psychology. *Psychological Science, 3*, 251–255.

Buunk, B. P., & Dijkstra, P. (2004). Men, women and infidelity: Sex differences in extradyadic sex and jealousy. In J. Duncombe, K. Harrison, G. Allan, & D. Marsden (Eds.), *The state of affairs: Explorations in infidelity and commitment* (pp. 103–120). Mahwah, NJ: Erlbaum.

Buunk, B. P., & Dijkstra, P. (2006). Temptations and threat: Extradyadic relations and jealousy. In A. L. Vangelisti & D. Perlman (Eds.), *The Cambridge handbook of personal relationships* (pp. 533–555). New York: Cambridge University Press.

Cancian, F. (1987). *Love in America: Gender and self-development*. New York: Cambridge University Press.

Cann, A., Mangum, J. L., & Wells, M. (2001). Distress in response to relationship infidelity: The roles of gender and attitudes about relationships. *Journal of Sex Research, 38*, 185–190.

Cherlin, A. J. (2004). The deinstitutionalization of American marriage. *Journal of Marriage and Family, 66*, 848–861.

Cramer, R. E., Abraham, W. T., Johnson, L. M., & Manning-Ryan, B. (2001). Gender differences in subjective distress to emotional and sexual infidelity: Evolutionary or logical inference explanation? *Current Psychology, 20*, 327–336.

DeSteno, D. A., Bartlett, M. Y., Salovey, P., & Braverman, J. (2002). Sex differences in jealousy: Evolutionary mechanism or artifact of measurement? *Journal of Personality and Social Psychology, 83*, 1103–1116.

DeSteno, D. A., & Salovey, P. (1996). Evolutionary origins of sex differences in jealousy? Questioning the "fitness" of the model. *Psychological Science, 7*, 367–372.

Feeney, J. A. (2005). Hurt feelings in couple relationships: Exploring the role of attachment and perceptions of personal injury. *Personal Relationships, 12*, 253–271.

Giddens, A. (1992). *The transformation of intimacy*. Cambridge: Polity Press.

Guerrero, L., Spitzberg, B. H., & Yoshimura, S. (2004). Sexual and emotional jealousy. In J. Harvey, A. Wenzel, & S. Sprecher (Eds.), *The handbook of sexuality in close relationships* (pp. 311–345). Mahwah, NJ: Erlbaum.

Haavio-Mannila, E., & Kontula, O. (2003). Single and double sexual standards in Finland, Estonia, and St. Petersburg. *Journal of Sex Research, 40*, 36–49.

Harris, C. R. (2003). A review of sex differences in sexual jealousy, including self-report data, psychophysiological responses, interpersonal violence, and morbid jealousy. *Personality and Social Psychology Review, 7*, 102–128.

Johnson, M. P. (1995). Patriarchal terrorism and common couple violence: Two forms of violence against women. *Journal of Marriage and the Family, 57*, 283–294.

Knapp, M. (2006). Lying and deception in close relationships. In A. L. Vangelisti & D. Perlman (Eds.), *The Cambridge handbook of personal relationships* (pp. 517–532). New York: Cambridge University Press.

Kontula, O., & Haavio-Mannila, E. (2004). Renaissance of romanticism in the era of increasing individualism. In J. Duncombe, K. Harrison, G. Allan, & D. Marsden (Eds.), *The state of affairs: Explorations in infidelity and commitment* (pp. 79–102). Mahwah, NJ: Erlbaum.

Laumann, E., Gagnon, J., Michael, R., & Michaels, S. (1994). *The social organization of sexuality: Sexual practices in the United States.* Chicago: University of Chicago Press.

Lawson, A. (1988). *Adultery: An analysis of love and betrayal.* New York: Basic Books.

Leary, M. R. (2001). Toward a conceptualization of interpersonal rejection. In M. R. Leary (Ed.), *Interpersonal rejection* (pp. 3–20). New York: Oxford University.

Leary, M. R., & Springer, C. A. (2001). Hurt feelings: The neglected emotion. In R. M. Kowalski (Ed.), *Behaving badly: Aversive behaviors in interpersonal relationships* (pp. 151–175). Washington, DC: American Psychological Association.

Leary, M. R., Springer, C., Negel, L., Ansell, E., & Evans, K. (1998). The causes, phenomenology, and consequences of hurt feelings. *Journal of Personality and Social Psychology, 74*, 1225–1237.

Olson, M. M., Russell, C. S., Higgins-Kessler, M., & Miller, R. B. (2002). Emotional processes following disclosure of an extramarital affair. *Journal of Marital and Family Therapy, 28*, 423–434.

Orbuch, T. (1992). A symbolic interactionist approach to the study of relationship loss. In T. Orbuch (Ed.), *Close relationship loss: Theoretical approaches* (pp. 192–204). New York: Springer-Verlag.

Reibstein, J., & Richards, M. (1992). *Sexual arrangements: Marriage and affairs.* London: Heinemann.

Richardson, L. (1985). *The new other woman: Contemporary single women in affairs with married men.* New York: Free Press.

Richardson, L. (1988). Sexual freedom and sexual constraint: The paradox for single women in liaisons with married men. *Gender and Society, 2*, 368–384.

Smock, P. (2004). The wax and wane of marriage: Prospects for marriage in the 21st century. *Journal of Marriage and Family, 66*, 966–973.

Treas, J., & Giesen, D. (2000). Sexual infidelity among married and cohabiting Americans. *Journal of Marriage and the Family, 62*, 48–60.

Vangelisti, A. L. (1994). Messages that hurt. In W. R. Cupach & B. H. Spitzberg (Eds.), *The dark side of interpersonal communication* (pp. 53–82). Hillsdale, NJ: Erlbaum.

Vangelisti, A. L. (2001). Making sense of hurtful interactions in close relationships. In V. Manusov & J. H. Harvey (Eds.), *Attribution, communication behavior and close relationships* (pp. 38–58). New York: Cambridge University Press.

Vangelisti, A. L., & Gerstenberger, M. (2004). Communication and marital infidelity. In J. Duncombe, K. Harrison, G. Allan, & D. Marsden (Eds.), *The state of affairs: Explorations in infidelity and commitment* (pp. 59–78). Mahwah, NJ: Erlbaum.

Weber, A. (1992). An account-making process: A phenomenological approach. In T. Orbuch (Ed.), *Close relationship loss: Theoretical approaches* (pp. 174–191). New York: Springer-Verlag.

Weeks, J., Heaphy, B., & Donovan, C. (2001). *Same sex intimacies: Families of choice and other life experiments.* London: Routledge.

Wellings, K., Fields, J., Johnson, A., & Wadsworth, J. (1994). *Sexual behaviour in Britain.* London: Penguin.

White, G. L. (1981). Jealousy and partner's perceived motives for attraction to a rival. *Social Psychology Quarterly, 44,* 24–30.

Wiederman, M. W. (1997). Extramarital sex: Prevalence and correlates in a national survey. *Journal of Sex Research, 34,* 167–174.

# 11

# Aggression, Violence, and Hurt in Close Relationships

BRIAN H. SPITZBERG

The fact that both physical and symbolic experiences are capable of instigating hurt is seldom more evident than in the context of intimate violence and aggression. Love and intimacy are not supposed to give way to aggression, and their peculiar union seems particularly poignant and potent. This chapter examines the topography of intimate partner aggression and its relationship to hurt and related phenomena.

Any and all attempts to chart a theoretical map of intimate violence are intrinsically selective in their attention to the existing literature. For example, it is relatively easy to find studies of the relationship between the experience of intimate violence and depression or anxiety but difficult to amass many studies of the attribution of who initiated physical aggression or the conditions under which violent couples emerge emotionally unscathed, or emotionally stronger, as a result of their aggressions. Consequently, the equation of violence and hurt often tends to be presumed rather than directly evidenced. Moreover, there is relatively little research on the possibilities that the hurtfulness of violence often may be (a) short lived and transient, (b) counterbalanced by co-occurring beneficial feelings or cognitions, or (c) an important phenomenological springboard to other more positive experiences.

To establish any claims regarding aggression and violence in close relationships, the cognate family of terms requires clarification. This is no mean task, as almost any attempt at definition risks "violence" against some ideological or intellectual altar. This is one of many conceptual hazards necessary to traverse. To set about this path, three grounding assumptions need to be articulated. First, although most of the evidence reviewed is relatively objective, the arguments and claims in which this evidence can be woven together entail some degree of ideological and political perspective, as is elaborated in the propositions that follow. Second, as much as *truths* can be assumed in the context of intimate violence, it is a truth that on the grand balance scales of hurt, in the context of intimate partner violence, women suffer disproportionately compared to men, in virtually every observable respect. Given these assumptions, however, it is still vital that intellectual space be provided for models that are more process and relationally based than most existing models. Third, in keeping with the available research on intimate violence, the term *hurt* in this chapter is generally considered an outcome, rather than a unique emotional state.

### COMING TO TERMS WITH TERMS

*Violence* is defined here as behavior intended to inflict physical harm (Sugarman & Hotaling, 1989). This definition is deceptively encompassing. The attribution of intent is often employed to differentiate *aggression* from violence, but here aggression includes processes that intend symbolic harm, physical harm, or both (Tedeschi & Felson, 1994). Kicking a sofa or throwing a plate at a wall during an argument may not intend physical harm to the partner, but it may well intend psychological harm. Either could be taken as a "harm-doing behavior" or a delivery of "noxious stimuli" (Tedeschi & Felson, 1994).

Establishing distinct vocabularies for distinguishing physical from psychological or verbal forms of aggression is important for several reasons. First, when struck physically, one has little choice in whether to experience some form of physical hurt – neurons are going to send signals of pain to the brain. A person has no choice but to bruise or experience broken bones when assaulted with sufficient physical force; despite individual differences in pain reactivity, the pain is physiological in nature, and some of the damage is objectively and observably registered. Symbolic attempts at causing harm, however, permit considerable discretion on the part of the target in how the behavior is appraised. As suggested by the "sticks and stones" aphorism of childhood, it is possible to nullify phenomenologically the impact of verbal assaults, even if few people are sufficiently inclined to achieve such discipline. Second, without such a distinction, research would be unable to identify the differential and combined effects of violence and symbolic aggression on identity and relationship outcomes. The two processes appear to play complex and interrelated roles in the initiation and continuation of relationships and in the interpretations the participants make of those relationships. Third, to equate verbal or symbolic acts of harm with physical acts of harm runs the risk of encroaching into constitutionally protected speech. For example, it is one thing to establish a policy of "automatic arrest" for perpetrators of physical violence, but such a policy seems inconceivable for verbal aggression. It is important to consider violence a separate interactional domain than verbal aggression, although both are integral to the study of hurt.

Intention is an important qualifier that separates harmful accidents from violence. It is important to recognize, however, that intent is a problematic criterion of violence (Tedeschi & Felson, 1994) on at least four counts. First, intent is not a very observable or objective phenomenon – it is linguistically and socially constructed and therefore open to wide latitudes of interpretation and reconstruction through discourse (Gergen, 1984). Second, those who are violent often refuse to admit or actively deny their intent (Ptacek, 1988). In one study, compared to husbands' self-attributions, "battered women were more likely to state that their husbands had intended to hurt them" (Bograd, 1988, p. 69). Third, the attribution of intent to another's harmful behavior often becomes an extremely important contested site in the negotiation of intimate conflict (Orvis, Kelley, & Butler, 1976), and such interpretations form a potential trigger to subsequent violence. Fourth, many actions are not proximally intended to hurt but may have extended, more distal, hurtful effects, which can complicate interpretations of actions, especially in the context of an ongoing long-term relationship in which interpretations of past actions can change over time.

Intent may be viewed as an interactant's valued expectation that aggression will produce a proximal outcome of punishment to the object of aggression (Tedeschi & Felson, 1994). Research does indicate that intent is a highly significant factor influencing the attribution of aggression (Björkqvist, Lindström, & Pehrsson, 2000), and the attribution of intent in turn directly predicts the experience of anger and violence (Betancourt & Blair, 1992). Even with this qualification, there are types of behavior that may qualify as violence, but to which a culture is reluctant to attach the label. For example, actions such as self-defense, parental discipline, judicial punishments, strategic deterrence, and so forth represent activities to which cultures have sought to ascribe distinct linguistic labels on the basis of their context or intent rather than their objective compositional behaviors. Many of these behaviors are clearly intentional, intend punishment to a person, and are nevertheless sanctioned and labeled separately from "violence" in given socially constructed contexts.

The qualifier "harm" also provides little delimitation. Under broad conceptions of harm, the term *violence* may "encompass verbal abuse, intimidation, physical harassment, homicide, sexual assault, and rape" (Dobash & Dobash, 1998, p. 4) and stalking (Cupach & Spitzberg, 2004). Many scholars therefore prefer the term *abuse*. Abuse generally is used herein to imply an aspect of chronicity. Thus, *abuse* can be defined as violence or aggression that occurs over extended periods of time, especially when it is (a) asymmetric in power or exploitation and (b) frequent, repetitive, or durable.

Regardless of intent, "violence is a form of interactive communication... motivated by a desire to communicate a message – often a demand for compliance – to the victim.... As a communicative tool, violence serves both instrumental and expressive purposes" (Anderson, Umberson, & Elliott, 2004, p. 630). There are many forms of interpersonal violence and abuse (Archer & Coyne, 2005). The nonintimate end of the continuum might include forms such as street hassling, grabbing, obscene phone calls, voyeurism, indecent exposure, gay-lesbian-bisexual-transgender baiting, sexual harassment, bullying, stranger stalking and rape, assault, and homicide. On the more intimate end of the continuum lie communicative aggression (aka "psychological abuse," "emotional abuse"), sexual coercion, child abuse and incest, intimate stalking, acquaintance/date/marital rape, partner or family physical violence and severe injury, and uxoricide or femicide.

This chapter focuses on intimate violence with an eye toward the relevance of communicative aggression, and the emphasis is on romantically intimate relationships. Violence itself is assumed to be a form of communication and interaction, although not all harmful communication is equated with violence. Specifically, *communicative aggression*, often referred to in the literature as psychological abuse, is defined as "any recurring set of messages that function to impair a person's enduring preferred self-image" (Dailey, Lee, & Spitzberg, 2007, p. 303). Such messages play an important role in the infliction of hurt in the context of intimate violence.

There is insufficient evidence on the scope of all these various types of violence and aggression. Research has, however, provided extensive evidence that physical violence and verbal aggression are relatively common experiences. If violence and aggression are likely to be hurtful, then an appreciation of their prevalence is in order.

## THE TOPOGRAPHY OF AGGRESSION IN CLOSE RELATIONSHIPS

All attempts to ascertain the prevalence of intimate violence involve a series of conceptual and methodological decisions and tradeoffs. Consequently, all estimates of intimate violence prevalence are controversial. Despite extensive debate regarding the challenges and implications of assessing intimate violence (e.g., Straus, 1999) and extensive evidence that different methods of assessment yield different estimates of the phenomenon (e.g., Johnson, 2001), there are no univocally accepted estimates.

### Physical Violence Prevalence and Forms

As testimony to the contested nature of assessing intimate violence, estimates of the occurrence of mutual hitting, pushing, or shoving range from 10% to 60% of all couples (Arriaga & Oskamp, 1999; Coker, Smith, McKeown, & King, 2000). Summarizing the past 25 years of couples survey research, Field and Caetano (2005) conclude that "approximately 20% of couples in the U.S. general population" report intimate partner violence (p. 465). The more conservative estimates generally derive from crime victimization studies that assess intimate violence as part of a larger survey on the experience of criminal events (Archer, 2000). The major ongoing systematic crime survey estimates that "on average each year from 1992 to 1996, about 8 in 1,000 women and 1 in 1,000 men age 12 or older experienced a violent victimization inflicted by a current or former spouse, girlfriend, or boyfriend" (Greenfeld et al., 1998, p. 3), including rape, sexual assault, robbery, aggravated assault, and simple assault. Overall, crime victimization surveys indicate that intimate violence is decreasing significantly in the United States (e.g., Catalano, 2006), although proportionately, severe intimate partner violence against women appears to be increasing or at least declining far more slowly (Campbell et al., 2007).

Men disproportionately represent victims of violence in society at large, but women disproportionately bear the brunt of *intimate* violence victimization (Catalano, 2006; Tjaden & Thoennes, 1998; cf. Dutton & Nicholls, 2005). Some non-crime-based (i.e., "couples") surveys corroborate that women are more likely than men to be victims of intimate violence. Tjaden and Thoennes (2000a, 2000b) found in a survey of 8,000 men and 8,000 women that women were more likely than men to be lifetime victims of rape (4.5% vs. 0.2%), physical assault (20.4% vs. 7.0%), and stalking (4.1% vs. 0.5%) in a current or former marital/opposite-sex cohabiting relationship. The majority of couples surveys, however, find that females are more likely to be violent in relationships than males (e.g., Archer, 2000, 2002; Straus, 1999), although these differences vary by setting and type of violence (Archer, 2004). This variation introduces a crucial qualification: women and men may be relatively equivalent in their *frequency of violence use* in relationships, but women are likely to suffer the consequences more, at least in terms of injury (Zlotnick, Kohn, Peterson, & Pearlstein, 1998).

Often lost in such statistics and comparisons, however, is that "mild" forms of violence tend to represent the vast majority of such prevalence estimates (Catalano, 2006). Tjaden and Thoennes (2000a) found in their large-scale study that of those experiencing physical assault, 41.5% of women and 20% of men reported injury from the violence, and 28% of the women's and 21.5% of the men's injuries were reported to require medical care. Of the types of injuries reported, more than three-quarters were reported as "scratch, bruise, welt"; more specifically, lacerations ($\cong$ 9%), broken or dislocated bones ($\cong$ 11%), head and spinal cord injury ($\cong$ 7%), sore, sprained, or strained muscles ($\cong$ 6.5%), broken teeth ($\cong$ 1%), burns ($\cong$ 1%), knocked unconscious ($\cong$ 1%), and internal injury (0.0%). According to the National Crime Victimization Survey, of the 4.5% of women who experienced serious injury as a result of non-fatal intimate violence, 0.1% incurred gunshot wounds, 0.6% knife wounds, 1% internal injuries, and 1.8% broken bones; 0.8% were knocked unconscious; 0.2% received other serious injuries, and 3.4% were victims of rape or sexual assault without any additional injuries (Catalano, 2006). Thus, although injuries are unfortunately too common and are more common among women than men, most intimate violence probably does not result in injury, and when injury does occur, the substantial majority of injuries are relatively minor.

The types of victimization overlap to varying degrees as well. Many victims experience one form of violence but not others, whereas a sizable minority experiences multiple forms (Campbell et al., 2003a; Walby & Allen, 2004). Research is only beginning to investigate the additive and differential effects of distinct types of violence (e.g., Basile, Arias, Desai, & Thompson, 2004; Coker, Smith, et al., 2000; Coker et al., 2002; Dutton, Kaltman, Goodman, Weinfurt, & Vankos, 2005; Pimlott-Kubiak & Cortina, 2003). The experience of hurt may well be differentiated based on the unique combinations of these types of victimization.

To the extent that hurt may reveal a direct linear relationship to violence, it is important to qualify prevalence estimates in terms of their stability or chronicity in relationships. The research on intimate violence reveals considerable instability over time and interactant. O'Leary et al. (1989) classified only 17% of the women and 8% of the men in their sample as "stably physically aggressive" (p. 266). Several studies indicated a desistance rate over time (typically 1–3 years) ranging between one-third (Bassuk et al., 2001; Hilton et al., 2004) to two-thirds (Campbell, Miller, Cardwell, & Belknap, 1994; Jacobson, Gottman, Gortner, Berns, & Shortt, 1996) among violent couples. In contrast, when multiple time periods are studied (typically 1 to 3 years), studies indicate that only 2% to 5% of couples experience violence at all time periods of the study (Bassuk et al., 2001; Riger, Staggs, & Schewe, 2004).

Collectively, therefore, although some people and relationships are relatively stable over time in their experience of violence, most violence in relationships is unstable across episodes and over time. When such instability is taken in the context of *cross-relational* exposure to violence, potential nonsummative relationships of exposure emerge, in which any given act of violence may disproportionately affect personal or relational outcomes. For example, Felitti et al. (1998) found that exposure to abusive childhood or dysfunctional family environments increased the probability of adult onset of "ischemic heart disease, cancer, chronic lung disease, skeletal fractures, and liver disease, as well as poor self-rated health," obesity, suicidality, depression, alcoholism, illicit drug use, smoking, sexually transmitted diseases (STDs), hepatitis, promiscuity, and engaging in intimate aggression and violence (see also Anda et al., 1999, 2006; Cohen et al., 2006; Dube, Felitti, Dong, Giles, & Anda, 2003). Large-scale studies (Briere & Elliott, 2003) and meta-analyses (Paolucci, Genuis, & Violato, 2001) also demonstrate sizable relationships between adult trauma and the experience of childhood physical and sexual abuse. Some research indicates importantly that, when lifetime exposure to violence is controlled for, men and women experience relatively similar large effects ($ds$ .49–.67) of psychological traumas (depression, drug use, health) from the same amount of exposure to violence (Pimlott-Kubiak & Cortina, 2003; see also Cohen et al., 2006; Dube et al., 2005; Dutton & Nicholls, 2005). Thus, the hurtfulness of violence may need to be contextualized not just in terms of a given relationship but also in terms of a lifetime exposure to violence and aggression.

## Verbal Aggression and Its Connections to Physical Violence

Verbal aggression, also commonly referred to as psychological abuse, appears far more prevalent than intimate physical violence. Studies indicate that more than 75% to 90% of individuals have experienced at least one act of verbal aggression from a past or current partner (e.g., Carey & Mongeau, 1996; Simonelli & Ingram, 1998). If the criterion for verbal aggression is stricter, requiring more behaviors or greater duration or frequency, findings vary, indicating that anywhere between 10% to 50% of people have experienced multiple acts of verbal aggression in an adolescent or adult pair-bonded relationship (Coker, Smith, et al., 2000; Coker et al., 2002; Murty et al., 2003). Among children, one-tenth to one-third appear to have experienced psychological abuse from a caregiver (e.g., Dube et al., 2005).

The vast majority of evidence indicates that intimate violence is almost always connected to verbal conflict (Cascardi & Vivian, 1995; Katz, Carino, & Hilton, 2002; Riggs, O'Leary, & Breslin, 1990; Stets, 1992). Communicative aggression often occurs without physical violence, but when physical violence or sexual aggression (e.g., Dutton et al., 1999) occurs, it generally co-occurs with communicative aggression.

Communicative aggression correlates strongly with physical assault victimization (e.g., 80%, Henning & Klesges, 2003; $r = .54$, Rhatigan & Street, 2005; $r = .78$, Watlington & Murphy, 2006). Furthermore, studies increasingly indicate that communicative aggression can be more harmful to quality of relationships or life (Follingstad, Rutledge, Polek, & McNeill-Hawkins, 1988) than physical violence or sexual abuse (Anda et al., 1999; Basile et al., 2004; Marshall, 1994; Rosen, Parmley, Knudson, & Fancher, 2002; Watlington & Murphy, 2006) and manifests effects above and beyond physical abuse (Coker, Smith, et al., 2000; Coker et al., 2002; Dailey et al., 2007; Marshall, 1994; Murty et al., 2003; Rosen et al., 2002; Straight, Harper, & Arias, 2003; Street & Arias, 2001). Similarly, childhood experience of emotional abuse seems to be a more potent predictor of adult depression, anxiety, and stress than the experience of domestic violence, physical abuse, or sexual abuse in the home (Cohen et al., 2006). As with physical violence, the aversiveness of communicative aggression is likely to depend on attributions of its intentionality, frequency, and severity (Dailey et al., 2007). Thus, although physical aggression is likely to be aversive, it does not seem to be as typically damaging in the long term as sustained psychological abuse, although when these processes are combined, the effects may be particularly aversive. Furthermore, the hurtfulness of physical violence may often be moderated or even mediated by the potency of the verbal aggression that accompanies it.

Intimate violence is not always severe, and it is not always stable, but relational violence in some form or another is nevertheless a relatively common experience. Given its relative ubiquity, it is important to understand its relationship to quality of life, and the experience of hurt and harm represents a useful window through which to examine this relationship. Two assumptions need to be addressed in discussing the relationship between violence and hurt. First, although statistically the vast majority of intimate violence tends to be mild, infrequent, and not particularly traumatizing, the darker sides of intimate violence are severe in their deleterious effects. Thus, although many claims regarding intimate violence tend toward the hyperbolic, there is no denying the import of understanding the process because the more severe forms are too damaging to ignore. Second, the links between violence and the emotional state experience of hurt must be largely assumed rather than demonstrated at this point in time. The very term *hurt* is strangely rare in its occurrence in the quantitative literature on intimate violence. There is, however, an extensive amount of research on the effects and correlates of intimate violence that may be viewed as proxies for or causally interconnected to the experience of hurt. The argument goes thusly: (a) Violence victimization causes various traumas, including, for example, depression, anxiety, and relationship dissatisfaction; (b) depression, anxiety, and relationship dissatisfaction cause, result from, or co-occur with feelings of hurt; therefore, (c) violence causes hurt feelings. This syllogism may or may not be entirely viable, given the difficulties of establishing the causal ordering of variables, but it is a very plausible starting point for discussing the links between intimate violence and hurt. Therefore, for the most part, it will be taken as a reasonable assumption that *trauma, harm,* and *hurt* are sufficiently synonymous to use interchangeably, even though the reasonableness of this assumption in regard to violence and aggression victimization is not sufficiently evidenced. When "hurt" is employed as an explicit feeling state, it is noted as such.

## AGGRESSION, VIOLENCE, AND HURT

There are obvious reasons to expect violence to be hurtful, and yet the term *hurt* is actually rare in the empirical literature on intimate aggression. Henton, Cate, Koval, Lloyd, and Christopher (1983) found that 57.5% of victims and 52.3% of aggressors claimed to feel "hurt" about their experience of violence in romantic relationships (the extent of overlap with feeling angry, scared, surprised, and sorry was not reported). When Matthews (1984) asked about the effect of the violence, nonspecific hurt was mentioned seventh in order of frequency of emotional effects. Similarly, Wells and Graham (2003) found that "hurt" was the sixth most frequently mentioned emotional effect after aggression. Jackson, Cram, and Seymour (2000) found that "relatively few students indicated that they felt guilty, unhappy, hurt, shocked, or scared," whereas anger and confusion were relatively common emotional reactions to dating violence. Despite how intuitive it seems that the implicit rejection and harm of intimate aggression and violence would result in phenomenologically ascribed "hurt," this appraisal seems more presumed than explicitly evidenced.

The vast majority of research examines a variety of psychosocial and individual reactions to intimate violence, all of which can be viewed as conceptual or empirical proxies for hurt. Emotional reactions such as emotional distress, social distrust, social distance, disenfranchisement, and disempowerment are common experiences associated with intimate violence (Amar & Alexy, 2005). Research has also begun to examine second-order and third-order types of harms resulting from intimate violence, such as the harm a given victim's trauma creates in his or her relationships with others, and the unique forms of trauma that those others experience as a result (Riger, Raja, & Camacho, 2002).

Given the varied forms that hurtful impacts may take, an organizing scheme is used here to facilitate their review. Cupach and Spitzberg (2004) developed a typology of effects through content analysis of symptoms or outcomes reported by victims of one form of interpersonal aggression: stalking. Approximately half of all stalking emerges from romantically intimate relationships, and about 30% to 50% of all stalking cases involve some degree of physical violence (Cupach & Spitzberg, 2004; Spitzberg & Cupach, 2007). Cupach and Spitzberg (2004) identified 10 clusters that are likely to encompass the various effects of all forms of intimate violence: (1) *general* (i.e., vague or diverse deleterious effects on quality of life), (2) *affective* health (i.e., changes in emotional quality of life – depression, sadness, anxiety, hurt feelings, etc.), (3) *cognitive* health (i.e., changes in volitional/rational quality of life – distrust, suspicion, lack of concentration, etc.), (4) *physical/physiological* health (i.e., changes in relational quality of life – sleep disorders, appetite disturbance, etc.), (5) *behavioral* health (i.e., interference in patterns of behavior, disruptions of employment routines, etc.), (6) *social* health (i.e., changes in relational quality of life – social isolation, strain on family relationships, etc.), (7) *resource* health (i.e., changes in property or economic quality of life – job loss, investments in home security, etc.), (8) *spiritual* health (i.e., changes in quality of faith-based belief systems – loss of faith in God, spiritual malaise, etc.), (9) *societal* health effects (i.e., cultivation effects and collective changes in societal belief systems – societal fear of crime, distorted stereotypes of victims and perpetrators, etc.), and (10) *resilience* effects (i.e., experiencing a sense of enhanced effects in any of the above categories – developing stronger family relationships, developing stronger self-confidence, etc.). The experience of hurt is likely to reside both within and across most of these categories. For example, a person could feel hurt physically, socially, emotionally, economically, and so forth. In general, it seems reasonable to posit that the closer or more important the relationship context, the greater the experience of hurt in any of these domains.

Research has identified effects of intimate violence across all of these arenas. *General trauma* has been associated with intimate violence victimization in the forms of general (total) trauma (Lerner & Kennedy, 2000), quality of life (Dutton et al., 2005), life dissatisfaction (Zlotnick, Johnson, & Kohn, 2006), and posttraumatic stress syndrome (PTSD) in particular (Basile et al., 2004; Cascardi, O'Leary, & Schlee, 1999; Cole, Logan, & Shannon, 2005; Dutton et al., 2005). This category overlaps significantly with experiences in the other categories, but it also functions as a composite *syndrome* entailing multiple symptoms of distress.

*Affective* harms have been associated with intimate violence victimization in the forms of depression (Boney-McCoy & Finkelhor, 1995; Bonomi et al., 2006; Cascardi et al., 1999; Dutton et al., 2005; Katz & Arias, 1999; Zlotnick et al., 2006), anxiety (Eagly & Steffen, 1986), sadness (Boney-McCoy & Finkelhor, 1995), grief (Campbell, 1989), and dissatisfaction with one's career (Doyle, Frank, Salzman, McMahon, & Fielding, 1999), relationships (Byrne & Arias, 1997; Rhatigan & Street, 2005; Rosen et al., 2002), and life (Zlotnick et al., 2006). The harms of this category may provide the most direct reflection of the emotional state of hurt.

Affective harms are often related to cognitive harms. *Cognitive* harms have been identified in the forms of dissociation (Lerner & Kennedy, 2000), loss of self-perceived autonomy (Lerner & Kennedy, 2000), suicidal ideation (Coker, McKeown, et al., 2000; Doyle et al., 1999), self-esteem (Campbell, 1989; Zlotnick et al., 2006), perceived guilt and harm (Eagly & Steffen, 1986), health perceptions (Straight et al., 2003), perceiving self as overweight (Doyle et al., 1999), cognitive impairment (Straight et al., 2003), and exaggerated social threat appraisal (Dutton et al., 2005).

A wide variety of *physical and physiological* types of symptoms could result from interpersonal violence. Some of the effects that have been demonstrated in the research include sleep disorders (Lerner & Kennedy, 2000; cf. Straight et al., 2003); chronic fatigue (Doyle et al., 1999), cigarette smoking (Bonomi et al., 2006; Doyle et al., 1999), substance use and abuse (Bonomi et al., 2006; Coker, Davis, et al., 2000; Coker, McKeown, et al., 2000; Coker et al., 2002; Doyle et al., 1999), physical health and disease (Bonomi et al., 2006; Coker, Davis, et al., 2000; Coker et al., 2002); sexual risk-taking (Coker, McKeown, et al., 2000), aggressive behavior (Coker, McKeown, et al., 2000), and physical and role limitations (Straight et al., 2003).

*Behavioral* symptoms of intimate violence victimization include any constraints or difficulties experienced in normal daily functioning. For example, teen victims are more likely to experience troubles with their teachers (Boney-McCoy & Finkelhor, 1995; Dutton & Spitzberg, 2007). Victims of physical violence appear less capable in daily functions such as caring for personal needs, household tasks, and work (Zlotnick et al., 2006). Stalking victims report a wide variety of disruptions in their daily routines, including changing their routes to and from work or school, getting a P.O. box and unlisted phone numbers, finding someone to accompany them in their movement in public spaces, enhancing home security, and sometimes changing jobs and residential locations (Cupach & Spitzberg, 2004; Spitzberg & Cupach, 2007).

A variety of *social and relational* harms have been associated with intimate violence victimization, including diminished relational (Lerner & Kennedy, 2000) or social functioning (Bonomi et al., 2006); stresses on help- and support-seeking (i.e., putting network members in harms way, straining members' financial resources) (Lerner & Kennedy, 2000); and miscellaneous deleterious effects on satisfaction with family life, friends (Coker, McKeown, et al., 2000), relationships, and on commitment (Rhatigan & Street, 2005). It is important to point out, however, that the causal direction of these relationships is not necessarily obvious. Some research indicates that declines in commitment and satisfaction may be the factors that increase the acceptability and use of violence, rather than the converse (Gaertner & Foshee, 1999). When contextual factors are taken into account, satisfaction may be relatively unrelated to violence. Roberts and Noller (1998) found that, when controlling for partner violence, "relationship satisfaction did not provide independent prediction of men's or women's use of violence.... However, couple communication successfully added to the prediction of both men's and women's use of violence, after controlling for satisfaction and partner violence" (pp. 337–338). Finally, several studies indicate that there are violent yet satisfied couples (e.g., O'Leary et al., 1989; Tonizzo, Howells, Day, Reidpath, & Froyland, 2000). Thus, although it seems reasonable to assume that violence victimization increases the likelihood of relational disaffection and harm, the relationship apparently is neither direct nor necessary.

*Resource* and societal harms have been investigated under multivariate formulas estimating economic "costs" of intimate violence victimization. These efforts take into account factors such as medical costs, mental health costs, victim and emergency response costs, productivity losses, lost quality of life, physical injuries, and less tangible psychological and societal costs to law enforcement, courts, health care, and insurance. Taking such direct and indirect costs into account, the Centers for Disease Control (CDC) estimated that in the United States intimate violence cost $5.8 billion in 1995 (National Center for Injury Prevention and Control, 2003, p. 2). These costs were analyzed further according to type of violence medical care costs, mental health care costs, lost productivity, and mortality costs for partner rapes ($320 million), physical assaults ($4.3 billion), stalking ($342 million), and murder ($893 million), which would total $8.3 billion in 2003 dollars (Max, Rice, Finkelstein, Bardwell, & Leadbetter, 2004). Although the category of resource and societal harms clearly is not directly related to individual experiences of hurt, it may reflect very indirect effects on the societal capacity for rendering protective or compensatory assistance to victims experiencing hurt. An overburdened health delivery system is less capable of providing a therapeutic response to victims of violence than a better resourced system.

*Spiritual* effects of victimization are not commonly investigated but may reflect a particularly important effect among those experiencing interpersonal trauma. Senter and Caldwell (2002) found that spirituality and faith were valuable resources for women who successfully ended relationships with their violent partners. One of the narrative themes was interpreted as "reaffirming faith-based beliefs and practices" (p. 556). Watlington and Murphy (2006) found spirituality, religious involvement, and religious coping did not correlate with either physical assault ($r = -.05$, .04, and .03, respectively) or psychological abuse victimization ($r = -.09$, $-.04$, and .09, respectively). In a U.S. probability sample, however, Bierman (2005) found that childhood abuse by mother or others outside the family had no effect, but abuse by a father significantly diminished the subsequent adult child's religious involvement, religious self-concept, and spiritual self-concept. Fathers may still more closely reflect the patriarchal aspects of religious belief systems, or they may be the primary source of insisting on child compliance with religious worship. The influence of violence on the link between parental socialization and subsequent adult spirituality may be more substantial than it is in contexts of adult-to-adult violence. Given the probable impact of parental influences on the child's religious socialization, children may be more susceptible than adults to the confusion resulting from the incongruity of a violent parent espousing a spiritual system of belief, especially if that belief system preaches pacifist and cooperative ethics.

Piecemeal reviews of these various types of effects (e.g., affective, cognitive, behavioral, etc.) indicate a diverse landscape, but one in which the predominant result of research is to indicate that victimization of physical violence in relationships is deleterious across several domains. For the most part, this conclusion is supported by more systematic attempts to demonstrate the harms of intimate violence. A meta-analysis by Weaver and Clum (1995) examined both childhood and adult experiences of interpersonal violence in relation to a variety of outcomes. Many of the outcomes reflected personality disorders as a possible result of childhood experience of violence. Although some of these effects clearly might be independent rather than dependent variables in adult populations, age of the sample was not a significant moderator of effect sizes. In addition to psychopathology and general adjustment, 16 other potential outcomes were examined: adjustment ($r = .17$), anxiety ($r = .19$), borderline personality disorder ($r = .63$), conduct disorder ($r = .16$), depression ($r = .21$), stress ($r = .24$), dissociative disorder ($r = .39$), drug abuse ($r = .24$), externalizing ($r = .28$), phobia/fear ($r = .17$), internalizing ($r = .27$), PTSD ($r = .20$), childhood deviant sexual behaviors ($r = .45$), social incompetence ($r = .45$), somatization ($r = .10$), and suicidal ideation ($r = .16$). Across all samples and outcomes, there was a small overall effect of interpersonal violence on measures of psychological distress ($r = .24$); this effect increased the greater the percentage of females in the sample (Weaver & Clum, 1995). Objective features of the violence (e.g., duration, physical injury, presence of weapon, etc.) accounted for only half of the effect ($r = .21$) that subjective features (e.g., general appraisal, self-blame, perceived safety) accounted for ($r = .40$).

The analysis of personality disorders as an "outcome" of violence among adults illustrates an important but still unresolved issue; specifically, the directionality of such causal relationships. For example, a nonviolent couple in which a member develops depression may have an increased likelihood of subsequent relational conflicts, stresses, and violence. Similarly, in their meta-analysis, Stith, Smith, Penn, Ward, and Tritt (2004) viewed fear, depression, and alcohol use as dispositional risk factors and marital dissatisfaction as a microsystem risk factor. That is, these factors were expected to increase the likelihood that stressors would be reacted to with violence. Among female victims, depression ($r = .28$), fear ($r = .27$), and alcohol use ($r = .13$) were related to the experience of aggression and violent behavior. Marital dissatisfaction was a risk factor of violence among male offenders ($r = .30$) and female offenders ($r = .25$), whereas depression ($r = .23$), jealousy ($r = .17$), and alcohol use ($r = .24$) were risk factors for male offenders. These types of effects illustrate the difficulty of causal interpretation, as marital dissatisfaction, depression, jealousy, and alcohol use may be considered risk factors, outcome factors, or reciprocally causal factors. Anda et al. (2006) make a strong case for the causal order between childhood adverse experiences, including being a victim or observer of verbal abuse and physical violence in one's family of origin, and later adverse adult health effects, but the case for causal direction in adult experiences of violence is not as easily made.

Finally, a meta-analysis by Golding (1999) examining the association between intimate violence and mental health indicators identified strong effects. Weighted mean prevalence was 47.6% for depression, 17.9% for suicidality, 63.8% for PTSD, 18.5% for alcohol abuse, and 8.9% for drug abuse. Although these prevalence estimates were variable, the increase in probability, adjusted by the size of the study sample (i.e., the weighted odds ratio), "ranged from 3.55 to 3.80 in studies of depression, suicidality, and PTSD and from 5.56 to 5.62 in studies of alcohol and drug abuse or dependence" (p. 327). These effects tended to be consistent across studies. Again, it is generally not possible in these kinds of analyses to determine which is the effect and which is the cause, but the "evidence is consistent with the hypothesis that intimate partner violence serves as a risk factor for mental health problems" (p. 128).

*Resilience* has not been studied as extensively as these other categories of negative effects. Resilience can be viewed as a personality trait enabling a person's sense of competence, and at least some research finds this trait unrelated to violence victimization (Humphreys, 2003). In contrast, resilience can be viewed as a set of adaptive beliefs and attitudes in reaction to hurt or victimization. Some research indicates that some victims are able to find silver linings to the dark clouds of their traumas. For example, McMillen, Zuravin, and Rideout (1995) found that almost half (46.8%) of the child sexual abuse victims were able to identify some benefit from their experience (e.g., protection of their own children, self-protection, increased knowledge of sexual abuse, etc.). Bogar and Hulse-Killacky (2006) found, in a small qualitative sample of women who had been sexually abused as children, five clusters of resilience: interpersonal skills (e.g., verbal ability, assertiveness, optimism), competence (e.g., academic excellence, creativity), self-regard (e.g., self-esteem, resistance to shame), spirituality (e.g., faith in God), and helpful life circumstances (e.g., managing challenges, resourcefulness). Spitzberg and Rhea (1999) found that a factor assessing various resilience symptoms (e.g., stronger relationships, stronger self-esteem, stronger family relationships, stronger coping skills) was significantly and positively correlated with frequency of experience of stalking behaviors. Senter and Caldwell (2002), in a small qualitative study, identified several narrative themes related to resilience among victims who successfully extricated themselves from a violent relationship: "letting go/releasing the unproductive," "awakening/rediscovery of the self," "reconnecting with/strengthening supportive relationships," "helping others/reaching out," and "embracing a new perspective of self, others, and life" (see also Draucker, 2003; Sheikh & Marotta, 2005).

To this point, the effects of intimate violence have been examined almost entirely in terms of the victim. Reflecting the biases of victimology, relatively few studies explicitly examine the traumas that the inflictor of violence may also experience, whether they be guilt, distorted identity, harms of retaliation, or even health effects. Any symptoms of victimization presumably may be manifest on any of the direct, relational, or partner levels of impact. Seldom considered is that those perpetrating violence may reap personal costs associated with such deviant or problematic behavior. For example, the mutuality of violence is so high in relationships that it might be reasonable to conjecture that *expressing* violence may be as correlated to adverse mental health characteristics as *receiving* violence (e.g., Simonelli & Ingram, 1998). Rosen et al. (2002) found that psychological symptoms correlated equally ($r = .27$) with both physical violence victimization and with violence inflicted. Related research indicates that hostility and engaging in hostile behaviors are related to ill health effects (e.g., Matthews, Gump, Harris, Haney, & Barefoot, 2004).

There is a strong conceptual basis to expect that intimate aggression tends to produce the experience of hurt, even if the term is not commonly evoked in the phenomenological language of victims and perpetrators. Intimate aggression represents a form of relational rejection, which has been linked psychologically (Leary, 2001) and physiologically (Eisenberger & Lieberman, 2004) to hurt. Many of life's valued outcomes depend on successful long-term relational attachments, and violence represents more than an episodic symbolic rejection of a partner; severe violence threatens the very potential to survive at all, much less in a particular relationship. Thus, it is a reasonable assumption that intimate violence carries the potential for hurtfulness, and the weight of evidence is that intimate violence increases the likelihood of hurt feelings – episodically, relationally, and individually. Less explored, however, is the possibility that people who are hurting may be more likely to interact in ways that initiate or elicit violent reactions in close relationships.

## REVISITING THE TRAUMA OF INTIMATE VIOLENCE

Given the many forms of harm that can be caused by interpersonal violence, there is no denying the seriousness of its consequences for many victims. A common misconception, however, is that all violence is perceived by victims as traumatic in its effects. Some research has found that around one-tenth to one-third of victims report their relationships as improving after an episode of violence, and a larger percentage of victims reports relatively little or no change in relationship status (Gryl, Smith, & Bird, 1991; Murphy, 1988). To the extent that violence is traumatizing to the relationship, it does not necessarily spell the end of the relationship. One-quarter to three-quarters of those experiencing violence appear motivated to continue their relationship or even to marry their partner (Dutton et al., 2005; Lo & Sporakowski, 1989; Roscoe & Benaske, 1985). Research also demonstrates that between one-fifth and one-third of relationships that have experienced violence are viewed by the partners as "satisfying" (Holtzworth-Munroe et al., 1992; O'Leary et al., 1989; Tonizzo et al., 2000; Wells & Graham, 2003). In summarizing such studies up to 1989, Sugarman and Hotaling concluded, "On average, the relationship has worsened because of the violence in about 40 percent of the cases, but in roughly six of every ten relationships that did not terminate, the violence is reported to have had no effect on, or to have actually improved, the relationship" (p. 14).

In one of the more sophisticated analyses of the traumatic effects of intimate violence, Lerner and Kennedy (2000) examined women who were in a violent relationship across four time periods after the end of a violent relationship, and they compared them to women still in a violent relationship. They examined sleep disturbance, dissociation, depression, postsexual abuse trauma, and anxiety. Women who were out of the relationship for less than 6 months tended to experience the highest level of symptoms. Indeed, women who were currently in a violent relationship did not differ in sleep disturbance, depression, abuse trauma, or anxiety from those out of the violent relationship, and they were actually less dissociated than those out of the relationship for less than 6 months. In general, "women who most recently left a violent relationship (within the previous 6 months) reported the highest level of specific trauma symptoms" (p. 228). These results could be evidence that getting out of a violent relationship involves its own sources of stress and distress. There may be many disruptions and barriers involved in departing a durable preexisting relationship over the short term. The hurt foregone by leaving the relationship may introduce new forms of hurt in the adjustment to relational independence. It is important to qualify these conjectures, however, by noting that relational disengagement is often a stimulus for estrangement violence, violence inflicted in the context of a partner's rejection, and imminent (attempted) departure (Calatano, 2006; Hannawa, Spitzberg, Wiering, & Teranishi, 2006). Such violence might continue in other distressing forms such as harassment or stalking even after the separation.

Collectively, therefore, for many couples, violence is a transitory, mutual, and relatively minor disruption to the relationship, producing relatively little enduring effect on the person's relational intentions, sense of relational quality, or personal well-being. A reasonable set of summary conclusions, therefore, is that (a) the majority of evidence indicates that physical violence and communicative aggression victimization significantly increase the likelihood of experiencing a wide variety of concurrent, short-term, and long-term traumas and harms, although (b) much intimate violence is neither particularly serious or traumatizing, (c) in a substantial proportion of episodes, there is relatively little perceived effect on the relationship, (d) most intimate violence is probably not as traumatizing as is the ongoing communicative aggression that tends to accompany the violence, and (e) in a sizable minority of cases, intimate violence is associated with perceived benefits.

Physical violence victimization does increase the risk of experiencing a host of deleterious psychological, emotional, behavioral, social, and spiritual effects. Despite such claims, however, relatively little is yet known about the many victims for whom such effects are relatively ephemeral. The processes by which violence and aggression lead to *enduring* hurt and harm are likely to depend on a variety of factors, including the personality of the victim, past victimization and its duration and severity, and, perhaps most important, how the processes of violence are negotiated in the meaning systems of the participants. The extent to which victims are made to feel helpless, worthless, responsible for their own victimization, and so forth may well moderate the hurtfulness of violence.

The interactional processes associated with the attributional meaning of and the responsibility and blame for violence in the context of relationships are receiving increasing attention (Sillars, Leonard, Roberts, & Dun, 2002; Tonizzo, et al., 2000). The ways in which these negotiations function to affect outcomes are not well understood. A number of studies have examined the accounting process in the wake of violence, as apologies, excuses, and justifications are likely to have a significant effect not only on the meanings attributed to the violence but also on the likelihood of forgiveness, reconciliation, and relational durability (Cascardi & Vivian, 1995; Mouradian, 2001; Stamp & Sabourin, 1995).

The finding that many female victims of violence tend to blame themselves, but women who are in later relational stages (Langhinrichsen-Rohling, Neidig, & Thorn, 1995) or no longer in abusive relationships are less inclined to blame themselves (Moore, Eisler, & Franchina, 2000), suggests that their blame attributions may be actively negotiated by the abuser, and when female victims are able to blame their partner, they are more likely to be dissatisfied

(Byrne & Arias, 1997) and more likely to leave (Pape & Arias, 2000). This possibility accords with research indicating that abusive men are particularly biased in blaming circumstances or their partner for their abusive behavior (Schweinle & Ickes, 2002; Tonizzo et al., 2000), in contrast to how female victims of abuse make such attributions (Langhinrichsen-Rohling et al., 1995). "The biased and vigilant outlook toward communication shown by aggressive husbands represents a reactive predisposition or 'hair-trigger' that tends to prompt a negative response to any perceived or real affront" (Sillars et al., 2002, p. 105). Whether such biases are indeed gender specific and the extent to which mutual negotiations collude to accentuate such biases remain important research questions. Until these negotiation processes are better understood, the relationships between the experience of hurt and the experience of physical violence and communicative aggression will not be well understood.

Intimate violence and aggression provide a useful lens through which hurt may be viewed. Actions that hurt physically do not always produce phenomenological hurt. In contrast, although sticks and stones may break bones, it appears that words often hurt in even deeper and more enduring ways. Hurt can be manifest and experienced in a variety of domains (e.g., social, cognitive, affective, etc.). Hurt can radiate interpersonally. It may overlap and co-occur with other similar phenomena (e.g., shame, sadness, anger). Hurt may also manifest ambivalence: An experience may hurt in the short term but lead to positive experiences in retrospect, or it may stimulate important growth experiences that are painful yet valued. Finally, the darker sides of intimate violence that victimize a definable population represent extraordinary interpersonal terrorism and, in some cases, suicide and murder (Campbell et al., 2003b). Thus, even if most violence is mild and not particularly hurtful, the proportion that is clearly harmful merits further scholarly inquiry. Despite all these lessons, the experience of hurt itself has not received much attention in the theory and research on intimate violence and aggression – an oversight clearly in need of correction.

## REFERENCES

Amar, A. F., & Alexy, E. M. (2005). "Dissed" by dating violence. *Perspectives in Psychiatric Care, 41*, 162–171.

Anda, R. F., Croft, J. B., Felitti, V. J., Nordenberg, D., Giles, W. H., Williamson, D. F. et al. (1999). Adverse childhood experiences and smoking during adolescence and adulthood. *Journal of the American Medical Association, 282*, 1652–1658.

Anda, R. F., Felitti, V. J., Bremner, J. D., Walker, J. D., Whitfield, C., Perry, B. D. et al. (2006). The enduring effects of abuse and related adverse experiences in childhood: A convergence of evidence from neurobiology and epidemiology. *European Archives of Psychiatry and Clinical Neuroscience, 256*, 174–186.

Anderson, K. L., Umberson, D., & Elliott, S. (2004). Violence and abuse in families. In A. L. Vangelisti (Ed.), *Handbook of family communication* (pp. 629–645). Mahwah, NJ: Erlbaum.

Archer, J. (2000). Sex differences in aggression between heterosexual partners: A meta-analytic review. *Psychological Bulletin, 126*, 651–680.
Archer, J. (2002). Sex differences in physically aggressive acts between heterosexual partners: A meta-analytic review. *Aggression and Violent Behavior, 7*, 313–351.
Archer, J. (2004). Sex differences in aggression in real-world settings: A meta-analytic review. *Review of General Psychology, 8*, 291–322.
Archer, J., & Coyne, S. M. (2005). An integrated review of indirect, relational, and social aggression. *Personality and Social Psychology Review, 9*, 212–230.
Arriaga, X. B., & Oskamp, S. (1999). The nature, correlates, and consequences of violence in intimate relationships. In X. B. Arriaga & S. Oskamp (Eds.), *Violence in intimate relationships* (pp. 3–16). Thousand Oaks, CA: Sage.
Basile, K., C., Arias, I., Desai, S., & Thompson, M. P. (2004). The differential association of intimate partner physical, sexual, psychological, and stalking violence and post-traumatic stress symptoms in a nationally representative sample of women. *Journal of Traumatic Stress, 17*, 413–421.
Bassuk, F. L., Dawson, R., Huntington, N., Salomon, A., Bassuk, S. S., & Browne, A. (2001). *Secondary data analysis on the etiology, course and consequences of intimate partner violence against extremely poor women* (NCJRS 188507). Washington, DC: U.S. Department of Justice.
Betancourt, H., & Blair, I. (1992). A cognition (attribution)-emotion model of violence in conflict situations. *Personality and Social Psychology Bulletin, 18*, 343–350.
Bierman, A. (2005). The effects of childhood maltreatment on adult religiosity and spirituality: Rejecting God the Father because of abusive fathers? *Journal for the Scientific Study of Religion, 44*, 349–359.
Björkqvist, K., Lindström, M., & Pehrsson, M. (2000). Attribution of aggression to acts: A four-factor model. *Psychological Reports, 87*, 525–530.
Bogar, C. B., & Hulse-Killacky, D. (2006). Resiliency determinants and resiliency processes among female adult survivors of childhood sexual abuse. *Journal of Counseling and Development, 84*, 318–327.
Bograd, M. (1988). How battered women and abusive men account for domestic violence: Excuses, justifications, or explanations? In G. T. Hotaling, D. Finkelhor, J. T. Kirkpatrick, & M. A. Straus (Eds.), *Coping with family violence: Research and policy perspectives* (pp. 60–77). Newbury Park, CA: Sage.
Boney-McCoy, S., & Finkelhor, D. (1995). Psychosocial sequelae of violent victimization in a national youth sample. *Journal of Consulting and Clinical Psychology, 63*, 726–736.
Bonomi, A. E., Thompson, R. S., Anderson, M., Reid, R. J., Carrell, D., Dimer, J. A. et al. (2006). Intimate partner violence and women's physical, mental, and social functioning. *American Journal of Preventative Medicine, 30*, 458–466.
Briere, J., & Elliott, D. M. (2003). Prevalence and psychological sequelae of self-reported childhood physical and sexual abuse in a general population sample of men and women. *Child Abuse & Neglect, 27*, 1205–1222.
Byrne, C. A., & Arias, I. (1997). Marital satisfaction and marital violence: Moderating effects of attributional processes. *Journal of Family Psychology, 11*, 188–195.
Campbell, J. C. (1989). A test of two competing explanatory models of women's responses to battering. *Nursing Research, 38*, 18–24.
Campbell, J. C., Garza, M. A., Gielen, A. C., O'Campo, P., Kub, J., Dienemann, J. et al. (2003a). Intimate partner violence and abuse among active duty military women. *Violence Against Women, 9*, 1072–1092.
Campbell, J. C., Glass, N., Sharps, P. W., Laughon, K., Yragui, N., & Sutherland, M. A. (2007). Research on intimate partner violence and femicide, attempted femicide, and

pregnancy-associated femicide. In K. A. Kendall-Tackett & S. M. Giacomoni (Eds.), *Intimate partner violence* (pp. 6.1–6.22). Kingston, NJ: Civic Research Institute.

Campbell, J. C., Miller, P. M., Cardwell, M. M., & Belknap, R. A. (1994). Relationship status of battered women over time. *Journal of Family Violence, 9*, 99–111.

Campbell, J. C., Webster, D., Koziol-McLain, J., Block, C., Campbell, D., Curry, M. A. et al. (2003b). Risk factors for femicide in abusive relationships: Results from a multisite case control study. *American Journal of Public Health, 93*, 1089–1097.

Carey, C. M., & Mongeau, P. A. (1996). Communication and violence in courtship relationships. In D. D. Cahn & S. A. Lloyd (Eds.), *Family violence from a communication perspective* (pp. 127–150). Thousand Oaks, CA: Sage.

Cascardi, M., O'Leary, K. D., & Schlee, K. A. (1999). Co-occurrence and correlates of posttraumatic stress disorder and major depression in physically abused women. *Journal of Family Violence, 14*, 227–249.

Cascardi, M., & Vivian, D. (1995). Context for specific episodes of marital violence: Gender and severity of violence differences. *Journal of Family Violence, 10*, 265–293.

Catalano, S. (2006). *Intimate partner violence in the United States.* Washington DC: Office of Justice Programs, U.S. Department of Justice. Retrieved January 3, 2007, from http://www.ojp.usdoj.gov/bjs/intimate/ipv.htm.

Cohen, R. A., Hitsman, B. L., Paul., R. H., McCaffrey, J., Stroud, L., Sweet, L. et al. (2006). Early life stress and adult emotional experience: An international perspective. *International Journal of Psychiatry in Medicine, 36*, 35–52.

Coker, A. L., Davis, K. E., Arias, I., Desai, S., Sanderson, M., Brandt, H. M. et al. (2002). Physical and mental health effects of intimate partner violence for men and women. *American Journal of Preventive Medicine, 23*, 260–268.

Coker, A. L., McKeown, R. E., Sanderson, M., Davis, K. E., Valois, R. F., & Huebner, E. S. (2000). Severe dating violence and quality of life among South Carolina High School Students. *American Journal of Preventive Medicine, 19*, 220–227.

Coker, A. L., Smith, P. H., McKeown, R. E., & King, M. J. (2000). Frequency and correlates of intimate partner violence by type: Physical, sexual, and psychological battering. *American Journal of Public Health, 90*, 553–559.

Cole, J., Logan, T. K., & Shannon, L. (2005). Intimate sexual victimization among women with protective orders: Types and associations of physical and mental health problems. *Violence and Victims, 20*, 695–715.

Cupach, W. R., & Spitzberg, B. H. (2004). *The dark side of relationship pursuit: From attraction to obsession to stalking.* Mahwah, NJ: Erlbaum.

Dailey, R. M., Lee, C., & Spitzberg, B. H. (2007). Psychological abuse and communicative aggression. In B. H. Spitzberg & W. R. Cupach (Eds.), *The dark side of interpersonal communication* (2nd ed., pp. 297–326). Mahwah, NJ: Erlbaum.

Dobash, R. E., & Dobash, R. P. (1998). Violent men and violent contexts. In R. E. Dobash & R. P. Dobash (Eds.), *Rethinking violence against women* (pp. 141–168). Thousand Oaks, CA: Sage.

Doyle, J. P., Frank, E., Salzman, L. E., McMahon, P. M., & Fielding, B. D. (1999). Domestic violence and sexual abuse in women physicians: Associated medical, psychiatric, and professional difficulties. *Journal of Women's Helath and Gender-Based Medicine, 8*, 955–965.

Draucker, C. B. (2003). Unique outcomes of women and men who were abused. *Perspectives in Phychiatric Care, 39*, 7–16.

Dube, S. R., Anda, R. F., Whitfield, C. L., Brown, D. W., Felitti, V. J., Dong, M. et al. (2005). Long-term consequences of childhood sexual abuse by gender of victim. *American Journal of Preventive Medicine, 28*, 430–438.

Dube, S. R., Felitti, V. J., Dong, M., Giles, W. H., & Anda, R. F. (2003). The impact of adverse childhood experiences on health problems: Evidence from four birth cohorts dating back to 1900. *Preventive Medicine, 37*, 268–277.

Dutton, M. A., Goodman, L. A., & Bennett, L. (1999). Court-involved battered women's responses to violence: The role of psychological, physical, and sexual abuse. *Violence and Victims, 14*, 89–104.

Dutton, M. A., Kaltman, S., Goodman, L. A., Weinfurt, K., & Vankos, N. (2005). Patterns of intimate partner violence: Correlates and outcomes. *Violence and Victims, 20*, 483–497.

Dutton, D. G., & Nicholls, T. L. (2005). The gender paradigm in domestic violence research and theory: Part 1 – The conflict of theory and data. *Aggression and Violent Behavior, 10*, 680–714.

Dutton, L. B., & Spitzberg, B. H. (2007). Stalking: Its nature and dynamics. In S. M. Giacomoni & K. Kendall-Tackett (Eds.), *Intimate partner violence*. Kingston, NJ: Civic Research Institute.

Eagly, A. H., & Steffen, V. J. (1986). Gender and aggressive behavior: A meta-analytic review of the social psychological literature. *Psychological Bulletin, 100*, 309–330.

Eisenberger, N. I., & Lieberman, M. D. (2004). Why rejection hurts: A common neural alarm system for physical and social pain. *Trends in Cognitive Science, 8*, 294–300.

Felitti, V. J., Anda, R. F., Nordenberg, D., Williamson, D. F., Spitz, A. M., Edwards, V., et al. (1998). Relationship of childhood abuse and household dysfunction to many of the leading causes of death in adults. *American Journal of Preventive Medicine, 14*, 245–257.

Field, C. A., & Caetano, R. (2005). Intimate partner violence in the U.S. general population. *Journal of Interpersonal Violence, 20*, 463–469.

Follingstad, D. R., Rutledge, L. L., Polek, D. S., & McNeill-Hawkins, K. (1988). Factors associated with patterns of dating violence toward college women. *Journal of Family Violence, 3*, 169–182.

Gaertner, L., & Foshee, V. (1999). Commitment and the perpetration of relationship violence. *Personal Relationships, 6*, 227–239.

Gergen, K. J. (1984). Aggression as discourse. In A. Mummendey (Ed.), *Social psychology of aggression: From individual behavior to social interaction* (pp. 51–68). New York: Springer-Verlag.

Golding, J. M. (1999). Intimate partner violence as a risk factor for mental disorders: A meta-analysis. *Journal of Family Violence, 14*, 99–132.

Greenfeld, L. A., Rand, M. R., Craven, D., Klaus, P. A., Perkins, C. A., Ringel, C., et al. (1998). *Violence by intimates: Analysis of data on crimes by current or former spouses, boyfriends, and girlfriends* (NCJ 167237). Washington, DC: U.S. *Department of Justice*.

Gryl, F. E., Stith, S. M., & Bird, G. W. (1991). Close dating relationships among college students: Differences by use of violence and by gender. *Journal of Social and Personal Relationships, 8*, 243–264.

Hannawa, A. F., Spitzberg, B. H., Wiering, L., & Teranishi, C. (2006). "If I can't have you, no one can": Development of a relational entitlement and proprietariness scale (REPS). *Violence and Victims, 21*, 539–560.

Henning, K., & Klesges, L. M. (2003). Prevalence and characteristics of psychological abuse reported by court-involved battered women. *Journal of Interpersonal Violence, 18*, 857–871.

Henton, J., Cate, R., Koval, J., Lloyd, S., & Christopher, S. (1983). Romance and violence in dating relationships. *Journal of Family Issues, 4*, 467–482.

Hilton, N. Z., Harris, G. T., Rice, M. E., Lange, C., Cormier, C. A., & Lines, K. J. (2004). A brief actuarial assessment for the prediction of wife assault recidivism: The Ontario domestic assault risk assessment. *Psychological Assessment, 16*, 267–275.

Holtzworth-Munroe, A., Waltz, J., Jacobson, N. S., Monaco, V., Fehrenbach, P. A., & Gottman, J. M. (1992). Recruiting nonviolent men as control subjects for research on marital violence: How easily can it be done? *Violence and Victims, 7*, 79–88.

Humphreys, J. (2003). Resilience in sheltered battered women. *Issues in Mental Health Nursing, 24*, 137–152.

Jackson, S. M., Cram, F., & Seymour, F. W. (2000). Violence and sexual coercion in high school students' dating relationships. *Journal of Family Violence, 15*, 23–36.

Jacobson, N. S., Gottman, J. M., Gortner, E., Berns, S., & Shortt, J. W. (1996). Psychological factors in the longitudinal course of battering: When do the couples split up? When does the abuse decrease? *Violence and Victims, 11*, 371–392.

Johnson, M. P. (2001). Domestic violence: It's not about gender — or is it? *Journal of Marriage and Family, 67*, 1126–1130.

Katz, J., & Arias, I. (1999). Psychological abuse and depressive symptoms in dating women: Do different types of abuse have differential effects? *Journal of Family Violence, 14*, 281–295.

Katz, J., Carino, A., & Hilton, A. (2002). Perceived verbal conflict behaviors associated with physical aggression and sexual coercion in dating relationships: A gender-sensitive analysis. *Violence and Victims, 17*, 93–109.

Langhinrichsen-Rohling, J., Neidig, P., & Thorn, G. (1995). Violent marriages: Gender differences in levels of current violence and past abuse. *Journal of Family Violence, 10*, 159–176.

Leary, M. R. (2001). Toward a conceptualization of interpersonal rejection. In M. R. Leary (Ed.), *Interpersonal rejection* (pp. 3–20). New York: Oxford.

Lerner, C. F., & Kennedy, L. T. (2000). Stay-leave decision making in battered women: Trauma, coping and self-efficacy. *Cognitive Therapy and Research, 24*, 215–232.

Lo, W. A., & Sporakowski, M. J. (1989). The continuation of violent dating relationships among college students. *Journal of College Student Development, 30*, 432–439.

Marshall, L. L. (1994). Physical and psychological abuse. In W. R. Cupach & B. H. Spitzberg (Eds.), *The dark side of interpersonal communication* (pp. 281–312). Hillsdale, NJ: Erlbaum.

Matthews, K. A., Gump, B. B., Harris, K. F., Haney, T. L., & Barefoot, J. C. (2004). Hostile behaviors predict cardiovascular mortality among men enrolled in multiple risk factor intervention trial. *Circulation, 109*, 66–70.

Matthews, W. J. (1984). Violence in college couples. *College Student Journal, 18*, 150–158.

Max, W., Rice, D. P., Finkelstein, E., Bardwell, R. A., & Leadbetter, S. (2004). The economic toll of intimate partner violence against women in the United States. *Violence and Victims, 19*, 259–272.

McMillen, C., Zuravin, S., & Rideout, G. (1995). Perceived benefit from child sexual abuse. *Journal of Consulting and Clinical Psychology, 63*, 1037–1043.

Moore, T. M., Eisler, R. M., & Franchina, J. J. (2000). Causal attributions and affective responses to provocative female partner behavior by abusive and nonabusive males. *Journal of Family Violence, 15*, 69–80.

Mouradian, V. E. (2001). Applying schema theory to intimate aggression: Individual and gender differences in representation of contexts and goals. *Journal of Applied Social Psychology, 31*, 376–408.

Murphy, J. E. (1988). Date abuse and forced intercourse among college students. In G. T. Hotaling, D. Finkelhor, J. T. Kirkpatrick, & M. A. Straus (Eds.), *Family abuse and its consequences: New directions in research* (pp. 285–296). Newbury Park, CA: Sage.

Murty, S. A., Peek-Asa, C., Zwerling, C., Stromquist, A. M., Burmeister, L. F., & Merchant, J. A. (2003). Physical and emotional partner abuse reported by men and women in a rural community. *American Journal of Public Health, 93*, 1073–1074.

National Center for Injury Prevention and Control. (2003). *Costs of intimate partner violence against women in the United States.* Atlanta: Centers for Disease Control and Prevention.

O'Leary, K. D., Barling, J., Arias, I., Rosenbaum, A., Malone, J., & Tyree, A. (1989). Prevalence and stability of physical aggression between spouses: A longitudinal analysis. *Journal of Consulting and Clinical Psychology, 57*, 263–268.

Orvis, B. R., Kelley, H. H., & Butler, D. (1976). Attributional conflict in young couples. In J. H. Harvey, W. J. Ickes, & R. F. Kidd (Eds.), *New directions in attribution research* (Vol. 1). Hillsdale, NJ: Erlbaum.

Paolucci, E. O., Genuis, M. L., & Violato, C. (2001). A meta-analysis of the published research on the effects of child sexual abuse. *Journal of Psychology, 135*, 17–36.

Pape, K. T., & Arias, I. (2000). The role of perceptions and attributions in battered women's intentions to permanently end their violent relationships. *Cognitive Therapy and Research, 24*, 201–214.

Pimlott-Kubiak, S., & Cortina, L. M. (2003). Gender, victimization, and outcomes: Reconceptualizing risk. *Journal of Consulting and Clinical Psychology, 71*, 528–539.

Ptacek, J. (1988). Why do men batter their wives? In K. Yllö & M. Bograd (Eds.), *Feminist perspectives on wife abuse* (pp. 133–157). Newbury Park, CA: Sage.

Rhatigan, D. L., & Street, A. E. (2005). The impact of intimate partner violence on decisions to leave dating relationships: A test of the investment model. *Journal of Interpersonal Violence, 20*, 1580–1597.

Riger, S., Raja, S., & Camacho, J. (2002). The radiating impact of intimate partner violence. *Journal of Interpersonal Violence, 17*, 184–205.

Riger, S., Staggs, S. L., & Schewe, P. (2004). Intimate partner violence as an obstacle to employment among mothers affected by welfare reform. *Journal of Social Issues, 60*, 801–818.

Riggs, D. S., O'Leary, K. D., & Breslin, F. C. (1990). Multiple correlates of physical aggression in dating couples. *Journal of Interpersonal Violence, 5*, 61–73.

Roberts, N., & Noller, P. (1998). The associations between adult attachment and couple violence: The role of communication patterns and relationship satisfaction. In J. A. Simpson & W. S. Rholes (Eds.), *Attachment theory and close relationships* (pp. 317–350). New York: Guilford.

Roscoe, B., & Benaske, N. (1985). Courtship violence experienced by abused wives: Similarities in patterns of abuse. *Family Relations, 34*, 419–424.

Rosen, L. N., Parmley, A. M., Knudson, K. H., & Fancher, P. (2002). Gender differences in the experience of intimate partner violence among active duty U.S. army soldiers. *Military Medicine, 167*, 959–963.

Schweinle, W. E., & Ickes, W. (2002). On empathic accuracy and husbands' abusiveness: The "overattibution bias." In P. Noller & J. A. Feeney (Eds.), *Understanding marriage: Developments in the study of couple interaction* (pp. 228–250). Cambridge: Cambridge University Press.

Senter, K. E., & Caldwell, K. (2002). Spirituality and the maintenance of change: A phenomenological study of women who leave abusive relationships. *Contemporary Family Therapy, 24*, 543–564.

Sheikh, A. I., & Marotta, S. A. (2005). A cross-validation study of the post-traumatic growth inventory. *Measurement and Evaluation in Counseling and Development, 38,* 66–77.

Sillars, A., Leonard, K. E., Roberts, L. J., & Dun, T. (2002). Cognition and communication during marital conflict: How alcohol affects subjective coding of interaction in aggressive and nonaggressive couples. In P. Noller & J. A. Feeney (Eds.), *Understanding marriage: Developments in the study of couple interaction* (pp. 85–112). Cambridge: Cambridge University Press.

Simonelli, C. J., & Ingram, K. M. (1998). Psychological distress among men experiencing physical and emotional abuse in heterosexual dating relationships. *Journal of Interpersonal Violence, 13,* 667–681.

Spitzberg, B. H., & Cupach, W. R. (2007). The state of the art of stalking: Taking stock of the emerging literature. *Aggression and Violent Behavior, 12,* 64–86.

Spitzberg, B. H., & Rhea, J. (1999). Obsessive relational intrusion and sexual coercion victimization. *Journal of Interpersonal Violence, 14,* 3–20.

Stamp, G. H., & Sabourin, T. C. (1995). Accounting for violence: An analysis of male spousal abuse narratives. *Journal of Applied Communication Research, 23,* 284–307.

Stets, J. E. (1992). Interactive processes in dating aggression: A national study. *Journal of Marriage and the Family, 54,* 165–177.

Stith, S. M., Smith, D. B., Penn, C. E., Ward, D. B., & Tritt, D. (2004). Intimate partner physical abuse perpetration and victimization risk factors: A meta-analytic review. *Aggression and Violent Behavior, 10,* 65–98.

Straight, E. S., Harper, F. W. K., & Arias, I. (2003). The impact of partner psychological abuse on health behaviors and health status in college women. *Journal of Interpersonal Violence, 18,* 1035–1054.

Straus, M. A. (1999). The controversy over domestic violence by women: A methodological, theoretical, and sociology of science analysis. In X. B. Arriaga & S. Oskamp (Eds.), *Violence in intimate relationships* (pp. 17–44). Thousand Oaks, CA: Sage.

Street, A. E., & Arias, I. (2001). Psychological abuse and posttraumatic stress disorder in battered women: Examining the role of shame and guilt. *Violence and Victims, 16,* 65–78.

Sugarman, D. B., & Hotaling, G. T. (1989). Dating violence: Prevalence, context, and risk markers. In M. A. Pirog-Good & J. E. Stets (Eds.), *Violence in dating relationships: Emerging social issues* (pp. 3–32). New York: Praeger.

Tedeschi, J. T., & Felson, R. B. (1994). *Violence, aggression, & coercive actions.* Washington, DC: American Psychological Association.

Tjaden, P., & Thoennes, N. (1998, November). *Prevalence, incidence, and consequences of violence against women: Findings from the National Violence Against Women Survey* (NCJ 172837). Washington, DC: U.S. Department of Justice, National Institute of Justice.

Tjaden, P., & Thoennes, N. (2000a). *Extent, nature, and consequences of intimate partner violence: Findings from the National Violence Against Women Survey* (NCJ 181867). Washington, DC: U.S. Department of Justice, Office of Justice Programs.

Tjaden, P., & Thoennes, N. (2000b). *Full report of the prevalence, incidence, and consequences of violence against women: Findings from the National Violence Against Women Survey* (NCJ 183781). Washington, DC: National Institute of Justice and Centers for Disease Control and Prevention.

Tonizzo, S., Howells, K., Day, A., Reidpath, D., & Froyland, I. (2000). Attributions of negative partner behavior by men who physically abuse their partners. *Journal of Family Violence, 15,* 155–167.

Walby, S., & Allen, J. (2004, March). *Domestic violence, sexual assault and stalking: Findings from the British Crime Survey.* London: Home Office Research, Development and Statistics Directorate.

Watlington, C. G., & Murphy, C. M. (2006). The roles of religion and spirituality among African American survivors of domestic violence. *Journal of Clinical Psychology, 62*, 837–857.

Weaver, T. L., & Clum, G. A. (1995). Psychological distress associated with interpersonal violence: A meta-analysis. *Clinical Psychology Review, 15,* 115–140.

Wells, S., & Graham, K. (2003). Emotional effects of physical aggression among adults in the general population in a Canadian province. *Psychological Reports, 92,* 218–222.

Zlotnick, C., Johnson, D. M., & Kohn, R. (2006). Intimate partner violence and long-term psychosocial functioning in a national sample of American women. *Journal of Interpersonal Violence, 21,* 262–275.

Zlotnick, C., Kohn, R., Peterson, J., & Pearlstein, T. (1998). Partner physical victimization in a national sample of American families. *Journal of Interpersonal Violence, 13,* 156–166.

# PART IV

# HURT IN RELATIONAL CONTEXTS

# 12

# Aggression and Victimization in Children's Peer Groups: A Relationship Perspective

NOEL A. CARD, JENNY ISAACS, AND ERNEST V. E. HODGES

Children's peer relations play an important role in their psychological, academic, and social development. Although peers offer many positive benefits, such as friendships and opportunities to enact and receive prosocial behavior, on occasion, they are the source of harmful influences that result in immediate hurt feelings as well as short- and long-term negative consequences. One of the more salient aspects of peer relations is the occurrence of aggression. Immediate consequences of this aggression include fear, sadness, humiliation, and diminished self-concept for the victim; in contrast, the aggressors often experience immediate positive affect (happiness, feeling powerful) from the aggression itself or the rewards it brings. This does not imply that the hurtfulness of childhood aggression is one-sided, however. Moving beyond the immediate affect in aggressive encounters, we next review evidence that these acts of aggression have negative psychological, academic, and social consequences for both the aggressors and victims. Consistent with the theme of this book, we then turn our focus to the dyadic relationships between aggressors and victims. In this chapter we describe the conceptual, empirical, and theoretical support for this relationship perspective and then review research showing that certain aggressor–victim relationships are especially hurtful. Given that this relationship approach to studying aggression is relatively novel, we conclude with a discussion of its opportunities and challenges and a call for future research.

## AGGRESSION AND VICTIMIZATION IN CHILDREN'S PEER GROUPS

Aggression is a common problem that negatively affects aggressors, their victims, and those witnessing the aggression. Prevalence estimates of aggression and victimization vary widely across studies because they use different measurement strategies (e.g., reliance on self-reports or nominations of peers, teacher reports, observations) and criteria for classification (e.g., many studies define a child as a victim if he or she is targeted about once a week or more, but others consider entire school years or lifetime incidents). Despite this variability across studies, it appears that about 10% to 20% of children and adolescents can be considered frequent aggressors (aggressing about once a week or more), 10% to 20% can be considered frequent victims (being victimized once a week or more), and 5% to 10% can be considered both aggressors and victims (sometimes called aggressive-victims). These prevalence estimates are remarkably consistent across countries, so it appears that aggression is a problem among schoolchildren worldwide (see Smith, Morita, Junger-Tas, Olweus, Catalano, & Slee, 1998). It is also worth noting that, although these prevalence estimates would suggest that most children (50% to 75%) are not directly involved as aggressors or victims on a regular basis, most play some role in aggressive incidents, often serving as assistants or reinforcers to aggressors or as defenders of victims (see Salmivalli, 2001). Thus, aggression is a salient aspect of most youths' development.

In the remainder of this section, we briefly review the extant literature on individual differences in aggression and victimization. Specifically, we describe the consequences and risk factors for both aggressors and victims, as well as the social-cognitive processes that support these roles.

## Aggression

*Consequences of Aggression*
Aggressive children are often disliked by their normative (nonaggressive) peers (see Newcomb, Bukowski, & Pattee, 1993) and affiliate with delinquent peers who solidify and expand their antisocial tendencies (e.g., Cairns, Cairns, Neckerman, Gest, & Gariépy, 1988; Dishion, Andrews, & Crosby, 1995; Hodges, Malone, & Perry, 1997). Aggressive children are also often disengaged from school, either by their own choice or because of negative teacher reactions, suspensions, and expulsions (e.g., Coie, Terry, Lenox, Lochman, & Hyman, 1995; Miles & Stipek, 2006; Moffitt, 1993). These negative consequences of childhood are often exacerbated over time, leading to further delinquency, substance use, and dropping out of school during adolescence, and to criminal behavior, poor marital relations, and unemployment/underemployment during adulthood (see Farrington, 1991).

Of course, these associations between aggressive behavior and maladjustment are not perfect, and most aggressive youths will discontinue, or at least decrease, their use of aggression with time and lead well-adapted lives. Unfortunately, the features that account for why some aggressors suffer negative short- and long-term outcomes, whereas others do not, are poorly understood, although numerous explanations have been proposed. For example, Hawley (2003; Hawley, Little, & Card, 2007; Hawley, Little, & Pasupathi, 2002) has argued that a subset of aggressive individuals who combine aggressive behavior with prosocial behavior ("Machiavellians" or bistrategic controllers) exhibit positive psychosocial adaptation. Others (Cillessen & Mayeux, 2004; Rodkin, Farmer, Pearl, & Van Acker, 2000; Rose, Swenson, & Waller, 2004) have shown that some aggressive youths are perceived as "cool" or popular by their peers and hence are presumably more interpersonally well adjusted than prior portrayals of aggressive youths as rejected social misfits. An extensive body of work on bullying and victimization commonly distinguishes between those who are aggressive only (i.e., bullies) and those who are both aggressive and victimized (i.e., aggressive-victims), and ample evidence suggests that aggressive children who are not victimized are more psychosocially adjusted than those who are also victimized (see Pellegrini, Bartini, & Brooks, 1999; Schwartz, 2000). Another consideration is the form of aggression used, with distinctions commonly made between direct (e.g., hitting or pushing) and indirect (e.g., gossiping or spreading rumors) forms of aggression (see Archer & Coyne, 2005). Although the two forms are highly intercorrelated, some have suggested that enacting forms that are considered "gender normative" (i.e., direct aggression by boys and indirect aggression by girls) is less strongly related to maladjustment than "gender nonnormative" forms (Crick, 1997; but see Card, Stucky, Sawalani, & Little, 2008). Finally, aggressive behavior can be distinguished according to function, typically by proactive (deliberate acts that are directed toward obtaining desired goals) versus reactive (angry, often emotionally dysregulated responses to perceived offenses or frustrations) aggression; evidence suggests that reactive aggression is more strongly related to maladjustment than is proactive aggression (Card & Little, 2006, 2007).

Although each of the explanations described in the preceding paragraph hold promise in understanding the variability in adjustment outcomes for aggressors, we believe that these explanations overlap both with one another and with the aggressor–victim relationship perspective offered later in the chapter.

*Risk Factors for Aggression*
Given the prevalence and negative consequences of aggression, a considerable body of literature has attempted to identify factors that heighten the likelihood that children will enact aggression (for a review see Hodges, Card, & Isaacs, 2003). In the home context, these risk factors include parental permissiveness or lack of monitoring (either not knowing about or not correcting aggressive behavior; e.g., Griffin, Botvin, Scheier, Diaz, & Miller, 2000), negativity or rejection (versus warmth and support; e.g., McHale, Johnson, & Sinclair, 1999), a pattern of inconsistent discipline (either one parent not consistently disciplining the child or multiple caregivers applying inconsistent standards; Snyder & Patterson, 1995), and exposure to aggression in the home (through interparental abuse, physical punishment of the child, or sibling aggression; Dodge, Bates, & Pettit, 1990; MacKinnon-Lewis, Starnes, Volling, & Johnson,

1997). In the peer context, peer rejection (e.g., Coie, Lochman, Terry, & Hyman, 1992; Dodge, 1983) and victimization (Egan, Monson, & Perry, 1998) by the peer group contribute to aggression, as do affiliation with aggressive friends and subsequent socializing with these friends (e.g., Dishion et al., 1995; Dishion, Spracklen, Andrews, & Patterson, 1996; Patterson, 1986). Many of these risk factors translate into aggressive behavior through the emergence of social cognitions supporting aggression (e.g., Dodge, Pettit, Bates, & Valente, 1995), which are described next.

*Social Cognitions and Aggression*
In this section we describe two social-cognitive models to explain individual differences in tendencies to enact aggressive behavior: social learning theory and a social information-processing model. They are two distinct theoretical approaches to explaining aggressive behavior.

Among the social learning theories, Bandura's (1973, 1986) social-cognitive learning theory has been most frequently applied to understanding childhood aggression. This theory describes three cognitive components underlying aggressive behavior: (a) self-efficacy for aggression (confidence in one's ability to enact aggression), (b) outcome expectations for aggression (beliefs that aggressive behavior will result in positive outcomes, such as a victim yielding his or her resources), and (c) outcome values for aggression (high valuation of outcomes obtained through the use of aggression). Research has shown that these various social-cognitive aspects are uniquely related to aggressive behavior (Boldizar, Perry, & Perry, 1989; Perry, Perry, & Rasmussen, 1986) and that these social cognitions predict increases in aggressive behavior over time (Egan et al., 1998).

A second social-cognitive model of childhood aggression derives from the information-processing perspective. The social information-processing model of childhood aggression (see Crick & Dodge, 1994; Gifford-Smith & Rabiner, 2004) posits six "on-line" steps to account for aggressive behavior: (a) encoding of cues (aggressive children tend to encode fewer cues and those more relevant to hostility), (b) interpretation of cues (aggressive children more often interpret others' ambiguous behavior as hostile in intent), (c) goal selection (aggressive children more often select goals based on domination rather than conciliation), (d) response access or construction (aggressive children more readily access or construct aggression as a potential response), (e) response decision (this step encompasses processes of Bandura's social-cognitive model), and (f) behavioral enactment (in which aggressive children ultimately enact aggressive behavior).

These two models of childhood aggression have some degree of both distinctness and overlap. As originally posited, social-cognitive learning theory describes aggression as a thoughtful process, whereas social information processing describes the more automatic, "in the moment" processes. For this reason, social-cognitive learning theory (and the later stages of social

# Aggression and Victimization in Children's Peer Groups

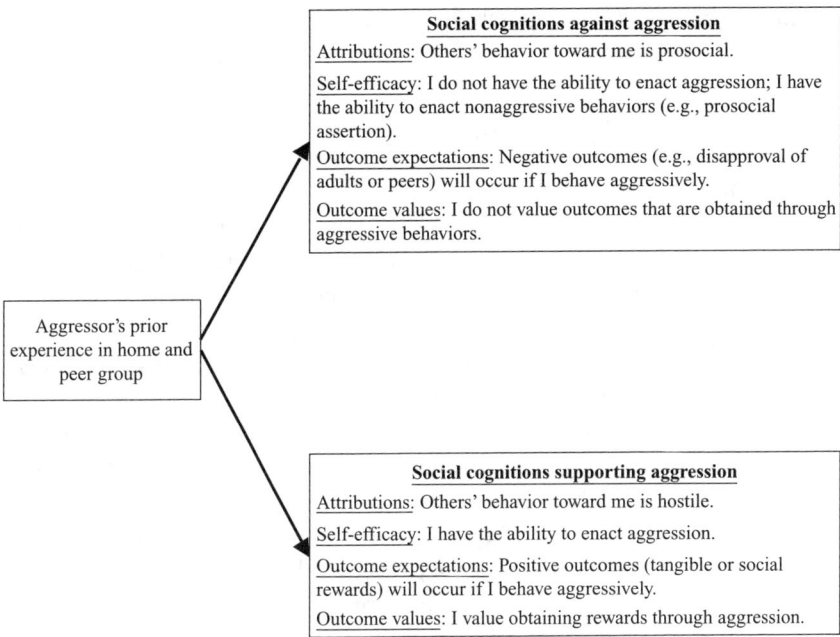

FIGURE 12.1. Schematic summary of social cognitions underlying nonaggressive and aggressive behaviors.

information-processing theory) is more often applied to research on proactive aggression, whereas social information-processing theory (especially the earlier stages) has been more often applied to reactive aggression (e.g., Crick & Dodge, 1996; see Card & Little, 2006). Despite these differences, current research has conceptualized and operationalized the social-cognitive mechanisms of each model in a way that has blurred the distinctions between them. Recent theoretical work in the social information-processing perspective on aggression has also focused increasing attention on the later stages of the model and on incorporating both impulsive and rational aggression (Fontaine & Dodge, 2006), further bridging the differences between these two models. In short, although we acknowledge that there may exist differences between the two theoretical perspectives (particularly in terms of the degree of automaticity of these processes), we consider research from both perspectives to contribute to a common picture of the social-cognitive mechanisms underlying children's aggressive behavior.

Figure 12.1 summarizes some of the social cognitions that result in children behaving nonaggressively versus aggressively toward their peers. Prior experiences in the home and peer group contribute to either cognitions against aggression or supporting aggression (of course, such a dichotomous view is not realistic, and there is likely a continuum of these cognitions and situations in which children hold some cognitions favoring aggression and others against aggression). It is expected that the upper pathway would lead to children behaving nonaggressively, whereas the lower pathway would lead to aggressive behavior.

## Victimization

*Consequences of Victimization*

As might be expected, victims of peer aggression suffer in numerous ways as a consequence of their abuse (for a review, see Card, Isaacs, & Hodges, 2007). Victimization often leads to diminished self-concept (Egan & Perry, 1998) and increases in internalizing problems (depression, anxiety, social withdrawal; Hodges, Boivin, Vitaro, & Bukowski, 1999; Hodges & Perry, 1999; Kochenderfer & Ladd, 1996; Vernberg, 1990). Victims also tend to have poorer academic adjustment, including lower grades, disliking of school, and truancy, relative to their nonvictimized peers (e.g., Juvonen, Nishina, & Graham, 2000; Kochenderfer & Ladd, 1996). Victimization also leads to poor social outcomes in the forms of having fewer friends, having friendships of poorer quality, and being disliked by most peers (Hodges et al., 1999; Hodges & Perry, 1999; Ladd & Troop-Gordon, 2003; Rigby, 2000; Vernberg, 1990). Although the empirical evidence is limited, that which is available indicates that these negative consequences, such as increased rates of depression and problematic romantic relationships in adulthood, are long lasting (e.g., Alsaker & Olweus, 2002; Gilmartin, 1987).

As with the consequences for aggressors, the consequences of victimization are not absolute. However, there has been limited theoretical or empirical attention to identifying the conditions under which victimization leads to greater or lesser negative consequences. One factor that has been found to moderate the consequences of victimization is the chronicity of abuse, with children who experience repeated victimization over time suffering more maladjustment than those experiencing victimization intermittently (Kochenderfer-Ladd & Wardrop, 2001). Although we noted earlier that victims often suffer low self-concept, it may be the case that those who have higher self-concept tend to suffer fewer negative consequences of victimization (in a concurrent study, in which directions of effect cannot be inferred, Grills & Ollendick [2002] found that high self-worth minimizes associations between victimization and anxiety for boys but not girls). More consistent support has been found for the buffering effect of friendships, especially high-quality friendships marked by support (Hodges et al., 1999; Prinstein, Boergers, & Vernberg, 2001; Vernberg, 1990). Similarly, family support may buffer the impact of victimization; for example, Isaacs, Salmivalli, and Hodges (2007) found that victimization in adolescence predicted increases in depression and decreases in self-esteem by young adulthood but only for adolescents who lacked a supportive family environment. Overall, much is still unknown about the factors that account for variability in the consequences of victimization.

*Risk Factors for Victimization*

As with aggressors, victims more often have experiences in the home context that place them at risk (for reviews see Card et al., 2007; Perry, Hodges, & Egan, 2001). These risk factors include low parental involvement, responsiveness, and support (e.g., Haynie et al., 2001; Ladd & Kochenderfer-Ladd, 1998); abuse (Duncan, 1999; Shields & Cicchetti, 2001); parental overenmeshment among boys and threats of rejection among girls (Finnegan, Hodges, & Perry, 1998); the development of preoccupied attachment (Finnegan, Hodges, & Perry, 1996; Troy & Sroufe, 1987); and exposure to community violence (Schwartz & Proctor, 2000). Many of these familial risk factors translate into victimization within the peer group via the emergence of personal and interpersonal risk factors, described next.

There are several personal characteristics that often place children at increased risk for victimization. As might be expected, children who are physically weak are more often victimized (Hodges et al., 1997; Hodges & Perry, 1999; Olweus, 1978; Pellegrini, 1995). Internalizing problems, such as depression, anxiety, and shy/withdrawn behaviors, are strongly associated with victimization (see Card, 2003) and predict increases in victimization over time (Boivin, Hymel, & Bukowski, 1995; Egan & Perry, 1998; Hodges et al., 1999; Hodges & Perry, 1999; Vernberg, 1990). The likely reasons for this association are that potential aggressors view these children as easy targets (who will not defend themselves) and are reinforced by the victims' displays of suffering when they do aggress against these children. This explanation might also account for findings that low self-concept contributes to increases in victimization over time (Egan & Perry, 1998). Externalizing problems are also related to victimization, although the magnitude of this association varies by the type of externalizing problem considered: Hyperactive and emotionally dysregulated behaviors are strongly related to victimization (e.g., Pope & Bierman, 1999; Shields & Cicchetti, 2001), delinquency and conduct problems exhibit a modest correlation with victimization (e.g., Prinstein et al., 2001), and aggression is essentially unrelated to victimization (e.g., Olweus, 1978; Perry, Kusel, & Perry, 1988). It is likely that hyperactive and dysregulated behaviors are especially annoying and provocative to aggressors, whereas other aspects of externalizing problems are either less provocative or simultaneously serve a deterring function (e.g., threat of retaliation).

In addition to these personal risk factors, victims often have social relations that place them at risk for peer victimization. Interpersonal risk factors at the group level include peer rejection and low peer acceptance; victims are often disliked by many peers and liked by few (e.g., Boulton, 1999; Hodges & Perry, 1999; Ladd & Troop-Gordon, 2003). Poor group-level relations may place children at risk for victimization because potential aggressors may expect that targeting these low-status students is unlikely to be negatively evaluated by the peer group. Similarly, victims are less likely to have reciprocal friendships than nonvictims (Boulton, Trueman, Chau, Whitehand, & Amatya, 1999; Hodges et al., 1999; Hodges & Perry, 1999; Salmivalli, Huttunen, & Lagerspetz, 1997), and the friends they do have tend to be themselves victimized (Haselager, Hartup, Van Lieshout, & Riksen-Walraven, 1998; Hodges et al., 1997; Salmivalli et al., 1997) or otherwise have characteristics that make them unable to provide protection (e.g., physical weakness, internalizing problems; Hodges et al., 1997). In other words, the absence of friends or having friendships only with children who are themselves at risk for or experience victimization places children at risk for themselves being victimized, presumably because potential aggressors do not fear retaliation from the target's friends. Finally, there is recent evidence of an association between victimization and the number of antipathetic relationships (i.e., relationships based on mutual dislike) children have (Card & Hodges, 2007; Parker & Gamm, 2003; Schwartz, Hopmeyer Gorman, Toblin, & Abou-ezzedine, 2003), especially if these antipathies are physically strong and aggressive (Card & Hodges, 2007). One possibility is that potential aggressors expect that their aggression will be supported or rewarded by these antipathies. A second possibility, discussed in more detail later, is that these antipathies themselves are sources of victimization.

It is worth noting that many of the personal and interpersonal risk factors for victimization were also described earlier as consequences of victimization. This is not a contradiction but rather representative of the cyclical nature of victimization. In other words, certain characteristics (e.g., depression, peer rejection) place children at risk for peer victimization, and the resulting peer victimization increases these characteristics (e.g., increased depression and peer rejection), resulting in further victimization, and so on. This vicious cycle may account for the high degree of stability in peer victimization across time and contexts.

*Social Cognitions and Victimization*
Two aspects of social cognitions are useful in understanding individual differences in peer victimization. The first involves the social cognitions held by peers toward victimized children, and the second involves the social cognitions about escaping the aggression held by the victims themselves.

Perry, Williard, and Perry (1990) examined the social cognitions that children in general (i.e., not just aggressors) hold toward children who are victimized. They found that children expect that aggressive behavior would result in more tangible rewards and more victim suffering and would be less likely to result in retaliation when directed toward peers viewed as highly victimized relative to those viewed as not victimized. These findings indicate that differences in how children are perceived by their peers (i.e., the social cognitions that peers have toward them) are related to being victimized by peers, presumably because at least some children are likely to act on these social cognitions.

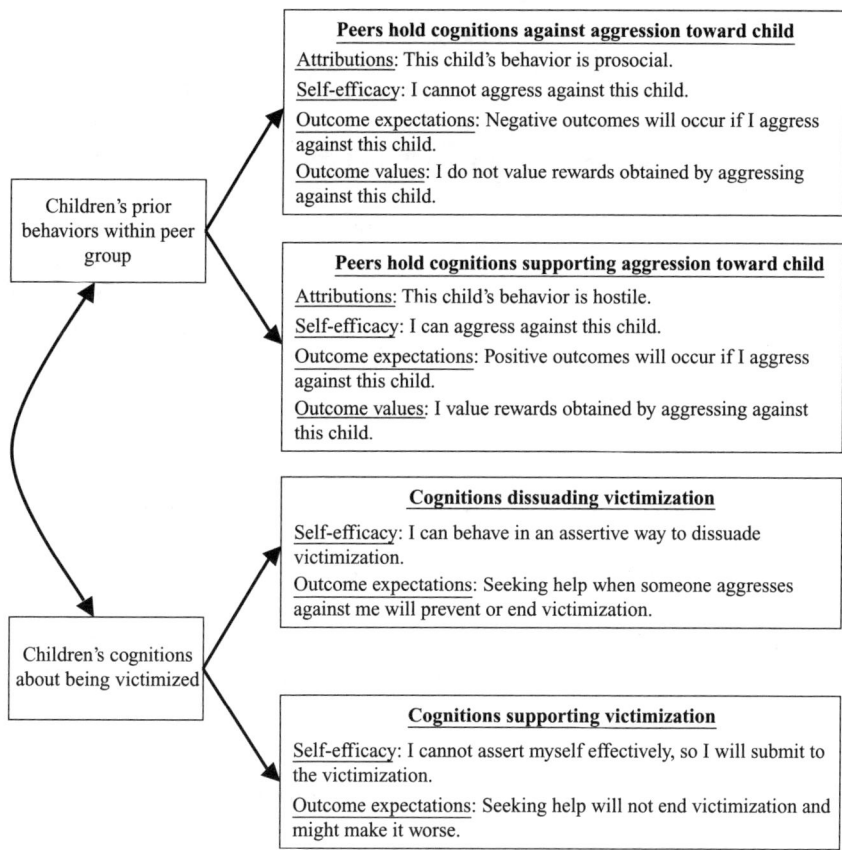

FIGURE 12.2. Schematic summary of social cognitions held by peers and child resulting in nonvictimization versus victimization.

Social cognitions held by the victims themselves seem to also contribute to their maltreatment by peers. There is some evidence that victims have low self-efficacy for assertion (see Camodeca & Goossens, 2005; Egan & Perry, 1998), leading them to behave submissively rather than assertively to aggressive overtures (Schwartz, Dodge, & Coie, 1993). Victims also often fail to seek help in preventing or countering aggression. For example, surveys have indicated that only about half of elementary school children report victimization to teachers, with this percentage falling even lower throughout middle and high school (e.g., O'Moore, Kirkham, & Smith, 1997; Smith & Shu, 2000). One reason for this failure to report victimization to teachers is that victims often believe such action will fail to improve and may even worsen their situation (Newman & Murray, 2005; Smith & Shu, 2000). Figure 12.2 summarizes some of the social cognitions held by children resulting in nonvictimization versus victimization.

## A RELATIONSHIP PERSPECTIVE ON AGGRESSION

Although the literature on the consequences and causes of individual differences in tendencies to enact or be the victim of aggression is valuable in understanding aggressors and victims, this approach is limited in several regards. One limitation of this individual-level focus is that the literatures on aggression and on victimization have progressed somewhat separately, with many theoretical and empirical investigations focusing on one aspect but not the other (e.g., studies of individual differences in aggression often do not consider individual differences in victimization and vice versa). More important, the focus on individual differences has resulted in a decontextualized perspective of the phenomena, investigating aggression as if it involved indiscriminant acts toward peers in general and victimization as if it were a form of mobbing imposed by an entire peer group on the unfortunate victims. In other words, the traditional focus on individual differences has failed to adequately consider the inextricable link between aggression and victimization. A consideration of aggressor–victim relationships overcomes these limits. Moreover, as we describe next, there are convincing conceptual and empirical reasons to adapt this relationship perspective, and we put forth a model that we believe represents a plausible (yet untested) model by which aggressor–victim relationships form.

### Conceptual Rationale for a Relationship Focus

With only a very few exceptions (e.g., self-injurious behavior, aggression toward animals or inanimate objects), aggressive behavior necessarily involves at least two individuals. This does not imply that aggression occurs only in the presence of a single aggressor and single victim. Instead, the presence of others during aggressive encounters can play influential roles in the occurrence or prevention of aggression, as these others can act as additional aggressors (e.g., two friends aggressing against a common target; Card & Hodges, 2006), assistants or reinforcers of the aggressor (e.g., by cheering on the aggressor or passing on rumors started by the aggressor), or defenders of the victim (e.g., by intervening on behalf of the victim; see Salmivalli, 2001). Nevertheless, aggressor–victim dyads represent the simplest interpersonal level for the consideration of acts of aggressive behavior.

### Empirical Rationale for a Relationship Focus

The empirical investigation of aggressor–victim relationships is limited, but the studies that have adopted this perspective provide convincing data for the importance of a relationship focus. The first study to demonstrate the saliency of aggressor–victim dyads was of 6- and 8-year-old boys in artificial play groups observed over multiple daily sessions (Dodge, Price, Coie, & Christopoulos, 1990). Results indicated that 50% of aggressive acts occurred within just 20% of dyads and that dyads in which aggression occurred in one play session tended to be the same dyads in which aggression occurred in other play sessions. These results provide evidence that a sizable percentage of aggressive behavior occurs within specific aggressor–victim dyads rather than as indiscriminant acts by aggressors or as the aggressive action of numerous peers toward certain victimized youths. A separate investigation (Coie et al., 1999) relying on observations of aggression in boys' artificial play groups used social relations modeling (SRM; see Kenny, 1994) to partition the variance of aggressive acts into that due to (a) individual differences among aggressors (tendencies for some children to enact frequent aggression whereas others enact little), (b) individual differences among victims (tendencies for some children to be victimized more frequently than others), and (c) stable relationship differences (tendencies for some dyads to consistently contain more aggression than others). Although individual differences in aggression and victimization were found to be statistically significant, stable aggressor–victim relationships accounted for greater variability in the occurrence of aggression. Further analyses indicated that the social cognitions held by specific aggressors about specific victims play a substantial role in accounting for this relationship effect (Hubbard, Dodge, Cillessen, Coie, & Schwartz, 2001).

Although these studies were valuable in demonstrating the importance of a dyadic focus on aggressor–victim relationships, they were also limited in focusing exclusively on boys' aggression within artificial play groups. A small amount of recent work has attempted to evaluate aggressor–victim relationships in naturalistic school contexts, and the results thus far also suggest the importance of a dyadic focus. For example, Card and Hodges (in press) evaluated a self-report instrument of directed aggression and received victimization, in which children identify specific peers they aggress against or are victimized by. They found that this instrument has adequate reliability and validity in identifying aggressor–victim relationships. These authors also conducted SRM variance partitioning procedures similar to Coie and colleagues (1999) and similarly found that relationship effects contributed the most variability in the occurrence of aggressive behaviors. These results indicate that aggressor–victim relationships are an important level of focus in naturally occurring settings such as school peer groups. Further findings from these data are discussed later.

## A MODEL OF THE FORMATION OF AGGRESSOR–VICTIM RELATIONSHIPS

In this section, we propose a model of how aggressor–victim relationships form. Although this model has not been empirically evaluated, we believe it

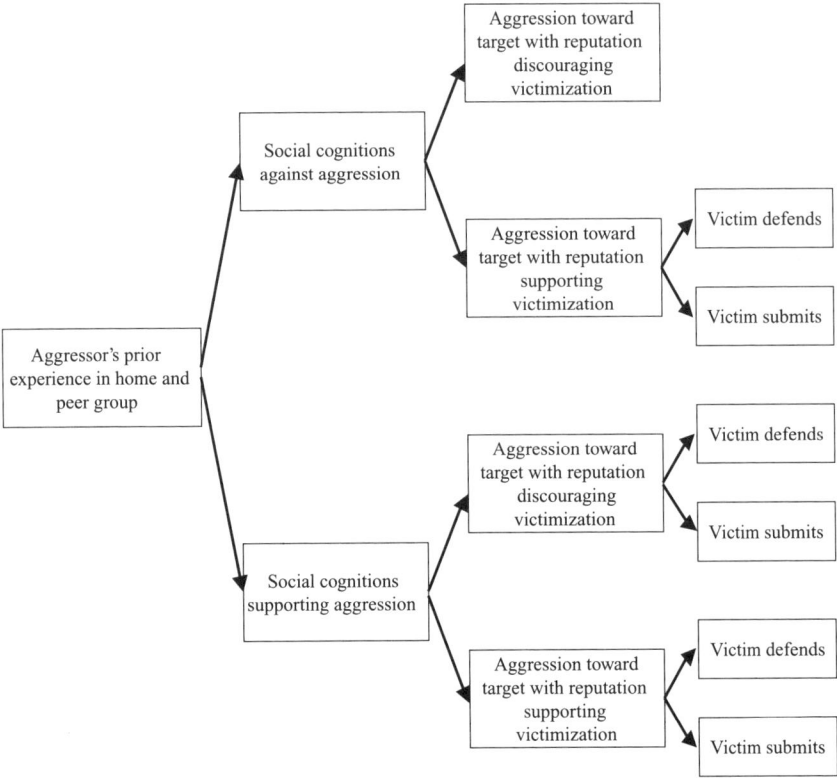

FIGURE 12.3. Schematic summary of interdependence of attackers and targets in the formation of aggressor–victim relationships.

represents a plausible model based on prior research on individual-level social cognitions of aggressors and social cognitions held by peers toward and by victims themselves. Although future research may disconfirm our speculations, we believe that consideration of this model illustrates why we view childhood aggression as a relationship, in which the outcomes for each individual are dependent on the actions of the partner.

We depict this model in Figure 12.3. Consider first the chain of events shown along the top of the figure. Here, we have depicted a situation in which a child's prior experiences in the home and peer group have led him or her to have social cognitions that do not support aggression (see also top portion of Fig. 12.1). The first potential outcome is that this child attempts to aggress against another child who does not have a reputation among peers that would encourage victimization (see top portion of Fig. 12.2). We consider this an unlikely occurrence and thus do not consider this situation further. The second pathway in the upper portion of Figure 12.3 involves this child with aggression-discouraging cognitions aggressing against another child who is generally viewed by peers as one who encourages victimization (e.g., the child is viewed as hostile or an easy target; upper portion of Fig. 12.2). In this instance, the targeted child might either successfully defend him- or herself or might submit to (or otherwise not defend against) the attack. If the targeted child successfully defends him- or herself, then it is likely that the attacker will not attempt further attacks on the target in the future, and this experience will likely further contribute to the attacker's aggression-discouraging cognitions. In contrast, if the victim submits, then the aggression toward this target is likely to be reinforced; this is likely to result in the formation of an aggressor–victim relationship, to contribute to increases in the attacker's social cognitions supporting aggression, and to lead to increasing peer group views of the target being susceptible to victimization. We might consider this pathway an instance of a victim-driven aggressor–victim relationship. Despite this terminology, we should keep in mind that this normally nonaggressive child found something uniquely provocative about this particular target (that was not experienced by other potential attackers). For example, the target may have exhibited behavior that the attacker found particularly aversive, there may have been an opportunity for rewards that the attacker found particularly desirable, or some relative characteristics between the attacker and target might have led the attacker to believe he or she could successfully aggress against this target. In short, we consider victim-driven aggressor–victim relationships to be relational rather than individual phenomena.

In the lower half of Figure 12.3, we consider attackers who have social cognitions that support aggression (see also lower portion of Fig. 12.1). These children are more likely to attempt aggression than children in the upper half of Figure 12.3, and we can consider two potential targets of their aggression: those whom the peer group views as unlikely victims (upward arrow) and those whom the peer group views as likely victims (downward arrow). Considering the first instance, we again present the possibilities that the target can either defend or submit (i.e., fail to defend), although of course this is an artificial dichotomy of what is likely to be a continuous range of outcomes. If the target successfully repels the attack then it is unlikely that an aggressor–victim relationship will form, the attacker is likely to consider other targets for aggression, and the target is likely to further encourage the peer groups' view that he or she is not a potential victim. However, if the target submits or is otherwise unable to defend him- or herself, then it is likely that an aggressor–victim relationship will emerge. This relationship could be considered aggressor-driven. Again, however, this terminology does not imply an individual rather than relational phenomenon, because it is likely that there were some characteristics that the attacker perceived as making the target a viable target for aggression more so than other potential targets (e.g., behaviors that the attacker found particularly provocative, potential weaknesses that the attacker felt able to exploit, or rewards that the attacker found possible and worthwhile).

Finally, we consider the lower portion of Figure 12.3, in which a child with aggression-encouraging cognitions attacks a target toward whom the peer group holds aggression-encouraging cognitions. This is likely the most common situation. The first possibility is that the target successfully repels the attack; if this occurs then the attacker is likely to attempt aggression again through different means (e.g., using a different form of aggression, gathering assistants for future attacks), seek other targets for aggression, or reduce cognitions about aggressive behavior (e.g., experience diminished self-efficacy for aggression). The second possibility is that the victim succumbs to the attack, resulting in an aggressor–victim relationship that is driven by both the characteristics of the aggressor and target. This outcome may lead the aggressor to attempt aggression toward targets similar to the victim and children similar to the aggressor to attempt attacks against the victim.

We should note that this model is an oversimplified representation of the processes that likely lead to the formation of aggressor–victim relationships. What makes the formation of aggressor–victim relationships far more complex is that these attacks are probably highly personal in some form. In other words, the reasons that a child attacks specific targets (e.g., because certain behaviors are particularly provocative, because potential rewards are particularly appealing), the characteristics of the attack itself (e.g., direct or indirect forms to serve proactive or reactive functions, occurring in different contexts), and the ability of the target to defend him- or herself (based on relative power between the attacker and target, the peer support available to the target in repelling the particular attacker, and the willingness to seek and be helped by adult intervention) create a much more complex picture than we have portrayed. In short, we believe that childhood aggression is personal – in that it involves numerous features of the attacker, victim, and context – and that the formation of aggressor–victim relationships is a highly interpersonal phenomenon.

## THE CONSEQUENCES OF AGGRESSOR–VICTIM RELATIONSHIPS

Conceptualizing aggressive behavior as a dyadic phenomenon allows for greater understanding of the variability (described later) in outcomes for aggressors and victims. Although full empirical investigation of the possibilities has not yet been conducted, we describe three ways of placing aggressor–victim relationships in the social context that offer promise in understanding the consequences of engagement in these relationships: (a) possibilities based on the place of the aggressor–victim relationship within the larger peer group, (b) the overlap of these aggressor–victim relationships with other dyadic relationships, and (c) the characteristics of the aggressor–victim relationships themselves.

### Place of Aggressor–Victim Relationship in the Peer Group

Various ways of subdividing children's peer groups have been proposed, including sociometric classification (i.e., popular, rejected, controversial, average, and neglected; see Cillessen & Bukowski, 2000; Coie, Dodge, & Coppotelli, 1982; DeRosier & Thomas, 2003; Newcomb et al., 1993), resource control strategies (i.e., prosocial, coercive, bistrategic, average, and noncontrolling; see Hawley, 2003; Hawley, Little, & Card, 2008; Hawley et al., 2002), and aggressor–victim status (i.e., aggressors, victims, aggressive-victims, uninvolved; see Pellegrini et al., 1999; Schwartz, 2000). Important questions that can be asked from each perspective include the following: How common is aggression by members of each group toward members of other (and the same) groups? What is the impact of aggressor–victim relationships between individuals in these different groups for the aggressors and for the victims?

To our knowledge, only one unpublished study has taken this approach to situating aggressor–victim relationships within the larger peer group. In this study (Card, 2001; Card, Isaacs, & Hodges, 2000) middle school students were classified as aggressive, aggressive-victims, victims, or uninvolved, and the frequency of aggressor–victim relationships among these different classifications was examined. Results indicated that aggressors (nonvictimized) directed their aggression primarily toward peers classified as victims or aggressive-victims. In contrast, aggressive-victims directed their aggression indiscriminately, reporting aggression approximately equally among peers in all four groups. Although we did not empirically evaluate this possibility, we speculate that the aggression by the aggressive-only group was more strategic (probably proactive) in being directed toward vulnerable peers and therefore less likely to yield negative consequences such as social condemnation; in contrast, the aggression by the aggressive-victims was probably less planful (reactive), was likely ineffectual (especially against more dominant aggressors; see also Perry, Perry, & Kennedy, 1992), and probably resulted in more negative consequences (e.g., aggression toward uninvolved peers likely resulted in peer rejection) than the aggression enacted by the aggressive-only group.

Although this study is limited by not formally assessing the outcomes of various aggressor–victim relationships and by speculating about outcomes only for aggressors (but not victims), we believe it represents the potential for considering the larger peer context in which aggressor–victim relationships lie. Clearly, there is considerable room for future research along these lines.

### Overlap of Aggressor–Victim Relationship with other Dyadic Relationships

Another potentially valuable approach to understanding aggressor–victim relationships is to consider their overlap with other dyadic relationships, such as friendships and antipathetic relationships. In one study in which college students were retrospectively interviewed about their peer relations during high school, participants reported that aggression and victimization were far more common in their relationships with antipathies than with friends or neutral acquaintances (Card, 2007). Findings that victimization is received disproportionately frequently within antipathetic relationships than in friendships or with neutral acquaintances were confirmed in a concurrent study of middle school children (Card & Hodges, 2007). Furthermore, victimization was especially likely within antipathetic relationships when these antipathies were aggressive, physically strong, and rarely victimized. Results also indicated that victimization within antipathetic relationships was more strongly linked to maladjustment (internalizing problems and low self-worth) than was victimization within friendships or neutral acquaintanceships. This latter finding illustrates the importance of the affective relationship context (e.g., mutual antipathy) in accounting for the variability in outcomes for victims.

The affective relationship context has also recently been demonstrated as being critical in children's thinking about aggression as well as their actual behavior. To assess relationship-specific attributions of hostile intent and behavioral strategies, Peets, Hodges, Kikas, and Salmivalli (2007) administered individually tailored vignettes in which each child was asked to think of their friend, neutral peer, or enemy (in separate vignettes) during peer provocation and rebuff situations. The overwhelming majority of the variance in children's thinking was due to relationship type, with more hostile intent attributed to and more hostile strategies proposed toward enemies than other relationship types. Moreover, Peets, Hodges, and Salmivalli (2008) demonstrated relationship-specific linkages between children's aggression-encouraging thought and behavior.

## Characteristics of Aggressor–Victim Relationships

Perhaps the most straightforward approach to understanding consequences for aggressors and their victims is to examine the qualities of the aggressor–victim relationship itself. Numerous qualities can readily be considered, including the forms (e.g., direct versus indirect) and functions (proactive versus reactive) that the aggression typically takes, the frequency and intensity of abuse, and the location in which aggression occurs. Another conceptually appealing quality of aggressor–victim relationships to consider is the magnitude of power differentials between aggressors and victims. It might be expected, for example, that relationships of unidirectional aggression commonly involve the aggressor being stronger, more popular, or having more friends than the targeted victims. Similarly, it might be expected that mutually aggressive relationships are characterized by discordance or "clashing" of some aspects of personality, behaviors, and social positions. These possibilities have not been empirically evaluated, so they are simply speculations at this point. However, we believe that these represent just a few of the many possibilities for better understanding aggressor–victim relationships and their consequences.

### CONCLUSION

We believe that a relationship perspective to studying children's aggression and victimization has several advantages over the traditional focus on individual differences in aggression and (separately) victimization. First, this relationship focus serves to integrate too-often separate bodies of literature on aggression and victimization. Second, this perspective has at its core the inherent interpersonal nature of aggressive behavior. Third, this approach contextualizes our investigation of aggressive behaviors, recognizing that the identity of the victim is important to the aggressor and vice versa. Finally, this approach allows for consideration of the features of aggressor–victim relationships as well as how they overlap with other dyadic relationships and are embedded within the larger peer group.

This relationship approach does not limit our attention to instances in which a single aggressor targets a single victim in the absence of peers. Such an approach would be unrealistic, as many occurrences of aggression occur in the presence of assistants or reinforcers to the aggressor or defenders of the victim (Salmivalli, 2001). Instead, this relationship focus represents the most fundamental unit of analysis for studying aggression. Once we better understand the aggressor–victim dyad, it is possible to build on this knowledge to study triads, networks or cliques, and larger peer groups. To provide one illustrative example, Card and Hodges (2006) studied the occurrence of two friends aggressing against a common victim; although this focus was on triads, it was approached by building up from dyadic levels of analysis (here, friendships and aggressor–victim relationships). Certainly, other possibilities exist when we start with dyads as the unit of analysis.

Given these advantages of a dyadic perspective, it seems fair to ask why more theory and research have not taken this approach. Calls for such an approach are not new; Pierce and Cohen argued persuasively for such an approach in 1995, and Dodge and colleagues empirically demonstrated the importance of aggressor–victim dyads in 1990. We believe that three challenges have limited the use of this approach.

First, one obstacle to a relationship approach to aggression and victimization might simply be that thinking about dyads is different from the traditional individual-level approach that has predominated in developmental science. Perhaps because of the strong influence of psychology, in which individual-differences approaches have historically dominated, our theoretical and empirical approaches to child development have focused primarily on mean-level age differences and individual differences around this mean. One obstacle to adapting a dyadic perspective, then, might simply be that this type of thinking is different from our usual approaches and will require new theories and research methods than we are accustomed to. We believe that a relationship perspective is both worthwhile and possible, as evidenced by the other chapters in this book, but will require developmental researchers to step outside of their typical comfort zones.

A second challenge to studying aggressor–victim relationships is that we need to develop new measures to assess these relationships. Although a wide variety of self-, peer-, teacher-, and parent-reported measures, as well as observational techniques, are available for measuring individual differences in aggression and victimization, new measurement strategies need to be developed to evaluate aggressor–victim relationships. In our own research, we have relied on self-reports of targets of aggression and sources of victimization, which therefore measure these relationships from the perspective of both the aggressors and victims, and this instrument has been shown to have adequate psychometric properties (Card & Hodges, 2009). Other measurement methods will likely be valuable in addressing different questions. For instance, observational methods might best allow us to understand the immediate affect experienced during instances of aggression, whereas self-reports of these relationships might be more strongly associated with more distal consequences for aggressors and victims. An important direction for future research is the development of ways to assess these relationships via various reporters (for a method of using peer reports, see Troop-Gordon & Brock, 2005) and to evaluate the overlap and differences in prevalence and consequences of these different assessment methods.

Finally, a third challenge to studying aggressor–victim relationships is the development of appropriate data analytic strategies. Traditional methods of inferential data analysis assume independence of observations, an assumption that is clearly violated when studying interdependent individuals in relationships. Techniques have been developed for appropriately analyzing dyads (e.g., the actor–partner interdependence model) and small groups (e.g., the social relations model; see Card, Selig, & Little, 2008; Kenny, Kashy, & Cook, 2006; Little & Card, 2005). However, aggressor–victim relationships represent a special challenge in that the dyads are partially overlapping (i.e., aggressors and victims are likely to each be in multiple dyads). This challenge should not deter us from studying aggressor–victim relationships, even in the absence of perfect methods for analyzing these data (existing methods are likely to yield unbiased results but diminished statistical power; see Little & Card, 2005). At the same time, development of these data analytic strategies will be valuable in aiding this emerging line of research.

We have described several directions for future research throughout this chapter, but it is worth noting that these represent only a small sample of the possibilities. Our hope is that future theory, research, and applications (e.g., prevention and intervention efforts) will continue to extend this focus on aggressor–victim relationships. This future work will allow us to better understand and prevent the hurt feelings and negative consequences that too many children experience in their social lives.

REFERENCES

Alsaker, F., & Olweus, D. (2002). Stability and change in global self-esteem and self-related affect. In T. M. Brinthaupt & R. P. Lipka (Eds.), *Understanding early adolescent self and identity: Applications and interventions* (pp. 193–223). Albany, NY: State University of New York Press.

Archer, J., & Coyne, S. M. (2005). An integrated review of indirect, relational, and social aggression. *Personality and Social Psychology Review, 9*, 212–230.

Bandura, A. (1973). *Aggression: A social learning analysis.* Englewood Cliffs, NJ: Prentice-Hall.

Bandura, A. (1986). *Social foundations of thought and action.* Englewood Cliffs, NJ: Prentice-Hall.

Boivin, M., Hymel, S., & Bukowski, W. M. (1995). The roles of social withdrawal, peer rejection, and victimization by peers in predicting loneliness and depressed mood in childhood. *Development and Psychopathology, 7*, 765–786.

Boldizar, J. P., Perry, D. G., & Perry, L. C. (1989). Outcome values and aggression. *Child Development, 60*, 571–579.

Boulton, M. J. (1999). Concurrent and longitudinal relations between children's playground behavior and social preference, victimization, and bullying. *Child Development, 70*, 944–954.

Boulton, M. J., Trueman, M., Chau, C., Whitehand, C., & Amatya, K. (1999). Concurrent and longitudinal links between friendships and peer victimization: Implications for befriending interventions. *Journal of Adolescence, 22*, 461–466.

Cairns, R. B., Cairns, B. D., Neckerman, H. J., Gest, S., & Gariépy, J. L. (1988). Social networks and aggressive behavior: Peer support or peer rejection? *Child Development, 65*, 1068–1079.

Camodeca, M., & Goossens, F. A. (2005). Aggression, social cognitions, anger and sadness in bullies and victims. *Journal of Child Psychology and Psychiatry, 46*, 186–197.

Card, N. A. (2001). *Who aggresses against whom?: An examination of aggressors and victims in a school setting.* Unpublished masters thesis, St. John's University.

Card, N. A. (2003, April). Victims of peer aggression: A meta-analytic review. In N. A. Card & A. Nishina (Chairs), *Whipping boys and other victims of peer aggression: 25 years of research, now where do we go?* Poster symposium presented at the biennial meeting of the Society for Research in Child Development, Tampa, FL.

Card, N. A. (2007). "I hated her guts!": Emerging adults' recollections of the formation, maintenance, and termination of antipathetic relationships during high school. *Journal of Adolescent Research, 22*, 32–57.

Card, N. A., & Hodges, E. V. E. (2006). Shared targets for aggression by early adolescent friends. *Developmental Psychology, 42*, 1327–1338.

Card, N. A., & Hodges, E. V. E. (2007). Victimization within mutually antipathetic peer relationships. *Social Development, 16*, 479–496.

Card, N. A., & Hodges, E. V. E. (in press). It takes two to fight in school too: A social relations model of the psychometric properties and relative variance of dyadic aggression and victimization in middle school. *Social Development.*

Card, N. A., Isaacs, J., & Hodges, E. V. E. (2000, March). Dynamics of interpersonal aggression in the school context: Who aggresses against whom? In J. Juvonen & A. Nishina (Chairs), *Harassment across diverse contexts.* Poster symposium presented at the biennial meeting of the Society for Research on Adolescence, Chicago.

Card, N. A., Isaacs, J., & Hodges, E. V. E. (2007). Correlates of school victimization: Recommendations for prevention and intervention. In J. E. Zins, M. J. Elias, & C. A. Maher (Eds.), *Bullying, victimization, and peer harassment: A handbook of prevention and intervention* (pp. 339–366). New York: Haworth.

Card, N. A., & Little, T. D. (2006). Proactive and reactive aggression in childhood and adolescence: A meta-analysis of differential relations with psychosocial adjustment. *International Journal of Behavioral Development, 30,* 466–480.

Card, N. A., & Little, T. D. (2007). The adaptivity of instrumental and reactive aggression. In P. H. Hawley, T. D. Little, & P. C. Rodkin (Eds.), *Aggression and adaptation: The bright side to bad behavior* (pp. 107–134). Mahwah, NJ: Erlbaum.

Card, N. A., Selig, J. P., & Little, T. D. (Eds.)(2008). *Modeling dyadic and interdependent data in developmental research.* New York: Routledge.

Card, N. A., Stucky, B. D., Sawalani, G. M., & Little, T. D. (2008). Direct and indirect aggression during childhood and adolescence: A meta-analytic review of intercorrelations, gender differences, and relations to maladjustment. *Child Development, 79,* 1185–1229.

Cillessen, A. H. N., & Bukowski, W. M. (Eds.). (2000). New directions in the measurement of acceptance and rejection in the peer system. *New Directions for Child and Adolescent Development, 88.* San Francisco: Jossey–Bass.

Cillessen, A. H. N., & Mayeux, L. (2004). From censure to reinforcement: Developmental changes in the association between aggression and social status. *Child Development, 75,* 147–163.

Coie, J. D., Cillessen, A. H. N., Dodge, K. A., Hubbard, J. A., Schwartz, D., Lemerise, E. A., & Bateman, H. (1999). It takes two to fight: A test of relational factors and a method for assessing aggressive dyads. *Developmental Psychology, 35,* 1179–1188.

Coie, J. D., Dodge, K. A., & Coppotelli, H. (1982). Dimensions and types of social status: A cross-age comparison. *Developmental Psychology, 18,* 557–570.

Coie, J. D., Lochman, J. E., Terry, R., & Hyman, C. (1992). Predicting early adolescent disorder from childhood aggression and peer rejection. *Journal of Consulting and Clinical Psychology, 60,* 783–792.

Coie, J. D., Terry, R., Lenox, K., Lochman, J., & Hyman, C. (1995). Childhood peer rejection and aggression as predictors of stable adolescent disorders. *Development and Psychology, 7,* 697–713.

Crick, N. R. (1997). Engagement in gender normative versus nonnormative forms of aggression: Links to social-psychological adjustment. *Developmental Psychology, 33,* 610–617.

Crick, N. R., & Dodge, K. A. (1994). A review and reformulation of social information-processing mechanisms in children's social adjustment. *Psychological Bulletin, 115,* 74–101.

Crick, N. R., & Dodge, K. A. (1996). Social information-processing mechanisms in reactive and instrumental aggression. *Child Development, 67,* 993–1002.

DeRosier, M. E., & Thomas, T. J. (2003). Strengthening sociometric prediction: Scientific advances in the assessment of children's peer relations. *Child Development, 74,* 1379–1392.

Dishion, T. J., Andrews, D. W., & Crosby, L. (1995). Antisocial boys and their friends in early adolescence: Relationship characteristics, quality, and interactional processes. *Child Development, 66,* 139–151.

Dishion, T. J., Spracklen, K. M., Andrews, D. M., & Patterson, G. R. (1996). Deviancy training in male adolescent friendships. *Behavior Therapy, 27,* 373–390.

Dodge, K. A. (1983). Behavioral antecedents of peer social status. *Child Development, 54,* 1386–1399.

Dodge, K. A., Bates, J. E., & Pettit, G. S. (1990). Mechanisms in the cycle of violence. *Science, 250,* 1678–1683.

Dodge, K. A., Pettit, G. S., Bates, J. E., & Valente, E. (1995). Social information-processing patterns partially mediate the effects of early physical abuse on later conduct problems. *Journal of Abnormal Psychology, 104*, 632–643.

Dodge, K. A., Price, J. M., Coie, J. D., & Christopoulos, C. (1990). On the development of aggressive dyadic relationships in boys' peer groups. *Human Development, 33*, 260–270.

Duncan, R. D. (1999). Maltreatment by parents and peers: The relationship between child abuse, bully victimization, and psychological distress. *Child Maltreatment, 4*, 45–55.

Egan, S. K., Monson, T. C., Perry, D. G. (1998). Social-cognitive influences on change in aggression over time. *Developmental Psychology, 34*, 996–1006.

Egan, S. K., & Perry, D. G. (1998). Does low self-regard invite victimization? *Developmental Psychology, 34*, 299–309.

Farrington, D. P. (1991). Childhood aggression and adult violence: Early precursors and life outcomes. In D. J. Pepler & K. H. Rubin (Eds.), *The development and treatment of childhood aggression* (pp. 5–29). Hillsdale, NJ: Erlbaum.

Finnegan, R. A., Hodges, E. V. E., & Perry, D. G. (1996). Preoccupied and avoidant coping during middle childhood. *Child Development, 67*, 1318–1328.

Finnegan, R. A., Hodges, E. V. E., & Perry, D. G. (1998). Victimization by peers: Associations with children's reports of mother–child interaction. *Journal of Personality and Social Psychology, 75*, 1076–1086.

Fontaine, R. G., & Dodge, K. A. (2006). Real-time decision making and aggressive behavior in youth: A heuristic model of Response Evaluation and Decision (RED). *Aggressive Behavior, 32*, 604–624.

Gifford-Smith, M. E., & Rabiner, D. L. (2004). Social information processing and children's social adjustment. In J. B. Kupersmidt & K. A. Dodge (Eds.), *Children's peer relations: From development to intervention* (pp. 61–79). Washington, DC: American Psychological Association.

Gilmartin, B. G. (1987). Peer group antecedents of severe love-shyness in males. *Journal of Personality, 55*, 467–489.

Griffin, K. W., Botvin, G. J., Scheier, L. M., Diaz, T., & Miller, N. L. (2000). Parenting practices as predictors of substance use, delinquency, and aggression among urban minority youth: Moderating effects of family structure and gender. *Psychology of Addictive Behaviors, 14*, 174–184.

Grills, A. E., & Ollendick, T. H. (2002). Peer victimization, global self-worth, and anxiety in middle school children. *Journal of Clinical Child and Adolescent Psychology, 31*, 59–68.

Haselager, G. J. T., Hartup, W. W, Van Lieshout, C. F. M., & Riksen-Walraven, J. M. (1998). Similarities between friends and nonfriends in middle childhood. *Child Development, 69*, 1198–1208.

Hawley, P. H. (2003). Prosocial and coercive configurations of resource control in early adolescence: A case for the well-adapted Machiavellian. *Merrill-Palmer Quarterly, 49*, 279–309.

Hawley, P. H., Little, T. D., & Card, N. A. (2007). The allure of a mean friend: Relationship quality and processes of aggressive adolescents with prosocial skills. *International Journal of Behavioral Development, 31*, 170–180.

Hawley, P. H., Little, T. D., & Card, N. A. (2008). The myth of the alpha male: A new look at dominance-related beliefs and behaviors among adolescent males and females. *International Journal of Behavioral Development, 32*, 76–88.

Hawley, P. H., Little, T. D., & Pasupathi, M. (2002). Winning friends and influencing peers: Strategies of peer influence in late childhood. *International Journal of Behavioral Development, 26*, 466–474.

Haynie, D. L., Nansel, T., Eitel, P., Crump, A. D., Saylor, K., Yu, K., & Simons-Morton, B. (2001). Bullies, victims, and bully/victims: Distinct groups of at-risk youth. *Journal of Early Adolescence, 21*, 29–49.

Hodges, E. V. E., Boivin, M., Vitaro, F., & Bukowski, W. M. (1999). The power of friendship: Protection against an escalating cycle of peer victimization. *Developmental Psychology, 35*, 94–101.

Hodges, E. V. E., Card, N. A., & Isaacs, J. (2003). Learning of aggression in the home and the peer group. In W. Heitmeyer & J. Hagan (Eds.), *International handbook of research on violence* (pp. 495–509). New York: Westview Press.

Hodges, E. V. E., Malone, M. J., & Perry, D. G. (1997). Individual risk and social risk as interacting determinants of victimization in the peer group. *Developmental Psychology, 33*, 1032–1039.

Hodges, E. V. E., & Perry, D. G. (1999). Personal and interpersonal consequences of victimization by peers. *Journal of Personality and Social Psychology, 76*, 677–685.

Hubbard, J. A., Dodge, K. A., Cillessen, A. H. N., Coie, J. D., & Schwartz, D. (2001). The dyadic nature of social information processing in boys' reactive and proactive aggression. *Journal of Personality and Social Psychology, 80*, 268–280.

Isaacs, J., Hodges, E. V. E., & Salmivalle, C. (2008). Long-term consequences of victimization by peers. *European Journal of Developmental Science, 2*, 387–397.

Juvonen, J., Nishina, A., & Graham, S. (2000). Peer harassment, psychological adjustment, and social functioning in early adolescence. *Journal of Educational Psychology, 92*, 349–359.

Kenny, D. A. (1994). *Interpersonal perception: A social relations analysis.* New York: Guilford.

Kenny, D. A., Kashy, D. A., & Cook, W. L. (2006). *Dyadic data analysis.* New York: Guilford.

Kochenderfer, B. J., & Ladd, G. W. (1996). Peer victimization: Cause or consequence of school maladjustment? *Child Development, 67*, 1305–1317.

Kochenderfer-Ladd, B., & Wardrop, J. L. (2001). Chronicity and instability of children's peer victimization experiences as predictors of loneliness and social satisfaction trajectories. *Child Development, 72*, 134–151.

Ladd, G. W., & Kochenderfer-Ladd, B. (1998). Parenting behaviors and parent-child relationships: Correlates of peer victimization in kindergarten? *Developmental Psychology, 34*, 1450–1458.

Ladd, G. W., & Troop-Gordon, W. (2003). The role of chronic peer difficulties in the development of children's psychological adjustment problems. *Child Development, 74*, 1344–1367.

Little, T. D., & Card, N. A. (2005). On the use of social relations and actor–partner interdependence models in developmental research. *International Journal of Behavioral Development, 29*, 173–179.

MacKinnon-Lewis, C. E., Starnes, R., Volling, B., & Johnson, S. (1997). Perceptions of parenting as predictors of boys' sibling and peer relations. *Developmental Psychology, 33*, 1024–1031.

McHale, J. P., Johnson, D., & Sinclair, R. (1999). Family dynamics, preschoolers' family representations, and preschool peer relationships. *Early Education and Development, 10*, 373–401.

Miles, S. B., & Stipek, D. (2006). Contemporaneous and longitudinal associations between social behavior and literacy achievement in a sample of low-income elementary school children. *Child Development, 77*, 103–117.

Moffitt, T. E. (1993). Adolescence-limited and life-course-persistent antisocial behavior: A developmental taxonomy. *Psychological Review, 100*, 674–701.

Newcomb, A. F., Bukowski, W. M., & Pattee, L. (1993). Children's peer relations: A meta-analytic review of popular, rejected, neglected, controversial, and average sociometric status. *Psychological Bulletin, 113*, 99–128.

Newman, R. S., & Murray, B. J. (2005). How students and teachers view the seriousness of peer harassment: When is it appropriate to seek help? *Journal of Educational Psychology, 97*, 347–365.

Olweus, D. (1978). *Aggression in the schools: Bullies and whipping boys.* Washington, DC: Hemisphere.

O'Moore, A. M., Kirkham, C., & Smith, M. (1997). Bullying behavior in Irish schools: A nationwide survey. *Irish Journal of Psychology, 18*, 141–169.

Parker, J. G., & Gamm, B. K. (2003). Describing the dark side of preadolescents' peer experiences: Four questions (and data) on preadolescents' enemies. In E. V. E. Hodges & N. A. Card (Eds.), *Enemies and the darker side of peer relations: New Directions for Child and Adolescent Development* (pp. 55–72). San Francisco: Jossey–Bass.

Patterson, G. R. (1986). Performance models for aggressive boys. *American Psychologist, 41*, 432–444.

Peets, K., Hodges, E. V. E., Kikas, E., & Salmivalli, C. (2007). Hostile attributions and behavioral strategies in children: Does relationship type matter? *Developmental Psychology, 43*, 889–900.

Peets, K., Hodges, E. V. E., & Salmivalli, C. (2008). Affect-congruent social-cognitive evaluations and behaviors. *Child Development, 79*, 170–185.

Pellegrini, A. D. (1995). A longitudinal study of boys' rough-and-tumble play and dominance during early adolescence. *Journal of Applied Developmental Psychology, 16*, 77–93.

Pellegrini, A. D., Bartini, M., & Brooks, F. (1999). School bullies, victims, and aggressive victims: Factors relating to group affiliation and victimization in early adolescence. *Journal of Educational Psychology, 91*, 216–224.

Perry, D. G., Hodges, E. V. E., & Egan, S. K. (2001). Determinants of chronic victimization by peers: A review and a new model of family influence. In J. Juvonen & S. Graham (Eds.), *Peer harassment in school: The plight of the vulnerable and victimized* (pp. 73–104). New York: Guilford.

Perry, D. G., Kusel, S. J., & Perry, L. C. (1988). Victims of peer aggression. *Developmental Psychology, 24*, 807–814.

Perry, D. G, Perry, L. C., & Kennedy, E. (1992). Conflict and the development of antisocial behavior. In C. U. Shantz & W. W. Hartup (Eds.), *Conflict in child and adolescent development* (pp. 301–329). New York: Cambridge University Press.

Perry, D. G., Perry, L. C., & Rasmussen, P. (1986). Cognitive social learning mediators of aggression. *Child Development, 57*, 700–711.

Perry, D. G., Williard, J. C., & Perry, L. C. (1990). Peers' perceptions of the consequences that victimized children provide aggressors. *Child Development, 61*, 1310–1325.

Pierce, K. A., & Cohen, R. (1995). Aggressors and their victims: Toward a contextual framework for understanding children's aggressor-victim relationships. *Developmental Review, 15*, 292–310.

Pope, A. W., & Bierman, K. L. (1999). Predicting adolescent peer problems and antisocial activities: The relative roles of aggression and dysregulation. *Developmental Psychology, 35*, 335–346.

Prinstein, M. J., Boergers, J., & Vernberg, E. M. (2001). Overt and relational aggression in adolescents: Social-psychological adjustment of aggressors and victims. *Journal of Clinical Child Psychology, 30*, 479–491.

Rigby, K. (2000). Effects of peer victimization in schools and perceived social support on adolescent well-being. *Journal of Adolescence, 23*, 57–68.

Rodkin, P., Farmer, T., Pearl, R., & Van Acker, R. (2000). Heterogeneity of popular boys: Antisocial and prosocial configurations. *Developmental Psychology, 36*, 14–24.

Rose, A. J., Swenson, L. P., & Waller, E. M. (2004). Overt and relational aggression and perceived popularity: Developmental differences in concurrent and prospective relations. *Developmental Psychology, 40*, 378–387.

Salmivalli, C. (2001). Group view on victimization: Empirical findings and their implications. In J. Juvonen & S. Graham (Eds.), *Peer harassment in school: The plight of the vulnerable and victimized* (pp. 398–419). New York: Guilford.

Salmivalli, C., Huttunen, A., & Lagerspetz, K. M. J. (1997). Peer networks and bullying in schools. *Scandinavian Journal of Psychology, 38*, 305–312.

Schwartz, D. (2000). Subtypes of victims and aggressors in children's peer groups. *Journal of Abnormal Child Psychology, 28*, 181–192.

Schwartz, D., Dodge, K. A., & Coie, J. D. (1993). The emergence of chronic peer victimization in boys' play groups. *Child Development, 64*, 1755–1772.

Schwartz, D., Hopmeyer Gorman, A. H., Toblin, R. L., & Abou-ezzedine, T. (2003). Mutual antipathies in the peer group as a moderating factor in the association between community violence exposure and psychosocial maladjustment. In E. V. E. Hodges & N. A. Card (Eds.), *Enemies and the darker side of peer relations: New directions for child and adolescent development* (pp. 39–54). San Francisco: Jossey-Bass.

Schwartz, D., & Proctor, L. J. (2000). Community violence exposure and children's social adjustment in the school peer group: The mediating roles of emotional regulation and social cognition. *Journal of Consulting and Clinical Psychology, 68*, 670–683.

Shields, A., & Cicchetti, D. (2001). Parental maltreatment and emotion dysregulation as risk factors for bullying and victimization in middle childhood. *Journal of Clinical Child Psychology, 30*, 349–363.

Smith, P. K., Morita, Y., Junger-Tas, J., Olweus, D., Catalano, R. F., & Slee, P. (Eds.). (1998). *The nature of school bullying: A cross-national perspective*. New York: Routledge.

Smith, P. K., & Shu, S. (2000). What good schools can do about bullying: Findings from a survey in English schools after a decade of research and action. *Childhood, 7*, 193–212.

Snyder, J. J., & Patterson, G. R. (1995). Individual differences in social aggression: A test of a reinforcement model of socialization in the natural environment. *Behavior Therapy, 26*, 371–391.

Troop-Gordon, W., & Brock, R. L. (2005, April). Peer-identified aggressor-victim dyads: Prevalence and associated adjustment outcomes. In N. A. Card & E. V. E. Hodges (Chairs), *Aggressor-victim relationships: Toward a dyadic perspective*. Paper symposium presented at the biennial meeting of the Society for Research in Child Development, Atlanta.

Troy, M., & Sroufe, L. A. (1987). Victimization among preschoolers: Role of attachment relationship history. *Journal of the American Academy of Child and Adolescent Psychiatry, 26,* 166–172.

Vernberg, E. M. (1990). Psychological adjustment and experiences with peers during early adolescence: Reciprocal, incidental, or unidirectional relationships? *Journal of Abnormal Child Psychology, 18,* 187–198.

## 13

## Haven in a Heartless World? Hurt Feelings in the Family

ROSEMARY S. L. MILLS AND CAROLINE C. PIOTROWSKI

Hurt feelings are ubiquitous in family relationships. The emotional investment that family members make in one another typically is intense and matched only by the emotional vulnerability it involves. In the ups and downs of daily life, irritation and conflict are frequent occurrences, and vulnerability heightens the potential for bruised feelings and sometimes agonizing emotional pain. Mothers of preschoolers experience an aversive event every few minutes, with major conflicts occurring as often as three times in an hour (Patterson, 1980), and although the rates decline with older children it is safe to say that parent–child interaction is rife with hurt feelings. Aversive interactions between young siblings may be even more frequent (Martin & Ross, 1996, 2005; Patterson, 1980). Aversive experiences that occur with such frequency must have a significant impact on the developing child, and a basic premise of research on children's relationships is that they are key learning experiences about self and social relationships and hence an important risk factor for development in these domains. Understanding the precise nature of these learning experiences has been a major aim of research on children's relationships with their parents and siblings. Our purpose in this chapter is to review research relevant to understanding the nature of these learning experiences and their effects on development.

We begin with the assumption that hurt feelings occurring during aversive interactions are central to the impact of these interactions. How people process the information that is available during interpersonal interactions constitutes the "raw data of social life" (Kenny & DePaulo, 1993). These information processes guide judgments about and responses to social interactions and are used like self-fulfilling prophecies to determine what to expect in new situations. They are also the input from which general beliefs and dispositions about self and others form and are changed over time. Thus, investigation of the immediate real-time processing of hurtful interactions in the family is critical to understanding the way in which early experiences in the family shape social and self development in childhood. Current models for understanding the impact of such experiences integrate processing and structural explanations.

## AN INTEGRATED SOCIAL INFORMATION-PROCESSING AND COGNITIVE STRUCTURAL PERSPECTIVE ON HURT FEELINGS IN THE FAMILY

Hurt feelings appear to be caused by acts of rejection or low relational evaluation – signs that one is less important, close, or valuable than one thought (Leary, 2001; Leary, Springer, Negel, Ansell, & Evans, 1998; Vangelisti, Young, Carpenter-Theune, & Alexander, 2005). Hurtful acts encompass acts both of commission (e.g., unkind comments) and omission (e.g., absence of warmth). Hurt feelings are the cognitive-affective processes that occur in immediate reaction to these acts. Models that integrate information processing and structural explanations (e.g., Arsenio & Lemerise, 2004; Fontaine, 2006; Hoyle, 2006) provide a way to understand the nature of these reactive processes and their effects, both short and long term.

People have a basic biological need for love and acceptance, and they expend considerable energy monitoring others' reactions to them for signs of rejection or low positive regard (e.g., Baumeister & Leary, 1995; Bowlby, 1969; Cooley, 1902). Cues of rejection or devaluation trigger appraisals of the self and others and associated affects that motivate efforts to restore a sense of being accepted (Leary, 2001; Pietrzak, Downey, & Ayduk, 2005). Hurt feelings are the immediate cognitive-affective reactions to perceived rejection or devaluation. They may involve distress, sadness, loneliness, jealousy, guilt and shame, embarrassment, and social anxiety (Leary, 2001) in varying degrees, depending on the situation and what it means. For example, a scolding may be highly shame-inducing when it occurs in public, but anger may be the dominant reaction when it occurs in private.

Social information-processing models specify the reactive processes or mental operations that are activated by social stimuli (Crick & Dodge, 1994; Huesmann, 1998; Lemerise & Arsenio, 2000). Some processing is controlled and reflective, but much of it is automatic and nonconscious. According to one model (Crick & Dodge, 1994), processing an event involves *encoding* it (attending to and perceiving internal and external cues in the situation), *interpreting* its meaning (e.g., causal attributions about the event, inferences about the other person's perspective, evaluations of self and other), *clarifying goals* (maintaining or changing the goals or desired outcomes for the situation), *accessing possible responses* to the situation (generating strategies for attaining the goal), *selecting a response* (e.g., evaluating alternative responses, assessing expected outcomes, evaluating self-efficacy, making a decision), and *enacting* the selected response. These operations are dynamic processes. Mental operations occur simultaneously and interactively. Even while retaliating against someone for a hurtful act, one may continue asking oneself how and why it occurred and what it means (Vangelisti et al., 2005). As well, some steps in processing affect others. When a hurtful act is attributed to hostility, hostile feelings may make other feelings less accessible.

Current information-processing models incorporate structural constructs and suggest that, in addition to the dynamic interplay among mental operations that occurs in processing social situations, there is a dynamic interplay between this processing and the mental representations or stored knowledge that individuals bring to the processing of social situations as a result of their past experiences and biological capabilities. According to this view, immediate reactive processes are reciprocally related via feedback loops to general social knowledge, beliefs, scripts, schemas, working models, and emotional dispositions. Thus, some immediate reactions are habitual or typical responses because they have occurred so often in the past due to temperamental characteristics or repeated experience that they have become habits or dispositions (e.g., Fischer, Shaver, & Carnochan, 1990). For example, being temperamentally reactive to stress may lower the threshold for perceiving hurtful acts, resulting in more frequent experiences of hurt, which thereby reinforce expectations of being hurt. In turn, the more often these reactions occur, the more habitual they become and the more they reinforce certain beliefs or dispositions. Repeated experiences of hurt feelings reinforce the appraisals of self, others, and relationships that occur each time and the choice of strategies for responding to these appraisals. This repetition leads to general beliefs about self, others, and relationships in general and to general styles of coping with rejection (e.g., Baldwin, 1992; Bowlby, 1969) that influence reactive processing in social situations experienced in the future. Thus, immediate reactions to hurtful messages can be viewed as the input or "raw data" that are assimilated into the "database" (Crick & Dodge, 1994) of general dispositions and cognitive schemas that guide processing in subsequent situations.

According to this integrated account, experiences of hurt are processed based on features of the hurtful event itself, dispositions that affect reactions to events, and prior experiences with those events. A hurtful act is more likely to elicit shame if the situation is potentially shame inducing (e.g., a critical comment), the individual is prone to self-condemnation, and many experiences of being shamed have occurred in the past. With this dynamic information-processing perspective as a guide, we turn to an examination of children's immediate reactive processing of hurtful parent–child and sibling interactions and their effects on children's cognitive-affective dispositions – that is, the general dispositions or beliefs that children develop about themselves, other people, and the nature of interpersonal relationships in the course of their development. We suggest that this reactive processing both influences and is influenced by general beliefs and dispositions and hence that hurtful interactions play a critical role in children's self and social development.

## PARENT–CHILD RELATIONSHIPS

Parent–child relationships operate simultaneously in separate domains that involve different goals and needs (Maccoby, 2000). Two domains in particular have been emphasized: an attachment domain in which the goal is to respond to the child's need for closeness and emotional support and a power domain in which the goal is to manage the competing interests of parent and child. Much theory and research have been devoted to understanding the effects on children of parental underresponsiveness in the attachment domain and overcontrol in the power domain. Although less attention has been paid to parents' needs in the domains of attachment and power (George & Solomon, 1999), parents are no less vulnerable to being hurt than are children. In this section, children's and parents' hurt feelings are addressed in turn.

### Children's Online Processing of Hurtful Interactions with Parents

For children as for adults, there are a myriad of ways in which feelings can be hurt. Rohner's parental acceptance–rejection theory (Khaleque & Rohner, 2002) suggests that parental acts of hostility, lack of affection, or indifference are the universal sources of perceived parental rejection. Children are likely to perceive these actions as reflecting a rejecting attitude and feel hurt by them. However, the bulk of research suggesting that these actions are hurtful consists of associations with children's adjustment over the long term rather than direct evidence that these behaviors precipitate hurt feelings at the time they occur.

*Perceiving Parental Acts as Hurtful*
Almost no research exists on hurtful parental acts as perceived by children. In one exception, school-aged children were asked to recall an instance when their mother had said or done something that hurt their feelings (Mills, Nazar, & Farrell, 2002). They recounted episodes of yelling, punishment (physical or otherwise), refusing permission, sibling favoritism, broken promises, disrespect, teasing, criticism, and distancing/rebuffing. These findings provide some indication of the types of interactions that are commonly hurtful to children. Interestingly, in the parenting literature many of these same parenting behaviors have been linked to child maladjustment, especially among children with temperamental characteristics that would be likely to amplify their effects (Bates & Pettit, 2007). However, there is limited evidence concerning the processes mediating these links. We suggest that children's online processing of hurtful parental acts plays a critical role by contributing to cognitive and emotional biases that put children at risk of maladaptive functioning.

PHYSICAL AGGRESSION. Children identified physical punishment as being hurtful (Mills et al., 2002). In the parenting literature, corporal punishment has been linked to various indicators of child maladjustment including aggression, delinquency, antisocial behavior, and depressive symptomatology (Gershoff, 2002). Hurt feelings may play a role in these outcomes. In an early analysis of the effects of discipline, Hoffman (1970) suggested that parental messages are important not only for their informational content but also their emotional intensity. Harsh punishment interferes with processing the parent's message about rules and expectations by arousing distress and overwhelming the child's ability to regulate his or her emotions. Hurt feelings may be an important component of such distress. Some research indicates that perceived parental rejection mediates the association between the frequency and severity of physical punishment and indices of maladjustment (Rohner, Kean, & Cournoyer, 1991). Repeated experiences of feeling hurt may gradually shape children's general expectations of what to expect from others and lead to the development of defenses for coping with these expectations. However, children's hurt feelings in response to physical punishment have yet to be directly assessed in research to date on the effects of physical punishment on children's adjustment.

PSYCHOLOGICAL AGGRESSION. When asked to recount hurtful experiences with their parents, children described several forms of psychological aggression: criticism, distancing/rebuffing, and expressions of disrespect. Psychological aggression has been defined as "parental behaviors that are intrusive and manipulative of children's thoughts, feelings, and attachments to parents" (Barber & Harmon, 2002, p. 15). These behaviors have been of some concern in the parenting literature. Expressions of love withdrawal, humiliation, disgust, and contempt have been singled out as prime forms of shaming because they are highly likely to convey a negative global attribution about the child (M. Lewis, 1992). They may also be considered hurtful acts because they communicate a message of rejection or devaluation. As circumstantial evidence for this idea, psychological control has been linked to adjustment problems (Barber & Harmon, 2002). However, as in the literature on physical aggression by parents, there has been no investigation of children's subjective perceptions of psychologically aggressive acts in research to date and thus no evidence as to whether children's hurt feelings mediate the link to adjustment.

TEASING. Children's recollections of hurtful interactions with their mother included episodes of teasing (Mills et al., 2002). Teasing is an ambiguous behavior that conveys a negative message in a kidding or playful way, but is nevertheless often perceived as hurtful (Keltner, Capps, Kring, Young, & Heerey, 2001; Kruger, Gordon, & Kuban, 2006). Research on parental teasing is rare, but by the school years children are able to discern the intentions behind teasing (Keltner et al., 2001). In an exception to the lack of research on parental teasing (Keery, Boutelle, van den Berg, & Thompson, 2005), 23% of school-aged girls reported appearance-related teasing by a parent. Moreover, parental teasing predicted symptomatology such as body dissatisfaction, low self-esteem, and depression. Again, it has yet to be determined whether these predictive relations are mediated by hurt feelings experienced during episodes of teasing.

PERCEIVED SIBLING FAVORITISM. The parent–child interactions directly involving the child are not the only ones that can be hurtful to children. Children also judge their importance and value to their parents by comparing the relationships they have with their parents to the relationships their parents have with other members of the family, most particularly their siblings. The perception of inequitable treatment by parents has been a focus of considerable attention, particularly because of its implications for sibling relationships (Boyle et al., 2004; Shebloski, Conger, & Widaman, 2005). When asked to recall a time their mother said or did something that hurt their feelings, some children recounted an event that made them feel their sibling was more important to their mother than they were (Mills et al., 2002). The importance of perceived sibling favoritism as a cause of hurt feelings is also suggested by retrospective research in which maladjustment in adults has been linked to perceived favoritism of siblings in childhood (Brody, Copeland, Sutton, Richardson, & Guyer, 1998; Gilbert & Gerlsma, 1999). The salience of these memories in adulthood suggests that childhood experiences of perceived favoritism are painful and make an indelible impression, possibly because of the intensity of the feelings they arouse.

Although the acts catalogued here may be the most common types of hurtful parental actions, they are not invariably perceived as hurtful. Children's emotional dispositions are likely to influence the extent to which they feel badly about themselves in response to negative parental messages and to perceive them as messages of rejection. For example, children who are temperamentally inhibited and characterized by involuntary constrained and rigid behavior in response to novel or challenging events reflecting a low threshold of arousal (Derryberry & Rothbart, 1997; Kagan, Reznick, & Snidman, 1987), are more likely than other children to experience internal cues of discomfort or distress in response to parental discipline and to blame themselves (Dienstbier, Hellman, Lehnhoff, Hillman, & Volkenaar, 1975; M. Lewis, 1992). Nor are all hurtful acts equally likely to signify rejection or devaluation. As noted earlier, acts of hostility, lack of affection, or indifference are considered to be the prototypical sources of perceived parental rejection (Khaleque & Rohner, 2002). Prime examples may include love withdrawal, expressions of disgust or contempt, and humiliation, which are highly likely to communicate a rejecting attitude (M. Lewis, 1992). However, further processing of the event to figure out why it occurred will determine the extent to which children feel hurt even by these acts. These appraisals will vary depending on the stored knowledge and beliefs children bring to the interpretation of new situations.

*Appraising Hurtful Parental Acts*

The perception that an interaction is hurtful initiates a process of appraisal. Why has the other person acted in a hurtful way? Is it because of something about the self, the other person, or the relationship? Hurtful interactions lead people to question themselves, the other person, and the relationship. The constellation of attributions and emotions associated with hurt feelings reflects this appraisal process. According to Rohner's parental acceptance–rejection theory (Khaleque & Rohner, 2002), perceived parental rejection arouses feelings of hurt, anxiety, insecurity, and anger and leads to the development of personality dispositions (e.g., hostility, dependence, impaired self-esteem, negative worldview) that reflect children's attempts to protect themselves against further hurt. From an integrated processing and structural perspective, the appraisals made online are the basis for these dispositions. People experience a drop in self-esteem and feel various rejection-related emotions depending on features of the rejecting event and their strategies for coping with stressful situations (Leary & Baumeister, 2000). According to some emotion theorists (Tomkins, 1987), shame is the master emotional response to perceived rejection, with other emotional reactions varying depending on the full meaning attached to the event. Although the issue of a master emotional response is open to debate, there seems to be wide agreement that hurt feelings involve a complex appraisal process concerned with the self, the other person, and the quality of the relationship. The prototypical emotional responses seem to be shame, anger, and feelings of alienation, but the extent to which they occur may depend critically on judgments of intentionality (Vangelisti, 2001; Vangelisti & Young, 2000).

SHAME, ANGER, AND ALIENATION. Research to date attests to the fact that adults and children alike evaluate themselves negatively and experience a constellation of emotional reactions to hurtful acts (Leary et al., 1998; Mills et al., 2002; Vangelisti, 2001; Vangelisti & Young, 2000). Hurtful acts judged to be deliberate evoke the strongest reactions, and the judgment of intentionality has a pervasive effect on the appraisal of hurtful exchanges (Vangelisti, 2001; Vangelisti & Young, 2000). Children's recollections of hurtful interactions (Mills et al., 2002) revealed that the more they felt rejected by their mother's hurtful actions or the more they blamed themselves for what had happened, the worse they felt about themselves. The more children thought their mother had deliberately hurt them, the more they felt rejected, the worse they felt about themselves, and the more they thought their feelings about their mother had changed as a result (Mills et al., 2002).

When hurtful acts are interpreted as having occurred unintentionally or are believed to be motivated by good intentions, the prototypical responses of shame, anger, and alienation may not occur or may be minimized. In keeping with this idea, weaker associations have been found between physical discipline and maladjustment in cultures in which physical punishment is normative

(Lansford et al., 2005; Rohner et al., 1991). These findings suggest that when physical discipline is valued and believed to be good parenting, children may acquire the same belief and interpret their parents' actions as a message of caring rather than rejection.

Children's cognitive-affective dispositions contribute to their online appraisal of hurtful interactions (Crick & Dodge, 1994). In a series of studies relevant to the appraisal of hurtful interactions, Dweck and colleagues (2000) demonstrated that children as young as 3½ years of age can be vulnerable to a "helpless" cognitive style characterized by self-blame, negative feelings, low expectancies, and impaired problem solving when they encounter failure or criticism. Children who are inclined to feel bad about themselves when they receive criticism are likely to have heightened sensitivity to hurtful messages; that is, they are more likely to interpret them as messages of rejection containing negative judgments of their worth or goodness. Thus, children with a helpless cognitive style are likely to make more negative inferences about themselves during hurtful interactions. Moreover, children given criticism reflecting on them as a whole person were subsequently more likely to respond to failure in a helpless-oriented manner (Kamins & Dweck, 1999). This finding suggests, in keeping with an integrated processing and structural perspective, that a history of experiences of hurtful criticism can foster the development of a helpless cognitive style.

*Responding to Hurtful Parental Acts*
When asked how they would respond to a hurtful act, children and adults alike describe various responses including acquiescing (e.g., apologizing, crying), withdrawing (e.g., leaving the room, hiding their feelings), and actively engaging the other person (arguing/defending, expressing anger or disappointment; Leary et al., 1998; Mills et al., 2002; Vangelisti, 1994). Because they signal the presence of a threat to the sense of acceptance by others, hurt feelings may be intrinsically connected to self-defensive reactions (MacDonald & Leary, 2005).

Aggressive and withdrawn interpersonal styles may define extreme ends of a continuum of children's self-defensive responses to hurtful parental acts. There is suggestive evidence for this in the general links that have been found between hurtful patterns of parent–child interaction and children's social behavioral styles. Physical and psychological aggression by parents have been linked to children's physical aggression against peers as well as relational aggression (i.e., acts that manipulate or damage social relationships; Casas et al., 2006; Gershoff, 2002; Hart, Nelson, Robinson, Olsen, & McNeilly-Choque, 1998). There also has been research linking psychological control to social withdrawal in children (Mills & Rubin, 1998). It remains to be established, however, whether children's online processing of hurtful interactions in the short term contributes to the development of these social behavioral styles over the long term.

The form that self-defense takes may vary from one person to another depending on features of the rejecting event and existing beliefs and dispositions that make certain response options more accessible and likely to be selected than others. Gender role-related socialization pressures and biologically based emotional dispositions may play a role in determining whether children tend to respond in an aggressive or a withdrawn/avoidant manner (Keenan & Shaw, 1997). For example, children who are temperamentally inhibited are more likely than other children to respond in an inhibited or withdrawn manner in stressful situations (Derryberry & Rothbart, 1997; Kagan et al., 1987), suggesting that they are more likely to acquiesce or withdraw when they feel hurt. In turn, repeated experiences of hurtful parent–child interactions would tend to reinforce this response tendency.

Parents' Online Reactive Processing of Hurtful Interactions with Children

There has been a marked shift in thinking about the nature of the relationship between parents and children over the past 40 years or so. The traditional unilateral model of the parent–child relationship as one of unequal power and influence has been replaced by a bilateral model that accommodates evidence that children themselves have power and influence. The attachment parents have to their children is one recognized source of children's power (Maccoby, 2000; Perlman, Siddiqui, Ram, & Ross, 2000). Although there still is an implicit assumption about the dominance of parents over children (Kuczynski & Lollis, 2001) and a belief that parents are relatively invulnerable to hurtful acts by their children, research has begun to challenge these assumptions.

*Perceiving Child Acts as Hurtful*
Mothers who were interviewed and asked to describe a time when their child had said or done something that hurt their feelings had no difficulty recalling such incidents (Mills et al., 2002). They described most commonly incidents of disparagement or disregard (disrespect, criticism, rebuff) and less commonly incidents of child misconduct. With some allowance for differences in their roles, it seems that mothers and children generally defined hurtful acts in much the same way, with disparagement/disregard and discipline being the most common contexts for hurt feelings. Moreover, the types of interactions they found hurtful were generally the same as those recounted in studies of adults (Leary et al., 1998; Vangelisti, 1994), suggesting that age and role have relatively little to do with the types of interpersonal behaviors perceived as rejecting.

*Appraising Hurtful Child Acts*
Mothers felt annoyed and angry when their child did something that hurt their feelings (Mills et al., 2002); in fact, these were among their strongest emotional reactions. The more hurt they felt, the worse they felt about

themselves. Mothers were not inclined to believe their child had deliberately meant to hurt them, but the more they thought their child's actions were deliberate, the more rejected they felt and the more they felt that their relationship with their child had been weakened at least temporarily. The more they felt they deserved what happened, the worse they felt about themselves. Thus, the processing dynamics of hurtful interactions seem to be the same for mothers as for children, and it appears that theories suggesting that experiences of perceived rejection induce shame and cause a drop in self-esteem (e.g., Leary & Baumeister, 2000) may apply broadly to any close relationship.

How mothers appraise hurtful child acts is likely to depend on beliefs, personality traits, and dispositions that influence their interpretation of new situations. Proneness to shame may be an important factor, given its likely association with heightened sensitivity to rejection (Downey, Khouri, & Feldman, 1997; H. B. Lewis, 1971). In a study examining this idea (Mills et al., 2007), mothers and fathers of preschool-aged children completed a measure of proneness to shame and were asked to rate their emotional reactions to hypothetical vignettes depicting hurtful acts by their child. Shame-prone parents reported feeling more hurt and angered by hurtful child acts than did other parents, possibly because proneness to shame heightens parents' vulnerability to their children's hurtful actions.

*Responding to Hurtful Child Acts*
Parents respond to children's hurtful actions in a variety of ways. In mothers' recollections of hurtful interactions with their school-aged children (Mills et al., 2002), their child's behavior was an important factor contributing to their response. Misconduct was more closely associated with a firm response of some kind (expressing anger/disappointment, disciplining the child) and disparagement/disregard was more closely associated with an expression of hurt feelings. Although hurtful child acts could be used as an occasion for teaching children how their actions affect other people, only 10% of mothers indicated that they told their child they felt hurt (Mills et al., 2002). This low percentage might reflect the methodological limitations of using mothers' recollections of hurtful interactions to study their reactions. This method depends on mothers' memory for events and the rules they may follow in narrating events. Because of these factors, the extent to which mothers actually talked to their child about how they felt may have been underestimated. Alternatively, it is possible that hurtful acts by children occasion little teaching because they are not regarded as wrong or are considered less objectionable than other types of interpersonal transgressions. Research on mothers' socialization in the area of peer aggression indicates that they do not regard relational aggression as seriously as physical aggression (e.g., Werner, Senich, & Przepyszny, 2006).

Another possibility is that hurt feelings interfere with parents' ability to turn hurtful interactions into teachable moments. When their feelings are hurt, parents may become preoccupied with feelings of anger and shame and efforts to manage their emotions. The stronger their emotional reactions, the less likely they are to manage them effectively. Mothers and fathers reporting stronger feelings of anger in reaction to hypothetical hurtful vignettes scored higher on a measure of psychological aggression (e.g., love withdrawal, shame/guilt induction; Walling, Mills, & Freeman, 2007), suggesting that hurt feelings may heighten the risk of parental aggression against children.

Some parents are especially likely to respond aggressively to hurtful child acts because of beliefs and dispositions that heighten their vulnerability to hurt and intensify their negative emotional reactions. In work on proneness to shame (Mills et al., 2007), negative reactivity to the child was found to mediate a link between parents' proneness to shame and critical/rejecting behavior toward the child (expressing disappointment, love withdrawal, shame/guilt induction, person-focused criticism). Parents' vulnerability to hurt and difficulty regulating the emotions involved may be important risk factors in parental aggression against children. They may also contribute, through repeated experiences of hurt, to a loss of parental self-efficacy. Evidence linking parental self-efficacy to parental competence (Jones & Prinz, 2005) raises the possibility that hurtful interactions could lead to a deterioration in parental competence mediated by a loss of confidence in the ability to be an effective parent.

*Hurtful versus Reparative Parent–Child Transactions*

When parents are vulnerable to hurt and prone to react negatively, a repetitive pattern of hurtful interaction may develop between parent and child, particularly if the child is also vulnerable to hurt and shares the same aggressive response style. These reciprocal hurtful interchanges may contribute to aversive cycles in parent–child interaction in which emotions intensify and retaliation occurs. In research on parent–child interactions in families of oppositional children, Patterson (1986) found significant relations between maternal perceptions of child aggressiveness and feelings of rejection toward the child and suggested that coercive cycles in parent–child interaction may lead parents to develop a negative, rejecting attitude to their child that helps worsen these cycles. Research on the role that hurt feelings may play in these escalating cycles is needed to better understand how escalation and deescalation occur and what enables some parent–child dyads to repair hurt feelings. On the parents' side, there is a substantial literature on the effects of personal concerns that intensify negative emotions and interfere with the ability to access emotions that serve a reparative function (Bugental & Lewis, 1999; Dix, 1992). There has been an emphasis on interpersonal power and the effects of perceived low power on parents' ability to regulate negative emotions toward the child and on the role of empathy in enabling parents to regulate their negative emotions and respond sensitively. Research is needed on the extent to which perceived low power may be a vulnerability factor and empathy a buffering factor in parents' experiences of hurt and the extent to which they may contribute to the escalation of hurtful interactions or their deescalation and repair.

SIBLING RELATIONSHIPS

Hurt feelings in the family are, of course, not restricted to parents and children; siblings also hurt each other and do so in an increasingly sophisticated and complex manner as they grow older. The sibling relationship is perhaps most notorious for feelings of rivalry; however, due to their intimate daily contact throughout childhood and adolescence, siblings can both cause and soothe hurt feelings in a myriad of ways.

As noted earlier, hurt feelings can be caused by either acts of omission (e.g., exclusion or neglect) or acts of commission (e.g., physical attack, teasing). Research on siblings includes studies of interactions that may be hurtful, typically focusing on conflict, physical aggression, and, most recently, relational aggression. To date, the emphasis has been on the nature and frequency of siblings' behaviors, rather than social information processing concerning their impact. However, some work has begun to address thoughts and feelings accompanying hurtful sibling interactions. We begin our discussion with a focus on interactions between siblings themselves, followed by the impact of parental involvement.

Perception and Appraisal of Hurtful Sibling Interactions

*Physical Aggression*
Physical aggression is commonly defined as physical harm or the threat of physical harm, and it has enormous potential to contribute to hurt feelings and affect perceptions of the self and the sibling. The sibling relationship is widely regarded as the most aggressive family relationship (Finkelhor & Dzubia-Leatherman, 1994; Finkelhor, Ormrod, Turner, & Hamby, 2005; Finkelhor, Turner, & Ormrod, 2006). Developmentally, siblings in early childhood are most likely to harm each other physically (Piotrowski, 1999), and although aggression declines throughout middle childhood it does not disappear (McGuire, Manke, Eftekhari, & Dunn, 2000). Longitudinal research has demonstrated that aggression by one sibling significantly predicts aggression by the other, both in the short term (Dunn & Munn, 1986b) and the long term (Compton, Snyder, Schrepferman, Bank, & Shortt, 2003). Naturalistic observations at home have indicated preschool-aged siblings hurt each other physically approximately 2.3 times per hour (Martin & Ross, 2005). As children grow older, sibling aggression has been linked with children's later maladjustment, including both externalizing (Fagan & Najman, 2003) and internalizing difficulties (Kim, Hetherington, & Reiss, 1999). And although

most mothers perceive sibling aggression as "not serious" (Piotrowski, 1999), children's perspectives can certainly differ in terms of impact.

An emerging literature on retrospective processing represents a first step toward better understanding of children's appraisals of physical aggression by siblings. Much of this work demonstrates that children have a strong self-serving bias, particularly when recounting physical harm (Kim et al., 1999; Ross, Smith, Spielmacher, & Recchia, 2004). Children tend to see their sibling as at fault while perceiving themselves as systemically less blameworthy. In fact, Wilson and her colleagues found that older siblings used their increasing cognitive sophistication to better justify their harmful behavior toward their younger sibling, whereas younger siblings relied more on denial (Wilson, Smith, Ross, & Ross, 2004). Other work on children's moral narratives about hurting or being hurt by a peer also feature a self-referential focus (Wainryb, Brehl, & Matwin, 2005). Taken together, these studies suggest that a cognitive bias involving negative interpretations of the other and positive interpretations of the self may serve a protective function against uncomfortable feelings such as guilt, shame, or negative self-evaluation and may help to preserve self-esteem and self-worth (Mills & Piotrowski, 2000; Ross, Smith et al., 2004; Wainryb et al., 2005).

Although different in some important respects, research on retrospective processing concerning bullying by peers is also helpful in understanding children's appraisals of aggression. Reports by sixth-grade students of their emotional reactions to daily physical harm or threats of harm by peers included feeling humiliated, ashamed, helpless, lonely, worried, scared, anxious, tense, and angry (Nishina & Juvonen, 2005). Other work has shown that bullying often contributes to low self-esteem and self-worth (Rigby, 2003). These reports highlight the intense hurt feelings that can accompany physical harm and point to the need for similar research investigating more immediate online processing after physical attack by siblings.

*Relational Aggression*
Relational aggression is a more recent area of study that has significant potential for investigating hurt feelings between siblings. Relational aggression can be defined as behaviors that damage a relationship or that threaten to damage a relationship (Crick, Casas, & Hu, 1999). It can consist of both direct and indirect actions, such as social exclusion, intentionally embarrassing or humiliating the other, betraying secrets, or telling lies about the other.

Developmentally, relational aggression seems to be a prominent feature of sibling interactions that begins in the preschool years (Ostrov, Crick, & Stauffacher, 2006) and continues to a lesser extent into middle childhood and adolescence (Ostrov et al., 2006; Updegraff, Thayer, Whiteman, Denning, & McHale, 2005). Preschool-aged siblings engage in relational aggression approximately once per minute on average; longitudinally, relational aggression between siblings tends to decline from the preschool years into middle childhood but not equally across gender combinations (Ostrov et al., 2006). It should be noted that, although parents indicate physical and relational aggression often occur simultaneously during the course of hurtful exchanges between siblings at home (Piotrowski, 1999), this co-occurrence has rarely, if ever, been addressed by researchers using naturalistic observation.

Some work has begun to address the impact of relational aggression on the sibling relationship. Updegraff and her colleagues found that greater relational aggression between adolescent siblings was associated with less intimacy and greater negativity reported by both siblings (Updegraff et al., 2005). Although this work did not investigate either retrospective or online processing, it does represent an important first step toward better understanding how unresolved hurt feelings can potentially undermine the quality of sibling relationships.

*Teasing and Tattling*
Teasing and tattling occur with relatively high frequency between siblings and can sometimes take on characteristics of relational aggression. Although teasing can be playful and is not always tied to negative outcomes, hostile teasing has been linked to hurt feelings and other negative consequences among children (see Keltner et al., 2001, for a review). For example, young siblings used teasing to upset or provoke older siblings and mothers (Dunn & Munn, 1986a). Girls in early adolescence who were teased about their physical appearance by older brothers had significantly lower self-esteem than girls who were not teased (Keery et al., 2005). These outcomes suggest that children's appraisals of sibling teasing, both hostile and friendly, deserve further research attention.

Tattling can also contribute to feeling hurt, especially if it occurs in the presence of a sibling (Ross & den Bak-Lammers, 1998). Tattling can harm the sibling relationship by undermining loyalty and trust as siblings typically tattle on each other's behavior rather than their own (den Bak & Ross, 1986). In a developmental analysis, Ross and den Bak-Lammers (1998) found that preschool-aged children tattled more often as they grew older and selectively chose to disclose certain acts, such as physical harm, more frequently than other misdeeds. Although appraisals and emotional consequences were not directly addressed, these findings suggest that tattling may be used at times for revenge and, if so, would have negative implications for the sibling relationship.

*Conflict*
It is important to note that not all sibling conflict is created equally. Destructive conflict is hurtful by definition; it causes hurt feelings through blaming, criticism, and defensiveness and leads to hurtful outcomes such as negative self-regard or relationship erosion. In contrast, constructive conflict, which consists mainly of negotiation and reasoning and can also involve expressions of empathy and support, may actually contribute to soothing

hurt feelings, in addition to facilitating individual growth and interpersonal intimacy.

Destructive sibling conflict has been studied more extensively than constructive conflict (Garcia, Shaw, Winslow, & Yaggi, 2000; Stocker, Burwell, & Briggs, 2002), although some researchers have investigated both types (Howe, Rinaldi, Jennings, & Petrakos, 2002). It has been reliably linked to negative self-regard (Stocker, 1994), more agonistic sibling relationships (Brody, 1998), as well as adjustment difficulties such as delinquency, anxiety, and depression (Garcia et al., 2000; Stocker et al., 2002). Interestingly, Howe et al. (2002) found that passive-aggressive strategies, such as ignoring, were also related to more hostile sibling relationships. Work by Stein and her colleagues (Stein & Albro, 2001) concerning online processing of conflict has confirmed that social goals are crucial in determining which conflict strategies are used; the degree to which an opponent was liked or disliked had clear implications for how conflicts were recalled as well as how they were resolved.

In light of these findings, it is not surprising that constructive conflict has been linked to warmer sibling relationships (Rinaldi & Howe, 1998). Constructive conflict has other potential benefits as well. Investigations of children's retrospective processing about sibling conflict found that children displayed a coherent understanding of their own and their opponent's goals (Ross, Siddiqui, Ram, & Ward, 2004) and an increasing use of justifications regarding their own actions with age (Wilson et al., 2004). Other work has linked perspective-taking during sibling conflict to preschool-aged children's developing theory of mind (Foote & Holmes-Lonergan, 2003). Therefore, it appears that conflict in which siblings consider opposing points of view and in which at least some reasoning occurs may be an important venue for the resolution or prevention of hurt feelings.

## Perceptions and Appraisals of Hurtful Triadic Interactions Involving Siblings and Parents

### Rivalry and Differential Treatment

Rivalry has long been a prominent theme in sibling relationships. According to Parrot (1991), jealous feelings are closely tied to feeling hurt because they represent the threat of potential loss of a relationship. Social comparison plays a role in that siblings evaluate themselves relative to other siblings in the family or parents compare sibling strengths and weaknesses unfavorably (Parrot, 1991; Tesser, 1980). Within a social information-processing framework, when comparison results in a negative self-evaluation on a valued dimension, consequences can include lower self-esteem and hostility toward the sibling (Cicirelli, 1985). Interestingly, recent work on the differentiation process between adolescent siblings has suggested that they avoid self-depreciating comparisons by developing talents and abilities as distinct from those of their sibling as possible (Fineberg, McHale, Crouter, & Cumsille, 2003).

Rivalry can also be fueled when one sibling is "treated better" by a parent (Brody et al., 1998). The nature and frequency of differential treatment, as well as its potential negative implications for individual adjustment and hostile sibling relationships, have been the subject of much research attention (Kowal, Krull, & Kramer, 2004, 2006; McHale, Updegraff, Shanahan, Crouter, & Killoren, 2005). Much like conflict, however, differential treatment of siblings is not necessarily hurtful; children's appraisals are of key importance. Given developmental differences between siblings, effective parenting may well require that each child be treated differently to best meet their individual needs. And it seems that when children understand the rationale for differential treatment and perceive it as fair, they are not as adversely affected (Kowal et al., 2004; McHale, Updegraff, Jackson-Newsom, Tucker, & Crouter, 2000). In recent work examining perceptions of differential treatment, agreement between siblings concerning the fairness of maternal differential treatment was linked with greater warmth and less agonism and rivalry in their relationship (Kowal et al., 2006). From an information-processing standpoint, these results suggest that investigating the *meaning* children attribute to parental behavior is crucial to better understanding how differential treatment contributes to hurt feelings in the family.

*Parental Responses to Aggression*
Parental responses to physical and relational aggression between siblings are of particular importance because these behaviors present parents with an opportunity not only to address misdeeds but also potentially to assuage hurt feelings and repair damaged relationships. However, findings indicate that parents tend to focus more on the transgression and less on individual comfort or relationship repair. Naturalistic observations of preschool-aged sibling aggression at home have found that parents tend to respond to about half of their children's acts of aggression, and they commonly do so with prohibition, particularly if the aggression is severe (Martin & Ross, 1996, 2005). When asked how they feel when their children hurt each other physically, most mothers reported feeling angry (Piotrowski, 1999) which may account, in part, for their focus on the transgression. However, parents are influenced by mitigating circumstances and are less likely to prohibit and more likely to ignore physical aggression in situations involving provocation, reciprocity, and lack of intent (Martin & Ross, 1996).

Less is known about parental responses to relational aggression. In one recent study, sibling relational aggression was linked to the quality of the parent–adolescent relationship. Updegraff and colleagues found that greater parental warmth and less differential treatment were linked to less relational aggression between siblings (Updegraff et al., 2005). These findings suggest that the quality of the parent–child relationship exerts an indirect influence on sibling relations and thereby on hurt feelings between siblings.

*Parental Responses to Conflict*
Parents of young children often intervene to stop aggressive behaviors that occur during destructive sibling conflict (Perlman & Ross, 1997). Constructive parent intervention strategies, such as prohibiting further acts of harm or requiring reasons or justifications, may function to ease or resolve hurt feelings (Perlman & Ross, 1997). It may also be the case that constructive intervention assists children in soothing their own or each others' hurt feelings, although these consequences have not yet been investigated.

Children often request parental involvement in their disputes through tattling (Ross & den Bak-Lammers, 1998). Invited or not, many parents choose not to become involved in constructive sibling conflicts, as they perceive their involvement as unnecessary interference and wish their children to work things through independently (Piotrowski, 1999). Others have argued that a lack of parental intervention into sibling conflict leads to hurtful consequences for both victims and perpetrators, in that it contributes to a pattern of domination on the part of the stronger and learned helplessness on the part of the weaker sibling. Interestingly, work examining parental response to conflict between adolescent siblings found that parents, especially mothers, refrain from involvement quite often (McHale, Updegraff, Tucker, & Crouter, 2000). In fact, these authors found parental involvement was associated with lower levels of sibling intimacy and higher levels of negativity. Developmentally, it may be the case that parents perceive conflict between preschool-aged siblings as a teaching opportunity, but refrain from involvement in conflicts between adolescent siblings because they possess many of the skills necessary to deal with their differences independently.

*Sibling Summary and Conclusions*
As noted with parent–child relationships, much is still not known about the appraisal of hurtful acts between siblings (but see Herzberger & Hall, 1993) or the implications of these appraisals for the self or the relationship. Even less is known about more covert means of causing hurt feelings, such as rejection or exclusion. Of equal importance are actions that soothe, repair, or prevent hurt feelings between siblings; a few innovative investigations have already begun to address some of these behaviors, such as reparation (Martin & Ross, 1996), apology (Schleien, Ross, & Ross, 2005), and conflict prevention strategies (DeHart, 1999; Fineberg et al., 2003). Unfortunately, this work is the exception rather than the rule. Finally, gaps also remain concerning how parents perceive their contributions to exacerbating hurt feelings between siblings. Differential

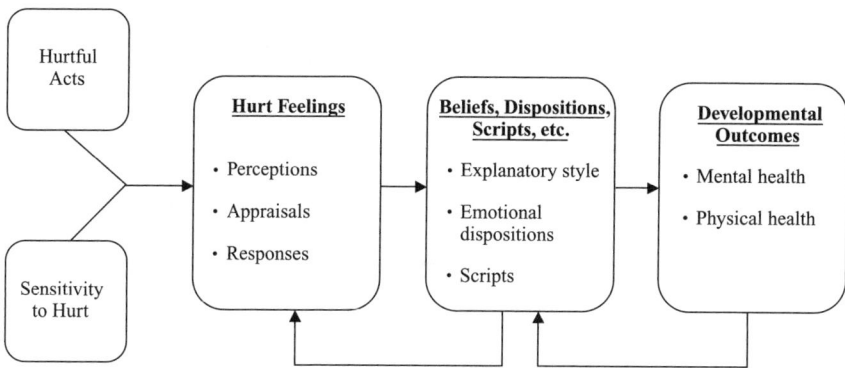

FIGURE 13.1. An integrated processing and structural organizing framework for research on the developmental effects of hurtful interactions in the family.

treatment stands out as one important avenue, but other aspects of parent behavior such as social comparison, alliances, and collusion remain open for future investigation.

### DIRECTIONS FOR FUTURE RESEARCH

Hurt feelings in parent–child and sibling interactions are significant experiences involving crucial judgments and emotions about self, others, and relationships that have consequences for the quality of the relationship and for children's self and social development. However, for the most part this conclusion is based on general associations between global patterns of interaction and outcomes assessed in some cases over a period of years. A critical next step is research from an integrated processing and structural perspective assessing the immediate information processing that occurs in real-time parent–child and sibling interactions and examining their impact on these relationships and on children's developing understanding (or misunderstanding) of self, others, and relationships.

Figure 13.1 shows a general organizing framework for research guided by an integrated perspective. Online processing of hurtful interactions is assumed to depend both on the joint interactive effects of the type of hurtful act that occurs and the individual's sensitivity to hurt. The *hurtful acts* children experience will have some effect on their online processing of hurtful interactions. The profile of emotions that children experience will vary depending on the specific meaning attached to the event. Acts of secrecy may make feelings of alienation most salient, whereas perceived favoritism may make jealousy the strongest emotion. Children's *sensitivity to hurt* also will have some effect on processing. Continual experiences of hurt in the past are likely to sensitize individuals to subsequent experiences (Cummings, Davies, & Campbell, 2000; Downey,

Lebolt, Rincon, & Freitas, 1998). People are more likely to perceive rejection as occurring if they have preexisting expectations that it will occur. Thus, children who are frequently subjected to hurtful acts will likely come to expect them and will be primed to perceive them. Temperamental characteristics also may affect sensitivity to hurt. As noted earlier, a low threshold of reactivity to novel or challenging events (Kagan, 1989; Kochanska, 1993) may heighten sensitivity. The more reactive children are to aversive interactions, the more likely they are to perceive these interactions as hurtful. Thus, whether children perceive negative acts as hurtful is a product of both the acts they experience and their sensitivity to these experiences. The hurt feelings they habitually experience – what they tend to feel, think, and decide to do – affect the *beliefs, dispositions, scripts, and the like* that are reinforced by repeated experiences of these interactions; that is, the way in which they tend to explain the causes of events, the emotional dispositions that become their habitual responses to events, and the scripts they acquire for responding to events. Children's current beliefs, dispositions, and scripts, in turn, affect the processing of subsequent interactions. Over the long term, *developmental outcomes* reflect the extent to which these cognitive-affective structures are adaptive or maladaptive. We provide two examples illustrating how this perspective can help contribute to a better understanding of the immediate processing of hurtful interactions and the dynamic interplay between this immediate processing and developing cognitive-affective structures.

## From Parental Shaming to Child Proneness to Shame

Shame is a key emotional barometer of a person's felt worth or value that motivates and regulates thinking, feeling, and behavior concerned with preserving acceptance by others (M. Lewis, 1992; Tangney & Fischer, 1995). States of shame are painful and aversive, involving self-condemnation, the desire to hide or disappear, difficulty sustaining social interaction, and even difficulty speaking fluently and thinking coherently. As such, they are potent experiences that play a role both in adaptive and maladaptive development. Shame is essential for normal development, helping motivate socially acceptable behavior and efforts to improve the self. When it becomes a dominant response tendency, however, it can be maladaptive (Barrett, 1998; Schore, 1996), and it has been implicated in the development of a wide range of mental and physical health problems (Dickerson, Gruenewald, & Kemeny, 2004; Tangney, Burggraf, & Wagner, 1995). Little research has been conducted on the factors that promote shame proneness in children. Parent–child interactions that arouse hurt feelings may play an important role.

Parental shaming may promote proneness to shame by causing hurt feelings in which shame is a prime component. Theories suggest that shame is precipitated by global negative self-attributions (i.e., attributions about the self as a whole for the failure to meet standards or expectations; H. B. Lewis, 1971; M. Lewis, 1992; Weiner, 1986). Global negative self-attributions may be precipitated directly by global negative attributional statements to the child, such as criticism or scolding that blames essential characteristics of the child, or indirectly by reflected appraisals communicated through negative treatment that generates such attributions by the child him- or herself (Campos, Thein, & Owen, 2004; M. Lewis, 1992). Love withdrawal, expressions of disgust or contempt, and humiliation are prime forms of shaming that are highly likely to lead to internal, global, negative attributions (M. Lewis, 1992). Repeated experiences of these hurtful acts and the feelings of shame they arouse may serve to reinforce a habit of making global negative self-attributions in response to negative events, leading to a self-blaming attributional style and increasing the risk of maladaptive functioning (M. Lewis, 1992). Research to date supports the link between parental shaming and child proneness to shame from early childhood and between shame proneness and mental and physical health problems beginning as early as the primary school years (see Mills, 2005, for a review). However, it has yet to be established that parental shaming induces feelings of shame at the time it occurs or that these experiences of shame contribute to the development of proneness to shame.

Evidence that parental shaming induces feelings of shame in young children may be obtained by observing parent–child interactions and assessing children's shame-expressive behavior in response to shaming acts. Other methods that could be used to study shame induction in older children include interviews conducted immediately after interactions to assess emotions and attributions during interactions. Individual differences in the online processing of parental shaming could be investigated by examining group differences in emotional-expressive responding as a function of past exposure to parental shaming, temperamental characteristics, current proneness to shame, and attributional style. A dyadic source of individual differences that warrants investigation is the extent to which hurtful parent–child interactions have typically been resolved or repaired in the past (Hoyt, Fincham, McCullough, Maio, & Davila, 2005; Worthington, 2005). Finally, a short-term longitudinal design could be used to determine whether observed shame responding during parent–child interaction mediates the association between children's exposure to parental shaming and their subsequent proneness to shame and attributional style.

### Sibling Bullying, Benign Neglect, and Maladjustment

An emerging literature has begun to note linkages between peer bullying at school and sibling bullying at home (Camodeca & Menesini, 2007). For example, Duncan (1999) found that children who self-identified as being both a bully and a victim with peers at school reported the highest frequency of sibling bullying and victimization at home (60% were bullied by siblings; 77% bullied their siblings). Similarly, more recent work found that more than half of children bullied by siblings were also involved in bullying at school and that these children were three times more likely to display behavior problems, even after controlling for sociodemographic factors (Wolke & Samara, 2004). These findings suggest that the combination of bullying by peers and by siblings can take a serious toll.

Shame may play an important role in maintaining these hurtful patterns of interactions between siblings. When harm becomes a typical pattern of sibling interaction because parents are not aware or do not stop it, victims may feel betrayed by the lack of protection and ashamed of their own inability to stop their victimization. "Blaming the victim" both by others and by victims themselves is a common psychological response to violent trauma rooted in shame and self-recrimination (Straus, Gelles, & Steinmetz, 2006; Wiehe, 1997). When parents do not stop sibling bullying, even for benign reasons such as the belief that children cannot inflict serious harm on one another (Finkelhor et al., 2006), victim appraisals may be more likely to include feelings of shame, incompetence, and resentment. Siblings who are compared unfavorably to one another, either by themselves or by their parents, may be particularly susceptible; as noted earlier, differential treatment by parents exacerbates both individual and relational maladjustment (Gilbert & Gerlsma, 1999). Retrospective work on physical harm has found that siblings often exchange victim and perpetrator roles (Hardy, 2001). Therefore, processes of shame, self-recrimination, resentment, and self-protection may be co-occurring to foster the continuing cycle of harm.

Although these processes are currently speculative, they can be tested empirically. As noted with parent–child processes earlier, observing interactions and assessing immediate behavioral and emotional responses would be an important first step. To capture online appraisals, conducting interviews during the replay of videotaped interactions would be invaluable. Last, short-term longitudinal research that investigates similarities and differences in online processing of intrafamily bullying with siblings in comparison to extrafamily bullying with peers would increase our understanding of the potential linkages among individual characteristics, family characteristics, and appraisal of and sensitivity to hurtful interactions across relationships.

REFERENCES

Arsenio, W. F., & Lemerise, E. A. (2004). Aggression and moral development: Integrating social information processing and moral domain models. *Child Development, 75*, 987–1002.

Baldwin, M. W. (1992). Relational schemas and the processing of social information. *Psychological Bulletin, 112*, 461–484.

Barber, B. K., & Harmon, E. L. (2002). Violating the self: Parental psychological control of children and adolescents. In B. K. Barber (Ed.), *Intrusive parenting: How psychological control affects children and adolescents* (pp. 15–52). Washington, DC: American Psychological Association.

Barrett, K. C. (1998). A functionalist perspective to the development of emotions. In M. F. Mascolo & S. Griffin (Eds.), *What develops in emotional development?* (pp. 109–133). New York: Plenum.

Bates, J. E., & Pettit, G. S. (2007). Temperament, parenting, and socialization. In J. E. Grusec & P. D. Hastings (Eds.), *Handbook of socialization: Theory and research* (pp. 153–177). New York: Guilford.

Baumeister, R. F., & Leary, M. R. (1995). The need to belong: Desire for interpersonal attachments as a fundamental human motivation. *Psychological Bulletin, 117,* 497–529.

Bowlby, J. (1969). *Attachment and loss: Vol. 1. Attachment.* Harmondsworth, UK: Penguin.

Boyle, M. H., Jenkins, J. M., Georgiades, K., Cairney, J., Duku, E., & Racine, Y. (2004). Differential-maternal parenting behavior: Estimating within- and between-family effects on children. *Child Development, 75,* 1457–1476.

Brody, G. H. (1998). Sibling relationship quality: Its causes and consequences. *Annual Review of Psychology, 49,* 1–24.

Brody, L. R., Copeland, A. P., Sutton, L. S., Richardson, D. R., & Guyer, M. (1998). Mommy and Daddy like you best: Perceived family favoritism in relation to affect, adjustment and family process. *Journal of Family Therapy, 20,* 269–291.

Bugental, D. B., & Lewis, J. C. (1999). The paradoxical misuse of power by those who see themselves as powerless: How does it happen? *Journal of Social Issues, 55,* 51–64.

Camodeca, M., & Menesini, E. (2007, April). *Is bullying just a school problem? Similarities and differences between siblings and peers.* Paper presented at the 33rd Biennial Meeting of the Society for Research in Child Development, Boston.

Campos, J. J., Thein, S., & Owen, D. (2004). A Darwinian legacy to understanding human infancy: Emotional expressions as behavior regulators. *Annals of the New York Academy of Sciences, 1000,* 1–26.

Casas, J. F., Weigel, S. M., Crick, N. R., Ostrov, J. M., Woods, K. E., Yeh, E. A. J., et al. (2006). Early parenting and children's relational and physical aggression in the preschool and home contexts. *Applied Developmental Psychology, 27,* 209–227.

Cicirelli, V. (1985). Sibling relationships throughout the life cycle. In L. L'Abate (Ed.), *The handbook of family psychology and therapy* (pp. 177–214). Homewood, IL: Dorsey Press.

Compton, K., Snyder, J., Schrepferman, L., Bank, L., & Shortt, J. (2003). The contribution of parents and siblings to antisocial and depressive behavior in adolescents: A double jeopardy coercion model. *Development and Psychopathology, 15,* 163–182.

Cooley, C. H. (1902). *Human nature and the social order.* New York: Scribner.

Crick, N. R., Casas, J. F., & Hu, H. (1999). Relational and physical forms of peer victimization in preschool. *Developmental Psychology, 35,* 376–385.

Crick, N. R., & Dodge, K. A. (1994). A review and reformulation of social information-processing mechanisms in chldren's social adjustment. *Psychological Bulletin, 115,* 74–101.

Cummings, E. M., Davies, P. T., & Campbell, S. B. (2000). *Developmental psychopathology and family process: Theory, research, and clinical implications.* New York: Guilford.

DeHart, G. (1999). Conflict and averted conflict in preschoolers' interactions with siblings and friends. In W. Collins & B. Laursen (Eds.), *Relationships as developmental* contexts: Festschrift in honor of Willard W. Hartup. Minnesota symposia on child psychology (Vol. 30, pp. 281–303). Hillsdale, NJ: Erlbaum.

den Bak, I., & Ross, H. (1986). I'm telling! The content, context and consequences of children's tattling on their siblings. *Social Development, 5*, 292–309.

Derryberry, D., & Rothbart, M. K. (1997). Reactive and effortful processes in the organization of temperament. *Development and Psychopathology, 9*, 633–652.

Dickerson, S. S., Gruenewald, T. L., & Kemeny, M. E. (2004). When the social self is threatened: Shame, physiology, and health. *Journal of Personality, 72*, 1191–1216.

Dienstbier, R. A., Hellman, D., Lehnhoff, J., Hillman, J. H., & Volkenaar, M. C. (1975). An emotion-attribution approach to moral behavior: Interfacing cognitive and avoidance theories of moral development. *Psychological Review, 82*, 299–315.

Dix, T. (1992). Parenting on behalf of the child: Empathic goals in the regulation of responsive parenting. In I. E. Sigel, A. V. McGillicuddy-DeLisi, & J. J. Goodnow (Eds.), *Parental belief systems: The psychological consequences for children* (2nd ed., pp. 319–346). Hillsdale, NJ: Erlbaum.

Downey, G., Khouri, H., & Feldman, S. I. (1997). Early interpersonal trauma and later adjustment: The mediational role of rejection sensitivity. In D. Cicchetti & S. L. Toth (Eds.), *Rochester Symposium on Developmental Psychopathology, Vol. 8: Developmental perspectives on trauma: Theory, research, and intervention* (pp. 85–114). Rochester, NY: University of Rochester Press.

Downey, G., Lebolt, A., Rincon, C., & Freitas, A. L. (1998). Rejection sensitivity and children's interpersonal difficulties. *Child Development, 69*, 1074–1091.

Duncan, R. D. (1999). Peer and sibling aggression: An investigation of intra and extrafamilial bullying. *Journal of Interpersonal Violence, 14*, 871–886.

Dunn, J., & Munn, P. (1986a). Sibling quarrels and maternal intervention: Individual differences in understanding and aggression. *Journal of Child Psychology and Psychiatry, 27*, 583–595.

Dunn, J., & Munn, P. (1986b). Sibling quarrels and maternal intervention: Individual differences in understanding and aggression. *Journal of Child Psychology and Psychiatry 27*, 583–595.

Dweck, C. S. (2000). *Self-theories: Their role in motivation, personality, and development.* Philadelphia: Psychology Press.

Fagan, A., & Najman, J. (2003). Association between early childhood aggression and internalizing behavior for sibling pairs. *Journal of the American Academy of Child and Adolescent Psychiatry, 42*, 1093–1100.

Fineberg, M., McHale, S., Crouter, A., & Cumsille, P. (2003). Sibling differentiation: Sibling and parent relationship trajectories in adolescence. *Child Development, 74*, 1261–1274.

Finkelhor, D., & Dzubia-Leatherman, J. (1994). Victimization of children. *American Psychologist, 49*, 173–183.

Finkelhor, D., Ormrod, R., Turner, H., & Hamby, S. (2005). The victimization of children and youth: A comprehensive, national survey *Child Maltreatment, 10*, 5–25.

Finkelhor, D., Turner, H., & Ormrod, R. (2006). Kid's stuff: The nature and impact of peer and sibling violence on younger and older children. *Child Abuse & Neglect, 30*, 1401–1421.

Fischer, K. W., Shaver, P. R., & Carnochan, P. (1990). How emotions develop and how they organise development. *Cognition and Emotion, 4*, 81–127.

Fontaine, R. G. (2006). Applying systems principles to models of social information processing and aggressive behavior in youth. *Aggression and Violent Behavior, 11*, 64–76.

Foote, R., & Holmes-Lonergan, H. (2003). Sibling conflict and theory of mind. *British Journal of Developmental Psychology, 21,* 45–58.

Garcia, M., Shaw, D., Winslow, E., & Yaggi, K. (2000). Destructive sibling conflict and the development of conduct problems in young boys. *Developmental Psychology, 36,* 44–53.

George, C., & Solomon, J. (1999). Attachment and caregiving: The caregiving behavioral system. In J. Cassidy & P. R. Shaver (Eds.), *Handbook of attachment: Theory, research and clinical applications* (pp. 649–670). New York: Guilford.

Gershoff, E. T. (2002). Corporal punishment by parents and associated child behaviors and experiences: A meta-analytic and theoretical review. *Psychological Bulletin, 128,* 539–579.

Gilbert, P., & Gerlsma, C. (1999). Recall of shame and favouritism in relation to psychopathology. *British Journal of Clinical Psychology, 38,* 357–373.

Hardy, M. S. (2001). Physical aggression and sexual behavior among siblings: A retrospective study. *Journal of Family Violence, 16,* 255–268.

Hart, C. H., Nelson, D. A., Robinson, C. C., Olsen, S. F., & McNeilly-Choque, M. K. (1998). Overt and relational aggression in Russian nursery-school-age children: Parenting style and marital linkages. *Developmental Psychology, 34,* 687–697.

Herzberger, S. D., & Hall, J. A. (1993). Children's evaluations of retaliatory aggression against siblings and friends. *Journal of Interpersonal Violence, 8,* 77–93.

Hoffman, M. L. (1970). Moral development. In P. H. Mussen (Ed.), *Carmichael's manual of child psychology* (Vol. 2, pp. 457–557). New York: Wiley.

Howe, N., Rinaldi, C., Jennings, M., & Petrakos, H. (2002). "No! The lambs can stay out because they got cozies": Constructive and destructive sibling conflict, pretend play and social understanding. *Child Development, 73,* 1460–1473.

Hoyle, R. H. (2006). Personality and self-regulation: Trait and information-processing perspectives. *Journal of Personality, 74,* 1507–1525.

Hoyt, W. T., Fincham, F. D., McCullough, M. E., Maio, G., & Davila, J. (2005). Responses to interpersonal transgressions in families: Forgivingness, forgivability, and relationship-specific effects. *Journal of Personality and Social Psychology, 89,* 375–394.

Huesmann, L. R. (1998). The role of social information processing and cognitive schema in the acquisition and maintenance of habitual aggressive behavior. In R. G. Geen & E. Donnerstein (Eds.), *Human aggression: Theories, research, and implications for social policy* (pp. 73–109). San Diego: Academic Press.

Jones, T. L., & Prinz, R. J. (2005). Potential roles of parental self-efficacy in parent and child adjustment: A review. *Clinical Psychology Review, 25,* 341–363.

Kagan, J. (1989). Temperamental contributions to social behavior. *American Psychologist, 44*(4), 668–674.

Kagan, J., Reznick, J. S., & Snidman, N. (1987). The physiology and psychology of behavioral inhibition in children. *Child Development, 58,* 1459–1473.

Kamins, M. L., & Dweck, C. S. (1999). Person versus process praise and criticism: Implications for contingent self-worth and coping. *Developmental Psychology, 35,* 835–847.

Keenan, K., & Shaw, D. (1997). Developmental and social influences on young girls' early problem behavior. *Psychological Bulletin, 121,* 95–113.

Keery, H., Boutelle, K., Van Den Berg, P., & Thompson, J. K. (2005). The impact of appearance-related teasing by family members. *Journal of Adolescent Health, 37,* 120–127.

Keltner, D., Capps, L., Kring, A. M., Young, R. C., & Heerey, E. A. (2001). Just teasing: A conceptual analysis and empirical review. *Psychological Bulletin, 127*, 229–248.

Kenny, D. A., & DePaulo, B. M. (1993). Do people know how others view them? An empirical and theoretical account. *Psychological Bulletin, 114*, 145–161.

Khaleque, A., & Rohner, R. P. (2002). Perceived parental acceptance-rejection and psychological adjustment: A meta-analysis of cross-cultural and intracultural studies. *Journal of Marriage and Family, 64*, 54–64.

Kim, J., Hetherington, M., & Reiss, D. (1999). Associations among family relationships, antisocial peers, and adolescents' externalizing behaviors: Gender and family type differences. *Child Development, 70*, 1209–1230.

Kochanska, G. (1993). Toward a synthesis of parental socialization and child temperament in early development of conscience. *Child Development, 66*, 325–347.

Kowal, A., Krull, J., & Kramer, L. (2004). How the differential treatment of siblings is linked to parent-child relationship quality. *Journal of Family Psychology, 18*, 658–665.

Kowal, A., Krull, J., & Kramer, L. (2006). Shared understanding of parental differential treatment in families. *Social Development, 15*, 276–295.

Kruger, J., Gordon, C. L., & Kuban, J. (2006). Intentions in teasing: When "just kidding" just isn't good enough. *Journal of Personality and Social Psychology, 90*, 412–425.

Kuczynski, L., & Lollis, S. (2001). Four foundations for a dynamic model of parenting. In J. R. M. Gerris (Ed.), *Dynamics of parenting* (pp. 445–462). Leuven, Belgium: Garant.

Lansford, J. E., Chang, L., Dodge, K. A., Malone, P. S., Oburu, P., Palmerus, K., et al. (2005). Physical discipline and children's adjustment: Cultural normativeness as a moderator. *Child Development, 76*, 1234–1246.

Leary, M. R. (2001). Toward a conceptualization of interpersonal rejection. In M. R. Leary (Ed.), *Interpersonal rejection* (pp. 3–20). New York: Oxford University Press.

Leary, M. R., & Baumeister, R. F. (2000). The nature and function of self-esteem: Sociometer theory. In M. P. Zanna (Ed.), *Advances in experimental social psychology* (Vol. 32, pp. 1–62). San Diego: Academic Press.

Leary, M. R., Springer, C., Negel, L., Ansell, E., & Evans, K. (1998). The causes, phenomenology, and consequences of hurt feelings. *Journal of Personality and Social Psychology, 74*, 1225–1237.

Lemerise, E. A., & Arsenio, W. F. (2000). An integrated model of emotion processes and cognition in social information processing. *Child-Development, 71*, 107–118.

Lewis, H. B. (1971). *Shame and guilt in neurosis.* New York: International Universities Press.

Lewis, M. (1992). *Shame: The exposed self.* New York: Free Press.

Maccoby, E. E. (2000). The uniqueness of the parent-child relationship. In W. A. Collins & B. Laursen (Eds.), *Relationships as developmental contexts* (pp. 157–175). Mahwah, NJ: Erlbaum.

MacDonald, G., & Leary, M. R. (2005). Why does social exclusion hurt? The relationship between social and physical pain. *Psychological Bulletin, 131*, 202–223.

Martin, J., & Ross, H. (1996). Do mitigating circumstances influence family reactions to physical aggression? *Child Development, 67*, 1455–1466.

Martin, J., & Ross, H. (2005). Sibling aggression: Sex differences and parents' reactions. *International Journal of Behavioral Development, 29*, 129–138.

McGuire, S., Manke, B., Eftekhari, A., & Dunn, J. (2000). Children's perceptions of sibling conflict during middle childhood: Issues and sibling (dis)similarity. *Social Development, 9*, 173–190.

McHale, S., Updegraff, K., Jackson-Newsom, J., Tucker, C., & Crouter, A. (2000). When does parents' differential treatment have negative implications for siblings? *Social Development, 9*, 149–172.

McHale, S., Updegraff, K., Shanahan, L., Crouter, A., & Killoren, S. (2005). Siblings' differential treatment in Mexican American families. *Journal of Marriage and Family, 67*, 1259–1274.

McHale, S., Updegraff, K., Tucker, C., & Crouter, A. (2000). Step in or stay out? Parents' roles in adolescent siblings' relationships. *Journal of Marriage and the Family, 62*, 746–760.

Mills, R. S. L. (2005). Taking stock of the developmental literature on shame. *Developmental Review, 25*, 26–63.

Mills, R. S. L., Freeman, W. S., Clara, I. P., Elgar, F. J., Walling, B. R., & Mak, L. (2007). Parent proneness to shame and the use of psychological control. *Journal of Child and Family Studies, 16*, 359–374.

Mills, R. S. L., Nazar, J., & Farrell, H. M. (2002). Child and parent perceptions of hurtful messages. *Journal of Social and Personal Relationships, 19*, 723–746.

Mills, R. S. L., & Piotrowski, C. C. (2000). Emotional communication and children's learning about conflict. In R. S. L. Mills & S. Duck (Eds.), *The developmental psychology of personal relationships* (pp. 71–90). Chichester, UK: Wiley.

Mills, R. S. L., & Rubin, K. H. (1998). Are behavioural and psychological control *both* differentially associated with childhood aggression and social withdrawal? *Canadian Journal of Behavioural Science, 30*, 132–136.

Nishina, A., & Juvonen, J. (2005). Daily reports of witnessing and experiencing peer harrassment in middle school. *Child Development, 76*, 435–450.

Ostrov, J. M., Crick, N. R., & Stauffacher, K. (2006). Relational aggression in sibling and peer relationships during early childhood. *Applied Developmental Psychology, 27*, 241–253.

Parrot, W. (1991). The emotional experiences of envy and jealousy. In P. Salovey (Ed.), *The psychology of jealousy and envy* (pp. 3–30). New York: Guilford.

Patterson, G. R. (1980). Mothers: The unacknowledged victims. *Monographs of the Society for Research in Child Development, 45*(5, Serial No. 186), 1–64.

Patterson, G. R. (1986). Maternal rejection: Determinant or product of deviant child behavior? In W. W. Hartup & Z. Rubin (Eds.), *Relationships and development* (pp. 73–94). Hillsdale, NJ: Erlbaum.

Perlman, M., & Ross, H. (1997). The benefits of parent intervention in children's disputes: An examination of concurrent changes in children's fighting styles. *Child Development, 68*, 690–700.

Perlman, M., Siddiqui, A., Ram, A., & Ross, H. S. (2000). An analysis of sources of power in children's conflict interactions. In R. S. L. Mills & S. Duck (Eds.), *The developmental psychology of personal relationships* (pp. 155–174). Chichester, UK: Wiley.

Pietrzak, J., Downey, G., & Ayduk, O. (2005). Rejection sensitivity as an interpersonal vulnerability. In M. W. Baldwin (Ed.), *Interpersonal cognition* (pp. 62–84). New York: Guilford.

Piotrowski, C. C. (1999). Keeping the peace or peace of mind? Maternal cognitions about sibling conflict & aggression. In P. D. Hastings & C. C. Piotrowski (Eds.), *Conflict as a context for understanding maternal beliefs about child-rearing and children's misbehavior* (Vol. 86, pp. 5–23). San Francisco: Jossey-Bass.

Rigby, K. (2003). Consequences of bullying in schools. *Canadian Journal of Psychiatry, 48*, 583–590.

Rinaldi, C., & Howe, N. (1998). Siblings' reports of conflict and the quality of their relationships. *Merrill-Palmer Quarterly, 44*, 404–422.

Rohner, R. P., Kean, K. J., & Cournoyer, D. E. (1991). Effects of corporal punishment, perceived caretaker warmth, and cultural beliefs on the psychological adjustment of children in St. Kitts, West Indies. *Journal of Marriage and the Family, 53*, 681–693.

Ross, H., & den Bak-Lammers, I. (1998). Consistency and change in children's tattling on their siblings: Children's perspectives on the moral rules and procedures of family life. *Social Development, 7*, 275–300.

Ross, H., Siddiqui, A., Ram, A., & Ward, L. (2004). Perspectives on self and other in children's representations of sibling conflict. *International Journal of Behavioral Development, 28*, 37–47.

Ross, H., Smith, J., Spielmacher, C., & Recchia, H. (2004). Shading the truth: Self-serving biases in children's reports of sibling conflict. *Merrill-Palmer Quarterly, 50*, 61–85.

Schleien, S., Ross, H., & Ross, M. (2005). *"I'm sorry, but": An analysis of sibling apologies*. Paper presented at the University of Waterloo Graduate Student Research Conference.

Schore, A. N. (1996). The experience-dependent maturation of a regulatory system in the orbital prefrontal cortex and the origin of developmental psychopathology. *Development and Psychopathology, 8*, 59–87.

Shebloski, B., Conger, K. J., & Widaman, K. F. (2005). Reciprocal links among differential parenting, perceived partiality, and self-worth: A three-wave longitudinal study. *Journal of Family Psychology, 19*, 633–642.

Stein, N., & Albro, E. (2001). The origins and nature of arguments: Studies in conflict understanding, emotion, and negotiation. *Discourse Processes, 32*, 113–133.

Stocker, C. (1994). Children's perceptions of relationships with siblings, friends, and mothers: Compensatory processes and links with adjustment. *Journal of Child Psychology and Psychiatry, 35*, 1447–1459.

Stocker, C., Burwell, R., & Briggs, M. (2002). Sibling conflict in middle childhood predicts children's adjustment in early adolescence. *Journal of Family Psychology, 16*, 50–57.

Straus, M. A., Gelles, R. J., & Steinmetz, S. K. (2006). *Behind closed doors: Violence in the American family*. Somerset, NJ: Transaction.

Tangney, J. P., Burggraf, S. A., & Wagner, P. E. (1995). Shame-proneness, guilt-proneness, and psychological symptoms. In J. P. Tangney & K. W. Fischer (Eds.), *Self-conscious emotions: The psychology of shame, guilt, embarrassment, and pride* (pp. 343–367). New York: Guilford.

Tangney, J. P., & Fischer, K. W. (Eds.). (1995). *Self-conscious emotions: The psychology of shame, guilt, embarrassment, and pride*. New York: Guilford.

Tesser, A. (1980). Self-esteem maintenance in family dynamics. *Journal of Personality and Social Psychology, 39*, 77–91.

Tomkins, S. S. (1987). Shame. In D. L. Nathanson (Ed.), *The many faces of shame* (pp. 133–161). New York: Guilford.

Updegraff, K., Thayer, S., Whiteman, S., Denning, D., & McHale, S. (2005). Relational aggression in adolescents' sibling relationships: Links to sibling and parent-adolescent relationship quality *Family Relations, 54*, 373–385.

Vangelisti, A. L. (1994). Messages that hurt. In W. R. Cupach & B. H. Spitzberg (Eds.), *The dark side of interpersonal communication* (pp. 53–82). Hillsdale, NJ: Erlbaum.

Vangelisti, A. L. (2001). Making sense of hurtful interactions in close relationships: When hurt feelings create distance. In V. Manusov & J. H. Harvey (Eds.), *Attribution, *communication behavior, and close relationships* (pp. 38–58). New York: Cambridge University Press.

Vangelisti, A. L., & Young, S. L. (2000). When words hurt: The effects of perceived intentionality on interpersonal relationships. *Journal of Social and Personal Relationships, 17*, 393–424.

Vangelisti, A. L., Young, S. L., Carpenter-Theune, K. E., & Alexander, A. L. (2005). Why does it hurt? The perceived causes of hurt feelings. *Communication Research, 32*, 443–477.

Wainryb, C., Brehl, B. A., & Matwin, S. (2005). Being hurt and hurting others: Children's narrative accounts and moral judgments of their own interpersonal conflicts. *Monographs of the Society for Research in Child Development, 70*(3, Serial No. 281), 1–122.

Walling, B. R., Mills, R. S. L., & Freeman, W. S. (2007). Parenting cognitions associated with the use of psychological control. *Journal of Child and Family Studies, 16*, 642–659.

Weiner, B. (1986). *An attributional theory of motivation and emotion.* New York: Springer-Verlag.

Werner, N. E., Senich, S., & Przepyszny, K. A. (2006). Mothers' responses to preschoolers' relational and physical aggression. *Applied Developmental Psychology, 27*, 193–208.

Wiehe, V. (1997). *Sibling abuse: Hidden physical, emotional and sexual trauma* (2nd ed.). Thousand Oaks, CA: Sage.

Wilson, A., Smith, M., Ross, H., & Ross, M. (2004). Young children's personal accounts of their sibling disputes. *Merrill-Palmer Quarterly, 50*, 39–60.

Wolke, D., & Samara, M. M. (2004). Bullied by siblings: Association with peer victimisation and behavior problems in Israeli lower secondary school children. *Journal of Child Psychology and Psychiatry, 45*, 1015–1029.

Worthington, E. L. (2005). *Handbook of forgiveness.* New York: Routledge.

# 14

## Hurt Feelings in Adult Friendships

BEVERLEY FEHR AND CHERYL HARASYMCHUK

When people are asked what gives their lives meaning or what gives them joy or happiness, friends are invariably near the top, if not at the top of the list (see Fehr, 1996). When people's day-to-day interactions are tracked and they are asked, at random times, to report on what they are doing at the moment, with whom, and how they feel, it is time with friends that is associated with the greatest enjoyment and pleasure – even more so than time spent with family or alone (Larson & Bradney, 1988). Although friendship has frequently been described as the "neglected relationship," the research that is accumulating clearly shows that friendships are cherished, valued, and of central importance in people's lives. Indeed, when Berscheid and colleagues (1989) asked undergraduate students to name "their closest, deepest, most involved, and most intimate relationship," 47% nominated a romantic relationship; a substantial 36% named a friend – family relationships, listed by only 14% of respondents, ranked third (Berscheid, Snyder, & Omoto, 1989). Thus, the dominant melody line in friendship is one of intimacy, closeness, happiness, and enjoyment. However, there is also another, contrasting melody line – a dark and lugubrious counterpoint. When Leary and colleagues (1998) asked undergraduate students to describe "a specific time when someone else said or did something that hurt your feelings," that "someone" was most likely to be a close friend (39%), followed by a romantic partner (32%); acquaintances (12%) and family members (10%) were listed much less frequently (Leary, Springer, Negel, Ansell, & Evans, 1998). Similar findings were obtained in Vangelisti's (1994) analysis of hurtful messages. In this research, romantic partners (39%) were most likely to have delivered a hurtful message, followed closely by friends (33%). Family members ranked a distant third (15%). Other research has shown that friends hurt, betray, deceive, ignore, and neglect one another (see Fehr, 1996). This darker side of friendship is the focus of this chapter. Specifically, our purpose is to examine the experience of hurt feelings in the context of adult friendships.

Hurt is defined as "a feeling that occurs as a result of a person being emotionally injured by another" (Vangelisti, Young, Carpenter-Theune, &

Alexander, 2005, p. 446). Scholars conceptualize hurt feelings as an explicitly interpersonal emotion that may entail, but is distinguishable from, other negative emotional states such as anger, guilt, and sadness (e.g., Leary et al., 1998; Vangelisti, 1994, 2006; Vangelisti & Crumley, 1998; Vangelisti & Sprague, 1998; Vangelisti et al., 2005). The experience of hurt feelings has been dissected into its component parts, including causes or eliciting events, cognitions (specifically, attributions), associated affect, responses to hurt feelings, as well as consequences for self and for the relationship. In this chapter, we review each of these elements of what could be construed as the "hurt feelings" script (Abelson, 1981). Most empirical investigations have focused on hurt feelings across relationship types rather than specifically focus on friendships. To further inform our analysis of hurt feelings in adult friendships, we drew on research in the related areas of anger, conflict, and dissatisfaction in friendships. Our intent was to extract those findings that might be useful in understanding hurt feelings in the context of friendships while acknowledging that the phenomenon of feeling hurt was not directly examined in these literatures.

Finally, we note that most of the research on friendship has been conducted with same-sex friends (see Fehr, 1996). Therefore, same-sex friendships are necessarily the focus of our chapter. However, where possible, we include findings for cross-sex friendships.

## CAUSES OF HURT FEELINGS IN ADULT FRIENDSHIPS

What kinds of behaviors cause hurt feelings in friendships? Research on elicitors of hurt feelings across relationship contexts shows that causes of hurt feelings range from cataclysmic events, such as betrayal, that have a major impact on the relationship to more minor, "garden variety" annoyance and irritations (e.g., Leary et al., 1998; Vangelisti, 1994; Vangelisti et al., 2005). In Leary and colleagues' (1998) analysis of hurt feelings, four major categories of eliciting events were identified: betrayal, criticism, active disassociation (social ostracism, explicit rejection), and passive disassociation (implicit rejection). As discussed later, Vangelisti and colleagues (2005) delineated 14 different elicitors of hurt feelings. Some of these elicitors of hurt, specifically betrayal, criticism, and rejection (active/passive disassociation), also have emerged in the friendship literature, particularly in research on conflict and anger. Thus, they are the focus here.

### Betrayal

When individuals are asked to recount an experience of hurt feelings, including the causal event, betrayal tends to be listed with high frequency (Leary et al., 1998; Vangelisti et al., 2005). Do betrayals plague friendships specifically, or are other relationships more vulnerable? Jones and Burdette (1994) examined experiences of betrayal and found that women were most likely to have been betrayed by their spouse (28.1%), followed by a same-sex friend (26.5%). Men reported fewer betrayal experiences overall, with coworkers being named most often (18.1%), followed by their spouse (14.3%) and then a friend (9.7%). When the focus shifted to being the perpetrator, rather than the victim, of betrayal, both women and men were most likely to report having betrayed their spouse. For women, a same-sex friend was the second most likely target.

In an investigation focused specifically on friendships, Davis and Todd (1985) asked participants whether their best or closest friend had ever "engaged in any action or failure to act that seemed a violation or betrayal of the relationship" (p. 31). More than one-third of the participants reported having experienced at least one betrayal or violation. A similar proportion (37%) admitted having committed such acts. In the same vein, Sias and colleagues identified betrayal as one of the causes of the deterioration of friendships in the workplace (Sias, Heath, Perry, Silva, & Fix, 2004). Thus, betrayals seem to be a potent cause of hurt feelings in friendships.

The nature of the betrayal also may be different in friendships than in other kinds of relationships. For example, there is some evidence that betrayals surrounding self-disclosure are more likely to plague friendships than romantic relationships.[1] As Feldman and colleagues put it, "Friendships typically involve a willingness to self-disclose and an understanding that such self-disclosure will be held in confidence" (Feldman, Cauffman, Jensen, & Arnett, 2000, p. 500). In fact, one of the basic rules of friendship is that friends "should trust and confide in each other" (Argyle & Henderson, 1984, p. 500). There is evidence that friends do feel betrayed when either of these expectations – that friends will engage in self-disclosure and that disclosures will be kept in confidence – is violated. For example, in a research program on the dialectics of loyalty versus betrayal in relationships, Baxter et al. (1997) found that friends reported greater difficulty managing the tension between openness versus closedness (e.g., "My friend wants me to disclose more information than I feel comfortable with") than did romantic partners. Given that women's same-sex friendships are based on intimate self-disclosure to a greater extent than men's (see Fehr, 1996, 2004), it is perhaps not surprising that women perceive failures to self-disclose as a greater betrayal than do men (e.g., Shackelford & Buss, 1996; see Crick et al., 2001, for similar findings in childhood and adolescent friendships).

Friends also are expected to maintain the confidentiality of self-disclosures. In Baxter et al.'s (1997) research, keeping confidences was found to be a greater dilemma for friendships than for romantic relationships. And, as might be expected, women regard the failure to keep self-disclosures confidential as a greater betrayal in a same-sex friendship than do men (e.g., Fehr, 1996, 2004).

---

[1] Shackelford and Buss (1996) predicted that a romantic partner or a close friend's failure to disclose intimate feelings would be perceived as a greater betrayal compared to a peer group member's failure to self-disclose. This prediction was supported.

For example, Feldman and colleagues (2000) found that women judged a friend's betrayal of confidence as more unacceptable than did men.

There are other acts of betrayal that are particularly impactful in friendships. One such act is the failure to defend a friend when others are saying something negative about him or her (e.g., Fehr, 2004). In Shackelford and Buss's (1996) research, failure to "stick up" for a friend in the face of public derogation was perceived as a greater betrayal than failure to defend one's romantic partner (failure to defend a peer group member was rated lowest). Finally, the ultimate act of betrayal is a friend's sexual or romantic involvement with one's romantic partner (Bleske & Shackelford, 2001; Shackelford & Buss, 1996). In fact, the most intense feelings of betrayal and upset are elicited when the "other" is a friend rather than a stranger or an enemy.

In short, several conclusions can be drawn from the literature on betrayal. First, it is clear that betrayal is an extremely hurtful event. In Leary et al.'s (1998) research, betrayal received the highest mean hurtfulness rating of all of the elicitors examined ($M = 4.41$ on a 5-point scale; Leary et al., 1998).[2] Second, friendships are not exempt from this extremely hurt-provoking event. According to Wiseman (1986), "the intimacy and closeness that is an integral part of friendship and creates mutual expectations makes both participants vulnerable to betrayals of trust" (p. 201). Nevertheless, when asked to report betrayal experiences, romantic partners are more likely to be named as perpetrators than are friends. It is not clear whether this difference reflects a lower incidence of betrayals in friendships or whether the same act is perceived differently, depending on whether the perpetrator is a romantic partner or a friend. In Shackelford and Buss's (1996) program of research, the highest betrayal ratings generally were assigned when the acts were attributed to a romantic partner, followed by a close same-sex friend. The least betrayal was perceived when the perpetrator was a same-sex peer group member (who was not a close friend). Finally, it also seems that betrayal takes a different form (e.g., breaches of confidence) in friendships than in romantic relationships. In short, when friends betray one another, feelings get hurt.

## Criticism

In Leary et al.'s (1998) phenomenological analysis of hurt feelings, criticism was listed with the greatest frequency (33%) and ranked second in terms of mean hurtfulness rating ($M = 3.78$ on a 5-point scale). Criticism of an individual's behavior or performance also emerged as a cause of hurt feelings in Vangelisti and colleagues' (2005) research. Corroboration of these findings can be found in the anger and conflict literatures. For example, personal criticism has been

---

[2] "Being unappreciated" actually received a higher mean hurtfulness rating in Leary et al.'s study, but this was a very low frequency response and therefore was not included as one of the major causes of hurt feelings.

identified as a major cause of anger in close relationships (e.g., Fehr & Baldwin, 1995; Fehr, Baldwin, Patterson, Collins, & Benditt, 1999). Because friendships were not singled out in these studies, it remains unknown whether criticism is a major cause of hurt feelings in this type of relationship. Interestingly, Argyle and Furnham (1983) found that criticism was a much less common reason for conflict in friendships than in marital or kin relationships. It is not clear whether this finding means that friends are less likely to engage in criticism (and therefore the issue does not arise as a source of conflict) or whether criticism has less of an impact in friendships when it does occur.

### Active Disassociation: Explicit Rejection/Social Ostracism

In Vangelisti et al.'s (2005) research, the most frequently listed cause of hurt feelings was rejection. This category included termination of the relationship, refusal to engage in future interaction, and social ostracism. Similarly, one of the major categories of elicitors of hurt identified by Leary et al. (1998) was active disassociation, defined as "explicit rejection, ostracism, or abandonment" (p. 1227). Social exclusion is also beginning to receive attention in the aggression literature, given that the perpetrators of extreme acts of aggression, such as school shootings, are often portrayed as socially ostracized individuals who eventually lash out at their peers (e.g., Aronson, 2000; Baumeister, DeWall, Ciarocco, & Twenge, 2005; Twenge, Baumeister, Tice, & Stucke, 2001). Most of this research has taken the form of experimental manipulations of social exclusion among groups of strangers in the laboratory. The study most relevant for the present purposes was conducted by Snapp and Leary (2001), who examined the role of closeness in predicting the degree of hurt feelings in response to social rejection. They found that social exclusion elicited more hurt when the perpetrator was an interaction partner in the laboratory to whom the participant had been induced to feel close than when the interaction partner was not close. Unfortunately, empirical investigations of social exclusion among established friendship pairs are rare; the research that has been conducted tends to focus on children's peer relationships (e.g., Crick et al., 2001; Pepler, Madsen, Webster, & Levene, 2005). These studies show that social exclusion is extremely hurtful.

### Passive Disassociation: Implicit Rejection

The fourth major class of causes of hurt feelings in Leary et al.'s (1998) research was passive disassociation, defined as "being ignored, not being included in others' activities and other instances of implicit rejection" (p. 1227).[3]

---

[3] We presented Williams' and colleagues research on social ostracism in the section on explicit rejection, although their definition of ostracism as "the act of being excluded or ignored" (Williams & Zadro, 2001, p. 28) seems to refer to both active and passive dissociation and therefore, could have been included in either the explicit rejection or the implicit rejection section.

Behaviors such as giving someone "the silent treatment" would be included in this category (e.g., Williams & Govan, 2005; Williams & Zadro, 2001). This cause of hurt feelings has received only limited empirical attention in the context of friendships, and again, the research that has been conducted has generally focused on children's peer relationships. A typical finding in this literature is that girls are more likely than boys to engage in implicit rejection. For example, girls are more likely to hurt someone by spreading rumors about him or her – a phenomenon that Crick et al. (2001) refer to as "I hurt you through the grapevine" (see also Pepler et al., 2005; Xie, Cairns, & Cairns, 2005).

The few studies on adult friendships have tended to focus on a particular form of passive disassociation, namely displacement of a friend by a romantic partner.[4] For example, in a large-scale analysis of sources of conflict between same- and cross-sex friends, *rival relationships* was one of 10 categories extracted from participants' accounts (Samter & Cupach, 1998). In the words of the researchers, "Typically, the threat centered around the fact that the rival relationship interfered with time spent together by the friends" (p. 120). For example, one respondent reported, "The conflict was about the girl I am currently dating. It was not that my friend cared so much about WHO I dated, but the fact that she [the friend] was neglected by me" (Samter & Cupach, 1998, p. 129). (Incidentally, the frequency with which this category of conflict was mentioned did not differ by gender nor by gender composition of the friendship pair.) Thus, it is not just blatant acts of social ostracism that produce hurt feelings but also more indirect, subtle forms of rejection.

## Other Causes

There are many other causes of hurt feelings in relationships. For example, as mentioned earlier, Vangelisti et al. (2005) identified 14 elicitors of hurt feelings. In addition to betrayal, criticism, and rejection (already discussed), hurt feelings were caused by moral affront (denigrating the victim's character or integrity), ill-conceived humor (inappropriate joking, excessive teasing), mistaken intent (misunderstanding or miscommunication), relational depreciation (discovering that the perpetrator does not value the relationship as much as the victim thought), indifference (lack of concern for the victim's feelings), personal attack (disparagement of the person), undermining of self-concept (provocation of feelings of inferiority), shattering of hopes (discouragement or disparagement of the victim's hopes, goals, or dreams), truth-telling (revelation of sensitive or embarrassing information), humiliation (public embarrassment), and, finally, inappropriate communication ("out of line" verbal or nonverbal behavior).

---

[4] Research on the dyadic withdrawal hypothesis confirms that as people's involvement with a romantic partner increases, their involvement with friends tends to decrease (e.g., Bendtschneider & Duck, 1993; Johnson & Leslie, 1982; Milardo, Johnson, & Huston, 1983).

It is unclear whether all of these causes (analyzed across relationship types) apply to friendships, although a few have surfaced in research on conflict in friendships. For example, in Samter and Cupach's (1998) analysis of conflict among same- and cross-sex friend pairs, one cause of conflict was *public transgressions*, which is similar to Vangelisti et al.'s *humiliation* category. Other research confirms that public humiliation evokes conflict and upset in friendships (e.g., Shackelford & Buss, 1996; Shulman & Laursen, 2002). Another cause of conflict identified in Samter and Cupach's research was *communication breakdown*, which resembles Vangelisti et al.'s *mistaken intent* category; both refer to misunderstandings and miscommunication.

In conclusion, hurt feelings are elicited by many different interpersonal events, including betrayal, criticism, and social rejection, to name a few. It is important to understand not only what causes hurt but also the way in which causal factors influence the intensity of hurt experienced. As mentioned earlier, in Leary et al.'s (1998) study, betrayal elicited the greatest intensity of hurt feelings. Implicit and explicit social rejection also received high hurtfulness ratings, whereas personal criticism elicited relatively less hurt (although the mean was still above the midpoint of the scale). Similarly, Vangelisti et al. (2005) found that the perceived causes of hurt feelings predicted the degree of hurt reported, even when controlling for variables such as relationship satisfaction, self-esteem, or perceptions of intent. More specifically, relational denigration (hurtful behavior that showed that the perpetrator did not value the relationship) was the strongest predictor of hurt feelings, followed by humiliation. None of the remaining six variables included in this analysis (e.g., aggression, mistaken intent) was associated with the degree of hurt, except for ill-conceived humor, which was negatively associated with hurt feelings.

It is also important to examine whether the causes of hurt feelings and the intensity of hurt reactions vary by type of relationship. Vangelisti and Crumley (1998), for example, found that hurtful messages from family members and romantic partners evoked more intense hurt than hurtful messages from a friend, acquaintance, or coworker (i.e., nonfamily/nonromantic relationship). This effect was not accounted for by differences in the quality of these relationships.

## ATTRIBUTIONS FOR HURT FEELINGS

How do people explain hurt feelings? Attributions for hurt feelings have been examined in a variety of ways. (Note that friendships have not been specifically targeted in these investigations.) Vangelisti (1994) asked participants to recall a situation in which someone said something that hurt their feelings. They were then asked whether they believed the other person intended to be hurtful and to explain why they thought the other person hurt them. The attributions were coded in terms of three dimensions: source (internal, external, interpersonal, relational), stability, and globality. Results indicated that hurtful messages were most likely to be attributed to internal, unstable, and specific factors.[5] In subsequent research, attributions for hurtful messages were coded in terms of perceived intent (Vangelisti & Young, 2000). Consistent with predictions, hurtful messages that were perceived as intentional elicited more intense hurt feelings than those that were perceived as unintentional. However, this difference became nonsignificant when controlling for relationship satisfaction and closeness, leading the authors to conclude that "differences in the intensity of people's hurt feelings may be due more to the quality of individuals' relationship with the person who hurt them than to perceived intent" (Vangelisti & Young, 2000, p. 407). A follow-up study revealed that messages were perceived as more hurtful when they were appraised as intentional and low, rather than high, in frequency. The authors suggest that, when hurtful messages are frequent, people may habituate to them or may develop coping strategies.

Finally, in Leary et al.'s (1998) research on hurt feelings, participants were asked to rate six possible reasons for why the perpetrator had committed the hurtful act. Results indicated that victims of hurt feelings lay the blame squarely on the shoulders of the perpetrator; the highest ratings were assigned to the reason, "the perpetrator was insensitive or inconsiderate." This was followed by "it was an accident," "the person was trying to hurt me," "the person was trying to get me back," and "the person thought he or she was being helpful," with the lowest ratings assigned to "I did something to hurt the person." Responses to a question about deservingness indicated that participants did not believe that they deserved to be hurt.

Interestingly, in Leary et al.'s study, the relation between attributions and the degree of hurt experienced was nonsignficant. In contrast, Vangelisti and Young (2000) found that intentional hurtful messages were perceived as producing more hurt than unintentional messages. However, as reported earlier, this relation became nonsignificant when controlling for relationship quality. Moreover, intentionality was not associated with the degree of hurt feelings reported in their second study (although intentionality did interact with the frequency of hurtful messages). Overall, the evidence suggests that people's attributions for hurt feelings do not play a major role in determining the degree of hurt experienced. However, as is seen next, the kinds of attributions that are made for hurt feelings do influence emotional responses to hurtful messages.

## AFFECT ASSOCIATED WITH HURT FEELINGS

How does it "feel" to be hurt? After describing an experience of feeling hurt, participants in Leary et al.'s (1998) study were asked to report on their emotions

---

[5] In this research, attributions made for hurt feelings also were compared to attributions made for anger and guilt. These findings are beyond the scope of the present chapter.

(positive and negative) and on their feelings of acceptance/rejection, their perception of how much the person who hurt their feelings liked/disliked them, and so on. In terms of emotions experienced, participants' ratings of how hurt they felt were strongly correlated with feelings of general distress (e.g., upset, distressed), moderately correlated with anxiety (e.g., nervous, jittery), and moderately negatively correlated with positive affect (e.g., proud, happy). In a regression analysis, the emotion variables accounted for 56% of the variance in hurt feelings, with few individual variables making a unique contribution. The authors concluded, "The subjective experience of hurt feelings appears to be characterized primarily by undifferentiated... affect as opposed to specific emotions such as hostility, anxiety, guilt" (p. 1229). Further analyses revealed that the experience of hurt feelings also was correlated with feelings of rejection, but not with perceptions of how much the perpetrator liked or disliked them. Other research has shown that hurt feelings are associated with sadness and anger (Leary, Koch, & Hechenbleikner, 2007) as well as agony, suffering, and anguish (Shaver, Schwartz, Kirson, & O'Connor, 1987).

Research that focused on a specific cause of hurt feelings, namely social exclusion, has shown that this experience is associated with a host of negative emotions, including social anxiety, jealousy, loneliness, depression, sadness, anger, feelings of isolation, loss of control, and so on (Eisenberger, Lieberman, & Williams, 2003; Leary, 1990; Parker, Low, Walker, & Gamm, 2005; Williams & Govan, 2005; Williams & Zadro, 2001). Moreover, these effects tend to be long term.

The emotional landscape of hurt feelings has not been examined specifically in the context of adult friendships. However, a study by Roth and Parker (2001) is relevant. These researchers focused on the experience of neglect from a friend whose attentions have turned to a dating partner. Participants reported that the experience made them feel hurt, angry, jealous, and surprised. There was also a gender difference such that female participants reported stronger negative emotions in response to neglect from a friend than did male participants. (When asked to imagine being in the role of perpetrator, participants were more likely to report feelings of guilt.)

Emotions also have been measured in the literature on conflict and aggression in children's and adolescents' friendships. For example, Whitesell and Harter (1996) presented participants with a scenario in which one child verbally attacked another child. The instigator was portrayed as either a classmate or a best friend. Preadolescents (ages 11–12) and adolescents (ages 13–15) reported that this behavior from a classmate would evoke anger; the same behavior from a close friend would evoke hurt feelings, sadness, and anger. Girls reported more extreme negative emotion in the best friend condition than in the classmate condition, whereas boys did not differentiate as strongly between conditions. The authors suggest that the more varied and intense emotional response to a friend's negative behavior may reflect the "multiplicity of concerns touched upon when a friend provokes anger. Concerns with the self, with the relationship, and with the friend whom one cares about are all brought into play" (Whitesell & Harter, 1996, p. 1356). In contrast, a classmate's negative behavior is more likely to affect only the self.

Finally, the emotions that people experience in response to hurt feelings also are affected by the attributions that are made for the hurt-eliciting event (Vangelisti, 1994). For example, in Leary et al.'s (1998) research, the attribution that "it was an accident" was negatively correlated with emotional distress. The attribution that "I did something to hurt the person" was linked with feelings of hostility, guilt, anxiety, and general distress.

One issue that is difficult to disentangle is whether negative emotions such as anger and sadness are feelings that accompany the experience of being hurt or whether these emotions define what hurt is. For example, Vangelisti and colleagues conceptualize hurt feelings as an emotion blend, specifically, a combination of sadness and fear – sadness about being emotionally wounded and fear of being vulnerable to harm (e.g., Vangelisti, 2006; Vangelisti & Sprague, 1998; Vangelisti & Young, 2000). Harter and colleagues (see Whitesell & Harter, 1996) conceptualize hurt feelings as a blend of anger and sadness. Others have suggested that hurt is a unique emotion (Feeney, 2005; Leary & Springer, 2001; see also Leary and Leder, Chapter 2, this volume). A challenge for future research will be to explore whether it is possible to separate the emotion(s) of feeling hurt from the emotions that tend to accompany the experience of hurt feelings. What is clear from the research that has been conducted is that feeling hurt is a negative emotional experience.

RESPONSES TO HURT FEELINGS

How do people respond when they feel hurt? Research addressing this question has, unfortunately, produced mixed results. In a program of research on reactions to hurt feelings across a number of relationship types, Vangelisti and Crumley (1998) identified 10 different responses that they then reduced to three factors. The first factor, *active verbal responses*, included attacking the other, sarcasm, defending oneself, and asking for or providing an explanation. The second factor was labeled *acquiescent responses* and included responses such as crying, conceding, and apologizing. The third factor, *invulnerable responses*, consisted of the responses of laughing, ignoring the message, and being silent. Overall, invulnerable responses were reported most frequently, followed by active verbal responses and then acquiescent responses. Importantly, responses to hurt feelings also depended on the degree of hurt that was experienced.[6] Specifically, participants who felt extremely hurt were more likely

---

[6] Responses to hurt feelings also are dependent on the eliciting event. For example, Vangelisti et al. (2005) found that hurt feelings caused by relational denigration and humiliation – elicitors that were rated as most hurtful – were likely to be responded to actively (although

to report acquiescent responses than those who were less hurt (Vangelisti & Crumley, 1998, study 1). (The extremity of hurt feelings did not influence the rate of endorsement of active verbal or invulnerable responses.) This finding was corroborated in a follow-up study in which the degree of hurt was positively correlated with endorsement of acquiescent responses, negatively correlated with invulnerable responses, and uncorrelated with active verbal responses (Vangelisti & Crumley, 1998, study 2).

In contrast, other researchers have found that people report active responses to hurt feelings. For example, in Leary et al.'s (1998) investigation, the most common reaction was "expressed anger" (80%), followed by "argue or defend oneself" (73%). Letting the other person know that one's feelings were hurt was also endorsed with high frequency (63%), as was responding with a critical or nasty remark. The remaining, more passive response categories, "cried in front of the person" and "cried later, when alone" were less common responses (33% and 42%, respectively). Interestingly, in this study, women's responses to feeling hurt did not differ as a function of gender of the perpetrator. However, men were less likely to express hurt feelings or cry when the perpetrator was a man than when the perpetrator was a woman.

It is not clear why participants in Leary et al.'s research tended to endorse active responses to feeling hurt, whereas those in Vangelisti and colleagues' studies were more likely to endorse passive responses.[7] Unfortunately, analyses by relationship type further cloud the issue in that some researchers have found evidence of more passive responses among friends than romantic partners, whereas others have found just the opposite. For example, Vangelisti and Crumley (1998, study 2) found greater acquiescence in romantic relationships than in familial and nonfamilial/nonromantic (e.g., friend, coworker, roommate) relationships. (This relation held even when controlling for relationship quality). Conversely, Healey and Bell (1990) found that friends reported the active response of exit, although only when a conflict was serious and if the social network did not oppose ending the friendship. Similarly, in Roth and Parker's (2001) study of the experience of neglect from a friend who has become absorbed in a dating relationship, the most common responses reported were active: voice followed by exit. The passive responses of neglect and loyalty were least likely.

These findings stand in contrast to much of the literature on conflict in relationships, in which it is generally found that friends respond more passively

---

this relation was positive for relational denigration and negative for humiliation). As Vangelisti (1994) pointed out, it is also the case that some hurtful messages (e.g., "I don't love you anymore") leave the recipient with few response options, whereas others (e.g., "You just told a lie") allow for a greater range of responses (e.g., denying the statement, explaining, excusing).

[7] It should be noted that most of the response options provided by Leary et al. were active. The only passive reaction on their list was crying.

than do romantic partners (see e.g., Creasey, Kershaw, & Boston, 1999; Fehr, 1996, for a review). For example, Sillars (1980a, 1980b) conducted a series of studies on conflict among college roommates. Three categories of conflict responses were extracted from the data. The *passive and indirect* strategy involved avoiding direct discussion of the conflict issue. The *distributive* strategy entailed a negative discussion of the issue in which the roommate was attacked and pressured to "give in." The final strategy, termed *integrative*, involved an open discussion of the issue in which the other person was not attacked nor were concessions demanded. Videotaped interactions of roommates describing problems or conflict issues revealed that avoidance was the most frequent response, whereas integrative tactics were least commonly used – even though they were most likely to result in satisfactory resolution of the conflict issue and restoration of the relationship (Sillars, 1980a, 1980b). Convergent evidence can be found in the literature on the exit-voice-loyalty-neglect model of responses to conflict (Drigotas, Whitney, & Rusbult, 1995; Rusbult & Zembrodt, 1983; Rusbult, Zembrodt, & Gunn, 1982). Research has consistently shown that friends are most likely to report passive responses (e.g., loyalty, neglect) to conflict and anger, whereas romantic partners are most likely to report active responses (e.g., voice, exit; Harasymchuk, 2001; Fehr & Harasymchuk, 2005). To give a final example, a recent study found that both same- and opposite-sex friends were more likely to respond to conflict with indirect aggression than were romantic partners. Conversely, romantic partners were more likely to use direct aggression than were friends (Richardson & Green, 2006). Thus, the overall picture is one of passivity in friendships, although there are notable exceptions.

There is also controversy over the relation between gender and gender composition of the friendship pair and the use of passive, avoidant responses to conflict.[8] For example, there is some evidence that women are more likely than men to use indirect approaches because of a concern that expressing anger and conflict would threaten a friendship (e.g., Richey & Richey, 1980; Tannen, 1990). Oliker (1989) interviewed a group of women (ranging in age from 20 to 50 years) and reported that "each of these women felt that suppressing conflict

---

[8] Other individual difference variables also play a role in friends' responses to conflict. For example, in a daily diary study of conflict between friends, Berry, Willingham, and Christine (2000) found that friends of participants who were high in positive affectivity were less likely to engage in neglect than friends of those who were lower in positive affectivity. Attachment style differences in responses to conflict among friends also have been examined (e.g., Bippus & Rollin, 2003; Creasey, Kershaw, & Boston, 1999; Gaines, Work, Johnson, Mary-Sue, & Lai, 2000). Unlike the literature on romantic relationships, few attachment style differences have been found. Developmental differences have received research attention as well. This research suggests that the tendency to respond with avoidance is more evident at lower developmental levels; with greater developmental maturity there is a tendency to respond with active, constructive discussion of conflict issues in friendships (e.g., von Salisch & Vogelgesang, 2005; Weinstock & Bond, 2000).

was the way to preserve harmony in the relationship, although for some it nonetheless left troubled feelings" (p. 164). However, others have found that men are more likely to respond with avoidance in both same-sex (Black, 2000) and cross-sex friendships (Blier & Blier-Wilson, 1989). To add further confusion, some researchers have found that the direct expression of emotions such as anger is more common in cross-sex, than in same-sex, friendships (e.g., Allen & Haccoun, 1976; Helgeson, Shaver, & Dyer, 1987).

Although the findings are somewhat variegated, overall, the research suggests that, when faced with hurt feelings in a friendship, people's natural inclination is to respond with passivity, avoidance, or other indirect strategies. There are several possible reasons for this tendency. One is that friendships are generally considered the most voluntary relationship (e.g., Canary, 1995; Fehr, 1996), and therefore, people can respond to conflict and hurt "by simply walking away from an adult friend" (Canary, 1995, p. 94). Based on a program of research on conflict among late adolescent friends and romantic partners, Laursen (1996) reached a similar conclusion. In his words, "When conflict arises, friends are apparently content to close off the dispute and leave well enough alone. Romantic relationships, however, engender special efforts to turn an episode fraught with costs into one that is ultimately rewarding" (p. 202).

It also has been suggested that people consider friendships to be less important and valuable than familial or romantic relationships and, therefore, not as deserving of active repair attempts when issues do arise (e.g., Canary, 1995; Fehr & Harasymchuk, 2005; Laursen, 1996). As Laursen (1996) put it, "Western culture endorses a relationship hierarchy that accords more status to romance than to friendship" (p. 203).

### CONSEQUENCES FOR THE SELF

Given that hurt feelings are associated with negative emotions, it seems reasonable to assume that the consequences for the self also would be negative. Indeed, Leary et al. (1998) found that hurt feelings were associated with negative effects on the self, such as lower self-esteem, worry that the event would recur, and so on. Moreover, the more rejected and emotionally hurt the participants felt, the more negative their self-ratings. Sadly, these effects appear to be long lasting. Leary and colleagues reported, "Overall, 93% of the respondents indicated that the event still evoked negative feelings for them; 33% characterized those feelings as either *strong* or *painfully negative*" (p. 1231). Similar negative effects on the self (e.g., emotional stress, inability to perform tasks) were documented by Sias et al. (2004) in their study on the effects of friendship deterioration in the workplace.

The extent to which hurt feelings affect the self depends on a number of factors, including what caused the hurt in the first place. In Vangelisti et al.'s (2005) research, four of eight causes examined were significantly associated with self-esteem. Specifically, relational denigration (hurtful message indicates that the perpetrator does not value the relationship), humiliation, and intrinsic flaw (perpetrator focuses on a personal defect of the victim) were associated with lowered self-esteem; shock (the hurtful interaction came as a surprise) was positively associated with self-esteem.

Crick et al. (2001) examined the effects of relational victimization (damaging a friendship through spreading rumors, withdrawing friendship, and social exclusion) among friend pairs. This kind of hurt was associated with a host of negative consequences for the self: "friend victimization was uniquely related for both boys and girls to social/psychological adjustment indices such as loneliness, psychological distress, internalizing and externalizing problems, social anxiety and avoidance, and lack of self restraint" (Crick et al., 2001, p. 207). In fact, victimization from a friend contributed to adjustment difficulties over and above victimization from the peer group. Thus, although little research has been done, the conclusion is clear: the experience of hurt feelings can have devastating effects on the self.

### RELATIONAL CONSEQUENCES OF HURT FEELINGS

What impact do hurt feelings have on the relationship between friends? The fact that friends generally respond with avoidance when feeling hurt might suggest that this experience has little impact on a friendship – that people "get over it and get on" with the relationship. However, the negative consequences for the self just discussed might be expected to carry over to the relationship. In Leary et al.'s (1998) research, two-thirds of the participants reported that the hurtful episode had weakened their relationship with the perpetrator "for a while afterward," and a substantial 42% indicated that it weakened the relationship permanently. Less than 5% of participants reported that the relationship was unaffected. A majority of participants (60%) also reported that the hurtful experience had eroded trust, and nearly half (44%) claimed that the situation caused them to dislike the perpetrator. As might be expected, the greater the intensity of hurt experienced by the victim, the greater the reported damage to the relationship (Leary et al., 1998). Similarly, Vangelisti and Young (2000) found that the degree of hurt that was experienced was positively correlated with relational distancing. In fact, Vangelisti (2006) has described relational distancing as the "action tendency associated with hurt" (p. 149).

Turning more specifically to friendships, according to research by Laursen and colleagues conducted with adolescents (see Laursen, 1996), disagreements between friends tend to have no impact on the relationship (63%) and sometimes even improve the relationship (23%). The least likely outcome is relationship deterioration (10% to 14%), leading Laursen (1996) to conclude that "positive outcomes for friends exceeded negative ones" (p. 201).

How closely these findings map onto hurt feelings is not clear, however, given that in this research, disagreements could range from "differences of opinion" to "quarrels and arguments." Research on relational victimization paints a grimmer picture. Crick et al. (2001) found that children who were victimized by a friend rated the friendship as more negative (i.e., higher aggression, conflict) and less positive (i.e., lower intimacy, caring, satisfaction) compared to the friendships of nonvictimized children. Similar findings were obtained by Davis and Todd (1985) in their research on violations in adult friendships (discussed in more detail later).

The relational consequences of hurt feelings are also dependent on a number of contextual variables, including *what* caused the hurt feelings, *who* caused them, attributions about *why* the hurtful behavior occurred, and *how* the hurt was responded to. With regard to the *what* issue, Vangelisti and colleagues (2005) examined the links between eight causal dimensions of hurt feelings and relationship satisfaction. Relational denigration was a significant negative predictor of relationship satisfaction. Surprisingly, humiliation was positively associated with satisfaction. The remaining six causes (e.g., aggression, ill-conceived humor) were not associated with relationship satisfaction. Parallel analyses were conducted with relational distancing as the dependent variable. In these analyses, relationship denigration and intrinsic flaw were significant predictors of relational distancing. There was also a significant, negative association between mistaken intent (hurt feelings caused by being misunderstood or questioned) and relational distancing. (The remaining five causes were not significantly associated with distancing.)

Research on friendships suggests that hurt that is caused by betrayal of trust has a particularly detrimental impact. Based on her research on problems in friendships, Wiseman (1986) commented, "Betrayal of trust can result in a complete (and sorrowful) recasting of the entire personality of the erring friend" (p. 201). In fact, distrust and betrayal are regarded as the most important reasons for terminating a friendship (e.g., Bleske-Rechek & Buss, 2001; Fehr, 1996), although perhaps not in children's friendships (Azmitia, Lippman, & Ittel, 1999).

With regard to the *who* question, there is evidence that the relational consequences of hurt feelings depend on whether one is the victim or the perpetrator. Perhaps not surprisingly, people report less damage to the relationship when they are on the inflicting, rather than the receiving, end of hurt feelings (Leary et al., 1998). Leary and colleagues also found that perpetrators tended to underestimate the extent to which trust and liking were eroded by the hurtful event. Similarly, Jones and Burdette (1994) found that the impact of betrayals (across a number of relationship types, including friendships) varied depending on who had perpetrated the betrayal. When self was to blame, 51% of men and 38% of women reported that the betrayal had resulted in the deterioration or termination of the relationship. Approximately 40% of the sample reported that the betrayal did not affect the relationship; the remaining 20% or so felt that the relationship had actually improved. However, a strikingly different picture emerged when self was the victim rather than the perpetrator. In this case, nearly all (93%) of the participants, male and female, reported that the betrayal had harmed the relationship. Finally, in Davis and Todd's (1985) analysis of relationship violations, when a friend was the perpetrator, the victim rated the friendship lower in viability (trust, respect, acceptance) and success compared to friendships in which a violation had not occurred. Friendships in which self committed a violation were rated as lower on intimacy, support, success, and stability than were no-violation friendships.

The attributions made for hurt feelings also influence relationship consequences. Vangelisti and Young (2000) found that, if a hurtful message was perceived as intentional, participants reported less satisfaction with the relationship, more distance, and less closeness than if it was perceived as unintentional. A follow-up study revealed that people are especially likely to distance themselves when they perceive the hurt as intentional and believe that the other person holds them in low regard (Vangelisti & Young, 2000, study 2). In the same vein, Vangelisti and colleagues (2005) found that people who interpreted a hurtful message as a denigration of the relationship or of themselves as a person were more likely to respond with relational distancing than those whose appraisals were more benign (e.g., mistaken intent, misunderstanding). Similarly, Leary and colleagues (1998) found that victims of hurt were more likely to report that the event had permanently weakened their relationship when they believed that the hurtful event was intentional and committed for a revenge motive.

Finally, how hurt feelings are responded to also determines their relational impact. In Vangelisti and Crumley's (1998) research described earlier, responses to hurt feelings were classified as active verbal (attacking the other, defending oneself), acquiescent (crying, conceding), and invulnerable (ignoring the message, being silent). It was found that "messages that had relatively little impact on the relationship were more often linked to *invulnerable reactions* than were messages that had a great deal of impact on the relationship" (Vangelisti & Crumley, 1998, p. 180). Analyses by relationship type revealed that hurtful messages were perceived as having a greater impact when they occurred in the context of a romantic relationship compared to familial and nonfamilial/nonromantic relationships (Vangelisti & Crumley, 1998, study 2). Feeney (2004) examined behavioral responses to hurt feelings in the context of romantic relationships. She found that destructive responses to hurt feelings (e.g., sarcasm, criticism) were associated with long-term, negative consequences for the relationship.

In conclusion, a number of different factors affect the relational consequences of hurt feelings. What caused the hurt feelings, who did the hurting, why the hurt occurred, and how it was responded to all play a role in determining the impact of hurt. Across these various factors there is a clear bottom line: people do not find it easy to "brush off" hurt feelings and carry on with a relationship. Hurt feelings extract a relational cost.

## GENERAL DISCUSSION AND FUTURE DIRECTIONS

The topic of hurt feelings is a relatively new area of investigation. However, this small body of work is rich in its contribution. The depth and breadth of the analyses of hurt feelings illuminate the complex and multifaceted nature of this emotion. The investigation of causes of hurt feelings, associated affect, cognitions, responses, and relational consequences can be construed as a script analysis, which we believe is a highly valuable approach to understanding this important human emotion. Not only have researchers such as Vangelisti and colleagues as well as Leary and colleagues documented the various elements of the hurt feelings script but they also have taken this research to the next level and explored relations among elements of the script (e.g., how the perceived causes of hurt feelings affect the attributions that people make, how attributions affect people's responses to hurt feelings, and so on). This is the kind of higher order analysis that prototype and script researchers have called for in other areas (e.g., Fehr & Russell, 1984; Fehr & Baldwin, 1995). The research on hurt feelings provides an exemplary model for prototype and script researchers interested in the study of interpersonal emotions.

Given that most of the analyses of hurt feelings have been conducted across relationship types, this research has produced what can be referred to as the "basic script" for hurt feelings. It will be important in future research to focus more specifically on relational variations in this script. Or, to use the terminology of Abelson (1981), to examine whether hurt feelings scripts follow different "tracks" in different relationships. Hurt feelings scripts may vary depending on relationship stage and length. The elicitors of, attributions for, and responses to hurt are probably quite different in the early stages of a relationship than in long-term relationships in which hurt feelings scripts have become solidified and entrenched ("You should have known that would hurt my feelings – for the past twenty years I've told you that I feel hurt when you point out I'm gaining weight"). The research on anger and conflict in friendships cited in this chapter suggests that the experience of hurt feelings may well differ in friendships compared to other kinds of relationships such as romantic and familial relationships. It would seem important, in future research, to flesh out hurt feelings scripts for each of these relationship types and to identify areas of commonality and points of difference.

Research focused specifically on hurt feelings in friendships may also help clarify some of the contradictions and inconsistencies between findings based on analyses of hurt feelings across relationship types and findings based on anger and conflict in friendships. To give one example, Vangelisti and colleagues (2005) found that friends responded more actively (i.e., with less acquiescence) to hurt feelings than did romantic partners. In contrast, research on responses to conflict and anger in friendships generally shows just the opposite – namely that friends are more passive and avoidant than romantic partners when problematic issues arise. It is possible that friends respond differently to hurt feelings than to anger and conflict. Furthermore, there may be different behavioral manifestations of active and passive responses in friendships than in romantic or other kinds of relationships. For example, Bell and Healey (1992) found that friends tended to buffer the impact of confrontation through the use of idioms. "You are hurting my peelings' was a humorous way of letting one's friend know that his words and action caused pain" (Bell & Healey, 1992, p. 312). Although a statement such as this might be considered an active response to hurt feelings, it could also be classified as indirect. A micro-level script analysis of hurt feelings specifically in friendships has the potential to flesh out these more subtle nuances of hurt feelings.

Another fruitful direction for research on hurt feelings is to further explore the underlying dimensions of this experience. According to Leary et al. (1998), "the common denominator in all instances of hurt feelings is the perception of *relational devaluation* – the perception that another individual does not regard his or her relationship with the person to be as important, close, or valuable as the person desires" (p. 1225). Vangelisti and colleagues (2005) disagree. Their factor analysis of 14 causes of hurt feelings yielded eight factors, leading the researchers to conclude that contrary to Leary et al.'s view, the experience of hurt feelings is multiply determined. Feeney (2005) combined Vangelisti and colleagues' findings with those of Leary and colleagues and came to the view that hurt (in the context of romantic relationships) is caused by relational transgressions, specifically transgressions that imply low regard for the relationship. Some of the underlying factors that have emerged in these investigations could be construed as proximal (e.g., aggression, ill-conceived humor), whereas others, such as relational denigration, might be more distal. It is also possible that one or more of these factors is a higher order construct that subsumes the others. It may be useful for future researchers to further specify and explore whether these different factors exist at different levels.

In research on social ostracism, Williams and colleagues (Williams & Govan, 2005; Williams & Zadro, 2007) have focused on the basic human needs that are threatened when people are ostracized. Specifically based on their program of research, they have concluded that social ostracism threatens four fundamental human needs – belonging, self-esteem, control, and meaningful existence. This kind of analysis has the potential to yield important insights if applied to hurt feelings. It may well be that the fundamental needs identified by Williams and colleagues also are threatened when people's feelings are hurt. It is also possible that which need is threatened depends on the cause of hurt feelings. For example, social rejection might be especially likely to threaten belonging needs; personal criticism might threaten self-esteem needs. And, of course, the need that is threatened most may vary depending on the relational context in which the hurtful act occurs.

Another intriguing issue that should be addressed in future research is whether the cloud of hurt feelings can have a silver lining. Certainly, the negative effects of having one's feelings hurt are well established. But can there be a positive side? In the social exclusion literature, recently researchers have moved beyond documenting the devastating effects of this experience to ask whether social exclusion might also motivate people to perform prosocial behaviors aimed at restoring social relations (e.g., Leary et al., 2007; Willams & Govan, 2005; Williams & Zadro, 2001). For example, in a recent investigation, Maner and colleagues (2007) found that participants who experienced social rejection expressed more interest in meeting new friends and perceived an interaction partner as nicer and more friendly than did nonrejected participants (Maner, DeWall, Baumeister, & Schaller, 2007). On a related note, Eisenberger et al. (2003) found that social exclusion was correlated with self-reported distress and with activation of neural regions of the brain associated with pain. However, social exclusion also activated regions of the brain associated with pain regulation

Whether hurt feelings have unmitigated negative effects versus potential positive outcomes may also depend on the "slice of time" that the researchers are examining. To refer again to the social ostracism literature, Williams and Zadro (2001) have documented that immediate effects of social ostracism are highly negative, including hurt feelings, anger, and worsened mood. However, these are followed by more positive reactions, such as attempting to strengthen social relationships, taking control, engaging in self-affirmation, and so on. Unfortunately, these more prosocial responses tend to be short-lived. The longer term consequences of social ostracism are highly damaging, including declining physical and psychological health, lower self-esteem, learned helplessness, isolation, and loss of meaning in life. It would seem important to examine whether other experiences of hurt feelings also are associated with efforts to restore interpersonal relations and whether it might be possible to sustain constructive emotion-regulation strategies.

Age or developmental differences in hurt feelings experiences should be explored in future research as well. Although friendships are important throughout the lifespan, people spend the most time with friends in young adulthood (see Fehr, 1996). It generally becomes more difficult to carve out time with friends as people assume greater family and work responsibilities. The vast majority of the friendship studies cited in this chapter were conducted with university students. The causes, attributions, affective reactions, and consequences of hurt feelings may differ at other life stages. A friend's hurtful actions may cause greater disruption in the life of a university student because she was accustomed to having coffee with her friend after class every day. On the other hand, a friend's hurtful action could cause more upset to a 50-year old woman because of the shock that a lifelong friend would commit a hurtful act. The frequency of hurt feelings might also differ by age. Leary et al. (1998) found that university students were most likely to have been hurt by a friend. It would be interesting to examine whether older adults would be more likely to report being hurt by a spouse or a child, for example. In short, the experience of hurt feelings at different phases of the lifespan warrants further investigation.

Finally, in future research it will be important to examine the role of culture in hurt feelings. Friendship has different meanings in different cultures (Krappmann, 1996). For example, in Western Africa, friends are seen as a source of harm to be regarded with caution and suspicion – more so than in the United States. In the United States, friendship is more likely to be defined in terms of trust and respect than in Western Africa (Adams & Plaut, 2003). These cultural differences in the construction of friendship are likely to affect the frequency, intensity, and nature of hurt feelings experiences. Similarly, the experience of hurt feelings may vary in different subcultures. For example, analyses of "street corner" friendships in the United States has shown that in some groups (e.g., Italian American adolescents living in an urban area), friendships are treated like kin relationships (see Krappman, 1996). These relationships are not likely to dissolve. However, in other groups of street corner friendships (e.g., certain African American groups), despite vows of loyalty and support, friendships crumble when conflict arises. Again, hurt feelings are likely to take a different form and have different consequences in these subcultures.

In conclusion, even though research on hurt feelings in friendships is in its infancy, the findings so far leave little doubt that friends hurt one another. It is perhaps not surprising, therefore, that the self-help book, *When Friendship Hurts: How to Deal with Friends Who Betray, Abandon, or Wound You* (Yager, 2002), has sold so many copies. This book was intended to have broad appeal as reflected by a statement on its cover: "For everyone who has ever wondered about friends who betray, hurt, or reject them, this authoritative book provides invaluable insights and advice to resolve the problem for once and for all." In our opinion, social scientists, too, should be wondering about friends who betray, hurt, and reject and should use scientific research as the tool for further understanding this potent human experience. Although we remain skeptical that there will be quick fixes that will "resolve the problem for once and for all," the greater our understanding of this experience, the greater the likelihood that interventions can be designed to reduce the incidence and impact of hurtful behaviors.

## REFERENCES

Abelson, R. P. (1981). Psychological status of the script concept. *American Psychologist, 36*, 715–729.
Adams, G., & Plaut, V. C. (2003). The cultural grounding of personal relationships: Friendship in North American and West African worlds. *Personal Relationships, 10*, 333–347.
Allen, J. G., & Haccoun, D. M. (1976). Sex differences in emotionality: A multidimensional approach. *Human Relations, 29*, 711–722.
Argyle, M., & Furnham, A. (1983). Sources of satisfaction and conflict in long-term relationships. *Journal of Marriage and the Family, 45*, 481–493.
Argyle, M., & Henderson, M. (1984). The rules of friendship. *Journal of Social and Personal Relationships, 2*, 211–237.
Aronson, E. (2000). *Nobody left to hate: Teaching compassion after Columbine*. New York: Worth/Freeman.
Azmitia, M., Lippman, D. N., & Ittel, A. (1999). On the relation of personal experience to early adolescents' reasoning about best friendship deterioration. *Social Development, 8*, 275–291.
Baumeister, R. F., DeWall, N. C., Ciarocco, N. J., & Twengem J. M. (2005). Social exclusion impairs self-regulation. *Journal of Personality and Social Psychology, 88*, 589–604.
Baxter, L. A., Mazanec, M., Nicholson, J., Pittman G., Smith, K., & West, L. (1997). Everyday loyalties and betrayals in personal relationships. *Journal of Social and Personal Relationships, 12*, 655–678.
Bell, R. A., & Healey, J. G. (1992). Idiomatic communication and interpersonal solidarity in friends' relational cultures. *Human Communication Research, 18*, 307–335.
Bendtschneider, L., & Duck, S. (1993). What's yours is mine and what's mine is yours: Couple friends. In P. J. Kalbfleisch (Ed.), *Interpersonal communication: Evolving interpersonal relationship* (pp. 169–186). Hillsdale, NJ: Erlbaum.
Berscheid, E., Snyder, M., & Omoto, A. M. (1989). The Relationship Closeness Inventory: Assessing the closeness of interpersonal relationships. *Journal of Personality and Social Psychology, 57*, 792–807.
Berry, D. S., Willingham, J.-K., & Christine, A. (2000). Affect and personality as predictors of conflict and closeness in young adults' friendships. *Journal of Research in Personality, 34*, 84–107.
Bippus, A. M., & Rollin, E. (2003). Attachment style differences in relational maintenance and conflict behaviors: Friends' perceptions. *Communication Reports, 16*, 113–123.
Black, K. A. (2000). Gender differences in adolescents' behavior during conflict resolution tasks with best friends. *Adolescence, 35*, 499–512.
Blier, M. J., & Blier-Wilson, L. A. (1989). Gender differences in self-rated emotional expressiveness. *Sex Roles, 21*, 287–295.
Bleske, A. L., & Shackelford, T. K. (2001). Poaching, promiscuity, and deceit: Combatting mating rivalry in same-sex friendships. *Personal Relationships, 8*, 407–424.
Bleske-Reshek, A. L., & Buss, D. M. (2001). Opposite-sex friendship: Sex differences and similarities in initiation, selection, and dissolution. *Personality and Social Psychology Bulletin, 27*, 1310–1323.
Canary, D. (1995). Conflict in friendship. In D. J. Canary, W. R. Cupach, & S. J. Messman (Eds.), *Relationship conflict: Conflict in parent–child, friendship, and romantic relationships* (pp. 77–97). Thousand Oaks, CA: Sage.

Creasey, G., Kershaw, K., & Boston, A (1999). Conflict management with friendship romantic partners: The role of attachment and negative mood regulation expectancies. *Journal of Youth and Adolescence, 28*, 523–544.

Crick, N. R., Nelson, D. A., Morales, J. R., Cullerton-Sen, C., Casa, J. F., & Hickman, S. E. (2001). Relational victimization in childhood and adolescence. In J. Juvonen & S. Graham (Eds.), *Peer harassment in school: The plight of the vulnerable and victimized* (pp. 196–214). New York: Guilford.

Davis, K. E., & Todd, M. J. (1985). Assessing friendship: Prototypes, paradigm cases, and relationship description. In S. Duck & D. Perlman (Eds.), *Understanding personal relationships: An interdisciplinary approach* (pp. 17–38). London: Sage.

Drigotas, S. M., Whitney, G. A., & Rusbult, C. E. (1995). On the peculiarities of loyalty: A diary study of responses to dissatisfaction in everyday life. *Personality and Social Psychology Bulletin, 21*, 596–609.

Eisenberger, N. I., Lieberman, M. D., & Williams, K. D. (2003). Does rejection hurt? An fMRI study of social exclusion. *Science, 302*, 290–292.

Feeney, J. A. (2004). Hurt feelings in couple relationships: Toward integrative models of the negative effects of hurtful events. *Journal of Social and Personal Relationships, 21*, 487–508.

Feeney, J. A. (2005). Hurt feelings in couple relationships: Exploring the role of attachment and a sense of personal injury. *Personal Relationships, 12*, 253–271.

Fehr, B. (1996). *Friendship processes*. Thousand Oaks, CA: Sage.

Fehr, B. (2004). Intimacy expectations in same-sex friendships: A prototype interaction pattern model. *Journal of Personality and Social Psychology, 86*, 265–284.

Fehr, B., & Baldwin, M. (1995). Prototype and script analyses of laypeople's knowledge of anger. In G. J. O. Fletcher & J. Fitness (Eds.), *Knowledge structures and interaction in close relations: A social psychological approach* (pp. 219–245). Hillsdale, NJ: Erlbaum.

Fehr, B., Baldwin, M., Collins, L., Patterson, S., & Benditt, R. (1999). Anger in close relationships: An interpersonal script analysis. *Personality and Social Psychology Bulletin, 25*, 299–312.

Fehr, B., & Harasymchuk, C. (2005). The experience of emotion in close relationships: Toward an integration of the emotion-in-relationships and interpersonal scripts models. *Personal Relationships, 12*, 181–196.

Fehr, B., & Russell, J. A. (1984). Concept of emotion viewed from a prototype perspective. *Journal of Experimental Psychology, 113*, 464–486.

Feldman, S. S., Cauffman, E., Jensen, L. A., & Arnett, J. (2000). The (un)acceptability of betrayal: A study of college students' evaluations of sexual betrayal by a romantic partner and betrayal of a friend's confidence. *Journal of Youth and Adolescence, 29*, 499–523.

Gaines, S. O., Work, C., Johnson, H., Mary-Sue, P., & Lai, K. (2000). Impact of attachment style and self-monitoring on individuals' responses to accommodative dilemmas across relationship types. *Journal of Social and Personal Relationships, 17*, 767–789.

Harasymchuk, C. (2001). *Responses to dissatisfaction in friendships and romantic relationships: An interpersonal script analysis*. Unpublished masters thesis, University of Manitoba.

Healey, J. G., & Bell, R. A. (1990). Effects of social networks on individuals' responses to conflicts in friendship. In D. D. Cahn (Ed.), *Intimates in conflict: A communication perspective* (pp. 121–150). Hillsdale, NJ: Erlbaum.

Helgeson, V. S., Shaver, P., & Dyer, M. (1987). Prototypes of intimacy and distance in same-sex and opposite-sex relationships. *Journal of Social and Personal Relationships, 4*, 195–233.

Johnson, M. P., & Leslie, L. (1982). Couple involvement and network structure: A test of dyadic withdrawal hypothesis. *Social Psychology Quarterly, 45,* 34–43.

Jones, W. H., & Burdette, M. P. (1994). Betrayal in relationships. In A. L. Weber & J. H. Harvey (Eds.), *Perspectives on close relationships* (pp. 243–262). Needham Heights, MA: Allyn & Bacon.

Krappmann, L. (1996). Amicitia, drujba, shin-yu, philia, freundschaft, friendship: On the cultural diversity of a human relationship. In W. M. Bukowski, A. F. Newcomb, & W. W. Hartup (Eds.), *The company they keep: Friendship in childhood and adolescence* (pp. 19–40). New York: Cambridge University Press.

Larson, R. W., & Bradney, N. (1988). Precious moments with family members and friends. In R. M. Milardo (Ed.), *Families and social networks* (pp. 107–126). Thousand Oaks, CA: Sage.

Laursen, B. (1996). Closeness and conflict in adolescent peer relationships: Interdependence with friends and romantic partners. In W. M. Bukowski, A. F. Newcomb, & W. W. Hartup (Ed.), *The company they keep: Friendship in childhood and adolescence* (pp. 186–210). New York: Cambridge University Press.

Leary, M. (1990). Responses to social exclusion: Social anxiety, jealousy, loneliness, depression, and low self-esteem. *Journal of Social and Clinical Psychology, 9,* 221–229.

Leary, M. R., Koch, E. J., & Hechenbleikner (2007). Emotional responses to interpersonal rejection. In M. R. Leary (Ed.), *Interpersonal rejection* (pp. 145–166). New York: Oxford University Press.

Leary, M. R., & Springer, C. A. (2001). Hurt feelings: The neglected emotion. In R. M. Kowalski (Ed.), *Behaving badly: Aversive behaviors in interpersonal relationships* (pp. 151–175). Washington, DC: American Psychological Association.

Leary, M. R., Springer, C., Negel, L., Ansell, E., & Evans, K. (1998). The causes, phenomenology, and consequences of hurt feelings. *Journal of Personality and Social Psychology, 74,* 1225–1237.

Maner, J. K., DeWall, N., Baumeister, R. F., & Schaller, M. (2007). Does social exclusion motivate interpersonal reconnection? Resolving the "porcupine problem." *Journal of Personality and Social Psychology, 92,* 42–55.

Milardo, R. M., Johnson, M. P., & Huston, T. L. (1983). Developing close relationships: Changing patterns of interaction between pair members and social networks. *Journal of Personality and Social Psychology, 44,* 964–976.

Oliker, S. J. (1989). *Best friends and marriage: Exchange among women.* Berkeley: University of California Press.

Parker, J. G., Low, , C. M., Walker, A. R., & Gamm, B. K. (2005). Friendship jealousy in young adolescents: Individual differences and links to sex, self-esteem, aggression, and social adjustment. *Developmental Psychology, 41,* 235–250.

Pepler, D. J., Madsen, K. C., Webster, C., & Levene, K. S. (2005). *The development and treatment of girlhood aggression.* Mahwah, NJ: Erlbaum.

Richardson, D. S., & Green, L. R. (2006). Direct and indirect aggression: Relationship as social context. *Journal of Applied Social Psychology, 36,* 2492–2508.

Richey, M. H., & Richey, H. W. (1980). The significance of best-friend relationships in adolescence. *Psychology in the Schools, 17,* 536–540.

Roth, M. A., & Parker, J. G. (2001). Affective and behavioral responses to friends who neglect their friends for dating partners: Influences of gender, jealousy and perspective. *Journal of Adolescence, 24,* 281–296.

Rusbult, C. E., & Zembrodt, I. M. (1983). Responses to dissatisfaction in romantic involvements: A multidimensional scaling analysis. *Journal of Experimental Social Psychology, 19,* 274–293.

Rusbult, C. E., Zembrodt, I. M., & Gunn, L. K. (1982). Exit, voice, loyalty, and neglect: Responses to dissatisfaction in romantic involvements. *Journal of Personality and Social Psychology, 43*, 1230–1242.

Samter, W., & Cupach, W. R. (1998). Friendly fire: Topical variations in conflict among same-and cross-sex friends. *Communication Studies, 49*, 121–138.

Shackelford, T. K., & Buss, D. M. (1996). Betrayal in mateships, friendships, and coalitions. *Personality and Social Psychology Bulletin, 22*, 1151–1164.

Shaver, P., Schwartz, J., Kirson, D., & O'Connor, C. (1987). Emotion knowledge: Further exploration of a prototype approach. In G. W. Parrot (Ed.), *Emotions in social psychology: Essential readings* (pp. 26–56). New York: Psychology Press.

Shulman, S., & Laursen, B. (2002). Adolescent perceptions of conflict in interdependent and disengaged friendships. *Journal of Research on Adolescence, 12*, 353–372.

Sias, P. M., Heath, R. G., Perry, T., Silva, D., & Fix, B. (2004). Narratives of workplace friendship deterioration. *Journal of Social and Personal Relationships, 21*, 321–340.

Sillars, A. L. (1980a). Attributions and communication in roommate conflicts. *Communication Monographs, 47*, 180–200.

Sillars, A. L. (1980b). The sequential and distributional structure of conflict interactions as a function of attributions concerning the locus of responsibility and stability of conflicts. In D. Nimmo (Ed.), *Communication Yearbook 4* (pp. 217–235). Edison, NJ: Transaction.

Snapp, C. M., & Leary, M. R. (2001). Hurt feelings among new acquaintances: Moderating effects of interpersonal familiarity. *Journal of Social and Personal Relationships, 18*, 315–326.

Tannen, D. (1990). Gender differences in topical coherence: Creating involvement in best friends' talk. *Discourse Processes, 13*, 73–90.

Twenge, J. M., Baumeister, R. F., Tice, D. M., & Stucke, T. S. (2001). If you can't join them, beat them: Effects of social exclusion on aggressive behavior. *Journal of Personality and Social Psychology, 81*, 1058–1069.

Vangelisti, A. L. (1994). Messages that hurt. In W. R. Cupach & B. H. Spitzberg (Eds.), *The dark side of interpersonal communication* (pp. 53–82). Hillsdale, NJ: Erlbaum.

Vangelisti, A. L. (2006). Hurtful interactions and the dissolution of intimacy. In M. A. Fine & J. H. Harvey (Eds.), *Handbook of divorce and relationship dissolution* (pp. 133–152). Mahwah, NJ: Erlbaum.

Vangelisti, A. L., & Crumley, L. P. (1998). Reactions to messages that hurt: The influence of relationship contexts. *Communication Monographs, 65*, 173–196.

Vangelisti, A. L., & Sprague, R. J. (1998). Guilt and hurt: Similarities, distinctions, and conversational strategies. In P. A. Andersen & L. K. Guerrero (Eds.), *Handbook of communication and emotion: Research, theory, applications, and contexts* (pp. 123–154). San Diego: Academic Press.

Vangelisti, A. L., & Young, S. L. (2000). When words hurt: The effects of perceived intentionality on interpersonal relationships. *Journal of Social and Personal Relationships, 17*, 393–424.

Vangelisti, A. L., Young, S. L., Carpenter-Theune, K. E., & Alexander, A. L. (2005). Why does it hurt?: The perceived causes of hurt feelings. *Communication Research, 32*, 443–477.

von Salisch, M., & Vogelgesang, J. (2005). Anger regulation among friends: Assessment and development from childhood to adolescence. *Journal of Social and Personal Relationships, 22*, 837–855.

Weinstock, J. S., & Bond, L. A. (2000). Conceptions of conflict in close friendships and ways of knowing among young college women: A developmental framework. *Journal of Social and Personal Relationships, 17*, 687–696.

Whitesell, N. R., & Harter, S. (1996). The interpersonal context of emotion: Anger with close friends and classmates. *Child Development, 67*, 1345–1359.

Williams, K. D., & Govan, C. (2005). Reacting to ostracism: Retaliation or reconciliation? In D. Abrams, M. A. Hogg, & J. M. Marques (Eds.), *The social psychology of exclusion* (pp. 47–62). New York: Psychology Press.

Williams, K. D., & Zadro, L. (2001). Ostracism. On being ignored, excluded, and rejected. In M. R. Leary (Ed.), *Interpersonal rejection* (pp. 21–53). New York: Oxford University Press.

Wiseman, J. P. (1986). Friendship: Bonds and binds in a voluntary relationship. *Journal of Social and Personal Relationships, 3*, 191–211.

Xie, H., Cairns, B. D., & Cairns, R. B. (2005). The development of aggressive behaviors among girls: Measurement issues, social function, and differential trajectories. In D. J. Pepler, K. C. Madsen, C. Webster, & K. S. Levene (Eds.), *The development and treatment of girlhood aggression* (pp. 105–136). Mahwah, NJ: Erlbaum.

Yager, J. (2002). *When friendship hurts: How to deal with friends who betray, abandon, or wound you.* New York: Simon & Schuster.

# 15

# When Love Hurts: Understanding Hurtful Events in Couple Relationships

JUDITH A. FEENEY

"Love is a battlefield," "love hurts," "love and other bruises": Popular songs are replete with references to the pain that may be associated with romantic love. This chapter begins by outlining the particular importance of hurt feelings in couple relationships. It then addresses issues concerning the nature of hurtful events between intimate partners, the consequences of these events for victims and relationships, and the differing perceptions of victims and perpetrators. The final section presents avenues for further research and implications for practice.

## WHY STUDY HURT IN COUPLE RELATIONSHIPS?

Researchers and lay people alike agree that personal relationships are crucial to physical and psychological well-being (e.g., Baumeister & Leary, 1995). Of particular importance in this regard are couple ("romantic") relationships. These relationships are fundamental to the structure of society and play a unique role in meeting individuals' needs for comfort, companionship, support, and security (Argyle, 1986; Weiss, 1991).

Although terms such as "comfort" and "support" imply *positive* affect, romantic partners' unique role as a source and target of strong emotion is a double-edged sword – as many song titles suggest, "love" often entails "hurt." The early stages of couple relationships involve considerable relational uncertainty, as partners know little about each other's hopes, intentions, and weaknesses. At the same time, they may experience intense physical attraction and the related features of physiological arousal, together with concerns about the extent to which these feelings are reciprocated (Hazan & Zeifman, 1999). In this emotionally charged context, a hurtful word or action may be enough to signal that the relationship is doomed.

Many couples, by contrast, go on to develop close, committed relationships; however, the very relational processes that draw these partners together create the potential for hurt and distress. For example, as intimate partners become privy to increasingly personal and sensitive information about one another, they gain access to more effective "weaponry" that can inflict intentional or unintentional hurt (Miller, 1997). Similarly, the high levels of interdependence that characterize committed couple bonds mean that each partner is strongly affected by the other – this ongoing process of mutual influence is likely to include hurtful episodes, especially given the high expectations of intimate partners in contemporary Western societies (Wallerstein & Blakeslee, 1995).

Two additional considerations further highlight the particular importance of hurt in couple relationships. First, couple bonds are communal relationships, which implies that partners should strive to meet each other's needs and protect each other's welfare. Indeed, most partners in committed couple relationships endorse this norm and try to follow it in their interactions with one another (Clark, Graham, & Grote, 2002). Hence, hurtful behavior by an intimate partner may be seen not only as inflicting a specific wound (e.g., by making an unjust accusation) but also, and more generally, as violating the communal norm. Second, and notwithstanding the considerable barriers to ending a committed partnership, couple bonds are essentially voluntary in nature. They may therefore be particularly susceptible to the effects of hurtful events, as partners can choose to end the relationship if the hurt is too severe (Vangelisti & Crumley, 1998).

In short, given that couple bonds involve interdependence and intense emotion, instances of hurt feelings may be both inevitable and distressing. What do empirical data tell us about the scope of this problem? Indirect evidence of the particularly sensitive nature of romantic relationships comes from studies of hurtful messages in two undergraduate samples (Vangelisti, 1994). In these studies, participants were asked to recall and describe a situation in which someone said something that hurt their feelings. Although Vangelisti did not explore in detail the effect of message *source* (romantic partner versus other), she noted that, in both samples, romantic relationships were the most commonly cited topic of hurtful messages (e.g., "He never liked you anyway").

More direct evidence of the sensitive nature of romantic relationships is provided by Leary, Springer, Negel, Ansell, and Evans (1998), who examined retrospective accounts of hurtful events across a range of relationship types. In this undergraduate sample, most hurtful episodes involved romantic partners or close friends; further, ratings of hurt and perceived rejection were highest when romantic partners were involved. Consistent with these findings, my own studies of undergraduates (Feeney, 2004) and of community samples of dating and married couples (Feeney & Hill, 2006) indicate that victims generally describe hurtful acts by romantic partners as "very" or "extremely" hurtful.

Most studies in this area have asked participants to describe a single hurtful event; hence, they shed light only on the severity of the *chosen* event (which may not be typical of hurtful events between intimates). Further, this method gives no information about the *frequency* with which hurtful events occur. The latter issue was addressed by my recent study of dating and married couples (Feeney & Hill, 2006), which included a diary component. In this part of the study, each partner was given a structured diary containing five pages for recording "victim events" (events in which the individual's feelings were hurt by the partner) and five for recording "perpetrator events" (events in which the individual hurt the partner's feelings). Participants were asked to record the date and time of each event and to give a brief description of what happened. They were instructed to return the diaries after recording all 10 events or after 3 weeks had elapsed (whichever occurred first). Not surprisingly, the number of hurtful events reported by couples varied widely. Among the 156 participants (78 couples) who returned the diaries, 12 explicitly noted that no such events had occurred in their relationship during the 3-week period; however, an equal number completed all 10 entries. Overall, respondents reported an average of about four hurtful events; more events were reported from the role of victim, rather than perpetrator, a point I revisit later.

In summary, both theory and research suggest that hurtful events occur relatively frequently in couple relationships and that victims experience at least some of these events as very distressing.

## WHAT EVENTS DO COUPLES FIND HURTFUL?

The emotional experience of hurt feelings remains controversial, with hurt being variously seen as a form of sadness (Shaver, Schwartz, Kirson, & O'Connor, 1987), an emotion blend (Vangelisti, 2001), and a unique emotion in its own right (Leary & Springer, 2001). Similarly, researchers are still grappling with two basic questions regarding the nature of hurtful events. First, what is the central (or defining) feature of events that are experienced as hurtful? And second, what are the major types of hurtful events?

### The Central Feature of Hurtful Events

A number of theoretical perspectives have been advanced regarding the first question, most of which apply to hurtful events generally (rather than to couple relationships specifically). For example, Leary (2001) proposed that the defining feature of hurtful events is perceived relational devaluation (or low relational evaluation); that is, the target perceives that the offender regards the relationship as less valuable, important, or close than the target would like. According to this perspective, people possess standards for assessing the extent to which others value relationships with them. These standards differ from person to person and from relationship to relationship; further, individuals differ in their readiness to "read" evidence of relational evaluation into specific behaviors (Leary, 2001). Hence, a given event may be experienced as hurtful by one individual, but not by another.

Vangelisti (2001) offered a somewhat different emphasis, proposing that the defining feature of hurt feelings is relational transgression. In this context, the term "transgression" refers to an act that inflicts emotional pain; targets of hurtful events perceive themselves as victims and as vulnerable and unprotected (Vangelisti, 2001; Vangelisti & Crumley, 1998). Similarly, Folkes (1982) discussed links between hurt feelings and a sense of harm, vulnerability, or wounding.

Both these perspectives highlight the importance of *appraisals* of behavior: hurt feelings result from the target's interpretation of the partner's actions. This focus is consistent with appraisal theories of emotion (e.g., Lazarus, 1991; Roseman & Smith, 2001), which view emotions as stemming from individuals' evaluations (appraisals) of particular situations. Further, the two perspectives are not inconsistent. After all, transgressions involve violating or infringing norms and rules, and such rules provide a widely accepted guide to appropriate relational behavior (Jones, Moore, Schratter, & Negel, 2001). Hence, most relational transgressions may be seen as implying that the offender devalues the relationship; conversely, acts that imply relational devaluation violate the norms of intimate relationships. In short, most hurtful events may involve both relational transgression and devaluation.

Recently, I proposed another perspective on the defining feature of hurtful events, focusing specifically on couple relationships (Feeney, 2005). This work built on previous research stressing the role of transgression (Vangelisti, 2001) and the evolutionary significance of monitoring one's relational standing (Leary, 2001). According to this perspective, hurt feelings are elicited by relational transgressions that evoke a sense of "personal injury," stemming from damage to mental models of attachment. In other words, hurt is associated with events that damage the victim's view of the self as worthy of love, or core beliefs about the availability and trustworthiness of others, or both.

This conceptualization of hurt is based on the argument that humans possess an innate attachment behavioral system that evolved through natural selection and that motivates them to establish and maintain intimate bonds (Bowlby, 1979). Although all humans are predisposed to form attachment bonds, attachment behavior shows individual differences that reflect working models (mental models) of attachment. That is, based on their unique history of interactions with attachment figures, individuals develop working models that embody their perceptions and expectations regarding two key questions: whether they themselves are worthy of love and attention (model of self) and whether attachment figures are generally available and dependable (model of others).

Although Bowlby's theory dealt primarily with the bonds between infants and their caregivers, attachment principles are also relevant to adults' romantic relationships. Romantic relationships fulfill needs for comfort and a sense of security, and positive models of self and others promote stable and satisfying relationships (Feeney, 1999; Rothbard & Shaver, 1994). Further, mental models of attachment carry crucial information about acceptance and rejection and shape responses to relational events (Downey & Feldman, 1996; Shaver & Mikulincer, 2002). For these reasons, events that compromise positive views of self or others are likely to be perceived as signaling a threat to safety and may be experienced as a kind of injury.

As noted earlier, this perspective builds on work linking hurt feelings with relational transgression and with evaluations of one's relational standing. Indeed, ratings by expert judges suggest that most hurtful events in couple relationships involve transgression and devaluation, as well as a perceived threat to working models (Feeney, 2005). However, the attachment perspective offers important advantages in studying couple relationships (Feeney, 2005). For example, attachment theory emphasizes the need for "felt security" and its basis in interactions with attachment figures. Hence, it helps explain the intense emotion that can result from threats to working models, and it fits with research demonstrating the visceral impact and lingering sense of pain associated with acts of betrayal by intimate partners (Fitness, 2001; Kowalski, 2001). In addition, attachment theory generates predictions about individual differences in responses to hurtful events. Adults who are anxious about their relationships, for example, may report high levels of hurt and fear, reflecting hyperactivation of the attachment system and the tendency to fear rejection (Shaver & Mikulincer, 2002). (Findings discussed later in this chapter support this prediction.)

Before leaving this question of the defining feature of hurtful events, it is worth noting recent work supporting the view that relational threats (whether conceptualized as devaluation, transgression, or compromised working models) are experienced as a kind of injury. Specifically, neuroimaging studies (Eisenberger, Lieberman, & Williams, 2003) indicate that the neural correlates of social exclusion are very similar to those observed in studies of physical pain. In addition, broader theoretical analyses suggest that physiological and behavioral responses to social pain parallel responses to physical pain (MacDonald & Leary, 2005).

## Typologies of Hurtful Events

The second question regarding the nature of hurtful events concerns the different *types* of events within this broad category. This question supplements the previous one by seeking to provide a concise summary of the major varieties of hurtful behavior.

In her studies of hurtful messages (across a range of relationships), Vangelisti (1994) found that the most frequent types were accusations (of a fault or offense), negative evaluations (of the target's value), and informative messages (disclosures of hurtful information, such as attractions to another). Less common types of hurtful messages included directives, threats, lies, and advice. This typology provides a useful summary of the diverse ways in which "words can hurt." However, as Vangelisti (1994) clearly acknowledged, verbal messages are not the only source of hurt; nonverbal behavior and acts of omission can also elicit hurt feelings.

Leary et al. (1998) provided a broader analysis of types of hurtful events in their retrospective study of hurt feelings across diverse relationships. Based on participants' accounts, these researchers proposed six categories of hurtful events: active disassociation (defined as explicit rejection, abandonment, or ostracism); passive disassociation (implicit rejection, such as being ignored); criticism; betrayal; teasing; and feeling unappreciated, used, or taken for granted. This typology provides another useful perspective on hurtful events, but two points require attention (Feeney, 2004).

First, "feeling unappreciated, used, or taken for granted" describes thoughts and feelings of targets rather than the behavior of offenders. Hence, this category does not clarify the nature of aversive relational behavior, and it creates difficulties in classifying specific events. For example, being abandoned by a lover involves active disassociation, but targets are also likely to feel unappreciated. In fact, most types of hurtful events may cause targets to feel unappreciated or taken for granted. Similarly, the term "rejection" may be of limited utility in classifying hurtful events. Researchers (e.g., Fitness, 2001; Jones et al., 2001) have argued that rejection refers to the way in which partner behaviors such as ostracism and betrayal are *cognized* (these behaviors are hurtful *because* they signal rejection). In short, it is crucial to distinguish between an actor's behavior and the target's responses to it.

Second, although broad-based typologies are useful for describing the full range of hurtful events, the relative frequencies of the various events may differ according to relationship type. As noted earlier, relational transgression is an important feature of hurtful events. Rules for relational behavior vary across relationships and should influence appraisals of hurt. For example, sexuality is a key feature of couple bonds, but not of other relationships; sexual involvement and exclusivity are highly endorsed rules for intimate partners (Argyle, Henderson, & Furnham, 1985; Baxter, 1986), and acts of fidelity are seen as indicators of love (Buss, 1988). Hence, sexual infidelity may be more hurtful than other acts of betrayal, such as lying. Conversely, teasing may not be a major source of hurt in couple relationships. Teasing is a complex behavior with different forms and motivations. It is most problematic when prolonged, aggressive, and condoned by others (Kowalski, Howerton, & McKenzie, 2001); these features may seldom apply to couple bonds, in which teasing often implies intimacy and positivity (Keltner, Young, Heerey, Oemig, & Monarch, 1998).

To clarify the types of events that couples experience as hurtful, a sample of undergraduate students was asked to describe, as victim, an experience of hurt feelings involving a dating partner or spouse (Feeney, 2004). Coding of the open-ended accounts yielded five categories: active disassociation (behaviors that explicitly signal disinterest in the partner, including relationship termination and the denial or retraction of feelings of love and commitment), passive disassociation (being ignored or excluded from the other's plans, activities, conversations, or disclosures), criticism (negative verbal comments about one's behavior, appearance, or personal characteristics), infidelity (extrarelationship sexual involvement), and deception (misleading acts, such as lying and breaking promises or confidences).

Although this typology is similar in several respects to the one developed by Leary et al. (1998), findings supported the notion that hurtful events are somewhat specific to relationship type. For example, no instances of teasing were reported, despite the relatively large sample ($N = 224$). Further, subdividing the broad category of "betrayal" into sexual infidelity and deception provided useful information, attesting to the particularly severe nature of sexual betrayals: sexual infidelity was rated as more hurtful than all other types of events and as affecting more negatively the couple relationship. Interestingly, however, the different types of hurtful events reported by participants did not represent a simple continuum of seriousness. Passive disassociation, for instance, was seen as less hurtful than infidelity and active disassociation, yet had more severe long-term effects on the victim. Further, despite these severe effects on the *victim* (as severe as those of infidelity), long-term effects on the *relationship* were less severe for passive disassociation than for infidelity. In short, different types of hurtful events have different patterns of short-term and long-term effects.

### RESPONSES TO AND CONSEQUENCES OF HURTFUL EVENTS

As the previous section highlights, hurtful events differ in their outcomes. Studies encompassing a range of relationship types have yielded several findings regarding these outcomes. Research by Vangelisti and Crumley (1998) revealed three broad responses to hurtful messages: active verbal (e.g., attacking the partner, requesting an explanation), acquiescent (e.g., crying, apologizing), and invulnerable (e.g., ignoring the message, laughing). These researchers noted that victims who felt extremely hurt were more likely to respond by acquiescing than those who felt less hurt, suggesting that people may feel that their relationships are vulnerable to the impact of reactions to major hurts. In addition, relationship satisfaction was related positively to active verbal responses and negatively to the degree of hurt experienced and the perceived impact of the incident on the relationship. Further, in their broad-based study of hurtful events, Leary et al. (1998) found that most victims reported responding assertively (e.g., by expressing anger or by defending themselves).

Surprisingly little research has examined, in depth, the varied effects of hurtful events in couple relationships. However, the available studies have produced noteworthy findings. For example, in a series of experiments, Murray and her colleagues (Murray, Rose, Bellavia, Holmes, & Kusche, 2002) examined individuals' responses to perceived rejection by dating partners by manipulating feedback about the partner's unspoken complaints or fault-finding. Findings indicated that low self-esteem participants tended to "read too much" into these relationship problems; that is, they interpreted the problems as a sign of partners' waning affection and commitment and, in response, tended to derogate the partner and report less relational closeness.

### Effects on Victims and on Couple Relationships

More complex models of the effects of hurtful events in couple relationships were reported recently (Feeney, 2004). In this study, victims described an incident in which an intimate partner had hurt their feelings. As well as giving an open-ended account of the event, respondents completed rating scales assessing their cognitive, emotional, and behavioral responses, as well as their perceptions of the long-term effects on themselves and on the couple relationship. The major analyses (using structural equations modeling) focused on predicting these long-term effects; after all, many hurtful events are resolved quickly to the satisfaction of both partners, but events that threaten individual or couple adjustment are particularly relevant to researchers and clinicians. Interestingly, the two outcome variables (effects on the victim and on the relationship) showed only a modest association. Hence, separate conceptual models were developed to predict each outcome variable.

Effects on the *victim* were defined in terms of reports of reduced self-confidence and continued worry about being hurt again. Given this focus on subjective discomfort, variables tapping aspects of initial distress were expected to provide good prediction. Four such variables were included: victims' overall level of immediate negative affect (distress, fear, etc.), negative self-perceptions (seeing the self as unworthy and undesirable), feeling rejected by the partner, and feeling less powerful and "in control" than the partner. Relationship anxiety was also included in the model; this dimension of attachment insecurity has been linked to hypervigilant monitoring of relationships for signs of negativity and rejection (Feeney, 1999).

Findings supported the proposed model. That is, victims who reported ongoing problems with self-confidence rated the event as more distressing, saw themselves as unworthy, felt rejected and powerless, and were anxious about their relationships generally. The strongest overall effects were for negative self-perceptions and relationship anxiety; the latter variable had a direct effect on victims' self-confidence, together with indirect effects through negative affect and self-perceptions. Of course, it is not surprising that events that elicit more distress in the short term are more problematic in the longer term. However, these findings suggest that both individual factors and relational dynamics influence the extent to which hurtful acts by romantic partners erode victims'

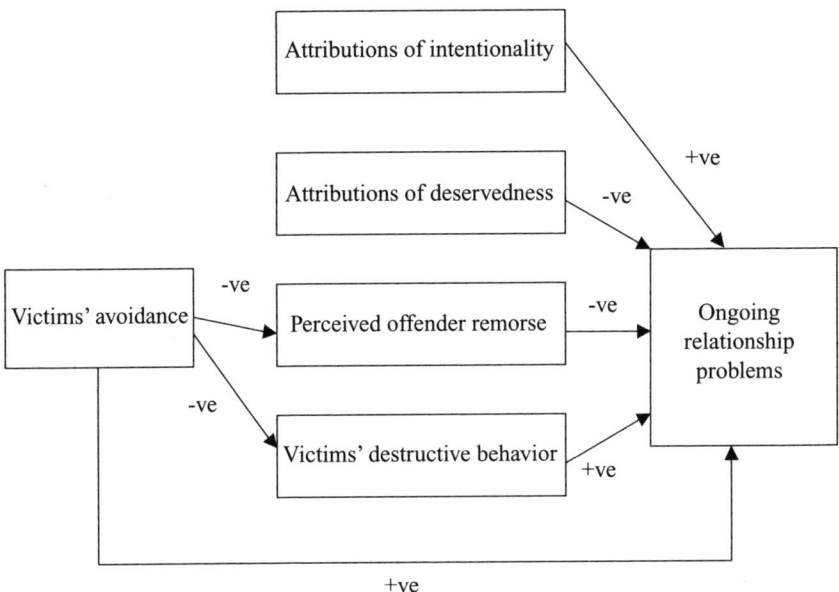

FIGURE 15.1. Predictors of ongoing negative effects of hurtful events on the couple relationship. *Note:* +ve indicates positive association; −ve indicates negative association.

self-confidence. Specifically, relevant issues include felt security, evaluations of acceptance or rejection, and threats to the balance of power. The importance of perceived power is highlighted by evidence that power imbalances underlie many instances of couple conflict and marital distress (Cahn, 1990).

As this chapter focuses on couple relationships, let us consider in some detail the predictors of ongoing *relationship problems*. The conceptual model predicting relationship problems incorporated variables tapping victims' behavior and victims' perceptions of the partner and relationship – these variables are likely to shape the course of couple interaction. Four constructs were proposed as predictors: attachment insecurity (which has been linked to negative perceptions of partners and destructive responses to conflict), victims' attributions for the event (e.g., was the hurt intentional? was it deserved?), perceptions of offender remorse (lack of remorse may impede relationship repair), and victims' behavioral reactions (aggressive and sarcastic responses are likely to fuel further conflict). Specifically, it was expected that ongoing relationship problems would be predicted by relationship anxiety and avoidance, distress-maintaining attributions, perceived lack of remorse, and destructive victim behavior; relationship anxiety and avoidance were proposed to have indirect effects through destructive victim behavior and perceived lack of remorse, respectively.

The final structural model is summarized in Figure 15.1. The results generally supported the proposed model, with two modifications. First, avoidance had a direct effect and an indirect (negative) effect through destructive behavior, as well as the proposed effect through perceptions of low offender remorse. Second, the proposed effect of relationship anxiety was of marginal significance and hence was not retained. As the figure shows, ongoing relationship problems were associated with avoidance, attributions of the act as intentional and as undeserved, perceived lack of remorse, and destructive victim behavior; the strongest effects were for avoidance and attributions of intentionality. Although these findings were based on the accounts of victims only, they highlight the interdependent roles of victim and offender in the process of relationship repair. As previous studies have noted, offenders can assist this process by engaging in sincere expressions of remorse and apology (Fitness, 2001; Jones et al., 2001). In addition, victims clearly shape the outcome of hurtful events and not simply by their overt behavior; victims' attributions (although undoubtedly linked to their behavior) seem to have direct effect effects on the state of the relationship.

Findings from this study (Feeney, 2004) also highlight the unique predictive power of each attachment dimension. Individuals who are anxious about their relationships tend to be very upset by hurtful partner behavior and to report long-term erosion of their self-confidence. Unlike avoidant individuals, however, they are not particularly likely to report ongoing relationship problems, perhaps because fears of rejection and abandonment drive them to try to restore the relationship and to reassure themselves of its viability.

### Insights from Couples: Barriers to Resolving Hurt and Issues Regarding Timing

More recently, responses to hurt feelings in couple relationships were investigated in samples of dating and married couples (Fitzgerald, 2005). As well as describing specific hurtful events that had occurred in their relationships, each couple in this study was asked to discuss how it generally dealt with episodes of hurt feelings in the current relationship. The purpose of this approach was to gather "insider" information (Noller & Guthrie, 1991) from couples regarding the resolution of relationship hurts, including their successes and failures; this approach acknowledges the value of participants' own insights into their relationship histories.

More specifically, participants were asked to reflect individually about factors they found helpful and unhelpful in resolving such episodes and factors they believed made resolution difficult or affected the partner's responses to hurt. A 5-minute videotape recording was made as the couple discussed these issues. Couples' comments were recorded verbatim and then coded for the major themes.

The present discussion addresses one aspect of these couple conversations, namely personal and situational factors that were seen as making resolution

TABLE 15.1. *Factors cited by couples as impeding resolution of hurt*

| Event-related | Contextual | Personal |
| --- | --- | --- |
| Strong emotions: anger, jealousy, fear (16%) | Distance: work hours, phone contact (12%) | Personality: moody, inexpressive (8%) |
| Sulking; refusing to talk or change (8%) | Presence of family, children, or friends (10%) | Hypersensitivity (6%) |
| Losing perspective; refusing to let go of issue (6%) | Influence of alcohol, drugs, fatigue, illness (6%) | |
| | "Baggage" from other relationships (5%) | |

*Note:* Percentages refer to couples, as coding was done at the couple level.

of hurtful events difficult. Participants offered a range of comments regarding these factors, which were coded into three broad categories: event related, contextual, and personal (see Table 15.1). In terms of the hurtful event itself, couples spoke of emotional, cognitive, and behavioral factors. Specifically, resolution was seen as more difficult when emotions ran very strong and when the victim "lost perspective" or refused to "move on." Again, the roles of both victim and offender were implicitly recognized: Resolution was impeded when the victim engaged in maladaptive behavior such as sulking or when the offender refused to discuss the issue or change his or her behavior.

Interestingly, however, contextual (situational) factors were mentioned almost as frequently as event-related factors. The most common contextual variables involved separation or physical distance (including long working hours and having to communicate by phone) and the presence of other people (family members or friends). Less common situational problems included the effects of having ingested alcohol or other substances, illness, fatigue, and "baggage" brought from previous relationships. Finally, some couples cited personal characteristics. That is, resolution of hurt was seen as more difficult if one or both partners were generally moody or inexpressive or seemed overly sensitive to criticism or rejection.

Although couples were not explicitly asked to discuss the appropriate *timing* of conversations about hurtful episodes, 63% of couples spontaneously raised this issue. Participants generally agreed that it was important for partners to talk about the episode; however, they varied in their opinions as to *when* that talk should take place. Importantly, both between-couple and within-couple differences were noted.

First, let us consider between-couple differences. On the one hand, some couples stated that the hurtful event should be given priority and addressed promptly. Some of these couples mentioned the proverb, "Don't let the sun go down on your wrath." They suggested that delaying discussion was risky because one partner, but not the other, might forget the matter. One wife described the risk of taking too much time to "cool off," as it often led to her thinking "weird stuff," such as doubting her partner's love for her; for this couple, prompt discussion was effective in interrupting the woman's inaccurate and distressing thoughts about her partner and their relationship.

By contrast, some couples emphasized the importance of taking time before talking over the issue. More specifically, these couples noted the value of calming down, thinking over what had happened, and evaluating the scope or significance of the incident. One husband's comment that he needed to "mow the lawn" before talking over hurtful issues was accompanied by good-humored laughter from his spouse; thus it appears that a mutually negotiated opportunity to calm down and consider the issues can contribute to effective discussion about hurtful events.

Within-couple differences also emerged and may be particularly important for those who seek to understand couple conflict. That is, some couples described a pattern whereby one partner wanted to resolve hurtful issues quickly, whereas the other wanted time to calm down and think before talking. The difficulty of dealing with this tension was evident in the couples' conversations. For example, one husband noted how distressed he became while waiting for his wife to talk ("I just *have* to know what I have done to upset you!"). His wife, however, said that she withdrew and sulked when hurt, and she needed time "to think her way out" of this state. Similarly, other couples indicated that one partner preferred time to think about the incident, whereas the other was ready to talk immediately. One husband said that it was unwise for him to talk immediately because he tended to say things that made matters worse; his wife, however, described her tendency to ruminate if he was silent and to "imagine the worst." Some husbands described how they needed to "leave the scene" to calm down – their wives said how disturbing they found this behavior, one suggesting that it felt like an enforced "time-out." The importance of this sort of "out-of-sync" communication is highlighted by literature on the destructive effects of the demand/withdraw pattern of couple communication (e.g., Eldridge & Christensen, 2002); this pattern is particularly problematic when the woman adopts the role of demander and the man adopts the role of withdrawer (a situation that exacerbates the differences inherent in traditional gender roles).

## VICTIM–PERPETRATOR DIFFERENCES IN PERCEPTIONS

Many studies of couple relationships focus on conflict, negativity, and hurt. Within this broad area, a growing body of work suggests that negative relationship events are evaluated differently by the two partners according to their *role* or perspective; that is, whether they are the victim or the perpetrator. Studies of role-related differences have addressed a range of transgressions, including events that are seen as hurtful (Leary et al., 1998), anger evoking (Baumeister, Stillwell, & Wotman, 1990; Zechmeister & Romero, 2002), conflict provoking

(Schutz, 1999), annoying or upsetting (Cameron, Ross, & Holmes, 2002), and unjust (Mikula, Athenstaedt, Heschgl, & Heimgartner, 1998). There is likely to be considerable overlap among these types of events; for example, acts of sexual betrayal tend to elicit both anger and hurt. Hence, the broad literature on role-related differences is briefly reviewed here, before turning specifically to recent studies of hurt feelings.

Researchers have obtained open-ended and structured data on various aspects of event-related perceptions, with findings generally supporting the effect of role. For example, in Leary et al.'s (1998) study of hurt feelings, victims reported feeling more rejection than perpetrators reported feeling toward their victims; further, victims rated hurtful behavior as less accidental and more intentional than did perpetrators. In Baumeister et al.'s (1990) study, each participant described two anger-evoking events, one from the perspective of victim and one from the perspective of perpetrator. Compared with perpetrator accounts, victim accounts were more likely to portray negative behavior as incomprehensible and immoral, and they were less likely to note mitigating factors. Zechmeister and Romero (2002) replicated aspects of Baumeister et al.'s (1990) methodology and reported comparable results. Further, Cameron et al. (2002) examined perceptions of upsetting incidents by randomly assigning dating partners to roles of victim and perpetrator; victims were less likely than perpetrators to minimize blame and to justify perpetrators' actions. Similarly, in autobiographical studies of conflict (Schutz, 1999) and lying (Kaplar & Gordon, 2004), participants gave fewer justifications and altruistic motivations for negative behavior when occupying the role of victim rather than perpetrator. Together, these findings suggest that victims perceive relational transgressions more negatively than do perpetrators.

Mikula et al. (1998) conducted more comprehensive studies of role-related differences, with somewhat mixed results. Participants in Studies 1 and 3 (married and "romantic" couples, respectively) described and evaluated one incident in which their partner had treated them unjustly and another in which they had treated their partner unjustly; they also evaluated the incidents selected by their partner. In Study 4 (involving married and cohabiting couples), the same method was applied to incidents involving hurt, anger, disappointment, or offense. (Study 2 employed friendship pairs and hence is not discussed here.) In Studies 1 and 4, victims rated the incidents as less justified, and the perpetrators as more responsible, than did perpetrators. Further, victims rated the incidents as more unjust and intentional than did perpetrators (Study 1 only) and as more controllable (Study 4 only). Study 3 yielded no main effects of role for any of these variables. In sum, specific findings differed across studies, but when role-related differences did emerge, they involved greater negativity on the part of victims.

Why does this pattern emerge? Researchers have suggested that role-related differences exist because both partners' accounts reflect *self-serving motivations*, linked to the different implications that wrongdoing carries for victims and perpetrators (e.g., Baumeister et al., 1990; Schutz, 1999). Specifically, victims may seek to reduce the unpleasant fate that the wrongdoing entails, to preserve their self-concept and social image, and to justify punishing the offender. Hence, victims may adopt an *accusing* stance, highlighting the unfair nature of the event. In contrast, perpetrators may be motivated to restore their image as just and moral people and to protect themselves from punishment and claims for restitution. Perpetrators may therefore adopt a *defensive* stance, denying intentional wrongdoing and downplaying the negativity of their actions.

Unfortunately, studies of role-related differences have suffered from several limitations that cloud interpretation of the results. First, some studies have employed small samples, and others have ignored the effects of relationship type; few have provided a detailed analysis of hurtful events in couple relationships. Second, in most studies, victims and perpetrators have reported on different events. Hence the results do not necessarily reflect genuine role-related differences, because victims and perpetrators may (for self-serving reasons) select qualitatively different events. Third, most studies have used a single method of data collection, such as unstructured, retrospective accounts. With this method, it is not clear whether the accounts reflect evaluations made when the event occurred or the effects of subsequent interactions (McGregor & Holmes, 1999). Finally, little is known about variables that may moderate role-related differences. Some evidence suggests that variables such as relationship quality and forgiveness may serve to reduce these differences (Mikula et al., 1998; Zechmeister & Romero, 2002), but methodological limitations again plague the interpretation of most findings.

## Recent Findings: Questionnaire and Diary Reports from Victims and Perpetrators

A recent study of hurt feelings in couple relationships (Feeney & Hill, 2006) addressed these issues. In this study, dating and married couples completed questionnaires and structured diaries. In the questionnaire component, victims and perpetrators gave retrospective accounts of the same events. Participants were first asked to think (individually) of hurtful events that had occurred in their relationship during the past year; a research assistant then facilitated a brief couple discussion in which partners jointly selected one male-perpetrated and one female-perpetrated event. Thus, each couple described one event in which the woman was the victim and one in which the man was the victim. Participants gave open-ended accounts of each event, which were scored for such variables as the extent to which the reporter highlighted or downplayed the severity of the event; they also completed rating scales assessing attributions, perceptions of offender remorse, and perceptions of long-term effects on the victim and the relationship (these variables are similar to those described in the study of victims' accounts of hurtful events; see Feeney, 2004). The diary component, outlined earlier, required participants to report up to five events as victim and five events as perpetrator.

The *questionnaire-based* analyses incorporated eight dependent variables: highlighting, downplaying, and contrition (derived from the open-ended accounts) and ratings of victim's immediate distress, attributed malice, remorse, and long-term effect on the victim and the relationship. All these variables yielded role-related effects, except for victim's immediate distress. The effects were generally consistent with self-serving biases. Specifically, victims' accounts were much more negative in general tone (i.e., showed more highlighting and less downplaying) and in reports of perpetrators' contrition than were those of perpetrators. Further, victims perceived perpetrators as more malicious and less remorseful than did perpetrators themselves. In contrast to the notion of self-serving biases, however, perpetrators perceived *more negative* effects on victims than victims themselves reported; similarly, sex-by-role interactions showed that male perpetrators perceived *particularly negative* effects on the couple relationship.

These varied effects suggest that, when respondents are asked to tell the story of a hurtful event and its immediate aftermath (what happened and why?), they focus on the nature and meaning of the injustice. Hence, as wrongdoing has different implications for victims and perpetrators, their accounts diverge in the expected (self-serving) direction. In contrast, when respondents are asked about *subsequent* effects of the event, different motivations may come into play. Perpetrators may choose to make concessions about the event that acknowledge its marked effects, without necessarily admitting personal culpability; similarly, victims may elect to show that they have "moved on," despite the injustice suffered (Feeney & Hill, 2006). Of course, victims also have unique access to their own emotional state; if the offender is told of the initial hurt but not of any subsequent "recovery," then role-related effects may run counter to those predicted by self-serving biases. In short, perceptions of relational events reflect the goals of particular communication acts (Sillars, 1998); some situations (e.g., telling the story to others) may inhibit understanding between partners, as the narrator shapes the account for the benefit of the self and the audience.

Feeney and Hill (2006) also assessed whether role-related effects were moderated by relationship status (dating, married), relationship satisfaction, or by the severity or forgiveness of the hurtful event. The only evidence of moderation was for forgiveness, with the effect of role being restricted to unforgiven events: Victims of unforgiven events were particularly negative in their attributions and their ratings of offender remorse and ongoing relationship problems. These role-by-forgiveness interactions remained significant when severity of the event was controlled. Overall, these findings suggest that role-related differences are quite robust. However, consistent with current models of forgiveness, these differences seem to be reduced by the forgiveness process, which involves change in variables such as empathy for the offender and attributions for the event (Gordon & Baucom, 1998; McCullough et al., 1998).

As already noted, Feeney and Hill (2006) also asked couples to complete *diary-based* interaction records of hurtful events; this feature provides relatively immediate evaluations of events. Participants (regardless of role) rated each event in terms of victim's hurt, intentionality of the hurt, offender remorse, openness of couple communication, and victim's satisfaction with the resolution. The diary reports also allowed us to compare events that were "matched" (i.e., reported by both partners) with those that were "unmatched" (reported by the victim only). This issue is relevant to misunderstandings about hurt feelings: Events that are acknowledged by victims only may be particularly detrimental to relationships, as the original offense is compounded by perpetrators' apparent failure to recognize the hurt.

The rating-scale data provided evidence of self-serving biases. Overall, victims rated events as more intentional and perpetrators as less remorseful than did perpetrators. As mentioned earlier, respondents also reported *more* events as victims than as perpetrators, despite the fact that both partners kept diaries for the same period of time. This finding is again consistent with self-serving biases, suggesting that perpetrators are more likely than victims to discount hurtful events.

Why were some hurtful events reported by *victims only*? This question was addressed in two ways. First, we compared participants' ratings of matched and unmatched events. We found that victims reported matched events as more hurtful than unmatched events and as involving more open communication. High levels of victim distress are, of course, more likely to be obvious to the partner; such distress may also act as a spur to couple communication, resulting in the offender becoming aware of the source and extent of the victim's hurt.

The second comparison of matched and unmatched events was based on literature illustrating the complex nature of couple communication (Sillars, Leonard, Roberts, & Dun, 2002). That is, intimate partners often engage in indirect and ambiguous communication while generally failing to recognize the subjective nature of their inferences about meanings and intentions. We expected that unmatched events would involve more indirect and ambiguous forms of communication, as coded from victims' reports: specifically, sins of omission (i.e., reports focused on what the offender *failed* to do, rather than on what he or she did), negative inferences (the offender implied something negative rather than saying it directly), conflict behavior (the hurtful behavior arose during the course of couple conflict), and humor (offender's playful or joking behavior was seen as hurtful). The findings, although gender specific, supported the prediction that these themes would be more characteristic of unmatched events; for females' reports (of males' transgressions), sins of omission and negative inference were more common in unmatched than matched events, and for males' reports (of females' transgressions), conflict was more commonly a trigger for unmatched than matched events.

In summary, offenders are more likely to *fail to report* an event as hurtful if the victim's hurt is less severe or if the issue is not discussed openly. Further, offenders may "miss" events that occur in an ongoing argument or do not involve overtly hurtful actions.

### FUTURE DIRECTIONS AND IMPLICATIONS FOR PRACTICE

Despite recent advances in the study of hurt feelings and their effects on couple relationships, important directions for further work can be identified. The following section outlines some of these directions, together with implications for practice.

### Linking Emotion, Cognition, and Behavior

The experience of hurt feelings seems to involve a complex set of emotions, cognitions, and behaviors. For example, hurt feelings are often accompanied by other negative emotions, such as anger and sadness (Feeney, 2004), and are usually linked to appraisals of relational transgression and to a sense of injury. Yet the nature of the link between psychological hurt and appraisals, in particular, remains unclear.

Appraisal theories of emotion suggest that the experience of a given emotion *follows* the evaluation (appraisal) of the associated event. However, as Planalp and Fitness (1999) noted, acts of betrayal may register affectively as hurt feelings before much conscious cognitive processing has occurred (although victims usually seek, at some point, to understand their causes and implications). Jones et al. (2001) further highlight the difficulty in disentangling the emotions and cognitions associated with psychological hurt, describing hurt and rejection as "cognitive-affective" variables that may be linked in a circular fashion. That is, events that involve rejection (real or perceived) elicit hurt feelings, and hurt feelings promote a sense of rejection. If this circular pattern of association applies, then emotional reactions and cognitive appraisals may be equally important targets of intervention efforts for distressed couples.

### Integrating Levels of Analysis

A second research imperative involves developing integrated models of the effects of hurtful events on victims and on couple relationships. To date, most studies in this area have focused on one or two key variables. Experimental studies by Murray and her colleagues (Murray et al., 2002) firmly established self-esteem as a "person variable" that helps explain individual differences in responses to rejection from intimate partners. Similarly, recent work suggests that attachment security affects individuals' perceptions of and responses to hurtful behavior (Feeney, 2005). However, given the likely overlap between such person variables as self-esteem, insecurity, rejection sensitivity (Downey & Feldman, 1996), and hurt proneness (Leary & Springer, 2001), more information is needed about the unique prediction afforded by each of these variables.

Work on person variables has been supplemented by some studies examining communicative responses to hurt feelings. A number of researchers have investigated the way in which victims communicate their hurt (e.g., Leary et al., 1998; Vangelisti, Young, Carpenter-Theune, & Alexander, 2005), but less is known about the varied ways in which offenders respond to these communications. It is important for researchers to conduct more work with samples of couples and to explore the complete process of dyadic communication relating to hurtful events. Given Fitzgerald's (2005) findings on the importance of partners' timing of discussion, it seems that demand/withdraw communication and associated issues of gender differences in communication may be particularly relevant. There is also a need for more comprehensive studies assessing the relative effects of person variables and dyadic communication, as well as the links between these types of variables.

However, theory and research suggest that incorporating person variables and dyadic variables will not tell the whole story. Couple relationships do not exist in a vacuum – rather, each partner is usually involved in a number of other close relationships that have an impact on the couple bond (Sprecher, Felmlee, Orbuch, & Willetts, 2002). As Fitzgerald's (2005) work highlights, the presence of friends or family members can interfere with the resolution of hurt feelings. In some cases, this interference stems from the simple fact that partners prefer not to discuss hurtful issues in the presence of others; hence, third parties delay the resolution process and allow hurt feelings to "simmer." In other cases, friends or family members may impede resolution more actively by taking sides or by giving unhelpful or unwanted advice. These issues concerning "social context effects" are understudied.

## Applying Attachment Principles

Recent work suggests that attachment theory provides a useful framework for studying hurt feelings in couple relationships. For example, attachment principles underpinned the conceptual work equating a sense of injury with threats to positive working models (Feeney, 2005). As noted earlier, this conceptualization was supported by expert judges' ratings of the characteristics of hurtful events.

Attachment theory also generates viable predictions about individual differences in reactions to romantic partners' hurtful behavior. Relationship anxiety predicts high levels of victim distress and self-perceptions as blameworthy and unlovable (Feeney, 2004); these findings fit with theoretical formulations linking relationship anxiety to negative models of self and to hyperactivation of the attachment system. In contrast, avoidance has been linked to ongoing problems in the couple relationship (as discussed earlier): This net effect (of increased problems) involved a direct positive effect, an indirect positive effect through perceptions of low offender remorse, and an indirect *negative* effect through less destructive victim behavior. These complex effects can be understood in terms of attachment principles; for example, the rather controlled interpersonal style of avoidant individuals may protect them, to some extent, from destructive expressions of anger and sarcasm (Feeney, 2004). An important extension of this work would be to examine the combined effects of both partners' attachment characteristics, an approach that has proved useful in the study of couple conflict (Feeney, 2003).

## Implications for Practice

Hurt feelings are clearly an important issue for clinicians who work with couples, whether in an educational or interventional role. As argued at the start of this chapter, hurt feelings are an inevitable part of all close relationships, but the high levels of emotionality and interdependence that characterize intimate partners make them particularly susceptible to this problem. Hence, a basic understanding of hurt feelings and of constructive and destructive responses may form a useful basis for education programs for couples (Fitzgerald, 2005).

In some instances, hurtful events can culminate in extreme withdrawal behavior or in relationship violence. The emotionally charged nature of responses to severe hurt has been established by recent research examining disclosures of extramarital affairs (Olson, Russell, Higgins-Kessler, & Miller, 2002). For some partners, the reaction is violent (e.g., throwing objects), whereas for others, it is "bottled up." Similarly, both the forgiveness literature (e.g., McCullough et al., 1998), and neuropsychological studies investigating the protection of self (Newberg, d'Aquili, Newberg, & de Marici, 2000) point to the tendency for hurt individuals to respond with either retaliation or avoidance.

Research findings to date suggest a number of intervention points relevant to distressed couples. (The importance of targeting both emotional and cognitive reactions has already been mentioned.) First, there has been a recent growth of interest in attachment-related interventions. For example, Johnson's (2003) work on attachment injuries acknowledges the traumatizing effects of rejection, the self-fulfilling nature of negative working models, and the therapeutic value of interventions that aim to build secure emotional ties. Second, given the pivotal role of communication between victim and perpetrator, it is vital for clinicians to consider how victims communicate hurt and how that communication is responded to. As noted earlier, issues pertaining to timing of discussion are particularly important, as are role-related differences in perceptions that may create misunderstandings between partners. Third, given the established role of forgiveness as a moderator of role-related differences, clinicians should find value in therapeutic models of the forgiveness process. These models focus on promoting empathy and benign attributions and reducing the tendencies to withdraw and retaliate. Together, these approaches to intervention should assist clients to deal constructively with their own hurt feelings and to be sensitive to those of their partner.

REFERENCES

Argyle, M. (1986). The skills, rules, and goals of relationships. In R. Gilmour & S. Duck (Eds.), *The emerging field of personal relationships* (pp. 23–39). Hillsdale, NJ: Erlbaum.

Argyle, M., Henderson, M., & Furnham, A. (1985). The rules of social relationships. *British Journal of Social Psychology, 24*, 125–139.

Baumeister, R. F., & Leary, M. R. (1995). The need to belong: Desire for interpersonal attachments as a fundamental human motivation. *Psychological Bulletin, 117*, 497–529.

Baumeister, R. F., Stillwell, A., & Wotman, S. R. (1990). Victim and perpetrator accounts of interpersonal conflict: Autobiographical narratives about anger. *Journal of Personality and Social Psychology, 59*, 994–1005.

Baxter, L. A. (1986). Gender differences in the heterosexual relationship rules embedded in break-up accounts. *Journal of Social and Personal Relationships, 3*, 289–306.

Bowlby, J. (1979). *The making and breaking of affectional bonds.* London: Tavistock.

Buss, D. M. (1988). Love acts: The evolutionary biology. In R. J. Sternberg & M. L. Barnes (Eds.), *The psychology of love* (pp. 100–118). New Haven, CT: Yale University Press.

Cahn, D. D. (1990). Intimates in conflict: A research review. In D. D. Cahn (Ed.), *Intimates in conflict: A communication perspective* (pp. 1–22). Hillsdale, NJ: Erlbaum.

Cameron, J. J., Ross, M., & Holmes, J. G. (2002). Loving the one you hurt: Positive effects of recounting a transgression against an intimate partner. *Journal of Experimental Social Psychology, 38*, 307–314.

Clark, M. S., Graham, S., & Grote, N. (2002). Bases for giving benefits in marriage: What is ideal? What is realistic? What really happens? In P. Noller & J. A. Feeney (Eds.), *Understanding marriage: Developments in the study of couple interaction* (pp. 150–176). Cambridge: Cambridge University Press.

Downey, G., & Feldman, S. I. (1996). Implications of rejection sensitivity for intimate relationships. *Journal of Personality and Social Psychology, 70*, 1327–1343.

Eisenberger, N. I., Lieberman, M. D., & Williams, K. D. (2003). Does rejection hurt? An fMRI study of social exclusion. *Science, 302*, 290–292.

Eldridge, K. A., & Christensen, A. (2002). Demand-withdraw communication during couple conflict: A review and analysis. In P. Noller & J. A. Feeney (Eds.), *Understanding marriage: Developments in the study of couple interaction* (pp. 289–322). Cambridge: Cambridge University Press.

Feeney, J. A. (1999). Adult romantic attachment and couple relationships. In J. Cassidy & P. R. Shaver (Eds.), *The handbook of attachment: Theory, research, and clinical applications* (pp. 355–377). New York: Guilford.

Feeney, J. A. (2003). The systemic nature of couple relationships: An attachment perspective. In P. Erdman & T. Caffery (Eds.), *Attachment and family systems: Conceptual, empirical and therapeutic relatedness* (pp. 139–163). New York: Brunner/Mazel.

Feeney, J. A. (2004). Hurt feelings in couple relationships: Towards integrative models of the negative effects of hurtful events. *Journal of Social and Personal Relationships, 21*, 487–508.

Feeney, J. A. (2005). Hurt feelings in couple relationships: Exploring the role of attachment and perceptions of personal injury. *Personal Relationships, 12*, 253–271.

Feeney, J. A., & Hill, A. (2006). Victim-perpetrator differences in reports of hurtful events. *Journal of Social and Personal Relationships, 23*, 587–608.

Fitness, J. (2001). Betrayal, rejection, revenge, and forgiveness: An interpersonal script approach. In M. R. Leary (Ed.), *Interpersonal rejection* (pp. 73–103). New York: Oxford University Press.

Fitzgerald, J. R. (2005). *Psychological hurt in couple relationships: Prevention and resolution.* Unpublished doctoral dissertation, University of Queensland, Australia.

Folkes, V. S. (1982). Communicating the reasons for social rejection. *Journal of Experimental Social Psychology, 18*, 235–252.

Gordon, K. C., & Baucom, D. H. (1998). Understanding betrayals in marriage: A synthesized model of forgiveness. *Family Process, 37*, 425–449.

Hazan, C., & Zeifman, D. (1999). Pair bonds as attachments: Evaluating the evidence. In J. Cassidy & P. R. Shaver (Eds.), *The handbook of attachment: Theory, research, and clinical applications* (pp. 336–354). New York: Guilford.

Johnson, S. M. (2003). Attachment theory: A guide for couple therapy. In S. M. Johnson & V. E. Whiffen (Eds.), *Attachment processes in couple and family therapy* (pp. 103–123). New York: Guilford.

Jones, W. H., Moore, D. S., Schratter, A., & Negel, L. A. (2001). Interpersonal transgressions and betrayals. In R. M. Kowalski (Ed.), *Behaving badly: Aversive behaviors in interpersonal relationships* (pp. 233–256). Washington, DC: American Psychological Association.

Kaplar, M. E., & Gordon, A. K. (2004). The enigma of altruistic lying: Perspective differences in what motivates and justifies lie telling within romantic relationships. *Personal Relationships, 11*, 489–507.

Keltner, D., Young, R. C., Heerey, E. A., Oemig, C., & Monarch, N. D. (1998). Teasing in hierarchical and intimate relations. *Journal of Personality and Social Psychology, 75*, 1231–1247.

Kowalski, R. M. (2001). The aversive side of social interaction revisited. In R. M. Kowalski (Ed.), *Behaving badly: Aversive behaviors in interpersonal relationships* (pp. 297–309). Washington, DC: American Psychological Association.

Kowalski, R. M., Howerton, E., & McKenzie, M. (2001). Permitted disrespect: Teasing in interpersonal interactions. In R. M. Kowalski (Ed.), *Behaving badly: Aversive behaviors in interpersonal relationships* (pp. 177–202). Washington, DC: American Psychological Association.

Lazarus, R. S. (1991). *Emotion and adaptation.* New York: Oxford University Press.

Leary, M. R. (2001). Toward a conceptualization of interpersonal rejection. In M. R. Leary (Ed.), *Interpersonal rejection* (pp. 3–20). New York: Oxford University Press.

Leary, M. R., & Springer, C. A. (2001). Hurt feelings: The neglected emotion. In R. M. Kowalski (Ed.), *Behaving badly: Aversive behaviors in interpersonal relationships* (pp. 151–175). Washington, DC: American Psychological Association.

Leary, M. R., Springer, C., Negel, L., Ansell, E., & Evans, K. (1998). The causes, phenomenology, and consequences of hurt feelings. *Journal of Personality and Social Psychology, 74*, 1225–1237.

MacDonald, G., & Leary, M. R. (2005). Why does social exclusion hurt? The relationship between social and physical pain. *Psychological Bulletin, 131*, 202–223.

McCullough, M. E., Rachal, K. C., Sandage, S. J., Worthington, E. L., .Jr, Brown, S. W., & Hight, T. L. (1998). Interpersonal forgiving in close relationships: II. Theoretical elaboration and measurement. *Journal of Personality and Social Psychology, 75*, 1586–1603.

McGregor, I., & Holmes, J. G. (1999). How storytelling shapes memory and impressions of relationship events over time. *Journal of Personality and Social Psychology, 76*, 403–419.

Mikula, G., Athenstaedt, U., Heschgl, S., & Heimgartner, A. (1998). Does it only depend on the point of view? Perspective-related differences in justice evaluations of negative incidents in personal relationships. *European Journal of Social Psychology, 28*, 931–962.

Miller, R. S. (1997). We always hurt the ones we love: Aversive interactions in close relationships. In R. M. Kowalski (Ed.), *Aversive interpersonal behaviors* (pp. 11–29). New York: Plenum Press.

Murray, S. L., Rose, P., Bellavia, G. M., Holmes, J. G., & Kusche, A. G. (2002). When rejection stings: How self-esteem constrains relationship-enhancement processes. *Journal of Personality and Social Psychology, 83*, 556–573.

Newberg, A. B., d'Aquili, E. G., Newberg, S. K., & de Marici, V. (2000). The neuropsychological correlates of forgiveness. In M. McCullough, K. Pargament, & C. Thoresen (Eds.), *Forgiveness: Theory, research and practice* (pp. 91–110). New York: Guilford.

Noller, P., & Guthrie, D. (1991). Studying communication in marriage: An integration and critical evaluation. In W. H. Jones & D. Perlman (Eds.), *Advances in personal relationships* (Vol. 3; pp. 37–73). London: Jessica Kingsley.

Olson, M. M., Russell, C. S., Higgins-Kessler, M., & Miller, R. B. (2002). Emotional processes following disclosure of an extramarital affair. *Journal of Marital and Family Therapy, 28*, 423–434.

Planalp, S., & Fitness, J. (1999). Thinking/feeling about social and personal relationships. *Journal of Social and Personal Relationships, 16*, 731–750.

Roseman, I. J., & Smith, C. A. (2001). Appraisal theory: Overview, assumptions, varieties, controversies. In K. R. Scherer, A. Schorr, & T. Johnstone (Eds.), *Appraisal process in emotion: Theory, methods, research* (pp. 3–19). London: Oxford University Press.

Rothbard, J. C., & Shaver, P. R. (1994). Continuity of attachment across the life span. In M. B. Sperling & W. H. Berman (Eds.), *Attachment in adults: Theory, assessment, and treatment* (pp. 31–71). New York: Guilford.

Schutz, A. (1999). It was your fault! Self-serving biases in autobiographical accounts of conflicts in married couples. *Journal of Social and Personal Relationships, 13*, 193–208.

Shaver, P. R., & Mikulincer, M. (2002). Attachment-related psychodynamics. *Attachment & Human Development, 4*, 133–161.

Shaver, P., Schwartz, J., Kirson, D., & O'Connor, C. (1987). Emotion knowledge: Further exploration of a prototype approach. *Journal of Personality and Social Psychology, 52*, 1061–1086.

Sillars, A. L. (1998). (Mis)understanding. In B. H. Spitzberg & W. R. Cupach (Eds.), *The dark side of close relationships* (pp. 73–102). Mahwah, NJ: Erlbaum.

Sillars, A., Leonard, K. E., Roberts, L. J., & Dun, T. (2002). Cognition and communication during marital conflict: How alcohol affects subjective coding of interaction in aggressive and nonaggressive couples. In P. Noller & J. A. Feeney (Eds.), *Understanding marriage: Developments in the study of couple interaction* (pp. 85–112). Cambridge: Cambridge University Press.

Sprecher, S., Felmlee, D., Orbuch, T. L., & Willetts, M. C. (2002). Social networks and change in personal relationships. In A. L. Vangelisti, H. T. Reis, & M. A. Fitzpatrick (Eds.), *Stability and change in relationships* (pp. 257–284). Cambridge: Cambridge University Press.

Vangelisti, A. L. (1994). Messages that hurt. In W. R. Cupach & B. H. Spitzberg (Eds.), *The dark side of interpersonal communication* (pp. 53–82). Hillsdale, NJ: Erlbaum.

Vangelisti, A. L. (2001). Making sense of hurtful interactions in close relationships. In V. Manusov & J. H. Harvey (Eds.), *Attribution, communication behavior, and close relationships* (pp. 38–58). New York: Cambridge University Press.

Vangelisti, A. L., & Crumley, L. P. (1998). Reactions to messages that hurt: The influence of relational contexts. *Communication Monographs, 65,* 173–196.

Vangelisti, A. L., Young, S. L., Carpenter-Theune, K. E., & Alexander, A. L. (2005). Why does it hurt? The perceived causes of hurt feelings. *Communication Research, 32,* 443–477.

Wallerstein, J. S., & Blakeslee, S. (1995). *The good marriage: How and why love lasts.* New York: Houghton Mifflin.

Weiss, R. S. (1991). The attachment bond in childhood and adulthood. In C. M. Parkes, J. Stevenson-Hinde, & P. Marris (Eds.), *Attachment across the life cycle* (pp. 66–76). London: Tavistock/Routledge.

Zechmeister, J. S., & Romero, C. (2002). Victim and offender accounts of interpersonal conflict: Autobiographical narratives of forgiveness and unforgiveness. *Journal of Personality and Social Psychology, 82,* 675–686.

# 16

## Hurt in Postdivorce Relationships

SANDRA METTS, DAWN O. BRAITHWAITE,
AND MARK A. FINE

The termination of any valued relationship through which individuals meet their needs for inclusion and affection and in which they have invested tangible and psychological resources is emotionally involving. The loss of a close friend, a dating partner, and even a coworker can evoke strong emotional responses. However, divorce and its emotional aftermath are unique experiences. Not only is the marriage union publicly recognized and officially validated, but its dissolution is likewise publicly recognized and officially recorded. Joint property must be redistributed and living space must be changed for one or both partners. Perhaps most problematic, when children are involved, decisions about custody, visitation, and coparenting must be negotiated. In short, a system of affective, identity-relevant, and structural connections must be explicitly acknowledged and realigned – a process that Emery (Sbarra & Emery, 2006) refers to as "renegotiating relationships" because partners who are also parents can never completely terminate their relationship.

Needless to say, the process of divorce and the subsequent challenges inherent in renegotiating postdivorce relationships involve the experience and expression of complex and often contradictory emotions. Depending on the proximate cause of the divorce (e.g., a critical event such as the discovery of an affair or simply a slow drifting apart), partners and children may experience social emotions such as embarrassment and shame; self-focused emotions such as guilt, sorrow, regret, and fear; or other-focused emotions such as anger and resentment. They may feel seemingly contradictory emotional states as indicated by the description of one man divorced for 3 years who participated in a study conducted by one of the authors: "Our conversations are very often hostile but I think that's because we are still in love" (Metts & Cupach, 1995, p. 241). On occasion, former spouses and children may even feel positive emotions such as relief, happiness, and hope for a "new beginning."

Our goal in this chapter is to narrow the lens of investigation to the emotion of hurt. Although hurt seldom exists alone, it is a powerful influence on the divorce process and on postdivorce relationships within the nuclear family (i.e., between former spouses and between parents and their children), as well as those between family members and their larger social network, including the extended family. If one or both spouses remarry and if children find themselves negotiating their roles within a stepfamily, hurt may again arise as a salient emotion in the process. Before discussing these relational contexts, we briefly discuss the nature of hurt: what it is, the functions served by its experience and expression, the challenges that hurt raises in the dissolution and postdivorce contexts, and the role of forgiveness and relationship redefinition in coping with these challenges.

## FORM, FUNCTIONS, AND CHALLENGES OF HURT

Hurt is a feeling of harm or injury felt in response to actions or messages from others that are perceived to devalue one's character, importance, or worth (Leary, Koch, & Hechenbleikner, 2001; May & Jones, 2005), to devalue the quality of the relationship and its importance (Leary, Springer, Negel, Ansell, & Evans, 1998), or to imply threat or injustice (Fine & Olson, 1997). Some cognitive theorists (Fine & Olson, 1997) have distinguished hurt from anger by noting that hurt stems from the perception that the provocation or transgression is somehow partly deserved or warranted, whereas anger stems from the perception that the provocation is not deserved. Further, these theorists have suggested that the tendency to experience hurt rather than anger is to some degree an individual difference variable, in that some individuals are prone to view provocations as being of their own doing, whereas others are prone to view provocations as being undeserved and unwarranted. In addition, as Johnston and Campbell (1988) suggest, the devaluation of self that so often occurs in marital dissolution may compound a lifelong pattern of feeling vulnerable to the actions of others.

Although a stranger's actions or comments may evoke hurt, the actions or comments from close others are far more likely to do so. Leary et al. (1998) note that, with strangers, we use the defense of unfamiliarity (e.g., a stranger may not realize what would be perceived as hurtful or may not know our "true" character or self). In close relationships, however, partners know (or "should" know) sensitive topics, concerns, or issues that may elicit hurt feelings, and violating these restrictive spaces reflects disregard for the person or the relationship or both. In addition, we expect to be treated positively by intimates and expect validation of our fundamental need to be valued and included (i.e., confirmation of positive face needs) (Metts, 2000).

Ironically, the need for felt security that motivates people to trust in romantic partners' regard for them (Murray, 2005) and the optimism (i.e., positive illusions) that contributes to relationship satisfaction (Murray, Holmes, & Griffin, 1996) are the very features that make partners vulnerable to hurt (Vangelisti & Young, 2000). In essence, partners are particularly vulnerable to being hurt in close relationships precisely because of the features that lead a relationship to be close: trust in the other person's inherent good judgment, kindness, integrity, and morality.

The events that trigger hurt in close relationships are particular families of relationship transgressions (Metts & Cupach, 2007) that imply personal and relational rejection (Fitness, 2001; Leary et al., 2001; Sommer, 2001). For example, Leary et al. (1998) describe six categories of events, actions, and messages that are likely to elicit hurt: active disassociation (e.g., explicit rejection); passive disassociation (e.g., implicit rejection, being ignored); criticism; betrayal; teasing; and feeling unappreciated, used, or taken for granted. Feeney (2004) offers an adapted version of these categories: active disassociation (e.g., relationship termination or retraction of love and commitment), passive disassociation (e.g., being ignored or excluded from other's plans, activities, or self-disclosure), criticism (e.g., negative comments about behavior, appearance, or characteristics), infidelity (e.g., extrarelationship sexual involvement), and deception (lying, breaking promises).

Although a commonly experienced emotion, hurt has received much less attention from emotion scholars than have the so-called primary emotions such as anger, fear, sadness, disgust, and joy. This oversight is due in part to the more situated and less universally recognized manifestations of hurt compared to the primary emotions, each of which has an identifiable motivational response (e.g., fear activates the body for flight) and characteristic facial display (e.g., the smile of joy). By comparison, hurt is considered a blended emotion, derived from the broader prototypes of sadness and fear (Shaver, Schwartz, Kirson, & O'Connor, 1987).

However, hurt also shares three important features with other emotions. First, the arousal that stimulates hurt is interpreted or appraised according to the relational and situational circumstances in which it occurs (Lazarus, 2006; Smith & Pope, 1992). During the appraisal process, primary appraisal provides the initial interpretation of arousal as negative (harmful) or positive (beneficial). Secondary appraisal quickly follows during which meaning (i.e., a label) is assigned to the arousal based on situational cues and resources for dealing with the situation or event are considered (Lazarus & Folkman, 1984). Finally, reappraisal is the process in which the original appraisal is reevaluated or reinterpreted.

Of particular relevance to the context of divorce is the fact that appraisal and reappraisal are not discrete, but rather are interdependent cognitive activities. Moreover, the appraisal process extends over undetermined periods of time, and initial responses may be influenced by subsequent events, which in turn reformulate the initial feelings of hurt. For example, when negative arousal is interpreted as hurt, the appraisal reflects an acknowledgment of personal vulnerability, and this appraisal is related to the intimacy level of one's close relationships (Fine & Olson, 1997).

Thus, partners who felt high levels of trust toward their spouse during marriage may experience a more intense level of hurt during dissolution, especially when the hurtful message or actions are perceived to be done intentionally (Vangelisti & Young, 2000). When an act is perceived to be intentional and when it is also done in public, the introspective qualities of sadness that accompany the appraisal of hurt are often replaced by retaliatory qualities of anger and blame (May & Jones, 2005). Indeed, the public nature of divorce and the reformulation of new families for one or both partners no doubt contribute to the complexity of emotional appraisals and reappraisals both during and after the dissolution process.

Second, like other emotions, both the experience and expression of hurt motivate actions that facilitate coping. The experience of emotion is fundamentally an adaptive response to the physical or social environment that signals the individual to respond in some way. Social and cultural norms may constrain the nature and extent of the response, but in general, response modes facilitate adaptation to environmental contingencies (Frijda, 1994; Frijda & Mesquita, 1994). Some emotions (e.g., guilt or embarrassment) are experienced by a person who has violated social or relational rules and motivate restoration behaviors through acts of restitution, contrition, and remorse (Frijda & Mesquita, 1994). By contrast, hurt is experienced by an offended person in response to the perceived devaluing actions of others and, consistent with the sadness/fear dimensions that comprise it, motivates withdrawal, disengagement, and distancing behaviors from the relationship and the offending partner. This response is especially likely when the action precipitating the hurt is serious (e.g., infidelity) (Feeney, 2004), is part of a pattern of such behavior (Vangelisti, 2006), and when the messages are expressed with intensity (e.g., via harsh and abrasive language) (Young, 2004). Withdrawing from the presence of partners who perform such actions is motivated by the need for emotional protection in much the same way that flight is motivated by the need for physical safety when fear is experienced.

Of course, there is also the possibility that the experience of excessive and enduring levels of hurt can promote physical and psychological withdrawal that eventually ceases to function as an effective coping strategy (see DeWall, Baumeister, & Masicampo, Chapter 7, this volume). Dispositionally sensitive or vulnerable individuals, for example, may be psychologically paralyzed both by the lingering pain of past hurt and the anticipation of future hurt to the point where they fail to maintain existing relationships and shy away from initiating new relationships. Lingering hurt may also make former spouses overly sensitive to possible hurtful comments made during their separation and relationship redefinition conversations. For example, Murray, Bellavia, Rose, and Griffin (2003) found in a diary study of married couples that spouses who felt chronic devaluation attributed more negativity to the partner's behavior, felt more hurt and rejection, and responded by being more "cold, critical, and rejecting" toward their spouse on the day after the hurtful assessment compared to those who felt a consistently high level of acceptance (p. 142). We speculate that, to the extent that some divorces entail significant personal devaluation for one or both partners and to the extent that some individuals experience particularly painful hurt, the patterns that Murray et al. identified in marriage are likely to emerge in dissolution and postdissolution interactions as well.

Whereas the experience of emotion functions to guide an individual's response to an environmental event, the expression of emotion functions to elicit certain types of responses from others (Ekman & Davidson, 1994; Frijda, 1994). The expression of sadness, for example, typically elicits sympathy, caretaking, and compassion from others (Izard & Ackerman, 2000). Expressing hurt to network members is likely to elicit similar responses. In fact, the interactive process of seeking and receiving emotional support facilitates emotional reappraisal of the hurtful event – a necessary first step in coping with the experience (Burleson & Goldsmith, 1998). Network support is most likely to be effective when messages reestablish or affirm the worth of the individual, thereby mitigating the sense of vulnerability that evoked the hurt.

In addition, although no research to date has tested the hypothesis, we reason that expressing hurt to the offending partner may serve a useful function as well. Specifically, it may function to elicit guilt that, as noted earlier, may then motivate the offending partner to perform acts of contrition and express his or her remorse. By contrast, the expression of anger and retaliatory emotions might activate symmetrical responses and escalate the negative affect. Ironically, however, in those circumstances where the expression of hurt would serve merely to confirm a former spouse's sense of control over the feelings of vulnerability that motivated the hurt, a moderate and controlled expression of anger may be necessary. The controlled expression of anger in such cases would function as an assertion of strength, communicating displeasure and desired corrective behaviors, thereby possibly reducing the frequency of hurtful messages in future interactions (Shaver et al., 1987).

Finally, hurt shares a third quality in common with other emotions: it is often vicariously experienced by others. Such empathic transference is typically explained as a result of social comparison or the result of emotional contagion. Social comparison theory, as adapted by Schachter (1959) and termed the "emotional similarity hypothesis," draws on the principles of appraisal theory to explain how we look to the experience of others in the same situation to obtain information about our own emotional state (Gump & Kulik, 1997). Emotional contagion is perhaps less cognitive and more visceral. According to Hatfield, Cacioppo, and Rapson (1992), it is the "tendency to automatically mimic and synchronize expressions, vocalizations, postures, and movements with those of another person's and, consequently, to converge emotionally" (pp. 153–154). Infants have been found to mimic their mothers' emotional expression and mothers to mimic their children's expression (Malatesta & Haviland, 1982). Research on nervousness and anxiety indicates that female participants waiting together in the same stressful situation supported both the emotional similarity hypothesis and the emotional contagion hypothesis; participants not only displayed behavioral mimicry but also reported similar levels of anxiety. Likewise, in older married couples dealing with one partner's loss of vision (Goodman & Shippy, 2002), emotional states converged for both partners, and in younger married couples facing the stress of the bar exam, anxiety converged until just before the exam when the nontesting spouse exhibited more calm and supportive emotions (Thompson & Bolger, 1999).

Although no systematic investigations of the generational transmission of hurt through emotional contagion are available, several studies indicate that a similar emotional complex, sadness and depression, is transferred to children from parents. For example, the communication of depressed parents tends to be marked by "negativity, hostility, complaining, and poor interpersonal problem solving" (Segrin, 1998, p. 221), a pattern evident even in mother–infant interactions (Bettes, 1988). As might be expected, children of depressed parents tend to reflect similar interaction patterns, displaying and expressing more negative affect than children of nondepressed parents (Kennedy-Moore & Watson, 1999).

At this juncture, it is important to make explicit the challenge inherent in the three qualities that hurt shares with all emotions: (a) it activates appraisal processes, (b) its experience and expression are functional and sometimes dysfunctional, and (c) it can be experienced empathically by close others. These three qualities constitute the emotional and interactional complexity at the center of hurt in postdivorce relationships. To the extent that events before and after the divorce are appraised as hurtful, withdrawal from the spouse may provide an opportunity for healing and reappraisal, unless the hurt is intense and inhibits social activity that would facilitate affirmation of one's worth or value. Likewise, talking about the hurt to others may help alleviate the intensity of the hurt through reappraisal and emotionally supportive communication. Unfortunately, if emotional contagion influences close others to experience empathic hurt or the more intense emotion of anger toward the offending spouse, they may no longer be able to serve as restorative resources.

Further, to the extent that parents include children in the network from which they seek comfort or confirmation, they may find that this "boundary enmeshment" induces even greater stress and discomfort for the children (for a review, see Afifi & Hamrick, 2006). The emotional strain on children may also be exacerbated if their parents inadvertently communicate the distress they experience as a result of their hurt or the children experience the hurt through emotional contagion. Even if parents attempt to mask their feelings of hurt by suppressing them and displaying positive emotions instead (Ekman & Friesen, 1975), the efforts to sustain the "performance" can be emotionally draining.

In sum, it is difficult to manage the challenges of negotiating the dissolution of a marriage and the reformulation of postdivorce relationships when hurt is a salient and prevalent emotion. Counseling intervention may help with reappraisal and adjustment to the dismantling of the family structure, but ultimately, one of the most functional options for coping is to forgive the person who caused the hurt (Gordon, Baucom, & Snyder, 2005). As Hall and Fincham (2006) concluded in their review of infidelity in relationship dissolution, "despite a couple's decision to break up or remain together, forgiveness can have significant emotional and physical health benefits" (p. 163).

These benefits arise from the transformative nature of forgiveness, the letting go of the hurt and resentment, the separating of the offense from the offender, and the emergence of sincere positive feelings toward the offender (Metts & Cupach, 2007). Whether overtly expressed or not, the liberating and empowering emotion of forgiveness is likely to be "caught" by close others and to facilitate both the peaceful dissolution of the marriage and the reformulation of separate family units. Even if more sustained intervention is required for children who are distressed by the divorce, research indicates that education that facilitates forgiveness toward their parents decreases anxiety and enhances feelings of hope (Freedman & Knupp, 2003).

Another way to manage hurt is to redefine the relationship from one of "couplehood" to one involving greater personal distance – "business partners" of sorts. This redefinition is especially advantageous when former spouses are coparenting children (Sbarra & Emery, 2006) and, in fact, postdivorce parents have even used this phrase in research interviews to describe their working relationship (Schrodt, Baxter, McBride, Braithwaite, & Fine, 2006). The business partner metaphor has both emotional and practical advantages for former partners. Redefining the marriage relationship from one of affectionate ties, intimacy, trust, and inherent personal and relational value to one of distance, formality, and task boundaries minimizes the vulnerability that evokes hurt. It is possible to become annoyed or angry with a business partner, but far less likely to be hurt by one. Redefining the relationship also has a practical advantage. It redefines conversations as business meetings in the sense that former spouses can organize their talk around a series of task-related topics, most often the children, rather than emotional issues. Such an agenda helps avoid sensitive topics that are likely to lead to conflict and hurtful messages (Schrodt et al., 2006).

Although former spouses may not explicitly organize their conversations as "business meetings," research suggests that spouses do, more or less consciously, keep their conversations focused on tasks related to parenting and legal (nonaffective) aspects of the divorce. For example, in their diary study of the interactions of parents, stepparents, and nonresidential parents who were coparenting children, Braithwaite, McBride, and Schrodt (2003) found little overt conflict between the adults in the 2-week period in which diaries were being kept. Rather, in the follow-up interviews the adults stressed that they focused their interactions on issues directly related to the children. Similarly, in her study of postdivorce communication about dating, Miller (2007) found that ex-spouses would make sure that their coparent knows they are dating, to keep potential conflict to a minimum, but would then quickly return the conversation to the topic of the children. In another study, Schrodt et al., 2006) found that one way some former spouses coped with postdivorce interactions was to invoke the divorce decree as a legal contract, very much following the "letter of the law" according to the decree. Others used the divorce decree as a more general guide and were able to reach agreement on child-rearing issues without resorting to the specific mandates of the divorce decree. Whatever they chose to do, most former spouses functioning as coparents seemed best served by brief businesslike interactions focused on issues related to children. Whether this form of communication reflects forgiveness or whether it might facilitate forgiveness is an empirical question that researchers should address.

We turn now to a more focused discussion of hurt and its role in the family system during and after divorce.

## HURT IN THE DISSOLUTION AND RESTRUCTURING OF FAMILY SYSTEMS

The transition from being married to being divorced is, of course, not a simple or linear process. Perhaps more important, it is not a process restricted to the couple alone. As with any system, the family system is characterized by interdependence among its members, is responsive to changes within and external to the family, manifests interactive complexity, and links in complex ways to other systems (Galvin, Dickson, & Marrow, 2006). Thus, change in a couple's marital status reverberates not only through the members of the immediate family such as the children but also through related systems beyond the nuclear family, including in-laws, grandparents, aunts, uncles, and other social network members. Here, we focus our discussion on the role of hurt in three broad arenas of change during and after divorce: spousal separation; reformulations of postdivorce family systems, including stepfamily reformulations; and changes in the extended family such as grandparent relationships.

### Spousal Separation

As spouses make the transition through various stages of relationship dissolution, they are likely to experience any number of the hurt-eliciting events described earlier: perceived slights, disconfirming messages, being excluded from plans and activities, criticism, deception, broken promises, and other provocations. Although the magnitude of the emotion experienced will vary depending on the nature of the eliciting event, the context in which it occurs, and the extent to which the individual tends to react with hurt rather than anger, these perceived devaluations are likely to lead to feelings of hurt. In addition, several aspects of the change in circumstances from being married to being single are specific sources of potential hurt.

First, running a household, caring for children's moment-to-moment needs, earning enough income to manage the household, maintaining the home, and so forth are considerably more challenging when there is only one adult in the home. These challenges are likely to be experienced as stressors. In some cases, these stressors elicit anger and resentment, especially when their cause is attributed to a former spouse's disregard for fairness and equality in accepting comparable responsibility. In other cases, however, these stressors elicit hurt, the combination of sadness and fear experienced when the tasks and activities that had formerly been shared as a couple are now the responsibility of one individual. For example, maintaining a home and caring for the children as a single parent may elicit fear that he or she cannot do this alone and be a persistent reminder that the "family" as previously constituted has been devalued by the partner who is no longer participating simultaneously in the activities.

Second, many divorcing spouses, particularly those who did not initiate the divorce, feel a sense of being rejected by their partner. From his ethnographic investigation of 40 people who were in the process of divorce, Hopper (2001) concluded that the partner who assumed the role of the initiator of the divorce has time to rewrite marital history – to redefine the quality of the marriage (e.g., flawed from the start) and to minimize his or her own culpability (someone had to end the bad situation). However, the noninitiator is seldom privy to the revision of his or her marital history and, as a consequence, may experience tremendous hurt when he or she hears messages such as these: "He told me that he didn't love me and that he never had" or "What she told me was that she married me without being in love with me" (p. 440).

Coupled with this sense of rejection is often a deep-rooted feeling of failure because many spouses, to varying degrees of conscious awareness, believe that they are responsible for the marriage ending. This sense of self-blame may bring to the surface and magnify feelings and thoughts of personal inadequacy that emerge during periods of perceived transgressions by others. Thus, it is not so much that divorce is the original cause of hurt feelings stemming from this sense of personal inadequacy, but divorce often brings this feeling to one's conscious awareness and may strengthen it.

Third, individuals going through a divorce often experience a change and a diminution in their social networks (Sprecher, Felmlee, Schmeeckle, & Shu, 2006). During the transition from being married to single, individuals are often excluded (often with no ill intent on the part of those who exclude them) from gatherings of married couples that they were routinely invited to before the divorce/separation. Much of our socializing is done with individuals who share the same marital/relationship status as we do, and divorced individuals often find themselves either as outsiders in social gatherings or they are not invited at all. Such a change in social relations can certainly lead to hurt feelings, particularly if the exclusion is taken personally as a message about one's worth as a social participant.

Fourth, individuals making the transition to being single find themselves to varying degrees and at different times engaged in what Rollie and Duck (2006) refer to as "resurrection processes," involving preparation for a different and improved future. One aspect of these resurrection processes is to once again be immersed in the "singles market." Eventually, most divorced individuals seek out another romantic partnership. In this process, they may find that they have to "sell" themselves and impress others in a way that they had not had to do for some time. This process of selling oneself may be hurtful, especially if one has difficulty finding romantic partners, feels rejected by potential partners, and feels resentful at even being in the situation in which one has to look for a partner. Further, being engaged in the process of finding a romantic partner may bring into conscious awareness perceived deficiencies that one did not have to confront in oneself when married.

Finally, hurt is commonly experienced by former spouses as they struggle to redefine their identity. "Considering the way in which marriage encompasses one's total personality, divorce cuts to the core of one's sense of self and dignity" (Hopper, 2001, p. 431). In the process of making the transition from being a married spouse to a divorced single individual, one's identity shifts dramatically (Adamsons & Pasley, 2006; Willen & Montgomery, 2006). When married, the state of being connected, being interdependent, being part of a larger whole becomes an integral aspect of one's identity; the legal termination of the relationship does not undo the psychological sense of "self as a spouse" with all that entails. Hurt arises when sadness and fear converge: Feelings of loss for "what was" in both affective and material terms evoke sadness, and feelings of apprehension about the future evoke fear. Thus, the loss of a social, sexual, and conversational companion and the loss of a sense of continuity and purpose combine with apprehension about future relationships, fear of loneliness, and so forth. To the extent that one was satisfied in one's marriage and did not want or initiate the divorce, these feelings of loss and fear are likely to evoke particularly intense hurt feelings.

In addition, the dissolution of a nuclear family often means an alteration in one's identity as parent and as spouse. Even when divorce is amicable and the custodial arrangement is equitable, one parent, usually the father, becomes a nonresidential parent. The struggle to be part of each other's lives, to maintain open and honest communication, and yet to recognize that family structures have changed can sometimes lead to hurt. As young adults of divorced parents described the challenges they encountered trying to maintain a relationship with their nonresidential parent, the potential for hurt was evident, even when not articulated (Braithwaite & Baxter, 2006). For example, one young woman said of her nonresidential father,

> I don't get to see him very much so that kinda puts constraints on our communication. But if I am talking about things I will say, "Oh, my parents..." meaning my mom and my stepdad, but really, he's my parent, too. I think that throws him for a loop. (p. 40)

Given our discussion here, we suspect that if the father were to rephrase his daughter's colloquial expression, "throws him for a loop," in his own words, it might well be, "Hearing my daughter refer to another man as her parent hurts me."

## Reformulation in the Postdivorce Family

Among the challenges that accompany the dissolution of a nuclear family is the need to manage not only lingering hurt but emergent hurt as well when one or both parents enter new relationships. Successful reformulation of the nuclear family requires both adults and children to negotiate new roles and effective communication within and between the new family units (Bokker, 2006; Coleman, Ganong, & Fine, 2000). For example, the nonresidential parent is important in the family equation as it is against this person that new partners and potential stepparents are compared (Ganong & Coleman, 2004). The relationship between the residential and nonresidential parent has the potential to affect all other postdivorce relationships, particularly in stepfamilies (Braithwaite & Baxter, 2006). Children are in danger of being caught between their parents as many parents tend to avoid direct communication and send messages via the children (Afifi, 2003; Braithwaite, Toller, Daas, Durham, & Jones, 2008), resulting in great potential for hurt. We turn now to more detailed discussion of a common family reformulation, the stepfamily.

### *The Stepfamily*

Several types of experiences can lead to hurt in stepfamilies. First, in the early stages of stepfamily formation, several possible hurts stem from the attempts to redefine, realign, or protect relationships. For example, children, particularly daughters, may become quite close to their single mothers and perhaps even become confidants (Ganong & Coleman, 2004; Hetherington, Hagan, & Anderson, 1989). As the single mother initiates and then nurtures the relationship with her new romantic partner (or spouse), she is likely to have less time to spend with her daughter, and even the nature of the mother–child interactions is likely to change (Braithwaite, Baxter, & Harper, 1998; Ganong & Coleman, 1994). Thus, the child may feel rejected, left out, devalued, and even abandoned – feelings often likely to be appraised as hurt.

Second, as the stepfamily becomes more stabilized and develops new routines and rituals, there is sure to be a sense of loss as "old" routines and rituals

from the original family(ies) are changed or abandoned (Braithwaite et al., 1998). Stepfamily members, as well as the stepfamily as a unit, experience multiple dilemmas, including one related to the adoption of new routines versus the temptations to stick with established patterns, routines, and rituals. Although stepfamily members are often advised to develop some rituals and routines in the new family, they are also advised to maintain remnants of the old ones as well, thus managing the tensions present in the loss of the old family and establishing the new family (Braithwaite et al., 1998). To the extent that individuals, especially stepchildren, feel that their old routines and traditions are devalued or "pushed aside" in favor of new ones, they are likely to be hurt – sad at the loss of the past and fearful of the future and the role they will play.

Third, the hurt that children feel over the breakup of their parent's marriage and the loss of the "old" or original family may carry over in the postdivorce and stepfamily stages. Children may experience a cacophony of different emotions during the breakup and remarriage of their parents (Coleman, Ganong, & Fine, 2004). As stepparents attempt to form relationships with stepchildren, they may find themselves recipients of the behavioral manifestations (e.g., acting out, resentment, hostility) of the children's hurt, even though it was not of the stepparents' own making. Stepparents are thus challenged to form relationships with children who are often still adjusting to the fact that their parents will not be getting back together; in fact, the stepparent may very well be the embodiment of the end of these dreams for children. Compounding stepchildren's hurt is the very common pattern of children from divorced families blaming themselves for the divorce to varying degrees, depending on their disposition, age, and experiences with their parents (Harvey & Fine, 2004). This sense of self-blame is often subtle and outside of children's conscious awareness, but it can lead to hurt, anger, and a variety of resulting behaviors.

Although researchers have not singled out hurt per se, certainly strong and often negative emotions can play a role in children's adjustment postdivorce and into the stepfamily years. Ganong, Coleman, Fine, and Martin (1999) found that stepparents who made efforts to establish affinity and a close relationship with their stepchildren and who sustained these efforts after the remarriage were more likely to develop close relationships with them. It may be that, for some stepchildren, a close relationship with a stepparent can help mitigate some of the hurt they have experienced (Harvey & Fine, 2004). However, applying a dialectical lens, Baxter, Braithwaite, Bryant, and Wagner (2004) interviewed young adult stepchildren and found that they wanted emotional closeness with their stepparent, but, at the same time, often rejected closeness out of loyalty to their nonresidential parent. For example, Braithwaite et al. (1998) heard this dynamic reflected as a stepdaughter explained how she became upset at a Father's Day outing with her stepfather; she reported that she told him, "I am not trading in dads this year" (p. 111). Similarly, children may experience hurt at being displaced in their close relationship with a parent following the postdivorce time they shared (Crosbie-Burnett & Giles-Sims, 1991; Golish, 2003). Scholars using clinical data have explained that stepchildren who feel anger over the loss of their old family or nonresidential parent may displace anger toward the new stepparent (Visher & Visher, 1979), especially in adolescence (Hetherington et al., 1989).

*Stepsiblings*
Of all the relationships in the stepfamily, the stepsibling relationship is the least studied (Coleman et al., 2004). Stepsiblings may find both the experience and expression of emotions difficult, especially in light of the loss of the old family and the various challenges associated with adjusting to the new stepfamily (Fitness & Duffield, 2004; Lamb, 2006; Rosenberg & Hajal, 1985). Although stepsiblings may experience positive emotions at the formation of the stepfamily, negative emotions such as hurt, anger, and jealousy are prevalent (Rosenberg & Hajal, 1985). Rosenberg and Hajal (1985) detailed many different changes that can lead to negative emotional experiences and expressions for stepsiblings, including losses caused by the divorce, lack of shared history, quick stepfamily formation, an increase in family size, changes in roles and expectations, and loss of parental attention. Lamb (2006) argued that there is a lack of empirical research on stepsibling relationships in general and on how their experience and expression of emotion change over time in the stepfamily specifically.

Certainly the potential for hurt among stepsiblings is great. Stepsiblings often find themselves in a situation that they neither expected nor wanted; at a time when their parents are happy in their new relationship, stepsiblings may find themselves struggling with hurt over the loss of their old life and of a close relationship with one or both of their parents, as well as the unwelcome addition of stepparents and stepsiblings into their lives (Coleman, Fine, Ganong, Downs, & Pauk, 2001). As are all stepkin, stepsiblings are affected by what Visher and Visher (1979) refer to as "stepfamily myths." One of these myths is that stepkin should instantly care for and love each other. Endorsing such a myth is likely to lead to frustration and hurt/anger, because it is unrealistic to expect and rare to find stepkin who immediately care for each other. Stepsiblings have described strong emotions, including hurt, as they experience competition with stepsiblings over attention from parents, affection, and resources (Coleman et al., 2001; Lamb, 2004).

EXTENDED FAMILY

To date, stepfamily researchers have focused primarily on various dyads and subsystems within the stepfamily home, most often the marital couple and the stepparent–stepchild dyad. Researchers have begun to argue for moving the focus on stepfamilies beyond the boundaries of a single household, accounting for the larger webs of individuals who live in different residences and comprise the stepfamily system (Braithwaite, Schrodt, & Baxter, 2006; Coleman et al., 2000). They have suggested that it is important to focus on the role of extended family in postdivorce families and stepfamilies – both the original extended family and the new extended family members added in the stepfamily years (Braithwaite et al., 1998).

Grandparents may be especially helpful to children during times of transition as they can provide some degree of stability and a sense of continuity during periods of change necessitated by the divorce. However, when a couple divorces and later as one or both partners enter into new relationships, in most cases, the level of contact with the extended family will be influenced heavily by the parental generation (Ganong & Coleman, 2004). In situations when custodial parents deny grandparents access to their grandchildren, in most states grandparents can exercise their legal right to see their grandchildren (Bartlett, 1999). The potential for divorced parents and their extended family members on their former spouses' side to experience hurt is reflected by Ganong and Coleman (2004) referring to these "former" family relationships postdivorce as "quasi-kin" (p. 172). Hurt may also extend to the divorcing parties; for example, one man we interviewed for a study reported the hurt he experienced when his own parents invited his ex-wife to visit their home one summer along with the grandchildren. For this man, who had a very acrimonious divorce, the invitation extended by his parents represented a personal betrayal.

Step-extended family members, especially grandparents or step-grandparents, are also understudied by scholars (Ganong & Coleman, 1994, 2004). In the families themselves, expectations for the role of stepkin are vague. Studying these relationships and the emotions and communication in them is important as Coleman et al. (2001) found that disagreements and disputes with extended family accounted for many serious conflicts in stepfamilies. Coleman and colleagues found that many of the family members in the immediate stepfamily handled these extended family conflicts by withdrawing both physically and emotionally. Our observation based on interviews with stepchildren is that in some cases, these children and stepgrandparents are virtual strangers to one another with little contact. When there is contact, the potential for sound relationships is there, provided that grandchildren perceive equity in the grandparents' treatment of grandchildren from different families. Inequity of treatment (real or perceived) by grandparents can lead to potential damage to the stepfamily and especially the stepsibling relationship(s). Coleman et al. (2001) also pointed out that is disagreement regarding the extent to which the nonresidential parent and extended family members should be active and involved stepfamily members exacerbates conflict with extended family members.

Finally, we should note that some stepchildren and extended family members, stepgrandchildren particularly, can form close bonds. For some children whose parent and stepparent divorce, the loss is compounded as their stepfamily disintegrates and they also likely lose their stepgrandparents (Coleman, Ganong, & Hans, 2006). For children who have experienced a good amount of change and loss, the risk of experiencing hurt feelings and possibly of more severe levels of dysfunction is magnified.

CONCLUSION

Our goal in this chapter was to examine the function of hurt in the postdivorce relationships of former spouses, their children, and their extended family. Clearly, hurt is a powerful emotion within a complex of other emotions that has salience in the divorce process as well as in families that form after the divorce. Especially when children are involved and former partners function as coparents, understanding the role of hurt in postdivorce communication and relationships is important. Based on our review, we offer the following suggestions for future research.

First, we encourage researchers to examine hurt as a process within dissolving relationships thereby augmenting the research on hurt evoked within single episodes, such as reactions to hurtful messages (Vangelisti & Young, 2000; Young, 2004). We know relatively little about how hurt unfolds and affects relational parties and members of their social networks over time. Studying hurt during and after divorce provides one context to examine hurt as a process. Systematic attempts to understand feelings of hurt, their verbal or nonverbal expression, and their influences on ongoing and new relationships are warranted. Of course, this is a daunting task, given that the reappraisal effects inherent in the coping process are typically reflected in retrospective, rather than prospective, self-reports. However, creative and nonintrusive methods to gather more contemporaneous information might be available through observations of support group meetings or analysis of online interactions or chatrooms.

Second, we argue that researchers should examine the influence of hurt on postdivorce communication and relationships beyond the dyad of the divorced couple. We have argued for examining the role of hurt among the couple's children, within the stepfamily(ies) formed postdivorce, and with extended family members. For example, we believe it is important for researchers to focus more specifically on the role of hurt in the stepparent–stepchild relationship, in the relationships of residential parents and their own children who may experience role change and loss when their parents remarry, and between nonresidential parents and their children. We also stress the need to examine potential effects of hurt on grandparents as well as between children and their stepgrandparents and other members of the new extended family.

We certainly recognize the ambitious scope of this call and the vast domain of interactions that it entails. However, the unique qualities of hurt necessitate extended investigation throughout the family system. Hurt is an inherently complicated emotion, and its expression is often ambiguous. More specifically, as noted previously, hurt is a blend of sadness and fear, experienced when we perceive or interpret the actions of others as devaluing us or the relationship and is particularly painful when these actions violate the trust and faith that we have placed in close others. An adult may be able to recognize and appraise these feelings as hurt and may be able to express them verbally. However, hurt also suggests vulnerability and motivates responses that provide a time for healing, often manifested in various degrees of relational distancing (Vangelisti, 2006). Thus, even adults may fail to clearly express their hurt, at least to the person they believe to be causing it.

For the child or adolescent who experiences hurt, both recognizing the emotion and distinguishing it from anger and related emotions may be particularly difficult. Further, gaining the ability to verbally express that hurt, rather than to withdraw or act out in anger, may be a greater challenge. Hence the child who experiences hurt during the divorce and postdivorce transitions may not be able to articulate these feelings and so may in turn withdraw from (or express anger toward) his or her parents, stepparents, stepsiblings, or grandparents. These recipients are distressed by the ambiguous expressions of what appears to be rejection, dislike, opposition, and so on, and in turn feel hurt. Like dominos, the effects of hurt not fully understood or clearly articulated continue to fall through the entire postdivorce family system.

Finally, we encourage researchers to examine the role of forgiveness on hurt in postdivorce and stepfamily relationships. Researchers have identified several important functions served by forgiveness during and after the circumstances associated with divorce. For example, forgiveness seems to mediate the effects of infidelity on both emotional and physical health for intact and divorcing relationships (Gordon et al., 2005; Hall & Fincham, 2006). Forgiveness also contributes to the likelihood of friendly relations between spouses who have divorced (Metts & Cupach, 2007) and to the likelihood that children will have stronger relationships with and more positive attitudes toward their parents after a divorce (Freedman & Knupp, 2003). We believe that a fuller understanding of the forgiveness process and its consequences for the experience of hurt in postdivorce relationships will benefit both researchers and practitioners. As Gordon et al. (2005) concluded from a review of the forgiveness research on couples therapy, forgiving an ex-spouse has an effect extending beyond the couple to their children by reducing the amount of conflict that the children have to witness. Thus, forgiveness and its impact on interaction and relationships within postdivorce families merit systematic investigation in future research on hurt in postdivorce relationships.

## REFERENCES

Adamsons, K., & Pasley, K. (2006). Coparenting following divorce and relationship dissolution. In M. A. Fine & J. H. Harvey (Eds.), *Handbook of divorce and relationship dissolution* (pp. 241–261). Mahwah, NJ: Erlbaum.

Afifi, T. D. (2003). "Feeling caught" in stepfamilies: Managing boundary turbulence through appropriate privacy coordination rules. *Journal of Social and Personal Relationships, 20,* 729–755.

Afifi, T. D., & Hamrick, K. (2006). Communication processes that promote risk and resiliency in postdivorce families. In M. A. Fine & J. H. Harvey (Eds.), *Handbook of divorce and relationship dissolution* (pp. 435–456). Mahwah, NJ: Erlbaum.

Bartlett, K. T. (1999). Improving the law relating to postdivorce arrangements for children. In R. A. Thompson & P. R. Amato (Eds.), *The postdivorce family: Children, parenting, and society* (pp. 71–102). Thousand Oaks, CA: Sage.

Baxter, L. A, Braithwaite, D. O., Bryant, L., & Wagner, A. (2004). Stepchildren's perceptions of the contradictions in communication with stepparents. *Journal of Social and Personal Relationships, 21,* 447–467.

Bettes, B. A. (1988). Maternal depression and motherese: Temporal and intonational features. *Child Development, 59,* 1089–1096.

Bokker, P. (2006). Factors that influence the relationships between divorced fathers and their children. *Journal of Divorce & Remarriage, 45,* 157–172.

Braithwaite, D. O., & Baxter, L. A. (2006). "You're my parent but you're not": Dialectical tensions in stepchildren's perceptions about communicating with the nonresidential parent. *Journal of Applied Communication Research, 34,* 30–48.

Braithwaite, D. O., Baxter, L. A., & Harper, A. (1998). The role of rituals in the management of the dialectical tension of "old" and "new" in blended families. *Communication Studies, 48,* 101–120.

Braithwaite, D. O., McBride, M. C., & Schrodt, P. (2003). Parent teams and the everyday interactions of co-parenting children in stepfamilies. *Communication Reports, 16,* 93–111.

Braithwaite, D. O., Schrodt, P., & Baxter, L. A. (2006). Communication in stepfamily relationships: Understudied and misunderstood. In K. Floyd & M. T. Morman (Eds.), *Widening the family circle: New research on family communication* (pp. 153–170). Thousand Oaks, CA: Sage.

Braithwaite, D. O., Toller, P., Daas, K., Durham, W., & Jones, A. (2008). Centered, but not caught in the middle: Stepchildren's perceptions of contradictions of the communication of co-parents. *Journal of Applied Communication Research, 36,* 33–55.

Burleson, B. R., & Goldsmith, D. J. (1998). How the comforting process works: Alleviating emotional distress through conversationally induced reappraisals. In P. A. Andersen & L. K. Guerrero (Eds.), *Handbook of communication and emotion: Research, theory, applications, and contexts* (pp. 245–280). San Diego: Academic Press.

Coleman, M., Fine, M. A., Ganong, L. G., Downs, K. M., & Pauk, N. (2001). When you're not the Brady Bunch: Identifying perceived conflicts and resolution strategies in stepfamilies. *Personal Relationships, 8,* 57–73.

Coleman, M., Ganong, L. H., & Fine, M. (2000). Reinvestigating remarriage: Another decade of progress. *Journal of Marriage and the Family, 62,* 1288–1307.

Coleman, M., Ganong, L. H., & Fine, M. (2004). Communication in stepfamilies. In A. L. Vangelisti (Ed.), *Handbook of family communication* (pp. 215–232). Mahwah, NJ: Erlbaum.

Coleman, M., Ganong, L. H., & Hans, J. (2006). Divorce as prelude to stepfamily living and the consequences of redivorce. In M. A. Fine & J. H. Harvey (Eds.), *Handbook of divorce and relationship dissolution* (pp. 409–434). Mahwah, NJ: Erlbaum.

Crosbie-Burnett, M., & Giles-Sims, J. (1991). Marital power in stepfather families: A test of normative-resource theory. *Journal of Family Psychology, 4,* 484–496.

Ekman, P., & Davidson, R. J. (1994). *The nature of emotion: Fundamental questions.* New York: Oxford University Press.

Ekman, P., & Friesen, W. V. (1975). *Unmasking the face.* Englewood Cliffs, NJ: Prentice-Hall.

Feeney, J. A. (2004). Hurt feelings in couple relationships: Toward integrative models of the negative effects of hurtful events. *Journal of Social and Personal Relationships, 21,* 487–508.

Fine, M. A., & Olson, K. (1997). Hurt and anger in response to provocation: Relations to aspects of adjustment. *Journal of Social Behavior and Personality, 12,* 325–344.

Fitness, J. (2001). Betrayal, rejection, revenge, and forgiveness: An interpersonal script approach. In M. R. Leary (Ed.), *Interpersonal rejection* (pp. 73–103). New York: Oxford University Press.

Fitness, J., & Duffield, J. (2004). Emotion and communication in families. In A. L. Vangelisti (Ed.), *Handbook of family communication* (pp. 473–494). Mahwah, NJ: Erlbaum.

Freedman, S., & Knupp, A. (2003). The impact of forgiveness on adolescent adjustment to parental divorce. *Journal of Divorce and Remarriage, 39,* 135–165.

Frijda, N. H. (1994). Emotions are functional, most of the time. In P. Ekman & R. J. Davidson (Eds.), *The nature of emotion: Fundamental questions* (pp. 113–122). New York: Oxford University Press.

Frijda, N. H., & Mesquita, B. (1994). The social roles and functions of emotions. In S. Kitayama & H. R. Markus (Eds.), *Emotion and culture: Empirical studies of mutual influence* (pp. 51–87). Washington, DC: American Psychological Association.

Galvin, K., Dickson, F., & Marrow, S. (2006). Systems theory: Patterns and (w)holes in family communication. In D. O. Braithwaite & L. A. Baxter (Eds.), *Engaging theories in family communication: Multiple perspectives* (pp. 309–324). Thousand Oaks CA: Sage.

Ganong, L. H., & Coleman, M. (1994). *Remarried family relationships.* Thousand Oaks, CA: Sage.

Ganong, L. H., & Coleman, M. (2004). *Stepfamily relationships: Development, dynamics, and interventions.* New York: Kluwer Academic.

Ganong, L. H., Coleman, M., Fine, M., & Martin, P. (1999). Stepparents' affinity-seeking and affinity-maintaining strategies with stepchildren. *Journal of Family Issues, 20,* 299–327.

Golish, T. D. (2003). Stepfamily communication strengths: Understanding the ties that bind. *Human Communication Research, 29,* 41–80.

Goodman, C. R., & Shippy, R. A. (2002). Is it contagious? Affect similarity among spouses. *Aging & Mental Health, 6,* 266–274.

Gordon, K. C., Baucom, D. H., & Snyder, D. K. (2005). Forgiveness in couples: Divorce, infidelity, and couples therapy. In E. L. Worthington, Jr. (Ed.), *Handbook of forgiveness* (pp. 407–421). New York: Routledge.

Gump, B. B., & Kulik, J. A. (1997). Stress, affiliation, and emotional contagion. *Journal of Personality and Social Psychology, 72,* 305–319.

Hall, J. H., & Fincham, F. D. (2006). Relationship dissolution following infidelity. In M. A. Fine & J. H. Harvey (Eds.), *Handbook of divorce and relationship dissolution* (pp. 153–168). Mahwah, NJ: Erlbaum.

Harvey, J. H., & Fine, M. A. (2004). *Children of divorce: Stories of loss and hope.* Mahwah, NJ: Erlbaum.

Hatfield, E., Cacioppo, J. T., & Rapson, R. L. (1992). Primitive emotional contagion. In M. S. Clark (Ed.), *Emotion and social behavior* (pp. 151–177). Newbury Park, CA: Sage.

Hetherington, E. M., Hagen, M. S., & Anderson, E. R. (1989). Marital transitions: A child's perspective. *American Psychologist, 44,* 303–312.

Hopper, J. (2001). The symbolic origins of conflict in divorce. *Journal of Marriage and Family, 63,* 430–445.

Izard, C. E., & Ackerman, B. P. (2000). Motivational, organizational, and regulatory functions of discrete emotions. In M. Lewis & J. M. Haviland-Jones (Eds.), *Handbook of emotions* (2nd ed., pp. 253–264). New York: Guilford.

Johnston, J. R., & Campbell, L. E. G. (1988). *Impasses of divorce.* New York: Free Press.

Kennedy-Moore, E., & Watson, J. C. (1999). *Expressing emotion: Myths, realities, and therapeutic strategies.* New York: Guilford.

Lamb, E. N. (2004, July). *The experience and expression of emotion within stepsibling relationships.* Presented at the meeting of the International Association for Relationship Research, Madison, WI.

Lamb, E. N. (2006). *The experience and expression of emotion within stepsibling relationships: How politeness of expression affects stepfamily functioning.* Unpublished manuscript, University of Nebraska-Lincoln.

Lazarus, R. S. (2006). Emotions and interpersonal relationships: Toward a person-centered conceptualization of emotions and coping. *Journal of Personality, 74,* 9–46.

Lazarus, R. S., & Folkman, S. (1984). *Stress, appraisal, and coping.* New York: Springer.

Leary, M. R., Koch, E. J., & Hechenbleikner, N. R. (2001). Emotional responses to interpersonal rejection. In M. R. Leary (Ed.), *Interpersonal rejection* (pp. 145–166). New York: Oxford University Press.

Leary, M. R., Springer, C., Negel, L., Ansell, E., & Evans, K. (1998). The causes, phenomenology, and consequences of hurt feelings. *Journal of Personality and Social Psychology, 74,* 1225–1237.

Malatesta, C. Z., & Haviland, J. M. (1982). Learning display rules: The socialization of emotion expression in infancy, *Child Development, 53,* 991–1003.

May, L. N., & Jones, W. H. (2005). Differential reactions to hurt. *Journal of Worry and Affective Experience, 1,* 54–59.

Metts, S. (2000). Face and facework: Implications for the study of personal relationship. In K. Dindia & S. Duck (Eds.), *Communication and personal relationships* (pp. 77–94). New York: Wiley.

Metts, S., & Cupach, W. R. (1995). Postdivorce relations. In M. A. Fitzpatrick & A. L. Vangelisti (Eds.), *Explaining family interactions* (pp. 232–251). Thousand Oaks, CA: Sage.

Metts, S., & Cupach W. R. (2007). Responses to relational transgressions: Hurt, anger, and sometimes forgiveness. In B. Spitzberg & W. R. Cupach (Eds.), *The dark side of interpersonal communication* (2nd ed., pp. 243–274). Mahwah, NJ: Erlbaum.

Miller, A. E. (2007, November). *Divorced coparents' strategies for disclosing post-divorce dating to one another.* Paper presented at the annual meeting of the National Communication Association, Chicago.

Murray, S. L. (2005). Regulating the risks of closeness: A relationship-specific sense of felt security. *Current Directions in Psychological Science, 14,* 74–78.

Murray, S. L., Bellavia, G. M., Rose, P., & Griffin, D. W. (2003). Once hurt, twice hurtful: How perceived regard regulates daily marital interactions. *Journal of Personality and Social Psychology, 84,* 126–147.

Murray, S. L., Holmes, J. G., & Griffin, D. (1996). The benefits of positive illusions: Idealization and the construction of satisfaction in close relationships. *Journal of Personality and Social Psychology, 70,* 79–98.

Rollie, S. S., & Duck, S. (2006). Stage models and their limitations. In M. A. Fine & J. H. Harvey (Eds.), *Handbook of divorce and relationship dissolution* (pp. 223–240). Mahwah, NJ: Erlbaum.

Rosenberg, E. B., & Hajal, F. (1985). Stepsibling relationships in remarried families. *Social Casework: The Journal of Contemporary Social Work, 66,* 287–292.

Sbarra, D. A., & Emery, R. E. (2006). In the presence of grief: The role of cognitive-emotional adaptation in contemporary divorce mediation. In M. A. Fine & J. H. Harvey (Eds.), *Handbook of divorce and relationship dissolution* (pp. 553–573). Mahwah, NJ: Erlbaum.

Schacter, S. (1959). *The psychology of affiliation.* Palo Alto, CA: Stanford University Press.

Schrodt, P., Baxter, L. A., McBride, C., Braithwaite, D. O., & Fine, M. A. (2006). The divorce decree, communication, and the structuration of co-parenting relationships in stepfamilies. *Journal of Social and Personal Relationships, 23,* 741–759

Segrin, C. (1998). Interpersonal communication problems associated with depression and loneliness. In P. A. Andersen & L. K. Guerrero (Eds.), *Handbook of communication and emotion: Research, theory, applications, and contexts* (pp. 215–242). San Diego: Academic Press.

Shaver, P., Schwartz, J., Kirson, D., & O'Connor, C. (1987). Emotion knowledge: Further exploration of a prototype approach. *Journal of Personality and Social Psychology, 52,* 1061–1086.

Smith, C. A., & Pope, L. K. (1992). Appraisal and emotion: The interactional contributions of dispositional and situational factors. In M. S. Clark (Ed.), *Emotion and social behavior* (pp. 32–62). Newbury Park, CA: Sage.

Sommer, K. (2001). Coping with rejection: Ego-defensive strategies, self-esteem, and interpersonal relationships. In M. R. Leary (Ed.), *Interpersonal rejection* (pp. 167–188). New York: Oxford University Press.

Sprecher, S., Felmlee, D., Schmeeckle, M., & Shu, X. (2006). No breakup occurs on an island: Social networks and relationship dissolution. In M. A. Fine & J. H. Harvey (Eds.), *Handbook of divorce and relationship dissolution* (pp. 457–478). Mahwah, NJ: Erlbaum.

Thompson, A., & Bolger, N. (1999). Emotional transmission in couples under stress. *Journal of Marriage and the Family, 61,* 38–48.

Vangelisti, A. L. (2006). Hurtful interactions and the dissolution of intimacy. In M. A. Fine & J. H. Harvey (Eds.), *Handbook of divorce and relationship dissolution* (pp. 133–152). Mahwah, NJ: Erlbaum.

Vangelisti, A. L., & Young, S. L. (2000). When words hurt: The effects of perceived intentionality on interpersonal relationships. *Journal of Social and Personal Relationships, 17,* 393–424.

Visher, E. B., & Visher, J. S. (1979). *Stepfamilies: A guide to working with stepparents and stepchildren.* New York: Brunner/Mazel.

Willen, H., & Montgomery, H. (2006). From marital distress to divorce: The creation of new identities for the spouses. *Journal of Divorce & Remarriage, 45,* 125–147.

Young, S. L. (2004). Factors that influence recipients' appraisals of hurtful communication. *Journal of Social and Personal Relationships, 21,* 291–303.

# PART V

# HURT IN APPLIED CONTEXTS

# 17

# The Physiology of Feeling Hurt

TIMOTHY J. LOVING, BENJAMIN LE, AND ERIN E. CROCKETT

For better or worse, the interdependency that defines close relationships grants one partner the ability to critically affect the other partner's outcomes. Perhaps nowhere are these double-edged effects better documented than in research on the link between close relationships and physical health or health-relevant physiological parameters; whereas satisfying intimate relationships procure a range of beneficial outcomes (e.g., Coan, Schaefer, & Davidson, 2006), they also have the ability to produce great harm (Robles & Kiecolt-Glaser, 2003). Without question, from the nasty remark to the unexpected breakup, intimate partners hold the power to hurt the feelings and subsequently the health outcomes of one another like few other individuals.

Interestingly, despite the prevalence of hurtful acts, writing a chapter on the physiological consequences of hurt feelings in close relationships presents unique challenges, given the surprising lack of empirical research that directly examines the link between feeling hurt and bodily responses. Ideally, we would review studies that deliberately incorporated stimuli-response designs such that physiological outcomes were assessed subsequent to hurtful acts (e.g., hormone responses when one partner belittles the other); however, few studies have been conducted with these explicit goals in mind. Fortunately, several lines of related research provide critical insight into why and how hurtful acts may "get under our skin." Specifically this chapter includes work assessing consequences of interpersonal dynamics and contexts that are conceptually similar to those producing hurt feelings that have been empirically linked to physiological parameters. Exploring these indirect links provides critical insights into the physiological outcomes associated with hurtful acts in close relationships and suggests specific biological pathways and associated health ramifications for individuals who have been hurt.

OVERVIEW

We begin the chapter by briefly reviewing what is meant by "feeling hurt" in close relationships. Next, we turn our attention to two specific forms of hurtful acts that range from active to passive. For *active hurt*, we focus on the physiological and health effects of emotional abuse. Subsequently, we review the marital interaction literature, with particular attention to the demand/withdraw interaction pattern and suggest that part of the reason the *passive act* of withdrawal leads to physiological consequences is because it is hurtful. This argument is bolstered by a brief review of research on rejection and ostracism, or "social hurt," and how this phenomenon results in endocrine, immunological, and neurophysiologic outcomes. Finally, we close with suggestions and ideas for future work. Although our focus is on how feeling hurt affects physiological outcomes, we do not dedicate significant space to reviewing the underlying biology of these physiological indices. Rather, we direct interested readers to a number of summaries of how the body's systems function and interact (Lovallo, 2005; Loving, Heffner, & Kiecolt-Glaser, 2006; Rabin, 1999). That said, we do discuss the potential health ramifications of specific indicators as warranted.

## WHAT IS "HURTFUL" BEHAVIOR?

Hurt refers to "a feeling that occurs as a result of a person being emotionally injured by another" (Vangelisti, Young, Carpenter-Theune, & Alexander, 2005, p. 446) and is tied to interpersonal causes or consequences of the interaction between two people (Vangelisti, 1994). Critical to this conceptualization of hurt is the notion that being hurt involves feelings of relational devaluation or rejection (Leary, Springer, Negel, Ansell, & Evans, 1998) that was caused by something somebody did or said (Vangelisti, 1994). For example, Vangelisti and colleagues (2005) noted that rejection was one of the two most frequently cited types of events that evoked hurt feelings (based on retrospective reports; betrayal was the other most-cited event). Leary and colleagues found that hurt feelings were preceded by events associated with the devaluation of the relationship and that the intensity of the reaction was directly related to feelings of rejection, which create the impression that the other desires to "disassociate from the individual by avoiding, excluding, or otherwise minimizing their interactions with him or her" (Leary et al., 1998, p. 1225).

Taken together, this conceptualization of hurt implies that acts carried out (or perceived to have been carried out) against another that devalue, push away, or otherwise limit interaction with another are perceived as hurtful. We believe there to be at least two forms of such devaluation, with each form occupying extremes of an active–passive continuum. On the active end of the continuum are those situations in which an individual is outwardly abusive toward another; situations whereby one individual withdraws from another reflect the passive end of the continuum. Although these actions manifest themselves very differently in overt behavior, available evidence suggests that each hurtful act is similar in its capability to profoundly influence physiological outcomes. We begin our review of physiological consequences of hurt by focusing on the active extreme form of relational devaluation – the undoubtedly hurtful relationship dynamic of emotional abuse.

### ACTIVE DEVALUATION: EMOTIONAL ABUSE

Emotional or psychological abuse is a complex construct that includes the occurrence of verbal abuse, misuse of power and control (e.g., threats), and humiliation (Arias, 1999; Coker et al., 2002). Although a number of studies have assessed both emotional abuse and physical health indicators, it is difficult to draw definitive conclusions regarding the physiological consequences of emotional abuse because it is highly comorbid with physical abuse, and researchers seldom distinguish between these two forms of abuse (Arias, 1999; Pimlott-Kubiak & Cortina, 2003; Sutherland, Bybee, & Sullivan, 2002). Furthermore, researchers have traditionally focused on physical abuse at the expense of emotional abuse because of the belief that physical abuse causes more harm (Arias, 1999). Mounting evidence suggests, however, that nonphysical abuse causes serious consequences above and beyond those of physical abuse (Arias & Pape, 1999; Coker et al., 2002; Spertus, Yehuda, Wong, Halligan, & Seremetis, 2003). That is, being "hurt" by emotional abuse has distinct physiological consequences from those stemming from physical violence.

### Health Consequences of Emotional Abuse

Emotional abuse is predictive of outcomes that are associated with physiological and health indicators, in addition to being directly related to specific physiological indicators themselves. For example, emotional abuse is predictive of lower self-esteem and is also associated with shame, depression, anxiety, and perceptions of helplessness (Arias, 1999; Coker et al., 2002; Spertus et al., 2003). Given the role that these various emotional and cognitive states play in physiological functioning and health (Dickerson, Kemeny, Aziz, Kim, & Fahey, 2004; Kiecolt-Glaser & Glaser, 2002; Lovallo & Thomas, 2000; Sanders, Iciek, & Kasprowicz, 2000; Wallston, 2001), it is not surprising that emotional abuse is also predictive of overall poorer health (Coker et al., 2002; Marshall, 1996; Spertus et al., 2003) and more frequent doctor visits (Marshall, 1996).

### Physiological Consequences of Emotional Abuse

Emotional abuse also has an impacts on physiological parameters, specifically those associated with immune functioning. This conclusion stems from reviewing research on the effects of posttraumatic stress disorder (PTSD). PTSD refers to the extreme stress experienced by individuals after undergoing particularly life-threatening or otherwise intense stressors (American Psychiatric Association, *Diagnostic and Statistical Manual of Mental Disorders*, 4th ed.,

1994). Several studies reveal an association between psychological abuse and PTSD, with this relationship holding even after controlling for levels of physical violence (Arias & Pape, 1999; Woods & Wineman, 2004; Woods et al., 2005). Importantly, PTSD and other forms of chronic stress are associated with a range of potentially detrimental immunological outcomes (Herbert & Cohen, 1993; Segerstrom & Miller, 2004). For example, males with PTSD demonstrate abnormally high leukocyte and T-cell counts compared to healthy individuals or individuals with other forms of mental illness (Boscarino & Chang, 1999). The results of these enumerative immune indices (Kiecolt-Glaser & Glaser, 1995), although not direct evidence of compromised immune function per se, do suggest that PTSD affects the normal functioning of the immune system. Leukocytes, which comprise the body's white blood cells, including T cells, are responsible for most of the body's immune responses such as antibody production and virus destruction (in the case of T cells). Results from studies of PTSD sufferers suggest an unregulated immune system, potentially increasing the likelihood of autoimmune and other disorders (Rogers & Brooks, 2001). Furthermore, given the prevalence of PTSD in victims of emotional abuse, it is likely that many of the negative health outcomes demonstrated by victims of psychological abuse result from compromised immune function (Woods et al., 2005).

Finally, there is evidence that emotional abuse is directly associated with weakened immune function. Woods and colleagues (2005) assessed the relationship among types of abuse, PTSD, and immune status in a sample of abused women compared to a subsample of matched controls. Emotional abuse was not only predictive of PTSD but also directly predicted decreased natural killer (NK) cell activity. These findings are notable because NK cells are implicated in a host of immune functions, including defense against cancers and viruses (Kiecolt-Glaser & Glaser, 1995).

Collectively, these studies provide evidence that emotional abuse, an extreme and active form of hurtful behavior in close relationships, is associated with physiological outcomes both directly (e.g., immune functioning) and indirectly (e.g., mediated by PTSD). Thus, the negative effects of emotional abuse are likely to be "felt," physiologically, by victims long after specific abusive acts have occurred.

## PASSIVE DEVALUATION: WITHDRAWAL

In 1983 Levenson and Gottman published data indicating that marital satisfaction diminished to the extent that spouses' physiological responses to a conflict discussion were "linked" (i.e., one spouse's physiological reactivity independently predicted the other's). In the decades subsequent to this seminal work, researchers have become intrigued by the processes in which characteristics of relationships, particularly marital interaction, contribute to changes in health-relevant physiological parameters (Ewart, Taylor, Kraemer, & Agras, 1991; Kiecolt-Glaser et al., 1993; Robles & Kiecolt-Glaser, 2003). Most work has used a problem-solving or conflict paradigm in which couple members are asked to resolve one or more areas of disagreement, with physiological indicators assessed before, during, and after the discussion (more recently, researchers have begun to assess interaction dynamics in nonconflict situations as well; Gonzaga, Turner, Keltner, Campos, & Altemus, 2006; Pasch, Bradbury, & Davila, 1997; Robles & Kiecolt-Glaser, 2003).

It is through these problem-solving studies that we can begin to gain insights into the ways that being hurt affects physiological responses. A number of negative or potentially hurtful behaviors, including criticizing, disagreeing, denying responsibility, interrupting, negative mind reading, and putting down the partner, are associated with an array of physiological outcomes. For example, negativity is predictive of increased blood pressure (Ewart et al., 1991), increased stress hormones (Kiecolt-Glaser et al., 1997; Malarkey, Kiecolt-Glaser, Pearl, & Glaser, 1994), decreased immune function (Kiecolt-Glaser et al., 1997), and delayed wound healing (Kiecolt-Glaser et al., 2005). In most of these studies, however, these discrete behaviors are combined into a general "negativity" behavioral code. As a result, the collapsed coding scheme makes it difficult to isolate effects resulting from more direct hurtful behaviors (e.g., putting down the partner) versus behaviors less clearly hurtful (e.g., interrupting). Fortunately, the demand/withdraw behavioral sequence has clear ramifications for understanding hurt feelings and is seldom aggregated with other coding categories.

The demand/withdraw communication pattern occurs when one couple member initiates a conversation about a problem in the relationship, subsequently causing the other person to avoid the issue by withdrawing from the conversation either emotionally (e.g., by not listening) or physically (e.g, by leaving the room). In other words, unlike emotional abuse, which involves actively inflicting hurt on another individual, withdrawal consists of not engaging with a relationship partner.

Our focus on behavioral withdrawal stems from three primary factors. First, as mentioned, most extant work considering physiological indicators tends to collapse several codes when creating a negative behavior index, making it difficult to provide definitive evidence of specific physiological consequences of specific hurtful behaviors. The demand/withdraw sequence, in contrast, is typically given attention as a unique behavior in dyadic interactions. Second, the concept of withdrawal has strong parallels in the social psychological and neuroendocrine literatures. Thus, although there is not a large amount of work that has assessed specific physiological consequences of withdrawal in marital interaction (with exceptions to be discussed shortly), we can extrapolate from related literatures and concepts to gain a better understanding of the psychological and physiological mechanisms that might be at play. Third, and perhaps most important, withdrawal is consistent with accepted definitions of what constitutes hurtful behaviors in intimate relationships. For example, Vangelisti and colleagues (2005), in their discussion of Leary et al.'s (1998) findings, note that "in some cases, perceptions of relational devaluation were obvious – individuals felt that the person who hurt them wanted to *avoid* [emphasis added] them or terminate their relationships" (p. 447). Consistent with this conceptualization, we suggest that the occurrence of withdrawal typically is hurtful because it (a) is easily perceived (Vangelisti, 1994) and (b) reflects a clear attempt at disassociation from the relationship or partner or both (Leary et al., 1998).

## Physiological Consequences of Withdrawal

Being withdrawn from negatively affects the cardiovascular system. For example, Denton and colleagues (Denton, Burleson, Hobbs, Von Stein, & Rodriguez, 2001) classified spouses as initiators (i.e., demand) or avoiders (i.e., withdraw) with respect to their general marital communication patterns. During a structured interview, spouses classified as avoiders (regardless of sex) demonstrated greater increases in systolic blood pressure (BP) than did initiators. Relevant to our discussion, husbands demonstrated greater diastolic and systolic BP when they interacted with an avoidant wife (versus an initiator wife), especially when the husband was classified as an initiator. Thus, being the victim of this form of hurt increases blood pressure, particularly for husbands. Importantly, a host of animal and human studies indicate that increased cardiovascular reactivity is associated with poor health outcomes (Blascovich & Katkin, 1993).

Being the target of withdrawal also affects endocrine outcomes for women. Kiecolt-Glaser and colleagues (1996) investigated physiological outcomes associated with interaction in 90 newlywed couples. Women whose husbands were more likely to withdraw had elevated cortisol, norepinephrine, and prolactin levels. Each of these hormones is stress-reactive and can dysregulate immune function (Rabin, 1999). For example, cortisol has multiple influences on immune function (Miller, 1998), including the trafficking of immune cells throughout the body and the ability of immune cells to kill antigen-infected cells, as well as the expression of latent viruses (Cacioppo et al., 2002), such as the Epstein-Barr virus responsible for mononucleosis.

Interestingly, it seems that withdrawal itself does not have to occur for physiological consequences to be present. In a study of 30 older couples, the wife demand/husband withdraw communication sequence during a conflict interaction was associated with increased cortisol responses in the wives (Heffner et al., 2006). But, when compared, spouses' *perceptions* of typical wife demand/husband withdraw patterns were predictive of increased cortisol responses, while actual demand/withdraw behavior was unrelated to cortisol reactivity. These findings provide preliminary evidence of a conditioning effect of being hurt and indicate that simply the expectation of rejection/withdrawal might be enough to create hurt feelings (and physiological consequences).

Collectively, these studies suggest that being the recipient of withdrawal or having one romantic partner reject another during a discussion has cardiovascular and hormonal implications (and likely concomitant immune effects as well). Why might this be the case? In other words, what is it about withdrawal that causes these physiological outcomes? We believe that, given its similarities with being withdrawn from, examining the mechanisms involved in social rejection may prove to be informative in building an understanding of the links between withdrawal-associated hurt and physiology.

## WHAT MAKES WITHDRAWAL-ASSOCIATED DEVALUATION HURTFUL?

One possible reason why withdrawal hurts is that it may serve as an indicator of social rejection or the phenomenologically similar construct of ostracism.[1] Ostracism, or being ignored or excluded by an individual or group (Williams, 2001), is an especially powerful experience because it violates the fundamental human need to belong (Baumeister & Leary, 1995). Social relationships are among the most pressing of all human goals, and from this perspective the motivation to form and maintain relationships is the objective behind many social behaviors. Importantly, studies of social ostracism among primates indicate that the hypothalamic, pituitary, adrenal, serotonin, and catecholamine systems may be engaged as a result of social rejection (see review by McGuire & Raleigh, 1986), although evidence for these effects with humans is not as clear.

We suggest that the ostracism and social rejection literature offers insight into how withdrawal during interactions results in physiological outcomes. One partner pulling away, particularly during a problem-solving discussion, serves as a sign that a partner is not willing to give the relationship the attention necessary to keep it functioning smoothly. Because of the crucial role that our close relationships play in terms of our identity (Aron & Aron, 1997; Baumeister & Leary, 1995), withdrawal during a conversation likely leads to a devaluation of the self and serves as a blatant indicator of separation (i.e., not belonging and a loss of self-worth). In other words, the act of withdrawing from another may induce physiological outcomes via the clear indication of social rejection, which is associated with physiological outcomes through at least two routes: (a) shared pathways with the physical pain system and (b) threats to the social self.

---

[1] Although there is a great deal of overlap between these constructs, they have often been examined separately in the literature. We treat them similarly here, given our goal of building a cohesive framework for understanding hurt feelings within demand/withdraw interactions as we draw from the few studies in these literatures that examine the physiological correlates of these similar concepts.

## Withdrawal and Social/Physical Pain

One reason dyadic social rejection, or withdrawal, might result in physiological outcomes is because it activates a "social pain" system within the body. Social pain refers to "a specific emotional reaction to the perception that one is being excluded from desired relationships or being devalued by desired relationship partners or groups" (MacDonald & Leary, 2005, p. 202). Pain overlap theory (Eisenberger & Lieberman, 2004, 2005; Lieberman & Eisenberger, 2006) proposes that this shared system reacts similarly to social loss or relationship threat as it does to physical injury and that the system serves the adaptive function of motivating the organism to remove itself from, or rectify, the situation that is causing the pain.

As previously noted, we suggest that, as one partner pulls away, the other is sensitive to the psychological distance being created within the dyad and the clear threat to the relationship. The discrepancy between the desired state (i.e., closeness) and current state (i.e., distance) should trigger the pain system (Eisenberger & Lieberman, 2004, 2005), resulting in the experience of negative affect by the partner being withdrawn from. Not surprisingly, just as physical pain promotes efforts to remove the self from the source of the painful stimuli, individuals attempt to remove or distance themselves from partners who show signs of rejecting the self or not valuing the relationship (Murray, Holmes, MacDonald, & Ellsworth, 1998). Indeed, the demand/withdraw pattern is associated with a range of deleterious relationship outcomes, including divorce (Christensen & Shenk, 1991) and decline in marital satisfaction (Gottman & Krokoff, 1989; Heavey, Christensen, & Malamuth, 1995).

Given the parallels between social and physical pain experiences, it is not surprising to find that the mechanisms underlying these experiences are shared (see DeWall, Baumeister, and Masicampo, Chapter 7, in this volume). The social and physical pain systems share specific neural structures such as the anterior cingulated cortex (ACC) and periaqueductal gray (PAG), as well as the opioid and oxytocin systems (see review by MacDonald & Leary, 2005). In particular, the dorsal anterior cingulate cortex (dACC) plays a central role in the experience of physical and social pain. For example, using fMRI imaging, Eisenberger and colleagues (2003) showed activation of the dACC when participants experienced an ostracism manipulation (i.e., being left out of an interactive computer game). Furthermore, the right ventral prefrontal cortex (RVPFC) was also active (and associated with reduced negative affectivity) and might serve to disrupt dACC activity, thus regulating the negative affect associated with social exclusion. In a sense, the dACC functions as a "neural alarm system" (Eisenberger & Lieberman, 2005) that is activated when goals are thwarted or unexpected events arise. Given that withdrawal tends to occur in response to one partner's attempts to achieve some resolution or discussion on a specific relationship topic, we would expect dACC activation in response to partner withdrawal behaviors as well.

Furthermore, the sensitivity of the dACC system may depend on individual differences, with those high in neuroticism having more sensitive systems. Experimental manipulations involving violations of expectancies (e.g., Stroop tasks) have been shown to make neurotics more reactive to social rejection, which corresponds to dACC activity (Eisenberger & Lieberman, 2005; Eisenberger, Lieberman, & Satpute, 2005). For example, after a Stroop task, individuals high in neuroticism demonstrated delayed reaction times to a lexical decision task involving words related to social rejection. These data indicate that unexpected events may make neurotic individuals particularly sensitive to issues regarding interpersonal abandonment (Eisenberger & Lieberman, 2005).

Importantly, neuroticism is also associated with an increased use of the demand/withdraw interaction sequence (Caughlin & Vangelisti, 2000). Therefore, we would expect to see a link between being the recipient of withdrawal and reports of pain. Work in the adult attachment literature suggests such a connection. Specifically, attachment anxiety, which is significantly associated with neuroticism (Shaver, 2006), is characterized by a concern for enhancing closeness with another coupled with a fear of abandonment. In one of nature's cruel twists, anxious individuals often find themselves involved with avoidant partners (Kirkpatrick & Davis, 1994), who are particularly likely to withdraw from these attempts at intimacy (i.e., demand/withdraw). Not surprisingly, given the nature of their relationships, individuals high in attachment anxiety report higher levels of physical pain (MacDonald & Kingsbury, 2006).

Altogether, this rejection–neurocognitive work provides reason to believe that the hurtful behavior of withdrawal during discussion likely elicits neurocognitive outcomes as well. Although much of what we suggest is highly speculative, we believe the application is theoretically consistent with research on social pain and offers potential insights into one possible mechanism for why being the target of withdrawal is hurtful. A second potential explanation arises from work on threats to the social self.

## Withdrawal and Threats to the Social Self

Relational devaluation also serves as one form of a "social self" threat (Dickerson, Gruenewald, & Kemeny, 2004). As noted, there seems to be clear evidence that withdrawal is associated with increased cortisol activity. Interestingly, in their seminal meta-analysis of cortisol responses to laboratory-based tasks, Dickerson and Kemeny (2004) found that threats to the social self are most likely to elicit hypothalamic-pituitary-adrenal axis activity (HPA; e.g., cortisol responses). Cortisol responses were particularly strong when individuals were in situations where the outcome of their performance was uncontrollable.

Conversations between coupled partners are by definition interdependent, creating a situation in which one partner has some degree of control over the other partner's outcomes (Kelley & Thibaut, 1978; Rusbult & Arriaga, 1997).

Thus, the withdrawal of one partner creates a lack of control, because it dictates the course of the interaction. As such, we would expect that HPA axis activity is greater to the degree that an individual lacks control (or perceives that he or she lacks control) over the outcome of the discussion. Indeed, there is evidence to support this hypothesis. In a sample of 72 newlywed couples, less powerful spouses (as indicated by relative levels of emotional involvement in the marriage) displayed elevated adrenocorticotropic hormone (ACTH) responses to a conflict discussion (Loving, Heffner, Kiecolt-Glaser, Glaser, & Malarkey, 2004). ACTH, one of the hormones comprising the HPA axis, is released by the pituitary gland and stimulates the adrenal gland to release cortisol. In this study, spouses' cortisol levels declined over time, except for wives who were less powerful and for husbands who shared power with their wives. The consistent evidence of cortisol reactivity to hurtful situations (i.e., withdraw, rejection) is noteworthy because, as noted earlier, cortisol can dysregulate immune function (Elenkov, Webster, Torpy, & Chrousos, 1999).

In line with these associations, threats to the social self are associated with proinflammatory cytokine production (Dickerson, Kemeny et al., 2004). Dickerson and colleagues manipulated self-blame and found that participants in an experimental group showed increases in shame and guilt, and those individuals reporting the greatest increases in shame also displayed the greatest increases in proinflammatory cytokine activity. Importantly, shame is believed to be a self-related emotion (Dickerson, Kemeny et al., 2004) that arises when an individual feels flawed or inferior. Thus, the feeling of rejection that accompanies perceptions of one's partner withdrawing from an interaction likely leads to additional immunological correlates via feelings of shame (Dickerson, Gruenewald et al., 2004). These findings are consistent with the social pain literature because proinflammatory responses should present themselves in reaction to tissue damage (i.e., actual physical pain; Glaser et al., 1999).

## Summary

Overall, it is likely that feeling hurt causes physiological outcomes; however, this claim would be bolstered by studies designed to deliberately assess the physical outcomes associated with agreed-on operationalizations of feeling hurt. We began by discussing the link between emotional abuse (what we suggest is an active form of hurt) and physical outcomes (direct and indirect); it is clear that living with an emotionally abusive partner is a risk factor for long-term poor health. The demand/withdraw sequence, an interaction dynamic not restricted to abusive relationships, is also foretelling of short-term (e.g., endocrine responses) and long-term (e.g., compromised immune function) physiological consequences, with the act of withdrawal (a passive form of hurt) being the principal culprit. Given the clear overlap between the conceptualization of this interaction sequence and operationalizations of hurt feelings, we believe scrutiny of this interaction pattern is particularly useful. We suggest that the reasons why withdrawal is hurtful come from examination of the social rejection literatures, with particular focus on the concepts of social pain and threats to the social self. These lines of inquiry suggest that withdrawal leads to neurological, endocrine, and immunological outcomes; however, there is still much to know and we believe our current knowledge is limited by (a) a lack of focus on cognitive and neurological mechanisms that underpin common hurtful intimate relationship dynamics (e.g., withdrawal) and (b) methodological practices that minimize our ability to draw definitive conclusions.

## SUGGESTIONS FOR FUTURE RESEARCH

As we noted in the previous section on social pain and reactions to social threat, the application of basic social psychological findings to complex interactions between couple members will likely provide valuable insights into the mechanisms that create hurt feelings. We believe a more holistic picture will be created by further work of this type. It would be useful to assess feelings of shame, for example, before and after couples discuss problem areas in their relationships. In addition, given the great advances in fMRI technology, we imagine it is only a matter of time before couples members are asked to carry on or reflect on a disagreement with their partner while undergoing an MRI (conceptually similar experiments now define the field of neuroeconomics). For example, does recalling a specific instance of a partner's withdrawal from the self lead to activation of the dACC? These approaches will certainly contribute volumes to our understanding of both how and why being hurt affect the body's cardiovascular, neuroendocrine, immune, and neurological systems.

Additionally, we encourage researchers to pay careful attention to how they define their constructs. For example, in the abuse literature, it is far too common to combine emotional and physical abuse; as a result, we are limited in our ability to draw definitive conclusions about which type of abuse results in specific health and physiological outcomes. Although great strides are beginning to be made in this regard, more attention is necessary.

Similarly, it is common for researchers to collapse several negative interaction behaviors into a single index of negativity. As a result, it is not feasible to examine the effects of specific acts (that may be more or less hurtful) on physiological parameters during couple interactions. Even if behaviors were not collapsed, the low base rate of many behaviors in "micro" coding systems would make it difficult to assess independent effects (see Heyman, 2001, for a review). A more precise behavioral coding system designed with conceptualizations of *hurt* in mind would allow for a more fine-grained assessment of consequences of specific behavioral sequences, whether it is by severity or other features (e.g., level of hurtfulness). For example, although not specifically designed to aid researchers interested in studying hurtful acts, the Rapid Martial Interaction Coding System (RMICS; Heyman, 2004) might prove particularly useful for this line of inquiry. The RMICS was developed in response to the issues noted earlier (and others) but maintains several coding categories directly relevant to feeling hurt, including verbal and nonverbal psychological abuse and withdrawal. In short, researchers interested in studying hurtful acts during couple interactions should attend carefully to the coding system employed to maximize their capabilities of conducting the necessary analyses to test their hypotheses.

Furthermore, we believe the physiological consequences of extreme forms of hurt, or emotional abuse, are worthy of significantly more empirical attention. We have provided indirect evidence that, not surprisingly, emotional abuse is predictive of a host of negative physical outcomes. However, these studies are often retrospective in nature, and their designs make it difficult to separate out potentially confounding variables. That said, conducting controlled stimulus-response investigations of emotional abuse are not possible given the ethical ramifications. One way to more succinctly isolate effects of hurtful acts would be to make use of daily diary methods; both the behaviors that comprise hurtful acts and physiological indicators (e.g., cortisol) are amenable to daily assessment. The hurtful acts recorded and subsequent feelings will vary in their degree of hurt, making it possible to gauge the level of day-to-day covariation of specific acts with acute and chronic physiological responses and to extrapolate to more extreme emotionally abusive relationships.

Finally, research that more explicitly ties together neural functioning (e.g., the dACC) with reactions in ongoing relationships may provide insight into the mechanisms involved in social pain, rejection, and hurt feelings. For example, whereas past studies have used cognitive or perceptual manipulations of expectancy violations, examining the effects of naturally occurring or primed interpersonal violations on hurt feelings would represent an exciting interface of physiological research within the context of interpersonal dynamics. In particular, this work should consider both the characteristics of relationships (e.g., interdependence) and of the individuals (e.g., attachment and neuroticism), because independently and together they may influence the extent to which relationship partners are reactive to withdrawal.

## CONCLUSIONS

Although to date there has been very little work that explicitly examines the physiological responses of individuals who have had their feelings hurt, reasonable inferences about the processes and mechanisms involved can be made based on related literatures. Specifically, research on the physiology of emotional abuse and demand/withdrawal behavioral sequences provides strong theoretical foundations that hint at the exciting possibilities that work on the physiology of hurt feelings may hold for the future. In particular, studies employing neuroimaging and assessing neuroendocrine function have clearly demonstrated links between physiological responses and constructs that are likely associated with hurt feelings. Future research explicitly linking these outcomes to the interpersonal dynamics that cause hurt feelings will prove to be valuable in building a comprehensive framework underlying mechanisms involved in hurt feelings. In addition, research arising from these literatures will further our understanding of the direct links between hurt feelings and physical health. The sensitive nature of the subject, particularly the more extreme forms of hurt such as emotional abuse, makes this a difficult topic to study. However, recent advances in technology and methodological tools will likely continue to provide new opportunities for enhancing our understanding of how and why feeling hurt results in physical outcomes.

### REFERENCES

American Psychiatric Association. (1994). *Diagnostic and statistical manual of mental disorders* (4th ed.). Washington, DC: Author.

Arias, I. (1999). Women's response to physical and psychological abuse. In X. B. Arriaga & S. Oskamp (Eds.), *Violence in intimate relationships* (pp. 139–161). Thousand Oaks, CA: Sage.

Arias, I., & Pape, K. T. (1999). Psychological abuse: Implications for adjustment and commitment to leave violent partners. *Violence and Victims, 14,* 55–67.

Aron, A., & Aron, E. N. (1997). Self-expansion motivation and including other in the self. In S. Duck (Ed.), *Handbook of personal relationships* (2nd ed., pp. 251–270). Hoboken, NJ: Wiley.

Baumeister, R. F., & Leary, M. R. (1995). The need to belong: Desire for interpersonal attachments as a fundamental human motivation. *Psychological Bulletin, 117,* 497–529.

Blascovich, J., & Katkin, E. S. (1993). *Cardiovascular reactivity to psychological stress & disease.* Washington, DC: American Psychological Association.

Boscarino, J. A., & Chang, J. (1999). Higher abnormal leukocyte and lymphocyte counts 20 years after exposure to severe stress: Research and clinical implications. *Psychosomatic Medicine, 61,* 378–386.

Cacioppo, J. T., Kiecolt-Glaser, J. K., Malarkey, W. B., Laskowski, B. F., Rozlog, L. A., Poehlmann, K. M., et al. (2002). Autonomic and glucocorticoid associations with the steady-state expression of latent Epstein-Barr virus. *Hormones and Behavior, 42,* 32–41.

Caughlin, J. P., & Vangelisti, A. L. (2000). An individual difference explanation of why married couples engage in the demand/withdraw pattern of conflict. *Journal of Social and Personal Relationships, 17,* 523–551.

Christensen, A., & Shenk, J. L. (1991). Communication, conflict, and psychological distance in nondistressed, clinic, and divorcing couples. *Journal of Consulting and Clinical Psychology, 59,* 458–463.

Coan, J. A., Schaefer, H. S., & Davidson, R. J. (2006). Lending a hand: Social regulation of the neural response to threat. *Psychological Science, 17,* 1032–1039.

Coker, A. L., Davis, K. E., Arias, I., Desai, S., Sanderson, M., Brandt, H. M., et al. (2002). Physical and mental health effects of intimate partner violence for men and women. *American Journal of Preventive Medicine, 23*, 260–268.

Denton, W. H., Burleson, B. R., Hobbs, B. V., Von Stein, M., & Rodriguez, C. P. (2001). Cardiovascular reactivity and initiate/avoid patterns of marital communication: A test of Gottman's psychophysiologic model of marital interaction. *Journal of Behavioral Medicine, 24*, 401–421.

Dickerson, S. S., Gruenewald, T. L., & Kemeny, M. E. (2004). When the social self is threatened: Shame, physiology, and health. *Journal of Personality, 72*, 1191–1216.

Dickerson, S. S., & Kemeny, M. E. (2004). Acute stressors and cortisol responses: A theoretical integration and synthesis of laboratory research. *Psychological Bulletin, 130*, 355–391.

Dickerson, S. S., Kemeny, M. E., Aziz, N., Kim, K. H., & Fahey, J. L. (2004). Immunological effects of induced shame and guilt. *Psychosomatic Medicine, 66*, 124–131.

Eisenberger, N. I., & Lieberman, M. D. (2004). Why rejection hurts: A common neural alarm system for physical and social pain. *Trends in Cognitive Sciences, 8*, 294–300.

Eisenberger, N. I., & Lieberman, M. D. (2005). Why it hurts to be left out: The neurocognitive overlap between physical and social pain. In K. D. Williams, J. P. Forgas, & W. von Hippel (Eds.), *The social outcast: Ostracism, social exclusion, rejection, and bullying* (pp. 109–127). New York: Psychology Press.

Eisenberger, N. I., Lieberman, M. D., & Satpute, A. B. (2005). Personality from a controlled processing perspective: An fMRI study of neuroticism, extraversion, and self-consciousness. *Cognitive, Affective, & Behavioral Neuroscience, 5*, 169–181.

Eisenberger, N. I., Lieberman, M. D., & Williams, K. D. (2003). Does rejection hurt? An fMRI study of social exclusion. *Science, 302*, 290–292.

Elenkov, I. J., Webster, E. L., Torpy, D. J., & Chrousos, G. P. (1999). Stress, corticotropin-releasing hormone, glucocorticoids, and the immune/inflammatory response: Acute and chronic effects. In M. Cutolo & A. T. Masi (Eds.), *Neuroendocrine immune basis of the rheumatic diseases* (Vol. 876, pp. 1–13). New York: New York Academy of Sciences.

Ewart, C. K., Taylor, C. B., Kraemer, H. C., & Agras, W. S. (1991). High blood pressure and marital discord: Not being nasty matters more than being nice. *Health Psychology, 10*, 155–163.

Glaser, R., Kiecolt-Glaser, J. K., Marucha, P. T., MacCallum, R. C., Laskowski, B. F., & Malarkey, W. B. (1999). Stress-related changes in proinflammatory cytokine production in wounds. *Archives of General Psychiatry, 56*, 450–456.

Gonzaga, G. C., Turner, R. A., Keltner, D., Campos, B., & Altemus, M. (2006). Romantic love and sexual desire in close relationships. *Emotion, 6*, 163–179.

Gottman, J. M., & Krokoff, L. J. (1989). Marital interaction and satisfaction: A longitudinal view. *Journal of Consulting and Clinical Psychology, 57*, 47–52.

Heavey, C. L., Christensen, A., & Malamuth, N. M. (1995). The longitudinal impact of demand and withdrawal during marital conflict. *Journal of Counsulting and Clinical Psychology, 63*, 797–801.

Heffner, K. L., Loving, T. J., Kiecolt-Glaser, J. K., Himawan, L. K., Glaser, R., & Malarkey, W. B. (2006). Older spouses' cortisol responses to marital conflict: Associations with demand-withdraw communication patterns. *Journal of Behavioral Medicine, 29*, 317–325.

Herbert, T. B., & Cohen, S. (1993). Depression and immunity: A meta-analytic review. *Psychological Bulletin, 113*, 472–486.

Heyman, R. E. (2001). Observation of couple conflicts: Clinical assessment applications, stubborn truths, and shaky foundations. *Psychological Assessment, 13*, 5–35.

Heyman, R. E. (2004). Rapid Marital Interaction Coding System. In P. K. Kerig & D. H. Baucom (Eds.), *Couple observational coding systems* (pp. 67–94). Mahwah, NJ: Erlbaum.

Kelley, H. H., & Thibaut, J. W. (1978). *Interpersonal relations: A theory of interdependence.* New York: Wiley.

Kiecolt-Glaser, J. K., & Glaser, R. (1995). Measurement of immune response. In S. Cohen, R. Kessler, & L. G. Gordon (Eds.), *Measuring stress* (pp. 213–229). New York: Oxford University Press.

Kiecolt-Glaser, J. K., & Glaser, R. (2002). Depression and immune function: Central pathways to morbidity and mortality. *Journal of Psychosomatic Research, 53,* 873–876.

Kiecolt-Glaser, J. K., Glaser, R., Cacioppo, J. T., MacCallum, R. C., Snydersmith, M., Kim, C., et al. (1997). Marital conflict in older adults: Endocrinological and immunological correlates. *Psychosomatic Medicine, 59,* 339–349.

Kiecolt-Glaser, J. K., Loving, T. J., Stowell, J. R., Malarkey, W. B., Lemeshow, S., Dickinson, S., et al. (2005). Hostile marital interactions, proinflammatory cytokine production, and wound healing. *Archives of General Psychiatry, 62,* 1377–1384.

Kiecolt-Glaser, J. K., Malarkey, W. B., Chee, M., Newton, T., Cacioppo, J. T., Mao, H., et al. (1993). Negative behavior during marital conflict is associated with immunological down-regulation. *Psychosomatic Medicine, 55,* 395–409.

Kiecolt-Glaser, J. K., Newton, T., Cacioppo, J. T., MacCallum, R. C., Glaser, R., & Malarkey, W. B. (1996). Marital conflict and endocrine function: Are men really more physiologically affected than women? *Journal of Consulting and Clinical Psychology, 64,* 324–332.

Kirkpatrick, L. A., & Davis, K. E. (1994). Attachment style, gender, and relationship stability: A longitudinal analysis. *Journal of Personality and Social Psychology, 66,* 502–512.

Leary, M. R., Springer, C., Negel, L., Ansell, E., & Evans, K. (1998). The causes, phenomenology, and consequences of hurt feelings. *Journal of Personality and Social Psychology, 74,* 1225–1237.

Levenson, R. W., & Gottman, J. M. (1983). Marital interaction: Physiological linkage and affective exchange. *Journal of Personality and Social Psychology, 45,* 587–597.

Lieberman, M. D., & Eisenberger, N. I. (2006). A pain by any other name (rejection, exclusion, ostracism) still hurts the same: The role of dorsal anterior cingulate cortex in social and physical pain. In J. T. Cacioppo, P. S. Visser, & C. L. Pickett (Eds.), *Social neuroscience: People thinking about thinking people* (pp. 167–187). Cambridge, MA: MIT Press.

Lovallo, W. R. (2005). *Stress & health: Biological and psychological interactions* (2nd ed.). Thousand Oaks, CA: Sage.

Lovallo, W. R., & Thomas, T. L. (2000). Stress hormones in psychophysiological research: Emotional, behavioral, and cognitive implications. In J. T. Cacioppo, L. G. Tassinary, & G. G. Berntson (Eds.), *Handbook of psychophysiology* (2nd ed., pp. 342–367). New York: Cambridge University Press.

Loving, T. J., Heffner, K. L., & Kiecolt-Glaser, J. K. (2006). Physiology and interpersonal relationships. In A. L. Vangelisti & D. Perlman (Eds.), *Cambridge handbook of personal relationships* (pp. 385–405). New York: Cambridge University Press.

Loving, T. J., Heffner, K. L., Kiecolt-Glaser, J. K., Glaser, R., & Malarkey, W. B. (2004). Stress hormone changes and marital conflict: Spouses' relative power makes a difference. *Journal of Marriage and Family, 66,* 595–612.

MacDonald, G., & Kingsbury, R. (2006). Does physical pain augment anxious attachment? *Journal of Social and Personal Relationships, 23,* 291–304.

MacDonald, G., & Leary, M. R. (2005). Why does social exclusion hurt? The relationship between social and physical pain. *Psychological Bulletin, 131,* 202–223.

Malarkey, W., Kiecolt-Glaser, J. K., Pearl, D., & Glaser, R. (1994). Hostile behavior during marital conflict alters pituitary and adrenal hormones. *Psychosomatic Medicine, 56,* 41–51.

Marshall, L. L. (1996). Psychological abuse of women: Six distinct clusters. *Journal of Family Violence, 11,* 379–409.

McGuire, M. T., & Raleigh, M. J. (1986). Behavioral and physiological correlates of ostracism. *Ethology and Sociobiology, 7,* 187–200.

Miller, A. H. (1998). Neuroendocrine and immune system interactions in stress and depression. *Psychiatric Clinics of North America, 21,* 443–463.

Murray, S. L., Holmes, J. G., MacDonald, G., & Ellsworth, P. C. (1998). Through the looking glass darkly? When self-doubts turn into relationship insecurities. *Journal of Personality and Social Psychology, 75,* 1459–1480.

Pasch, L. A., Bradbury, T. N., & Davila, J. (1997). Gender, negative affectivity, and observed social support behavior in marital interaction. *Personal Relationships, 4,* 361–378.

Pimlott-Kubiak, S., & Cortina, L. M. (2003). Gender, victimization, and outcomes: Reconceptualizing risk. *Journal of Consulting and Clinical Psychology, 71,* 528–539.

Rabin, B. S. (1999). *Stress, immune function, and health: The connection.* New York: Wiley-Liss.

Robles, T. F., & Kiecolt-Glaser, J. K. (2003). The physiology of marriage: Pathways to health. *Physiology and Behavior, 79,* 409–416.

Rogers, M. P., & Brooks, E. B. (2001). Psychosocial influences, immune function, and the progression of autoimmune disease. In R. Ader, D. L. Felten, & N. Cohen (Eds.), *Psychoneuroimmunology* (3rd ed., Vol. 2, pp. 399–419). San Diego: Academic Press.

Rusbult, C. E., & Arriaga, X. B. (1997). Interdependence theory. In S. Duck (Ed.), *Handbook of personal relationships: Theory, research and interventions* (2nd ed., pp. 221–250). Hoboken, NJ: Wiley.

Sanders, V. M., Iciek, L., & Kasprowicz, D. J. (2000). Psychosocial factors and humoral immunity. In J. T. Cacioppo, L. G. Tassinary, & G. G. Berntson (Eds.), *Handbook of psychophysiology* (2nd ed., pp. 425–455). New York: Cambridge University Press.

Segerstrom, S. C., & Miller, G. E. (2004). Psychological stress and the human immune system: A meta-analytic study of 30 years of inquiry. *Psychological Bulletin, 130,* 601–630.

Shaver, P. R. (2006). The dynamics of romantic love: Comments, questions, and future directions. In M. Mikulincer & G. S. Goodman (Eds.), *Dynamics of romantic love: Attachment, caregiving, and sex* (pp. 423–456). New York: Guilford.

Spertus, I. L., Yehuda, R., Wong, C. M., Halligan, S., & Seremetis, S. V. (2003). Childhood emotional abuse and neglect as predictors of psychological and physical symptoms in women presenting to a primary care practice. *Child Abuse and Neglect, 27,* 1247–1258.

Sutherland, C. A., Bybee, D. I., & Sullivan, C. M. (2002). Beyond bruises and broken bones: The joint effects of stress and injuries on battered women's health. *American Journal of Community Psychology, 30,* 609–636.

Vangelisti, A. L. (1994). Messages that hurt. In W. R. Cupach & B. H. Spitzberg (Eds.), *Dark side of interpersonal communication* (pp. 53–82). Hillsdale, NJ: Erlbaum.

Vangelisti, A. L., Young, S. L., Carpenter-Theune, K. E., & Alexander, A. L. (2005). Why does it hurt?: The perceived causes of hurt feelings. *Communication Research, 32,* 443–477.

Wallston, K. A. (2001). Conceptualization and operationalization of perceived control. In A. Baum, T. A. Revenson, & J. E. Singer (Eds.), *Handbook of health psychology* (pp. 49–58). Mahwah, NJ: Erlbaum.
Williams, K. D. (2001). *Ostracism: The power of silence.* New York: Guilford.
Woods, S. J., & Wineman, N. M. (2004). Trauma, posttraumatic stress disorder symptom clusters, and physical health symptoms in postabused women. *Archives of Psychiatric Nursing, 18,* 26–34.
Woods, S. J., Wineman, N. M., Page, G. G., Hall, R. J., Alexander, T. S., & Campbell, J. C. (2005). Predicting immune status in women from PTSD and childhood and adult violence. *Advances in Nursing Science, 28,* 306–319.

# 18

# Hurt and Psychological Health in Close Relationships

SCOTT R. BRAITHWAITE, FRANK D. FINCHAM,
AND NATHANIEL M. LAMBERT

> Where there is love, there is pain.
> – Spanish proverb

Experiencing hurt is an inevitable part of being in a close relationship. The depth of feeling and emotion that come from loving another brings with it in equal measure the potential for pain and anguish. This conundrum is arguably the most frequently explored theme in art, literature, and religious thought. Despite the pain that inexorably follows love, the vast majority of individuals in Western culture continue to invest themselves in love, marriage, and family (Gallup, 2006). The happiness associated with loving relationships such as marriage is substantial and is well documented in psychological research. However, the hurt associated with love is also substantial, and its sequelae have also been documented. This hurt born of love often goes beyond temporary feelings of sadness or disappointment and is linked to psychological distress.

The first section of the chapter examines the relationship between experiencing hurt in close relationships and mental health. We discuss experienced hurt in relation to chronic and discrete transgressions and provide prototypes to illustrate how reactions to each type of event may be related to psychological health. In the second section, we propose a conceptual model in which forgiveness mediates the relationship between hurtful events and mental health. We also explore some potential moderators that may influence the forgiveness process. Finally, we make suggestions for future research.

## CLOSE RELATIONSHIPS AND MENTAL HEALTH: THE BEST OF TIMES ... THE WORST OF TIMES

Close relationships are a blessing and a burden when it comes to mental health and well-being. Marital status is one of the most powerful demographic predictors of mental health. Empirical research consistently shows that married individuals enjoy better mental health than persons in all other types of close relationships (e.g., dating and cohabiting relationships). In fact marital status is a better predictor of mental health than other key demographic factors such as socioeconomic status, level of education, age, ethnicity, or childhood background (e.g., Gove, Hughes, & Style, 1983). In comparison to their unmarried counterparts, married individuals experience less depression (Beach, Fincham, & Katz, 1998) and more happiness and general mental well-being (for a review see Waite & Gallagher, 2000). Recently, Simon (2002) using longitudinal data from a large nationally representative sample showed that the transition to marriage is associated with increases in mental health and that transitions out of marriage are associated with declines in mental health. In sum, across clinical and nonclinical samples and across a wide range of variables and indices of mental health, the well-being associated with marital status is well documented (Gotlib & McCabe, 1990).

This conclusion, however, needs to be interpreted in the light of two observations. First, many studies confuse the ideas of happiness/satisfaction with mental health, and it therefore behooves us to distinguish between them. Second, although initial studies on the link between marital status and mental health looked mostly at demographic factors, research has moved beyond simply looking at marital status and has found that the quality of relationships moderates the association between marital status and mental health. Specifically, individuals in supportive, satisfying relationships are most likely to experience mental health benefits, whereas those in low-quality, conflictual relationships are less likely to experience the beneficial effects of close relationships and are, in some instances, at increased risk for mental health problems. Thus, problematic relationships with spouses are among the most powerful predictors of personal distress (Dohrenwend, Krasnoff, Askenasy, & Dohrenwend, 1978), and recent longitudinal data provide evidence for the well-established association between marital discord and the onset of clinical levels of psychopathology (Overbeek et al., 2006). Several studies document an association between marital distress and psychopathology across various inpatient and outpatient populations (e.g., Bauserman, Arias, & Craighead, 1995; Coyne, Thompson, & Palmer, 2002) and with specific disorders, including depression (e.g., Horwitz, McLaughlin, & White, 1998; Whisman & Bruce, 1999), mood disorders (e.g., Bauserman et al., 1995), anxiety disorders (Chambless et al., 2002), and substance use disorders (e.g., Fals-Stewart, Birchler, & O'Farrell, 1999; O'Farrell & Birchler, 1987). Thus, the hurt that can be experienced in marriage and other close relationships is significant and can exert significant influence on the mental health of those involved (Whisman & Uebelacker, 2006).

### HURT IN CLOSE RELATIONSHIPS: HURT IS NOT HURT IS NOT HURT

One of the difficulties in trying to understand the association between hurt experienced in relationships and mental health arises from the complex nature of "hurt" in close relationships. Hurt in close relationships can appear in many different forms and degrees, ranging from what might be considered small offenses such as a thoughtless criticism to more serious offenses such as infidelity or abuse. Leary, Springer, Negel, Ansell, and Evans (1998) suggest that the common theme of all hurtful experiences within close relationships is relational devaluation. In intimate relationships, the victim often feels that the transgressor does not regard the relationship as important, close, or valuable as a result of the transgression. Note the dual referent implicit in this idea: Hurt refers both to a characteristic of experience and to a feature of events, and consequent inferences about relationship devaluation are likely a function of both elements. Whatever the precise referent, the degree and impact of hurt experienced can be moderated by a panoply of different factors such as the victim's attributions (Leary et al., 1998), degree of familiarity with the transgressor (Snapp & Leary, 2001), and the relational history between partners (Overbeek et al., 2006). Therefore, operationalizing hurt in a way that captures its inherent complexity (as a potential emotion, characteristic of an event, and inference about the relationship) is difficult. Researchers have approached this problem from different perspectives using studies ranging from teasing (Kowalski, 2000), to being excluded (MacDonald & Leary, 2005), to infidelity (Hall & Fincham, 2006). Despite the manifest variability, however, researchers have implicitly tended to focus on hurt as a feature of events.

What mechanism mediates the relationship between hurt experienced in relationships and psychopathology? The assumption found in most studies is that personal vulnerabilities (diatheses), in combination with the stress associated with marital problems, leads to the onset of psychopathology. In other words a *diathesis–stress* model is assumed. Recognition of this assumption is helpful in understanding experienced hurt in that it ceases to be the sole property of individuals or events but is rather a function both of the individual (specifically his or her vulnerabilities) and the stressors (potentially hurtful events) to which he or she is exposed. A useful way of conceptualizing stressors is to distinguish chronic from discrete stressors. Chronic stressors represent "persistent or recurrent demands which require readjustments over prolonged periods of time," whereas discrete stressors represent "acute changes which require major behavioral readjustments within a relatively short period of time" (Thoits, 1995, p. 54). These distinctions have been found to moderate outcomes across a wide range of variables such as physical and mental health (for a review, see Thoits, 1995). Although researchers have examined the impact of chronic and discrete stressors in the context of other negative life events or as external factors that may influence a marriage (Neff & Karney, 2004), to our knowledge no one has applied that distinction to the study of hurt experienced within romantic relationships. In this section, we therefore examine the literature on the impact of chronic and discrete hurtful events on the mental health and well-being of individuals in close relationships.

Rather than reviewing all possible "hurts," we consider serious transgressions that represent a prototype of either chronic or discrete hurtful events. In the stress literature, researchers have struggled to develop well-demarcated boundaries for chronic and discrete social stressors (Coyne & Downey, 1991), and similar dilemmas present themselves in applying this distinction to hurtful events within close relationships. Nonetheless we believe that the distinction serves a useful heuristic function. Although it is impossible to perfectly capture and categorize the protean nature of hurtful events, it is possible to understand a prototypical example that captures much of the complexity of a type of transgression.

This prototype approach has been advanced in attempting to understand other psychological concepts. For example, Lilienfeld and Marino (1995, 1999) suggest that mental disorders have inherently fuzzy boundaries and that they are best codified in a system that takes a prototype approach. This is a logical and realistic approach to developing a categorical system for psychological constructs if that system seeks to map on to reality. For if our goal is to "carve nature at the joints," we may come to the frustrating realization that nature's joints are not as neatly defined as we wish them to be. Consequently, we propose that our understanding of hurtful events can be advanced by identifying and understanding prototypes of transgressions. As an exemplar of a chronic transgression, we have chosen alcohol abuse, and for a discrete transgression we consider infidelity. Although choosing any prototype of a hurtful event has its advantages and disadvantages (e.g., it is clearly possible that each of these transgressions could in some instances represent the opposite of its current chronic or discrete categorization – for infidelity, an ongoing affair), these prototypes were chosen because they have been studied extensively and robustly linked to divorce. This latter feature is a crucial consideration because divorce represents an important and objective consequence of hurtful transgressions. In most instances, relationship dissolution represents the final response to a serious hurt; therefore, understanding the hurtful event that leads to relationships dissolution can provide insight into the relative impact of chronic versus discrete hurtful events in relationships as they are exemplified by alcohol abuse and infidelity, respectively.

INFIDELITY AS A PROTOTYPICAL DISCRETE HURTFUL EVENT

Infidelity is a source of deep relational distress. Although it is possible for an affair to last for years, its modal duration is much shorter (6 months; see, e.g., Allen, 2001), and there are many instances of "one-night stands." We chose infidelity as a prototype of a discrete hurt because the revelation of an affair tends to occur all at once rather than in a continuous fashion (people either know for sure that their significant other is having an affair or they do not). It should be noted that there are surely instances where one partner continues to engage in an ongoing affair with the other's full knowledge, and clearly such a situation would be correctly termed a chronic hurtful event rather than a discrete event. This speaks to the limitations of choosing a prototype approach to classifying psychological constructs; however, science is generally interested in understanding the rule before exploring the inevitable exceptions to the rule. Notice that in the present case what makes the hurt discrete is not the duration or frequency of the hurtful actions. Rather, it is defined by the tendency of the victim's sure knowledge of the infidelity to occur in a discrete ("all or none") manner and, more important, for the transgression to cease on the victim partner's discovery of it, thereby giving it the appearance of a "discrete event" in contrast to an ongoing situation.

Research has established that the typical response to hurt in the form of infidelity includes feelings of betrayal, rejection, abandonment, devastation, loneliness, shame, jealousy, anger, isolation, and humiliation, as well as loss of self-esteem (e.g., Schneider, 2003). Even though more than 90% of the general public agreed that it is "always" or "almost always" wrong to be unfaithful to one's romantic partner (Smith, 1994), the bulk of scientific research suggests that the prevalence of infidelity is quite high. Over the course of marriage, approximately 25% of men and 15% of women report having had sex with someone other than their spouse (Laumann, Gagnon, Michael, & Michaels, 1994; Wiederman, 1997), a number that soars to 65% to 75% of persons in a serious dating relationship (Shackelford, LeBlanc, Drass, 2000). Considering its high prevalence rate, its consequences, and its typically isolated nature, infidelity is a promising prototype of discrete hurt within romantic relationships.

## Discrete Hurts as a Cause of Mental Health Problems or Relational Distress or Both

Infidelity exacts a toll on the mental health and well-being of the partners of those who are unfaithful. Cano and O'Leary (2000) found that women who experienced marital stressors that involved humiliation or devaluation (e.g., their husband's infidelity) were six times more likely to be diagnosed with major depression. And Gordon and colleagues (Gordon, Baucom, & Snyder, 2004) noted that the discovery of extramarital sex often resulted in interpersonal reactions resembling the posttraumatic stress symptoms seen in the victims of catastrophic events.

In addition to its impact on mental health, data suggest that infidelity is the number one cause of divorce (e.g., Amato & Previti, 2003), and it often precipitates domestic abuse (Daly & Wilson, 1988). For example, infidelity is cited as the most frequent cause of wife battery and wife killing in the United States (Buss, 1994; Daly & Wilson, 1988). Such consequences of infidelity are obviously significant, but the direction of effects in the association between infidelity and psychopathology has not been unequivocally established. We therefore turn to consider discrete hurts as a consequence rather than cause of mental health problems.

### Discrete Hurts as a Consequence of Mental Health Problems, Relational Distress, or Both

Several scholars believe that infidelity may also be a consequence rather than simply a cause of personal and relational distress. For example, it has been hypothesized that individuals engage in extramarital sexual relationships to boost their self-esteem (e.g., Sheppard, Nelson, & Andreoli-Mathie, 1995), and Atwood and Seifer (1997) found that individuals reported entering into affairs at a time when they felt emotionally vulnerable. Not surprisingly, a common assumption among therapists is that psychological distress puts partners at risk for infidelity (e.g., Buunk & van Driel, 1989).

As regards relationship characteristics, low satisfaction has been linked to discrete hurts such as infidelity (Prins, Buunk, & Van Yperpen, 1993). It is a truism that illicit liaisons are not usually formed in the midst of happy unions. In fact, infidelity primarily occurs when relationship quality is low (Buss & Shackelford, 1997; Treas & Giesen, 2000; Waite & Joyner, 2001), which may indicate that discrete hurt in the form of infidelity is a consequence of previously experienced hurt that is reflected in relational distress. For example, persons who report their relationships as "not too happy" are four times more likely to engage in infidelity than those who characterize them as "very happy" (Atkins, Jacobson, & Baucom, 2001). Additionally, Prins et al. (1993) also found that people in unhappy relationships expressed a greater desire for extramarital sex, as well as an increased involvement in such relationships. Further, Previti and Amato (2004) found that most individuals form extramarital relations only after seriously considering a divorce. In a similar vein, extramarital sex is more common among individuals who report that marital sexual intercourse is low in frequency or quality (Buss & Shackelford, 1997; Lui, 2000; Treas & Giesen, 2000). Low frequency or quality of sexual intercourse may be a sign that one or both partners are experiencing unresolved hurt feelings. Finally, marital conflict is linked to higher susceptibility to an extramarital affair (Buss & Shackelford, 1997). Thus, research suggests that it may be a history of prior experienced hurt that has contributed to a distressed relationship that predicts increased probability of the discrete hurt of infidelity within romantic relationships.

Most likely, there are bidirectional effects between infidelity and mental health problems, relational distress, or both. Understanding discrete hurts such as infidelity is important because if infidelity is primarily a cause of psychological distress, then future intervention research should focus on how to reduce its prevalence directly. However, if infidelity is primarily a consequence of mental health problems or prior relational hurt, prevention efforts are better focused on promoting individual and relational adjustment.

In light of the conceptual and practical importance of determining direction of effects, Hall and Fincham (2007) conducted the first prospective, longitudinal study investigating infidelity, psychological distress, and relationship functioning. Using a sample of persons from exclusive dating relationships, they found that infidelity and psychological distress were, as expected, concurrently related. However, infidelity did not predict subsequent psychological distress, a finding that could reflect the fact that the study focused on perpetrators, rather than victims, of infidelity or that persons in dating relationships experience less distress in the aftermath of infidelity than individuals in more committed relationships (i.e., married individuals). However, the researchers did find that initial levels of psychological distress predicted later infidelity. Thus, it appears that psychological distress might be a precursor of infidelity.

### ALCOHOL ABUSE AS A PROTOTYPICAL CHRONIC HURTFUL EVENT

Alcohol abuse is a relatively common problem in the United States and is a source of serious hurt in close relationships (see Marshal, 2003). The abuser's drinking may precipitate a host of problems for the drinker's romantic partner (both acts of commission and of omission), and continuing to drink in full knowledge of these problems constitutes a chronic hurt for the nonabusing partner. Recent research suggests that approximately one-third of those requiring marital counseling reported alcohol abuse problems in the relationship (e.g., Halford & Osgarby, 1993; Malet et al., 2003). Alcohol abuse can often become a vicious cycle of perpetuating hurt in a marriage: a nonabusing spouse may attempt to reduce the partner's drinking through periodic aversive means like nagging, threatening, and criticizing; these aversive techniques are usually ineffective and most often perpetuate existing marital conflict patterns (Thomas & Ager, 1993) and further alcohol abuse (Halford, Bouma, Kelly, & Young, 1999). Thus, through this and other means, the alcohol abuse problem is perpetuated and becomes a chronic hurt in the relationship. Note also that continued engagement in the hurtful event in the face of partner objections serves to support the inference that the relationship is indeed devalued.

#### Chronic Hurt as a Cause of Mental Health Problems, Relational Distress, or Both

The chronic hurt represented by alcohol abuse may create many stressors such as financial problems, embarrassing incidents, poor parenting, job problems, verbal and physical abuse, and poor sexual functioning. These stressors, often accompanied by repeatedly broken promises to change, usually exact a heavy toll on both the nonabusing partner and the relationship. As regards individual functioning, it has been shown that being married to an alcohol abuser is not only a risk factor for mental health problems but is also a danger to physical health in that (a) more frequent and more severe domestic violence is related to the use of alcohol (Fals-Stewart, 2003) and (b) male alcohol abusers are more likely than nonabusers to engage in unprotected extramarital sex (often with high-risk populations like prostitutes or other substance abusers) and to then engage in unprotected sex with their spouse without informing her of his extramarital activity (Hall, Fals-Stewart & Fincham, 2008).

Needless to say, alcohol abuse is likely to create an atmosphere of mistrust and anger, as well as a reduction in positive shared activities between spouses (O'Farrell & Bayog, 1986). Some studies have also shown that alcohol use predicts subsequent marital dissatisfaction (Locke & Newcomb, 2003). This relationship may be due in part to the fact that couples in which one partner has a problem are often characterized by high rates of negative affect expression, withdrawal during conflict, few supportive and constructive responses (Jacob & Leonard, 1992), and frequent and intense arguments (Blankfield & Maritz, 1990). In addition, heavy drinking interferes with a family's everyday functioning as it distracts spouses from their responsibilities. These and other findings may explain why Amato and Previti (2003) found that problematic drinking is the third most commonly cited reason for divorce.

## Chronic Hurts as a Consequence of Mental Health Problems, Relational Distress, or Both

Chronic hurts like alcohol abuse when manifest at sufficiently high levels are themselves considered to be mental health problems. Alcohol abuse (requiring a pattern of maladaptive drinking leading to clinically significant impairment) and alcohol dependence (which requires a more intense pattern of use and impairment marked by an increased need for alcohol) are both included in the *Diagnostic and Statistical Manual of Mental Disorders*. In addition, these disorders are frequently comorbid with other disorders, and it is widely acknowledged that people can use alcohol to self-medicate as a way of coping with stressors, or psychopathology, or both. In light of such observations it is perhaps axiomatic that this particular exemplar of a chronic hurt – alcohol abuse – can reflect a preexisting mental health problem. But it is not ipso facto a poor exemplar. Mental health problems can and do impair judgment, and so it is not far-fetched to imagine that persistent engagement in a behavior that is hurtful to the partner may reflect the actor's maladjustment/mental health.

Marital problems have been shown to stimulate excessive drinking (Davis, Berenson, Steinglass, & Davis, 1974) and are predictive of a poor prognosis in programs that treat alcohol problems (Billings & Moos, 1983). In addition, conflict in marriage has been identified as a cause of relapse by abstinent alcoholics in a retrospective study (Maisto, O'Farrell, Connors, McKay, & Pelcovits, 1988), and has been identified as a risk for relapse in prospective studies (Maisto, McKay, & O'Farrell, 1998; O'Farrell, Hooley, Fals-Stewart, & Cutter, 1998). In a follow-up study, Whisman, Uebelacker, and Bruce (2006) report that, compared with satisfied spouses, individuals dissatisfied with marriage were 3.7 times more likely to report alcohol use disorders. These findings seem to indicate that a chronic transgression like alcohol abuse may be perpetuated by other types of relational hurt. In this regard, alcohol abuse seems to be no different from other chronic hurts.

### THE IMPACT OF DISCRETE VERSUS CHRONIC HURTFUL EVENTS

Does the impact of hurtful transgressions differ based on their discrete versus chronic nature? At a conceptual level, we have noted that chronic transgressions, especially when perpetrated over partner objections, have the potential to make it very difficult to overlook devaluation of the relationship, and thereby they potentially deepen the hurt experienced. In contrast, discrete hurts as one-time events may be more easily attributed to a lapse in judgment. Whether this difference matters when fundamental relationship rules are violated (as in the case of infidelity) is open to question. Such uncertainties cannot easily be resolved by appeal to extant data as shown by our preceding review; however, the characterization of hurtful events as discrete or chronic seems to moderate the impact of these transgressions on mental health outcomes. There is some support for the idea that discrete transgressions may have a more immediate impact on mental health than the enduring, yet expected chronic transgression. As previously mentioned, Gordon and colleagues (2004) found that the discovery of an affair often resulted in interpersonal reactions resembling post-traumatic stress symptoms. Discrete transgressions like infidelity may be more predictive of mental health problems given that Amato and Previti (2003) found extramarital sex to be the number one cause of divorce, an outcome associated with decreases in mental health (Simon, 2002). In fact, the impact of extramarital sex on divorce was more than twice as large as any other cited reason for divorce in their study.

However, whether a serious, discrete hurtful event such as infidelity continues to have a larger impact on mental health over time than a chronic transgression is doubtful. It is conceivable that the victims of a chronic transgression may come to view themselves as responsible, in part, for the hurt they experience by staying in the relationship, and this attribution could end up exacting a toll on their mental health at some point. In contrast, the victims of a serious acute hurtful event might, by virtue of being able to dissociate themselves from playing any role in causing the hurt experienced, be able to more quickly recover from its impact. In any event, the precise nature of the discrete and chronic transgressions might be important, as illustrated by considering our two chosen exemplars. The question of which type of hurtful event has more impact on mental health is somewhat confounded in the case of our examples by the fact that alcohol abuse predicts infidelity (Atkins et al., 2005). Despite this fact, research clearly suggests that it is the act of infidelity itself that creates hurt sufficient to initiate the largest number of divorces (Amato & Previti, 2003).

Difficulty in distinguishing discrete from chronic events is not new and has been confronted in the stress literature, which can provide guidance in applying this distinction to transgressions (e.g., Cohen et al., 1995). Notwithstanding the challenges it entails, conceptualizing transgressions into these two categories seems to be a useful and intuitive way to organize future research on the topic of hurt in close relationships.

### FORGIVENESS: MOVING BEYOND HURT

Because of the inevitability of experiencing hurt in close relationships, it is important to know what can be done to attenuate its impact on the mental health of those in close relationships. One transformative process that has great potential to help individuals recover from the damage caused by hurtful events in close relationships is forgiveness (Fincham, Stanley, & Beach, 2007). Forgiveness provides one critical means whereby couples can move past vengeful and hurt feelings following a transgression. In fact, it is widely believed that forgiveness can be instrumental for couples in dealing with existing difficulties and preventing future problems (e.g., Worthington & DiBlasio, 1990), and several researchers and clinicians believe that forgiveness is the cornerstone of a successful marriage (e.g., Worthington, 1994).

In this section we explore the meaning of forgiveness and how it may be used to address hurt feelings experienced in relationships. We then propose a model in which forgiveness mediates the relationship between hurtful events and mental health. In addition, we discuss the relationship between hurtful events and forgiveness in terms of several factors that may moderate this relationship, including severity of transgression, self-esteem, rumination, and attribution. Finally, we review some of the literature that demonstrates a link between forgiveness and mental health and discuss how forgiveness may be a mediator in this model.

### What Is Forgiveness?

First, it is important to clarify what is meant by forgiveness. A number of definitions have been offered to capture this concept, including (a) a motivational transformation in which the desire to seek revenge and to avoid contact with the transgressor is lessened (McCullough et al., 1998), (b) the cancellation of a debt (Exline, & Baumeister, 2000), (c) an altruistic gift (e.g., Enright, Freedman, & Rique, 1998), or (d) an "intraindividual, prosocial change toward a perceived transgressor that is situated within a specific interpersonal context" (McCullough, Pargament, & Thoresen, 2000, p. 9). Although forgiving is usually recognized as a positive act, several misconceptions about forgiveness portray it as being undesirable. For example, some laypersons perceive forgiving as sign of weakness (Kearns & Fincham, 2004). Instead, forgiving requires strength in that it requires the victim to acknowledge the poor treatment and to overcome subsequent negative feelings. Others perceive forgiveness as potentially dangerous because it could make the victim vulnerable to further mistreatment (Kearns & Fincham, 2004). This perspective portrays forgiveness as condoning a negative behavior, essentially giving permission to the transgressor to repeat the hurtful behavior. However, forgiving is not inconsistent with a clear communication of hurt and prevention of future hurt from the transgressor.

## How Can Forgiveness Help an Individual Overcome a Hurtful Event?

As noted, hurtful events are complex, and each individual may react in a different manner to a particular hurtful event. Nonetheless, it seems that forgiveness may help an individual overcome, at least in part, the pain of a transgression despite its severity or chronic nature. Much of the literature on this subject focuses on the marital relationship; however, the principles discussed may also be applicable to other close relationships.

Several empirically tested models have been developed to assist individuals in working through the pain of a hurtful event and moving toward forgiveness. For example, Gordon, Baucom, and Snyder (2000) developed a model that seems most appropriate for those couples that have undergone an "interpersonal trauma" like infidelity. Gordon and colleagues posit a three-stage model that begins with coping with the impact of the offense, finding meaning for the transgression, and finally moving forward with a new set of beliefs about the relationship. They found couples who followed these steps had less marital distress and increased forgiveness after an affair (Gordon et al., 2004).

Similarly, Enright and Fitzgibbons (2000) suggest a four-phase model. In the first phase, termed the "uncovering phase," an individual focuses on exploring the hurt that he or she has experienced. In the next, "decision phase," an individual commits to attempting to forgive the offender. In the third, "work phase," the focus is shifted to the transgressor in an attempt to gain understanding and insight. Finally, in the "deepening phase" the individual moves toward resolution by becoming aware that he or she is not alone, has been the recipient of others' forgiveness, and discovers meaning and purpose in the forgiveness process. The forgiveness process described here may be used as a tool for processing and resolving a hurtful event.

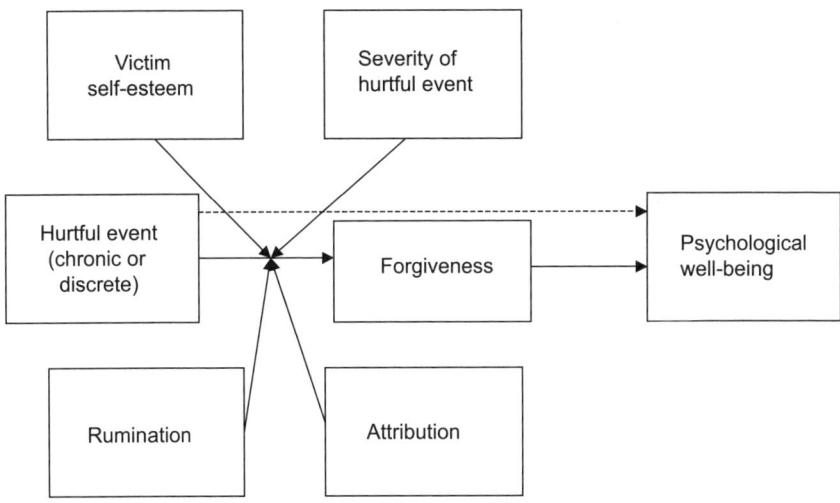

FIGURE 18.1. Forgiveness as a mediator of hurtful events and psychological well-being.

These are two examples of empirically tested methods by which individuals may work through a hurtful event and achieve forgiveness. They contain several important principles that may be applied by all individuals who have experienced hurtful events to attain forgiveness.

## FORGIVENESS AS A MEDIATOR OF HURTFUL EVENTS AND PSYCHOLOGICAL HEALTH: A CONCEPTUAL MODEL

We earlier reviewed some of the literature that demonstrates a link between hurtful events and psychological health, and we have shown how forgiveness may be applied in overcoming the effects of a hurtful event. In this section we illustrate these relationships with a conceptual model and suggest some factors that may moderate the relationship between hurtful events and forgiveness (see Fig. 18.1).

### Hurtful Event: Chronic versus Discrete

Both discrete and chronic transgressions possess qualities that present unique obstacles to forgiveness. The prior occurrence or a history of hurt is an important factor that influences the forgiveness process in close relationships. In the case of chronic transgressions, forgiveness may not pertain only to a particular transgression but rather to an accumulation of prior, equivalent acts. The transgressed party may be frequently reminded of the initial hurt by a partner's similar behavior that could be perceived as the same transgression.

Conversely, although a discrete transgression may not carry as much baggage, it also has the potential to influence an individual's achieved forgiveness. For example, discrete transgressions are often more severe by nature and are often unanticipated, likely altering the level of forgiveness achieved. Moreover, it is worth noting an added complexity for both types of events: Specifically, the transgressed party's past experience with a similar or the same transgression in other close relationships can also factor into the interpretation of the current transgression.

As previously noted, discrete transgressions may become habitual, such as the case with many online cybersex romances (Schneider, 2003), or certain chronic transgressions may reach a level of severity more typical of discrete transgressions. Nonetheless, the type of hurtful event, whether discrete or chronic, likely influences forgiveness. In addition, we would expect the relative contributions of each moderator to be different based on whether the event is chronic or discrete.

### Possible Moderators of Hurtful Events and Forgiveness

Experts agree that forgiveness is a challenging but necessary part of the healing process for major relationship transgressions such as infidelity (Gordon & Baucom, 1999), and it seems to be important for less hurtful events as well. Several barriers to forgiveness moderate the inclination to forgive discrete and chronic transgressions. These potential moderators include the severity of the transgression, the self-esteem of the victim, the type of hurtful event (chronic versus discrete), rumination, and attribution.

*Level of Severity*

Severe transgressions tend to affect a victim's life more profoundly and may have more enduring consequences and therefore may be harder to forgive than less severe transgressions. Not surprisingly, the severity of a partner transgression is negatively related to forgiveness (e.g., Boon & Sulsky, 1997). More specifically, Fincham, Jackson, and Beach (2005) found that both subjective and objective ratings of severity predicted forgiveness. In the case of infidelity, the severity of the transgression may be partially related to the identity of the extramarital lover. For instance, Cann and Baucom (2004) found that, when sexual infidelity took place with a former partner, both men and women thought of the injury as more severe and found it more difficult to forgive.

Similarly, the type of infidelity seems to affect its level of severity. Respondents in Thompson's (1984) study ranked affairs that were classified as both emotional and sexual as being the most harmful and emotion-only affairs as being the least harmful. In such a case, a spouse may have a much easier time forgiving the partner for having an emotional affair, whereas if intercourse were involved it would likely be much more difficult for him or her to forgive the partner. The length of the affair and the manner in which it is disclosed – whether accidentally (or intentionally) discovered by the noninvolved spouse or confessed – are also factors that determine the severity of the transgression. Although it is now well documented that more severe transgressions are harder to forgive (see Fincham, Jackson, & Beach, 2005), additional research is needed to determine the exact impact of severity on forgiveness.

*Self-Esteem*
Transgressions usually communicate relational devaluation that injures the transgressed individual's self-image. Balswick and Balswick (1999) noted that a typical response of someone with an unfaithful partner was to be torn by questions of self-doubt and inadequacy and to wonder whether he or she was attractive and adequate as a sex partner. Accordingly, the degree to which the transgressed party feels devalued may be related to the forgiveness process. Fincham (2000) hypothesized that forgiveness for an individual with low self-esteem may not be as difficult to achieve because the harm may be seen as consistent with the victim's view of what he or she deserves. Similarly, because individuals with high self-esteem may not be as susceptible to emotional injury, they also may have an easier time forgiving. However, a person with intermediate levels of self-esteem may struggle the most to forgive because the hurt may be more keenly felt by such an individual. This hypothesis should be tested in future studies to determine the role of self-esteem as it relates to forgiveness in general and specifically as it relates to self-esteem-altering discrete transgressions like infidelity.

*Rumination*
People who frequently think about a transgression are less likely to forgive, and as rumination lessens over time, people become more forgiving (McCullough et al., 1998). Thus, the amount of time an individual spends ruminating about a hurtful event will likely moderate that person's forgiveness of the perpetrator. Kachadourian, Fincham, and Davila (2005) found that ambivalence toward one's spouse was negatively related to forgiveness only when the husband or wife thought frequently about the partner's transgression. In light of these findings, chronic transgressions may be more difficult to forgive because continued, repeated offenses may keep a transgression at the forefront of the injured party's mind and not allow for enough time between incidents for decreased rumination, which facilitates forgiveness.

Conversely, the abrupt and unexpected nature of a discrete transgression may catch individuals by surprise and leave them feeling like the rug has been pulled out from underneath them. This unexpectedness may affect victims differently than the predictable offenses that comprise a chronic transgression. For instance, Riskind (1997) has proposed that injurious events that seem to rapidly change, grow, or escalate are often far more disturbing than injurious events of equal magnitude that do not have a rapid rate of change. These former types of events create a sense of "looming vulnerability," as Riskind terms it, that increases the probability of experiencing anxiety in the future (Riskind, 1997). Consequently, the nature of discrete transgressions may actually trigger more rumination than an expected chronic transgression, and this idea should be explored by future research. This is a good example of the type of difference in the moderating variables we would expect based on the nature of the transgression (discrete or chronic).

*Attribution*
There is empirical evidence to show that the way in which the offended party cognitively processes the transgression influences forgiveness (e.g., Boon & Sulsky, 1997). Forgiveness varies as a function of judgments of responsibility, blame, and perceived intentionality. Some data show that attributing more responsibility and blame to the offending partner makes forgiveness more difficult to achieve (Fincham & Beach, 2001). In a similar vein, Fincham, Paleari, and Regalia (2002) found that more benign attributions both directly and indirectly predicted forgiveness by decreasing emotional reactions to the transgression and by increasing empathy. In the case of the chronic transgression of alcohol abuse, a partner's attribution of responsibility could significantly influence forgiveness. For example, a wife may think, "My husband drinks because drinking runs in his family," or she may think, "My husband drinks because he's irresponsible and doesn't care about me or the kids." Clearly, the former attribution would be much more likely to facilitate forgiveness than the latter.

As regards intentionality, Vangelisti and Young (2000) found that intentional hurt was linked to more hostility, making the forgiveness process more difficult. Perceived intentionality is likely to influence an individual's likelihood of forgiving a transgression. "He hit me because he's drunk and isn't in control," as opposed to "He hit me because he despises me and thinks I'm worthless," is an example of how perceived intentionality may influence forgiveness in a case of domestic abuse. These four moderators are likely to interact with the hurtful event (be it chronic or discrete) to alter the course of achieved forgiveness.

## Forgiveness and Psychological Health

Forgiveness is associated with positive mental health outcomes in numerous studies. Mauger, Perry, Freeman, Grove, and McKinney (1992) found that forgiveness of self and others was inversely related to indicators of psychopathology, and Touissant, Williams, Musick, and Everson (2001) showed that forgiveness of others was inversely related to psychological distress. Moreover, forgiveness interventions improve existential well-being and lower levels of anxiety, depression, and anger (Freedman & Enright, 1996; Rye & Pargament, 2002). Although each of these moderators would likely affect the degree to which full forgiveness is achieved, we suggest that any amount of forgiveness is likely to reduce the negative effects of a hurtful event on an individual's mental health.

Barron and Kenney (1986) suggest that for mediation to take place an independent variable must be significantly correlated both to the dependent variable and to the mediator variable. In our case, the mediator variable (forgiveness) must be significantly correlated with both the independent (hurtful event) and dependent variables (psychological health). We have cited several studies that demonstrate such relationships and propose that, conceptually, forgiveness should fully mediate the relationship between hurtful events and mental health. Future research could profitably test the associations specified in the proposed model.

Appreciation of the potential benefits of forgiveness for mental health should not blind us to the possibility that under certain conditions forgiving might be detrimental to the forgiver's well-being. This might be the case, for example, in physically or emotionally abusive relationships and might also occur in the case of serial infidelity or repeated transgressions, whatever their specific nature. Finally, forgiveness born of felt obligation (e.g., to conform to the tenets of the forgiver's religious beliefs) or of social pressure is unlikely to promote well-being. In any event, delineating the conditions under which forgiveness is unrelated or negatively related to mental health is among the important tasks for future research.

## FUTURE DIRECTIONS

Our examination of the literature relevant to experienced hurt and psychological health in close relationships prompts us to call for additional research on the heuristic value of the discrete/chronic distinction, as well as on the role of forgiveness as a potential mediator between hurt and psychological health. In addition we focus on two linchpins for advancing understanding in this domain: theory development and greater methodological sophistication.

### Discrete versus Chronic Paradigm

Although the distinction between chronic and discrete events is neither new nor always cut and dry, it has been found to moderate outcomes across a wide range of variables, including physical and mental health (Thoits, 1995). However, this paradigm has not yet been applied to the study of hurtful events in close relationships, and future research in this area could be beneficial to researchers and therapists alike. For example, it can be hypothesized that habituation processes, if found, are limited to chronic transgressions, whereas sensitization may occur in relation to both chronic and discrete hurts. Increased attention to this paradigm also has the potential to improve the sensitivity and effectiveness of interventions that address hurt experienced in response to a transgression.

## The Role of Forgiveness

Although there is a documented link between forgiveness and mental health and evidence to show how forgiveness may be used in overcoming hurt experienced after a transgression, the role of forgiveness in mediating the effects of hurtful events on psychological health is vastly understudied. Our conceptual model provides several questions that ought to be addressed by future research. For example, how might severity, rumination, attribution, and victim self-esteem affect the hypothesized mediating role accorded to forgiveness when it comes to mental health? To what extent does the specific level of achieved forgiveness affect psychological health? And how might discrete versus chronic hurtful events differentially affect an individual's level of achieved forgiveness? These are a few of the many questions that need to be addressed by future research.

## Nothing as Practical as Good Theory

Although numerous studies have investigated the association between hurt experienced in close relationships and psychopathology, there is little theory pertaining to this association, an omission that begs for attention. As noted, an assumption in the literature is that stress associated with hurtful events in close relationships interacts with a preexisting vulnerability or diathesis for a given mental health problem, resulting in elevated clinical symptoms. This assumption is a useful point of departure as future research could begin by examining whether a stress–diathesis model is the best way of conceptualizing the relationship between hurt in relationships and psychopathology.

As mentioned previously, however, it is possible that the direction of effects is in the opposite direction and that individuals with preexisting psychopathology create contexts propitious to getting hurt by intimate others. This observation points to the possibility of adapting Hammen's (2006) stress-generation theory of depression to study the association between hurt in relationships and mental health. The perspective offered by this theory points to the need to examine the extent to which victims of transgression play a role in facilitating future transgressions from partners, an issue that has not yet received attention. The obvious points of contact with existing theoretical frameworks bode well for the future of this applied research area as "there is nothing so practical as a good theory" (Lewin, 1951, p. 169).

## Good Theory Is Not Enough: The Need for Greater Methodological Sophistication

Two characteristics of extant research on transgressions in close relationships necessarily limit its contribution to understanding the relation between hurt and psychological well-being in such relationships. The first is the almost exclusive reliance on self-reports (for exceptions, see Battle & Miller, 2005; Fincham et al., 2005). This reliance is important because it inevitably means that measures of hurt and psychological well-being are confounded (e.g., when self-report is used, both could reflect the respondent's level of neuroticism or negative affectivity, a variable that has independently been related to both experienced hurt and indicators of psychological distress, such as depression). A further consequence is that it is not possible to tease apart contexts in which the partner transgression is dependent, either wholly or partly, on the respondent's behavior. Such concerns in the study of depression led the sociologist George Brown (Brown & Harris, 1978) to develop an interview-based contextual threat method for assessing stressors. Hammen (1991), building on this approach, has developed episodic and chronic stress assessments that could be easily used in future research on transgressions, thereby yielding objective, observer-based ratings of hurt. The potential advances promised by doing so make this a recommendation that merits immediate attention.

The second characteristic of extant research that limits its contribution is the emphasis on concurrent relations at the expense of prospective, longitudinal studies. Two observations are worth making in this regard. First, the finding that marital conflict is inversely related to marital satisfaction, but positively related to future marital satisfaction (see Fincham & Beach, 1999), points to the danger of extrapolation from concurrent to longitudinal relations. Second, given the widely accepted premise that causes precede effects, longitudinal studies provide stronger data for causal inferences. This is particularly important in a field where practical and ethical considerations limit experimental manipulation of the construct under study (hurt). The need is imperative for prospective longitudinal studies on hurt in close relationships and psychological distress to examine direction of effects.

Consideration of the temporal dimension of experienced hurt also highlights the fact that we know nothing about the natural course of hurt in close relationships and points to a further research need. The emergence of growth curve modeling in recent years provides the necessary tool to fulfill this need, and initial steps in this direction have been taken (see McCullough, Fincham, & Tsang, 2003; Tsang, McCullough, & Fincham, 2006). One might reasonably expect the distinction between discrete and chronic transgressions to moderate the trajectory of hurt. However, the nature of any impact on the trajectory is unclear as we do not know whether chronic transgressions lead to habituation or sensitization to the hurt. Again this is an empirical question that cries out for data.

## SUMMARY AND CONCLUSION

We have traversed a great deal of ground in this chapter. Starting with the observation that relationship status is associated with mental health, we went on to identify relationship well-being as a critical moderator of this relationship.

Central to relationship well-being are hurt and how partners deal with the inevitable hurt experienced in close relationships. After making explicit the diathesis–stress model that informs research in this area, we distinguished discrete from chronic transgressions and went on to explore this distinction's implication for the association between hurt and mental health in close relationships.

Next, we demonstrated the plausibility of forgiveness as a mediator of hurtful events and psychological health. We also explored self-esteem, severity of transgression, type (chronic vs. discrete), attribution, and rumination as potential moderators of the relationship between hurtful events and forgiveness. The chapter then concluded by calling for more theory and outlining several methodological changes needed in future research on hurt and mental health in close relationships.

## REFERENCES

Allen, E. S. (2001). *Attachment styles and their relation to patterns of extradyadic and extramarital involvement.* Unpublished doctoral dissertation, University of North Carolina, Chapel Hill.

Amato, P., & Previti, D. (2003). People's reasons for divorcing: Gender, social class, the life course, and adjustment. *Journal of Family Issues, 24*, 602–626.

Atkins, D. C., Jacobson, N. S., & Baucom, D. H. (2001). Understanding infidelity: Correlates in a national random sample. *Journal of Family Psychology, 15*, 735–749.

Atkins, D. C., Yi, J., Baucom, D. H., & Christensen, A. (2005). Infidelity in couples seeking marital therapy. *Journal of Family Psychology, 19*, 470–473.

Atwood, J. D., & Seifer, M. (1997). Extramarital affairs and constructed meanings: A social constructionist therapeutic approach. *American Journal of Family Therapy, 25*(1), 55–75.

Balswick, J. K., & Balswick, J. O. (1999). Extramarital affairs: Causes, consequences, & recovery. *Marriage & Family: A Christian Journal, 2*(4), 419–426.

Barron, R. M., & Kenny D. A. (1986). The moderator-mediator variable distinction in social psychological research: Conceptual, strategic, and statistical considerations. *Journal of Personality and Social Psychology, 51*, 1173–1182.

Battle, C. L., & Miller, I. W. (2005). Families and forgiveness. In E. L. Worthington (Ed.), *Handbook of forgiveness* (pp. 227–242). New York: Routledge.

Bauserman, S. A. K., Arias, I., & Craighead, W. E. (1995). Marital attributions in spouses of depressed patients. *Journal of Psychopathology and Behavioural Assessment, 17*, 231–249.

Beach, S. R., Fincham, F. D. & Katz, J. (1998). Marital therapy in the treatment of depression: Toward a third generation of outcome research. *Clinical Psychology Review, 18*, 635–661.

Billings, A., & Moos, R. (1983). Psychosocial processes of recovery among alcoholics and their families: Implications for clinicians and program evaluators. *Addictive Behavior, 8*, 205–218.

Blankfield, A., & Maritz, J. S. (1990). Female alcoholics: IV. Admission problems and patterns. *Acta Psychiatrica Scandinavica, 82*, 445–450.

Boon, S. D., Sulsky, L. M. (1997). Attributions of blame and forgiveness in romantic relationships: A policy-capturing study. *Journal of Social Behavior and Personality, 12*, 19–44.

Brown, G. W., & Harris, T. (1978). *Social origins of depression.* London: Free Press.

Buss, D. M. (1994). *The evolution of desire.* New York: Basic Books.
Buss, D. M., & Shackelford, T. K. (1997). Susceptibility to infidelity in the first year of marriage. *Journal of Research in Personality, 31,* 193–221.
Buunk, B. P., & van Driel, B. (1989). *Variant lifestyles and relationships.* Newbury Park, CA: Sage.
Cann, A., & Baucom, T. R. (2004). Former partners and new rivals as threats to a relationship: Infidelity type, gender, and commitment as factors related to distress and forgiveness. *Personal Relationships, 11,* 305–318.
Cano, A., & O'Leary, K. D. (2000). Infidelity and separation precipitate Major Depressive Episodes and symptoms of non-specific depression and anxiety. *Journal of Consulting and Clinical Psychology, 68,* 774–781.
Chambless, D. L., Fauerbach, J. A., Floyd, F. J., Wilson, K. A., Remen, A. L., & Renneberg, B. (2002). Marital interaction of agoraphobic women: A controlled, behavioral observation study. *Journal of Abnormal Psychology, 111,* 502–512.
Cohen, S., Kessler, R. C., & Gordon, L.V. (1995). *Measuring stress: A guide for health and social scientists.* USA: Oxford University Press.
Coyne, J. C., & Downey, G. (1991). Social factors and psychopathology: Stress, social support, and coping processes. *Annual Review of Psychology, 42,* 401–425.
Coyne, J. C., Thompson, R., & Palmer, S. C. (2002). Marital quality, coping with conflict, marital complaints, and affection in couples with a depressed wife. *Journal of Family Pscychology, 16,* 26–37.
Daly, M., & Wilson, M. (1988). *Homicide.* Hawthorne, NJ: Aldine de Gruyter.
Davis, D. I., Berenson, D., Steinglass, P., & Davis, S. (1974). The adaptive consequences of drinking. *Psychiatry: Interpersonal & Biological Processes, 37,* 209–215.
Dohrenwend, B. S., Krasnoff, L., Askenasy, A. R., & Dohrenwend, B. P. (1978). Exemplification of a method for scaling life events: The peri life events scale. *Journal of Health and Social Behavior, 19*(2), 205–229.
Enright, R. D., & Fitzgibbons, R. P. (2000). *Helping clients forgive: An empirical guide for resolving anger and restoring hope.* Washington, DC: American Psychological Association.
Enright, R. D., Freedman, S., & Rique, J. (1998). The psychology of interpersonal forgiveness. In R. D. Enright & J. North (Eds.), *Exploring forgiveness* (pp. 46–62). Madison: University of Wisconsin Press.
Exline, J. J., & Baumeister, R. F. (2000). *Expressing forgiveness and repentance: Benefits and barriers.* In M. McCullough, K. Pargament, & C. Thoresen (Eds.), *Forgiveness: Theory, research, and practice* (pp. 133–155). New York: Guilford.
Fals-Stewart, W. (2003). The occurrence of partner physical aggression on days of alcohol consumption: A longitudinal diary study. *Journal of Consulting and Clinical Psychology, 71,* 41–45.
Fals-Stewart, W., Birchler, G. R., & O'Farrell, T. J. (1999). Drug-abusing patients and their intimate partners: Dyadic adjustment, relationship stability, and substance use. *Journal of Abnormal Psychology, 108,* 11–23.
Fincham, F. D. (2000). The kiss of the porcupines: From attributing responsibility to forgiving. *Personal Relationships, 23,* 1–23.
Fincham, F. D., & Beach, S. R. (1999). Marital conflict: Implications for working with couples. *Annual Review of Psychology, 50,* 47–77.
Fincham, F. D. & Beach, S. R. (2001). Forgiving in close relationships. *Advances in Psychology Research, 7,* 163–198.
Fincham, F. D., Jackson, H., & Beach, S. R. H. (2005). Transgression severity and forgiveness: Different moderators for objective and subjective severity. *Journal of Social and Clinical Psychology, 24,* 860–875.

Fincham, F. D., Paleari, G., & Regalia, C. (2002). Forgiveness in marriage: The role of relationship quality, attributions and empathy. *Personal Relationships, 9*, 27–37.

Fincham, F. D., Stanley, S., & Beach, S. R. H. (2007). Transformative processes in marriage: An analysis of emerging trends. *Journal of Marriage and Family, 69*, 275–292.

Freedman, S., & Enright, R. D. (1996). Forgiveness as an intervention goal with incest survivors. *Journal of Consulting and Clinical Psychology, 64*, 938–922.

Gallup. (2006). *Americans have complex relationship with marriage*. Retrieved May 30, 2006 from http://www.galluppoll.com/content/?ci=23041&pg=1.

Gordon, K. C., & Baucom, D. H. (1999). A multitheoretical intervention for promoting recovery from extramarital affairs. *Clinical Psychology: Science & Practice, 6*, 382–399.

Gordon, K. C., Baucom, D. H., & Snyder, D. K. (2000). The use of forgiveness in marital therapy. In M. McCullough, K. Pargament, & C. Thoresen (Eds.), *Forgiveness: Theory, research, and practice* (pp. 203–227). New York: Guilford.

Gordon, K. C., Baucom, D. H., & Snyder, D. K. (2004). An integrative intervention for promoting recovery from extramarital affairs. *Journal of Marital and Family Therapy, 30*, 213–246.

Gotlib, I. H., & McCabe, S. B. (1990). *Marriage and psychopathology*. In F. D. Fincham & T. N. Bradbury (Eds.), *The psychology of marriage: Basic issues and applications* (pp. 226–257). New York: Guilford.

Gove, W. R., Hughes, M., & Style, C. B. (1983). Does marriage have positive effects on the psychological well-being of the individual? *Journal of Health and Social Behavior, 24*(2), 122–131.

Halford, W. K., Bouma, R., Kelly, A., & Young, R. M. (1999). Individual psychopathology and marital distress. *Behavior Modification, 23*, 179–216.

Halford, W. K., & Osgarby, S. (1993). Alcohol abuse in clients presenting with marital problems. *Journal of Family Psychology, 6*, 1–11.

Hall, J. H., Fals-Stewart, W., & Fincham, F. D. (2008). Risky sexual behavior among married alcoholic men. *Journal of Family Psychology, 22*, 287–292.

Hall, J. H., & Fincham, F. D. (2006). Relationship dissolution following infidelity: The roles of attributions and forgiveness. *Journal of Social and Clinical Psychology, 25*, 508–522.

Hall, J. H., & Fincham, F. D. (2007). *Psychological distress: Precursor or consequence of dating infidelity?* Manuscript submitted for publication.

Hammen, G. (1991). Generation of stress in the course of unipolar depression. *Journal of Abnormal Psychology, 100*, 555–561.

Hammen, C. (2006). Stress generation in depression: Reflections on origins, research and future directions. *Journal of Clinical Psychology, 62*, 1065–1082.

Horwitz, A. V., McLaughlin, J., & White, H. R. (1998). How the negative and positive aspects of partner relationships affect the mental health of young married people. *Journal of Health and Social Behavior, 39*(2), 124–136.

Jacob, T., & Leonard, K. E. (1992). Sequential analysis of marital interactions involving alcoholic, depressed and nondistressed men. *Journal of Abnormal Psychology, 101*, 647–656.

Kachadourian, L. K., Fincham, F. D., & Davila, J. (2005). Attitudinal ambivalence, rumination and forgiveness of partner transgressions in marriage. *Personality and Social Psychology Bulletin, 31*, 334–342.

Kearns, J. N., & Fincham, F. D. (2004). A prototype analysis of forgiveness. *Personality and Social Psychology Bulletin, 30*, 838–855.

Kowalski, R. M. (2000). "I was only kidding!": Victims' and perpetrators' perceptions of teasing. *Personality and Social Psychology Bulletin, 26*, 231–241.

Lauman, E. O., Gagnon, J. H., Michael, R. T., & Michaels, S. (1994). *The social organization of sexuality: Sexual practices in the United States*. Chicago: University of Chicago Press.

Leary, M., Springer, C., Negel, L., Ansell, E., & Evans, K. (1998). The causes, phenomenology, and consequences of hurt feelings. *Journal of Personality and Social Psychology, 74*, 1225–1237.

Lewin, K. (1951). *Field theory in social science: Selected theoretical papers*. New York: Harper & Row.

Lilienfeld, S. O., & Marino, L. (1995). Mental disorder as a Roschian concept: A critique of Wakefield's "harmful dysfunction" analysis. *Journal of Abnormal Psychology, 104*, 411–420.

Lilienfeld, S. O., & Marino, L. (1999). Essentialism revisited: Evolutionary theory and the concept of mental disorder. *Journal of Abnormal Psychology, 108*, 400–411.

Liu, C. (2000). A theory of marital sexual life. *Journal of Marriage and the Family, 62*, 363–374.

Locke, T. F., & Newcomb, M. D. (2003). Psychological outcomes of alcohol involvement and dysphoria in women: A 16-year prospective community study. *Journal of Studies on Alcohol, 64*, 531–547.

MacDonald, G., & Leary, M. R. (2005). Why does social exclusion hurt? The relationship between social and physical pain. *Psychological Bulletin, 131*, 202–223.

Maisto, S. A., McKay, J. R., & O'Farrell, T. J. (1998). Twelve-month abstinence from alcohol and long-term drinking and marital outcomes in men with severe alcohol problems. *Journal of Studies on Alcohol, 59*, 591–598.

Maisto, S. A., O'Farrell, T. J., Connors, G. J., McKay, J. R., & Pelcovits, M. (1988). Alcoholics' attributions of factors affecting their relapse to drinking and reasons for terminating relapse episodes. *Addictive Behaviors, 13*, 79–82.

Malet, L., Llorca, P.-M., Boussiron, D., Schwan, R., Facy, F., & Reynaud, M. (2003). General practitioners and alcohol use disorders: Quantity without quality. *Alcoholism: Clinical and Experimental Research, 27*(1), 61–66.

Marshal, M. P. (2003). For better or for worse? The effects of alcohol use on marital functioning. *Clinical Psychology Review 23*, 959–997.

Mauger, P. A., Perry, J. E., Freeman, T., Grove, D. C., & McKinney, K. E. (1992). The measurement of forgiveness: Preliminary research. *Journal of Personality and Christianity, 11*, 170–180.

McCullough, M. E., Fincham, F. D., & Tsang, J. (2003). Forgiveness, forbearance, and time: The temporal unfolding of transgression-related interpersonal motivations. *Journal of Personality and Social Psychology, 84*, 540–557.

McCullough, M., Pargament, K. T., & Thoreson, C. E. (2000). *Forgiveness: Theory, research, and practice*. New York: Guilford.

McCullough, M., Rachal, K., Sandage, S., Worthington, E., Brown, S., & Hight, T. (1998). Interpersonal forgiving in close relationships: II. Theoretical elaboration and measurement. *Journal of Personality and Social Psychology, 75*, 1586–1603.

Neff, L. A., & Karney, B. R. (2004). How does context affect intimate relationships? Linking external stress and cognitive processes within marriage. *Personality and Social Psychology Bulletin, 30*, 134–148.

O'Farrell, T. J., & Bayog, R. D. (1986). Antabuse contracts for married alcoholics and their spouses: A method to insure Antabuse taking and decrease conflict about alcohol. *Journal of Substance Abuse Treatment, 3*, 1–8.

O'Farrell, T. J., & Birchler, G. R. (1987). Marital relationship of alcoholic, conflicted, and nonconflicted couples. *Journal of Marital and Family Theory, 13*, 259–274.

O'Farrell, T. J., Hooley, J., Fals-Stewart, W., & Cutter, H. Q. (1998). Expressed emotion and relapse in alcoholic patients. *Journal of Consulting and Clinical Psychology, 66*, 744–752.

Overbeek, G., Vollebergh, W., de Graaf, R., Scholte, R., de Kemp, R., & Engels, R. (2006). Longitudinal associations of marital quality and marital dissolution with the incidence of DSM-III-R disorders. *Journal of Family Psychology, 20*, 284–291.

Previti D., &. Amato, P. R. (2004). Is infidelity a cause or a consequence of poor marital quality? *Journal of Social and Personal Relationships, 21*, 217–230.

Prins, K. S., Buunk, B. P., & Van Yperen, N. W. (1993). Equity, normative disapproval and extramarital relationships. *Journal of Social and Personal Relationships, 10*, 39–53.

Riskind, J. H. (1997). Looming vulnerability to threat: A cognitive paradigm for anxiety. *Behaviour Research and Therapy, 35*(8), 685–702.

Rye, M. S., & Pargament, K. I. (2002). Forgiveness and romantic relationships in college: Can it heal the wounded heart? *Journal of Clinical Psychology, 54*, 419–441.

Schneider, J. P. (2003). The impact of compulsive cybersex behaviors on the family. *Sexual and Relationship Therapy, 3*(18), 329–354.

Shackelford, T. K., LeBlanc, G. J., & Drass, E. (2000). Emotional reactions to infidelity. *Cognition and Emotion, 14*, 643–659.

Sheppard, V. J., Nelson, E. S., & Andreoli-Mathie, V. (1995). Dating relationships and infidelity: Attitudes and behaviors. *Journal of Sex and Marital Therapy, 21*, 202–212.

Simon, R. W. (2002). Revisiting the relationships among gender, marital status, and mental health. *American Journal of Sociology, 107*, 1065–1096.

Smith, T. W. (1994). Attitudes towards sexual permissiveness: Trends, correlates, and behavioral connections. In A. S. Rossi (Ed.), *Sexuality across the life course* (pp. 63–97). Chicago: University of Chicago Press.

Snapp, C. M., & Leary, M. R. (2001). Hurt feelings among new acquaintances: Moderating effects of interpersonal familiarity. *Journal of Social and Personal Relationships, 18*, 315–326.

Thoits, P. A. (1995). Stress, coping, and social support processes: Where are we? What next? *Journal of Health and Social Behavior, (Extra Issue)*, 53–79.

Thomas, E. J., & Ager, R. D. (1993). *Unilateral family therapy with the spouses of uncooperative alcohol abusers.* In T. J. O'Farrell (Ed.), *Marital and family therapy in alcohol treatment.* New York: Academic Press.

Thompson, A. P. (1984). Emotional and sexual components of extramarital relations. *Journal of Marriage and the Family, 10*, 35–42.

Toussaint, L. L., Williams, D. R., Musick, M. A., & Everson, S. A. (2001). Forgiveness and health: Age differences in a U.S. probability sample. *Journal of Adult Development, 8*, 249–257.

Treas, J., & Giesen, D. (2000). Sexual infidelity among married and cohabitating Americans. *Journal of Marriage and the Family, 62*, 48–60.

Tsang, J., McCullough, M., & Fincham, F. D. (2006). Forgiveness and the psychological dimension of reconciliation: A longitudinal analysis. *Journal of Social and Clinical Psychology, 25*, 404–428.

Vangelisti, A. L., & Young, S. L. (2000). When words hurt: The effects of perceived intentionality on interpersonal relationships. *Journal of Social and Personal Relationships, 17*, 395–425.

Waite, L. J., & Gallagher, M. (2000). *The case for marriage: Why married people are happier, healthier, and better off financially*. New York: Doubleday.

Waite, L. J., & Joyner, K. (2001). Emotional satisfaction and physical pleasure in sexual unions: Time horizon, sexual behavior, and sexual exclusivity. *Journal of Marriage and Family, 63*, 247–64.

Whisman, M. A., & Bruce, M. L. (1999). Marital dissatisfaction and incidence of major depressive episode in a community sample. *Journal of Abnormal Psychology, 108*, 674–678.

Whisman, M. A., & Uebelacker, L. A. (2006). Impairment and distress associated with relationship discord in a national sample of married or cohabiting adults. *Journal of Family Psychology, 20*, 369–377.

Whisman, M. A., Uebelacker, L. A., & Bruce, M. L. (2006). Longitudinal association between marital discord and alcohol use disorders in a community sample. *Journal of Family Psychology, 20*, 164–167.

Wiederman, M. W. (1997). Extramarital sex: Prevalence and correlates in a national survey. *Journal of Sex Research, 34*(2), 167–174.

Worthington, E. L. (1994). Marriage counseling: A Christian approach. *Journal of Psychology and Christianity, 13*(2), 166–173.

Worthington, E. L., & DiBlasio, F. (1990). Promoting mutual forgiveness within the fractured relationship. *Psychotherapy: Theory, Research, Practice, Training, 27*, 219–223.

# 19

## Technology and Hurt in Close Relationships

MONICA WHITTY

Although it is acknowledged here that there are numerous ways technology can be used to hurt people, this chapter focuses solely on one type of technology – that being cyberspace. "It is generally understood that cyberspace is the space generated by software within a computer that produces a virtual reality" (Whitty, 2003a, p. 343). However, an alternative view is that cyberspace existed before the Internet in the form of telephone calls. Others would even contend that the telegraph is another example of communications in cyberspace (see Whitty & Carr, 2006, for a more detailed discussion). For the purposes of this chapter cyberspace is taken to mean the Internet and SMS text messaging.

It is noteworthy that the Internet was not first set up as a communication tool. Rather it was originally set up by the U.S. Defense Department in the 1960s as a system for their workers to share data. This original system, which was called the Arpanet, soon changed as the individuals using the system quickly reshaped it to meet their personal and social needs. Friendships began to blossom online and so too did romances, which often led to face-to-face meetings and sometimes even marriage. In the early days of the Internet, scholars held much hope for this new arena. Turkle (1995), for instance, argued that cyberspace was a kind of utopia where individuals could feel free to explore their identities without judgment. In my own work, I have argued that cyberspace can be very liberating, especially for those who feel awkward and shy when it comes to initiating relationships or exploring one's sexuality (Whitty, 2003a, 2004; Whitty & Buchanan, in press; Whitty & Carr, 2003). Although I still maintain that there are many benefits for people interacting within cyberspace, this chapter only considers the ways individuals can be hurt by electronic communication. In particular, it focuses on how electronic communication might be used to hurt those close to us. Additionally, it examines how our own interactions online might hurt those close to us offline.

## HURT CAUSED BY STRANGERS IN CYBERSPACE

Many of the original studies and theories about the Internet presupposed that individuals are anonymous online and that they communicate with people unknown to them offline. This anonymity made these types of relationships quite different from typical relationships formed in face-to-face settings. Before moving on to consider how technology can hurt individuals close to us, it is instructive to present a brief overview of the negative effects of communicating with strangers online.

### HomeNet Study

It was Kraut et al. (1998) in their well-known HomeNet Study who first raised the concern that "weak ties" (that is, relationships formed with strangers online) might be psychologically unhealthy. These researchers conducted a longitudinal study in which they gave households that had never accessed the Internet before the study a computer, free telephone line, and free access to the Internet. During the course of the study they tracked changes in psychological states over time. Alarmingly, Kraut et al. (1998) found a significant relationship between heavy Internet usage and loneliness. These researchers concluded that Internet usage was taking up time that could be better used for more psychologically beneficial interactions offline.

Kraut et al.'s (1998) HomeNet Study has been widely criticized. Two of the major criticisms were that they only used three items from the UCLA loneliness scale to measure loneliness and their Cronbach's alpha of .54 was clearly poor (Grohol, 1998). Morahan-Martin (1999) also pointed out that the sample size was too small and not randomly selected. Perhaps a more important criticism, however, is that Kraut et al.'s findings might only explain novice Internet users (LaRose, Eastin, & Gregg, 2001). Moreover, as LaRose et al. (2001) have maintained, self-efficacy might be an important variable to consider. The individuals who spent more time online in Kraut et al.'s study might have been simply ineffective users of the Internet, and the stress in trying to work out how to use this new technology might have caused them to become more depressed (Whitty & McLaughlin, 2007).

Interestingly, in the 3-year follow-up to the HomeNet Study the same researchers found that almost all of the previously reported negative effects had dissipated (Kraut et al., 2002). Instead, higher levels of Internet use were positively correlated with measures of social involvement and psychological well-being. Such results might be explained by LaRose et al.'s (2001) claim that it is also important to consider self efficacy. As Whitty and McLaughlin (2007) have suggested, it might be that the participants in the HomeNet study became savvier over time, which, in turn, altered the way they used the Internet.

## Flaming

Although it is debatable as to whether weak ties are psychological unhealthy, one thing we know for certain is that some individuals can be quite aggressive in their electronic communications. Aggressive talk online is referred to as "flaming." Individuals often flame in spaces such as discussion groups and chat rooms to incite a reaction. Theorists have argued that some people are more likely to speak aggressively online compared to their face-to-face conversations because the people they talk to online are strangers whom they never intend to meet offline. Moreover, those who flame can remain anonymous by using a screen name and e-mail address that does not give away their offline identity.

The dearth of social cues is another feature of cyberspace that arguably promotes aggressive talk. The social context cues theory first proposed by Sproull and Kiesler (1986) states that online and face-to-face communication differ in the amount of available social information. Social context cues, such as those conveyed by aspects in the physical environment, as well as nonverbal cues are typically unavailable online. Given the absence of these social context cues, there is an increase in excited and uninhibited online communication. One example of uninhibited online communication is flaming. Flaming therefore is not restricted to communication among strangers. Individuals known to us sometimes communicate with us in a more aggressive manner than they would in face-to-face settings (e.g., loved ones and work colleagues). Moreover, if we subscribe to the social context cues theory, we would predict that individuals are likely to prefer to end a relationship via electronic communication.

## HURT CAUSED BY CLOSE RELATIONSHIP PARTNERS

### Deception

What about other unsavory forms of communication such as lying? If the person who lies is caught, a lie can hurt its target, especially when the lie comes from someone close. When it comes to lying in cyberspace, the results to date are mixed. Whitty (2002) has found that lying is a ubiquitous phenomenon in chat rooms: In this study, 28% of male users and 18% of female users lied about their gender, 63% of men and 60% of women lied about their age, 56% of men and 42% of women lied about their occupation, 40% of men and 25% of women lied about their education, and 44% of men and 28% of women lied about their income. Cornwell and Lundgren (2001) found that 28% of their respondents lied online about their physical attractiveness, 23% about their age, 18% about their background, and 15% about their interests. Utz (2005) found that online attractiveness deception was deemed more severe than gender switching and identity concealment. Interestingly, Caspi and Gorsky

(2006) found that 84% of their sample experienced enjoyment from telling a lie online.

Whitty has found that people using online dating sites are quite likely to deceive potential dates (see Whitty, 2008; Whitty & Carr, 2006). The most common way in which individuals misrepresent themselves is in regard to their physical appearance. In fact 68% of the participants she interviewed stated that they had met face to face with people from the online dating site who had lied about their looks. For example, they had described themselves as more attractive than they were, used outdated photographs, or even used a photograph of a different person. Forty-two percent of the participants said they had met up with people who lied about their weight or size (women were more likely to do this than men). Seventeen percent stated they met people who lied about their height (men were more likely to do this compared to women). Online daters also told lies about their personality, interests/hobbies, age, intentions (e.g., lying about wanting a relationship when they were just hoping for a one-night stand), socioeconomic status, having children, and being a nonsmoker.

Researchers have also been interested in examining how much people lie in cyberspace compared to face to face and over the telephone. In a diary study consisting of 28 participants, Hancock, Thom-Santelli, and Ritchie (2004) found that people are most likely to lie on the phone, followed by face-to-face settings and, finally, least in e-mail. In this study Hancock et al. (2004) argued that their results do not support earlier theories on computer-mediated communication (CMC) such as the social distance hypotheses and media richness theory. Social distance theory argues that, because lying makes individuals feel uncomfortable, they will choose less rich media to maintain social distance between themselves and the person to whom they are lying. In respect to the four types of media Hancock et al. (2004) examined, individuals would lie most in e-mail, followed by instant messenger, phone, and face to face. In contrast, media richness theory suggests that because lying is highly equivocal individuals elect to lie more in rich media, which includes multiple cue systems, immediate feedback, natural language, and message personalization. Hence, this theory would predict that individuals would lie in face-to-face situations more, followed by phone, instant messenger, and e-mail.

Given the results yielded from their study, Hancock and colleagues (2004) developed a new theory to explain lying across different media. They suggest that researchers need to consider other dimensions besides richness and distance. In their new feature-based theory, the additional dimensions they included were synchronous, recordless, and distributed (i.e., not co-present) communication. This theory proposes that the more synchronous and distributed, but the less recordable a medium is, the more frequently lying should occur. One lies more in synchronous interactions, because the majority of lying is spontaneous and hence synchronous communication should present more opportunities to lie. In recorded communication one is aware that one's conversation is potentially kept or stored (e.g., in a saved e-mail) and can be referred to in future conversations; hence, people are less likely to lie if they are aware that there is proof of their lie that can be referred to later. In media where participants are not distributed deception should be constrained to some degree as some lies can be immediately obvious (e.g., it is easier to lie in e-mail saying one is writing a report when really one is actually playing a computer game). Therefore, because telephone conversations are distributed, synchronous, and recordless, the most amount of lying should take place in this media, as supported by their results. In contrast, e-mail is distributed, but not synchronous or recordless and, therefore, as supported by their study, had the lowest rate of deception.

One of the criticisms that can be made about Hancock et al.'s work is that they did not examine the type of lie being told or the target of the lie. When it comes to offline lying, DePaulo and Kashy (1998) found that their participants reported telling fewer lies to people they were close to and felt uncomfortable when they did lie to these people. In addition, they found that relatively more of the lies told to best friends and friends were altruistic rather than self-serving. Given this research Whitty and Carville (2008) decided to examine self-oriented lies and other-oriented lies to strangers and to people considered close to the liar across three types of media: face to face, telephone, and e-mail. This study found that individuals were much more likely to tell self-serving lies in every media to individuals not well known to them compared to those to whom they felt close. They argued that this is because it is more risky and challenging to get away with telling a self-serving lie to individuals one is close to. Individuals who are close typically have more information about each others' daily lives. In line with Goffman's (1959) theory, Whitty and Carville (2008) contend that if people are caught telling a self-serving lie, they are not only going to be judged negatively for the lie they told but their entire character could also be brought into question.

In the same study, Whitty and Carville (2008) found that individuals are more likely to tell other-oriented lies to people close to them than to strangers. Other-oriented lies are often told to protect the feelings of the target of the lie. Given this, these theorists surmised that individuals might feel more compelled to lie to a person close to them to protect his or her feelings rather than saying the truth, which could possibly cause them upset or distress. People are perhaps less motivated or concerned to protect the feelings of those less well known to them.

Whitty and Carville's (2008) study challenges Hancock et al.'s (2004) feature-based theory, finding more evidence to support the "social distance" model. For self-serving lies told to both people close to participants as well as strangers, individuals stated they were more likely to tell a lie in e-mail, followed by phone and, last, face to face. These theorists argue that they obtained this result because lying makes people feel uncomfortable and that having distance between the liar and the target makes the liar more at ease with executing the lie. Self-serving lies are arguably more likely to make the liar feel uncomfortable and apprehensive, and so e-mail is not surprisingly the ideal place to tell such a lie. E-mail has the extra bonus of being an asynchronous form of media, which gives individuals time to think about how they will best tell their lie. Phone provides the distance and eliminates some of the nonverbal cues that might give away the lie.

### Unrequited Love: Harassment in Cyberspace

Individuals have been known to hurt others online whom they would like to be close to or falsely believe they are close to. Sometimes this hurt can take the form of cyberstalking. Bocij (2004) defines cyberspace as follows:

> A group of behaviors in which an individual, group of individuals, or organization uses information and communications technology to harass another individual, group of individuals, or organization. Such behaviors may include, but are not limited to, the transmission of threats and false accusations, identity theft, damage to data or equipment, computer monitoring, solicitation of minors for sexual purposes, and any form of aggression. Harassment is defined as a course of actions that a reasonable person, in possession of the same information, would think causes another reasonable person to suffer emotional distress. (p. 14)

Importantly, a number of countries have rewritten their legislation on harassment to ensure that cyberharassment and cyberstalking are deemed as crimes.

There are a variety of reasons why individuals or groups of people are motivated to harass and stalk others online, and these reasons are similar to those for why individuals stalk and harass others offline (Whitty & Carr, 2005a). Not all stalking is about pursuing and harassing an unrequited love interest, although much of it is (Whitty & Carr, 2006). Individuals might begin to cyberstalk after a romantic relationship has ended and they obsess about its continuation. Another reason might be that the stalkers are not able to comprehend that their romantic and sexual advances are unwanted or inappropriate, so much so that they might frighten or terrify their victim. A further cause might be that the stalkers do comprehend that their affections are not reciprocated and consequently set out to hurt their victim or ensure that their victim is unable to be involved romantically with any other partners. Barak (2005) points out three types of sexual harassment that can take place in cyberspace: gender harassment, unwanted sexual attention, and sexual coercion. He argues that gender harassment and unwanted sexual attention are the more common types of online sexual harassment.

There have been a number of reported cases of horrendous incidences of cyberstalking. Here is one example:

> David Cruz in 1993 was given a prison sentence of five months for cyberstalking Chloe Easton. Cruz met Easton through friends and he quickly became infatuated with her. Chloe Easton was going through a messy divorce and she found that Cruz was very supportive throughout the process. When David Cruz made romantic advances towards Easton she made it clear that she wanted the relationship to remain platonic. This angered Cruz who proceeded to launch a campaign of harassment over six months against Chloe and her family. Throughout most of the harassment, David Cruz pretended to be a concerned friend and tried to help Chloe find her stalker. Some of the harassment included sending a pornographic video in an e-mail attachment to Chloe's father – the video showed a woman who looked very similar to Chloe, engaged in group sex. Chloe was also sent up to 30 sexually explicit text messages a day with "disgusting sexual connotations." (Wilkins, 2003)

### Revenge Web Sites

The harm caused by cyberstalking and cyberharassment can be more severe than any similar offline acts (Bocij, 2003, 2004). This is especially the case when it comes to destroying someone's reputation. Web sites can be viewed by a large audience and are easily accessible. In fact there have been Web sites designed to intentionally hurt and destroy an ex-partner's reputation. Revenge sites, such as http://www.formergirlfriends.com/index.php and http://www.outmyex.com/, display naked photographs (often unflattering) of ex-partners posted together with negative comments about them. Table 19.1 shows an extract from outmyex.com, which indicates one woman's thoughts about her ex-boyfriend.

### Monitoring a Loved one's Activities

Cyberstalking and placing damning information about ex-partners online clearly have the potential to cause a great deal of harm, but what about monitoring a current partner's activities? Using technology to check on the whereabouts of a romantic partner and the conversations he or she has had may not be as harmless an activity as it first seems.

Using the Internet to find out information about people online has became such a common activity that "to Google someone" is now a common phrase in our everyday language. If someone is connected to software such as instant messenger or Skype those linked up to the contact can monitor when that person is logged in. People can fairly easily and covertly check what text messages their partner has been sending and receiving. Affordable software

TABLE 19.1. *Extract from a revenge Web site*

| My Ex | |
|---|---|
| Tell us what they're TRULY like in bed! Don't hold back! | Lazy lover, I had to do all the work. Predictable. Predictable. Predictable. You would think, that with all that practice with the others, he'd have some moves. |
| Is your Ex a LIAR?? | DICKHEAD NEVER TOLD THE TRUTH! |
| Is your Ex a CHEATER?? | Hell yes! Caught that DICKHEAD CHEATING! |
| Your Ex's love making rating! | They kissed like a camel on crack and sucked in the sack!! |
| Girls, tell us how many times you FAKED it! | Every single time that Tic Tac tried to do some damage – poor lil weiner bastard! |
| Girls, tell us how BIG it REALLY is! | Looks like a Tic Tac |
| Your warning to others about your Ex that they should KNOW! | He may have been seeing and lying to as many as four girls at once, so be careful you might be one of them ... (Bonnie, Bose, Pumpkin Nose ...) Does "You're the only one I'm sleeping with." sound familiar? He marks his women with a Tiffany's heart pendant. He's lazy, non-committal, arrogant, and LIES LIES LIES ... |
| Describe Your Ex | Egotistic, manipulating asshole with no conscience. Thinks he's hot shit. Can lie like a sociopath. Short, short man ... He is always concerned about his appearance and how others see him. Snores like a lawn mower. Interests limited to watching football, gambling, and women, he doesn't deserve. |

packages can be purchased to record individuals' computer activity. They can view and record people's e-mails, chat messages, Web sites visited, as well as monitor and record keystrokes and even individuals' passwords. So it is not too difficult to spy on a loved one's online conversations. A program called 007 Spy Software (n.d) advertises the following:

> 007 Spy Software is a stealthy computer monitoring software which allows you to secretly record all activities of computer users and automatically deliver logs to you via Email or FTP, including all areas of the system such as email sent, Web sites visited, every keystroke (including login/password of ICQ, MSN, AOL, AIM, and Yahoo Messenger or Webmail), file operations, online chat conversation, and take screen snapshots at set intervals just like a surveillance camera directly point at the computer monitor.

Companies advertising these types of software promote them as a way for employers to monitor their employees, as well as for individuals to check on family members in the home, including children or a spouse. Moreover, some companies suggest that their software is an ideal tool to use if people suspect their spouse is cheating on them.

Researchers have found that using the Internet to find out information about others and to monitor their lives is common practice (e.g., Andrejevic, 2006). In an international study Andrejevic (2006) found that 75% of individuals admitted to having used the Internet to search for information about others. The people they were most likely to seek out information about were their friends (67%), significant others (36%), former friends (33%), new acquaintances (30%), and former significant others (28%). In the main, they were looking for photographs of these people (55%), contact information (50%), personal information (45%), and where they lived and worked (35%).

So can this monitoring potentially hurt others close to us? Monitoring of others could signify a desire to learn more about that person. However, that particular person might be concerned with why he or she was not simply asked to provide that information. More important, monitoring of others could signify a lack of trust. Imagine that you find out that your partner had been reading your e-mails and checking your text messages even though you had nothing to hide from them. How would you feel? Once trust is broken in a relationship it can be quite difficult to restore.

## Internet Infidelity

Sometimes there might be a good reason why individuals might want to check up on their spouse's online activities. As Whitty (2003b, 2005) has noted, online infidelity is a genuine form of infidelity that can hurt spouses and even lead to the breakup of relationships. So what is Internet infidelity and why might it lead to the ending of a relationship?

Before defining Internet infidelity let us consider what we typically mean by offline infidelity. Infidelity occurs when a partner breaks the rules of the relationship. Not every couple has the same rules. However, in the main, research has found, at least when it comes to offline interactions, falling in love with or having sex with someone other than one's spouse is considered an act of infidelity. Some researchers have found that other behaviors such as spending time with a different partner, kissing, flirting, petting, sexual fantasies, sexual attraction, and romantic attraction are also deemed by some to be acts of infidelity (Roscoe, Cavanaugh, & Kennedy, 1988; Yarab, Sensibaugh, & Allgeier, 1998). Arguably for many couples "mental exclusivity" is as important as "sexual exclusivity" (Yarab et al. 1998).

Given this understanding of traditional offline infidelity, it should not come as a surprise that some types of online interactions are deemed relationship transgressions. People can fall in love and engage in sexual acts online even if there is no real penetrative sex. There are Web sites for married people to engage in cybersex with other married people and for married people to find another person to engage in an offline affair. For example, Philanderers.com is an online service that is an introductory agency for people seeking extramarital offline relationships. This description of its services is on its Web site:

> Why you are here is our main concern. Helping you sort out your thoughts, provide some direction for your extramarital affair, and a safe, secure outlet for your extramarital desires is our mission.
>
> We are not a sex or personals site that provides empty promises. Our clientele are well educated and informed before they become members. We are not "the biggest," "the best" or the "most popular" – we don't want to be. We are honest, forthright and caring. Three things that we value in our extramarital web-relations.
>
> Come in and explore. Learn why you may want to pursue an extramarital affair and what you can do about it. Find out the reasons why this may be just the right place for you. Find out how you can fulfill your extramarital desires.

Researchers have consulted participants about their opinions on whether certain Internet activities might be deemed as relationship transgressions (e.g., Mileham 2007; Parker & Wampler 2003; Whitty 2003b, 2005). These researchers have concluded that some online sexual (e.g., cyberflirting and cybersex) and emotional activities (e.g., sharing intimate secrets and falling in love) are thought to be acts of online betrayal.

In one of the first studies in this area, Whitty (2003b) surveyed 1,117 participants about their attitudes toward both online and offline infidelity. The study considered acts such as sexual intercourse, cybersex, hot chatting, emotional disclosure, and pornography. It found that participants believed that behaviors such as cybersex posed a greater threat than other behaviors such as downloading pornography. The study also found that emotional infidelity was deemed as much as an act of betrayal online as it is offline.

In a follow-up qualitative study, Whitty (2005) examined individuals' representations of Internet infidelity. In this study 234 participants were asked to write a fictitious story in response to a cue relating to Internet infidelity. Most people (86%) wrote a story that suggested that Internet infidelity is a real form of betrayal. Reasons given for why it was an act of infidelity included the idea that one cannot have a relationship with more than one person, that it was emotional infidelity, that it was sexual infidelity, or that the relationship was kept a secret. Interestingly, the stories stressed emotional infidelity as much as sexual infidelity. Moreover, when participants discussed sexual infidelity they referred to sexual acts such as cybersex, cyberflirting, and hotchatting. Rarely did the participants write about participants moving the relationship offline to engage in penetrative sex. Participants included in their stories the kind of impact that cybercheating had on the relationship. Sixty-five percent of the participants wrote that the aggrieved had been hurt or upset by the virtual encounter. Some participants wrote about how this form of betrayal led to a loss of trust and about the pain and upset it caused the aggrieved. Of further interest is that some wrote that the relationship would break up as a consequence, and others wrote about the type of revenge the aggrieved would carry out.

In another study on attitudes toward Internet infidelity, Parker and Wampler (2003) asked 242 undergraduate students to rate whether they believed certain scenarios were acts of infidelity. The scenarios included the following: meeting someone in a hotel room to have sex, interacting in adult chat rooms, having cybersex, having telephone sex, becoming a member of an adult Web site, engaging in cybersex various times, visiting adult chat rooms but not interacting, and visiting various adult Web sites. These researchers found that all of the sexual activities they included in their survey, except for (a) visiting adult chat rooms but not interacting and (b) visiting adult Web sites, were seen as acts of infidelity.

## Gender Differences

Evolutionary theorists argue that men have evolved to be more upset by sexual infidelity and women by emotional infidelity (e.g., Buss, Larsen, Westen, & Semmelroth, 1992; Shackelford & Buss, 1996). These theorists believe that men should be more likely than women to react with greater jealousy to sexual infidelity because of paternal uncertainty. In contrast, women should be more likely to react with greater jealousy than men to emotional infidelity because they would perceive it as a greater threat to paternal investment. Evidence has been found for this claim when respondents are forced to choose whether sexual or emotional infidelity is most upsetting to them (Shackelford & Buss, 1996). It is, however, noteworthy that both men and women report extradyadic sexual behavior to be more unacceptable and a greater betrayal than extradyadic emotional behavior (Shackelford & Buss 1996).

Not all researchers agree with the evolutionary theorists' claims. Many argue that the methodology used by evolutionary theorists to test out their claims is not sound. Researchers have found that gender differences are not always found when individuals are asked to rate scenarios but are typically found when individuals are forced to choose among them (DeSteno, Bartlett, Braverman, & Salovey, 2002). Sociocognitive theorists, in contrast to evolutionary theorists, believe that instead it is important to understand what men and women read into their spouses' infidelity. DeSteno and Salovey (1996) have developed the double-shot hypothesis and Harris and Christenfeld (1996) have developed the two-for-one hypothesis to explain how men and women understand sexual and emotional infidelity. These hypotheses contend that a man feels doubly upset when thinking about his female partner having sex with another man as he holds the belief that to do so she is probably also in love with this man. In contrast, women become doubly upset by their male partner falling in love with another woman because they believe that emotional infidelity implies sexual infidelity.

So what of gender differences when it comes to Internet infidelity? Consistent with previous research on offline infidelity, Whitty (2005) found that women were more likely than men to mention emotional betrayal in their fictitious stories about online betrayal. Also, in line with previous research on offline betrayal (e.g., Amato & Previti 2003), this study found that women were more likely than men to write that they would end the relationship if they found out their partner was having an Internet affair. Interestingly, as with some research on offline infidelity, when participants are presented with scenarios separately with rating scales, the gender difference has been found to occur in the opposite direction. Parker and Wampler's (2003) study, which considered sexual online activities, found that women viewed these activities more seriously than men did. Whitty's (2003) study found that women overall were more likely to believe that sexual acts were an act of betrayal than men did.

In more recent research, Whitty and Quigley (2008) examined the double-shot hypothesis with regard to online infidelity. This study did not find any support for it, as no gender differences were found. Moreover, participants were much less likely to believe that cybersex implied love or that online love implied cybersex than they were to believe that sexual intercourse implied love or that love implied sexual intercourse. Whitty and Quigley argue that there could be a number of reasons for the lack of support for this hypothesis. First, given that previous research has found that most people have not engaged in online sexual activities (e.g., Whitty, 2003b), making connections between love and cybersex might not be easy for them to do. Second, given that cybersex is qualitatively different from sexual intercourse, although individuals might still perceive it as a relationship transgression, they might not necessarily link it with love in the same way they would offline relationship transgressions. Importantly, this research highlights that we still have much to learn about online transgressions and the real threat they present to offline relationship.

## Internet Addiction

Another form of online behavior that can hurt others close to us is online addiction. It was Ivan Goldberg in the mid-1990s who first proposed the notion that a new disorder has emerged as a consequence of the Internet: "Internet addiction disorder" (IAD; see Whitty & Carr, 2006). Although he first proposed this as a joke people wrote to him discussing their IADs. Since that time theorists have argued that online relationships do have a seductive appeal (Whitty & Carr, 2006). Young (1998) has argued that people can be addicted to cybersex. Similarly, Griffiths (2000) believes that although the Internet is a place for some addicts to fuel the addictions they already had offline (e.g., gambling addict, sex addict), some individuals are addicted per se to the Internet.

Some studies have been conducted to determine which types of people are more likely to be addicted to the Internet. For example, Cooper, Delmonico, and Burg (2000) examined a group of "cyber-sexually compulsive" Internet users. They came to the conclusion that there is a small proportion of individuals whose online sexual behavior is clearly compulsive behavior. They also identified some demographic variables that they believe put an individual at greater risk for cybersex compulsivity. Both women and gay men were more highly represented in the cybersex compulsive group. The propensity to be a risk-taker in both sexual and nonsexual behavioral domains was also more common in cybersex compulsives. Finally, using chat rooms and spending more time online were more indicative of the cybersex compulsives.

As with any addiction, an individual with an online addiction typically withdraws from others to spend more time on his or her addiction. Moreover such an individual's mood often changes. To witness someone close to us change to become more negative in mood and increasingly more unavailable can be quite a stressful event. Moreover, it is even more hurtful for a spouse whose partner's addiction is an online relationship or engaging in cybersex.

## CONCEPTUALIZING CYBERSPACE: A SPACE BETWEEN REALITY AND FANTASY

In understanding how people's interactions and activities online might affect their offline relationships, it is important to conceptualize cyberspace. Early theorists pointed out that in many online interactions individuals remain anonymous and are typically communicating with strangers. This type of behavior, however, is not so typical these days. People connect and communicate with offline friends in spaces such as Facebook, Bebo, and Myspace. Moreover, many individuals' online interactions are with colleagues and friends (via e-mail and IM). Early theories about the Internet, such as the social context cues theory, pointed out that traditional nonverbal cues are absent online. Although this is to some degree still the case, nonverbal cues can be present these days via webcams, videos, avatars, and sophisticated emoticons. So what is it about online interactions that might be different from offline interactions?

Research has found that individuals often do communicate and develop relationships differently online. The research reported in this chapter demonstrates that people can be more aggressive and deceive more online, and there is a greater potential for harassment to occur in this space than offline. It has also been found that the Internet can have a seductive appeal, so much so that some individuals are addicted to the Internet. In addition we find that although online infidelity can cause "real" hurt, it is not always considered as hurtful as offline betrayals. Given these results it is arguably important to consider how cyberspace might be different from face-to-face contexts.

Whitty (2003a) has drawn from object relations theory to explain how researchers might best conceptualize cyberspace. In particular, she has drawn from Winnicott's (1971) notions of potential space and transitional objects. Winnicott was very interested in the potential space between the mother and the infant. He understood potential space to be the space where connections may be maintained between an external world and an internal conception of self; it is the space between the subject and object, where play takes place. As he stated, potential space "is not inner psychic reality. It is outside the individual, but it is not the external world. . . . Into this play area the child gathers objects or phenomena from external reality and uses these in the services of . . . inner or personal reality" (Winnicott, 1971, p. 51). Although Winnicott referred a great deal to the potential space between the mother and infant, he did state that this space is not confined to the experience of infants. For example, he proposed that such spaces could exist between patient and analyst.

In line with Winnicott's theory, Whitty has argued that cyberspace could be understood as potential space (see for example, Whitty 2003a; Whitty & Carr, 2005b, 2006). Cyberspace is often perceived to be a space somewhere outside the individual but is still not the external world. Therefore many of the interactions that take place in this space might appear to the individual as more playful than in ordinary face-to-face interactions. This perception can lead to both positive and negative experiences. More positively, it allows individuals to be creative and in turn explore new identities and learn more about themselves (see Whitty & Carr, 2006 for a more extensive discussion). The real impact, however, on others who are online and offline might not be fully appreciated because of the nature of the space. It is interesting that in cyberspace, even when individuals know the people offline and the site has been set up with a number of cues and immediate feedback systems, people can still behave differently than they ordinarily do and in a manner that would often be considered socially unacceptable if were to be performed offline.

## CONCLUSION

The Internet has become a part of many people's everyday lives across the globe. We work online, talk to offline friends, and develop new friendships and romances online. We shop online, conduct our banking online, and are regularly entertained by online content. Given this, as this chapter illustrates, any discussion on hurt and close relationships needs to also consider cyberspace.

Understanding what role the Internet plays in romantic relationships is a must. Do some spouses spend too much time online and neglect their partner and their family? Is the Internet a useful tool in bringing people closer together – especially when working hours are increasing and leisure time is decreasing?

Researchers need to learn more about how partners talk to one another and whether their communication is acceptable or hurtful. Being more aware of the negative aspects of cyber-relating will surely help improve the quality of our relationships both online and offline.

Learning more about what types of flirtatious and emotional encounters individuals engage in online is also critical. As this chapter elucidated, sometimes the line is fuzzy between online acceptable behavior and infidelity. How people's online relationships affect their offline relationships should be of interest to researchers.

On a concluding note, the Internet is constantly evolving. If researchers learn how the Internet works best in people's lives, then it can be restructured to improve their quality of life and the quality of their close relationships.

REFERENCES

Amato, P. R., & Previti, D. (2003). People's reasons for divorcing: Gender, social class, the life course, and adjustment. *Journal of Family Issues, 24*, 602–626.

Andrejevic, M. (2006). *Monitoring survey*. Unpublished raw data.

Barak, A. (2005). Sexual harassment on the Internet. *Social Science Computer Review, 23*(1), 77–92.

Bocij, P. (2003). *Victims of cyberstalking: An exploratory study of harassment perpetrated via the Internet*. Retrieved November 20, 2005, from http://firstmonday.org/issues/issue8_10/bocij/

Bocij, P. (2004). *Cyberstalking: Harassment in the internet age and how to protect your family*. Westport, CT: Praeger.

Buss, D. M., Larsen, R., Westen, D., & Semmelroth, J. (1992). Sex differences in jealousy: Evolution, physiology, and psychology. *Psychological Science, 3*, 251–255.

Caspi, A., & Gorsky, P. (2006). Online deception: Prevalence, motivation and emotion. *CyberPsychology & Behavior, 9*(1), 54–59.

Cooper, A., Delmonico, D. L., & Burg, R. (2000). Cybersex users, abusers, and compulsives: New findings and implications. *Sexual Addiction & Compulsivity, 7*, 5–29.

Cornwell, B., & Lundgren, D. C. (2001). Love on the Internet: Involvement and misrepresentation in romantic relationships in cyberspace vs. realspace. *Computers in Human Behavior, 17*, 197–211.

De Paulo, B. M., & Kashy, D. A. (1998). Everyday lies in close and casual relationships. *Journal of Personality and Social Psychology, 74*, 147–167.

DeSteno, D., Bartlett, M. Y., Braverman, J., & Salovey, P. (2002). Sex differences in jealousy: Evolutionary mechanism or artifact of measurement? *Journal of Personality and Social Psychology, 83*, 1103–1116.

DeSteno, D., & Salovey, P. (1996). Evolutionary origins of sex differences in jealousy? Questioning the "fitness" of the model. *Psychological Science, 7*, 367–371.

Goffman, E. (1997). *The presentation of self in everyday life*. In C. Lemert & A. Branaman (Eds.), *The Goffman reader*. New York: Doubleday Anchor. (Original work published in 1959)

Griffiths, M. (2000). Internet addiction – Time to be taken seriously? *Addiction Research, 8*, 413–418.

Grohol, J. M. (1998). Response to the HomeNet study, *PsychCentral*. Retrieved October, 27, 2004, from http://psychcentral.com/homenet.htm

Hancock, J., Thom-Santelli, J., & Ritchie, T. (2004). Deception and design: The impact of communication technologies on lying behavior. *Proceedings of the Conference on Computer Human Interaction, 6*(1), 130–136.

Harris, C. R., & Christenfeld, N. (1996). Gender, jealousy, and reason. *Psychological Science, 7*, 364–366.

Kraut, R., Kiesler, S., Boneva, B., Cummings, J., Helgeson, V., & Crawford, A. (2002). Internet paradox revisited. *Journal of Social Issues, 58*, 49–74.

Kraut, R., Patterson, M., Lundmark, V., Kiesler, S., Mukopadhyay, T., & Scherlies, W. (1998). Internet paradox: A social technology that reduces social involvement and psychological well-being? *American Psychologist, 53*, 1017–1031.

LaRose, R., Eastin, M., & Gregg, J. (2001). Reformulating the Internet paradox: Social cognitive explanations of Internet use and depression. *Journal of Online Behavior, 1*(2). Retrieved October 27, 2004, from http://www.behavior.net/JOB/v1n2/paradox.html

Mileham, B. L. A. (2007). Online infidelity in Internet chat rooms: An ethnographic exploration. *Computers in Human Behavior, 23*(1), 11–31.

Morahan-Martin, J. (1999). The relationship between loneliness and Internet use and abuse. *Cyberpsychology & Behavior, 2*, 431–439.

Out my ex.com.(n.d.). Retrieved November 20, 2005, from http://www.outmyex.com

Parker, T. S., & Wampler, K. S. (2003). How bad is it? Perceptions of the relationship impact of different types of internet sexual activities. *Contemporary Family Therapy, 25*(4), 415–429.

Philanderers.com (n.d.). Retrieved October 31, 2005, from http://www.philanderers.com

Roscoe, B., Cavanaugh, L., & Kennedy, D. (1988). Dating infidelity: Behaviors reasons, and consequences. *Adolescence, 23*, 35–43.

Shackelford, T., & Buss D. (1996). Betrayal in mateships, friendships, and coalitions. *Journal of Personality and Social Psychology, 22*, 1151–1164.

Sproull, L., & Kiesler, S. (1986). Reducing social context cues: Electronic mail in organizational communication. *Management Science, 32*, 1492–1512.

Turkle, S. (1995). *Life on the screen: Identity in the age of the Internet.* London: Weidenfeld & Nicolson.

Utz, S. (2005). Types of deception and underlying motivation: What people think. *Social Science Computer Review, 23*(1), 39–48.

Whitty, M. T. (2002). Liar, liar! An examination of how open, supportive and honest people are in chat rooms. *Computers in Human Behavior, 18*, 343–352.

Whitty, M. T. (2003a). Cyber-flirting: Playing at love on the Internet. *Theory and Psychology, 13*(3), 339–357.

Whitty, M. T. (2003b). Pushing the wrong buttons: Men's and women's attitudes towards online and offline infidelity. *CyberPsychology & Behavior, 6*(6), 569–579.

Whitty, M. T. (2004). Cyber-flirting: An examination of men's and women's flirting behaviour both offline and on the Internet. *Behaviour Change, 21*(2), 115–126.

Whitty, M. T. (2005). The 'realness' of cyber-cheating: Men and women's representations of unfaithful Internet relationships. *Social Science Computer Review, 23*(1), 57–67.

Whitty, M. T. (2008). Revealing the 'real' me, searching for the 'actual' you: Presentations of self on an internet dating site. *Computers in Human Behavior, 24*(4), 1707–1723.

Whitty, M. T., & Buchanan, T. ( in press). Looking for love in so many places: Characteristics of online daters and speed daters. *Interpersona: An International Journal on Personal Relationships.*

Whitty, M. T., & Carr, A. N. (2003). Cyberspace as potential space: Considering the web as a playground to cyber-flirt. *Human Relations, 56,* 861–891.

Whitty, M. T., & Carr, A. N. (2005a). Electronic bullying in the workplace. In B. Fisher, V. Bowie, & C. Cooper (Eds.), *Workplace violence.* (pp. 103–115). Devon, UK: Willan Publishing.

Whitty, M. T., & Carr, A. N. (2005b). Taking the good with the bad: Applying Klein's work to further our understandings of cyber-cheating. *Journal of Couple and Relationship Therapy, 4*(2/3), 103–115.

Whitty, M. T., & Carr, A. N. (2006). *Cyberspace romance: The psychology of online relationships.* Basingstoke: Palgrave Macmillan.

Whitty, M. T., & Carville, S. E. (2008). Would I lie to you? Self-serving lies and other-oriented lies told across different media. *Computers in Human Behavior, 24*(3), 1021–1031.

Whitty, M. T., & McLaughlin, D. (2007). Online recreation: The relationship between loneliness, internet self-efficacy and the use of the internet for entertainment purposes. *Computers in Human Behavior, 23,* 1435–1446.

Whitty, M. T., & Quigley, L. (2008). Emotional and sexual infidelity offline and in cyberspace. *Journal of Marital and Family Therapy, 34,* 461–488.

Wilkins, L. (2003, May 20). Stalker had sophisticated cyber plan. *BBC News, UK edition.* Retrieved March, 2, 2005, from http://news.bbc.co.uk/1/hi/uk/3040623.stm

Winnicott, D. W. (1971). *Playing and reality.* New York: Basic Books.

Yarab, P. E., Sensibaugh, C. C., & Allgeier, E. (1998). More than just sex: Gender differences in the incidence of self-defined unfaithful behavior in heterosexual dating relationships. *Journal of Psychology & Human Sexuality, 10*(2), 45–57.

Young, K. S. (1998). Internet addiction: The emergence of a new clinical disorder. *CyberPsychology & Behavior, 1,* 237–244.

# 20

## Hurt Feelings and the Workplace

MICHAEL R. CUNNINGHAM, ANITA P. BARBEE, AND
ESHITA MANDAL

In Western societies in the first decade of the 21st century, a majority of adults spend nearly half of their waking hours working as paid employees in private or public organizations. From the moment that an individual applies for a job to the moment that the person moves on to another opportunity, is terminated from the position, or retires, there are abundant opportunities for hurt feelings.

We define hurt feelings as a form of emotional distress that may be experienced predominantly as sadness and depression but also may include sensations of anger, anxiety, and guilt. May and Jones (2007) distinguished between introjective hurt (feeling sad, engaging in self-blame, and wondering what one did wrong) and retaliatory hurt (yelling at, blaming, confronting, and feeling angry toward the offender) and suggested the two types have different dynamics. Yet, such feelings may be mixed, as we discuss later. The central element of hurt feelings is a sense that another person devalues the relationship (Leary, Springer, Negell, Ansell, & Evans, 1998), has rejected the self (Fitness, 2001), or has transgressed (Vangelisti, 2001).

Hurt feelings can be painful in any type of relationship, but hurt feelings may have particular intensity in the workplace. Although workplace relationships tend to be less close and personal than romantic relationships or friendships formed elsewhere, social acceptance in the workplace is associated with material as well as emotional well-being. A sense of rejection in the workplace not only can affect an individual's feelings of social desirability and self-confidence but also may have a tangible impact on the individual's career prospects and likelihood of maintaining a stable income, which can ripple through many domains of life. In addition, people may find their feelings hurt by institutional policies, as well as by individuals. This chapter reviews various sources of hurt feelings at work, looking first at institutional causes and then at interpersonal causes and responses.

## HURT FEELINGS DURING RECRUITMENT AND THE ON-BOARDING PROCESS

Hurt feelings at work involve a complex combination of actions, attributions, and emotions. Although work-related hurt feelings have not been the focus of a great deal of direct empirical examination, principles derived in other domains may be applied to this context. This application might be illustrated with an example. Suppose a young woman has just graduated from college with a bachelor of arts degree in communication, has acquired marketable skills but has thousands of dollars of debt, and seeks employment in a major corporation. The usual job-seeking process involves meeting a campus interviewer or submitting a resume by mail or online. By requesting a job, the individual has just put her self-respect on the line, and each day that goes by without a response may cause a downward click on the sociometer (Leary, Tambor, Terdal, & Downs, 1995). However, the hurt caused by the absence of immediate enthusiasm from employers depends on the new graduate's expectations. If the delay is seen as preventable, the employee-to-be may feel angry, whereas if she starts to question her own marketability, she may begin to feel depressed (Weiner, 1986). If the prospect regards the delay as normal, she may feel nothing but anticipation. Similar expectations may influence each step of the on-boarding process.

Imagine that our new graduate is invited to meet with the organization to discuss her qualifications. Preemployment interviewing and testing ask questions of job applicants to probe their competence, job-relevant attitudes, and ethics. In a meta-analysis of 86 studies, the applicants' gender, age, and ethnic background had no relation to their perceptions of selection procedures. Yet, applicants responded more favorably to interview procedures (which have low reliability and validity) than to cognitive ability tests, which were perceived more favorably than personality inventories and integrity tests (Hausknecht, Day, & Thomas, 2004). Because both preemployment cognitive and integrity tests have substantial validity in predicting performance, their use is justifiable (Arnold, 1991; Cunningham, Wong, & Barbee, 1995; Ones, Viswesvaran, & Schmidt, 1993). Nonetheless, if a job applicant has the expectation that because she graduated from college she should be exempt from testing, then her feelings may be hurt. Interestingly, applicants who hold positive perceptions about the selection process are more likely to view the organization favorably to report stronger intentions to accept job offers and to recommend the employer to other people (Hausknecht et al., 2004). Such results suggest that those who are unruffled by preemployment testing make better employees than those whose feelings are easily hurt by the selection process.

In many aspects of the workplace, a thick skin can be an asset. However, the opposite trend may be on the rise. A recent study of 16,475 college students who completed the Narcissistic Personality Inventory between 1982 and 2006 indicated a 30% increase on that trait (Twenge, 2006). Narcissists tend to feel a sense of uniqueness and entitlement, react aggressively to criticism, lack empathy, and favor self-promotion over helping others. These characteristics can cause problems when such graduates are disappointed by being offered a starting salary that affords little discretionary spending and are assigned to a work station in an unglamorous cubicle. Not only will their feelings be hurt by the quality of the job situation that they receive but also the combination of their narcissistic personalities and feeling undervalued may cause them to hurt the feelings of their coworkers as they function in a workplace that they despise. The combination of high expectations and reduced economic opportunities may set the stage for individuals to find themselves in work situations in which their feelings are repeatedly being hurt, but they have little recourse (Hess, 2000, 2006). As a consequence it is useful to briefly examine the historical dynamics that led to the current structures that influence expectations for relations within the modern workplace.

## EXPECTATIONS FOR COMMUNAL RELATIONSHIPS IN THE WORKPLACE

Family and friendship bands operating as hunter-gatherers formed the earliest economic organizations (Farb, 1968) and generally functioned on the basis of norms of communal sharing (Fiske, 1991). In a communal relationship, loyalty and compassion are essential values. The primary means of securing resources and services in a communal relationship is by asking or pleading for them. The communal norm expectation is that the other person will respond to the expressed need with helpfulness and generosity, downplaying equity considerations (Clark & Mills, 1979). If basic requests fail, people may convey their needs by expressing distress and complaints.

Employers often encourage the perception that workers are part of a big "family" that shares communal norms. Employees may wish to adopt that belief, because it allows them to feel that they are valued and secure. They may be subtly encouraged by administrators to hope that, if they disavow the power to unionize and negotiate, then management will accept the communal norm of the responsibility to protect and care for them, as if they were beloved sons and daughters. To maintain that impression and avoid hurt feelings, managers generally tell individual workers who request additional pay, benefits, or safety equipment that the company cannot afford it rather than that the employee simply has a low priority for such resources.

### Exchange Relationships and Hurt Feelings

Face-to-face relations among people who frequently interact together often follow communal norms, but decisions at other levels of a workplace organization tend to be based on exchange relationship norms. In an exchange relationship, individuals operate on the basis of norms of proportionality and market equity, distributing favors and rewards on the basis of the recipient's status and opportunity to pursue other options while competitively exploiting those with poor alternatives (Rusbult, Insko, Lin, & Smith, 1990).

Disclosures of individual needs and displays of expressive behaviors may influence one's coworker or immediate supervisor, but such communal norm communications seldom serve as persuasive arguments that can be passed up the administrative hierarchy to produce decisions by executives supporting enhanced compensation or improved working conditions for workers whom they have not met. Rejection of such requests may cause hurt feelings if the individual expected the executives to be more communally responsive. Yet, despite administrators' use of "family" language, such expectations may be misplaced. In fact, most desirable workplace benefits, such as paid family leave, were not granted because employers had a communal orientation and recognized employed parents' needs to take care of newborn children. Instead, such benefits were first granted in parts of Europe with strong union traditions, and then introduced in U.S. industries, such as information technology, in which there was a labor shortage and employees had ample opportunities to take their services elsewhere. In other words, communal relationship benefits were granted as a result of exchange relationship business necessities.

The primary means of acquiring resources in an exchange relationship is negotiation. Executives can negotiate individually for their salaries, because their boards of directors usually see them as unique, rather than as easily replaced (Cao, Maruping, & Takeuchi, 2006). Indeed, a chief executive officer (CEO) or organization president may have a communal relationship with members of the board of directors or board of trustees that determine his or her compensation packages, because the CEO or president contributed to their selection. CEOs substantially increased their wages and benefits since the late 1980s. In 1980, CEOs earned 42 times more than the average worker; in 2005, CEOs earned 411 times the pay of their subordinates, according to the Institute for Policy Studies – United for a Fair Economy. By contrast, the employee minimum wage remained unchanged in the United States from 1997 to 2007.

Managers and other workers who receive disproportionately lower salaries than the executives above them may experience hurt feelings because they believe that they are undervalued and unjustly treated (Wade, O'Reilly, & Pollock, 2006). Their hurt feelings may be compounded by the managers' recognition that the CEO and other top executives receive substantial company stock holdings and other personal incentives that are contingent on holding down employees' wages, benefits, and expenses such as investments in safety equipment. Such structures require that enlightened CEOs, who recognize the long-term economic benefits for their organization of a stable, high morale workforce, act contrary to their own short-term economic self-interest.

## Union Organizing and Hurt Feelings

To deal with the realities of exchange norms in the workplace, which conveyed the pervasively hurtful message that workers had few options and could easily be replaced, labor unions developed in the 19th century. The economic benefit of unionization was the opportunity it provided for collective bargaining, or negotiating as a group of workers who could not all easily be replaced. The emotional benefit of unionization was its encouragement of an atmosphere of acceptance, individual value, and communal feeling, which extended to the use of fraternal and sororal terminology. The union movement addressed some forms of hurt feelings, but ran the risk of creating others.

Although trade unions were successful in outlawing child labor, instituting an 8-hour work day, increasing wages, and securing seniority, pension, and medical benefits, unionization efforts have been minimally successful in the United States. Currently, Sweden has twice the proportion of unionists as Great Britain and Germany, which have twice the proportion of unionists as the United States; the percentage of union members among the U.S. workforce has decreased from a high of 35% to approximately 7% ("The Right to Organize," 2007). In the United States, antiunion propaganda linking unions with Communism, infiltration of some labor unions by organized crime, threats and intimidation of nonunion workers by union members, illegal retaliation against employees seeking unionization by employers, and federal laws favorable to offshore expansion have all taken their toll. For example, the United Auto Workers thrived after a successful sit-down strike at the General Motors factory in Flint, Michigan, in 1937, but General Motors exported the jobs to Mexico in the 1980s and closed the factory (Moore, 1989). Many American employees, including Wal-Mart workers, pharmacists, engineers, and university professors, refuse to organize and likely receive lower wages and benefits than they could obtain through collective bargaining.

A portion of U.S. employees' resistance to union organizing may be caused by a misapplication of communal relationship norms to an exchange relationship context. Unionization requires the adoption of an adversarial exchange orientation toward the workplace, as well as a burning sense of unjust treatment, which may be uncomfortable for those who prefer communal relationships (Blader, 2007). Employees who attempt to recruit their coworkers to join them in union activities may threaten their pleasant communal worldview. As a consequence, coworkers who feel social pressure to join a union may experience hurt feelings because their tranquility and autonomy are not being respected by the union organizers. Conversely, an employee who supports unionization and encounters resistance from coworkers may experience hurt feelings because of their implicit rejection of solidarity and apparent unwillingness to identify with the group and to work together for improved pay, benefits, and working conditions. Such hurt feelings may be compounded if the employee seeking unionization is relatively disadvantaged, such as a part-time faculty member, and the employee who rejects it is relatively advantaged, such as a tenured professor.

Professionals with advanced degrees also may be reluctant to participate in unionization activities because of their identity concerns. Such identity concerns include seeing involvement in a labor union as conveying working-class status and interchangeability with coworkers rather than reinforcing higher status and individuality. A request to join a union risks hurting the feelings of self-respecting professionals, who do not wish to see themselves as economically vulnerable employees. Similar dynamics operate in efforts to organize graduate students. Identification with the union-organizing group is a prerequisite for support for union certification (Blader, 2007).

Resistance to unionization by professionals also may stem from devotion to their work and distaste for conflict that could injure innocent third parties, such as students and pharmacy patients who could be adversely affected by labor actions such as a strike. Such altruistic attitudes may reduce employees' ability to negotiate effectively, because they eliminate the threat to withhold services. Ironically, the feelings of such professionals may be hurt because third-party beneficiaries seldom show appreciation for the professionals' unilateral disarmament and acceptance of poor compensation. The feelings of professionals may be further hurt when their spouse and children complain about their relatively modest pay and benefits.

The recent business trend toward a looser, less militaristic organizational hierarchy, with informal language (no longer addressing the supervisor as "sir" or "ma'am"), mixed genders in the workplace, casual workplace dress (fewer suits, ties, and dresses), options for telecommuting, and flexible vacation scheduling (Bailyn, 2006, Belson, 2007) may enhance workers' expectations for a communal relationship with their employer. These changes also may deepen the employee's feelings of hurt and betrayal when an executive makes an adverse decision based on cold exchange relationship considerations.

This discussion is not meant to imply that unionization is the only means of attaining equitable pay, benefits, and working conditions. Enlightened management could always adopt a generous and communal, rather than a penurious and exchange, relationship approach toward such decisions. Costco CEO Jim Segal reportedly takes a salary that is only 12 times that of his floor workers and pays salaries to them that are 40% higher than employees receive at competitors such as Sam's Club. As a consequence, Costco's turnover is five times lower than its chief rival, Wal-Mart (Goldberg & Ritter, 2006). Unfortunately, even in nonprofit organizations such as charitable organizations and universities, progress toward enlightened decision making is uneven.

At this point in history, people can no longer be captured and legally sold as slaves, but the companies in which they work can be sold without their input or consent. Such buyouts have major implications for employees' feelings of self-respect and for the quality of their working lives. Western corporate law currently conveys specific shareholder rights to the investment of money, but the investment of a career's worth of time and energy conveys almost no stakeholder standing (Uchitelle, 2006). Because most companies are acquired using leveraged funds, some staff members may be terminated and others may be forced to work longer and harder for the same salary, just to allow the new owners to pay interest to their bankers and investors (Bogle, 2005). Consequently, being part of a company that is sold may cause dislocation and diminished economic prospects for the workers. Being put in that uncomfortable position can certainly hurt workers' feelings, and that reaction is multiplied if the employee is terminated in the downsizing. The mafia slogan: "It's not personal, it's business" is cold comfort. A law that required that a company buyout compensate employees for their time investment could be a remedy for such lesses.

Employees' feelings also are hurt if the company is sold or dissolved because of the questionable management or malfeasance of the prior owners. Despite their personal innocence, employees feel shame for having been involved with stigmatized companies like Enron, Arthur Anderson, and WorldCom. Laws that actually protect corporate whistle-blowers and organizational policies that truly encourage the flow of suggestions and decision making upward as well as downward could prevent such business debacles, truncated careers, and the hurt feelings of thousands of employees.

## LEADERSHIP STYLE AND HURT FEELINGS

Senior business executives seldom seem troubled about making decisions that have adverse consequences for others. John F. Welch, chairman and CEO of General Electric (GE) from 1982 to 2000, reportedly had a practice of firing the bottom 10% of his managers and a comparable proportion of his lower level employees each year. CEOs at other companies imitated the GE downsizing policy. Although such policies enhanced stock prices, they also demoralized workers and led managers to engage in illegitimate actions to boost their division's profits and thereby avoid the ax (O'Boyle, 1999).

Termination from employment is the ultimate expression of devaluation of the person in the workplace. Bizarrely, employment termination became a spectator sport in the early 2000s, through the popularity of "reality" television shows, such as NBC's *The Apprentice*, which has aired for seven seasons to date. In that show, 18 employees are put in competitive situations, and one is fired by Donald Trump each week until only one remains. Demonstrating the impact of situational stress on employee behavior, the contestants engaged in many hurtful actions toward each other.

Pioneering social psychologist Kurt Lewin conducted influential experiments that contrasted the impact of authoritarian leaders, such as Welch and Trump, with democratic and laissez-faire leaders on both productivity and worker relations (Lewin, Lippett, & White, 1939). The studies were conducted with 10-year-old boys who participated in Saturday morning hobby activity clubs with adult leaders. The authoritarian leader established all of the policies and work assignments, emphasized the completion of tasks, and criticized boys who did not produce, obey, or measure up in other ways. The democratic leader worked with the group to set an agenda while trying not to dominate the group discussion and left decisions about specific assignments up to the group. Finally, the laissez-faire leader was relatively passive, facilitating group processes only when the group requested them and leaving decisions up to the group.

The experiments demonstrated that situational factors, such as the leadership and organizational structure, can have side effects on coworker hurt and hurtfulness. The boys produced the most crafts under the authoritarian leader, but they worked hard only when he was watching. Their work dropped off when he left the room. Boys under the direction of the authoritarian leader also tended to act aggressively toward each other, presumably directing the tension created by the leader against their peers. In the laissez-faire approach to management, the workers were unproductive, and members were dissatisfied both with the leader and with each other, presumably because of the absence of success experiences. Finally, the democratic leader was the most popular, producing a moderately high level of productivity and cordial group relations, because of the cooperation and task success achieved.

Subsequent research confirmed Lewin et al.'s (1939) original findings but added some important distinctions. Fiedler's (1958) contingency theory suggested that authoritarian leaders might be more successful than democratic leaders in poorly structured situations with ambiguous tasks and poor intergroup relations, whereas democratic leaders may be more successful when the tasks are predictable and intergroup relations already are pleasant. Vroom and Jago (1988) suggested that effectiveness of participatory leadership depends on the relationships among group members. Hersey and Blanchard's (1993) situational leadership theory suggested that mature groups may function quite well under a "delegating" style, which resembles laissez-faire leadership.

Many industries that are based on creativity and innovation, such as entertainment and high technology, emphasize a democratic leadership style and consensus building among peers. Google's CEO Eric Schmidt stated, "We adhere to the view that the 'many are smarter than the few,' and solicit a broad base of views before reaching any decision.... Building a consensus sometimes takes longer, but always produces a more committed team and better decisions." Consensus is sought not only about the directions to be taken in projects, but even about hiring. Schmidt added, "Virtually every person who interviews at Google talks to at least half-a-dozen interviewers, drawn from both management and potential colleagues. Everyone's opinion counts... One reason for extensive peer interviews is to make sure that teams are enthused about the new team member. Many of our best people are terrific role models in terms of team building, and we want to keep it that way" (Schmidt & Varian, 2005). Consensus building is an excellent way to avoid the hurt feelings that comes from stifled opinions. Similarly, having likely coworkers participate in the hiring process can reduce the stress that comes from having to associate with disliked new coworkers (Hess, 2000, 2006). Unfortunately, most organizations still seem to function in the authoritarian model, even when they meet the criteria for more mature approaches.

## MICRO-CULTURES AND THE ORGANIZATIONAL SOCIOMETER

Just as workplace organizations are influenced by the larger culture, each workplace organization is itself a mini-culture, influenced by the personality, goals, and preferences of the top leadership. Within each organization mini-culture are micro-cultures, influenced by the values and style of the department supervisor, coworkers, and the functions of that part of the organization. The new communication studies graduate described earlier would have a very different experience if hired by a small, family-owned company rather than a large multinational corporation. Suppose our new graduate is hired by a medium-sized private business. She might be assigned to the sales department, and have direct customer contact, or to the marketing department to design Web pages. The values, norms, and modal behaviors of the two departments may differ substantially. The two departments work under very different compensation systems, have different reporting structures, and face different challenges in meeting their work goals. A marketing employee who needs help on a project can ask a supervisor or peer for it, and someone who is not on a tight deadline will usually be available to provide assistance. Although salespeople are just as sociable as marketing staff, the sales force works for commission under a tight quota system and often has little uncommitted time.

A new employee who does not recognize those situational demands and micro-cultural norms and who asks a salesperson for a favor may have her feelings hurt, and her sociometer might decline when the salesperson refuses or fails to follow through. To avoid hurt feelings caused by such misunderstandings, it would be helpful if the new employee had a mentor who would clarify expectations and thereby reduce the impact of minor slights. Unfortunately, many organizations do not permit their employees to choose mentors who can devote their work time to individual training.

Even nonemployees can be hurt by workplace policies and practices. Some organizations have strict policies prohibiting employees from receiving phone calls or visits from relatives or friends while at work, and office staff may be quite rude to nonemployees who try to contact the employee during work time. A spouse who is hurt by a curt rebuff by a receptionist may, in turn, express displeasure to the employee, who then feels a downward click on the sociometer caused by affiliation with such an unpleasant organization.

Interpersonal tension and hurt feelings also can occur when the employer makes a precipitous reduction or change in an employee's work or vacation schedule. Such changes may ripple through the employee's family, affecting domestic arrangements for child care and cooking, involvements in voluntary organizations and sports teams, travel reservations, and the spouse's vacation schedule. If the changes cannot be helped and the organization is apologetic, then most employees and their families graciously make accommodations. But if the organization adopts a "take it or quit" attitude and there are no better employment alternatives, then the employee's feelings are likely to be hurt by such cold and uncivil treatment, which is compounded by the family's adverse reaction.

The institutional style of the modern workplace remains largely hierarchical and based on competitive, exchange norms. Consequently, there are ample opportunities for individuals to feel undervalued by the organization and to have their feelings hurt by institutional policies. Because employees have little discretion in the choice of their departments, offices, supervisors, and coworkers, they also have the opportunity to be hurt by individuals from whom they have little chance to avoid or escape.

## Hurtful Types of Employees

A popular approach for discussing hurt within the workplace is to classify offending people into categories or types. Bramson (1981), for example, offered colorful labels to describe his informal observations about "difficult" coworkers, including Sniper, Compleat Complainer, Unresponsive Person, Super-Agreeable, Wet Blanket, Know-it-All, and Indecisive Staller. The tradition continues with Sutton's (2007) description of coworkers and bosses whom he described as "assholes." Because such approaches are subjective, it is not clear whether all employees fall into or recognize such types.

By contrast, Harden Fritz (2002) took an empirical approach to "troublesome others at work," studing 744 undergraduate and graduate students, plus their parents, at a northeastern U.S. university. She asked respondents to select a work associate with whom they typically had unpleasant or negative experiences and to rate that person on 54 descriptive items using a 7-point rating scale (1 = not at all, 7 = very much or very often). A slim majority nominated peers ($n = 328$) as the most troublesome, followed by supervisors ($n = 223$) and subordinates ($n = 104$). Harden Fritz (2002) factor analyzed the responses both across and within status levels. She extracted 11 factors, not all of which applied to each status level: (a) *Lording Power* (the person wants his or her own way; the person likes to boss people around), which was largely the same for boss and subordinate but decomposed into two factors in the peer analysis – *controlling and bossy* and *self-promotion* (the person wants to be "number one"); (b) *Busybody Behavior* (the person butts into my conversations); (c) *Backstabbing* (the person bad mouths me to a third party or parties); (d) *Different from Me* (the person and I have different styles of communicating); (e) *Sexual Harassment* (the person gives others unwanted romantic attention); (f) *Poor Work Ethic* (the person performs incompetently); (g) *Unprofessional Focus of Attention* (the person brings personal problems to work); (h) *Distracting* (the person's personality is irritating); (i) *Defensiveness* (the person sees me as a threat to his or her job); (j) *Unethical* (the person takes credit for my work), which was apparent for bosses but not peers or subordinates; and (k) *Excessive Demands* (the person asks me to do tasks that are not related to work), which was evident for bosses and peers but not for subordinates.

There are some limitations to the analysis by Harden Fritz (2002). It is not clear that so many factors are required to effectively describe troublesome others, and criteria for factor extraction, such as minimum eigenvalues, were not reported. As a consequence, it is not clear whether it was crucial to retain a two-item factor, such as Excessive Demands. Other factors were composed of items that appear to have redundant or overlapping content. The Busybody factor, for example, included separate items about "butting into my busines," "butting into other people's business," "butting into my conversations," and "butting into other people's conversations." Had those four items been incorporated into a single statement, such as "the person butts into people's affairs," the item likely would have landed on another factor rather than defining an independent dimension. Finally, rather than describing concrete behaviors some items were vague or involved making inferences, such as "the person's personality is irritating," "the person and I have different styles of communicating," and "the person sees me as a threat to his or her job."

Harden Fritz (2002) also used the respondents' ratings to perform cluster analyses to identify six types of bosses, eight types of peers, and five types of subordinates. Harden Fritz (2006) conducted a replication study using 751 university students and their parents while employing the same 54 items as in the earlier study. This time, she extracted 9 boss factors, 10 peer factors, and 8 subordinate factors, but they were not always the same ones. Approximately half of the troublesome types, including two of six boss types, six of nine peer types, and one of five subordinate types were replicated from the first study of troublesome others. The two reliable boss types were the *Taskmaster*, who was characterized by control and excessive task demands that were sometimes unrelated to work and was believed to flout workplace ethical standards, and the *Okay Boss*, who exhibited very low levels of negative attributes. The replicated troublesome peer types included the *Soap Opera Star*, who was distracted by and distracted others by discussing personal problems in the workplace and was seen as somewhat incompetent, self-centered, and interfering with others' business. The *Bully* insisted on work being done his or her own way, got others to do work he or she should be doing, and took credit for that work, whereas the *Adolescent* was fearful of losing the job, sometimes screamed and yelled, and was demanding, self-promoting, distracting, and controlling. The *Independent Other* was troublesome only in rejecting the legitimate role-based authority of coworkers and was seen as being different in work style and interaction from the respondent. The *Mild Annoyance* was not a very problematic coworker, with low scores on all negative attribute factors. But the *Abrasive, Incompetent Harasser* fit the profile of someone who commits sexual harassment, was incompetent, unprofessional (yelling and screaming), distracting, and bossy and feared job loss. Finally, the reliable subordinate type was the *Incompetent Renegade*, who was portrayed as incompetent, resistant to orders, and distracting to others.

It was interesting that the peer types were particularly replicable, but it was unclear whether that was because peer relations were more consistent in form and content than superior–subordinate relations across the different times of the two studies or because the two peer samples were the largest, making them more robust than the other samples. Although those workplace types were fascinating, a question can be raised about the virtues of linking disparate qualities into types. The Abrasive, Incompetent Harasser was observed in both of the peer samples and the first subordinate samples, but should the conclusion be drawn that there are no harassers who are smooth and competent? Readers also may wonder which troublesome type causes the most hurt in the workplace, but that question was outside the scope of Harden Fritz's (2002, 2006) studies.

Another problem with typologies of employees is the dispositional presumption, which is that certain individuals have toxic personalities or fatal character flaws. An implication is that such warped employees should be socially rejected or discharged from the workplace. Certainly, personality and character issues may influence an employee's actions, providing ample justification for preemployment screening. But once an individual has been hired, it may be more prudent to focus on his or her overt behaviors than on presumed underlying traits. Such a focus encourages more objective feedback because it allows for the possibility that unacceptable actions may have situational rather than dispositional origins. Such feedback, in turn, may lead to less reactance and more change. Consequently, some researchers have focused on problematic communication and actions.

### Hurtful Behaviors: Incivility

Andersson and Pearson (1999) defined workplace incivility as "low-intensity deviant behavior with ambiguous intent to harm the target, in violation of workplace norms for mutual respect. Uncivil behaviors are characteristically rude and discourteous, displaying a lack of regard for others"(p. 457). Pearson, Andersson, and Wegner (2001) found that workers who felt they had been targets of workplace incivility reported experiencing a negative affective state after the experience. A limitation of their study was that employees used their own definitions of incivility, so some may have reported about more serious forms of conflict (cf. Keashly, 2001).

Pearson, Andersson, and Porath (2005) recounted popular interpretations for perceived increases in incivility in general, such as "absentee parenting, poor schools, media fascination with the dark side, and a relentless quest for individuality" (p. 181). They expanded that analysis to discuss both social contextual shifts and organizational pressures. Social contextual shifts include a general trend toward irreverence in society and an altered psychological contract with employers, described as "shifts in loyalty, retention, entitlement, short-term profitability, and informality. With minimal investment or trust in the long term, some employees will focus sharply on taking care of themselves, while neglecting the needs and desires of colleagues" (pp. 181–182). If employees are expected to think of the workplace as an informal communal environment, and modern family members periodically display backstage habits and express rude, impulsive, domineering, or selfish behavior, then such behaviors also may occur in the workplace.

Pearson et al. (2000) noted that shifting demographics may contribute to uncivil behavior, because communicating with those with different values could require additional time and effort. However, race and gender differences may matter less than the mixing of regional cultures caused by geographical mobility. A white and an African American coworker who both grew up in Savannah may have more in common with each other than either has with a white coworker from the Upper West Side of Manhattan or an African American from south central Los Angeles.

Pearson et al. (2005) suggested that organizational pressures, including downsizing, restructuring, mergers, and outsourcing, may contribute to a labor force that is unwilling to internalize organizational norms. Further, intraorganizational communication technology such as e-mail and voicemail can facilitate impersonal contact, including expressions that are not moderated by perceiving their immediate nonverbal impact on the recipient. Additional issues mentioned by Pearson et al. (2000, 2005) include inferior leadership caused by the promotion of technically rather than socially skilled managers and compressed time and deadlines. Some organizations have been forced to become "lean and mean" as a result of external pressures, such as increased fuel costs or price undercutting by government-subsidized foreign companies. Cost-control pressures that cause a reduction in the size of the workforce result in more responsibilities for those who remain and produce a more stressful, tiring, and longer workday. Unfortunately, most workers are not beneficiaries of a profit-sharing plan and are never compensated for their extra labor. Instead, they are expected to further increase their productivity to enhance the company's stock prices. Overworked and frustrated employees often become irritable and aggressive toward one another (Pearson et al., 2000, 2005).

## Measurements of Incivility

Cortina, Magley, Williams, and Langhout (2001) surveyed 1,662 employees in a federal court system about their experiences of workplace incivility using the seven-item Workplace Incivility Scale (WIS). The WIS measured the frequency of participants' experience of seven examples of disrespectful, rude, or condescending behaviors from superiors or coworkers in the past 5 years:

1. Put you down or was condescending to you?
2. Paid little attention to your statement or showed little interest in your opinion?
3. Made demeaning or derogatory remarks about you?
4. Addressed you in unprofessional terms, either publicly or privately?
5. Ignored or excluded you from professional camaraderie?
6. Doubted your judgment on a matter over which you have responsibility?
7. Made unwanted attempts to draw you into a discussion of personal matters?

The investigators reported that 71% of the respondent experienced some level of incivility in the workplace: 39% had encountered uncivil behavior an average of "once or twice," 25% experienced incivility "sometimes," and 6% endured the behavior "often" or "many times" (Cortina et al., 2001, p. 70). Respondents who reported more frequent experiences of incivility also reported less job satisfaction. After controlling for demographics and job stress, a higher frequency of reported incivility was still associated with lower satisfaction with coworkers, supervisors, promotion opportunities, work, and pay/benefits, in that order. In this study, incivility had a negligible impact on job withdrawal. Questions can be raised about the use of a 5-year reporting period and imprecise response intervals (i.e., how many times must an event occur in 5 years to be rated "sometimes"?). It is possible that generalized disgruntlement produced a negative halo that affected responses to both the incivility items, such as "excluded you from professional camaraderie," and specific forms of dissatisfaction, such as pay/benefits. Lim and Cortina (2005) conducted a subsequent study using four items from the WIS and reported that incivility often co-occurs with sexual harassment.

Martin and Hine (2005) sought to improve the assessment of workplace incivility with the development of the Uncivil Workplace Behavior Questionnaire (UWBQ). They generated a pool of items and then evaluated them for their conceptual consistency in terms of a priori categories of communication, nonverbal behavior, use of facilities, obstructionism, abuse of power, and exclusionary behavior. They further reduced their item pool to achieve clarity and conciseness, producing a pilot set of 124 items. Then, 339 Australian respondents indicated how frequently the uncivil behaviors occurred in the past year, using a 5-point Likert scale (1 = *never*, 2 = *rarely*, 3 = *occasionally*, 4 = *often*, 5 = *very often*.). Principal components analyses with oblimin rotation were conducted, using the stringent criterion of 60 item loading. This approach resulted in four factors, consisting of 20 items:

1. Hostility
   a. Raised their voice while speaking to you.
   b. Used an inappropriate tone when speaking to you.
   c. Spoke to you in an aggressive tone of voice.
   d. Rolled their eyes at you.
2. Privacy Invasion
   a. Took stationery from your desk without later returning it.
   b. Took items from your desk without prior permission.
   c. Interrupted you while you were speaking on the telephone.
   d. Read communications addressed to you, such as e-mails or faxes.
   e. Opened your desk drawers without prior permission.
3. Exclusionary Behavior
   a. Did not consult you in reference to a decision you should have been involved in.
   b. Gave unreasonably short notice when canceling or scheduling events you were required to be present for.
   c. Failed to inform you of a meeting you should have been informed about.
   d. Avoided consulting you when they would normally be expected to do so.
   e. Was excessively slow in returning your phone messages or e-mails without good reason for the delay.
   f. Intentionally failed to pass on information which you should have been made aware of.
   g. Was unreasonably slow in seeing to matters on which you were reliant on them without good reason.
4. Gossiping
   a. Publicly discussed your confidential personal information.
   b. Made snide remarks about you.
   c. Talked about you behind your back.
   d. Gossiped behind your back.

Although the labeling of factors is clearly an art rather than a science, the labels that Martin and Hine (2005) applied to their factors seem a bit stronger and more extreme than many of the behaviors within the factors; we use them here to illustrate a larger point about perspective. For example Hostility may be too polarized a label for rolled eyes or raised voice; Gruffness might be more accurate. Similarly, Privacy Invasion may apply to reading e-mails and opening desk drawers, but "invasion" seems a bit inflammatory to describe the majority of items, including taking stationery, taking other items from one's desk, or interrupting a conversation. Boundary Intrusion might better capture that disparate set of behaviors. Finally, Exclusionary Behavior suggests an overt effort to ostracize a person. Although two of the items in that factor convey such active behaviors, the majority of the items are relatively passive; Neglect-Disregard Behavior might be closer to the mark.

The labeling of behaviors, such as those in the Martin and Hines study, may depend on whether the investigator takes a victim or a perpetrator perspective (Stillwell & Baumeister, 1997) on the uncivil behaviors in question. The recipient of behaviors such as rolled eyes or a raised voice, for example, may experience the action as extremely uncivil and perhaps bullying, whereas the perpetrator may see the same actions as conveying only mild annoyance. It may be tempting to assume that the middle ground between the perspectives of the victim and the perpetrator represents objectivity, but that may be inaccurate. Since Heider's (1958) and Jones and Davis's (1965) pioneering work, psychologists have recognized that individuals who are personally affected by an action tend to make extreme attributions about the dispositions of the person who performed it. In the best of circumstances, the author of a communicative act may be the best interpreter of its meaning. A raised voice should be classified as hostile if the person who is yelling feels strongly aggressive and intends hurtful consequences for the target of the yelling. However, the raised voice should be classified merely as gruff if the person who is yelling simply feels irritated and wishes the recipient to be aware of being the cause of such annoyance. Unfortunately, if queried later, the "yeller" may not recall his or her emotions at the precise time of the action. In addition, because of motives ranging from self-deception to saving face to avoiding disciplinary consequences, one who does an allegedly uncivil action may not honestly and forthrightly recount its meaning. As a consequence, it can be difficult to gain consensus on characterizations of uncivil behavior. Of course, studies of hurt feelings may focus only on the victim's perspective, but it should be recognized that the recipient of an uncivil action may have completely misunderstood the coworker's behavior or may have been narcissistically oversensitive to mild negativity. In that light, Martin and Hines' (2005) factor labels may represent a strong victim perspective on uncivil workplace behaviors.

Returning to Martin and Hines's (2005) results, three of the four dimensions of the UWBQ correlated $r = .64$ or higher with the Workplace Incivility Scale, but Privacy Invasion (Boundary Intrusion) correlated only $r = .28$. Other factors had coherent relations with the outcome measures. Exclusionary

Behavior (Neglect-Disregard) ($r = -.33$, $\beta = -.17$; based on controlling for demographics in regression step 1, job stress in step 2, then entering the four UWBQ factors in step 3) and Gossiping ($r = -.36$; $\beta = -.17$) predicted low coworker satisfaction. Exclusionary Behavior (Neglect-Disregard) ($r = -.32$; $\beta = -.16$) and Hostility (Gruffness) ($r = -.36$; $\beta = -.24$) were negatively associated with supervisor satisfaction. Such results seem reasonable, in the sense that being ignored by either coworkers or supervisors can be unsettling, but coworkers are likely to engage in indirect aggression in the form of Gossiping, whereas supervisors are more likely to engage in direct aggression through Hostility (Gruffness). Gossiping ($r = -.24$; $\beta = -.18$) was negatively associated with health satisfaction, suggesting that being the victim of indirect aggression can be hazardous to one's health. Exclusionary Behavior (Neglect-Disregard) ($r = -.23$; $\beta = -.20$) was negatively associated with psychological well-being. Active or passive rejection is a major cause of hurt feelings, so the relationship of such behaviors with low psychological well-being is particularly interesting.

Respondents in the Martin and Hine (2005) study were not queried whether the uncivil behaviors were performed by one coworker or by different coworkers. Some uncivil actions, such as Gossiping by a group or Privacy Invasions (Boundary Intrusion) involving things missing from the desk without a known perpetrator, can cause employees to feel that the workplace as a whole is uncivil. Consequently, it was intriguing that Gossiping ($r = .25$; $\beta = -.24$) and Privacy Invasions (Boundary Intrusion) ($r = .17$; $\beta = -.13$) were associated with work withdrawal or neglecting tasks and reducing productivity. In the regression analysis, none of the four UWBQ factors was a significant predictor of job withdrawal (thoughts of leaving the organization), but each factor was individually correlated with job withdrawal, as was the total UWBQ scale ($r = .31$).

### Hurtful Behaviors: Social Allergy Processes

The incivility literature seems to lack a process theory for explaining how actions become hurtful (Feeny, 2005; Phillips & Smith, 2003; Plank, McDill, McPartland, & Jordan, 2001) and the role of receiver characteristics on the interpretation of uncivil messages and behaviors. By contrast, the social allergy model (Cunningham, Barbee, & Druen; 1997; Cunningham, Shamblen, Barbee, & Ault, 2005) offers a theoretically based, empirically validated analysis of the objectively minor but emotionally major incivilities of social life that grate on people's nerves like a pebble in a shoe.

A social allergen is defined as a behavior or situation created by another person that may be seen as unpleasant, but not as unbearably aversive, by objective observers. Through repeated exposure at periodic intervals, or through extreme or prolonged initial contact, a social allergen may produce a social allergy in the individual. A social allergy is a reaction of hypersensitive annoyance, disgust, or sadness in response to a social allergen. The social allergy model suggests that relatively minor uncivil behaviors affect a person emotionally in a manner that resembles how physical allergens function immunologically. The first experience with a physical allergen, such as poison ivy, is likely to produce a small negative reaction. With repeated contact with poison ivy, however, sensitivity tends to increase and the negative response becomes stronger. The same repetition–sensitization response may occur in response to a coworker's uncivil behavior.

Many uncivil behaviors that occur once or twice are gracefully tolerated and quickly forgotten (Kowalski, 2001). However, repeated exposures may increase the magnitude of the unpleasant feelings. For example, suppose our new employee in the marketing department discovers that a coworker has used up all of the paper in the photocopier and failed to replenish it, contrary to posted company norms. The first time that happens, she is likely to be slightly irritated. Each additional time it happens, her annoyance may become stronger, consistent with the repetition–sensitization process. This annoyance may accelerate if the employee jumps to the conclusion that the coworker does not care about inconveniencing her because she has such low rank, which then hurts her feelings.

Social allergies seem to be common experiences. In one study, 150 university students were asked about "people whom you cannot stand to be around, who drive you crazy without them necessarily intending to do so . . . situations in which you have such strong feelings toward a person that it takes very little for the person to irritate, offend you, or cause physical symptoms" (Cunningham et al., 1997). Every respondent was able to name at least one person who got under his or her skin; the average was one relative and three nonrelatives. When asked to identify the one person who generated the strongest negative feelings, 18% nominated coworkers and 17% noted superiors. Thus, at least one-third of social allergies were work related; the remaining nominations went to relatives, friends, and romantic partners. Relationships that are largely involuntary, such as with supervisors and coworkers, could be particularly aversive (Hess, 2000, 2006).

*Social Allergy Typology*
Initial efforts to classify allergenic behaviors were conducted using a grounded theory approach, followed by an assessment of interrater reliability (Cunningham et al., 1997). Subsequent research demonstrated the coherence of the typology in three samples using principal components analysis (Cunningham et al., 2005; Shamblen, 2004). In these studies, allergenic behaviors were reliably factored into four major categories that varied on the relatively orthogonal dimensions of personalism (Jones & Davis, 1965) and intentionality (Heider, 1958; Vangelisti & Young, 2000). Personalism refers to whether

the coworker's behaviors are personally directed toward the individual who is affected by them, as opposed to behaviors of the coworker that do not specifically focus on the affected observer. The more personally directed the action, the more the victim attributes it to dispositions within the actor (Jones & Davis, 1965). Intentionality involves behaviors that are perceived by the observer as being done on purpose, as opposed to behaviors that are performed habitually, accidentally, or without mindful thought. Note that this distinction focuses on the intentionality of the action rather than the consequences. Intentional actions may produce unintended negative consequences. However, the more intentional an act is perceived to be and the more harm that is created, the more anger that the victim feels (Weiner, 1986).

The intersection of the intentionality and personalism dimensions produces four categories of allergens. *Uncouth Habits* are uncivil coworker behaviors that are neither intentional nor personally directed, such as displaying poor grooming or frequently leaving one's things in others' work space. *Inconsiderate Acts* are egocentric behaviors that are unintentional but seem personally focused, such as not offering help when it is needed or being vague and indecisive in direct discussions. *Intrusive Behaviors* are obnoxious actions that are both intentional and personally directed, such as being critical, giving commands without having legitimate authority, or expressing prejudicial attitudes about a group. *Norm Violations* are intentional actions that violate the observer's standards of civil propriety but are not personally directed, such as doing unethical things to get ahead or lying to other people. Norm Violations are a violation of sociomoral expectations (Phillips & Smith, 2003). Honest people tend to deplore dishonest behavior in other people, even if such behavior does not affect them personally (Cunningham, 1990; Cunningham & Ash, 1988).

In essence, a social allergy may occur whenever the self-expression or convenience needs of one employee interfere with the personal boundaries, propriety, or comfort needs of another employee. A person who performs a vulgar, insensitive, pushy, or proscribed behavior not only introduces a negative element of incivility into a relationship but also suggests the lack of expected positive relationship elements, such as mutual esteem and consideration (Barbee, Cunningham, Druen, & Yankeelov, 1996). Consistency in the occurrence of allergenic behaviors over time may create a perception of character flaws in the perpetrator and reflect a lack of respect by the perpetrator for the offended party and a perceived deficiency in the organization's culture. For example, allergic reactions to uncouth habits may include both coworker and workplace attributions. An employee who is irritated by a coworker's loud, off-key humming in an adjacent cubicle may simultaneously resent the inherent unpleasantness of the sound, the coworker's apparent indifference to others, and the CEO's poor decisions about the physical layout and soundproofing of the office. Similarly, a coworker's norm violations may suggest an asocial or antisocial character in the perpetrator and the human resource department's indifference to such deviancy, as indicated by hiring that employee. In the same vein, inconsiderate actions and intrusive behaviors suggest the perpetrator's egocentrism and a lack of respect for the recipient, as well as the supervisor's inattentiveness to the coworker's personality flaws. Each repetition of the allergenic action may seem to confirm the victim's negative attributions (Fincham & Bradbury, 1987) and increase the hurt feelings. Such feelings may be magnified if the victim said something about the issue to the perpetrator or the perpetrator's supervisor, but the offending action continues nonetheless.

The original description of social allergy processes was based on studies of close relationships but is compatible with research on incivility in the workplace. The two research fields are similar in recognizing that aversive interpersonal behaviors have the potential to spiral out of control, leading to overtly hostile interactions (Andersson & Pearson, 1999; Kowalski, 2001, 2003), with adverse effects on the morale of other coworkers (Robinson & Greenberg, 1998) and the organization as a whole. However, social allergy research has diverged from the approach taken by Martin and Hine (2005) on uncivil workplace behavior, which included acts of omission, such as "*Was excessively slow in returning your phone messages or e-mails.*" When research on social allergies began more than a decade ago, a decision was made to emphasize overt behaviors performed by the other party rather than perceptions that the other person should have performed a behavior but did not do so. There were several theoretical grounds for this position. The first was that an individual could have expectations for a partner that never were communicated. Although the individual could grow increasingly resentful at the partner's repeated failures to perform as expected, responsibility for the cause of the negative emotions may lie more with the individual than with the partner. To avoid such causal ambiguities, it seemed appropriate to conduct initial examinations of repetition–sensitization processes using overt behaviors. A second reason for excluding nonperformance from the initial social allergen typology was the issue of the controllability of the remedy. An unintentional uncouth or egocentric behavior generates internal stimuli that can be monitored by the perpetrator and stifled as they are occurring, if desired. But a forgotten action generates no sensations. As a consequence, it may be more difficult for a perpetrator to force him- or herself to remember to perform a desired behavior than to curtail an undesirable action. For those reasons, social allergy analyses, both in close relationships and in the workplace relationships, focused on unpleasant commissions rather than omissions.

## Social Allergens in the Workplace

We conducted a survey of the experience of social allergies in current employees. The sample consisted of 112 adults (61 males, 51 females) from a wide variety of occupations and industries in Louisville, Kentucky. The majority of participants were full-time employees recruited from the community ($n = 80$, employed full time an average of 8.31 years, including 3.66 years with the current employer) and the rest were full-time employees ($n = 32$, employed full time an average of 4.38 years, including 1.47 years with the current employer) recruited from social science classes at a large southeastern U.S. university. The males and females did not significantly differ in age (male = 28.28; female = 27.61), length of full-time employment ($m = 6.59; f = 8.45$), tenure with the same employer ($m = 2.94; f = 3.14$), or education ($m = 16.12; f = 15.46$). The sample was ethnically diverse, with 46.3% white, 41.1% Asian including the Indian subcontinent, 3.6% African American, and 9% participants who reported "Other Ethnicity."

After signing an informed consent statement, respondents reported background information, such as demographics and their tenure with the company. Next, respondents were asked to identify the coworker with whom they interacted most frequently; his or her relative rank, age, and gender; and the number of hours spent in the same room with the coworker. All subsequent questions focused on the behavior of that coworker, asking for reports of the frequency of allergenic behaviors by that coworker and the employee's perceptions of that coworker's organizational citizenship behaviors. Finally, employees were asked to rate their own intrinsic and extrinsic job satisfaction and their turnover intentions. This approach had the virtue of specifying a single source for a social allergy, but deliberately ignored unpleasant behavior by other coworkers. Because this study did not seek to capture the full range of social allergens or other workplace stresses to which an employee might be subjected, small to moderate correlations were expected between reports of social allergens from a single coworker and the employee's job satisfaction and turnover intentions.

*Coworker Allergy Inventory (CAI)*
After specifying the coworker with whom they spent the most time, respondents were asked to report how frequently the coworker performed 48 behaviors. The 48 behaviors were derived from the Cunningham et al. (1997) study, in which respondents nominated acts that they found aversive, as well as additional items suggested by the incivility literature (Cortina et al., 2001; Johnson & Indvik, 2001a,b; Pearson, Andersson, & Porath, 2000) and from personal observation. Ratings of behavior frequencies were made on a 9-point scale, ranging from 0 = *never* to 9 = *two or more times per day*. The participants also were asked to rate how annoying the behaviors were on a 9-point scale (0 = *not at all annoying* to 9 = *extremely annoying*).

Twenty-eight items were retained based on varimax rotation (minimum eigenvalue = 1, minimum .40 for loading on primary factor, and .10 difference between loading on a primary and secondary factor). The typology of social allergens that was initially validated with dating couples was also supported in this study of organizational relationships and included the following:

1. Uncouth Habits (unintentional and not personal, $\alpha = .72$)
   a. The coworker acts in an inappropriately sexual fashion at work.
   b. The coworker uses jargon that makes it difficult to understand him/her.
   c. The coworker forgets to share work information with you.
   d. The coworker smells unpleasant due to poor hygiene.
   e. The coworker uses too much tobacco, alcohol or drugs.
   f. The coworker leaves his/her things in your space.
   g. The coworker does not dress appropriately for the job.
2. Inconsiderate Acts (unintentional and personal, $\alpha = .81$)
   a. The coworker becomes highly anxious with minor problems.
   b. The coworker is vague and indecisive.
   c. The coworker does not work hard.
   d. The coworker often complains about mundane things.
   e. The coworker does not show the essential team spirit skills.
   f. The coworker does not exhibit the necessary skills for the job.
   g. The coworker allows other people to strongly influence his/her actions.
   h. The coworker does not offer to help when you obviously need it.
3. Intrusive Behaviors (intentional and personal, $\alpha = .91$)
   a. The coworker turns down a reasonable request without explaining why.
   b. The coworker is rigid and does not accept your suggestions.
   c. The coworker is arrogant and treats you like you are inferior.
   d. The coworker tells you what to do without having appropriate authority.
   e. The coworker forgets to reciprocate favors to you.
   f. The coworker does not let you take a turn in the conversation.
   g. The coworker imposes his/her thoughts and opinion on you.
   h. The coworker expresses prejudicial attitudes about a group without thinking about you being a member (i.e., comments about a political party, religion, ethnic group, gender, etc.).
   i. The coworker is critical of you.
   j. The coworker is stubborn and refuses to compromise with you.
   k. The coworker is unable to say and do things to support you when you are feeling upset.
   l. The coworker is cool and distant to you.
   m. The coworker asks you questions that are overly personal.
4. Norm Violations (intentional and not personal, $\alpha = .88$)
   a. The coworker criticizes others publicly.
   b. The coworker criticizes people who are in a position of authority.
   c. The coworker says nasty things about other people.
   d. The coworker has lied to other people.

e. The coworker creates obstacles for more successful people.
f. The coworker frequently expresses anger to other people.

Inconsiderate Acts were the most frequently observed allergenic behaviors ($M = 2.34$), occurring significantly more often than Uncouth Habits (1.08), Intrusive Behaviors (1.48), or Norm Violations (1.45), which did not differ in frequency. A similar pattern was observed with respect to emotional responses to the allergens. When Inconsiderate Acts occurred, they produced significantly greater emotional reaction than Uncouth Habits ($M = 2.30$ vs. 1.25) and Intrusive Behaviors (1.82) and marginally more emotional reaction than Norm Violations (1.52). The repetition–sensitization hypothesis, which suggested that more frequent allergens tended to produce more intense emotional responses, was tested by correlating the mean frequency of occurrence of each allergen with the mean emotional response to each allergen. Across all allergens, the correlation was $r = .83$, indicating that the more often an allergen occurred, the more intense was the emotional reaction to it. As a consequence, the primary variable explored in this investigation was *social allergy impact*, which consisted of the product of the frequency that the coworker performed an allergen and the intensity of the respondent's emotional reaction to that allergen. Earlier studies of social allergies (Cunningham et al., 2005) reported significant agreement between observers' and actors' reports of the frequency of allergen performance; thus, the responses are presumably based on fairly accurate estimates of behavioral frequencies.

ORGANIZATIONAL CITIZENSHIP, JOB SATISFACTION, TURNOVER INTENTIONS, AND COPING. Respondents also completed Posdakoff and Mackenzie's (1994) Organizational Citizenship Behavior (OCB) scale, which was modified by asking respondents to report about their *coworker's* behaviors rather than their own. The scale originally consisted of 14 items that measure six dimensions: courtesy, cheerleading, peacemaking, civic virtue, altruism, and unsportsmanship. Principal components analysis in our sample produced three factors. The *Courteous* factor included 6 items ($\alpha = .87$) stressing courtesy, peacemaking, cheerleading, and altruism. The second factor, titled *Complaining*, consisted of the four "unsportsmanlike" items ($\alpha = .84$), such as making demoralizing comments. The third factor, *Participating*, involved four items ($\alpha = .77$) assessing the willingness to volunteer for optional activities. The Courteous and Participating factors were strongly correlated ($r = .56$, $p < .001$), but those two variables were less closely related to Complaining ($r = -.46, p < .01; r = -.24, p < .05$). In fact, Complaining had a lower average correlation with the other OCB factors (mean $r = -.35$) than with the Social Allergy factors (mean $r = .45$), such as Inconsiderate ($r = .58$) and Intrusive ($r = .49$). Therefore, it appeared that the Complaining factor was a measure of social allergens rather than Organizational Citizenship.

In addition, respondents completed the Minnesota Satisfaction Scale (MSQ; Weiss, Davis, England, & Lofquist, 1967). Principal components analysis indicated two intrinsic and three extrinsic sources of job satisfaction. *Skill Use* involved five items ($\alpha = .80$) based on satisfaction stemming from using one's abilities and doing different activities. *Power* consisted of three items ($\alpha = .75$) involving satisfaction from influencing and helping people and having steady employment. Three factors involved extrinsic sources of satisfaction. *Social Environment* consisted of three items ($\alpha = .65$) asking about how coworkers get along, the behavior of the most frequently seen coworker, and the general environment. The *Pay* factor involved three items ($\alpha = .73$) measuring satisfaction with compensation, chances for advancement, and company politics. The final factor, labeled *Boss Quality*, consisted of two items ($\alpha = .82$) involving satisfaction with one's immediate superior. Those dimensions are quite similar to Baehr and Renck's (1958) findings for the determinants of employee morale, which reported factors concerning Friendliness and Cooperation of Fellow Employees, Personal Rewards, Immediate Supervision, Job Performance Satisfaction, and Integration in the Organization.

Based on such study fundings, it seemed appropriate to focus our analyses of the impact of coworker behaviors on satisfaction with the social environment of the job while recognizing that other components of job satisfaction, such as pay and skill use also could predict turnover intentions. Respondents reported their turnover intentions using three questions ($\alpha = .73$) that asked about thoughts about leaving, plans to look for another job, and willingness to choose the current job again (Michigan Organizational Assessment Questionnaire, Camman, Fichman, Jenkins, & Klesh, 1979, cited in Cook, Hepworth, Wall, & Warr, 1981).

Finally, employees were asked three questions about their efforts to cope with the allergenic coworker. They were asked to what extent they avoid the coworker (0 = *Never avoid* to 9 = *Avoid as much as possible*). They also were asked about the extent to which they talked to the coworker about what annoyed them (*Never talked to the coworker* = 0 to *Talked three or more times* = 3). Finally, employees reported the extent to which they talked to other people about the coworker, using the same response scale.

*Gender Effects on Contact and Social Allergens*
Males had their most frequent work interactions with other male coworkers (83.6%), and females were more likely to interact with other females (66.7%). A series of ANOVAs were conducted on the impact of the respondent's gender, which indicated that female participants reported experiencing greater allergy impact (allergen frequency * emotional response) than men to Inconsiderate Acts, Intrusive Behaviors, and Norm Violations but not to Uncouth Habits. This outcome is consistent with prior reports that females were more sensitive to negative interpersonal communication and relationship problems than men (Anderson, 1998).

To explore these effects, additional analyses were conducted on gender differences in perceived allergen frequency and emotional reaction. Female respondents reported that their coworkers performed a higher frequency of Norm Violations than males reported (1.87 vs. 1.09) and a marginally higher frequency of Intrusive Acts (1.80 vs. 1.17) but not a higher frequency of Inconsiderate Acts (2.56 vs. 2.12) or Uncouth Habits (1.39 vs. 1.16). In addition, female coworkers (as observed by both female and male respondents) were perceived to produce marginally more Norm Violations (1.83 vs. 1.17). Specifically, female coworkers were seen as more likely to engage in publicly criticizing others (1.95 vs. .97) and were marginally more likely to criticize those in positions of authority (2.84 vs. 1.91), say nasty things about other people (2.00 vs. 1.29), and express anger to other people (2.14 vs. 1.39). Female coworkers were not perceived to perform more Intrusive Behaviors (1.60 vs. 1.38), Uncouth Habits (.95 vs. 1.24), or Inconsiderate Acts, (2.41 vs. 2.27), nor were there any interactions between respondent and coworker gender.

Continuing to explore the determinants of allergy impact, females reported stronger emotional reactions than men to the occurrence of Intrusive Behaviors (2.28 vs. 1.39) and marginally greater reactions to Inconsiderate Acts (2.76 vs. 2.05) and Norm Violations (1.88 vs. 1.20), but no difference in response to Uncouth Habits (1.45 vs. 1.15). Examining the specific behaviors that constituted Intrusive Behaviors, females were more upset than men when the coworker was critical of them and expressed prejudicial attitudes without thinking; females were and marginally more annoyed when the coworker was stubborn and refused to compromise with them, told them what to do without having appropriate authority, was cool and distant to them, was unable to say and do things to support them when they were upset, and imposed thoughts and opinions on them. Thus, gender differences in allergy impact may be attributed to a greater frequency of the female coworkers' verbally aggressive Norm Violations to the employee and to the female employees' greater emotional reactivity to the coworkers' critical, dominant, or cold Intrusive behavior.

*Organizational Rank Effects on Contact and Social Allergens*
Respondents interacted most frequently with peers (51.38%) and were less likely to report that the fellow employee with whom they interacted most frequently was a superior (33.03%) or subordinate (15.60%). Coworker rank in the organization had an effect on Intrusive Behavior impact, such that equal-status peers produced a marginally stronger impact on Intrusive Behavior (M = 10.61) than either upper status (4.99) or lower status (2.66) coworkers, who did not differ. Perhaps superiors were not seen as more Intrusive than others because they were evaluated using different criteria than peers or subordinates. Peers who engaged in Intrusive Behaviors may have been seen more negatively than superiors who engaged in the same actions, because the latter had organizational legitimacy.

There were no significant effects of coworker ethnic group on perceived allergens nor any interactions with subject gender, coworker gender, or rank. No significant correlations were obtained between the reported frequency of social allergens and the respondent's status as a full-time or part-time employee, the respondent's tenure with the organization, or the education or ethnic group to which he or she belonged. The respondent's gender was unrelated to the perception of the coworker in terms of the OCB dimension of Courteous or Participating. The OCB dimensions also were unrelated to coworker gender, coworker rank, or coworker ethnicity. As a consequence, the demographic variables were disregarded for the remainder of the analyses.

*Relation of Social Allergy Impact to Coworker Organizational Citizenship, Job Satisfaction, and Turnover*

The four Social Allergy impact scores were significantly negatively correlated with perception of the coworker's performance on the two OCB dimensions (mean $r = -.40$). The four Social Allergy impacts also were each negatively correlated with the Social Environment component of job satisfaction (mean $r = -.35$). The Courteous and Participating OCB dimensions also were positively correlated with Social Environment job satisfaction (mean $r = .35$). Neither social allergies nor OCBs correlated with the Skill Use, Power, or Pay components of job satisfaction. However, satisfaction with Boss Quality was higher with the perception that the coworker displayed a high level of Courteous ($r = .29$) and a low level of Complaining OCBs ($r = -.22$). Thus, it appears that both the coworker's negative social allergy behaviors and the positive organizational citizenship behaviors affected satisfaction with the social environment dimension of the job but did not appear to undermine other aspects of job satisfaction. Such results indicate that research participants were responding thoughtfully to the items and not letting a general feeling of negativity or positivity color their reactions.

Although it was only one component of job satisfaction, the importance of the social environment factor should not be minimized, because it was significantly negatively correlated with turnover intention ($r = -.30$; when corrected for predictor and criterion unreliability, $r = -.44$). The other four sources of satisfaction especially pay and skill use also were correlated with turnover intention (mean $r = -.42$). In addition, greater allergy impacts from Norm Violations ($r = .19$) and Complaining ($r = .20$) were positively correlated with turnover intentions.

## Attempts to Buffer the Impact of Social Allergies

*Coping by Talking to the Coworker*

Greater allergy impact was associated with more coping effort. The greater the allergy impact of the coworker's Uncouth Habits ($r = .26$), Inconsiderate

Acts ($r = .29$), Intrusive Behavior ($r = .34$), and Norm Violations ($r = .25$), the greater the likelihood that the employee talked to the coworker about the problem. There were no gender differences in speaking with the coworker about the problem (1.12 vs. .97) nor in the willingness to speak to a peer vs. a subordinate (1.26 vs. 1.06). However, employees were more willing to talk to a peer than to talk to a superior when the coworker's behavior annoyed them (1.26 vs. .69). Of the 81% of employees whose coworker displayed allergenic behavior once every 2 months or more often, 65.4% (53% of the total sample) had spoken with the coworker about the problem. Most such conversations did not stop the problem, however, because discussing the issue was positively, rather than negatively, correlated with total allergen frequency ($r = .40$) and total emotional intensity ($r = .36$). Perhaps as a result of the ineffectiveness of the effort, talking with the coworker about the problem did not improve job satisfaction with the social environment ($r = -.42$), nor did it reduce thoughts of turnover ($r = -.07$). Yet, there were some hints of communication success, because 19% of the sample reported that the coworker with whom they interacted most frequently currently displayed allergenic behavior less than once every 2 months or never. Some of those coworkers may have never caused an annoyance, but 42% of the employees whose coworker currently displayed allergenic behavior less than once every 2 months or never (8% of the full sample) had spoken to the coworker about an annoying behavior. Consequently, some of the coworkers who were currently displaying a low frequency of allergens likely curtailed their aversive actions as a result of the talk. Less frequent displays of a behavior and rapid changes in behavior when confronted may point to a situational rather than dispositional reason for the behavior. Those who perform a behavior more frequently and are unresponsive to feedback, may, in fact, behave based on internal personality or value traits that are resistant to change. A more formal or prolonged intervention may be needed for such individuals. A longitudinal study would provide more definitive information on this issue.

*Coping by Avoidance*
The employees also reported more avoidance of the coworker as a function of stronger allergy impact from the coworker's Uncouth Habits ($r = .54$), Inconsiderate Acts ($r = .65$), Intrusive Behavior ($r = .73$), and Norm Violations ($r = .60$). Females reported a higher level of avoidance than males (2.44 vs. 1.52). Employees tended to avoid unpleasant peers more than they avoided their subordinates (2.29 vs. 1.00). They also tended to avoid their bosses marginally more than their subordinates (1.84 vs. 1.00), but avoidance of bosses did not differ from avoidance of peers (1.84 vs. 2.29). Avoidance was not particularly successful, however, because it was associated with *lower* satisfaction with the social environment at work ($r = -.42$) and did *not* reduce turnover intentions ($r = .11$). One reason why avoidance may not have been an effective coping

strategy is that the constraints of the workplace did not permit the employee to avoid the coworker for a sufficient length of time for the social allergy to abate. In fact, employees who were above the median on reported effort to avoid the coworker did *not* spend significantly fewer hours with the offending party than those who were below the median on reported effort to avoid their fellow employee (4.67 vs. 5.48).

*Coping by Seeking Social Support*
Finally, employees were more likely to talk to other employees about the coworker as a function of the magnitude of their allergy to the coworker's Uncouth Behaviors ($r = .28$), Inconsiderate Acts ($r = .46$), Intrusive Behavior ($r = .44$), and Norm Violations ($r = .24$). Among the employees whose coworker performed allergenic behaviors once every 2 months or more often, 67.9% (54.5% of the total sample) talked about the coworker's behavior with other people. Females were marginally more likely than males to talk to others about their annoying coworker (1.40 vs. 1.07). Employees were more likely to complain to others about a peer than a subordinate (1.37 vs. .65) and marginally more likely to discuss a boss than a subordinate (1.27 vs. .65), whereas rates of talking about a peer and boss did not differ. It is possible that employees did not complain to others about their subordinates because it could imply a lack of supervisory influence over the offending worker. In this sample, reports of talking to others about the coworker were marginally negatively related to satisfaction with the social environment of the job ($r = -.20$) but significantly inversely related to reduced turnover intentions ($r = -.32$). Thus, talking to fellow employees did not reduce the component of job dissatisfaction that was caused by an allergen-producing coworker, but having other people who were willing to provide understanding and solutions appeared to reduce thoughts of quitting.

*Latent Variable Path Model*
The bivariate correlation analyses could not determine whether the negative Social Allergy and positive OCB behaviors had independent effects on satisfaction turnover or were merely alternate measures of the same underlying construct. To clarify the correlation results, LISREL (Joreskog & Sorbom, 1993) analyses were conducted to examine the paths from Social Allergy impact and Organizational Citizenship Behavior frequency through social environment job satisfaction to turnover intentions.

The correlation results indicated that the four Social Allergy impact measures, plus Complaining, had comparable effects on coping, job satisfaction, and turnover intention. A latent trait of Social Allergy impact was indicated by Uncouth Habits, Inconsiderate Acts, Intrusive Behavior, and Norm Violations allergy impacts, plus the frequency of coworker Complaining. The latent Social Allergy variable negatively predicted the social environment

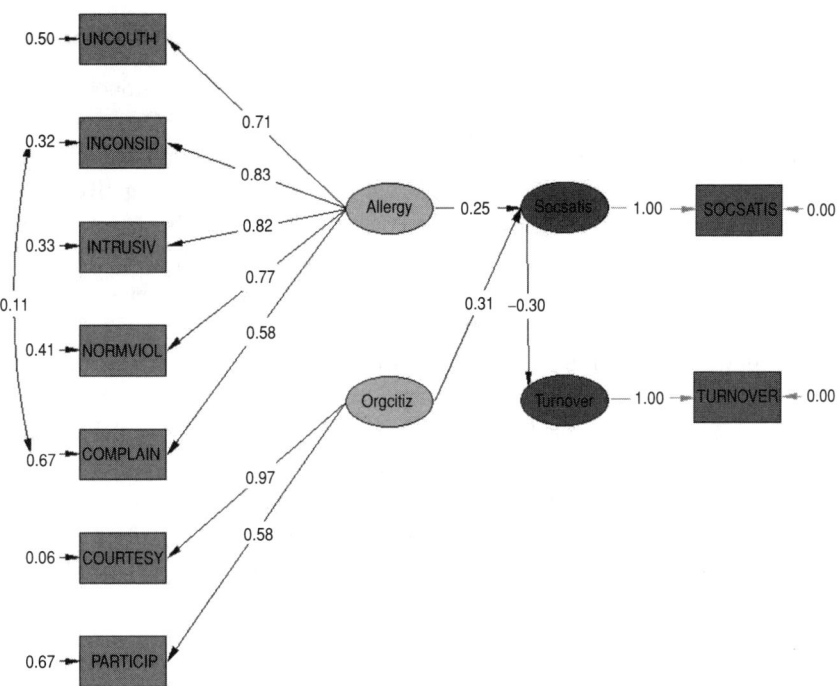

FIGURE 20.1. Structural equation model of the relation of social allergies and coworker organizational citizenship behaviors to satisfaction with the social environment of the job and turnover intentions. Uncouth = impact of Uncouth Habit social allergies; Inconsid = Inconsiderate Acts; Intrusiv = Intrusive Behaviors; Normviol = Norm Violations; Courtesy = courteous organizational citizenship behaviors; Particip = participatory organizational citizenship behaviors; Orgcitz = coworker organizational citizenship behavior; Socsatis = satisfaction with the social environment of the job; Turnover = turnover intention.

component of job satisfaction. The errors of Complaining and Inconsiderate were correlated. The latent trait of OCB was indicated by Courtesy and Participation, and OCB positively predicted the social environment component of job satisfaction. The latent traits of Social Allergy and Organizational Citizenship Behavior both made significant independent contributions to social environment job satisfaction. Social environment job satisfaction was inversely related to turnover intentions. In addition, the Social Allergy latent trait influenced talking to others about the annoying coworker, which independently reduced turnover intentions. The reduced model had an excellent fit [$\chi2(24) =$ 28.56, $p < .24$; AGFI = .90] and is presented in Figure 20.1. Other tested models had substantially poorer fits. Thus, the structural equation results indicate that separate assessments of social allergies and of coworker organizational citizenship behaviors both contribute to employees' satisfaction with the social environment of their job, which, in turn, affects their turnover intentions.

### Observations, Limitations, and Extensions of the Coworker Allergy Study

It was particularly interesting that the impact of the coworker's Social Allergens on the employee, and the frequency of the coworkers' Organizational Citizenship Behavior, were independent predictors of satisfaction with the social environment of the job. It appears that a reduction of negative workplace behaviors, indexed by social allergens, and an increase in positive workplace actions, indicated by organizational citizenship behaviors, might both be important strategies to enhance productivity and reduce turnover.

In this study, only the participants' recollection and report of their coworker were assessed rather than the coworkers' own self-reports or independent observations of the coworker's behavior. Yet, the employees' perceptions of coworkers' behaviors likely have some validity. In a study of social allergies in dating couples, the individual's perceptions of the frequency of allergenic behaviors were significantly correlated with the partner's own self-reports of having performed such behavior (Cunningham et al., 2005). Nonetheless, future research could attempt to measure both the self-reported behavior and the personality of the coworker who performs allergenic behaviors. It would be informative to know if allergen-emitting coworkers were more narcissistic or lower in self-monitoring than their peers.

The possibility of a negative halo effect cannot be completely excluded, because there were no unique relations between specific allergens and specific coworker organizational citizenship behaviors. But that outcome may reflect reality, in that coworkers who display high levels of any allergen may display low levels of each type of organizational citizenship behavior. Also arguing against a halo effect, research participants displayed careful responding in differentiating their feelings about the social environment of work from other elements of their job satisfaction.

This study assessed the employees' use of three types of strategies to cope with social allergies. There were hints that talking to the fellow employee had a positive effect in some instances, although the problems continued in many others. Efforts to avoid the coworker did not appear to be effective, although this could have been due to job constraints that required the employee to frequently interact with the allergy-inducing coworker. If an allergic employee could avoid the allergenic coworker for weeks at a time, rather like a trial separation in a troubled marriage, there might be more allergy abatement.

The strategy that seemed to be most successful for coping with social allergies was talking to other employees about the allergenic coworker. Seeking social support from peers offered both the prospect of short-term emotional solace and long-term problem-solving advice (Barbee & Cunningham, 1995, Cunningham & Barbee, 2000). Seeking social support was associated with reduced turnover intentions. However, there are two drawbacks to consulting with other employees about an annoying coworker. The first downside is that the time that the employee spends soliciting support for a social allergy from a peer reduces the work productivity of both employees, unless such discussions are strictly restricted to lunch or off-hours. The second problem with seeking social support is that the employee with the original allergy may create an allergy in the second employee, either to the perpetrator or to the complaining victim, who may display whining, helplessness, or unresponsiveness to proposed solutions that could become aversive to the support provider. Perceiving that the coworker frequently says nasty things ($r = .24$), expresses anger ($r = .21$), and criticizes others publicly ($r = .18$) all may stimulate the supportive peer to have thoughts of leaving the organization. If the allergenic person hears about the support seeking, he or she may interpret the conversations as gossip and feel hurt or harassed. Thus, social allergenic behavior can stimulate a ripple of negative feeling that reduces productivity and enhances a negative social environment throughout the organization. Future studies might use more extensive measures of employee coping and through longitudinal assessment of coping and of actual turnover rather than cross-sectional measurement of coping and turnover intentions.

Social allergy items were excluded if they loaded on more than one allergy factor, so some common and aversive allergies were not present in the final measures. That approach does not undermine the current findings, but it probably underestimated allergy impact and attenuated the relation among allergies, satisfaction, and turnover. In addition, as noted earlier, this study asked about the coworker with whom the employee interacted most frequently rather than about the total frequency of uncivil behaviors in the workplace. That approach was useful in examining the impact of a single allergenic coworker, but it did not account for the impact of a clique of unpleasant coworkers or of an out-of-control workplace that tolerates widespread bullying or sexual harassment. Future investigations might use both the Coworker Allergy Inventory and the Unpleasant Workplace Behavior Questionnaire to assess group and individual sources of disagreeable behaviors.

Allergy impact was measured as the product of the frequency and the affective aversiveness of the allergen. Aversiveness was measured globally, by asking respondents how annoying, disgusting, or upsetting a behavior was, without separating out the specific nature of the emotional reaction, attributions about the intentionality of the action, or attributes about the character of the actor. Research indicates that anger is greater the more that the action is perceived to be intentional (Vangelisti & Young, 2000). In addition, hurt feelings are greater the more that the act conveys a devaluation of the relationship (Feeny, 2005; Leary et al., 1998), and rejection of the antagonist is greater the more that the action is perceived to be due to stable internal qualities, such as an uncivil disposition (Fincham & Bradbury, 1987). Consequently, future research might measure such mediating emotions and cognitions, especially the workplace behaviors that cause the specific reaction of hurt feelings.

Another limitation of the study was that we did not systematically sample either job types or industries. Our sample represented a diverse range of industries, but it would be helpful to test the results of the present study in replications using large sample of employees at different levels of each organization in a range of industries and regions of the country. As noted earlier, it is possible that some allergens are both expected and tolerated in some industries. Yelling and profanity, for example, seem much more acceptable in the military than in the civilian world and more acceptable in manufacturing plants than in offices. In addition, because norms of civility may vary from culture to culture, it would be helpful to test these findings in organizations based in cultures outside the United States.

Some employees may not need to depend on coping and social support but instead may have natural or acquired indifference to certain social allergens. Individuals who are emotionally stable demonstrate less sensitivity and emotional response to social allergens than those who are more neurotic (Cunningham et al., 1997), although the precise patterning of individual emotional responses to social allergens, such as amplitude and duration, remains to be charted. Individuals with higher social intelligence may be better able than others to cope with social allergies and to avoid causing them in others. Such predictions could be tested using a measure of emotional intelligence as an ability (Salovey, Kokkonen, Lopes, & Mayer, 2004) or as self-reported personality quality (Goleman, 1999).

An independent replication and extension of the current findings on workplace allergens was reported by Henderson (2005). That study confirmed the factor structure of the four social allergy dimensions and that peers were the most frequent sources of social allergies rather than supervisors or subordinates. In addition, it found that employees who felt that they had less control over the allergens perceived them as more aversive than employees who felt they had more control over the allergens. The study also confirmed that employees with neurotic personalities experienced more frequent allergens and more intense allergies than their coworkers. In contrast to the current results, it did not find significant relationships between the social allergen exposure and the use of coping strategies, including problem solving, seeking support, avoidance, and venting of emotions. But Henderson (2005) acknowledged that her study used a general purpose coping measure that included items that were inappropriate for workplace coping, such as "Watched television more than usual." In addition, the use of each coping strategy was assessed on a 3-point scale (1 = *a lot*, 2 = *a little*, 3 = *not at all*), which might not have allowed sufficiently fine-grained assessment to track subtle variations in the use of the various coping strategies as a function of allergen frequency. Consequently, Henderson's findings that confirmed and extended the present findings seem compelling, whereas the inconsistent outcomes seem understandable.

Additional adaptive and maladaptive forms of coping should be assessed in future studies. Our study did not assess admissions of retaliatory aggression toward an allergen-emitting coworker. This aggression may take the form of informal acts of social rejection or sabotage, loud direct confrontation, aggression through a third party, or a formal grievance. Because few company policies accept grievances for mild irritations, such as a coworker who does not let one take a turn in the conversation or who leaves his or her things in one's space, an allergic employee has few options. We have heard of cases of employees who have filed bogus complaints of sexual harassment and "creating a hostile workplace" against coworkers to whom they were allergic as a result of nonsexual behaviors. The availability of meditational services to address ordinary irritations and hurtful behaviors at work might reduce such charges.

### APPLIED RECOMMENDATIONS

Organizations may enhance employee morale, reduce turnover costs, and reduce unwarranted sexual harassment complaints by developing and implementing programs to reduce the frequency of hurtful behaviors and social allergens and increase the frequency of organizational citizenship behaviors. These efforts may begin with job advertisements, job descriptions, and personnel selection programs that are designed to hire new employees who are low in the likelihood of emitting social allergens and high in civility and the likelihood of performing organizational citizenship behaviors. Prospective employees who are regularly passed over by such selection programs might have the option of participating in sponsored workshops to improve their behavior in these domains.

In addition, the use of anonymous 360 feedback procedures as part of a yearly personnel review process could allow current employees to inform their coworkers that some of their behaviors are allergenic and demoralizing. This type of yearly feedback could warn people of the bad habits that annoy others so they could make efforts to change their behavior patterns and keep peace in the workplace. Protocols could be developed such that if someone continues to be offended, he or she must tell the allergen-emitting person. If the perpetrator does not stop being allergenic after being warned, the victim should have the option of asking the perpetrator if both of them could meet with a trained counselor as part of the organization's Employee Assistance Program (EAP). The counselor could encourage the victim to express the distress and the perpetrator to explain his or her intentions and work on strategies for change.

In our view, the counselor should discourage blaming and dispositional attributions and encourage change in both the perpetrator's behavior and in the victim's emotional reaction. Acceptance of the victim's perspective is the norm in charges of sexual harassment, but it is questionable whether similar weight should be given to that perspective in the evaluation of uncivil behaviors. Perpetrators are often surprised by the intensity of the victim's reactions and may defensively deny that the offensive behavior occurs as frequently or as intensely as what is claimed by the victim (Stillwell & Baumeister, 1997). Inducing a perpetrator to recognize and change uncivil behavioral patterns may require that feedback be delivered using language that approximates the perpetrator's own understanding of the nature of the actions. It may hurt the perpetrator's feelings less if his or her yelling is described as "gruff" rather than hostile.

The victim's hurt feelings might be assuaged if the coworker makes a sincere apology for the offensive behavior and avows that maintaining cordial relations with the injured employee is really important, thereby alleviating the relationship derogation component of social allergies (Bachman & Guerrero, 2006; Risen & Gilovich, 2007). At the same time, the victim should recognize that it might be difficult for the perpetrator to promptly change old habits and that the victim could make a parallel effort to forgive the perpetrator and modify his or her own ruminations and angry reactions if the offensive behavior happens to occur again (McCullough, Bono, & Root, 2007). Such emotion changes in the victim might be aided by systematic desensitization and other therapeutic techniques.

Employers would be wise to monitor their employees for signs of social allergies so they can intervene before thoughts of retaliation or turnover are acted on. Although managers may be reluctant to intervene after minor acts of incivility, a parallel can be drawn to the "broken windows" theory of urban decay and crime (Wilson & Kelling, 1982). This theory recommends fixing misbehavior problems when they are small, before they can escalate. In the case of hurtful behavior and social allergies, such escalation could take the form of overt hostility, precipitous turnover, or, in the worse case, a violent rampage in the workplace.

Employers may choose to adopt a policy and promote an organizational culture in which employees are (a) encouraged to be respectful, civil, and pleasant as much as humanly possible, regardless of personal feelings or judgments about a coworker; (b) instructed that some people are more sensitive than others and that everyone should be careful to protect the feelings of the more sensitive; (c) discouraged from gossiping, so as to decrease chances of spreading misperceptions and rejection; (d) encouraged to recognize a social allergy and to use EAP procedures to address it, if it should develop; and (e) warned that a social allergy could cause them to respond harshly or inappropriately to an offending coworker, which could cause them end up in more trouble than the irritating party. In extreme cases, courtesy and etiquette consultants might be engaged to help teach civility and appropriate workplace social behaviors to employees. Such recommendations need not be limited to the paid workplace, but might be useful to guide people at work in other settings, such as students in school and volunteers in charities.

## Organizational Turnover and Hurt Feelings

Employees can be hurt by coworkers who take their services elsewhere. Whenever a coworker voluntarily resigns, the employees who remain behind may feel somewhat hurt and rejected. After all, a peer's decision to quit implicitly means that the value of their relationships with colleagues was lower than that of other considerations. In addition, the resignation causes the coworkers to forfeit their investment in training, help, or friendship with the employee who is leaving. Finally, a peer's decision to move on may cause unpleasantly dissonant thoughts in the coworkers, such as they should seek better opportunities themselves. To avoid such hurt feelings, coworkers who take positions elsewhere may engage in a complex dance of reluctance and regret, making it appear that they did not seek the new job offer and that they really hoped management would top it so they would not have to leave (Frances, 2007).

Although employees who find a better fit should be wished well, progressive executives recognize the value of providing incentives to retain key employees who have other job offers, even if it means that they also have to increase the salaries of some other employees to maintain equity. There is a growing recognition that companies and countries should regard their social capital as important as their financial capital (Putnam, 2001). Social capital is the accumulated network of relationships and positive feelings created through the fair treatment of employees, gracious dealings with customers, and civic engagement in the community. If social capital were given the same standing as financial capital, then adverse workplace decisions that cause hurt feelings by violating reasonable communal expectations might be less likely.

An emphasis on increasing organizational citizenship and decreasing social allergens and hurtful behavior in the workplace is part of a general cultural evolutionary trend toward a morality based on democracy and compassion, rather than dominance and distributive inequality. That trend has led to international laws against slavery and genocide and national laws establishing minimum wages and rights for the disabled. The transformation is far from complete, but progressive executives are beginning to recognize that an organization's effectiveness in maintaining effective working relationships can have a profound influence on its overall success. Positive mood increases creativity (Isen, 2004), cordial group relations facilitate teamwork and productivity (Lewin et al., 1939), and low rates of social allergens and high rates of organizational citizenship behaviors reduce thoughts of turnover, with its associated recruitment and training expenses (Johnson & Indvik, 2001a, 2001b). With a new generation of employees coming on board, with strong talent and high expectations like our communications graduate, a focus on reducing hurt feelings in the workplace makes excellent business sense. Ensuring that allergenic behaviors are minimized and civility is maximized should become an important goal for the lean, but not-so-mean, 21st-century workplace.

REFERENCES

Anderson, P. A. (1998). Researching sex differences within sex similarities. The evolutionary consequences of sex differences. In D. J. Canary & K. Dindia (Eds.), *Sex differences and similarities in communication* (pp. 83–100). Mahwah, NJ: Erlbaum.

Andersson, L. M., & Pearson, C. M. (1999). Tit for tat? The spiraling effect of incivility in the workplace. *Academy of Management Review, 24*, 452–471.

Arnold, D. W. (1991). To test or not to test: Legal issues in integrity testing. *Forensic Reports, 4*, 213–224.

Bachman, G. F., & Guerrero, L. K. (2006). Forgiveness, apology, and communicative responses to hurful events. *Communication Reports, 19*, 45–56.

Baehr, M. E., & Renck, R. (1958). The definition and measurement of employee morale. *Administrative Science Quarterly, 3*, 157–184.

Bailyn, L. (2006). *Breaking the mold: Redesigning work for productive and satisfying lives.* Ithaca, NY: Cornell University Press.

Barbee, A. P., & Cunningham, M. R. (1995). An experimental approach to social support: Interactive coping in close relationships. *Communication Yearbook, 18*, 381–413.

Barbee, A. P., Cunningham, M. R., Druen, P. B., & Yankeelov, P. A. (1996). Loss of passion, intimacy and commitment: A conceptual framework for relationship researchers. *Journal of Personal and Interpersonal Loss, 1*, 93–108.

Belson, K. (2007, August 31). At I.B.M., a vacation anytime, or maybe none. *The New York Times.*

Blader, S. L. (2007). What leads organizational members to collectivize? Injustice and identification as precursors of union certification. *Organization Science, 18*, 108–126.

Bogle, J. C. (2005). *The battle for the soul of capitalism.* New Haven, CT: Yale University Press.

Bramson, R. M. (1981). *Coping with difficult people.* New York: Anchor Books/ Doubleday.

Cao, Q., Maruping, L., & Takeuchi, R. (2006). Disentangling the effects of CEO turnover and succession on organizational capabilities: A social network perspective. *Organization Science, 17*, 563–576.

Camman, C., Fichman, M., Jenkins, D., & Klesh, J. (1979). *The Michigan Organizational Assessment Questionnaire.* Unpublished manuscript. University of Michigan, Ann Arbor.

Clark, M. S., & Mills, J. (1979). Interpersonal attraction in exchange and communal relationships. *Journal of Personality and Social Psychology, 37*, 12–24.

Cook, J. D., Hepworth, S. J., Wall, T. D., & Warr, P. B. (1981). *The experience of work.* New York: Academic Press.

Cortina, L. M., Magley, V. J., Williams, J. H., & Langhout, R. D. (2001). Incivility in the workplace: Incidence and impact. *Journal of Occupation Health Psychology, 6*, 64–80.

Cunningham, M. R. (1990). Test-taking motivations and outcomes on a standardized measure of on-the-job integrity. *Journal of Business and Psychology, 4*, 119–127.

Cunningham, M. R., & Ash, P. (1988). The structure of honesty: Factor analysis of the Reid Report. *Journal of Business and Psychology, 3*, 54–66.

Cunningham, M. R., & Barbee, A. P. (2000). Social support in close relationships. In C. Hendrick & S. Hendrick (Eds.), *Close relationships: A sourcebook* (pp. 273–285). Thousand Oaks, CA: Sage.

Cunningham, M. R., Barbee, A. P., & Druen, P. B. (1997). Social allergens and the reaction that they produce: Escalation of annoyance and disgust in love and work. In R. M. Kowalski (Ed.), *Aversive interpersonal behavior* (pp. 190–214). New York: Plenum.

Cunningham, M. R., Shamblen, S. R., Barbee, A. R., & Ault, L. K. (2005). Social allergies in romantic relationships: Behavioral repetition, emotional sensitization, and dissatisfaction in dating couples. *Personal Relationships, 12,* 273–295.

Cunningham, M. R., Wong, D. T., & Barbee, A. P. (1994). Self-presentation dynamics on overt integrity tests: Experimental studies of the Reid Report. *Journal of Applied Psychology, 79,* 643–658.

Farb, M. (1968). *Man's rise to civilization, as shown by the Indians of North America from primeval times to the coming of the industrial state.* New York: E. P. Dutton.

Feeney, J. A. (2005). Hurt feelings in couple relationships: Exploring the role of attachment and perceptions of personal injury. *Personal Relationships, 12,* 253–271.

Fiedler, F. E. (1958). *Leader attitudes and group effectiveness.* Oxford, England: University of Illinois Press.

Fincham, J. D., & Bradbury, T. N. (1987). Cognitive process and conflict in close relationships: An attribution–efficacy model. *Journal of Personality and Social Psychology, 53,* 1106–1118.

Fiske, A. P. (1991). *The structures of social life: The four elementary forms of human relations.* New York: Free Press.

Fitness, J. (2001). Betrayal, rejection, revenge, and forgiveness: An interpersonal script approach. In M. R. Leary (Ed.) *Interpersonal rejection* (pp. 73–103). New York: Oxford University Press.

Frances, M. (2007, July 13). Can we still be friends? *Chronicle of Higher Education,* pp. 1, 4.

Goldberg, A. B., & Ritter, B. (2006, August 2). Costco CEO finds pro-worker means profitability. *ABC 20/20.*

Goleman, D. (1998). *Working with emotional intelligence.* New York: Bantam.

Harden Fritz, J. M. (2002). How do I dislike thee? Let me count the ways. *Management Communication Quarterly, 15,* 410–438.

Harden Fritz, J. M. (2006). Typology of troublesome others at work: A follow-up investigation. In. J. M. Harden Fritz & B. L. Omdahl (Eds.), *Problematic relationships in the workplace* (pp. 21–46). New York: Peter Lang.

Hausknecht, J. P., Day, D. V., & Thomas, S. C. (2004). Applicant reactions to selection procedures: An updated model and meta-analysis. *Personnel Psychology, 57,* 639–683.

Heider, F. (1958). *The psychology of interpersonal relations.* New York: Wiley.

Henderson, L. (2005). *My coworker stinks: How personality affects coping strategies used to deal with annoying work associates.* Unpublished masters thesis, Minnesota State University, Mankato, MN.

Hersey, P., & Blanchard, K. H. (1993). *Management of organizational behavior: Utilizing human resources* (6th ed.). Upper Saddle River, NJ: Prentice-Hall.

Hess, J. A. (2000). Maintaining nonvoluntary relationships with disliked partners: An investigation into the use of distancing behaviors. *Human Communication Research, 26,* 458–488.

Hess, J. A. (2006). Distancing from problematic coworkers. In J. M. Harden Fritz & B. L. Omdahl (Eds.), *Problematic relationships in the workplace* (pp. 205–232). New York: Peter Lang.

Isen, A. M. (2004). Some perspectives on positive feelings and emotions: Positive affect facilitates thinking and problem solving. In A. S. R. Manstead, N. Frijda, & A. Fischer (Eds.), *Feelings and emotions: The Amsterdam symposium* (pp. 263–281). New York: Cambridge University Press.

Johnson, P. R., & Indvik, J. (2001a). Slings and arrows of rudeness: Incivility in the workplace. *Journal of Management Development, 20*, 705–713.

Johnson, P., & Indvik, J. (2001b). Rudeness at work: Impulse over restraint. *Public Personnel Management, 30*, 457–465.

Jones, E. E., & Davis, K. E. (1965). From acts to dispositions: The attribution process in person perception. In L. Berkowitz (Eds.), *Advances in experimental social psychology* (Vol. 2, pp. 219–266). New York: Academic Press.

Joreskog, K. G., & Sorbom, D. (1993). *LISREL 8: User's reference guide*. Chicago: Scientific Software International.

Keashly, L. (2001). Interpersonal and systemic aspects of emotional abuse at work: The target's perspective. *Violence and Victims, 16*, 233–268.

Kowalski, R. M. (2001). *Behaving badly: Aversive behaviors in interpersonal relationships*. Washington, DC: American Psychological Association.

Kowalski, R. M. (2003). *Complaining, teasing, and other annoying behaviors*. New Haven, CT: Yale University Press.

Leary, M. R., Springer, C., Negel, L., Ansell, E., & Evans, K. (1998). The causes, phenomenology, and consequences of hurt feelings. *Journal of Personality and Social Psychology, 74*, 1225–1237.

Leary, M. R., Tambor, E. S., Terdal, S. K., & Downs, D. L. (1995). Self-esteem as an interpersonal monitor: The sociometer hypothesis. *Journal of Personality and Social Psychology, 68*, 518–530.

Lewin, K., Lippitt, R., & White, R. (1939). Patterns of aggressive behaviour in experimentally created "social climates." *Journal of Social Psychology, 10*, 271–299.

Lim, S., & Cortina, L. M. (2005). Interpersonal mistreatment in the workplace: The interface and impact of general incivility and sexual harassment. *Journal of Applied Psychology, 90*, 483–496.

Martin, R. J., & Hine, D. W. (2005). Development and validation of the Uncivil Workplace Behavior Questionnaire. *Journal of Occupational Health Psychology, 10*, 477–490.

May, L. N., & Jones, W. H. (2007). Does hurt linger? Exploring the nature of hurt feelings over time. *Current Psychology: Developmental, Learning, Personality, Social, 25*, 245–256.

McCullough, M. E., Bono, G., & Root, L. M. (2007). Rumination, emotion, and forgiveness: Three longitudinal studies. *Journal of Personality and Social Psychology, 92*, 490–505.

Moore, M. (1989). *Roger & Me*. [Motion Picture]. Warner Home Video.

*The New York Times*. The right to organize (2007, March 6). Editorial.

O'Boyle, T. F. (1999). *At any cost: Jack Welch, General Electric, and the pursuit of profit*. New York: Vantage Books.

Ones, D. S., Viswesvaran, C., & Schmidt, F. L. (1993). Comprehensive meta-analysis of integrity test validities: Findings and implications for personnel selection and theories of job performance. *Journal of Applied Psychology, 78*, 679–703.

Pearson, C. M., Andersson, L. M., & Porath, C. L. (2000). Assessing and attacking workplace incivility. *Organizational Dynamics, 29*, 123–137.

Pearson, C. M., Andersson, L. M., & Porath, C.L. (2005). Workplace incivility. In S. Fox & P. E. Spector (Eds.), *Counterproductive work behavior* (pp. 177–200). Washington, DC: American Psychological Association.

Pearson, C. M., Andersson, L. M., & Wegner, J. W. (2001). When workers flout convention: A study of workplace incivility. *Human Relations, 54*, 1387–1419.

Phillips, T., & Smith, P. (2003). Everyday incivility: Towards a benchmark. *Sociological Review, 51*, 85–108.

Plank, S. B., McDill, E. L., McPartland, J. M., & Jordan, W. J. (2001). Situation and repertoire: Civility, incivility, cursing, and politeness in an urban high school. *Teachers College Record, 103*, 504–524.

Posdakoff, P. M., & MacKenzie, S. B. (1994). Organizational citizenship behavior and sales unit effectiveness. *Journal of Marketing Research, 3*(1), 351–363.

Putnam, R. D. (2001). *Bowling alone: The collapse and revival of American community.* New York: Touchstone.

Risen, J. L., & Gilovich, T. (2007). Target and observer differences in the acceptance of questionable apologies. *Journal of Personality and Social Psychology, 92*, 418–433.

Robinson, S., & Greenberg, J. (1998). Employees behaving badly: Dimensions, determinants and dilemmas in the study of workplace deviance. In C. L. Cooper & D. M. Rousseau (Eds.), *Trends in organizational behavior* (Vol. 5, pp. 1–30). New York: Wiley.

Rusbult, C. E, Insko, C. A., Lin, Y. W., & Smith, W. J. (1990). Social motives underlying rational selective exploitation: The impact of instrumental versus social-emotional allocator orientation on the distribution of rewards in groups. *Journal of Applied Social Psychology, 20*, 984–1025.

Salovey, P., Kokkonen, M., Lopes, P. N., & Mayer, J. D. (2004). Emotional intelligence: What do we know? In A. S. R. Manstead, N. Frijda, & A. Fischer (Eds.), *Feelings and emotions: The Amsterdam symposium* (pp. 321–340). New York: Cambridge University Press.

Schmidt, E., & Varian, H. (2005, December 2). Google: Ten golden rules. *Newsweek.*

Shamblen, S. R. (2004). My partner wasn't so disgusting when we first started dating, what happened? An exploration of change processes in close relationships and their causes. *Dissertation Abstracts International: Section B: The Sciences and Engineering, 65*, 2697.

Stillwell, A. M., & Baumeister, R. F. (1997). The construction of victim and perpetrator memories: Accuracy and distortion distortion in role-based accounts. *Personality and Social Psychology Bulletin, 23*, 1157–1172.

Sutton, R. I. (2007). *The no asshole rule: Building a civilized workplace and surviving one that isn't.* New York: Elsevier.

Twenge, J. (2006). *Generation me: Why today's young Americans are more confident, assertive, entitled – and more miserable than ever before.* New York: Free Press.

Uchitelle, L. (2006). *The disposable American: Layoffs and their consequences.* New York: Vintage Press.

Vangelisti, A. L. (2001). Making sense of hurtful interactions in close relationships: When hurt feelings create distance. In V. Manusov & J. H. Harvey (Eds.), *Attribution, communication behavior, and close relationships* (pp. 38–58). New York: Cambridge University Press.

Vangelisti, A. L., & Young, S. L. (2000). When words hurt: The effects of perceived intentionality on interpersonal relationships. *Journal of Social and Personal Relationships, 17*, 393–424.

Vroom, V. H., & Jago, A. G. (1988). *The new leadership: Managing participation in organizations.* Upper Saddle River, NJ: Prentice-Hall.

Wade, J. B., O'Reilly III, C. A., & Pollock, T. G. (2006). Overpaid CEOs and underpaid managers: Fairness and executive compensation. *Organization Science, 17,* 527–544.

Weiner, B. (1986). Attribution, emotion, and action. In R. M. Sorrentino & T. E. Higgins (Eds.), *Handbook of motivation and cognition: Foundations of social behavior* (pp. 281–312). New York: Guilford.

Weiss, D. J., Davis, R. V., England, G. W., & Lofquist, L. H. (1967). *Manual for the Minnesota Satisfaction Questionnaire:* Minneapolis: Industrial Relations Center, University of Minnesota.

Wilson, J. Q., & Kelling, G. L. (1982). Broken windows. *Atlantic Monthly, 269,* 29–38.

# 21

## Cultural Influences on the Causes and Experience of Hurt Feelings

ROBIN M. KOWALSKI

The purpose of this chapter is to examine cultural influences on the antecedents, phenomenology, and expression of hurt feelings. Most research on hurt feelings has been conducted in Western cultures, with relatively little attention paid to the ways in which the experience and expression of hurt feelings might vary cross-culturally. Furthermore, research on hurt feelings, relative to other emotions, is in its infancy. A key issue is the degree to which hurt feelings represent a distinct emotional state as opposed to the degree to which hurt feelings are simply a blend of other emotions. Although people who experience hurt feelings may also be sad, angry, or fearful – all emotions that have received fairly extensive attention from cross-cultural researchers – we cannot simply assume that findings from research on sadness, anger, and fear directly apply to hurt feelings (Vangelisti, Young, Carpenter-Theune, & Alexander, 2005). In addition, other emotions that often accompany hurt feelings are caused by other, different appraisals in the situation. If a rejection event that produces hurt feelings seems unjustified, a person might feel angry; if the rejection event involves a loss, he or she might feel sad. But these are separate from the appraisals that cause hurt per se (see Leary & Leder, Chapter 2, this volume). To the degree that cross-cultural research has been useful in helping us delineate emotions other than hurt feelings, particularly given differences in appraisals of some situations across, for example, individualistic and collectivist cultures, examining cultural influences on hurt feelings should aid us in advancing our knowledge of this underresearched emotion.

Mesquita's (2003; see also Mesquita & Frijda, 1992; Mesquita & Markus, 2004) cultural model of emotion provides the organizing framework for this chapter. Most emotions, including hurt feelings, arise from interpersonal interactions and relationships, so it is not surprising that cultural differences in patterns of interacting and the meaning attached to those interactions influence the experience of and expression of particular emotions. Attributions of intentionality, appraisals of the hurtfulness of another's behavior or words, and correlates of hurt feelings would be expected to vary with cultural models and prevailing social norms. After providing a brief overview of hurt feelings, I apply Mesquita's cultural model of emotion to examine cultural similarities and differences in the experience and expression of hurt feelings. Then, the chapter closes by examining two unexplored questions regarding hurt: What is meant by "empathic hurt feelings?" What steps do people take to *actively avoid* hurting another person's feelings?

## OVERVIEW OF HURT FEELINGS

Certainly, no one in any part of the world is immune to having his or her feelings hurt. An intentional put-down by an abusive partner or an unintentional slight by a friend can both be perceived as hurtful. A partner who has an affair and a friend who forgets your birthday both yield hurt feelings. But what does it really mean to have one's feelings hurt? According to Young and Bippus (2001, p. 36), hurt is "a feeling that occurs as a result of an individual being emotionally injured or wounded by another." Others have defined hurt feelings as "the acute emotional distress felt in response to relational devaluation" (MacDonald & Leary, 2005, p. 202; see also Leary & Springer, 2001). This latter definition is the working definition of hurt feelings used in this chapter.

Typically, people are more likely to be hurt by close others than by strangers. In an early investigation of hurt feelings, Leary and his colleagues (Leary, Springer, Negel, Ansell & Evans, 1998) asked participants to recount an episode in which their feelings had been hurt. Most of the accounts that participants reported were perpetrated by someone whom participants knew well. In almost 40% of the cases, the person who hurt their feelings was a close friend. In a related study, Whitesell and Harter (1996) had children hear stories in which a close friend or a classmate called the child a name. In ratings of the degree to which their feelings would be hurt, the children said their feelings would be hurt more when called a name by a close friend than by a classmate.

However, in an interesting twist on the "we only hurt the ones we love" theme, Snapp and Leary (2001) found that participants actually reported significantly more hurt when they were ignored by a confederate they had just met than when they were ignored by someone with whom they were slightly more familiar. Snapp and Leary offered several explanations for these counterintuitive findings. First, being rejected and ignored by someone who barely knows you suggests a strong, immediate aversive reaction that signals even greater relational devaluation than might be indicated by a familiar other forgetting one's birthday. In addition, because of people's investments in long-term, established relationships, familiar relationships may buffer people against the bite of hurt feelings. The fact that both unfamiliar and close others have the potential to produce strong feelings of hurt led Snapp and Leary to conclude that the relationship between hurt feelings and familiarity may be curvilinear. Thus, people who are closest to us and people with whom we are unfamiliar have the capacity to hurt our feelings more than those with whom we share a casual relationship.

As with other emotions, intrapersonal, interpersonal, and contextual variables determine the extent to which hurt feelings are both experienced and expressed. For example, the attributions that people make for events determine whether they experience hurt feelings or some other emotion, such as anger, sadness, or shame (Vangelisti, 1994). Research over the last several years has examined people's attributions for hurt feelings and the situations most likely to give rise to hurt feelings, a point we return to shortly. Research on hurt feelings has failed to examine, however, one of the most salient contextual variables that influences the experience and expression of emotions – culture.

## CULTURE AS A CONTEXTUAL VARIABLE

Much has been written about cultural variations in the experience of emotions, with a particular focus on the universal, biological aspects of emotions as opposed to sociocultural factors underlying emotions (Mesquita & Walker, 2003). However, virtually no research attention has been devoted to cross-cultural similarities and differences in the experiences of hurt feelings. There is little reason to doubt, however, that current theories of culture and emotion as they apply to emotions other than hurt feelings would apply any less well to hurt feelings. Research by Scherer (1997) suggested a great deal of cross-cultural consistency in the appraisal of particular eliciting situations and thus the type of emotions experienced. Nevertheless, Scherer acknowledged that there is still room for some "culture-specific modulations of appraisal patterns, variations around a universal theme" (p. 146).

Most process theories of emotion suggest that emotions consist of a series of components that follow from one another: the precipitating or eliciting event, appraisal, action readiness, physiological changes (e.g., autonomic nervous system activity), action tendencies and behaviors, and regulation (Mesquita & Walker, 2003; Planalp, 1999). Each component is influenced by intrapersonal and situational variables that may vary from one situation or one culture to another. Thus, the situational and contextual variables that set the stage for eliciting hurt feelings in one culture may differ from those variables in another culture.

Because of cross-cultural variability in emotions, Mesquita, Frijda, and Scherer (1997) have drawn a distinction between *emotional practices*, the actual emotions that people experience and express, and *emotion potentials*, the emotions that people are capable of having. Mesquita et al. (1997) suggested that cultural differences in emotions lie primarily at the emotional practices level. "Emotional practices differ across cultures when there are cultural differences in the likelihood that certain outputs are selected. For example, Americans tend to appraise positive as well as negative events in terms of personal agency

(Mesquita & Ellsworth, 2001). Agency is less prevalent in cultures that stress fate and multi-determination" (Mesquita & Walker, 2003, p. 779). Using this framework, people in all cultures are capable of having hurt feelings. The extent to which they actually experience and express hurt feelings, however, should vary with dominant cultural models.

## A PROCESS THEORY OF HURT FEELINGS

As noted earlier, process theories suggest that emotions follow from a sequence of steps, each of which is multiply determined by intrapersonal, interpersonal, and contextual variables. Adapting Mesquita's (2003) cultural theory of emotion, the process theory of hurt feelings involves antecedent events, appraisal, physiological changes, action tendencies, and emotional regulation.

### Antecedent Events

An emotion, such as hurt feelings, is experienced as the result of an antecedent or a triggering event. Something has to occur that will ultimately be appraised as indicative of relational devaluation and emotionally painful to cause hurt feelings. The triggers for hurt feelings are clearly interpersonal events. Several studies have looked specifically at the nature of messages that produce hurt feelings (Leary & Springer, 2001; Leary et al., 1998; Vangelisti, 1994). Events that ultimately lead to the experience of hurt feelings involve rejection, betrayal, and, more broadly, relational devaluation, or feeling that someone does not value you as much as he or she once did or as much as you would like him or her to (see Leary & Leder, Chapter 2, this volume).

In one of the earliest studies investigating hurt feelings, Vangelisti (1994) asked participants to recall a hurtful message that someone else said to them and to write about the events occurring immediately before the hurtful message, the hurtful message itself, and their response to the message. The most commonly cited hurtful messages were accusations (e.g., "You're a liar"), evaluations ("Going out with you was the biggest mistake of my life"), and informative messages ("You aren't a priority in my life"). Vangelisti found that, although the events listed were all hurtful to participants, some were more hurtful than others. Comments made about aspects of oneself that can be changed and that may simply be annoying to someone else tend to be less hurtful than comments made about more enduring aspects of oneself, such as one's personality. For example, people accused of being a spendthrift can counter with examples of times when they have been very thrifty. Those who are told that their partner no longer loves them, however have little to offer in their own defense.

Using a similar methodology, Leary and his colleagues (1998; see also Leary & Springer, 2001) asked participants to recount an episode in which their feelings had been hurt. Participants then completed a questionnaire examining their feelings about the event and the attributions they made for the event. Events that individuals indicated led them to feel hurt included criticism, betrayal, rejection, being unappreciated, and being teased. Leary et al. (1998) suggested that underlying all of these instances of hurt feelings was relational devaluation – "the perception that another individual does not regard his or her relationship with the person to be as important, close, or valuable as the person desires" (Leary et al., 1998, p. 1225; see also Fitness, 2001).

In a 2005 study, Vangelisti et al. again asked participants to describe a situation in which their feelings had been hurt and to describe what about the situation made them feel hurt. Two of the most frequently mentioned categories were rejection and betrayal. Although these antecedent events are consistent with the idea that hurt feelings arise from relational devaluation, Vangelisti et al. (2005) suggested that relational devaluation may be only one of several causes of hurt feelings. For example, another frequently mentioned cause of hurt feelings was "undermining of self-concept... the interaction they described made them doubt their confidence or self-worth" (p. 449). The argument could be made, of course, that events that lead us to doubt our self-worth also involve things that cause us to feel low relational value (e.g., Leary & Baumeister, 2000). Indeed, in an examination of hurt feelings within the context of close relationships, Feeney (2005) found that events appraised as hurtful implied relational devaluation and threatened the positive self-view that an individual had of him- or herself.

The occurrence of certain antecedent events is not sufficient, however, to induce hurt feelings. Additional situational and dispositional variables interact with these antecedent events to determine whether hurt feelings are actually experienced. Thus, the experience of hurt feelings in response to a particular set of circumstances may differ from one time to another (Vangelisti et al., 2005) and as a function of the cultural context.

Whether the elicitors of hurt feelings are universal or culturally specific is, as yet, an unexplored question. Some events are likely to trigger hurt feelings among people living in virtually any culture, although the expression of hurt may vary with the culture. Beyond these universal precipitators of hurt feelings, however, which events trigger hurt feelings in different cultures likely depends on the norms and cultural models operating in that particular culture. That is one reason why it is easy to offend and to get our feelings hurt when visiting in a foreign country – we are often unaware of the norms in cultures other than our own.

Research has shown that other people's actions are the most reported triggers for emotions including anger, disgust, sadness, happiness, and fear (Oatley & Duncan, 1992; Scherer, Wallbott, Matsumoto, & Kudoh, 1988). Hurt feelings are no exception here. Partial support for universality in the elicitors of emotions was found by Scherer and Wallbott (1994; see also Wallbott &

Scherer, 1988) in a study of emotion elicitors in 37 countries. They found greater variation in emotional elicitors across emotions than across countries. One of the most notable cultural differences concerned the emotions of shame and guilt. In individualistic cultures, shame and guilt seemed to be triggered by similar events, usually of an immoral nature. In collectivist cultures, the events precipitating guilt were evaluated as more immoral than those precipitating shame. Overall, Scherer's research suggests cultural universality for certain emotions, such as sadness, anger, and fear, but more variability for other emotions such as shame and guilt (Ekman & Davidson, 1994). Although hurt feelings can accompany any of these emotions, they are more likely to co-occur with sadness, anger, and fear, suggesting that there might be some cross-cultural consistency in the elicitors of hurt feelings.

Variability in emotional practices and emotion elicitors may be caused by different cultural emphases placed on particular emotions (Dalai Lama, 2002; Mesquita & Walker, 2003). As Heelas (1996) observed, "emotion talk functions as a kind of spotlight.... Emotional elements which have no light thrown on them remain in the dark. And emotions which are focused on become enriched and highlighted or experienced" (p. 192). Planalp (1999) discussed the anthropological distinction between hypercognized emotions, or those emotions that are emphasized, written about, and talked about in a culture, and hypocognized emotions, those emotions that are infrequently mentioned within a culture (Levy, 1984). Within Western cultures, for example, love is a hypercognized emotion, whereas shame is hypocognized. Within a given culture, one way to differentiate hyper- from hypocognized emotions is to see which emotions are most understood by a young child (Shaver, Wu, & Schwartz, 1992). Different patterns of emotional socialization will be reflected in different levels of familiarity with different emotions (Planalp, 1999).

To date we have no data on the degree to which hurt feelings are a hyper-cognized or a hypocognized emotion in particular cultures. We also do not know at what age hurt feelings are socialized within certain cultures. Within Western culture, at least, children as young as 3 or 4 years of age seem to have at least a rudimentary understanding of what it means to have their feelings hurt, and children as young as 1 to 2 years of age demonstrate a basic understanding of compassion (Davidson & Harrington, 2002). However, we know that cultures promote situations and events that will likely lead to desired emotions, and they discourage situations and events in which undesired emotions might emerge (Mesquita & Walker, 2003). Although most people would consider hurt feelings to be an undesired emotion, the experience of hurt feelings may be effective in leading people to modify behavior that is producing relational devaluation.

Cultural models may structure antecedent events in such a way that the frequency of hurt feelings varies across cultures. I suspect that, like other emotions, there is cross-cultural variability in both the frequency with which particular antecedent events occur that make hurt feelings likely and, consequently, the frequency with which hurt feelings themselves are experienced and expressed. That said, however, I also believe that hurt feelings are a universal emotion, experienced by members of every cultural group. Irrespective of cultural group, people's need to belong is a fundamental human need, and threats to that need to belong are emotionally damaging (Baumeister & Leary, 1995). Thus, the potential for perceived relational devaluation and hurt feelings is inherent in all relationships. The meaning that is attached to the hurt differs, however, which brings us to the next stage in the process model of emotions: appraisal.

## Appraisal

Appraisals refer to individuals' beliefs about the situations or circumstances with which they are confronted and the implication of those circumstances for their own personal goals (Lazarus & Smith, 1988; Smith, 1991). The ways in which individuals appraise events determine the emotions that they feel. The appraisals then affect how quickly individuals cope with the hurt feelings and how they respond to the hurt feelings, a point we return to later.

Generally, the appraisal process can be broken down into two phases: primary appraisals and secondary appraisals. Primary appraisals involve assessments of the degree to which events or situations interfere with current life goals (Planalp, 1999). The more that an event disrupts, positively or negatively, one's life goals or plans or gives one cause for concern, the more likely it is that positive or negative emotions, respectively, will be triggered. Thus, to the degree that another's actions have implications for one's inclusionary status, financial security, self-concept, and so on, emotions of hurt feelings, fear, and anxiety are more likely to be triggered. Having one's feelings hurt in a culture, group, or relationship in which relational ties are critical and desired has more serious implications than having one's feelings hurt in a culture, group, or relationship in which such ties are less important.

Secondary appraisals involve an individual's assessment of his or her ability to cope with or handle the demands imposed by the event. Secondary appraisals account for the fact that two individuals can be exposed to the same hurtful communication yet interpret and react to it in very different ways. Even if both individuals perceive that the communication hurts their feelings and has implications for their relationship with the source of the message and for their long-term goals, one individual may feel that he or she can handle the stressor, whereas another may feel anxiety and depression, in addition to hurt feelings.

Some researchers add a third component to the appraisal process: reappraisals (Mesquita & Frijda, 1992). Reappraisals, or reevaluations of a situation, can occur as a test to see how well one has coped with a situation. In addition, reappraisals in the form of reframing can occur. Thus, after an initial set of appraisals, a second set of primary and secondary appraisals (i.e., the reappraisal) occur that involve reevaluating events so that they are not perceived as hurtful as they originally were or the person's motivations not as malevolent as one originally thought.

Not surprisingly, the attributions that people make for why someone would hurt their feelings influence their feelings toward the individual who hurt them and guide their behavioral response. Should they attribute their hurt feelings to an accidental oversight on the part of the perpetrator, both their perceptions of the perpetrator and their behavioral response are more favorable than if they believe the source intentionally set out to hurt their feelings (Vangelisti & Young, 2000).

People's desire to understand the causes of events increases with the negativity of the experience (Wong & Weiner, 1981). Thus, people's attributions for hurt feelings vary with the degree of hurt they feel. The more hurt they feel, the more likely they are to make not only internal, intentional attributions to the source but also intentional malevolent attributions (Vangelisti et al., 2005).

In general, research has shown significant, although slight in some cases (Matsumoto, Kudoh, Scherer, & Wallbott, 1988), cross-cultural variations in the ways in which people appraise events, with the outcomes of these appraisals producing different emotional experiences (Mesquita & Frijda, 1992). In Western cultures, agency attributions, or being able to attribute the cause for an event to either oneself or another person, are important (Mauro, Sato, & Tucker, 1992). Agency attributions are less important in many non-Western cultures. In some non-Western cultures, for example, agency attributions are either made to other sources, such as magic or spirits, or they are simply not viewed as relevant. Because individuals in these cultures are more likely to externalize the behaviors of others, feelings of hurt caused by the actions of those others should be attenuated. Even if hurt feelings are experienced, an individual might say, "The person didn't mean to hurt me, it was an accident."

This externalization of responsibility fits nicely with the emphasis in interdependent, collectivist cultures on the maintenance of relationships. "The need or desire to maintain a close relationship may encourage participants to make attributions that minimize the intentionality they attach to hurtful messages" (Vangelisti, 1994, p. 66). In interdependent, collectivist cultures, where maintaining close relationships is more central to the culture's core value structure, one would anticipate that the tendency to make attributions assigning intentionality for hurtful actions would be lower. However, it also is possible, given the emphasis on concern for the welfare of others and for the group, that actions that are hurtful may be perceived as counternormative, and thus, attributions of intentionality may be increased.

Additionally, because of the emphasis on connection and relations with others, the *potential* for the experience of hurt feelings should be greater in cultures with interdependent than in those with independent self-construals.

Lebra (1976) described Japanese culture as an "ethos of social relativism" to reflect its "constant concern for belongingness" (Markus & Kitayama, 1991, p. 228). According to Lebra, one of the most feared experiences among the Japanese is exclusion, an indication of relational devaluation. Although exclusion is a universal fear, there seems to be cross-cultural variability in the magnitude of anxiety and hurt feelings associated with it.

Although the *potential* for hurt feelings caused by the intense fear of exclusion and rejection may be greater in interdependent than independent cultures, the actual experience of hurt feelings may be lower because of the attributions made for the rejection. People with interdependent self-construals (Markus & Kitayama, 1991) are more likely to blame themselves as the source of the rejection and exclusion, believing that they have done something to deserve being ostracized by the group. "Among the Japanese, the awareness to be responsible for an unpleasant event not only is elicited by one's own wrongdoings but also is elicited by taking the responsibility for another person's faults" (Mesquita & Frijda, 1992, p. 187). Thus, the emotions experienced would, in all likelihood, be hurt plus sadness and shame. People with independent self-construals, in contrast, would be less likely to internalize the cause of the rejection and would, therefore, be more likely to experience hurt feelings. So, using Mesquita and Frijda's (1992) distinction between potential and practice, the potential for hurt feelings would seem to be greater in cultures that emphasize interdependent self-construals, but the practice and expression of hurt feelings in those cultures would be less than in those cultures with independent self-construals.

## Physiological Changes

Everyone is familiar with the "pain" associated with hurt feelings. When people's feelings are hurt, they describe the physical feeling by saying things such as "it cut to the quick," "it was like being hit in the gut," "I felt like I had been stabbed with a knife," "I thought I was going to be sick," or "he broke my heart." Clearly, the emotional experience of hurt feelings is linked to physiological sensations.

The theorized relationship between physiology and emotion has changed with time and technology. Arousal theories of emotion suggested that physiological changes are the defining feature of emotions, which would imply universal patterns of physiological reactivity for different emotions across cultures. In support of this, Wallbott and Scherer (1988; see also, Scherer & Wallbott, 1994) found more variability in descriptors of physiological changes accompanying emotions across emotions than across cultures. In other words, the descriptors that people from different cultures used to describe emotions – such as anger, happiness, sadness, and fear – showed remarkable consistency across cultures, although they varied from one emotion to another.

However, additional research found some cross-cultural variability in the physiological responses participants reported with particular emotions. For example, in one study, relative to American and European participants, Japanese participants reported fewer physiological reactions accompanying emotions (Scherer et al., 1988; see also Mesquita & Frijda, 1992). Mesquita and Frijda (1992) offered a number of explanations for this difference, among which is the idea that physiological symptoms may be more noticeable in some cultures than others. To this I would add that a period of emotional habituation may occur that may attenuate some physiological reactions over time. Viewed from this perspective, emotions such as hurt feelings may produce more physiological changes when they are first experienced, such as in the early stages of an abusive relationship, than after a year of being emotionally abused. How likely it is that emotional habituation would occur should vary with the attention given to certain emotions in a particular culture, as noted earlier (Heelas, 1996).

Most of the cross-cultural research on emotions relies on self-report data and gross measures of physiological arousal that do not always distinguish among emotions. More recently, though, neuroscientific evidence obtained using fMRI scans, has shown specific patterns of brain activation for specific emotions (Eisenberger, Lieberman, & Williams, 2003). This neuroscientific evidence has been used to show a link between physical pain and social pain, such as that experienced with hurt feelings. MacDonald and Leary (2005) defined social pain as "a specific emotional reaction to the perception that one is being excluded from desired relationships or being devalued by desired relationship partners or groups" (p. 202). Hurt feelings are only one of several emotions (e.g., embarrassment, shame, jealousy) that can be subsumed within a broader category of social pain.

As is discussed in the next section, events associated with social pain produce very specific approach/avoidance reactions. Just as physically painful stimuli lead someone to avoid coming into contact with the source of pain again, sources of social pain may also be avoided to decrease the likelihood of experiencing hurt feelings again. MacDonald and Leary (2005) suggested that events that connote relational devaluation and that trigger hurt feelings activate the physiological system associated with the avoidance of physical pain (see also Eisenberger & Lieberman, 2005; Eisenberger et al., 2003). Empirical support for this neuropsychological link between physical and social pain systems is detailed in MacDonald, Kingsbury, and Shaw (2005).

The physiological mechanisms underlying social pain would be expected to vary little cross-culturally. However, this again brings up the distinction between the *experience* and the *expression* of particular emotions. Just as there are individual and cultural variations in the extent to which people manifest physical pain sensations, so too are there variations across people and cultures in the manifestation of social pain, even when the physical and emotional magnitude of the pain experienced are equal. Cultural models regarding appropriate and inappropriate expressions of pain, whether physical or social, determine the extent to which people express their painful feelings.

## Action Tendencies, Action, and Expression

Action tendencies reflect the urge we have to act or not act in particular situations. They are so endemic to emotions that Frijda (1986) felt that the *urge to act* was more characteristic of emotion than *action* itself. Interestingly, action tendencies and actions are often not the same thing. We may have the urge to respond one way, yet act a completely different way depending on personal, social, and cultural norms that constrain our behavior in a particular situation.

According to Vangelisti and Crumley (1998), how people respond when their feelings are hurt provides four types of information. First, the response identifies core relational themes or how they view themselves in relation to others in their environment. Second, the response provides clues about the target's goal hierarchy or the things that the individual perceives to be valuable or important. People who respond strongly when their feelings are hurt show that the hurtful message was important to them relative to those who offer a weak or no response to a hurtful communication. Third, responses to hurt feelings reveal information about the target's "beliefs about self and world" (Vangelisti & Crumley, 1998, p. 175). Last, behavioral and emotional reactions indicate how the individual has appraised the situation – for example, whether he or she believes that the other person intentionally hurt his or her feelings. Cultural models could influence any or all of these four types of information. Important relational themes may vary cross-culturally as may a target's goal hierarchies and that target's beliefs about the self and the world. These beliefs will, in all likelihood, drive appraisals used to evaluate situations in which hurt feelings arise. What is valued or important to an individual or a group and, thus, what can most easily be used to connote relational devaluation will vary from one culture to another.

To examine people's specific responses to hurt feelings, Vangelisti and Crumley (1998) coded participants' responses to hurtful communications. They found that the most frequent responses were silence, attack, defend, and concede. In a second phase of this study, a different group of participants rated each of these responses for the degree to which it was likely they would respond in that manner if someone hurt their feelings. A factor analysis of these ratings yielded three factors. The first, *acquiescent responses*, included behaviors such as apologizing and crying and represented a cautious approach. The second factor, *invulnerable responses*, included behaviors such as ignoring the person who hurt them to avoid further hurt or laughing. At an emotional level, this response could include emotional numbness (DeWall & Baumeister, 2006;

see DeWall, Baumeister, & Masicampo, Chapter 7, this volume). The third factor, *active verbal responses*, involved behaviors such as verbally attacking the source of the hurt feelings or reacting sarcastically.

A number of variables should influence the type of response that people offer to hurt feelings. First, the nature of the relationship between the source of hurt and the target determines the target's response (Vangelisti & Crumley, 1998). People in both satisfying and dissatisfying relationships get their feelings hurt, but as discussed by Vangelisti (1994), people in satisfying relationships attribute negative interpersonal behaviors to unstable, specific causes, whereas those in dissatisfying relationships attribute those same events to stable, global causes. Importantly, Vangelisti also noted that aversive behaviors or communications in satisfying or dissatisfying relationships may be evaluated as equally hurtful. However, the divergent pattern of attributions for the event leads to more or less distancing in the dissatisfying and satisfying relationships, respectively. Consistent with Bradbury and Fincham's (1992; Fincham, Harold, & Gano-Phillips, 2000) research on relationship-enhancing and distress-maintaining attributions in close relationships, in dissatisfying relationships, a spiral of hurt feelings is set in motion from which it becomes difficult for the involved parties to extricate themselves.

Second, according to Lazarus (1991), the way in which people appraise the cause of events determines their behavioral and emotional responses to those events. Not surprisingly, people have different responses to hurtful comments made by others (Vangelisti & Crumley, 1998). Not everyone responds to the same hurtful message in the same way, and a single person will respond differently to different types of hurtful communications. For example, Vangelisti et al. (2005) found that participants reported intense feelings of hurt when the cause of hurt was perceived to be relational denigration or humiliation. However, whereas relational denigration led the hurt individual to engage in an active verbal response, humiliation led to few active verbal responses. Differences in responding may also stem from variations in secondary appraisals. People who feel hurt because of another's ill-conceived humor may feel they have adequate resources to handle the situation. People who feel that the hurt is caused by humiliation may feel they have few resources to deal with the situation (Vangelisti et al., 2005).

Relatedly, appraisals of the intentionality of the hurtful communication affect people's responses. People who believe the source of a hurtful communication intentionally hurt their feelings engage in more relational distancing than those who perceive that the hurtful communication was unintentional. Furthermore, among those who believe that the source intentionally hurt them, those who perceive that he or she did it to help them in some way (for example, to teach them a beneficial lesson) engage in less relational distancing than those who evaluate the intentional motivation as malevolent (Bourgeois & Leary, 2001; Vangelisti & Young, 2000).

Third, the presence of other appraisals influences the behaviors offered in response to hurt feelings. Other behaviors that follow from being hurt depend on the presence or absence of appraisals associated with other emotions. For example, when someone hurts our feelings, we may have the urge to hurt that person back or to strike out at that person aggressively, assuming that appraisals are also present that lead us to feel anger. Interestingly, social rejection, an antecedent condition for hurt feelings, is considered to be one of the leading precursors of aggression, as an examination of the school shootings over the past several years can attest (Leary, Kowalski, Smith, & Phillips, 2003; Leary, Twenge, & Quinlivan, 2006).

Fourth, cultural models should also determine the nature of responses that people offer when their feelings are hurt. One would expect cultural variation in the tendency for there to be discrepancies between action tendencies and actions or between behavioral intentions and behaviors. A greater mismatch would be expected in collectivist as opposed to individualistic cultures because people would be more inclined to squelch their personal behavioral tendencies and desires. For example, as suggested earlier, some people who have been hurt engage in relational distancing (Vangelisti et al., 2005) – moving away, physically, or emotionally, or both from the individual who hurt them. Although many people across cultures may feel the desire to engage in relational distancing to protect themselves from further hurt, we would not necessarily expect this response to be universal. People in collectivist cultures may feel that they cannot engage in relational distancing because the costs of doing so may exceed the pain of hurt feelings. Should the source of hurt feelings be a coworker or a family member, individuals in collectivist cultures may feel compelled to "forgive and forget" to a greater degree than people in individualistic cultures.

Mesquita and her colleagues (cited in Mesquita, 2003) conducted a study examining cultural differences in emotional expression and behavior. European-American, Mexican, and Japanese participants were interviewed about emotional situations they had experienced, including situations involving "offense" and "humiliation." The participants were asked about their behavioral responses in these situations. Among the Americans, the most common behavioral responses were blaming, aggression, and relational distancing, with the goal being to maintain individuality. Mexican participants reported blaming, moving away, and distancing, partly to hurt the person who hurt them and partly as a means of avoiding conflict. The Japanese individuals were more likely to blame themselves and attempted to justify the actions of the offending party. Thus, their focus was on maintaining the relationship with the other individual.

In another study, Mesquita (1993, cited in Mesquita, 2003) found that Surinamese and Turkish participants who had been hurt by another person responded by showing indifference. Because of the importance of interpersonal engagement in these cultures, to respond with indifference was tantamount to an act of aggression in responding. This study highlights the importance of understanding prevalent cultural models as a backdrop for interpreting the meaning of behavioral responses to hurt feelings. Of course, the tendency is to use one's own cultural milieu as the fabric within which to interpret everyone's behavior. But the actions of people in other cultures are cut from a different pattern.

## Regulation of Emotions

Inherent in the idea that we often do not act on our urges is that we engage in emotional regulation. Often occurring at an unconscious, automatic level, emotional regulation operates at each of the component levels of emotion: precipitating event, appraisal, physiology, and action tendency. In other words, people can regulate their emotions by changing the antecedent conditions, changing their appraisals (e.g., reappraisal), attempting to control their physiological responses, and modifying their behavioral reactions. Applied to hurt feelings, the ability of people to regulate their emotions is influenced by whether they have experienced relational devaluation by being rejected or excluded. Specifically, people who have been excluded or rejected show decrements in both cognitive functioning and the ability to self-regulate (Baumeister & DeWall, 2005). Sadly, these deficiencies as a result of relational devaluation set them up for further rejection and hurt feelings.

Cultures that promote peace and harmony, such as some Southeast Asian cultures, evidence more emotional self-regulation than many Western cultures, for example (Mesquita, 2003). Research by Stephan and his colleagues found that people in individualistic cultures felt more comfortable expressing negative emotions than those in collectivist cultures because the negative emotions interfered with cultural models of harmony (Stephan, Stephan, & De Vargas, 1996; Stephan, Stephan, Saito, & Barnett, 1998).

Mesquita (2003) provided a detailed analysis of cross-cultural variations in emotional regulation. However, no research has examined cultural differences in the regulation of hurt feelings. Given that hurt is a negative emotion that can lead to relational distancing, one would expect greater attempts at controlling the expression of hurt feelings in collectivist as opposed to individualistic cultures to sustain harmony. Toward this end, individuals in collectivist cultures may alter their appraisals so that events that have the potential to produce hurt feelings are reframed in a less hurtful manner, look for alternative explanations for their partner's betrayal or disrespectful behavior, or, as mentioned earlier, assume more responsibility for engaging in behaviors that "deserve" relational devaluation.

Unfortunately, research on self-regulation suggests that the more self-control people exercise in one arena, the less reserve they have to devote to other arenas. For example, Muraven, Tice, and Baumeister (1998) found that participants who had regulated their emotions gave up sooner on a task requiring physical stamina than those who had not been required to engage in affect regulation. Similarly, suppressing thoughts led participants to be less able to control their affective responses to a comedy video. Extrapolating from this finding, emotional self-control exercised to bring one's emotions and behaviors in line with cultural models and expectations may come at a cost. First, the cognitive resources needed to reappraise situations might be better allocated toward other tasks (Cacioppo, 2003). The time and effort given to reappraisal take attentional resources away from other tasks and activities. In addition, the more effort people expend trying to regulate the emotional experience of having their feelings hurt, the less able they are to control other behaviors, such as impulses to aggress in response to having their feelings hurt. There are also negative health consequences associated with the suppression of negative emotions (Gross & Levenson, 1997). Notable among these are the link between the suppression of negative emotion and the elevated risk of developing cancer and having that cancer progress once it has developed (Giese-Davis & Spiegel, 2003).

## CULTURE AND HURT FEELINGS REVISITED

Because research on hurt feelings is in its early stages, many questions remain unanswered. In addition to testing elements of Mesquita's (2003) cultural model of emotions as it relates to hurt feelings, future research is needed to explore untapped areas, two of which are briefly discussed here.

### Empathic Hurt Feelings

I have 6-year-old identical twin boys. Although they fight like all siblings do, they are extremely close. At golf camp this summer, one of them received a trophy for the coach's award, an award for the best all-around player as exemplified by potential, attitude, and behavior. As soon as he sat down after receiving his award, he immediately looked at his brother with an almost apologetic look. His brother then began to cry. I have never felt my heart break as much as I did at that moment. Although I'm sure it won't be the last time that I experience that type of heartbreak, the pain that I felt for my child who was hurting was unlike any pain I have ever felt before – to the point of almost taking my breath away. It haunted me for days afterward each time I thought about it.

What I experienced that day at golf camp was *empathic hurt feelings* – hurting for other people who are hurting. Although they are closely related to compassion, I believe empathic hurt feelings and compassion are not the same thing. I have compassion for other people's children whose feelings are hurt or for animals that have been hit by a car and are in need of assistance. But I do not hurt for those other children or for those animals in the same way that I hurt for my son at golf camp. Just as I wanted to alleviate his suffering, I also want to alleviate the suffering of an animal that has been injured or another child who has been teased. But what I feel for that animal or child differs from what I feel for my own child.

Curiously, the pain associated with empathic hurt feelings seems more intense than personally experienced hurt feelings. I would rather have my own feelings hurt any day than have my children's feelings hurt. One reason is that, when the hurt feelings are experienced by someone else, there is very little that we can do about them. Unlike when our own feelings are hurt, we cannot do the cognitive work for someone else that is needed to reappraise a hurtful situation or to cope with the hurtful situation. Although my son who did not win the trophy did receive an award for accuracy, in his 6-year-old mind it wasn't a trophy and wasn't as good as what his brother had received.

Additionally, our gut-wrenching feelings of hurt at the hurt that others experience are, in all likelihood, more likely to be tinged with a host of other negative emotions, such as fear, anxiety, anger, and sadness. Imagine your own feelings of hurt on finding out that your child's withdrawal, social isolation, and unexplained crying stemmed from being a victim of persistent bullying at school. In addition to the pain associated with your own empathic feelings of hurt, you will also experience fear and anxiety that the bullying will happen again, anger that someone would treat your child this way, and sadness that your child has suffered for months without your knowledge. Certainly, these emotions also often accompany our own feelings of hurt, albeit typically not to the same degree.

We know very little about cross-cultural similarities and differences in empathy and compassion, two variables related to empathic hurt feelings that have received empirical research attention. Snyder and Lopez (2007) suggested that compassion may be a more natural response for someone from a collectivist as opposed to an individualistic culture and that this might translate into a higher frequency of prosocial behaviors among members of the collectivist culture. Extrapolating from this suggestion, we can speculate about the possible relationship between culture and the experience of empathic hurt feelings, arguing that empathic hurt feelings may emerge more readily among members of collectivist as opposed to individualistic cultures. More than likely, however, the experience of empathic hurt feelings is a function more of the nature of the relationship between two individuals rather than a particular cultural model. The closer and more connected two people are, regardless of the independent versus interdependent nature of the culture, the greater the likelihood that empathic hurt feelings will occur. Of course, cultures that emphasize close relational ties and the maintenance of those ties through close connections with family members may be more likely to have the types of relationships that would engender empathic hurt feelings.

Close ties and empathic hurt feelings would also be expected the more similar that individuals perceived themselves to be to one another. In one of the few studies looking at empathy and culture, researchers found that participants reported less empathy for targets in distress who appeared to be operating from cultural norms different from their own. Feelings of sympathy and compassion were also reduced when the target's behaviors reflected divergent cultural norms (Nelson & Baumgarte, 2004).

## Avoidance of Hurt Feelings

Most of us do not make a habit of intentionally hurting someone else's feelings. On those occasions when we do hurt someone else, we feel bad about it, but we do not belabor the point and we do not spend a great deal of time dwelling on how we can prevent a similar situation from arising in the future. That said, there are times, perhaps more so for some people than others, when we take steps to actively avoid hurting someone else's feelings. Research has not examined the steps by which people intentionally *avoid* hurting another person's feelings, such as biting one's tongue or walking away from a potentially volatile situation. Yet, much of what we do and do not do is, in all likelihood, motivated at least in part by a desire to avoid hurting someone's feelings. People may visit their relatives and in-laws so that no one gets their feelings hurt and harmonious relations are maintained. It would be interesting to know how many more people than desired are invited to weddings because people worry that someone will "get their feelings hurt."

Although the list of actions people take to avoid hurting others' feelings is probably limitless, the motivations for doing so are much more constrained. Some people actively avoid hurting others' feelings because they have empathy for those people and do not want them to experience any type of negative feelings. Moreover, because hurtful communications often threaten the "face" of the other individual, we may actively avoid hurting others' feelings as a means of helping them save face. Perhaps more likely, however, is the self-serving motivation that we actively avoid hurting other people's feelings because we want to avoid the negative consequences that we ourselves may face if we make someone else feel as if we do not sufficiently value their relationship.

The frequency with which people actively avoid hurting someone else's feelings and the means by which they do so should vary according to dominant cultural models. At the most general level, people in individualistic cultures, operating from independent self-construals, should be less constrained about hurting another's feelings than those from collectivist cultures with an interdependent frame of reference. People in collectivist cultures would have less desire to fracture relationships by conveying relational devaluation and may have more concerns with helping others maintain face than people in individualistic cultures (Cocroft & Ting-Toomey, 1994; Ting-Toomey et al., 1991).

Clearly there are within-cultural variations in this as well as between-cultural differences. Nevertheless, the investigation of cross-cultural similarities and differences in active avoidance of hurt feelings will be an interesting area of future research.

CONCLUSION

As happens any time uncharted waters are traversed, writing this chapter about the relationship between culture and hurt feelings raises more questions than it answers. The link between hurt feelings and related emotions, such as sadness, gives us a good starting point for examining cross-cultural consistency and variability in the experience and expression of hurt feelings. Mesquita's (2003) cultural model of emotion provides a useful heuristic for examining ways in which cultures may be similar to and different from one another in relation to hurt feelings. Antecedent events leading to hurt feelings, appraisals of those events and the meaning attached to hurtful communications, physiological underpinnings of the social pain of hurt feelings, action tendencies and behaviors, and self-regulation of emotion each provide avenues for future research into culture and hurt feelings. Without additional empirical evidence, however, we can only speculate on the degree to which independent and interdependent self-construals, individualism and collectivism, affect the experience and expression of hurt feelings. Additional research is also needed to examine the relationship between compassion and empathic hurt feelings. What type of person is most likely to experience empathic hurt feelings and for whom? Are our own recollections of empathic hurt feelings also identified as such when heard by others? In other words, how objective or subjective is the experience of empathic hurt feelings? Under what situations are we most likely to engage in behaviors intended to actively avoid hurting another person's feelings? Are the steps that we take to avoid hurting others' feelings similar to the steps we take to avoid having our own feelings hurt?

Importantly, research on cultural influences on hurt feelings will not only inform us about cross-cultural variations in the experience and expression of this particular emotion but it will also inform us about the topic of hurt feelings. We clearly have much to learn about hurt feelings as a construct, particularly when compared to the wealth of research on other emotions. Our understanding of the antecedents and consequences of hurt feelings will certainly benefit from casting the research net as broadly as we can in the samples we are investigating.

REFERENCES

Baumeister, R. F., & Leary, M. R. (1995). The need to belong: Desire for interpersonal attachments as a fundamental human motivation. *Psychological Bulletin, 3*, 497–529.

Baumeister, R. F., & DeWall, C. N. (2005). The inner dimension of social exclusion: Intelligent thought and self-regulation among rejected persons. In K. D. Williams, J. P. Forgas, & W. von Hippel (Eds.), *The social outcast: Ostracism, social exclusion, rejection, and bullying* (pp. 53–73). New York: Psychology Press.

Bourgeois, K. S., & Leary, M. R. (2001). Coping with rejection: Derogating those who choose us last. *Motivation and Emotion, 25,* 101–111.

Bradbury, T. N., & Fincham, F. D. (1992). Attributions and behavior in marital interaction. *Journal of Personality and Social Psychology, 63,* 613–628.

Cacioppo, J. (2003). Introduction: Emotion and health. In R. J. Davidson, K. R. Scherer, & H. H. Goldsmith (Eds.), *Handbook of affective sciences* (pp. 1047–1052). New York: Oxford University Press.

Cocroft, B., & Ting-Toomey, S. (1994). Facework in Japan and the United States. *International Journal of Intercultural Relations, 18,* 469–506.

Dalai Lama. (2002). Understanding our fundamental nature. In R. J. Davidson & A. Harrington (Eds.), *Visions of compassion* (pp. 66–80). New York: Oxford University Press.

Davidson, R. J., & Harrington, A. (2002). *Visions of compassion.* New York: Oxford University Press.

DeWall, C. N., & Baumeister, R. F. (2006). Alone but feeling no pain: Effects of social exclusion on physical pain tolerance and pain threshold, affective forecasting, and interpersonal empathy. *Journal of Personality and Social Psychology, 91,* 1–15.

Eisenberger, N. I., & Lieberman, M. D. (2005). The neurocognitive overlap between physical and social pain. In K. D. Williams, J. P. Forgas, & W. von Hippel (Eds.), *The social outcast: Ostracism, social exclusion, rejection, and bullying* (pp. 109–127). New York: Psychology Press.

Eisenberger, N. I., Lieberman, M. D., & Williams, K. D. (2003). Does rejection hurt? An fMRI study of social exclusion. *Science, 302,* 290–292.

Ekman, P., & Davidson, R. J. (1994). Afterward: How is evidence of universals in antecedents of emotion explained? In P. Ekman & R. J. Davidson (Eds.), *The nature of emotion* (pp. 176–177). New York: Oxford University Press.

Feeney, J. A. (2005). Hurt feelings in couple relationships: Exploring the role of attachment and perceptions of personal injury. *Personal Relationships, 12,* 253–271.

Fincham, F. D., Harold, G. T., & Gano-Phillips, S. (2000). The longitudinal association between attributions and marital satisfaction: Direction of effects and role of efficacy expectations. *Journal of Family Psychology, 14,* 267–285.

Fitness, J. (2001). Betrayal, rejection, revenge, and forgiveness: An interpersonal script approach. In M. R. Leary (Ed.), *Interpersonal rejection* (pp. 73–103). New York: Oxford University Press.

Frijda, N. H. (1986). *The emotions.* Cambridge: Cambridge University Press.

Giese-Davis, J., & Spiegel, D. (2003). Emotional expression and cancer progression. In R. J. Davidson, K. R. Scherer, & H. H. Goldsmith (Eds.), *Handbook of affective sciences* (pp. 1053–1082). New York: Oxford University Press.

Gross, J. J., & Levenson, R. W. (1997). Hiding feelings: The acute effects of inhibiting negative and positive emotions. *Journal of Abnormal Psychology, 106,* 95–103.

Heelas, P. (1996). Emotion talk across cultures. In R. Harre & W. G. Parrott (Eds.), *The emotions* (pp. 171–199). London: Sage.

Lazarus, R. S. (1991). *Emotion and adaptation.* New York: Oxford University Press.

Lazarus, R. S., & Smith, C. A. (1988). Knowledge and appraisal in the cognition-emotion relationship. *Cognition and Emotion, 2,* 281–300.

Leary, M. R., & Baumeister, R. F. (2000). The nature and function of self-esteem: Sociometer theory. In M. P. Zanna (Ed.), *Advances in experimental social psychology* (pp. 1–62). San Diego: Academic Press.

Leary, M. R., Kowalski, R. M., Smith, L., & Phillips, S. (2003). Teasing, rejection, and violence: Case studies of the school shootings. *Aggressive Behavior, 29,* 202–214.

Leary, M. R., & Springer, C. (2001). Hurt feelings: The neglected emotion. In R. M. Kowalski (Ed.), *Aversive interpersonal behaviors* (pp. 151–175). Washington, DC: American Psychological Association.

Leary, M. R., Springer, C., Negel, L., Ansell, E., & Evans, K. (1998). The causes, phenomenology, and consequences of hurt feelings. *Journal of Personality and Social Psychology, 74,* 1225–1237.

Leary, M. R., Twenge, J. M., & Quinlivan, E. (2006). Interpersonal rejection as a determinant of anger and aggression. *Personality and Social Psychology Review, 10,* 111–132.

Lebra, T. S. (1976). *Japanese patterns of behavior.* Honolulu: University of Hawaii Press.

Levy, R. I. (1984). The emotions in comparative perspective. In K. R. Scherer & P. Ekman (Eds.), *Approaches to emotion* (pp. 397–412). Hillsdale, NJ: Erlbaum.

MacDonald, G., Kingsbury, R., & Shaw, S. (2005). Adding insult to injury: Social pain theory and response to social exclusion. In K. D. Williams, J. P. Forgas, & W. von Hippel (Eds.), *The social outcast: Ostracism, social exclusion, rejection, and bullying* (pp. 77–90). New York: Psychology Press.

MacDonald, G., & Leary, M. R. (2005). Why does social exclusion hurt? The relationship between social and physical pain. *Psychological Bulletin, 131,* 202–223.

Markus, H. R., & Kitayama, S. (1991). Culture and the self: Implications for cognition, emotion, and motivation. *Psychological Review, 98,* 224–253.

Matsumoto, D., Kudoh, T., Scherer, K., & Wallbott, H. (1988). Antecedents of and reactions to emotions in the United States and Japan. *Journal of Cross-Cultural Psychology, 19,* 267–286.

Mauro, R., Sato, K., & Tucker, J. (1992). The role of appraisal in human emotions: A cross-cultural study. *Journal of Personality and Social Psychology, 62,* 301–317.

Mesquita, B. (2003). Emotions as dynamic cultural phenomena. In R. J. Davidson, K. R. Scherer, & H. H. Goldsmith (Eds.), *Handbook of affective sciences* (pp. 871–890). New York: Oxford University Press.

Mesquita, B., & Ellsworth, P. (2001). The role of culture in appraisal. In K. R. Scherer & A. Schorr (Eds.), *Appraisal processes in emotion: Theory, methods, research* (pp. 233–248). New York: Oxford University Press.

Mesquita, B., & Frijda, N. H. (1992). Cultural variations in emotions: A review. *Psychological Bulletin, 112,* 179–204.

Mesquita, B., Frijda, N. H., & Scherer, K. R. (1997). Culture and emotion. In P. Dasen & T. S. Saraswathi (Eds.), *Handbook of cross-cultural psychology* (Vol. 2, pp. 255–297). Boston: Allyn & Bacon.

Mesquita, B., & Markus, H. R. (2004). Culture and emotion: Models of agency as sources of cultural variation in emotion. In A. S. R. Manstead, N. Frijda, & A. Fischer (Eds.), *Feelings and emotions: The Amsterdam symposium* (pp. 341–358). New York: Cambridge University Press.

Mesquita, B., & Walker, R. (2003). Cultural differences in emotions: A context for interpreting emotional experiences. *Behaviour Research and Therapy, 41,* 777-793.

Muraven, M., Tice, D. M., & Baumeister, R. F. (1998). Self-control as a limited resource: Regulatory depletion patterns. *Journal of Personality and Social Psychology, 74,* 774–789.

Nelson, D. W., & Baumgarte, R. (2004). Cross-cultural misunderstandings reduce empathic responding. *Journal of Applied Social Psychology, 34*, 391–401.

Oatley, K., & Duncan, E. (1992). Incidents of emotion in daily life. In K. T. Strongman (Ed.), *International review of studies on emotion* (Vol. 2, pp. 249–293). Hoboken, NJ: Wiley.

Planalp, S. (1999). *Communicating emotion: Social, moral, and cultural processes*. Paris: Cambridge University Press.

Scherer, K. R. (1997). Profiles of emotion-antecedent appraisal: Testing theoretical predictions across cultures. *Cognition & Emotion, 11*, 113–150.

Scherer, K. R., & Wallbott, H. G. (1994). Evidence for universality and cultural variation of differential emotion response patterning. *Journal of Personality and Social Psychology, 66*, 310–328.

Scherer, K. R., Wallbott, H. G., Matsumoto, D., & Kudoh, T. (1988). Emotional experience in cultural context: A comparison between Europe, Japan, and the United States. In K. R. Scherer (Ed.), *Faces of emotions* (pp. 5–30). Hillsdale, NJ: Erlbaum.

Shaver, P. R., Wu, S., & Schwartz, J. C. (1992). Cross-cultural similarities and differences in emotion and its representation: A prototype approach. In M. S. Clark (Ed.), *Emotion* (pp. 175–212). Newbury Park, CA: Sage.

Smith, C. A. (1991). The self, appraisal, and coping. In C. R. Snyder & D. R. Forsyth (Eds.), *Handbook of social and clinical psychology* (pp. 116–137). New York: Pergamon.

Snapp, C. M., & Leary, M. R. (2001). Hurt feelings among new acquaintances: Moderating effects of interpersonal familiarity. *Journal of Social and Personal Relationships, 18*, 315–326.

Snyder, C. R., & Lopez, S. J. (2007). *Positive psychology: The scientific and practical explorations of human strengths*. Thousand Oaks, CA: Sage.

Stephan, W. G., Stephan, C. W., & De Vargas, M. (1996). Emotional expression in Costa Rica and the United States. *Journal of Cross-Cultural Psychology, 27*, 147–160.

Stephan, C. W., Stephan, W. G., Saito, I., & Barnett, S. M. (1998). Emotional expression in Japan and the United States: The nonmonolithic nature of individualism and collectivism. *Journal of Cross-Cultural Psychology, 29*, 728–748.

Ting-Toomey, S., Gao, G., Trubisky, P., Yang, Z., Kim, H. S., Lin, S. L., & Nishida, T. (1991). Culture, face maintenance, and styles of handling interpersonal conflict: A study in five cultures. *International Journal of Conflict Management, 2*, 275–296.

Vangelisti, A. L. (1994). Messages that hurt. In W. R. Cupach & B. H. Spitzberg (Eds.), *The dark side of interpersonal communication* (pp. 53–82). Hillsdale, NJ: Erlbaum.

Vangelisti, A. L., & Crumley, L. P. (1998). Reactions to messages that hurt: The influence of relational contexts. *Communication Monographs, 65*, 173–196.

Vangelisti, A. L., & Young, S. L. (2000). When words hurt: The effects of perceived intentionality on interpersonal relationships. *Journal of Social and Personal Relationships, 17*, 393–424.

Vangelisti, A. L., Young, S. L., Carpenter-Theune, K. E., & Alexander, A. L. (2005). Why does it hurt? The perceived causes of hurt feelings. *Communication Research, 32*, 443–477.

Wallbott, H. G., & Scherer, K. (1988). How universal and specific is emotional experience? Evidence from 27 countries and five continents. In K. R. Scherer (Ed.), *Facets of emotion* (pp. 31–56). Hillsdale, NJ: Erlbaum.

Whitesell, N. R., & Harter, S. (1996). The interpersonal context of emotion: Anger with close friends and classmates. *Child Development, 67*, 1345–1359.

Wong, P. T. P., & Weiner, B. (1981). When people ask "why" questions, and the heuristics of attributional search. *Journal of Personality and Social Psychology, 40,* 650–663.

Young, S. L., & Bippus, A. M. (2001). Does it make a difference if they hurt you in a funny way? Humorously and non-humorously phrased hurtful messages in personal relationships. *Communication Quarterly, 49,* 35–52.

## 22

# Hurt Feelings: The Last Taboo for Researchers and Clinicians?

LUCIANO L'ABATE

The purpose of this chapter is threefold: (a) to note that researchers and clinicians, like most of us human beings, have avoided dealing directly with hurt feelings in their research and practice, (b) to provide researchers and clinicians a way to identify and conceptualize hurt through a theoretical model, and (c) to offer researchers and clinicians ideas about how to help people deal with their hurt feelings in positive ways.

The relevance of hurt feelings to personality socialization and to close relationships has been validated repeatedly in relationship research by Feeney (2004b, 2005) and by Vangelisti (1994; Vangelisti & Young, 2000), among others. Although this work has demonstrated the importance of hurt feelings to relationships, especially intimate relationships, researchers in psychology have not attended to this evidence, creating a gap between psychological theories of feelings and emotions and research results in relationship science. A perusal of most psychological treatises on feelings and emotions failed to yield the term *hurt*. At best, the term *distress* was cited in passim, but it was never defined or introduced as being relevant to theories and models of feelings and emotions. This is not surprising given that most of these theories and models are based on intrapersonal self-report, paper-and-pencil tests, or contrived laboratory experiments rather than on direct observations of hurt feelings in intimate relationships (Niedenthal, Krauth-Gruber, & Ric, 2006).

Hurt feelings are at the bottom of our existence. If left covered, pushed down, and avoided they can produce dangerous personal and interpersonal outcomes. It is doubtful whether scholars and clinicians in psychology can continue to ignore these feelings. Hurt feelings are too important to psychological functioning to be overlooked by the scientific and professional communities. Of course, as we shall see, there are plenty of related (but not synonymous) terms in the relevant psychological literature. In addition to examining these terms, the current chapter describes a multilayered, integrative model of feelings and emotions built on hurt feelings and offers means for coping with hurt feelings.

## THE IMPORTANCE OF HURT FEELINGS IN PERSONALITY SOCIALIZATION AND INTIMATE RELATIONSHIPS

The importance of hurt feelings in psychological functioning and personality socialization was initially suggested 30 years ago (L'Abate, 1977), leading to a verification of their presence and relevance in couples conflict resolution (Frey, Holly, & L'Abate, 1979) and in couple intimacy (L'Abate & McHenry, 1983). Emotionality and hurt feelings were described as "the primary basis – the structure – of intimate relationships" (p. 144) and as regulating "distances between and among individuals" (L'Abate, 1986, p. 145).

Intimacy, in turn, was defined as the sharing of joys and hurts and fears of being hurt. When intimacy is defined in this fashion, it is found in functional relationships, whereas its absence denotes dysfunctionality (Feeney, 2004a, 2005; L'Abate, 1994, 1997, 1999a, 2003a, 2005, 2008b, in press; L'Abate & Cusinato, 2007; L'Abate & De Giacomo, 2003; Vangelisti, 2006; Vangelisti & Beck, 2007). As such, this definition became part of written homework assignments in systematic family therapy (L'Abate, 1986) and led to various preventive and psychotherapeutic applications (L'Abate, 1999b, 1999c, 2000a, 2000b; L'Abate & De Giacomo, 2003). Eventually, hurt feelings were included in a relational theory of personality development (L'Abate, 1976, 1994) that evolved into theories of personality socialization in the family (L'Abate, 1997, 2002, 2003a) and in intimate relationships and psychopathology (L'Abate, 2005).

## AVOIDANCE OF HURT FEELINGS IN RESEARCH AND PRACTICE PARALLELS THE SAME AVOIDANCE IN OURSELVES

Many metaphors, analogies, and similes have been used in the literature to avoid dealing directly with the bottom line of our existence: experiencing, expressing, and sharing joys, hurt, and fears of being hurt within the context of intimate relationships. These relationships are called "intimate" because they are characterized by (a) *emotional closeness* or being communally available in a reciprocal fashion to loved ones, in addition to being instrumentally available in problem solving and negotiating; (b) *commitment* to keeping and enhancing the relationship in sickness and health, and in poverty and riches; (c) *interdependence* or reciprocal dependence rather than unrealistic independence or actual dependence between the parties involved; and (d) involvement in the *prolongation* of relationships that have withstood the test of time (L'Abate, 1997, 2003a, 2005; 2008b, in press; L'Abate & Cusinato, 2007; L'Abate & De Giacomo, 2003).

The neglect of hurt feelings in theories and models of feelings and emotions is evidenced by a recent scholarly review of the literature (Niedenthal et al., 2006). This review, for instance, supported the traditional model of five fundamental emotions: anger, disgust, fear, joy, and sadness. Hurt feelings, and related constructs like distress or injury, were included in the texts, but were not considered as being part of traditional classifications of feelings and emotions. The consistent neglect of hurt feelings in the literature is caused in part by the remnants of an intrapsychic orientation in most psychological theories and models of feelings and emotions. It also may be caused by the tendency, on the part of most humans, to treat hurt feelings as a taboo. We try to avoid (deny, repress, suppress) hurt feelings because they are very unpleasant. The consequences of such avoidance and the subsequent failure to express and share these feelings with loved ones are costly to us as well as to our intimate relationships. This avoidance might be responsible for many psychosomatic and physical illnesses, in spite of their absence in relevant treatises on these topics (Thomas & Cummings, 2000; Van Dyke, Temoshock, & Zegans, 1984).

In the next section are two lists of terms that have been used to indirectly describe toxic, hurtful internal states that supposedly are responsible for external behavior and for dysfunctional human relationships. Both lists are characterized by the same progression, starting with unspecified, vague, and encompassing constructs and ending with more specific and detailed constructs. Taken together, the terms represent a widespread academic and even clinical avoidance of hurt feelings. By avoiding these feelings as a major component of personal and intimate relationships, both the academic and clinical literatures have paralleled a process that occurs in human relationships: *strong avoidance of hurt feelings and even stronger avoidance of approaching them through sharing them with loved ones or, in the absence of a loved one, with helpful others* (Vangelisti, 2006; Vangelisti & Beck, 2007). Avoiding these feelings is the root of many dysfunctional relationships, whereas approaching them is central to functional ones (Higgins, 1998; L'Abate, 2003a, 2005).

## Terms Used to Deal with Underlying Hurt

An important characteristic of terms used to deal indirectly with underlying hurt is their intrapsychic rather than relational nature. Another interesting characteristic of these terms is that they usually are not clearly defined. Of course, there are quite a few words that are related to hurt, like anguish, bereavement, and grief, among others. Rather than review all of them, some representative terms are used to illustrate the scholarly and professional avoidance of hurt feelings.

### *Anger*
The construct of hurt feelings came into being in reaction to Mace's (1976) conceptualization of anger as a feeling basic to marital intimacy and as the bottom line to whatever is relevant to couple relationships (L'Abate, 1977). Anger is, and can be, a real distracter and detractor from hurt feelings, both intra- and interpersonally. One could even say that anger is used by individuals

as a strategy to avoid coming to terms with their hurt feelings. The initial arguments put forth by Mace and L'Abate were followed by a pilot study (Frey et al., 1979) that found that couples prefer to share their hurt feelings over other rational conflict resolution strategies.

*Distress*

Distress is discussed at length in various references. It sometimes is referred to as "personal distress" or "self-directed empathy" (Batson, 1991; Eisenberg, 1986; Thomas & Cummings, 2000). More often than not, the term *distress* is left undefined, but it usually represents an internal state that results from unpleasant or painful experiences (Jones, Kugler, & Adams, 1995; Tangney & Fisher, 1995). The literature is so littered by the use of this term that only few representative examples are presented here.

  a. Segrin and Givertz (2003) used this term in relation to "marital distress" (p. 149).
  b. Burleson (2003) used the same term (p. 552) in "affective distress" and in "emotional distress . . . and . . . distress cues" (p. 558).
  c. Kelly, Fincham, and Beach (2003) used it in "marital distress" (p. 732) and "distressed couples" (p. 733).
  d. Horowitz (2004) went as far as to suggest various methods "to avoid other forms of emotional distress" (p. 33), using as an example of this avoidance John Steinbeck's (1939) *The Grapes of Wrath*. In addition, Horowitz cited Higgins' (1987) research to illustrate various "Types of Resulting Distress," from discrepancies among actual, ideal, and ought selves (pp. 90–91).

*Sorrow*

This is a frequently used term associated with hurt, grief, loss, or bereavement. One work on this subject (Levine, 2005) interestingly enough, gives a list of intrapsychic (i.e., internal) suggestions on how to deal with grief or "unattended sorrow." These suggestions do not deal with how to share sorrow with loved ones. The author notes, for example, that people experiencing sorrow should try (a) keeping a grief journal; (b) using breathing exercises "to aid in healing sorrow"; (c) becoming aware of the three stages of working with mental and physical sorrow, according to the late Elisabeth Kubler-Ross; (d) adopting and adapting a new positive mindset on sorrow as an ability to feel and to be alive; (e) using mindfulness to become more aware of bodily sensations and reactions that lead to greater intellectual awareness; (f) spending more time in singing, or in silence, or in mindful walking; (g) connecting with the lost one through "heart speech"; and (h) recognizing the importance of unattended sorrow of the survivor after an accident or disaster.

It is important to note that these suggestions, if followed to the letter, would not allow individuals who are hurt to achieve intimacy with loved ones because there is no recommendation to share hurt feelings with anyone else. Again, this is an exemplary illustration of a monadic view of personality – a view that assumes that people grow and live in a vacuum, apart from nurturing relationships with loved ones.

*Negative Feelings/Emotions*
Perhaps one of the most deleterious misnomers for hurt is "negative feelings," where anguish, distress, grief, and so on are all lumped together with feelings like anger and hostility without any distinction among them. The use of this misnomer is based on two fallacies. One fallacy lies in not differentiating *feelings*, which are receptive and experiential, from *emotions*, which are expressive (Watson, 2000). Here, feelings and emotions are equated rather than treated as two separate aspects of the same affective process or, at least, as a continuum with receptive experiencing input on one end and expressive output on the other end (L'Abate, 1994, 1997, 2003a, 2005).

The second fallacy derives from the first one and lies in applying negative versus positive connotations to feelings. This value judgment is misleading and unnecessary. What makes anger or hurt negative? Who decides whether anger is negative or positive? Is anger more negative or positive than hurt? Feelings are feelings. To connote them negatively implies that people should avoid them. Of course feelings – including hurt – cannot be avoided. They happen to us as a result of what is going on inside and outside of us. If we have any control, it involves how those feelings, whatever they may be, are expressed outwardly and become emotions.

There are myriad ways in which people can express feelings, whether hurtful or otherwise. For instance, individuals can express their feelings in conjunctive or disjunctive ways. They can express anger as a way of coming together, or they can use anger to blame, insult, or abuse whoever provoked it. David and Vera Mace noted, in a personal communication (too long ago to remember its date), that they used the conjunctive expression: "Sweetheart, I have a problem with my anger; can you help me?" Of course, there are plenty of examples of how anger is used disjunctively. No need to repeat them here.

We are all hurt human beings to some degree or another and in some ways. Although most of us can choose whether and how to express and share those hurt feelings, it is important to note that some of us cannot. Some people have no choice about whether they even feel hurt, as in alexthymia. Others have been so hurt before they could even speak that they have no words or memories to access their feelings. As a result, they may express their feelings motorically, through physical movements, as in the case of impulsively acting out criminality and other forms of aggression and abuse. Alternatively they may keep their hurt inside and become ruminative schizophrenics, completely unable to deal with feelings and emotions (L'Abate, 2005).

## Disclosure

Ever since Jourard's (1971) pioneering work, the term *disclosure* has been a favored construct to describe what happens when someone speaks about supposedly painful or traumatic experiences (i.e., "negative feelings"; see Stroebe, Schut, & Stroebe, 2005). In most cases, disclosure is described as a behavior engaged in by individuals, rather than as a communication pattern that occurs between relational partners. But, of course, disclosure occurs in the context of a relationship. It happens between people. In fact, there is some evidence that a partner's response to disclosure predicts intimacy above and beyond the effect of disclosure (Laurenceau, Feldman-Barrett, & Revine, 2005).

Instead of "disclosure," which implies a relatively abstract, one-way process, it may be preferable to use terms like *sharing*, which implies a specific and concrete two-way reciprocal process between caring partners, among loving family members, or with intimate others (L'Abate, 2005; L'Abate & De Giacomo, 2003; Vangelisti, 2006).

## Support

Although researchers have argued that support is important to close, prolonged relationships (e.g., Bertera, 2005; Franks, Wendorf, Gonzales, & Ketterer, 2004), the term *support*, like the term *disclosure*, typically describes a one-way process. That is, one hurt person, the vulnerable one, reveals abuses, traumas, accidents, and physical upheavals to someone who is supposedly not hurt as much and therefore not as vulnerable. This latter person serves as the source of support (Stroebe et al., 2005). No wonder that the outcome of these interactions sometimes is negative, because the disclosure that occurs need not be reciprocal. Without reciprocity there is no intimacy. The support is temporary, short-lived, and limited to the occurrence of a specific event. Without a lasting intimate relationship, support is not only a one-way-street but also a temporary emotional Band-aid. It covers the hurt but without a specific, long-lasting remedy, it may allow the hurts to fester, grow, and not go away.

### AN INTEGRATED MODEL OF HURT FEELINGS AND EMOTIONS

Given the tendency of researchers and clinicians to avoid hurt feelings, it is not surprising that these feelings, when discussed, are not always well defined. Before constructing and presenting a model of hurt feelings and emotions, hurt should be defined.

Hurt feelings are subjectively painful and unpleasant feelings based on antecedent conditions such as abandonment, abuse, betrayal, and the loss of loved ones (L'Abate, 1997; Vangelisti, 2006). When the hurt associated with these conditions is not expressed and shared with loved ones, the ultimate outcome is psychopathology within individuals and with intimate and nonintimate others. Hurt is not inflicted or received in an interpersonal vacuum. It occurs most of the time within intimate relationships (Perris,

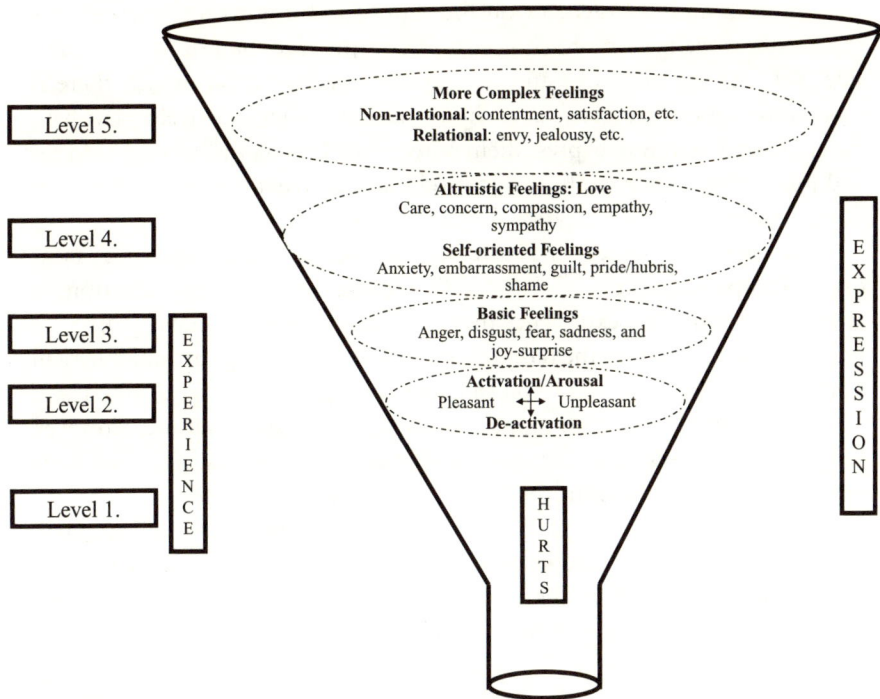

FIGURE 22.1. A multilayered model of the experience and expression of hurt feelings.

Arrindell, & Eisemann, 1994). Indeed, as noted by Feeney (2004a, 2004b), "Psychological hurt is emerging as an important topic for relationship researchers.... Hurt is a relational phenomenon, and the outcomes or hurtful events undoubtedly depend on the thoughts, feelings, and behaviors of both partners" (p. 349).

In addition to defining hurt, it is important to acknowledge that all people do not deal with hurt in the same way. For instance, cultural stereotypes depict women as tending to cry more than men to express their hurt, whereas men may become angry and act out more often than women. Yet, there are some commonalities in the ways people deal with hurt feelings and in the associations between hurt and other emotions that enable the construction of a model that should be useful to researchers and clinicians.

## A Multilayered Model

The model presented here is multilayered and two dimensional (see Fig. 22.1). Hurt feelings are conceived as the narrow, speaking side of a funnel or a megaphone, underneath anger, anxiety, sadness, joy, fear, and disgust (L'Abate, 2003a, 2005; L'Abate & De Giacomo, 2003). On the expressive side, where the voice comes out amplified, the volume is increased because the widening allows a progressive movement from compression at the receptive input side to an amplification and enlargement on the expressive output side. This analogy explains how we have more choices on the expressive than on the receptive side. Between the receptive and the expressive ends of the model, there is rationality. Rationality allows us to choose how to deal with the feelings we have experienced and how to express them outwardly, constructively, conjunctively, and proactively or reactively, disjunctively, and destructively. The latter sorts of expressions occur when rationality is defective.

The model presented in Figure 22.1 is based on Tomkins' (1962, 1963) original amplification model. Hurt feelings move upward from the bottom of an upright funnel. We experience these feelings as inflicted on us by intimate others or by ourselves on the receptive input side, with an upward enlargement of emotions on the expressive output side. Strangers may hurt us physically, and those wounds and their emotional sequels may last a lifetime. However, only intimate others have the power to hurt us deeply and lastingly. The same power applies to us: We hurt those who love us the most (Jones et al., 1995).

The model consists of at least five levels. If necessary, a supraordinate sixth level could be added. These levels range from simple at the narrow bottom, moving up from experiencing receptive feelings such as hurts to increasingly complex feelings at higher levels. As noted earlier, feelings are experienced; emotions are expressed (L'Abate, 2005). Four criteria differentiate feelings along the five supraordinate levels of this model: (a) depth or vertical up–down direction; (b) width or horizontal narrow–wide direction; (c) complexity, including subtlety and indirection; and (d) stages of maturation starting from (1) early dependency in childhood to (2) denial of dependency in adolescence to (3) interdependency in adulthood and finally to (4) a return to dependency in old age.

## Model Levels

*Level 1.* Hurt feelings as subjectively unpleasant and painful experiences lie at the bottom of our existence, instigated by phenomena such as physical, sexual, and verbal abuses; bereavements; betrayals; grieving; losses; put-downs; and rejections, among others (Feeney, 2005, 2006; L'Abate, 1997; Vangelisti, 2006, Vangelisti & Beck, 2007). If left uncovered, unspoken, and unexpressed, these feelings can produce untold negative consequences to individuals and to their intimate relationships. Psychopathology and psychosomatic illnesses indeed could be conceived as the outcome of avoided, unexpressed hurt feelings (L'Abate, 1986, 1994, 1997, 2000a, 2003a, 2005; L'Abate & De Giacomo, 2003; Thomas & Cummings, 2000; Van Dyke et al., 1984).

*Level 2.* This level is composed of the two major dimensions of emotional experience: (1) activation/arousal – deactivation and (2) pleasantness–unpleasantness. These two orthogonal dimensions serve as gatekeepers to allow (approach) or not allow (avoid) hurt feelings to "seep out" and expand at higher levels of expression or to keep them inside, invisible and unspoken.

We approach who and what is pleasant and avoid who and what is unpleasant. We discharge or express when we want to get something that is inside of us outside. We delay or deny and therefore avoid whatever we are afraid of or unable to express and share. Approach/avoidance occurs in a dimension of space and distance. Discharge/delay occurs in a dimension of time and control. These two dimensions of space and time are basic to our process of socialization in intimate relationships (L'Abate, 1994, 1997, 2002, 2003a, 2005; L'Abate & De Giacomo, 2003). A third dimension of powerfulness–powerlessness may be part of the process of gatekeeping, but this conceptual possibility needs to be explored further elsewhere.

*Level 3.* The extant literature consistently describes the existence of a group of basic feelings: joy/surprise, anger, fear, disgust, and sadness, plus or minus a couple of other feelings. Hence, at this level, the number of fundamental feelings is circumscribed by scientific consensus to a handful (Niedenthal et al., 2006) or, at best, to circumplex models of personality and emotions (Plutchik & Conte, 1997).

*Level 4.* At this level, one can include more complex feelings such as altruistic (love) feelings (e.g., care, concern, compassion, empathy, and sympathy), as well as self-oriented feelings (e.g., anxiety, embarrassment, guilt, pride/hubris, shame, and worry; Tangney & Fischer, 1995).

*Level 5.* Here one can include even more complex and subtle feelings such as nonrelational feelings (e.g., in contentment and satisfaction) and relational feelings (e.g., envy and jealousy).

The multileveled model proposed here integrates feelings and emotions in ways that may solve the raging controversy about how many feelings and emotions there are (Niedenthal et al., 2006). If this model is valid, instead of being considered at the same level of analysis and interpretation, feelings and emotions can be considered at various levels of depth, width, complexity, and age progression. Supposedly, the more differentiated the range of feelings people experience, the more functional they might be.

The five levels suggest a developmental and perhaps age-related progression moving upward from Level 1, as the most basic stage of socialization, to a wider range of feelings and emotions at higher levels. Possibly, these levels might represent stages of personality socialization, with progressively more articulate and advanced stages in the experience and expression of feelings. Consequently, we need to distinguish among different stages of personality socialization in terms of how feelings are kept and retained and how they are expressed and shared with loved ones. At least four stages of socialization of feelings and emotions can be distinguished.

## Model Stages

*Stage 1.* The fully functioning personality is or should be able to experience feelings of hurt, such as sadness, fear, guilt, shame, and embarrassment (Tangney &

Fischer, 1995). At this level of personality functioning, hurt can be experienced, expressed positively, and shared constructively with loved ones. Receptive feelings are distinguished from how those feelings are expressed through rational thought processes. The introduction of this rational process allows individuals to modulate, modify, and mediate the bridge between their feelings (i.e., hurt) on one receptive end of the model and emotions on the other expressive end (L'Abate, 2005).

*Stage 2.* People with internalizing personality disorders, such as depression (and other disorders in Axis II, Cluster C of the *Diagnostic Statistical Manual of Mental Disorders IV* [DSM-IV]), are likely to wallow in guilt, shame, or embarrassment, blaming themselves and exculpating others for whatever hurt they may have experienced. Here hurt feelings are kept inside and are not expressed except through self-blaming and rationalized exculpation of others. The initial outcome of this process is emotional suicide. Ultimately, the outcome may be actual suicide (L'Abate, 2005).

*Stage 3.* Individuals with externalizing personality disorders, such as antisocial, narcissistic, histrionic, and obsessive personalities (those represented by Axis II, Cluster B in the DSM-IV), tend to discharge physically and verbally whatever hurt feelings are experienced. In these disorders, acting out without the interposition of rationality means going from hurt feelings directly and immediately into action, blaming others for whatever hurt feelings may have been elicited or produced. These personalities would tend to express any perceived or real hurts by immediate and direct discharge or even attack, either verbal or physical or both, without reflection or rational consideration of the potential consequences of their behavior. The obsessive-compulsive personality, for instance, would discharge hurt feelings through the repetition of inappropriate actions that seem completely unrelated to the original hurt feelings. When an addiction is present, one can pretty well predict that it is a form of self-medication to avoid dealing directly with any felt hurt (L'Abate, 1994, 2005; Meyer. 1986).

*Stage 4.* In severe psychopathology, as in severe depression, schizophrenias, and borderline personality disorders (those in Cluster A of Axis II and disorders of Axis I in the DSM-IV), there can be extreme, contradictory, and inconsistent ways of dealing with hurt feelings. These can range from keeping those hurt feelings bottled inside, as is the case for many with schizophrenia, to expressing them inappropriately, as in the persecutory ideation and often destructive behavior of those who are paranoid. This is why there is positive relationship between expressed emotions (EE) and relapse in schizophrenia. In cases where severe hurt occurs, when a child can talk and think but cannot express him- or herself, as in sexual abuse, the outcome may be dissociative identity disorders. When intense hurt occurs in adulthood and is not shared, posttraumatic stress disorders may be the outcome (L'Abate, 2005).

At least three cognitive processes are required to access, approach, acknowledge, accept, express, and share our hurt feelings with those we love and who love us. These include awareness and acknowledgment of (a) our *neediness* to be close reciprocally with someone who is important to us, (b) our *fallibility* in hurting the very ones we love and who love us (L'Abate, 1999a), and (c) our *vulnerability* to being hurt by those we love and who love us (Jones et al., 1995). As noted, we may be physically hurt by strangers, and those wounds may last a lifetime. Nonetheless, we are more vulnerable to being hurt by loved ones because, by being important to us, they have the power to hurt us more than anybody else.

The three aforementioned processes are included as an expansion of this model in spite of being cognitive rather than emotional in nature (L'Abate, 1999a, 2005). Although they are not emotional, they may represent sine qua non conditions for our being able to eventually share hurt feelings with loved ones. To experience and express hurt appropriately with loved ones, it may be necessary to reach an interdependent stage mentioned earlier. Hence, mainly very articulate, well-functioning individuals who possess in some degree these three qualities can express and share deep feelings of hurt in a reciprocal fashion with loving partners, caring family members, and long-time friends. People have to allow themselves to be "weak" in order to be "strong" enough to admit being needy, vulnerable, and fallible to share their hurts with loved ones.

In a similar vein, individuals need to be willing and able to share hurt feelings with the very persons who hurt them if they are to experience and practice forgiveness. Sharing hurt feelings is the conditio sine qua non for forgiveness to occur (Fincham, 2000; Fincham & Beach, 2002; Root & McCullough, 2007).

Finally, the relationship between the extent and nature of hurt feelings and physiological, neurological, and even chemical functions in the biological system needs to be evaluated. The possibilities of this connection are infinite and mind-boggling.

## THE IMPROVEMENT OF HURT FEELINGS

Once we accept the premise that most of us have been hurt in one way or another and that hurts are at the bottom line of our existence, then what? There is no way we can help all the people who are hurt through face-to-face, talk-based psychotherapy. This process is expensive and limited to those who need it and who can afford it. If all of us are hurt, what other choices do we have to deal with our hurts, outside of psychotherapy? This section suggests ways of helping people improve their feelings and emotions to promote health and avoid sickness (L'Abate, 2007b). Without denying the contribution of one or two sessions of brief psychotherapy a la Nicholas Cummings (Thomas & Cummings, 2000), talk should not be viewed as the only medium for communication and healing. For instance, another vehicle for communication and healing (on a large scale) can be found in distance writing (Esterling, L'Abate, Murray, & Pennebaker, 1999; L'Abate, 2001a, 2002, 2003b, 2004a, 2004b; L'Abate & De Giacomo, 2003).

## Structured Talk-Based Interventions in Psychotherapy

*Identifying Dysfunctional Patterns in Individuals*
If indeed anger, hostility, and rage are outcomes of hurt feelings, then we must consider those external manifestations of underlying hurts. Those external manifestations are the smoke that often distracts us from the fire of hurt feelings. If this position is valid, then most criminal acting-out personality disorders, and even murderers, oriented toward immediate discharge are the outcome of avoided (denied, repressed, or suppressed) hurt feelings received through past abuses and neglects. Consequently, these external manifestations lead to the first identifying question: "How were you hurt in the past?" From this initial question clinicians can go on to identify past experiences, and usually abusive or neglectful traumas, that were experienced by the individual.

Of course, in addition to taking an oral history of anger, hostility, and aggression, there are numerous paper-and-pencil self-report tests that evaluate individuals' level of anger and acting out, and there is at least one measure to evaluate hurt and intimacy that is consistent with the views put forth in this chapter (Stevens & L'Abate, 1989).

*Identifying Dysfunctional Patterns in Couples and Families*
As a first step, couples might be encouraged to check which positive activities they are involved in individually, dyadically, and multirelationally. Positive activities can be prescribed to improve their relationship. Then, to evaluate the hurt feelings that may underlie a variety of dysfunctional patterns (see Gottman, 1994; L'Abate, 2005), partners can be advised to (a) define the patterns (using a dictionary), (b) provide one or two examples of each pattern, and (c) rank order those patterns according to how much they influence partners or family members. After completing this assignment, couples can either complete standard measures to evaluate their hurt or deal with their most dysfunctional patterns through face-to-face talk with a professional helper (L'Abate, 2006).

What can we do to help people become more emotionally articulate both when they experience and express their hurt feelings? The control and regulation of emotions have been considered at great length in the literature from an intrapsychic rather than from a relational viewpoint (Baumeister & Vohs, 2004; Blankstein, Pliner, & Polivy, 1980). Very few concrete suggestions have been introduced on how to help individuals achieve more appropriately positive and interpersonally relevant experiences of feelings and expressions of emotions. Unfortunately, as long as theorists and clinicians persist in distinguishing between positive and negative feelings (Averill, 1980), and as long as hurt feelings are labeled as negative, options for helping people deal with hurt effectively may be limited.

With this said, an important step in dealing verbally with hurt in participants lies in a positive reframing of hurt feelings as happening to people who are sensitive and caring: "Only sensitive and caring people like you are able to feel hurt because there are many people in hospitals and jails who cannot," "If you hurt, it means that you can also feel guilty, ashamed, and embarrassed. Is that right?" "If you hurt, it means that you are able to feel deeply what many other people cannot." "Feeling, expressing, and sharing our hurts like you do is a blessing, not a curse."

## Prescriptions in Couple and Family Therapy

There are at least two direct model-derived techniques or prescriptions that can be administered in unstructured, talk-based interventions in face-to-face counseling and psychotherapy (L'Abate, 2005). The first is hugging, holding, huddling, and cuddling. Even though this prescription does not deal directly with feelings and emotions, it is general enough to help couples and families learn to be physically available to each other through extended physical nonerotic contact, thereby establishing a more favorable emotional context for sharing pleasant and unpleasant feelings and emotions (L'Abate, 2001b; L'Abate & De Giacomo, 2003). The second is sharing of hurts in couples and families. This is a straightforward technique to help partners learn to share hurt feelings first in the professional helper's office and later in the privacy of their home. Partners initially are asked to hold hands and to describe how they feel about holding hands. After this prologue, they are asked to concentrate on their own hurt until they feel "butterflies in their stomach" and the need to express and share their hurt. As soon as one or both partners become aware of their hurt (i.e., they "get in touch with their feelings"), they are asked to complete the stem "I am hurting..." or "I hurt because..." (L'Abate, 1986, 1994, 1997, 1999b, 2000b, 2005; L'Abate & De Giacomo, 2003). When there is a match in sharing hurts, often this match leads to crying together. Conceivably, this technique could be used at a distance through the Internet and via television. Verbatim instructions for these prescriptions are available in L'Abate and Cusinato (2007).

What is important in this process lies in who is able to express hurt feelings and who cannot or does not want to express them. In an anecdotal sample of clinical couples, women tended to express their hurts quite a bit more often than did men (L'Abate, 1999b). About one-third of the men did express their hurt feelings, sharing them with their partners appropriately and constructively. Perhaps another third of this sample of men tended to play the role of the stoic, "strong" unexpressive male. About another third had reactions of anger or showed signs of being "upset" and "troubled" by the interaction. In a few extreme cases, not knowing what to do or how to cope with this expression of feelings, the men got up and walked out of the therapy office. Consequently, this exercise is also diagnostic in that it helps reveal who can and who cannot express hurt feelings. Such information is grist for the diagnostic and healing mill. Indeed, when this exercise was conducted in a workshop on intimacy with professional therapists (mostly women who brought their partners with them, as required by the nature of the workshop), it was interesting to find that these couples had as much trouble sharing hurt as did clinical couples!

## Distance Writing and Structured Self-Help Mental Health Protocols or Workbooks

Instead of face-to-face, talk-based confrontation, another direct way to deal with hurt is through writing (L'Abate, 2001a, 2002, 2003b; L'Abate & De Giacomo, 2003). Once writing is used as an additional or alternative way to help and heal hurt people, new vistas and possibilities open up. For instance, writing can be directed specifically toward people's hurt, as in Pennebaker's expressive writing paradigm (Kacewicz, Slatcher, & Pennebaker, 2007). Using this paradigm, individuals are required to write about their unexpressed traumas for 15 to 20 minutes a day for 4 consecutive days. If couples are involved, both partners could follow the basic script and then convene to compare and contrast their writings.

Another approach, mostly programmed, consists of workbooks directly focused on intimacy or, more generally, on feelings and emotions. For instance, one workbook, based on the model of intimacy described in this chapter, includes most of the components of hurt sharing, such as seeing the good, forgiveness, and sharing hurt (L'Abate, 1986). Another workbook also deals with hurt (L'Abate & Hewitt, 2000a, 2000b). A third, about planned parenting, includes most aspects of the model described in Figure 22.1 including, of course, intimacy and sharing joys, hurt, and fears of being hurt (L'Abate, 2009).

Indirect distance writing approaches that, in one way or another, provoke or elicit hurt feelings, are exemplified by journals (Levine & Calvanio, 2007) and autobiographies (Demetrio & Borgonovi, 2007). After reading information from these written sources, professional helpers can develop a list of questions to specify further what needs to be shared about hurt feelings.

Last, but not least, among the tools that can be used to encourage writing about hurt is the Internet. This medium provides a ready-made source for sharing hurts through chat rooms, specific support groups, and structured programs (Pulier, Mount, McMenamin, & Maheu, 2007).

More research is needed about the effectiveness of these various tools. To illustrate, a meta-analysis of the effectiveness of mental and physical health workbooks found an effect size of .44 for the former and .25 for the latter (Smyth & L'Abate, 2001). These findings suggest a literature that is somewhat mixed. For example, in one study, L'Abate and Goldstein (2007) administered a problem-solving workbook to a group of hospitalized women with personality disorders. They found that, in comparison to a control group that did not receive the workbook, the experimental group cut the length of their hospitalization in half and significantly decreased the frequency of relapse

(L'Abate & Goldstein, 2007). These results, however, were not supported by another study that found that self-help workbooks administered as homework during psychotherapy with individuals, couples, and families actually were associated with an increase in the number of therapy sessions (L'Abate, L'Abate, & Maino, 2005). Contradictory findings such as these, of course, need further evaluation as they raise questions about the nature and interaction among specific protocols, levels of functioning in participants, and settings.

### The Dictionary as the First Step in Dealing with Hurts

The dictionary is the most readily available source of information that can be used to improve individuals' experience and expression of feelings and emotions. In addition to being available in libraries and on the Internet, it is readable because it consists of brief sentences and it usually gives synonyms and antonyms. However, the use of a dictionary makes no sense unless it is directed toward a specific topic, in this case emotional experience and expression. This direction is available in self-help protocols or workbooks about feelings and emotions, as noted earlier (L'Abate, 2007a, 2009; also see Kazantzis & L'Abate, 2007).

It would be very easy to build a workbook or to create interactive practice exercises related specifically to hurt, similar to the workbooks and exercises on intimacy and planned parenting developed years ago (L'Abate, 1986, 2009). For instance, one could ask participants to define (again with a help of a dictionary) a number of the terms related to hurt, including abandonment, abuse, anger, anguish, anxiety, bereavement, betrayal, grief, loss, put-down, rejection, and sorrow. Two or three blank spaces could be added to the end of the list of terms to allow participants to add whatever terms apply to them that were not listed earlier. After participants generate their definitions, they could be asked to give two examples to illustrate each term. Then, participants could be asked to rank order the terms according to how well they apply to their own particular experience, from most to least applicable. From that point on, practice exercises could be administered for each term based on the rank ordering it received. Standard practice exercises about the history, development, nature, or intensity of any term as well as the frequency and rate with which any term is used can be found in L'Abate's work (2007c).

## CONCLUSION

The road to dealing with hurt feelings conceptually, clinically, and empirically has been very interesting and rewarding, if not tortuous. I cannot help but wonder what would have happened if such a term had not been introduced and eventually supported by research. This volume is the outcome of years of initial neglect by scholars and clinicians crowned by eventual growth in theory and research and acceptance of hurt feelings. One can only be proud of such achievement. Perhaps one day scholars and professionals in psychology will become aware of hurt feelings in themselves, apply them to their own intimate relationships, and learn to explore their functions in the laboratory and in their therapy and prevention offices.

ACKNOWLEDGMENT

I am indebted to Raj Kidambi for his help in drawing Figure 22.1.

REFERENCES

Averill, J. R. (1980). On the paucity of positive emotions. In K. R. Blankstein, K. P. Pliner, & J. Polivy, (Eds.), *Assessment and modification of emotional behavior* (pp. 7–45). New York: Plenum Press.

Batson, C. D. (1991). *The altruism question: Toward a social-psychological answer.* Mahwah, NJ: Erlbaum.

Baumeister, R. F., & Vohs, K. D. (Eds.). (2004). *Handbook of self-regulation: Research, theory, and applications.* New York: Guilford.

Bertera, E. M. (2005). Mental health in U.S. adults: The role of positive social support and social negativity in personal relationships. *Journal of Social and Personal Relationships, 22,* 33–48.

Blankstein, K. R., Pliner, P., & Polivy, J. (Eds.). (1980). *Assessment and modification of emotional behavior.* New York: Plenum Press.

Burleson, B. R. (2003). Emotional support skills. In J. O. Greene & B. R. Burleson (Eds.), *Handbook of communication and social interaction skills* (pp. 551–594). Mahwah, NJ: Erlbaum.

Demetrio, D., & Borgonovi, C. (2007). Teaching to remember ourselves: The autobiographical methodology. In L. L'Abate (Ed.), *Handbook of low-cost interventions to promote physical and mental health: Theory, research, and practice* (pp. 251–270). Mahwah, NJ: Erlbaum.

Eisenberg, N. (1986). *Altruistic emotion, cognition, and behavior.* Hillsdale, NJ: Erlbaum.

Esterling, B. A., L'Abate, L., Murray, E., & Pennebaker, J. M. (1999). Empirical foundations for writing in prevention and psychotherapy: Mental and physical outcomes. *Clinical Psychology Review, 19,* 79–96.

Feeney, J. A. (2004a). Adult attachment and relationship functioning under stressful conditions: Understanding partners' responses to conflict and challenge. In W. S. Rholes & J. A. Simpson (Eds.), *Adult attachment: Theory, research, and clinical applications* (pp. 339–364). New York: Guilford.

Feeney, J. A. (2004b). Hurt feelings in couple relationships: Toward integrative models of the negative effects of hurtful events. *Journal of Social and Personal Relationships, 21,* 487–508.

Feeney, J. A. (2005). Hurt feelings in couple relationships: Exploring the role of attachment and perceptions of personal injury. *Personal Relationships, 12,* 253–271.

Fincham, F. D. (2000). The kiss of porcupines: From attributing responsibility to forgiving. *Personal Relationships, 7,* 1–23.

Fincham, F. D., & Beach, S. R. H. (2002). Forgiveness in marriage: Implications for psychological aggression and constructive communication. *Personal Relationships, 9,* 239–251.

Franks, M. M., Wendorf, C. A., Gonzales, R., & Ketterer, M. (2004). Aid and influence: Health promoting exchanges of older married partners. *Journal of Social and Personal Relationships, 21*, 431–445.

Frey, J., III, Holley, J., & L'Abate, L. (1979). Intimacy is sharing hurt feelings: A comparison of three conflict resolution models. *Journal of Marriage and Family Therapy, 5*, 35–41.

Gottman, J. M. (1994). *What predicts divorce? The relationship between marital processes and marital outcomes.* Hillsdale, NJ: Erlbaum.

Higgins, E. T. (1987). Self-discrepancy: A theory relating self and affect. *Psychological Review, 94*, 319–340.

Higgins, E. T. (1998). Promotion and prevention: Regulatory focus of a motivational principle. *Advances in Experimental Social Psychology, 30*, 1–46.

Horowitz, L. M. (2004). *Interpersonal foundations of psychopathology.* Washington, DC: American Psychological Association.

Jones, W. H., Kugler, K., & Adams, P. (1995). You always hurt the one you love: Guilt and transgressions against relationship partners. In J. P. Tangney & K. W. Fischer (Eds.), *Self-conscious emotions: The psychology of shame, guilt, embarrassment and pride* (pp. 301–321). New York: Guilford.

Jourard, S. M. (1971). *Self-disclosure: An experimental analysis of the transparent self.* New York: Wiley.

Kacewicz, E., Slatcher, R., & Pennebaker, J. M. (2007). Expressive writing: An alternative to traditional methods In L. L'Abate (Ed.), *Handbook of low-cost interventions to promote physical and mental health: Theory, research, and practice* (pp. 272–284). Mahwah, NJ: Erlbaum.

Kazantzis, N., & L'Abate, L. (Eds.). (2007). *Handbook of homework assignments in psychotherapy: Theory, research, and prevention.* New York: Springer.

Kelly, A. B., Fincham, F. D., & Beach, S. R. H. (2003). Communication skills in couples: A review and discussion of emerging perspectives. In J. O. Greene & B. R. Burleson (Eds.), *Handbook of communication and social interaction skills* (pp. 723–751). Mahwah, NJ: Erlbaum.

L'Abate, L. (1976). *Understanding and helping the individual in the family.* New York: Grune & Stratton.

L'Abate, L. (1977). Intimacy is sharing hurt feelings: A reply to David Mace. *Journal of Marriage and Family Counseling, 3*, 13–16.

L'Abate, L. (1986). *Systematic family therapy.* New York: Brunner/Mazel.

L'Abate, L. (1994). *A theory of personality development.* New York: Wiley.

L'Abate, L. (1997). *The self in the family: Classification of personality, psychopathology, and criminality.* New York: Wiley.

L'Abate, L. (1999a). Being human: Loving and hurting. In A. C. Richards & T. Schumrum (Eds.), *Invitations to dialogue: The legacy of Sidney Jourard* (pp. 81–90). Dubuque, IO: Kent/Kendall.

L'Abate, L. (1999b). Increasing intimacy in couples through distance writing and face-to-face approaches. In J. Carlson & L. Sperry (Eds.), *The intimate couple* (pp. 328–340). Philadelpha: Brunner/Mazel.

L'Abate, L. (1999c). Structured enrichment and distance writing for couples. In R. Berger & T. Hannah (Eds.), *Preventative approaches in couples therapy* (pp. 106–124). Philadelphia: Taylor & Francis.

L'Abate, L. (2000a). Hurt feelings and personality socialization in the family. *Psicologia: Teoria e Pesquisa, 16*, 113–123.

L'Abate, L. (2000b). Psycho-educational strategies. In J. Carlson & L. Sperry (Eds.), *Brief therapy strategies with individuals and couples* (pp. 396–346). Phoenix: Zeig/Tucker.

L'Abate, L. (Ed.). (2001a). *Distance writing and computer-assisted interventions in psychiatry and mental heath.* Westport, CT: Ablex.

L'Abate, L. (2001b). Hugging, holding, huddling, and cuddling (3HC): A task prescription in couples and family therapy. *Journal of Clinical Activities, Assignments, & Handouts in Psychotherapy Practice, 1,* 5–18.

L'Abate, L. (2002). *Beyond psychotherapy: Programmed writing and structured computer-assisted interventions.* Westport, CT: Ablex.

L'Abate, L. (2003a). *Family psychology III: Theory-building, theory-testing, and psychological interventions.* Lanham, MD: University Press of America.

L'Abate, L. (2003b). Treatment through writing: A unique new direction. In T. L. Sexton, G. Weeks, & M. Robbins (Eds.), *The handbook of family therapy* (pp. 397–409). New York: Brunner-Routledge.

L'Abate, L. (2004a). *A guide to self-help workbooks for clinicians and researchers.* Binghamton, NY: Haworth.

L'Abate, L. (Ed.). (2004b). *Using workbooks in mental health: Resources in prevention, psychotherapy, and rehabilitation for clinicians and researchers.* Binghamton, NY: Haworth.

L'Abate, L. (2005). *Personality in intimate relationships: Socialization and psychopathology.* New York: Springer.

L'Abate, L. (2007a). A completely preposterous proposal: The dictionary as an initial vehicle for behavior change in the family. *Family Psychologist, 23,* 39–42.

L'Abate, L. (Ed.). (2007b). *Low-cost approaches to promote physical and mental health: Theory, research, and practice.* New York: Springer.

L'Abate, L. (2008a). A proposal for including distance writing in couples therapy. *Journal of Couple and Relationship Therapy, 7,* 337–362.

L'Abate, L. (2008b). Applications of relational competence theory to prevention in psychotherapy. In K. Jordan (Ed.), *The quick theory references guide* (pp. 475–492). New York: Nova Science.

L'Abate, L. (2009). Sourcebook of interactive exercises in mental health. New York: Springer.

L'Abate, L. (in press). *Hurt feelings: Theory, research, and applications in intimate relationships.* New York: Cambridge University Press.

L'Abate, L., & Cusinato, M. (2007). Linking theory with practice: Theory-derived interventions in prevention and family therapy. *The Family Journal: Counseling and Therapy for Couples and Families, 15,* 318–327.

L'Abate, L., & De Giacomo, P. (2003). *Intimate relationships and how to improve them: Integrating theoretical models with preventive and psychotherapeutic applications.* Westport, Ct: Praeger.

L'Abate, L., Frey, J., & Holly, J. (1979). Intimacy is sharing hurt feelings: Comparison of three conflict resolution methods. *Journal of Marriage and Family Therapy, 5,* 35–41.

L'Abate, L., & Goldstein, J. (2007). Workbooks to promote mental health and life-long learning. In L. L'Abate (Ed.), *Low-cost approaches to promote physical and mental health: Theory, research, and practice* (pp. 285–302). New York: Springer.

L'Abate, L., & Hewitt, D. W. (2000a). Avoiding the seven deadly sins of communication. In C. G. Waugh, W. I. Golden, & K. M. Golden (Eds.), *Let's talk: A cognitive skills approach to interpersonal communication* (pp. 358–360). Dubuque, IO: Kendall-Hunt.

L'Abate, L., & Hewitt, D. W. (2000b). How to respond to emotionally provocative comments. In C. G. Waugh, W. I. Golden, & K. M. Golden (Eds.), *Let's talk: A cognitive skills approach to interpersonal communication* (pp. 363–365). Dubuque, IO: Kendall-Hunt.

L'Abate, L., L'Abate, B. L., & Maino, E. (2005). A review of 25 years of part-time professional practice: Workbooks and length of psychotherapy. *American Journal of Family Therapy, 33*, 19–31.

L'Abate, L., & McHenry, S. (1983). *Handbook of marital interventions.* New York: Grune & Stratton.

Laurenceau, J. P., Feldman-Barrett, L., & Rovine, M. J. (2005). The interpersonal process of intimacy in marriage: A daily-diary and multilevel modeling approach. *Journal of Family Psychology, 19*, 314–323.

Levine, S. (2005). *Unattended sorrow: Recovering from loss and reviving the heart.* Emmaus, PE: Rodale Press.

Levine, M., & Calvanio, R. (2007). Recording of personal information as an intervention and as electronic health support. In L. L'Abate (Ed.), *Handbook of low-cost interventions to promote physical and mental health: Theory, research, and practice* (pp. 227–250). Mahwah, NJ: Erlbaum.

Lewin, K. (1935). *A dynamic theory of personality.* New York: McGraw-Hill.

Mace, D. (1976). Marital intimacy and the deadly love-anger cycle. *Journal of Marriage and Family Counseling, 2*, 131–137.

Meyer, R. E. (1986). *Psychopathology and addictive disorders.* New York: Guilford.

Niedenthal. P. M., Krauth-Gruber, S., & Ric, F. (2006). *Psychology of emotions: Interpersonal, experiential, and cognitive approaches.* New York: Psychology Press.

Perris, C., Arridell, W. A., & Eisemann, M. (1994). *Parenting and psychopathology.* New York: Wiley.

Plutchik, R., & Conte, H. R. (Eds.). (1997). *Circumplex models of personality and emotions.* Washington, DC: American Psychological Association.

Pulier, M., Mount, T. G., McMenamin, J. P., & Maheu, M. M. (2007). Computers and the Internet. In L. L'Abate (Ed.), *Handbook of low-cost interventions to promote physical and mental health: Theory, research, and practice* (pp. 303–319). Mahwah, NJ: Erlbaum.

Reis, H. T., & Shaver, P. (1988). Intimacy as an interpersonal process. In S. Duck (Ed.), *Handbook of personal relationships* (pp. 367–389). Chichester, UK: Wiley.

Root, L. M., & McCullough, M. E. (2007). Low-cost interventions for promoting forgiveness. In L. L'Abate (Ed.), *Low-cost interventions to promote physical and mental health: Theory, research, and practice* (pp. 415–434). New York: Springer.

Segrin, C., & Givertz, M. (2003). Methods of social skills training and development. In J. O. Greene & B. R. Burleson (Eds.), *Handbook of communication and social interaction skills* (pp. 135–176). Mahwah, NJ: Erlbaum.

Smyth, J. M., & L'Abate, L. (2001). A meta-analytic evaluation of workbook effectiveness in physical and mental health. In L. L'Abate (Ed.), *Distance writing and computer-assisted interventions in psychiatry and mental heath* (pp. 77–90). Westport, CT: Ablex.

Stevens, F. E., & L'Abate, L. (1989). Validity and reliability of theory-derived measures of intimacy. *American Journal of Family Therapy, 17*, 359–368.

Stroebe, W., Schut, H., & Stroebe, M. S. (2005). Grief work, disclosure and counseling: Do they help the bereaved? *Clinical Psychology Review, 25*, 395–414.

Tangney, J. P., & Fischer, K. W. (Eds.). (1995). *Self-conscious emotions: The psychology of shame, guilt, embarrassment and pride.* New York: Guilford.

Thomas, J. L., & Cummings, J. L. (Eds.). (2000). *The collected papers of Nicholas A. Cummings: Vol. 1. The value of psychological treatment.* Phoenix: Zeig/Tucker.

Tomkins, S. S. (1962). *Affect, imagery, and consciousness: Vol. 1. The positive effects.* New York: Springer-Verlag.

Tomkins, S. S. (1963). *Affect, imagery, and consciousness: Vol. 2. The negative effects.* New York: Springer-Verlag.

Van Dyke, C., Temoshock, L., & Zegans, L. S. (Eds.). (1984). *Emotions in health and illness: Applications to clinical practice.* Orlando, FL: Grune & Stratton.

Vangelisti, A. L. (1994). Messages that hurt. In W. R. Cupach & B. H. Spitzberg (Eds.), *The dark side of interpersonal communication* (pp. 53–82). Hillsdale, NJ: Erlbaum.

Vangelisti, A. L. (2006). Hurtful interactions and the dissolution of intimacy. In M. A. Fine & J. H. Harvey (Eds.), *Handbook of divorce and relationship dissolution* (pp. 133–152). Mahwah, NJ: Erlbaum.

Vangelisti, A. L., & Beck, G. (2007). Intimacy and fear of intimacy. In L. L'Abate (Ed.), *Low-cost approaches to promote physical and mental health: Theory, research, and practice* (pp. 395–414). New York: Springer.

Vangelisti, A. L., & Young, S. L. (2000). When words hurt: The effects of perceived intentionality on interpersonal relationships. *Journal of Social and Personal Relationships, 17,* 393–424.

Watson, D. (2000). *Mood and temperament.* New York: Guilford.

# AUTHOR INDEX

Abelson, R. P., 289, 304, 308
Abou-ezzedine, T., 242, 258
Abraham, W. T., 197, 206
Abramson, L. Y., 116
Ackerman, B. P., 340, 354
Adams, G., 307, 308
Adams, P., 482, 486, 489, 495
Adamsons, K., 345, 351
Afifi, T. D., 341, 346, 352
Afifi, W. A., 60, 65, 70
Ager, R. D., 382, 398
Agras, W. S., 363, 372
Ainsworth, M. D. S., 92, 96, 116
Albro, E., 274, 286
Alexander, A. L., 3, 11, 23, 26, 33, 39, 42, 44, 49, 59, 60, 72, 98, 108, 119, 145, 149, 155, 165, 175, 190, 261, 262, 287, 289, 291, 292, 293, 294, 297, 300, 303, 305, 311, 330, 335, 360, 374, 457, 461, 464, 468, 469, 477
Alexander, T. S., 362, 375
Alexy, E. M., 217, 225
Allan, G., 191, 194, 195, 200, 206
Allen, E. S., 192, 194, 199, 200, 202, 206, 379, 394
Allen, J., 214, 231
Allen, J. G., 300, 308
Allgeier, E., 408, 416
Allison, C. J., 109, 116
Alloy, L. B., 107, 116
Alsaker, F., 240, 252
Altemus, M., 363, 372
Amar, A. F., 217, 225
Amato, P. R., 195, 206, 352, 380, 381, 383, 384, 385, 394, 398, 411, 414
Amatya, K., 242, 253
Anda, R. F., 214, 215, 221, 225, 227, 228
Andersen, S. M., 46, 47
Anderson, E. R., 346, 348, 353

Anderson, K. L., 211, 225
Anderson, M., 218, 219, 226
Anderson, P. A., 440, 452
Andersson, L. M., 428, 429, 430, 436, 437, 452, 454, 455
Andrejevic, M., 408, 414
Andreoli-Mathie, V., 381, 398
Andrews, D. W., 236, 238, 254
Ang, J., 45, 49
Ansell, E., 3, 4, 5, 6, 8, 10, 16, 17, 24, 26, 27, 29, 32, 38, 44, 48, 59, 61, 62, 63, 64, 66, 71, 73, 74, 90, 98, 105, 107, 108, 112, 118, 144, 145, 146, 163, 173, 174, 189, 192, 207, 261, 266, 267, 268, 284, 288, 289, 291, 292, 294, 295, 297, 298, 300, 301, 302, 303, 305, 307, 310, 314, 318, 319, 324, 325, 330, 333, 337, 338, 354, 360, 364, 373, 378, 397, 417, 447, 454, 458, 460, 461, 476
Ansfield, M. E., 182, 188
Archer, J., 211, 212, 213, 226, 237, 253
Argyle, M., 290, 292, 308, 313, 318, 332
Arias, I., 214, 215, 218, 225, 226, 227, 229, 230, 231, 361, 362, 371, 372, 377, 394
Arnett, J., 290, 291, 309
Arnold, D. W., 418, 452
Arnold, M., 35, 36, 37, 47
Aron, A., 365, 371
Aron, E. N., 365, 371
Aronson, E., 292, 308
Arriaga, X. B., 212, 226, 367, 374
Arridell, W. A., 485, 497
Arsenio, W. F., 261, 280, 284
Ash, P., 435, 452
Asher, S. R., 124, 135, 139, 140
Askenasy, A. R., 377, 395
Athenstaedt, U., 64, 71, 325, 326, 334
Atkins, D. C., 192, 194, 199, 200, 202, 206, 381, 385, 394

Atwood, J. D., 381, 394
Ault, L. K., 433, 434, 439, 446, 453
Averill, J. R., 490, 494
Ayduk, O., 73, 79, 81, 88, 90, 261, 285
Aziz, N., 361, 368, 372
Azmitia, M., 302, 308

Bachman, G. F., 92, 116, 450, 452
Baehr, M. E., 440, 452
Bailey, D. C., 161, 165
Bailyn, L., 422, 452
Bain-Chekal, J., 149, 164
Baldwin, M. W., 78, 80, 88, 89, 262, 280, 292, 304, 309
Balswick, J. K., 389, 394
Balswick, J. O., 389, 394
Banai, E., 101, 116
Bancroft, J. H., 125, 139
Bandura, A., 238, 253
Bank, L., 271, 281
Barak, A., 405, 414
Barbee, A. P., 417, 418, 433, 434, 435, 437, 439, 446, 448, 452, 453
Barber, B. K., 264, 281
Bardwell, R. A., 219, 229
Barefoot, J. C., 222, 229
Barling, J., 214, 230
Barnett, S. M., 470, 477
Barr, G. A., 127, 142
Barrett, K. C., 278, 281
Barrett, L. F., 17, 21, 31
Barron, R. M., 391, 394
Barry, W. A., 157, 164
Bartels, J. M., 124, 135, 138, 142
Bartholomew, K., 109, 110, 116, 119
Bartini, M., 237, 249, 257
Bartlett, K. T., 349, 352
Bartlett, M. Y., 198, 206, 410, 414
Basile, K. C., 214, 215, 218, 226
Bassuk, E. L., 214, 226
Bassuk, S. S., 214, 226
Bateman, H., 245, 254
Bates, J. E., 237, 238, 251, 254, 255, 263, 281
Batson, C. D., 131, 132, 135, 136, 139, 482, 494
Battle, C. L., 393, 394
Baucom, D. H., 192, 194, 199, 200, 202, 206, 328, 333, 342, 351, 353, 380, 381, 384, 385, 386, 388, 394, 396
Baucom, T. R., 388, 395
Baumeister, R. F., 31, 38, 42, 48, 64, 70, 99, 116, 123, 124, 125, 127, 128, 129, 130, 131, 134, 135, 136, 137, 138, 139, 140, 142, 261, 266, 269, 281, 284, 292, 306, 308, 310, 311, 313, 324, 325, 326, 332, 339, 365, 366, 371, 386, 395, 432, 450, 455, 461, 463, 467, 468, 470, 474, 475, 476, 490, 494
Baumgarte, R., 473, 477
Bauserman, S. A. K., 377, 394
Bavelas, J. B., 187, 188
Baxter, L. A., 157, 159, 162, 290, 308, 318, 332, 342, 343, 346, 347, 349, 352, 355
Bayog, R. D., 383, 397
Beach, S. R. H., 82, 89, 147, 149, 151, 155, 156, 160, 162, 377, 385, 388, 389, 390, 392, 393, 394, 395, 396, 482, 489, 494, 495
Bean, N. J., 126, 141
Bechara, A., 135, 140
Beck, G., 480, 481, 486, 498
Becker, D. V., 197, 199, 206
Beckes, L., 100, 116
Beitz, K., 108, 117
Belknap, R. A., 214, 227
Bell, K. L., 175, 181, 188
Bell, R. A., 298, 305, 308, 309
Bellavia, G. M., 76, 78, 81, 90, 148, 159, 164, 320, 329, 334, 339, 340, 354
Belson, K., 422, 452
Benaske, N., 223, 230
Benditt, R., 292, 309
Bendtschneider, L., 293, 308
Bennett, L., 215, 228
Berenson, D., 383, 395
Berns, S., 214, 229
Berntson, G. G., 124, 140, 141
Berry, D. S., 147, 161, 299, 308
Berscheid, E., 288, 308
Bertera, E. M., 484, 494
Betancourt, H., 211, 226
Bettes, B. A., 341, 352
Bierman, K. L., 220, 226, 241, 258
Billings, A. G., 384, 394
Bippus, A. M., 299, 458, 478
Birchler, G. R., 377, 395, 398
Bird, G. W., 223, 228
Birnbaum, G., 99, 105, 118
Bishop, G. D., 45, 49
Bishop, P., 126, 139, 141
Björkqvist, K., 211, 226
Black, A., 187, 188
Black, K. A., 300, 308
Blader, S. L., 421, 422, 452
Blair, I., 211, 226
Blair, R. J. R., 137, 140
Blakeslee, S., 314, 335
Blanchard, K. H., 424, 453
Blankfield, A., 383, 394
Blankstein, K. R., 490, 494
Blascovich, J., 364, 371
Blass, E. M., 127, 141

Bledsoe, K. L., 117
Blehar, M. C., 92, 96, 116
Bleske, A. L., 291, 308
Bleske-Rechek, A. L., 302, 308
Blier, M. J., 300, 308
Blier-Wilson, L. A., 300, 308
Block, C., 214, 227
Bloom, B. L., 124, 140
Blumberg, S. J., 130, 141
Bocij, P., 405, 406, 414
Boden, J. M., 182, 188
Boekhout, B. A., 199, 200, 206
Boergers, J., 240, 241, 258
Bogar, C. B., 222, 226
Bogle, J. C., 423, 452
Bograd, M., 211, 226
Boivin, M., 240, 241, 242, 253, 256
Bokker, P., 346, 352
Boldizar, J. P., 238, 253
Boldry, J., 76, 80, 86, 89, 104, 116
Bolger, N., 76, 82, 83, 86, 87, 88, 89, 90, 341, 355
Bond, L. A., 71, 311
Boneva, B., 401, 415
Boney-McCoy, S., 218, 226
Bono, G., 450, 454
Bonomi, A. E., 218, 219, 226
Boon, S. D., 388, 390
Borgonovi, C., 492, 494
Boscarino, J. A., 362, 371
Boston, A., 299, 309
Botvin, G. J., 237, 255
Boulton, M. J., 241, 242, 253
Bouma, R., 382, 396
Bourgeois, K. S., 23, 26, 31, 468, 475
Boussiron, D., 382, 397
Boutelle, K., 264, 273, 283
Bowlby, J., 39, 47, 92, 95, 96, 97, 99, 101, 102, 103, 116, 261, 262, 281, 316, 332
Boyle, M. H., 265, 281
Bradbury, T. N., 82, 88, 89, 145, 149, 151, 155, 161, 163, 363, 374, 436, 447, 453, 468, 475
Bradney, N., 288, 310
Braithwaite, D. O., 336, 342, 343, 346, 347, 349, 352, 355
Braithwaite, S. R., 376
Bramson, R. M., 426, 452
Brandt, H. M., 214, 215, 218, 227, 361, 372
Branje, S. J. T, 85, 89
Brauer, M., 80, 90
Braverman, J., 198, 206, 410, 414
Brehl, B. A., 143, 165, 272, 287
Bremner, J. D., 214, 215, 221, 225
Brennan, K. A., 96, 116
Breslin, F. C., 215, 230
Brewer, M. B., 123, 125, 133, 141

Briere, J., 214, 226
Briggs, M., 274, 286
Brock, R. L., 252, 258
Brody, G. H., 274, 281
Brody, L. R., 265, 275, 281
Brooks, E. B., 362, 374
Brooks, F., 237, 249, 257
Brown, D. W., 214, 215, 227
Brown, G. W., 393, 394
Brown, P., 50, 51, 52, 55, 56, 57, 70, 71
Brown, S. W., 132, 141, 328, 331, 334, 386, 389, 397
Browne, A., 214, 226
Bruce, M. L., 377, 384, 399
Bryant, L., 347, 352
Bryant, R. A., 214, 215, 227
Buchanan, T., 400, 415
Bucholtz, I., 85, 90
Buckley, K. E., 26, 31, 123, 124, 125, 140
Bugental, D. B., 270, 281
Buhrmester, D., 147, 163
Bukowski, W. M., 135, 140, 236, 240, 241, 242, 248, 253, 254, 256, 257
Burdette, M. P., 289, 302, 310
Burg, R., 412, 414
Burggraf, S. A., 278, 286
Burleson, B. R., 153, 154, 155, 159, 160, 161, 162, 340, 352, 364, 372, 482, 494
Burleson, M. H., 124, 141
Burmeister, L. F., 215, 230
Burwell, R., 274, 286
Bush, G., 126, 140
Buss, D. M., 191, 197, 198, 206, 290, 291, 294, 302, 308, 311, 318, 332, 381, 395, 410, 414, 415
Butler, D., 211, 230
Buunk, B. P., 191, 196, 197, 198, 206, 381, 395, 398
Bybee, D. I., 361, 374
Byrne, C. A., 218, 225, 226

Cacioppo, J. T., 124, 140, 141, 142, 340, 353, 363, 364, 371, 373, 471, 475
Caetano, R., 212, 228
Cahn, D. D., 321, 332
Cairney, J., 265, 281
Cairns, B. D., 236, 253, 293, 312
Cairns, R. B., 236, 253, 293, 312
Caldwell, D. F., 149, 164
Caldwell, K., 220, 222, 230
Calvanio, R., 492, 497
Camacho, J., 217, 230
Camden, C., 168, 188
Cameron, J. J., 64, 71, 325, 332
Camman, C., 440, 452
Camodeca, M., 243, 253, 279, 281

Campbell, D., 214, 227
Campbell, J. C., 213, 214, 218, 225, 226, 227, 362, 375
Campbell, L., 76, 80, 86, 89, 104
Campbell, L. E. G., 337, 354
Campbell, S. B., 277, 281
Campos, B., 363, 372
Campos, J. J., 279, 281
Canary, D. J., 145, 148, 149, 151, 152, 162, 165, 300, 308
Cancian, F., 192, 206
Cann, A., 198, 206, 388, 395
Cano, A., 380, 395
Cao, Q., 420, 452
Capps, L., 264, 273, 284
Card, N. A., 235, 236, 237, 239, 240, 241, 242, 244, 245, 249, 251, 252, 253, 254, 255, 256
Cardwell, M. M., 214, 227
Carey, C. M., 160, 166, 215, 227
Carino, A., 215, 229
Carnochan, P., 93, 117, 262, 282
Carpenter-Theune, K. E., 3, 11, 23, 26, 33, 39, 42, 44, 49, 59, 60, 72, 98, 108, 119, 145, 149, 155, 165, 175, 190, 261, 262, 287, 288, 289, 291, 292, 293, 294, 297, 300, 303, 305, 311, 330, 335, 360, 374, 457, 461, 464, 468, 469, 477
Carr, A. N., 400, 403, 405, 411, 413, 416
Carrell, D., 218, 219, 226
Carrere, S., 150, 163
Carson, C. L., 59, 60, 71
Carstensen, L. L., 145, 156, 162
Carville, S. E., 404, 416
Casas, J. F., 267, 272, 281, 290, 292, 293, 301, 302, 309
Cascardi, M., 215, 218, 224, 227
Caspi, A., 402, 414
Cassidy, J., 5, 6, 92, 96, 109, 110, 114, 117
Catalano, R. F., 213, 227, 236, 258
Catalano, S., 224
Catanese, K. R., 124, 125, 142
Cate, R., 216, 228
Cauffman, E., 290, 291, 309
Caughlin, J. P., 143, 147, 149, 156, 159, 162, 163, 164, 367, 371
Cavanaugh, L., 408, 415
Chambless, D. L., 377, 395
Chang, J., 362, 371
Chang, L., 267, 284
Charlesworth, R., 135, 141
Chau, C., 242, 253
Chee, M., 363, 373
Chen, S., 46, 47
Cherlin, A. J., 192, 201, 206
Cheung, C. K. T., 125, 142
Choi, W., 125, 142

Chovil, N., 187, 188
Christenfeld, N., 410, 415
Christensen, A., 324, 332, 366, 371, 372, 385, 394
Christine, A., 299, 308
Christopher, S., 216, 228
Christopoulos, C., 245, 255
Chrousos, G. P., 368, 372
Cialdini, R. B., 132, 141
Ciarocco, N. J., 123, 124, 135, 138, 139, 142, 292, 308
Cicchetti, D., 241, 258
Cicirelli, V., 274, 281
Cillessen, A. H. N., 237, 245, 248, 254, 256
Clara, I. P., 269, 270, 285
Clark, C. L., 35, 48, 96, 116
Clark, G., 3, 11
Clark, L. A., 17, 18, 19, 21, 22, 28, 33
Clark, M. S., 314, 332, 419, 452
Clore, G. L., 23, 32
Cloven, D. H., 145, 162
Clum, G. A., 220, 232
Coan, J. A., 150, 163, 359, 371
Cobb, R. J., 88, 89
Cocroft, B., 473, 475
Cohen, J., 128, 134, 140
Cohen, R., 251, 257
Cohen, R. A., 214, 215, 227
Cohen, S., 83, 89, 362, 372
Coie, J. D., 135, 139, 140, 236, 238, 243, 245, 248, 254, 255, 256, 258
Coker, A. L., 212, 214, 215, 218, 219, 227, 361, 372
Cole, D. A., 147, 162
Cole, J., 218, 227
Coleman, M., 346, 347, 348, 349, 350, 352, 353
Collins, A., 23, 32
Collins, L., 292, 309
Collins, N. L., 35, 38, 48, 80, 87, 89, 102, 107, 117
Compton, K., 271, 281
Conger, K. J., 265, 286
Conner, R., 126, 139, 141
Connors, G. J., 384, 397
Consadine, J., 68, 71
Conte, H. R., 487, 497
Cook, J. D., 440, 452
Cook, W. L., 252, 256
Cooley, C. H., 261, 281
Cooper, A., 412, 414
Copeland, A. P., 265, 275, 281
Coppotelli, H., 248, 254
Cormier, C. A., 214, 229
Cornell, D. G., 137, 140
Cornwell, B., 402, 414
Cortina, L. M., 214, 230, 361, 374, 430, 437, 452, 454
Cournoyer, D. E., 264, 267, 286

Cox, C. L., 117
Coy, D. H., 126, 141
Coyne, J. C., 77, 78, 89, 90, 377, 379, 395
Coyne, S. M., 211, 226, 237, 253
Craig, A. D., 127, 140
Craighead, W. E., 377, 394
Cram, F., 216, 229
Cramer, R. E., 197, 206
Craven, D., 213, 228
Crawford, A., 401, 415
Creasey, G., 299, 309
Crick, N. R., 237, 238, 239, 254, 261, 262, 267, 272, 273, 281, 285, 290, 292, 293, 301, 302, 309
Crocker, J., 104, 119
Crockett, E. E., 73, 359
Croft, J. B., 214, 225
Crosbie-Burnett, M., 348, 352
Crosby, L., 236, 238, 254
Crouter, A., 275, 276, 282, 285
Crumley, L. P., 63, 71, 289, 294, 297, 298, 303, 311, 314, 316, 319, 335, 467, 468, 477
Crump, A. D., 241, 256
Cruz, M. G., 105, 118
Cullerton-Sen, C., 290, 292, 293, 301, 302, 309
Cummings, E. M., 277, 281
Cummings, J., 401, 415
Cummings, J. L., 481, 482, 486, 489, 497
Cumsille, P., 275, 276, 282
Cunningham, M. R., 417, 418, 433, 434, 435, 437, 439, 446, 448, 452, 453
Cupach, W. R., 59, 60, 71, 211, 217, 218, 227, 231, 293, 294, 311, 336, 338, 342, 351, 354
Curry, M. A., 214, 227
Cutrona, C. E., 82, 89
Cutter, H. Q., 384, 398

Daas, K., 346, 352
Dailey, R. M., 212, 215, 227
Dalai Lama, 462
Daly, M., 380, 381, 395
Damasio, A., 135, 140
Damasio, H., 135, 140
Dandeneau, S. D., 80, 88, 89
d'Aquili, E. G., 331, 334
Davidson, R. J., 340, 352, 359, 371, 462, 475
Davies, P. T., 277, 281
Davila, J., 88, 89, 111, 118, 160, 162, 163, 279, 283, 363, 374, 389, 396
Davis, A., 83, 88
Davis, D., 108, 109, 117
Davis, D. I., 383, 395
Davis, K. E., 214, 215, 218, 219, 227, 290, 302, 303, 309, 361, 367, 372, 373, 432, 434, 435, 454
Davis, R. V., 440, 456

Davis, S., 383, 395
Dawson, R., 214, 226
Day, A., 219, 223, 224, 225, 231
Day, D. V., 418, 453
De Giacomo, P., 480, 484, 485, 486, 487, 489, 491, 492, 496
de Graaf, R., 377, 378, 398
de Kemp, R., 377, 378, 398
de Marici, V., 331, 334
de Rivera, J., 92, 117
De Vargas, M., 470, 477
DeHart, G., 276, 281
Dehle, C., 86, 89
Delmonico, D. L., 412, 414
Demetrio, D., 492, 494
den Bak, I., 273, 282
den Bak-Lammers, I., 273, 276, 286
Denning, D., 272, 273, 276, 286
Denton, W. H., 364, 372
DePaulo, B. M., 167, 168, 170, 175, 181, 182, 185, 186, 188, 189, 260, 284, 404, 414
DeRosier, M. E., 248, 254
Derryberry, D., 265, 268, 282
Desai, S., 214, 215, 218, 226, 227, 361, 372
DeSteno, D. A., 198, 206, 410, 414
DeWall, C. N., 123, 124, 127, 128, 129, 130, 131, 134, 135, 136, 137, 138, 139, 140, 142, 292, 306, 308, 310, 339, 366, 467, 468, 470, 475
Diaz, T., 237, 255
DiBlasio, F., 385, 399
Dickerson, S. S., 278, 282, 361, 367, 368, 372
Dickinson, S., 363, 373
Dickson, F., 343, 353
Dienemann, J., 225, 226
Diener, E., 15, 31
Dienstbier, R. A., 265, 282
Dijkstra, P., 191, 196, 197, 198, 206
Dimer, J. A., 218, 219, 226
Diong, S. M., 45, 49
Dishion, T. J., 236, 238, 254
Dix, T., 270, 282
Dobash, R. E., 211, 227
Dobash, R. P., 211, 227
Dodge, K. A., 135, 140, 237, 238, 239, 243, 245, 248, 251, 254, 255, 256, 258, 261, 262, 267, 281, 284
Dohrenwend, B. P., 377, 395
Dohrenwend, B. S., 377, 395
Dong, M., 214, 215, 227, 228
Donovan, C., 202, 208
Donovan-Kicken, E., 50, 150
Dostrovsky, J. O., 127, 140
Downey, G., 43, 44, 47, 48, 73, 74, 75, 77, 78, 79, 81, 88, 89, 90, 261, 269, 277, 282, 285, 317, 330, 332, 379, 395

Downs, D. L., 418, 454
Downs, K. M., 348, 349, 352
Doyle, J. P., 218, 227
Drass, E., 380, 398
Drigotas, S. M., 299, 309
Druen, P. B., 433, 434, 435, 437, 448, 452, 453
Dube, S. R., 214, 215, 221, 225, 227, 228
Duck, S., 293, 308, 345, 354
Duffield, J., 348, 353
Duku, E., 265, 281
Dun, T., 147, 151, 152, 153, 165, 224, 225, 231, 328
Duncan, E., 461, 477
Duncan, R. D., 241, 255, 279, 282
Dunn, E., 130, 142
Dunn, J., 271, 273, 282, 284
Durham, W., 346, 352
Dutton, D. G., 213, 214, 228
Dutton, L. B., 218, 228
Dutton, M. A., 214, 215, 217, 218, 223, 228
Dweck, C. S., 267, 282, 283
Dyer, M., 300, 309
Dzubia-Leatherman, J., 271, 282

Eagly, A. H., 218, 228
Eastin, M., 401, 415
Eckenrode, J., 86, 88
Eckert, V., 146, 163
Edgley, C., 168, 189
Edwards, K., 43, 48
Edwards, V., 214, 228
Eftekhari, A., 271, 284
Egan, S. K., 238, 240, 241, 243, 255, 257
Eisemann, M., 485, 497
Eisenberg, N., 482, 494
Eisenberger, N. I., 21, 23, 26, 31, 99, 101, 106, 117, 124, 126, 134, 137, 140, 222, 228, 296, 306, 309, 317, 332, 366, 367, 372, 373, 466, 475
Eisler, R. M., 224, 229
Eitel, P., 241, 256
Ekman, P., 15, 31, 92, 95, 117, 340, 342, 352, 353, 462, 475
Eldridge, K. A., 324, 332
Elenkov, I. J., 368, 372
Elgar, F. J., 269, 270, 285
Elliott, D. M., 214, 226
Elliott, S., 211, 225
Ellsworth, P. C., 23, 28, 31, 32, 36, 37, 40, 43, 47, 48, 366, 374, 460, 476
El-Sheikh, M., 147, 166
Emery, R. E., 336, 342, 355
Engels, R., 377, 378, 398
Engl, J., 146, 163
England, G. W., 440, 456
Enkelmann, H. C., 45, 49
Enright, R. D., 386, 390, 395, 396

Epstein, J. A., 168, 189
Esterling, B. A., 489, 494
Evans, K., 3, 4, 5, 6, 8, 10, 16, 17, 24, 26, 27, 29, 32, 38, 44, 48, 59, 61, 62, 63, 64, 66, 71, 73, 74, 90, 98, 105, 107, 108, 112, 118, 144, 145, 146, 163, 173, 174, 189, 192, 207, 261, 266, 267, 268, 284, 288, 289, 291, 292, 294, 295, 297, 298, 300, 301, 302, 303, 305, 307, 310, 314, 318, 319, 324, 325, 330, 333, 337, 338, 354, 360, 364, 373, 378, 397, 417, 447, 454, 458, 460, 461, 476
Everson, S. A., 390, 398
Ewart, C. K., 363, 372
Exline, J. J., 386, 395

Facy, F., 382, 397
Fagan, A., 271, 282
Fahey, J. L., 361, 368, 372
Falato, W. L., 60, 65, 70
Fals-Stewart, W., 377, 383, 384, 395, 396, 398
Fancher, P., 215, 218, 222, 230
Farb, M., 419, 453
Farmer, T., 237, 258
Farrell, H. M., 3, 10, 27, 32, 65, 71, 263, 264, 265, 266, 267, 268, 269, 285
Farrington, D. P., 236, 255
Farris, K. R., 117
Fauerbach, J. A., 377, 395
Feeney, B. C., 87, 89
Feeney, J. A., 3, 4, 5, 6, 8, 10, 22, 23, 26, 27, 29, 31, 35, 39, 40, 42, 44, 46, 47, 59, 60, 61, 62, 63, 65, 67, 71, 74, 90, 92, 93, 97, 98, 99, 103, 104, 105, 106, 107, 112, 113, 114, 117, 144, 145, 146, 158, 162, 184, 189, 192, 193, 206, 297, 303, 305, 309, 313, 314, 315, 316, 317, 318, 320, 322, 326, 327, 328, 329, 330, 331, 332, 333, 338, 339, 353, 433, 447, 453, 461, 475, 479, 480, 485, 486, 494
Fehr, B., 69, 78, 88, 288, 289, 290, 291, 292, 299, 300, 302, 304, 306, 309
Fehrenbach, P. A., 223, 229
Feldman, R. S., 185, 186, 189, 190
Feldman, S. I., 43, 44, 47, 73, 74, 75, 78, 79, 89, 269, 282, 317, 330, 332
Feldman, S. S., 290, 291, 309
Feldman-Barrett, L., 484, 497
Felitti, V. J., 214, 215, 221, 225, 227, 228
Felmlee, D., 330, 335, 344, 355
Felson, R. B., 210, 211, 231
Fichman, M., 440, 452
Fiedler, F. E., 424, 453
Field, C. A., 212, 228
Fielding, B. D., 218, 227
Fields, J., 191, 208
Fincham, F. D., 82, 89, 111, 118, 145, 147, 149, 151, 155, 156, 160, 161, 162, 163, 279, 283, 342, 351, 353, 376, 377, 378, 382, 383, 385, 386, 388, 389,

390, 393, 394, 395, 396, 397, 398, 436, 447, 453, 468, 475, 482, 489, 494, 495
Fine, M. A., 5, 10, 336, 337, 338, 342, 343, 346, 347, 348, 349, 352, 353, 355
Fineberg, M., 275, 276, 282
Finkelhor, D., 218, 226, 271, 280, 282
Finkelstein, E., 219, 229
Finnegan, R. A., 241, 255
Fischer, K. W., 93, 117, 262, 278, 282, 286, 482, 487, 497
Fiske, A. P., 419, 453
Fitness, J., 34, 37, 38, 40, 42, 43, 45, 46, 47, 48, 107, 317, 318, 322, 329, 333, 334, 338, 348, 353, 417, 453, 461, 475
Fitzgerald, J. R., 322, 330, 331, 333
Fitzgibbons, R. P., 386, 395
Fitzpatrick, M. A., 143, 144
Fix, B., 290, 300, 311
Fletcher, G. J. O., 37, 40, 45, 47
Florian, V., 85, 90, 99, 105, 118
Floyd, F. J., 146, 163, 377, 395
Folkes, V. S., 3, 10, 150, 162, 188, 189, 316, 333
Folkman, S., 94, 95, 118, 338, 354
Follette, W. C., 108, 117
Follingstad, D. R., 215, 228
Fonagy, P., 100, 117
Fontaine, R. G., 239, 255, 261, 282
Foote, R., 274, 283
Forgas, J. P., 153, 162
Foshee, V., 219, 228
Fox, J. A., 213, 228
Fraley, R. C., 96, 104, 117
Frances, M., 451, 453
Franchina, J. J., 224, 229
Frank, E., 218, 227
Franks, M. M., 484, 495
Freedman, S., 342, 351, 353, 386, 390, 395, 396
Freeman, T., 390, 397
Freeman, W. S., 269, 270, 285, 287
Freitas, A. L., 44, 47, 77, 78, 89, 278, 282
Frey, J., 480, 482, 495, 496
Friesen, W. V., 342, 353
Frijda, N. H., 23, 31, 37, 47, 145, 146, 156, 162, 339, 340, 353, 457, 459, 463, 464, 465, 466, 467, 475, 476
Froyland, I., 219, 223, 224, 225, 231
Frye, V., 214, 227
Fuentes, J. A., 127, 141
Fujita, K., 82, 90
Furnham, A., 292, 308, 318, 332

Gaertner, L., 219, 228
Gagnon, J. H., 191, 197, 201, 207, 380, 397
Gaines, S. O., Jr., 73, 110, 117, 299, 309
Gallagher, M., 377, 398

Gallup, 376, 396
Galvin, K., 343, 353
Gamm, B. K., 242, 257, 296, 310
Ganong, L. H., 346, 347, 348, 349, 350, 352, 353
Gano-Phillips, S., 468, 475
Gao, G., 473, 477
Garcia, B. F., 117
Garcia, M., 274, 283
Gardner, K. A., 82, 89
Gardner, W. L., 123, 125, 133, 141
Gariépy, J. L., 236, 253
Garner, J., 68, 71
Gary, F., 214, 227
Garza, M. A., 225, 226
Gelles, R. J., 280, 286
Gencoz, F., 76, 90
Gencoz, T., 76, 90
Genuis, M. L., 214, 230
George, C., 263, 283
George, L. J., 149, 163
Georgiades, K., 265, 281
Gergen, K. J., 211, 228
Gerlsma, C., 265, 280, 283
Gershoff, E. T., 264, 267, 283
Gerstenberger, M., 196, 207
Gerzi, S., 101, 117
Gest, S., 236, 253
Giddens, A., 201, 206
Gielen, A. C., 225, 226
Giese-Davis, J., 471, 475
Giesen, D., 191, 202, 207, 381, 398
Gifford-Smith, M. E., 238, 255
Gilbert, D. T., 130, 131, 141, 142
Gilbert, P., 265, 280, 283
Giles, W. H., 214, 215, 221, 225, 227, 228
Giles-Sims, J., 348, 352
Gill, M. J., 130, 141
Gillath, O., 103, 112, 118
Gilmartin, B. G., 240, 255
Gilovich, T., 450, 455
Giovino, G. A., 214, 225
Givertz, M., 482, 497
Glaser, R., 361, 362, 363, 364, 368, 372, 373, 374
Glass, N., 213, 214, 226, 227
Glass, S. P., 192, 194, 199, 200, 202, 206
Glazer, J. A., 135, 141
Goffman, E., 50, 51, 52, 53, 54, 55, 56, 63, 66, 67, 71, 404, 414
Goldberg, A. B., 422, 453
Goldberg, L. R., 85, 90
Golding, J. M., 221, 228
Goldsmith, D. J., 50, 51, 69, 71, 150, 153, 154, 155, 157, 159, 160, 161, 162, 340, 352
Goldstein, J., 492, 493, 496

Goleman, D., 448, 453
Golish, T. D., 348, 353
Gonzaga, G. C., 363, 372
Gonzales, R., 484, 495
Goodman, C. R., 341, 353
Goodman, L. A., 214, 215, 217, 218, 223, 228
Goodness, K., 147, 163
Goodwin, G. A., 127, 142
Goossens, F. A., 243, 253
Gordon, A. K., 186, 189, 325, 333
Gordon, C. L., 264, 284
Gordon, E., 214, 215, 227
Gordon, K. C., 192, 194, 199, 200, 202, 206, 328, 333, 342, 351, 353, 380, 384, 386, 388, 396
Gorsky, P., 402, 414
Gortner, E., 214, 229
Gotlib, I. H., 377, 396
Gottman, J. M., 143, 145, 146, 149, 150, 156, 159, 162, 163, 214, 223, 229, 362, 366, 372, 373, 490, 495
Govan, C., 293, 296, 305, 306, 312
Gove, W. R., 377, 396
Graham, K., 216, 223, 232
Graham, S., 240, 256, 314, 332
Granrose, C. S., 117
Green, L. R., 299, 310
Greenberg, J., 436, 455
Greenfeld, L. A., 213, 228
Gregg, J., 401, 415
Griffin, D. W., 80, 90, 148, 159, 164, 337, 339, 340, 354
Griffin, K. W., 237, 255
Griffiths, M., 411, 414
Grills, A. E., 240, 255
Grohol, J. M., 401, 414
Gross, J. J., 17, 21, 31, 471, 475
Grote, N., 314, 332
Grove, D. C., 390, 397
Gruenewald, T. L., 278, 282, 367, 368, 372
Gryl, F. E., 223, 228
Guadagno, R. E., 197, 199, 206
Guerrero, L. K., 92, 105, 110, 116, 118, 196, 206, 450, 452
Gump, B. B., 222, 229, 340, 353
Gunn, L. K., 299, 311
Gunstad, J., 214, 215, 227
Guthrie, D., 322, 334
Guyer, M., 265, 275, 281

Haavio-Mannila, E., 191, 196, 201, 206, 207
Haccoun, D. M., 300, 308
Hagen, M. S., 346, 348, 353
Hahlweg, K., 146, 163
Hajal, F., 348, 355
Halberstadt, J. B., 18, 32

Halford, W. K., 382, 396
Hall, J. A., 276, 283
Hall, J. H., 342, 351, 353, 378, 382, 383, 396
Hall, R. J., 362, 375
Halligan, S., 361, 374
Hamby, S., 271, 282
Hammen, C., 392, 393, 396
Hample, D., 168, 189
Hamrick, K., 341, 352
Hancock, J., 403, 404, 415
Haney, T. L., 222, 229
Hannawa, A. F., 224, 228
Hans, J., 350, 352
Harasymchuk, C., 288, 299, 300, 309
Harden Fritz, J. M., 426, 427, 428, 453
Hardy, M. S., 280, 283
Harmon, E. L., 264, 281
Harold, G. T., 468, 475
Harper, A., 346, 347, 349, 352
Harper, F. W. K., 215, 218, 231
Harrington, A., 462, 475
Harris, C. R., 191, 197, 198, 207, 410, 415
Harris, G. T., 214, 229
Harris, K. F., 222, 229
Harris, T., 393, 394
Harrison, K., 191, 194, 200, 206
Hart, C. H., 267, 283
Harter, S., 296, 297, 312, 458, 477
Hartup, W. W., 135, 141, 242, 255
Harvey, J. H., 347, 353
Haselager, G. J. T., 242, 255
Hatfield, E., 340, 353
Hausknecht, J. P., 418, 453
Haviland, J. M., 341, 354
Hawk, G., 137, 140
Hawkley, L. C., 124, 140, 141
Hawley, P. H., 236, 249, 255, 256
Haynie, D. L., 241, 256
Hazan, C., 92, 103, 109, 118, 119, 313, 333
Healey, J. G., 298, 305, 308, 309
Heaphy, B., 202, 208
Heath, R. G., 290, 300, 311
Heavey, C. L., 366, 372
Hechenbleikner, N. R., 28, 31, 296, 306, 310, 337, 338, 354
Heelas, P., 462, 466, 475
Heerey, E. A., 264, 273, 284, 318, 333
Heffner, K. L., 360, 364, 368, 372, 373
Heider, F., 432, 434, 453
Heimgartner, A., 64, 71, 325, 326, 334
Helgeson, V. S., 300, 309, 401, 415
Hellman, D., 265, 282
Henderson, L., 448, 453
Henderson, M., 290, 308, 318, 332
Hendrick, C., 199, 200, 206

Hendrick, S. S., 199, 200, 206
Henning, K., 215, 228
Henton, J., 216, 228
Hepworth, S. J., 440, 452
Herbert, T. B., 362, 372
Herman, B. H., 126, 139, 141
Hersey, P., 424, 453
Hertel, R. K., 157, 164
Herzberger, S. D., 276, 283
Heschgl, S., 64, 71, 325, 326, 334
Hess, J. A., 419, 425, 434, 453, 454
Hesse, E., 100, 118
Hetherington, E. M., 346, 348, 353
Hetherington, M., 271, 272, 284
Hewitt, D. W., 492, 496
Heyman, R. E., 369, 370, 372, 373
Hickman, S. E., 290, 292, 293, 301, 302, 309
Higgins, E. T., 481, 482, 495
Higgins-Kessler, M., 191, 199, 200, 204, 207, 331, 334
Higgitt, P., 100, 117
Highberger, L., 131, 132, 139
Hight, T. L., 328, 331, 334, 386, 389, 397
Hill, A., 67, 71, 314, 315, 326, 327, 328, 333
Hillman, J. H., 265, 282
Hilton, A., 215, 229
Hilton, N. Z., 214, 229
Himawan, L. K., 364, 372
Hine, D. W., 430, 431, 432, 433, 436, 454
Hitsman, B. L., 214, 215, 227
Hobbs, B. V., 364, 372
Hodges, E. V. E., 235, 236, 237, 240, 241, 242, 244, 245, 249, 250, 251, 252, 253, 255, 256, 257
Hoffman, M. L., 264, 283
Holley, J., 480, 482, 495, 496
Holmes, J. G., 23, 32, 38, 48, 64, 71, 76, 78, 80, 81, 90, 320, 325, 326, 329, 332, 334, 337, 354, 366, 374
Holmes-Lonergan, H., 274, 283
Holtzworth-Munroe, A., 223, 229
Hooley, J., 384, 398
Hopmeyer Gorman, A. H., 242, 258
Hopper, J., 344, 345, 354
Horowitz, L. M., 482, 495
Horwitz, A. V., 377, 396
Hotaling, G. T., 210, 223, 231
Houts, R. M., 149, 163
Howe, N., 274, 283, 286
Howell, F. M., 82, 91
Howells, K., 219, 223, 224, 225, 231
Howerton, E., 318, 333
Hoyle, R. H., 261, 283
Hoyt, W. T., 279, 283
Hrubes, D., 186, 189

Hsee, C. K., 135, 141
Hu, H., 272, 281
Hubbard, J. A., 245, 254, 256
Huebner, E. S., 218, 219, 227
Huesmann, L. R., 261, 283
Hughes, M., 377, 396
Hulse-Killacky, D., 222, 226
Humphreys, J., 221, 229
Hunsley, J., 19, 31
Huntington, N., 214, 226
Huston, T. L., 149, 159, 162, 163, 164, 293, 310
Huttunen, A., 242, 258
Hyman, C., 236, 238, 254
Hymel, S., 241, 253

Iciek, L., 361, 374
Ickes, W., 225, 230
Ifert, D. E., 145, 146, 164
Iida, M., 73, 82, 90
Indvik, J., 437, 451, 454
Ingram, K. M., 215, 222, 231
Innes-Ker, A. H., 80, 90
Insko, C. A., 420, 455
Isaacs, J., 235, 237, 240, 249, 253, 256
Isen, A. M., 451, 454
Ittel, A., 302, 308
Izard, C. E., 15, 23, 31, 92, 95, 118, 340, 354

Jackson, H., 388, 389, 392, 395
Jackson, S. M., 216, 229
Jackson-Newsom, J., 275, 285
Jacob, T., 383, 396
Jacobson, N. S., 214, 223, 229, 381, 394
Jafar, E., 225, 226
Jago, A. G., 424, 456
Jang, S. A., 110, 118
Janoff-Bulman, R., 107, 118
Jansen-Nawas, C., 147, 164
Jenkins, D., 440, 452
Jenkins, J. M., 265, 281
Jenkins, S. R., 147, 163
Jennings, M., 274, 283
Jensen, L. A., 290, 291, 309
Johnson, A., 191, 208
Johnson, D., 237, 256
Johnson, D. M., 217, 218, 232
Johnson, H., 299, 309
Johnson, K. L., 151, 157, 163, 164
Johnson, L. M., 197, 206
Johnson, M. P., 197, 207, 212, 229, 293, 310
Johnson, P. R., 437, 451, 454
Johnson, S., 237, 256
Johnson, S. M., 331, 333
Johnston, J. R., 337, 354

Johnstone, T., 15, 32
Joiner, T. E., 76, 78, 90, 137, 141
Jones, A., 346, 352
Jones, A. S., 225, 226
Jones, E. E., 432, 434, 435, 454
Jones, S. M., 153, 154, 159, 163
Jones, T. L., 270, 283
Jones, W. H., 289, 302, 310, 316, 318, 322, 329, 333, 337, 339, 354, 417, 454, 482, 486, 489, 495
Jordan, W. J., 433, 455
Joreskog, K. G., 444, 454
Jourard, S. M., 484, 495
Joyner, K., 381, 399
Junger-Tas, J., 236, 258
Juvonen, J., 240, 256, 272, 285

Kacewicz, E., 492, 495
Kachadourian, L. K., 111, 118, 160, 163, 389, 396
Kagan, J., 265, 268, 278, 283
Kaltman, S., 214, 217, 218, 223, 228
Kamins, M. L., 267, 283
Kang, N. J., 73
Kaplar, M. E., 186, 189, 325, 333
Kappas, A., 35, 37, 47
Karney, B. R., 149, 163, 378, 397
Kashy, D. A., 76, 80, 86, 89, 104, 116, 168, 170, 189, 252, 256, 404, 414
Kasprowicz, D. J., 361, 374
Kastin, A. J., 126, 141
Katkin, E. S., 364, 371
Katz, J., 215, 218, 229, 377, 394
Kazantzis, N., 493, 495
Kean, K. J., 264, 267, 286
Kearns, J. N., 386, 396
Keashly, L., 429, 454
Keedian, E., 78, 88
Keelan, J. P. R., 88
Keenan, K., 268, 283
Keery, H., 264, 273, 283
Kehoe, P., 127, 141
Kelley, D. L., 63, 72
Kelley, H. H., 211, 230, 367, 373
Kelling, G. L., 450, 456
Kelly, A. B., 382, 482, 495
Keltner, D., 43, 48, 264, 273, 284, 318, 333, 363, 372
Kelvin, P., 5, 10
Kemeny, M. E., 278, 282, 361, 367, 368, 372
Kennedy, D., 408, 415
Kennedy, E., 249, 257
Kennedy, L. T., 217, 218, 219, 223, 229
Kennedy-Moore, E., 341, 354
Kenny, D. A., 245, 252, 256, 260, 284, 391, 394
Kershaw, K., 299, 309
Ketterer, M., 484, 495

Khader, M., 45, 49
Khaleque, A., 263, 265, 266, 284
Khouri, H., 44, 47, 75, 77, 78, 89, 269, 282
Kiecolt-Glaser, J. K., 124, 142, 359, 360, 361, 362, 363, 364, 368, 371, 372, 373, 374
Kiesler, S., 401, 402, 415
Kikas, E., 250, 257
Killoren, S., 275, 285
Kim, C., 363, 373
Kim, H. S., 473, 477
Kim, J., 271, 272, 284
Kim, K. H., 361, 368, 372
Kim, M., 81, 88
King, M. J., 212, 214, 215, 227
Kingsbury, R., 32, 367, 373, 466, 476
Kirby, L. D., 151, 165
Kirkendol, S. E., 168, 182, 188, 189
Kirkham, C., 243, 257
Kirkpatrick, L. A., 367, 373
Kirson, D., 4, 5, 6, 10, 15, 16, 18, 32, 92, 93, 94, 95, 96, 97, 105, 107, 108, 119, 145, 146, 165, 296, 311, 315, 334, 338, 340, 355
Kitayama, S., 465, 476
Klaus, P. A., 213, 228
Klein, R. C. A., 160, 163
Klein, T. R., 131, 132, 139
Klesges, L. M., 215, 228
Klesh, J., 440, 452
Knapp, M., 199, 207
Knobe, J., 155, 163
Knobloch, L. K., 105, 118, 147, 163
Knowles, M., 133, 141
Knudson, K. H., 215, 218, 222, 230
Knupp, A., 342, 351, 353
Kobak, R. R., 85, 90, 96, 117
Koch, E. J., 28, 31, 296, 306, 310, 337, 338, 354
Kochanska, G., 278, 284
Kochenderfer, B. J., 240, 256
Kochenderfer-Ladd, B., 240, 241, 256
Kohn, R., 213, 217, 218, 232
Kohut, H., 97, 101, 118
Kokkonen, M., 448, 455
Kontula, O., 191, 196, 201, 206, 207
Koss, M. P., 214, 228
Koval, J., 216, 228
Kowal, A., 275, 284
Kowalski, R. M., 48, 63, 71, 317, 318, 333, 378, 397, 434, 436, 454, 457, 469, 476
Koziol-McLain, J., 214, 227
Kraemer, H. C., 363, 372
Kramer, L., 275, 284
Krappmann, L., 307, 310
Krasnoff, L., 377, 395
Kraut, R., 401, 415
Krauth-Gruber, S., 479, 480, 487, 497

Kring, A. M., 264, 273, 284
Krokoff, L. J., 366, 372
Krouth-Gruber, S., 487
Kruger, J., 264, 284
Krull, D. S., 78, 91
Krull, J., 275, 284
Kub, J., 225, 226
Kuban, J., 264, 284
Kuczynski, L., 268, 284
Kudoh, T., 461, 464, 466, 476, 477
Kugler, K., 482, 486, 489, 495
Kuipers, P., 145, 146, 156, 162
Kulik, J. A., 340, 353
Kurdek, L. A., 82, 90
Kurtz, J., 130, 142
Kusche, A. G., 76, 78, 81, 90, 320, 329, 334
Kusel, S. J., 241, 257

L'Abate, B. L., 493, 497
L'Abate, L., 3, 4, 10, 479, 480, 481, 482, 483, 484, 485, 486, 487, 488, 489, 490, 491, 492, 493, 494, 495, 496, 497
Ladd, G. W., 240, 241, 256
Lagerspetz, K. M. J., 242, 258
Lai, K., 299, 309
Lakey, B., 85, 90
Lakey, S. G., 148, 162
Lamb, E. N., 348, 354
Lambert, N. M., 376
Landers, J. E., 86, 89
Lange, C., 214, 229
Langhinrichsen-Rohling, J., 224, 225, 229
Langhout, R. D., 430, 437, 452
Lansford, J. E., 267, 284
LaRose, R., 401, 415
Larsen, R. J., 15, 31, 191, 197, 198, 206, 410, 414
Larson, J. R., Jr., 187, 189
Larson, R. W., 288, 310
Lashley, S. L., 143, 145, 156, 164
Laskowski, B. F., 364, 368, 371, 372
Laughon, K., 213, 214, 226, 227
Laumann, E. O., 191, 197, 201, 207, 380, 397
Laurenceau, J. P., 484, 497
Laursen, B., 294, 300, 301, 310, 311
Lavy, S., 5, 6, 92
Lawson, A., 194, 207
Lazarus, R. S., 23, 27, 31, 37, 48, 93, 94, 95, 108, 118, 145, 151, 152, 153, 156, 160, 163, 316, 333, 338, 354, 463, 468, 475
Le, B., 73, 359
Leadbetter, S., 219, 229
Leary, M. R., 3, 4, 5, 6, 8, 10, 15, 16, 17, 21, 23, 24, 26, 27, 28, 29, 30, 31, 32, 34, 35, 38, 40, 41, 42, 43, 44, 48, 59, 61, 62, 63, 64, 66, 71, 73, 74, 90, 98, 99, 105, 106, 107, 108, 112, 113, 116, 118, 123, 124, 125, 126, 127, 130, 131, 134, 137, 139, 140, 141, 144, 145, 146, 163, 173, 174, 175, 189, 192, 193, 207, 222, 229, 261, 266, 267, 268, 269, 281, 284, 288, 289, 291, 292, 294, 295, 296, 297, 298, 300, 301, 302, 303, 304, 305, 306, 307, 310, 311, 313, 314, 315, 316, 317, 318, 319, 324, 325, 330, 332, 333, 337, 338, 354, 360, 364, 365, 366, 371, 373, 374, 378, 397, 398, 417, 418, 447, 454, 457, 458, 460, 461, 463, 466, 468, 469, 474, 475, 476, 477
LeBlanc, G. J., 380, 398
Lebolt, A., 278, 282
Lebra, T. S., 465, 476
Leder, S., 15, 106, 144, 297, 457, 460
Lee, C., 212, 215, 227
Lee, G. P., 135, 140
Lehnhoff, J., 265, 282
Lemerise, E. A., 245, 254, 261, 284
Lemeshow, S., 363, 373
Lenox, K., 236, 254
Leonard, K. E., 81, 91, 147, 151, 152, 153, 165, 224, 225, 231, 328, 383, 396
Lerner, C. F., 217, 218, 219, 223, 229
Leslie, L., 293, 310
Leven, K. S., 292, 293, 310
Levenson, R. W., 143, 145, 156, 162, 163, 362, 373, 471, 475
Levine, M., 492, 497
Levine, S., 482, 497
Levine, T. R., 110, 118, 186, 189
Levinson, S., 50, 51, 52, 55, 56, 57, 70, 71
Levy, R. I., 462, 476
Lewin, K., 392, 397, 424, 451, 454, 497
Lewis, H. B., 269, 279, 284
Lewis, J. C., 270, 281
Lewis, M., 264, 265, 278, 279, 284
Lieberman, M. D., 21, 26, 31, 99, 101, 106, 117, 124, 126, 134, 137, 140, 222, 228, 296, 306, 309, 317, 332, 366, 367, 372, 373, 466, 475
Lilienfeld, S. O., 379, 397
Lim, S., 430, 454
Lin, S. L., 473, 477
Lin, Y. W., 420, 455
Lindström, M., 211, 226
Lines, K. J., 214, 229
Lippard, P. V., 168, 185, 189
Lippitt, R., 424, 451, 454
Lippman, D. N., 302, 308
Little, T. D., 45, 236, 237, 239, 249, 252, 254, 255, 256, 278
Liu, C., 381, 397
Llorca, P. M., 382, 397
Lloyd, S., 216, 228
Lo, W. A., 223, 229

Lochman, J. E., 236, 238, 254
Locke, T. F., 383, 397
Loewenstein, G. F., 130, 135, 141, 142
Lofquist, L. H., 440, 456
Logan, T. K., 218, 227
Lollis, S., 268, 284
London, B. E., 79, 90
Lopes, P. N., 448, 455
Lopez, S. J., 472, 477
Lovallo, W. R., 360, 361, 373
Loving, T. J., 73, 359, 360, 363, 364, 368, 372, 373, 495
Low, C. M., 296, 310
Lubin, B., 19, 33
Luce, C. L., 132, 141
Lundgren, D. C., 402, 414
Lundmark, V., 401, 415
Lutz, C. J., 85, 90
Luu, P., 126, 140

MacCallum, R. C., 363, 364, 368, 372, 373
Maccoby, E. E., 263, 268, 284
MacDonald, G., 6, 10, 21, 23, 30, 32, 34, 41, 48, 124, 126, 127, 130, 131, 134, 137, 139, 141, 267, 284, 317, 333, 366, 367, 373, 374, 378, 397, 458, 466, 476
Mace, D., 481, 482, 483, 497
MacFarlane, A., 214, 215, 227
MacGeorge, E. L., 154, 162
MacKenzie, S. B., 439, 455
MacKinnon-Lewis, C. E., 237, 256
Madsen, K. C., 292, 293, 310
Magley, V. J., 430, 437, 452
Maguire, K. C., 3, 11, 60, 72, 158, 165
Maheu, M. M., 492, 497
Maino, E., 493, 497
Maio, G., 279, 283
Maisto, S. A., 384, 397
Mak, L., 269, 270, 285
Malamuth, N. M., 366, 372
Malarkey, W. B., 363, 364, 368, 371, 372, 373, 374
Malatesta, C. Z., 341, 354
Malet, L., 382, 397
Malis, R. S., 147, 162
Malishkevich, S., 99, 105, 118
Malle, B. F., 155, 163
Malone, J., 214, 230
Malone, M. J., 236, 241, 242, 256
Malone, P. S., 267, 284
Mandal, E., 417
Maner, J. K., 132, 141, 306, 310
Manganello, J., 214, 227
Mangum, J. L., 198, 206
Manke, B., 271, 284
Manning-Ryan, B., 197, 206

Mao, H., 363, 373
Marino, L., 379, 397
Maritz, J. S., 383, 394
Markman, H. J., 146, 159, 163
Marks, J. S., 214, 228
Markus, H. R., 457, 465, 476
Marrow, S., 343, 353
Marshal, M. P., 382, 397
Marshall, L. L., 215, 229, 361, 374
Martin, J., 260, 271, 275, 276, 284
Martin, P., 347, 353
Martin, R. J., 430, 431, 432, 433, 436, 454
Marucha, P. T., 368, 372
Maruping, L., 420, 452
Mary-Sue, P., 299, 309
Masicampo, E. J., 123, 339, 366, 468
Maston, C., 213, 228
Matsumoto, D., 461, 464, 466, 476, 477
Matthews, K. A., 222, 229
Matthews, W. J., 216, 229
Matwin, S., 143, 165, 272, 287
Mauger, P. A., 390, 397
Mauro, R., 464, 476
Max, W., 219, 229
May, L. N., 337, 339, 354, 417, 454
May, W. H., 95, 119
Mayer, J. D., 448, 455
Mayeux, L., 237, 254
Mazanec, M., 290, 308
McBride, M. C., 342, 343, 352, 355
McCabe, S. B., 377, 396
McCaffrey, J., 214, 215, 227
McCornack, S. A., 186, 189
McCullough, M. E., 279, 283, 328, 331, 334, 386, 389, 393, 397, 398, 450, 454, 489, 497
McDill, E. L., 433, 455
McFarlane, J., 214, 227
McGregor, I., 326, 334
McGuire, M. T., 365, 374
McGuire, S., 271, 284
McHale, J. P., 237, 256
McHale, S., 272, 273, 275, 276, 282, 285, 286
McHenry, S., 480, 497
McKay, J. R., 384, 397
McKenzie, M., 318, 333
McKeown, R. E., 212, 214, 215, 218, 219, 227
Mckinney, K. E., 390, 397
McLaren, R. M., 3, 10, 152, 155, 164
McLaughlin, D., 401, 416
McLaughlin, J., 377, 396
McMahon, P. M., 218, 227
McMenamin, J. P., 492, 497
McMillen, C., 221, 229
McNeill-Hawkins, K., 215, 228

McNeilly-Choque, M. K., 267, 283
McPartland, J. M., 433, 455
McPherson, A. E., 147, 162
Menesini, E., 279, 281
Merchant, J. A., 215, 230
Mesquita, B., 17, 21, 31, 339, 353, 457, 458, 459, 460, 462, 463, 464, 465, 466, 469, 470, 471, 474, 476
Metalsky, G. I., 76, 90, 107, 116
Metts, S., 66, 71, 157, 158, 164, 168, 185, 189, 336, 337, 338, 342, 351, 354
Meyer, B., 105, 118
Meyer, R. E., 488, 497
Michael, R. T., 191, 197, 201, 207, 380, 397
Michaelis, B., 44, 47, 77, 78, 89
Michaels, S., 191, 197, 201, 207, 380, 397
Mickelson, K. D., 104, 119
Mikula, G., 64, 71, 325, 326, 334
Mikulincer, M., 5, 6, 39, 45, 48, 85, 90, 92, 93, 95, 96, 97, 99, 101, 102, 103, 104, 105, 107, 108, 109, 110, 111, 112, 115, 116, 118, 119, 317, 334
Milardo, R. M., 160, 163, 293, 310
Mileham, B. L. A., 409, 415
Miles, S. B., 236, 257
Millar, K. U., 184, 189
Miller, A. E., 343, 354
Miller, A. H., 364, 374
Miller, C. W., 3, 67, 71, 145, 147, 164
Miller, G. E., 362, 374
Miller, I. W., 393, 394
Miller, K. I., 68, 71
Miller, L. E., 143
Miller, N. L., 237, 255
Miller, P. J., 159, 164
Miller, P. M., 214, 227
Miller, R. B., 191, 199, 200, 204, 207, 331, 334
Miller, R. S., 314, 334
Millevoi, A., 197, 199, 206
Mills, J., 419, 452
Mills, R. S. L., 3, 10, 27, 32, 65, 71, 260, 263, 264, 265, 266, 267, 268, 269, 270, 279, 285, 287
Miron, M. S., 95, 119
Mischel, W., 76, 90
Moffitt, T. E., 236, 257
Monaco, V., 223, 229
Monarch, N. D., 318, 333
Mongeau, P. A., 215, 227
Monson, T. C., 238, 255
Montgomery, H., 345, 355
Moore, D. S., 316, 318, 322, 329, 333
Moore, M., 421, 454
Moore, T. M., 224, 229
Moos, R., 384, 394
Morahan-Martin, J., 401, 415
Morales, J. R., 290, 292, 293, 301, 302, 309

Moran, G. S., 100, 117
Morita, Y., 236, 258
Morris, W. L., 167
Motley, M. T., 168, 188
Mougios, V., 79, 90
Mount, T. G., 492, 497
Mouradian, V. E., 224, 229
Mukopadhyay, T., 401, 415
Mullett, J., 187, 188
Munn, P., 271, 273, 282
Muraven, M., 470, 476
Murphy, C. M., 215, 220, 232
Murphy, J. E., 223, 229
Murray, B. J., 243, 257
Murray, E., 489, 494
Murray, S. L., 23, 32, 38, 48, 76, 78, 80, 81, 90, 148, 159, 160, 164, 319, 320, 329, 334, 337, 339, 340, 354, 366, 374
Murty, S. A., 215, 230
Musick, M. A., 390, 398

Najman, J., 271, 282
Nansel, T., 241, 256
Naranjo, J. R., 127, 141
Nazar, J., 3, 10, 27, 32, 65, 71, 263, 264, 265, 266, 267, 268, 269, 285
Neckerman, H. J., 236, 253
Neff, L. A., 378, 397
Negel, L. A., 3, 4, 5, 6, 8, 10, 16, 17, 24, 26, 27, 29, 32, 38, 44, 48, 59, 61, 62, 63, 64, 66, 71, 73, 74, 90, 98, 105, 107, 108, 112, 118, 144, 145, 146, 163, 173, 174, 189, 192, 207, 261, 266, 267, 268, 284, 288, 289, 291, 292, 294, 295, 297, 298, 300, 301, 302, 303, 305, 307, 310, 314, 316, 318, 319, 322, 324, 325, 329, 330, 333, 337, 338, 354, 360, 364, 373, 378, 397, 417, 447, 454, 458, 460, 461, 476
Neidig, P., 224, 229
Nelson, D. A., 267, 283, 290, 292, 293, 301, 302, 309
Nelson, D. W., 473, 477
Nelson, E. E., 126, 141
Nelson, E. S., 381, 398
Neuberg, S. L., 132, 141
*New York Times*, 421, 455
Newberg, A. B., 331, 334
Newberg, S. K., 331, 334
Newcomb, A. F., 135, 140, 236, 248, 257
Newcomb, M. D., 383, 397
Newell, S. E., 144, 164
Newman, R. S., 243, 257
Newton, T., 363, 364, 373
Niaura, R., 214, 215, 227
Nicastle, L. D., 197, 199, 206
Nicholls, T. L., 213, 214, 228

Nicholson, J., 290, 308
Niedenthal, P. M., 18, 32, 80, 90, 479, 480, 487, 497
Nishida, T., 473, 477
Nishina, A., 240, 256, 272, 285
Noller, P., 23, 31, 219, 230, 322, 334
Nordenberg, D., 214, 225, 228
Notarius, C. I., 143, 145, 156, 159, 163, 164
Nuss, C. K., 123, 124, 125, 140

Oatley, K., 461, 477
O'Boyle, T. F., 423, 454
Oburu, P., 267, 284
O'Campo, P., 225, 226
Ochsner, K. N., 17, 21, 31
O'Connor, C., 4, 5, 6, 10, 15, 16, 18, 32, 92, 93, 94, 95, 96, 97, 105, 107, 108, 119, 145, 146, 165, 296, 311, 315, 334, 338, 340, 355
Oemig, C., 318, 333
O'Farrell, T. J., 377, 383, 384, 397, 398
O'Keefe, B. J., 156, 164
O'Leary, K. D., 214, 215, 218, 219, 223, 227, 230, 380, 395
Oliker, S. J., 299, 310
Olivier, L., 105, 118
Ollendick, T. H., 240, 255
Olmstead, G., 168, 189
Olsen, S. F., 267, 283
Olson, K., 5, 10, 337, 338, 353
Olson, M. M., 191, 199, 200, 204, 207, 331, 334
Olweus, D., 236, 240, 241, 252, 257, 258
O'Moore, A. M., 243, 257
Omoto, A. M., 288, 308
Ones, D. S., 418, 454
Oram, G., 137, 140
Orbach, I., 104, 118
Orbuch, T. L., 200, 207, 330, 335
O'Reilly, C. A., 420, 456
Ormrod, R., 271, 280, 282
Ortony, A., 23, 32
Orvis, B. R., 211, 230
Osgarby, S., 382, 396
Osgood, C. E., 95, 119
Oskamp, S., 212, 226
Ostrov, J. M., 267, 272, 273, 281, 285
Overall, N., 45, 47
Overbeek, G., 377, 378, 398
Owen, D., 279, 281

Page, G. G., 362, 375
Paleari, G., 390, 396
Palmer, S. C., 377, 395
Palmerus, K., 267, 284
Panksepp, J., 126, 127, 139, 141
Paolucci, E. O., 214, 230

Pape, K. T., 225, 230, 361, 362, 371
Pargament, K. I., 386, 390, 398
Park, L. E., 104, 119
Parker, J. G., 242, 257, 296, 298, 310, 411
Parker, T. S., 409, 410, 415
Parkinson, B., 45, 48
Parks, M. R., 156, 164
Parmley, A. M., 215, 218, 222, 230
Parrot, W., 274, 285
Pasch, L. A., 363, 374
Pasley, K., 345, 351
Pasupathi, M., 236, 256
Pattee, L., 236, 248, 257
Patterson, G. R., 237, 238, 254, 257, 258, 260, 270, 285
Patterson, M., 401, 415
Patterson, S., 292, 309
Pauk, N., 348, 349, 352
Paul, R. H., 214, 215, 227
Pearl, D., 363, 374
Pearl, R., 237, 258
Pearlstein, T., 213, 232
Pearson, C. M., 428, 429, 430, 436, 437, 452, 454, 455
Peek-Asa, C., 215, 230
Peets, K., 250, 257
Pehrsson, M., 211, 226
Pelcovits, M., 384, 397
Pelham, B. W., 78, 91
Pellegrini, A. D., 237, 241, 249, 257
Penn, C. E., 221, 231
Pennebaker, J. W., 154, 164, 489, 492, 494, 495
Pepler, D. J., 292, 293, 310
Perkins, C. A., 213, 228
Perlman, M., 268, 276, 285
Perris, C., 485, 497
Perry, B. D., 214, 215, 221, 225
Perry, D. G., 236, 238, 240, 241, 242, 243, 249, 253, 255, 256, 257
Perry, J. E., 390, 397
Perry, L. C., 238, 241, 242, 249, 253, 257
Perry, T., 290, 300, 311
Peterson, J., 213, 232
Petrakos, H., 274, 283
Pettit, G. S., 237, 238, 251, 254, 255, 263, 281
Phillips, D., 105, 119
Phillips, S., 469, 476
Phillips, T., 433, 435, 455
Pickett, C. L., 123, 125, 133, 141
Pierce, G. R., 82, 91
Pierce, K. A., 251, 257
Pietrzak, J., 261, 285
Pike, G. R., 159, 164
Pimlott-Kubiak, S., 214, 230, 361, 374
Pine, D., 137, 140

Pinel, E. C., 130, 141
Piotrowski, C. C., 260, 271, 272, 273, 275, 276, 285
Pittman, G., 290, 308
Planalp, S., 37, 42, 43, 46, 48, 329, 334, 459, 462, 463, 477
Plank, S. B., 433, 455
Plaut, V. C., 307, 308
Pliner, P., 490, 494
Plutchik, R., 15, 32, 487, 497
Poehlmann, K. M., 364, 371
Polek, D. S., 215, 228
Polivy, J., 490, 494
Pollock, T. G., 420, 456
Pontari, B. A., 187, 189
Pope, A. W., 241, 258
Pope, L. K., 338, 355
Porath, C. L., 429, 430, 437, 454, 455
Posdakoff, P. M., 439, 455
Posner, M. I., 126, 140
Previti, D., 195, 206, 380, 381, 383, 384, 394, 398, 411, 414
Price, J. M., 245, 255
Prins, K. S., 381, 398
Prinstein, M. J., 240, 241, 258
Prinz, R. J., 270, 283
Proctor, L. J., 241, 258
Przepyszny, K. A., 269, 287
Ptacek, J., 211, 230
Pulier, M., 492, 497
Purdie, V., 81, 90
Putnam, R. D., 451, 455

Quigley, L., 411, 416
Quinlivan, E., 469, 476

Rabin, B. S., 360, 364, 374
Rabiner, D. L., 238, 255
Rachal, K. C., 328, 331, 334, 386, 389, 397
Racine, Y., 265, 281
Rafaeli, E., 83, 88
Raja, S., 217, 230
Raleigh, M. J., 365, 374
Ram, A., 268, 274, 285, 286
Rand, M. R., 213, 228
Rapson, R. L., 340, 353
Rasmussen, P., 238, 257
Raush, H. L., 157, 164
Recchia, H., 272, 286
Regalia, C., 390, 396
Reibstein, J., 194, 207
Reid, R. J., 218, 219, 226
Reidpath, D., 219, 223, 224, 225, 231
Reis, H. T., 82, 91, 117, 497
Reiss, D., 271, 272, 284

Remen, A. L., 377, 395
Renck, R., 440, 452
Renneberg, B., 377, 395
Repetti, R. L., 147, 164
Reynaud, M., 382, 397
Reznick, J. S., 265, 268, 283
Rhatigan, D. L., 215, 218, 219, 230
Rhea, J., 222, 231
Rholes, W. S., 105, 119
Ric, F., 479, 480, 487, 497
Rice, D. P., 219, 229
Rice, M. E., 214, 229
Richards, M., 194, 207
Richardson, D. R., 265, 275, 281
Richardson, D. S., 299, 310
Richardson, L., 195, 207
Richardson, R., 123, 125, 142
Richey, H. W., 299, 310
Richey, M. H., 299, 310
Rideout, G., 221, 229
Rigby, K., 240, 258, 272, 285
Riger, S., 214, 217, 230
Riggs, D. S., 215, 230
Riksen-Walraven, J. M., 242, 255
Rinaldi, C., 274, 283, 286
Rinck, C. M., 19, 33
Rincon, C., 278, 282
Ringel, C., 213, 228
Rios, D. I., 117
Rique, J., 386, 395
Risen, J. L., 450, 455
Riskind, J. H., 389, 398
Ritchie, T., 403, 404, 415
Ritter, B., 422, 453
Rivara, F. P., 218, 219, 226
Roberts, L. J., 147, 151, 152, 153, 165, 224, 225, 231, 328
Roberts, N., 23, 31, 219, 230
Robin, L., 90
Robinson, C. C., 267, 283
Robinson, S., 436, 455
Robles, T. F., 359, 363, 374
Rodkin, P., 237, 258
Rodriguez, C. P., 364, 372
Rodriguez, S., 73
Rogers, M. P., 362, 374
Rohner, R. P., 263, 264, 265, 266, 267, 284, 286
Rollie, S. S., 345, 354
Rollin, E., 299, 308
Roloff, M. E., 3, 10, 67, 71, 145, 146, 147, 151, 157, 160, 162, 163, 164, 166
Romero, C., 65, 72, 324, 325, 326, 335
Romero-Canyas, R., 44, 48
Root, L. M., 450, 454, 489, 497
Roscoe, B., 223, 230, 408, 415

Rose, P., 76, 78, 81, 90, 148, 159, 164, 237, 258, 320, 329, 334, 339, 340, 354
Roseman, I. J., 36, 40, 42, 48, 316, 334
Rosen, L. N., 215, 218, 222, 230
Rosen, S., 187, 189
Rosenbaum, A., 214, 230
Rosenberg, E. B., 348, 355
Ross, H., 260, 268, 271, 272, 273, 274, 275, 276, 282, 284, 285, 286, 287
Ross, M., 64, 71, 272, 274, 276, 286, 287, 325, 332
Roth, D. A., 105, 118
Roth, M. A., 296, 298, 310
Rothbard, J. C., 317, 334
Rothbart, M. K., 265, 268, 282
Rovine, M. J., 484, 497
Rowatt, W. C., 147, 161, 164
Rozlog, L. A., 364, 371
Rubin, K. H., 267, 285
Rusbult, C. E., 117, 299, 309, 310, 311, 367, 374, 420, 455
Russell, C. S., 191, 199, 200, 204, 207, 331, 334
Russell, D. W., 82, 89
Russell, J. A., 15, 32, 95, 119, 304, 309
Rutledge, L. L., 215, 228
Rye, M. S., 390, 398

Sabourin, T. C., 224, 231
Sachs, C., 214, 227
Sagarin, B. J., 132, 141, 197, 199, 206
Saito, I., 470, 477
Salmivalli, C., 236, 240, 242, 244, 250, 251, 256, 257, 258
Salomon, A., 214, 226
Salovey, P., 46, 48, 198, 206, 410, 414, 448, 455
Salzman, L. E., 218, 227
Samara, M. M., 280, 287
Samter, W., 293, 294, 311
Sandage, S. J., 328, 331, 334, 386, 389, 397
Sanders, V. M., 361, 374
Sanderson, M., 214, 215, 218, 219, 227, 361, 372
Sanford, K., 147, 161, 164
Sarason, B. R., 82, 91
Sarason, I. G., 82, 91
Sato, K., 464, 476
Satpute, A. B., 367, 372
Sawalani, G. M., 237, 254
Saylor, K., 241, 256
Sbarra, D. A., 336, 342, 355
Sceery, A., 85, 90
Schaap, C., 147, 164
Schachner, D. A., 104, 119
Schachter, S., 340, 355
Schaefer, H. S., 359, 371
Schaller, M., 306, 310
Scharfe, E., 110, 119

Scheier, L. M., 237, 255
Scher, S. J., 125, 140
Scherer, K. R., 15, 32, 36, 46, 47, 48, 459, 461, 462, 464, 465, 466, 476, 477
Scherlies, W., 401, 415
Schewe, P., 214, 230
Schilling, E. A., 76, 87, 89
Schlee, K. A., 218, 227
Schleien, S., 276, 286
Schlenker, B. R., 187, 189
Schmeeckle, M., 344, 355
Schmidt, E., 425, 455
Schmidt, F. L., 418, 454
Schneider, J. P., 380, 388, 398
Schollenberger, J., 214, 227
Scholte, R., 377, 378, 398
Schore, A. N., 278, 286
Schorr, A., 15, 32
Schratter, A., 316, 318, 322, 329, 333
Schrepferman, L., 271, 281
Schrodt, P., 342, 343, 349, 352, 355
Schroth, H. A., 149, 164
Schut, H., 484, 497
Schutz, A., 64, 65, 71, 325, 326, 334
Schwan, R., 382, 397
Schwartz, D., 237, 241, 242, 243, 245, 249, 254, 256, 258
Schwartz, J., 4, 5, 6, 10, 15, 16, 18, 32, 92, 93, 94, 95, 96, 97, 105, 107, 108, 119, 145, 146, 165, 296, 311, 315, 334, 338, 340, 355, 462, 477
Schweinle, W. E., 225, 230
Scott, A. M., 143
Scott, J. P., 126, 139, 141
Seeman, T. E., 147, 164
Segerstrom, S. C., 362, 374
Segrin, C., 341, 355, 482, 497
Seidel, M., 78, 88
Seidman, G., 82, 90
Seifer, M., 381, 394
Selig, J. P., 252, 254
Semmelroth, J., 191, 197, 198, 206, 410, 414
Senchak, M., 81, 91
Senich, S., 269, 287
Sensibaugh, C. C., 408, 416
Senter, K. E., 220, 222, 230
Seremetis, S. V., 361, 374
Seymour, F. W., 216, 229
Shackelford, T. K., 290, 291, 294, 308, 311, 380, 381, 395, 398, 410, 415
Shaffer, P., 161, 165
Shamblen, S. R., 433, 434, 439, 446, 453, 455
Shanahan, L., 275, 285
Shannon, L., 218, 227
Sharps, P. W., 213, 214, 226, 227

Shaver, P. R., 4, 5, 6, 10, 15, 16, 18, 32, 35, 39, 45, 48, 82, 91, 92, 93, 94, 95, 96, 97, 99, 101, 102, 103, 104, 105, 107, 108, 109, 111, 112, 115, 116, 117, 118, 119, 145, 146, 165, 262, 282, 296, 300, 309, 311, 315, 317, 334, 338, 340, 355, 367, 374, 462, 477, 497
Shaw, D., 268, 274, 283
Shaw, L. L., 131, 132, 139
Shaw, S., 32, 466, 476
Shebloski, B., 265, 286
Shenk, J. L., 366, 371
Sheppard, V. J., 381, 398
Shields, A., 241, 258
Shippy, R. A., 341, 353
Shoda, Y., 73, 76, 79, 88, 90
Shortt, J. W., 214, 229, 271, 281
Shrout, P. E., 82, 90
Shu, S., 243, 258
Shu, X., 344, 355
Shulman, S., 294, 311
Sias, P. M., 290, 300, 311
Siddiqui, A., 268, 274, 285, 286
Siegert, J. R., 147, 165
Sillars, A. L., 147, 148, 149, 151, 152, 153, 159, 164, 165, 224, 225, 231, 299, 311, 327, 328, 334
Silva, D., 290, 300, 311
Simkin, S., 125, 139
Simon, R. W., 377, 384, 398
Simonelli, C. J., 215, 222, 231
Simons-Morton, B., 241, 256
Simpson, J. A., 76, 80, 81, 86, 89, 100, 104, 105, 116, 119
Sinclair, R., 237, 256
Skrimshire, A. M., 125, 139
Slatcher, R., 492, 495
Slav, K., 102, 111, 119
Slee, P., 236, 258
Smith, C. A., 23, 28, 31, 32, 36, 40, 48, 151, 165, 316, 334, 338, 355, 463, 475, 477
Smith, D. B., 221, 231
Smith, J., 272, 286
Smith, K., 290, 308
Smith, L., 469, 476
Smith, M., 243, 257, 272, 274, 287
Smith, P., 433, 435, 455
Smith, P. H., 212, 214, 215, 218, 227
Smith, P. K., 236, 243, 258
Smith, S., 149, 163
Smith, S. W., 110, 118
Smith, T. W., 380, 398
Smith, W. J., 420, 455
Smock, P., 201, 207
Smyth, J. M., 492, 497
Snapp, C. M., 26, 32, 61, 71, 292, 311, 378, 398, 458, 477

Snidman, N., 265, 268, 283
Snyder, C. R., 472, 477
Snyder, D. K., 192, 194, 199, 200, 202, 206, 342, 351, 353, 380, 384, 386, 396
Snyder, J. J., 237, 258, 271, 281
Snyder, M., 288, 308
Snydersmith, M., 363, 373
Solomon, D. H., 3, 10, 105, 118, 147, 152, 155, 163, 164
Solomon, J., 263, 283
Sommer, K., 338, 355
Sorbom, D., 444, 454
Spertus, I. L., 361, 374
Spiegel, D., 471, 475
Spielmacher, C., 272, 286
Spitz, A. M., 214, 228
Spitzberg, B. H., 196, 206, 209, 211, 212, 215, 217, 218, 222, 224, 227, 228, 231
Sporakowski, M. J., 223, 229
Spracklen, K. M., 238, 254
Sprague, R. J., 146, 165, 289, 297, 311
Sprecher, S., 82, 91, 330, 335, 344, 355
Springer, C. A., 3, 4, 5, 6, 8, 10, 16, 17, 24, 26, 27, 29, 31, 32, 35, 38, 40, 42, 43, 44, 48, 59, 61, 62, 63, 64, 66, 71, 73, 74, 90, 98, 105, 107, 108, 112, 118, 126, 141, 144, 145, 146, 163, 173, 174, 189, 192, 193, 207, 261, 266, 267, 268, 284, 288, 289, 291, 292, 294, 295, 297, 298, 300, 301, 302, 303, 305, 307, 310, 314, 315, 318, 319, 324, 325, 330, 333, 337, 338, 354, 360, 364, 373, 378, 397, 417, 447, 454, 458, 460, 461, 476
Sproull, L., 402, 415
Sroufe, L. A., 241, 259
Stafford, E., 137, 140
Staggs, S. L., 214, 230
Stamp, G. H., 147, 165, 224, 231
Stanley, S., 146, 163, 385, 396
Starnes, R., 237, 256
Stauffacher, K., 272, 273, 285
Steele, H., 100, 117
Steele, M., 100, 117
Steffen, V. J., 218, 228
Stein, N., 274, 286
Steinglass, P., 383, 395
Steinmetz, S. K., 280, 286
Stephan, C. W., 470, 477
Stephan, W. G., 470, 477
Sternglanz, R. W., 185, 186, 189
Stets, J. E., 215, 231
Stevens, F. E., 490, 497
Stillwell, A. M., 64, 70, 324, 325, 326, 332, 432, 450, 455
Stipek, D., 236, 257
Stith, S. M., 221, 223, 228, 231
Stocker, C., 274, 286

Storaasli, R., 146, 163
Storm, C., 16, 17, 32
Storm, T., 16, 17, 32
Stowell, J. R., 363, 373
Straight, E. S., 215, 218, 231
Straus, M. A., 212, 213, 231, 280, 286
Street, A. E., 215, 218, 219, 230, 231
Stroebe, M. S., 484, 497
Stroebe, W., 484, 497
Stromquist, A. M., 215, 230
Stroud, L., 214, 215, 227
Stucke, T. S., 123, 124, 125, 127, 128, 142, 292, 311
Stucky, B. D., 237, 254
Stutman, R. K., 144, 164
Style, C. B., 377, 396
Sugarman, D. B., 210, 223, 231
Sullivan, C. M., 361, 374
Sullivan, D. J., 143, 145, 156, 164
Sulsky, L. M., 388, 390
Summers, K. J., 78, 91
Summers, S., 117
Sutherland, C. A., 361, 374
Sutherland, M. A., 213, 226
Sutton, L. S., 265, 275, 281
Sutton, R. I., 426, 455
Swain, M. A., 157, 164
Swann, W. B., 78, 91
Swanson, C., 150, 163
Sweet, L., 214, 215, 227
Swenson, L. P., 237, 258

Tafoya, M., 148, 165
Takeuchi, R., 420, 452
Tambor, E. S., 418, 454
Tangney, J. P., 46, 48, 278, 286, 482, 487, 497
Tannen, D., 299, 311
Taylor, C. B., 363, 372
Taylor, S. E., 147, 164
Tedeschi, J. T., 210, 211, 231
Tellegen, A., 15, 33
Temoshock, L., 481, 486, 498
ter Schure, E., 145, 146, 156, 162
Teranishi, C., 224, 228
Terdal, S. K., 418, 454
Terry, R., 236, 238, 254
Tesser, A., 184, 187, 189, 274, 286
Testa, A., 73, 88
Thayer, S., 272, 273, 276, 286
Thein, S., 279, 281
Thibaut, J. W., 367, 373
Thoennes, N., 213, 231
Thoits, P. A., 378, 391, 398
Thomas, E. J., 382, 398
Thomas, J. L., 481, 482, 486, 489, 497
Thomas, S. C., 418, 453

Thomas, T. J., 248, 254
Thomas, T. L., 361, 373
Thompson, A., 341, 355
Thompson, A. P., 388, 398
Thompson, J. K., 264, 273, 283
Thompson, M. P., 214, 215, 218, 226
Thompson, R., 377, 395
Thompson, R. S., 218, 219, 226
Thom-Santelli, J., 403, 404, 415
Thomson, D. W., 78, 88
Thoresen, C. E., 386
Thorn, G., 224, 229
Thurnmaier, F., 146, 163
Tice, D. M., 123, 124, 125, 127, 128, 140, 142, 292, 311, 470, 476
Ting-Toomey, S., 473, 475, 477
Tjaden, P., 213, 231
Toblin, R. L., 242, 258
Todd, M. J., 290, 302, 303, 309
Toller, P., 346, 352
Tomkins, S. S., 15, 32, 42, 48, 266, 286, 486, 498
Tong, E. M. W., 45, 49
Tonizzo, S., 219, 223, 224, 225, 231
Torpy, D. J., 368, 372
Toussaint, L. L., 390, 398
Treas, J., 191, 202, 207, 381, 398
Tritt, D., 221, 231
Troop-Gordon, W., 240, 241, 252, 256, 258
Troy, M., 241, 259
Trubisky, P., 473, 477
Trueman, M., 242, 253
Tsang, J., 393, 397, 398
Tucker, C., 275, 276, 285
Tucker, J., 464, 476
Turkle, S., 400, 415
Turner, H., 271, 280, 282
Turner, R. A., 363, 372
Turner, R. E., 168, 189
Turner, T. J., 23, 32
Twenge, J. M., 123, 124, 125, 127, 128, 131, 135, 138, 139, 140, 142, 292, 308, 311, 419, 455, 469, 476
Tyler, J. M., 185, 186, 189, 190
Tyree, A., 214, 230

Uchino, B. N., 124, 142
Uchitelle, L., 423, 455
Uebelacker, L. A., 377, 384, 399
Ulrich, Y., 214, 227
Umberson, D., 211, 225
Updegraff, K., 272, 273, 275, 276, 285, 286
Utz, S., 402, 415

Valente, E., 238, 255
Valois, R. F., 218, 219, 227

Van Acker, R., 237, 258
van Aken, M. A. G., 85, 89
Van Boven, L., 130, 142
van den Berg, P., 264, 273, 283
van Driel, B., 381, 395
Van Dyke, C., 481, 486, 498
Van Lieshout, C. F. M., 85, 89, 242, 255
Van Yperen, N. W., 381, 398
Vangelisti, A. L., 3, 4, 5, 6, 8, 10, 11, 16, 23, 26, 32, 33, 38, 39, 40, 42, 44, 49, 51, 59, 60, 61, 62, 63, 64, 65, 66, 71, 72, 73, 74, 91, 98, 105, 108, 119, 143, 144, 145, 146, 147, 149, 150, 152, 155, 158, 159, 162, 165, 175, 190, 192, 193, 196, 207, 261, 262, 266, 267, 268, 286, 287, 288, 289, 291, 292, 293, 294, 295, 297, 298, 300, 301, 302, 303, 304, 305, 311, 314, 315, 316, 317, 318, 319, 330, 335, 337, 339, 350, 351, 355, 360, 364, 367, 371, 374, 390, 398, 417, 434, 447, 455, 457, 459, 460, 461, 464, 467, 468, 469, 477, 479, 480, 481, 484, 486, 498
Vankos, N., 214, 217, 218, 223, 228
Varian, H., 425, 455
Vernberg, E. M., 240, 241, 258, 259
Vernon, M. L., 108, 117
Vilberg, T., 126, 141
Violato, C., 214, 230
Visher, E. B., 348, 355
Visher, J. S., 348, 355
Viswesvaran, C., 418, 454
Vitaro, F., 240, 242, 256
Vivian, D., 215, 224, 227
Vogelgesang, J., 299, 311
Vohs, K. D., 490, 494
Volkenaar, M. C., 265, 282
Vollebergh, W., 377, 378, 398
Volling, B., 237, 256
von Salisch, M., 299, 311
Von Stein, M., 364, 372
Vroom, V. H., 424, 456

Wade, C. K., 82, 91
Wade, J. B., 420, 456
Wade, N. G., 159, 161, 165
Wadsworth, J., 191, 208
Wagner, A., 347, 352
Wagner, P. E., 278, 286
Wainryb, C., 143, 165, 272, 287
Waite, L. J., 377, 381, 398, 399
Walby, S., 214, 231
Waldron, V. R., 63, 72
Walker Wilson, M. J., 186, 189
Walker, A. R., 296, 310
Walker, J. D., 214, 215, 221, 225
Walker, R., 459, 460, 462, 476
Wall, S., 92, 96, 116

Wall, T. D., 440, 452
Wallbott, H. G., 461, 464, 465, 466, 476, 477
Waller, E. M., 237, 258
Wallerstein, J. S., 314, 335
Walling, B. R., 269, 270, 285, 287
Wallston, K. A., 361, 375
Waltz, J., 223, 229
Wampler, K. S., 409, 410, 411, 415
Warburton, W. A., 34, 46, 49
Warchol, G., 213, 228
Ward, D. B., 221, 231
Ward, L., 274, 286
Wardrop, J. L., 240, 256
Warr, P. B., 440, 452
Warren, J., 137, 140
Waters, E., 92, 96, 116
Watlington, C. G., 215, 220, 232
Watson, D., 15, 17, 18, 19, 21, 22, 28, 33, 483, 498
Watson, J. C., 341, 354
Watts, R., 51, 72
Weaver, T. L., 220, 232
Weber, A., 205, 207
Weber, E. U., 135, 141
Webster, C., 292, 293, 310
Webster, D., 214, 227
Webster, E. L., 368, 372
Weeks, J., 202, 208
Wegner, J. W., 429, 455
Weigel, S. M., 267, 281
Weiner, B., 107, 119, 279, 287, 418, 435, 456, 464, 478
Weiner, J. L., 60, 65, 70
Weinfurt, K., 214, 217, 218, 223, 228
Weinstock, J. S., 299, 311
Weisberg, J., 148, 165
Weiss, D. J., 440, 456
Weiss, R. L., 78, 91
Weiss, R. S., 313, 335
Welch, N., 135, 141
Wellings, K., 191, 208
Wells, J. G., 82, 91
Wells, M., 198, 206
Wells, S., 216, 223, 232
Wendorf, C. A., 484, 495
Wenzlaff, R. M., 78, 91
Werner, N. E., 269, 287
West, L., 290, 308
Westen, D., 191, 197, 198, 206, 410, 414
Wetzel, C., 186, 189
Wexler, M. O., 117
Weylin Sternglanz, R., 167
Wheatley, T., 130, 141, 142
Whisman, M. A., 377, 384, 399
White, G. L., 81, 91, 208

White, H. R., 377, 396
White, R., 424, 451, 454
White, S. W., 124, 140
Whitehand, C., 242, 253
Whiteman, S., 272, 273, 276, 286
Whitesell, N. R., 296, 297, 312, 458, 477
Whitfield, C. L., 214, 215, 221, 225, 227
Whitney, G. A., 299, 309
Whitson, S., 147, 166
Whitty, M. T., 400, 401, 402, 403, 404, 405, 408, 409, 411, 413, 415, 416
Why, Y. P., 45, 49
Widaman, K. F., 108, 117, 265, 286
Wiedenmayer, C. P., 127, 142
Wiederman, M. W., 191, 197, 208, 380, 399
Wiehe, V., 280, 287
Wiering, L., 224, 228
Wilkins, L., 406, 416
Willams, K. D., 306
Willen, H., 345, 355
Willetts, M. C., 330, 335
Williams, D. R., 390, 398
Williams, J. H., 430, 437, 452
Williams, K. D., 21, 26, 31, 46, 49, 99, 101, 106, 117, 123, 124, 125, 126, 134, 137, 140, 142, 292, 293, 296, 305, 306, 309, 312, 317, 332, 365, 366, 372, 375, 466, 475
Williamson, D. F., 214, 225, 228
Williard, J. C., 242, 257
Willingham, J. K., 147, 161, 299, 308
Wills, T. A., 83, 89
Wilson, A., 168, 188, 272, 274, 287
Wilson, J. Q., 450, 456
Wilson, K. A., 377, 395
Wilson, L. L., 160, 166
Wilson, M., 380, 381, 395
Wilson, T. D., 130, 131, 141, 142
Wilt, S. A., 214, 227
Wineman, N. M., 362, 375
Winke, J., 143, 144
Winkel, R. E., 26, 31, 123, 124, 125, 140
Winnicott, D. W., 413, 416
Winslow, E., 274, 283
Wirtz, J. G., 153, 154, 159, 163
Wiseman, J. P., 291, 302, 312
Wolf, E. S., 101, 119
Wolke, D., 280, 287
Wong, C. M., 361, 374
Wong, D. T., 418, 453

Wong, P. T. P., 464, 478
Woods, K. E., 267, 281
Woods, S. J., 362, 375
Work, C., 299, 309
Worthington, E. L., Jr., 159, 161, 165, 279, 287, 328, 331, 334, 385, 386, 389, 397, 399
Wotman, S. R., 64, 70, 324, 325, 326, 332
Wu, S., 462, 477
Wyer, M. M., 168, 189

Xie, H., 293, 312

Yager, J., 307, 312
Yaggi, K., 274, 283
Yang, Z., 473, 477
Yankeelov, P. A., 435, 452
Yarab, P. E., 408, 416
Yeh, E. A. J., 267, 281
Yehuda, R., 361, 374
Yen, Y., 73, 88
Yi, J., 385, 394
Yoshimura, S., 196, 206
Youn, M. S., 117
Young, K. S., 411, 416
Young, R. C., 264, 273, 284, 318, 333
Young, R. M., 382, 396
Young, S. L., 3, 4, 5, 11, 16, 23, 26, 32, 33, 38, 39, 42, 44, 49, 59, 60, 61, 62, 64, 66, 72, 98, 105, 108, 119, 144, 145, 149, 150, 152, 155, 165, 166, 175, 190, 261, 262, 266, 287, 288, 289, 291, 292, 293, 294, 295, 297, 300, 301, 303, 305, 311, 330, 335, 337, 339, 350, 355, 360, 374, 390, 398, 434, 447, 455, 457, 458, 461, 464, 468, 469, 477, 478, 479, 498
Yragui, N., 213, 226
Yu, K., 241, 256

Zadro, L., 123, 125, 142, 292, 293, 296, 305, 306, 312
Zechmeister, J. S., 65, 72, 324, 325, 326, 335
Zegans, L. S., 481, 486, 498
Zeifman, D., 313, 333
Zembrodt, I. M., 299, 310, 311
Zlotnick, C., 213, 217, 218, 232
Zu, Z., 214, 227
Zuckerman, A., 76, 87, 89
Zuckerman, M., 19, 33
Zuravin, S., 221, 229
Zwerling, C., 215, 230

# SUBJECT INDEX

action tendencies, 42, 108, 301, 470. *See also* responses to hurt
active devaluation, 360–361. *See also* emotional abuse
active disassociation. *See also* social exclusion
   as a cause of hurt, 26, 29, 63, 192–193, 318, 338
   in couple relationships, 319
   in friendships, 292
adolescents, 147, 236, 240, 307
adults
   and friendships, 288–307
   as parents, 263–268
   as separated spouses, 343–348
affairs. *See* infidelity
aggression. *See also* childhood aggression
   communicative, 215–216
   and hurt, 216–223
   intimate violence and, 223–225
   online. *See* flaming
   parental responses to, 275–276
   physical violence and, 212–216, 264, 271–272
   psychological, 264
   relational, 272–273
aggressor–victim relationships, 235, 237
   consequences of, 248–250
   formation of, 245–248
alcohol abuse, 221, 379, 382–385, 390
alienation, 266, 277
anger
   appraisals during hurtful episodes, 28, 41–42, 266–267
   and attachment, 105. *See also* attachment anxiety
   and culture, 447, 459
   in emotion blend, 92, 105–106, 296–297, 472, 481–482
   as an expression of hurt, 145–147, 324–325, 447, 469, 483–485, 490–491
   factors that predict hurt vs., 28–29, 337
   and multilayered model of hurt, 485–489
   negative affect, 483–484
   as a term to describe hurt, 481–482
antipathetic relationship, 249–250
anxiety
   appraisals of, 43
   and emotional contagion, 341
   forgiveness and levels of, 342, 390
   relationship, 320, 330–331. *See also* attachment anxiety
   threat of emotional harm and, 28
   and vulnerability, 389
appraisals, 16, 23, 28, 338
   of anger, 41–42
   of anxiety, 43
   and culture, 457
   and hurt, 38–40, 316
   and rejection-related emotions, 27–28
   role of, in emotion, 35–38
   of sadness, 43
   of shame, 46
   of social interaction and hurt, 34
attachment anxiety, 96, 104–113. *See also* attachment security; attachment style
   and appraisals of hurtful behavior, 104
   and neuroticism, 367
   and physical pain, 367
   and responses to hurt feelings, 105, 330–331
   and vulnerability to hurt feelings, 104
attachment behavior system, 95, 316–317, 330–331
attachment security. *See also* attachment anxiety; attachment style
   in couple relationships, 320–322, 330–331

attachment security (*cont.*)
   in emotion regulation, 96–101
   and healthy narcissism, 101
   in parent–child relationships, 263–264
attachment style
   and appraisals during hurtful interaction, 42, 101–105
   attributional tendencies and, 107
   in couple relationships, 320–322
   differences in cognitive and behavioral responses to hurt, 108–111
   emotion regulation and, 95–97
   rejection sensitivity and, 44–45, 78–82
attributions
   and attachment style, 107
   and childhood aggression, 239, 243. *See also* childhood aggression
   and conflict, 145–146
   and culture, 457, 464–465
   and facework, 54–55, 67–69
   in friendships, 294–295, 302–303
   of intentionality, 155–156, 210–211, 321–322, 464
   self, 278–279
   and violence, 224–225
avoidance
   of conflict as a response to hurt, 145–146
   as coping strategy, 443–444
   in couple relationships as a response to hurt feelings, 321–322
   culture and, of hurt feelings, 473–474
   deception and, of hurt feelings, 171–175
   in friendships as a response to hurt feelings, 299–301
   interpersonal. *See* relational distancing
   motivations to avoid hurting people's feelings, 175–179
   of research on hurt feelings, 480–484

basic emotion, 22–23, 105–106, 480–481
betrayal
   as a cause of hurt, 144, 289, 318
   in couple relationships, 319
   in friendships, 289–291
   and infidelity, 199
   as source of conflict, 144
blended emotion model, 16. *See also* blended emotions
blended emotions, 4–6, 92, 105–106, 297, 315, 338, 351
Brown, Penelope, 50, 55–58

CAI. *See* Coworker Allergy Inventory

causes of hurt. *See also* hurtful behavior; hurtful events; hurtful messages
   face threats as, 58
   perceived, 26, 39, 303
   relational evaluation and, 24–29, 360, 461
   relational rule violations as, 39
   relational transgression. *See* relational transgression
CDC. *See* Centers for Disease Control
Centers for Disease Control (CDC), 137, 219
childhood aggression. *See also* victimization
   aggressor–victim relationships, 235, 237, 245–250
   consequences of, 236–237
   prevalence of, 235–236
   a relationship perspective on, 244–245
   risk factors for, 237–238
   social cognitions and, 238–240
children
   aggression. *See* childhood aggression
   conflict between, 296. *See also* childhood aggression; sibling relationships
   online processing of hurtful interactions, 263–271. *See also* parent–child relationships
   sensitivity to hurt, 277
   stepchildren, 346–348
chronic hurt, 147, 379–391. *See also* discrete hurt
cognitions
   affect, 295–297, 483
   appraisals and hurt feelings, 38–43. *See also* appraisals
   attitudes about self and other, 6, 44
   attributions. *See* attributions
   childhood aggression and social, 238–240. *See also* childhood aggression
   cognitive-affective schemas for responding to hurt, 43
   expectations. *See* expectations
   hurt-eliciting, 35–40
   hurt feelings and conflict, 145
   self- and other-schemas, 39–40
   scripts, 278, 289, 304
   shared qualities between hurt and other emotions, 338–340, 417. *See also* anger; fear; sadness
common negative affect model, 16–17
communal relationships, 314, 419–423
communicative aggression, 212, 215–225. *See also* emotional abuse; violence
conceptualization of hurt, 3–6, 105–107
   distinct emotion, 4–5, 17–22, 35, 105–106
   emotion blend, 4–6, 16–17, 92, 105–106. *See also* blended emotions

emotional injury, 3–5, 50, 360
face threat, 58–67
interpersonal phenomenon, 5
personal injury, 5, 39, 98, 106, 193, 316
relational devaluation, 5, 98, 102–104. *See also* relational devaluation
relational transgression, 5, 98. *See also* relational transgression
threat to safety and security, 5, 98–99. *See also* attachment anxiety
threat to mental models of attachment, 5, 98, 316. *See also* personal injury
confession, 194. *See also* extradyadic relationships
conflict
  alleviating hurt during, 152–157
  and anger, 145–147
  avoidance as consequence of hurt, 145–146
  bidirectional association between hurt and, 148
  in children's peer groups, 296
  as a consequence of hurt, 144–145
  in couple relationships, 321–326
  demand/withdraw pattern of, 147, 159
  discussion about hurtful, 157–159
  discussion with third parties for hurt and, 160–161
  forgiveness in managing hurt caused from, 160
  in friendships, 289–294
  hurt diminished by, 147–148
  intimate violence and, 215
  leading to hurt, 146–147
  and psychological health, 381–384
  physiological effects of, 362–364
  in postdivorce relationships, 342–343, 349–351
  relationship quality moderating impact of hurt, 159–160
  responses to, 298–300
  in sibling relationships, 273–274
  strategies for preventing hurt, 148–152
contemporaneous reports, 18–21
couple relationships
  aggression in, 212–215
  and attachment, 316–317
  attributions of hurtful events in, 322, 326–329
  chronic hurt in, 339, 382–385
  conflict in, 321–326
  demand/withdraw pattern in, 363–365
  effects of hurt on, 320–322
  effects of hurt on victim in, 320–322
  forgiveness as moderator of hurt, 327
  hurtful events in romantic, 26, 318–319

infidelity in, 199–203
public vs. private hurt in, 60
resolving hurt in, 322–324
responses to hurt in, 299
role-related effects of hurt in, 326–329, 331
victim–perpetrator perceptions of hurt in, 324–326
Coworker Allergy Inventory (CAI), 437–449
criticism
  as a cause of hurt, 76, 82, 291, 318
  and face threat, 59
  in friendships, 291–292
  lying to shield other from, 174–175
  in romantic relationships, 193, 319
culture
  action tendencies, 467–470
  and antecedent events, 460–463
  appraisals and, 463–465
  avoidance of hurt feelings, 473–474
  as a contextual variable, 459–460
  empathic, 471–473
  micro-cultures, 425–426
  physiological changes, 465–467
  regulation of emotions, 470–471
  and responses to infidelity, 196
  and sexual exclusivity, 201–202
cyberspace. *See* technology
cyberstalking, 405–406

dACC. *See* dorsal anterior cingulated cortex
deception
  and attachment, 110
  to avoid hurting people's feelings, 175–179
  as a cause of hurt feelings, 98, 158, 193, 319, 338
  in close relationships, 184–187
  in cyberspace, 402–405
  equivocation when caught between truth and, 187–188
  in everyday life, 168–175
  by implication, 170–171, 180
  motivations for, 186–187
  and the MUM effect, 187
  rates of outright lying, 179
  role of relationship devaluation, 173–175
  self-centered vs. other-oriented lies, 169–170; 183–185
    affection and, 181–182
    relationship context and, 185
    social distance model and, 404–405
  serious lies, 182–184
  sex differences in, 185
  in between truth-telling and, 179–180

demand/withdraw
  adverse effects of, 147
  in couple relationships, 324, 330, 363–366
  and impact of hurt on relationships, 159
  and neuroticism, 367
  physiological outcomes of, 366–367
depression
  and mental health, 377, 380, 392, 393
  rejection sensitivity and, 75–79
  violence and, 216, 217, 218
devaluation. *See* relational devaluation
diathesis–stress model, 378, 392
direct strategies, 6–7
disclosure
  exclusion from, and hurt, 193. *See also* passive disassociation
  and facework, 65
  in friendships, 290
  and hurt research, 484
  hurtful, 144, 318, 319. *See also* hurtful events; hurtful messages
discrepancy and relational value, 24–28. *See also* relational devaluation
discrete emotion, 15, 16, 21–22, 35, 40–43, 92, 95
discrete hurt, 384–391. *See also* chronic hurt
distance writing protocols, 492–493
distancing, relational. *See* relational distancing
distinct emotion model, 4–5, 15, 17, 22, 106
distress, as a term to describe hurt, 482
distributive strategy, 299
divorce. *See also* postdivorce relationships
  as a consequence of hurtful transgressions, 379–383
  as a consequence of infidelity, 195, 200, 380–385
  and demand/withdraw, 366
  and reformulation of the family, 346–348
  spousal separation and, 343–346
dorsal anterior cingulated cortex (dACC), 126, 366–367

ECRI. *See* Experiences in Close Relationships Inventory
embarrassment. *See also* social affront
  face threat as link between hurt and, 60
emotion blend. *See* blended emotions
emotion regulation, 93–97
  and attachment, 95–97
  and culture, 470–471
emotional abuse, 370–371
  health consequences of, 361
  physiological consequences of, 361–362
emotional injury, 3–5, 360
  and social insult, 50
emotional insensitivity, 123–125, 131, 134–135

emotional numbness. *See* emotional insensitivity
empathy/empathic
  as a buffering factor in parent experiences of hurt, 270–271
  and culture, 471–473
  and emotional insensitivity, 130–134
  hurt, 340–341
  promoting, 332
  and prosocial behavior, 135–136
  social exclusion, 131–135
employees, 426–428
enemy. *See* antipathetic relationship
evolution, 38, 123, 139, 198, 410–411
exchange relationships, 419–421
expectations
  anxious, of rejection, 75–79. *See also* rejection sensitivity
  betrayal as a violation of, 144
  frequency of hurt and development of, 264
  of hurt, 262
  outcome, and childhood aggression, 238–239, 243
  and physical aggression, 264
  in stepfamilies, 348, 349
  of support, 84–85
  and victimization, 243
Experiences in Close Relationships Inventory (ECRI), 112
extended family, 348–350
extradyadic relationships, 191–195, 199–200. *See also* affairs; infidelity
  emotional responses to, 191–193
  as form of betrayal, 144
  and the study of hurt, 205
extramarital sex, 196, 380–381, 383. *See also* extradyadic relationships

face/facework
  definition of, 52, 54
  face-threatening acts (FTAs), 56–58
  features of, 52–53
  social order and, 53–55
  strategies, 54–55
  threat and hurt, 58–67
face wants, 56
family relationships
  aggressive, 271–273
  dissolution and reformation of. *See* postdivorce relationships
  dysfunctional patterns in, 490
  extended. *See* extended family
  hurtful events in, 288
  impact of hurt on, 217

## Subject Index

an integrated perspective on hurt in the, 261–263, 277
parent–child. *See* parent–child relationships
therapy for, 491–492
siblings. *See* sibling relationships
spouses. *See* couple relationships
and violence, 214, 219
fantasy, 412–413
fear
appraisals of, during hurtful episodes, 28
in emotion blend (hurt), 4, 15, 16, 17, 19, 105–106, 345, 472. *See also* blended emotions
and multilayered model of hurt, 485–489
of rejection, 109, 317, 322. *See also* attachment anxiety
and withdrawal, 339
feature–based theory, 403–405
features of hurt, distinguishing, 3–6, 98–99. *See also* conceptualization of hurt
flaming, 402. *See also* technology
fMRI. *See* Functional Magnetic Resonance Imaging
forgiveness, 63–64, 111, 385–391
in managing hurt caused from conflict, 160
in postdivorce relationships, 351
friendships
affect in, 295–297
attributions for hurt feelings in, 294–295, 302–303
causes of hurt in, 289–294
conflict in, 289–294, 298–300
consequences of hurt for self in, 300–301
public vs. private conflict in, 294
relational consequences of hurt in, 301–304
responses to hurt feelings in, 297–300
scripts of hurt feelings in, 289, 304
Functional Magnetic Resonance Imaging (fMRI), 126, 366, 466
functions of hurt, 6–8
informative, 6
persuasive, 6
supportive, 7
future alone, 127–132, 136
future belonging, 127–132, 136

gender differences
and deception, 185
in demand/withdraw pattern, 330
and intimate partner violence, 209, 212–214
and jealousy, 196–199
and online infidelity, 410–411
and social allergens, 441
Goffman, Erving, 50–55

guilt
affect associated with, 17, 21, 261
appraisals during hurtful episodes, 28
and avoidance, 110
and culture, 462
about involvement in extradyadic relationships, 194–195
and multilayered model of hurt, 487–488
violations of standards and, 28

harassment
online, 405–406. *See also* cyberstalking
sexual, 427–428, 430, 447, 449, 450
health. *See also* physiology
chronic hurt and, 382–384
and close relationships, 376–377
consequences of emotional abuse, 361
discrete hurt and, 380–382
forgiveness and, 390–391
and intimate violence, 217–220
mental. *See* mental health
hostility
affect shared with hurt, 16–17, 21
attributing hurtful acts to, 263
as a source of parental rejection, 263, 265
in the workplace, 431–433
humiliation
as a cause of hurt, 98, 109, 113, 293–294, 468
and hurtful acts of parents, 264, 265
and self-esteem, 44, 380
hurtful behavior. *See also* hurtful events; hurtful messages
acts of commission, 76–82, 261
acts of omission, 82–87, 261, 318
expression of, 62–64
as an indicator of relational quality, 6
as an influence technique, 6–7. *See also* functions of hurt
responses to, 63–64. *See also* responses to hurt feelings
as supportive, 7
hurtful events. *See also* hurtful behavior; hurtful messages
active disassociation, 29. *See also* active disassociation
and attachment, 98–99
betrayal, 29. *See also* betrayal
criticism, 29. *See also* criticism
frequency of, 315, 318
infidelity, 318. *See also* infidelity
lack of appreciation, 318
passive disassociation, 29. *See also* passive disassociation
in romantic relationships, 26, 29, 98, 192–193. *See also* couple relationships

hurtful events (*cont.*)
  teasing, 28, 318. *See also* teasing
  types/categories of, 26, 29, 98, 317–318, 338, 460–461
hurtful messages (speech acts), 60–61, 314. *See also* hurtful behavior; hurtful events
  and face threat, 59
  frequency of, 460
  intensity of, 60–61
  types of, 59, 317–318

incivility, 428–433
indirect strategies, 7, 299. *See also* avoidance
individual differences
  attachment, 316, 330–331
  narcissism, 418–419
  neuroticism, 367
  positive affectivity, 299
  proneness to hurt vs. anger, 337
  rejection sensitivity, 73. *See also* rejection sensitivity
infidelity
  and betrayal, 199
  hurt and, 192–194, 318–319
  as a hurtful event, 379–382
  Internet, 408–410
  involvement in an affair, 194–195
  jealousy as a result of, 196–199
  loss as a result of, 199–201
  methodological issues, 203–205
  responses to discovery of, 195–196
integrative strategy, 261–263, 484–489
intensity (hurtfulness)
  and ability to respond to hurtful message, 60–61
  in different contexts, 61–62
  and relationship evaluation appraisals, 28
intentionality
  attributions of, 55, 66, 321–322
  and intensity of hurt feelings, 42–43, 66
  and negative impact on relationships, 152, 155–156

jealousy
  gender differences, 196–199, 410
  and rejection sensitivity, 76

leadership style, 423–425
Levinson, Stephen, 50, 55–58
loneliness, 261, 272, 296, 301, 345, 380, 401
loss
  of identity, 199–200
  irrevocable, 27
  relationship, 5–6, 200–201

love. *See also* couple relationships
  absence of, and hurt, 102, 338
  infidelity and, 408–411
  and multilayered model of hurt, 485
low relational evaluation. *See* relational devaluation
lying. *See* deception

MAACL-R. *See* Multiple Affect Adjective Check List-Revised
marriage, 192, 342, 347, 377. *See also* couple relationships
media richness theory, 403
mental health
  chronic hurt and, 382–385
  and close relationships, 376–379
  discrete hurt and, 380–382
  and distance writing, 492–493
  forgiveness and, 390–391
  infidelity and, 379–380
  and suicide, 137
micro-culture, 425–426
misfortune control, 127, 129, 134
Multiple Affect Adjective Check List-Revised (MAACL-R), 19–22
MUM effect, 187

narcissism, 488
  healthy, 97, 101, 115
  in the workplace, 418–419
neuroticism, 367

organizational turnover, 451–452

pain
  consequences of psychological/emotional, 43
  emotional, 34, 316, 460
  evoked by threats to security, 100–101
  feeling another's, 131–134. *See also* empathy
  neural pathways associated with emotional and physical, 21
  physical, 126–127, 210, 317, 366–367, 466
  predicting future, 130–131, 134
  regulation of, 306
  threshold, 128–129
PANAS-X. *See* Positive and Negative Affect Schedule – Expanded Form
parent–child relationships
  appraisals of hurtful child acts, 268–269
  appraisals of hurtful parental acts, 266–267
  attachment and, 263–264
  hurtful vs. reparative transactions in, 270–271
  low relationship evaluation in, 27

## Subject Index

perceiving child acts as hurtful, 268
perceiving parental acts as hurtful, 263–266
public vs. private hurtful episodes in, 60
responses to hurtful child acts, 269–270
responses to hurtful parental acts, 267–268
shaming in, 278–280
passive devaluation, 360–361. *See also* withdrawal
passive disassociation
  as a cause of hurt, 193, 318, 292
  in couple relationships, 318–319
  in friendships, 292–293
passive strategy, 299. *See also* avoidance
patriarchal terrorism, 197
personal injury, 5, 39, 98–99, 106, 193, 316–317
physical aggression. *See* violence
physical insensitivity, 125, 129–131
physiology. *See also* health
  and emotional abuse, 361–364
  and social exclusion, 126–131
  and withdrawal, 364–368
politeness
  expected pattern violation of, 58
  strategies, 56–58
  variation of expressing hurtful content and, 62–64
politeness theory, 50–51, 55–58
Positive and Negative Affect Schedule – Expanded Form (PANAS-X), 17–22
postdivorce relationships
  extended family and, 348–350
  forgiveness and hurt in, 351
  managing transition from divorce to, 339–343
  reformulation in the family, 346–348
  spousal separation transition, 343–346
  stepfamilies, 346–348
  stepsiblings, 348
post-traumatic stress disorder (PTSD), 361–362. *See also* emotional abuse
primary appraisal, 37
priming, security, 111–115
prosocial behavior, 135–136
psychological abuse. *See* emotional abuse
psychological control, 264, 267
psychopathology, 377, 378, 488
PTSD. *See* post-traumatic stress disorder

Rapid Marital Interaction Coding System (RMICS), 370
reactions to hurt. *See* responses to hurt feelings
ready perceptions
  of acts of commission, 79–80
  of support, 85–86

recruitment, 418–419
rejection
  emotions and appraisals related to, 27–28
  explicit. *See* active disassociation
  implicit. *See* passive disassociation
  parental, 266–267
  peer, 241–242
  physical insensitivity, 129–135
  and psychological pain, 34
  sensitivity. *See* rejection sensitivity
  social. *See* withdrawal
  social exclusion. *See* social exclusion
rejection sensitivity, 73–87
  and acts of commission, 76–82
  and acts of omission, 82–87
  and appraisals, 44
  and attachment style, 44–45, 78–82
  definition of, 44, 74
  and depression, 75
  and hostility, 75
  and hurt feelings, 76
  and hurt sensitivity, 43
  and self-esteem, 74–75
relational aggression, 267, 269, 272–273. *See also* childhood aggression; violence
relational contexts, 61–62. *See also* couple relationships; family relationships; friendships; parent–child relationships; postdivorce relationships; sibling relationships
relational devaluation. *See also* relational transgression
  and attachment, 98–105
  and culture, 462–473
  and deception, 173–175
  definition of, 24
  as a distinguishing feature of hurt, 5, 98, 193, 305, 315–317, 378, 417
  emotions elicited by, 27
  forms of, 7, 360–364
  and self-esteem, 389
  in the workplace, 423, 447
relational distancing
  appraisals and, 108, 468
  and culture, 469–470
  in response to hurt, 23, 66, 107–108, 110, 301–302
relational evaluation hypothesis, 23–27
relational transgression. *See also* relational devaluation
  and attachment, 98–105
  as defining feature of hurt, 5, 98, 193, 305, 315–317, 378, 417
  online, 408–411
  and personal injury, 193, 316–317

relational transgression (*cont.*)
   and self-esteem, 389
   and vulnerability, 5
resilience, 217, 221–222
responses to hurt feelings
   from acts of commission, 80–82
   attachment and, 44, 108–111, 330–331
   categories of, 297–298, 303, 319
   cognitive and behavioral, 107–111
   and discovery of lies, 184
   in friendships, 297–300
   in parent–child relationships, 267–270
   and politeness, 63–64
   from support omission, 86–87
retrospective reports, 17–18
revenge web sites, 406
rivalry, 273–275, 293
RMICS. *See* Rapid Marital Interaction Coding System
rumination, 387, 389–390

sadness
   appraisals of, during hurtful episodes, 28, 42–43
   and culture, 461–462
   in emotion blend (hurt), 105–106, 296–297, 315
   and hurt, 16, 30, 344, 345
   and multilayered model of hurt, 485–487
secondary appraisal, 37, 338, 463–465. *See also* appraisals
security. *See also* attachment security
   physical pain resulting from threats to, 100–101
   priming, 111–115
self-esteem
   and appraisals of hurt, 44
   and attachment style, 44
   and demand/withdraw, 147
   and rejection sensitivity, 74–75
   and the sociometer, 44
self-fulfilling prophecy, 75, 78, 260
self-presentation, 64–66, 184
separation, 202, 367
sexual exclusivity, 199, 201–202
shame, 46, 278, 485, 488
   parental shaming and proneness to, 278–279
sibling relationships
   bullying in, 279–280
   conflict in, 273–274
   differential treatment, 274–275
   parental responses to aggression in, 275–276
   parental responses to conflict in, 276
   physical aggression in, 271–272

   relational aggression in, 272–273
   rivalry in, 274–275
   role of shame in, 278–280
   teasing and tattling in, 273
social accountability, 66–67
social affront, 59–61
social allergies
   Coworker Allergy Inventory (CAI), 437–440
   typology, 434–436
   workplace and, 436–449
social distance theory, 403
social exclusion. *See also* rejection
   and affective forecasting, 130–131
   clinical implications of, 136–138
   emotional insensitivity produced by, 123–125, 131, 134–135
   empathy and, 131–135
   future alone, 127–132, 136
   future belonging, 127–132, 136
   misfortune control, 127, 129, 134
   and physical insensitivity, 129–131
   and physical pain, 126–129
   reduced prosocial behavior as a result of, 135–136
   threat of, 124–126
social ostracism, 126, 292, 305–306, 365. *See also* social exclusion
social learning theory, 238
sociometer
   definition of, 44
   organizational, 425–426
   and self-esteem, 44
sorrow, 482–483
stepfamily, 346–348. *See also* postdivorce relationships
stonewalling, 179–180
support, 484

taboo, 479, 481
talk-based therapy, 490–491
teasing
   as a cause of hurt, 28, 318
   in family relationships, 264–265
   and politeness, 62–63
   in romantic relationships, 318
   in sibling relationships, 273
technology
   conceptualizing cyberspace, 412–413
   cyberstalking, 405
   deception in cyberspace, 402–405
   feature-based theory, 403–405
   flaming, 402
   gender differences and online fidelity, 410–411

HomeNet study, 401
Internet addiction, 411–412
Internet infidelity, 408–410
monitoring another's activities, 406–408
revenge Web sites, 406
social distance theory, 403
unrequited love in cyberspace, 405–406
transgression. *See* relational transgression
trust, 193
infidelity and, 199–200
in postdivorce relationships, 338–339
truth. *See also* deception
in between deception and, 179–180
equivocation when caught between deception and, 187–188
rates of telling the, 177–178

undifferentiated negative affect, 16, 21. *See also* common negative affect model
unions (labor), 421–423
unrequited love, 405–406. *See also* cyberstalking

verbal aggression. *See* communicative aggression
victimization. *See also* childhood aggression; violence
consequences of, in children's peer groups, 240
intimate violence, 212–215, 217–222
risk factors for, in children's peer groups, 241–242
social cognitions and, in children's peer groups, 242–243
types of, and violence, 213–214
violence
aggression, hurt, and, 216–223
and communicative aggression, 212
definition of, 210
gender differences and intimate partner, 209, 212–214
intention and, 210–211
intimate, 223–225
prevalence and forms of physical, 212–214
verbal aggression and physical, 215–216. *See also* communicative aggression
vulnerability
as a distinguishing feature of hurt, 4–6
in the family, 260
to hurt, 35, 338–339

withdrawal
demand/withdraw pattern and passive devaluation, 362–364
and feeling hurt, 365–367
physiological consequences of, 362–365
from the relationship. *See* relationship distancing
and social rejection, 365–367
and threats to the social self, 367–368
workbooks, 492–493
workplace
Coworker Allergy Inventory, 437–440
communal relationships in the, 419–423
exchange relationships in the, 419–422
hurtful employees, types of, 426–428
incivility, 428–433
leadership style and hurt feelings, 423–425
micro-cultures in the, 425–426
organizational sociometer, 425–426
organizational turnover, 451–452
recruitment and hurt feelings, 418–419
relational devaluation in the, 423, 447
social allergy processes and hurt in the, 433–449
union organizing and hurt feelings, 421–423